W9-CRK-768

The Undermining of Austria-Hungary

*Also by Mark Cornwall*

THE LAST YEARS OF AUSTRIA-HUNGARY: Essays in Political and Military History, 1908–1918 (*editor*)

# The Undermining of Austria-Hungary

## The Battle for Hearts and Minds

Mark Cornwall

First published in Great Britain 2000 by
**MACMILLAN PRESS LTD**
Houndmills, Basingstoke, Hampshire RG21 6XS and London
Companies and representatives throughout the world

A catalogue record for this book is available from the British Library.

ISBN 0–333–80452–X

First published in the United States of America 2000 by
**ST. MARTIN'S PRESS, INC.,**
Scholarly and Reference Division,
175 Fifth Avenue, New York, N.Y. 10010

ISBN 0–312–23151–2

Library of Congress Cataloging-in-Publication Data
Cornwall, Mark.
The undermining of Austria-Hungary : the battle for hearts and minds / Mark Cornwall.
p. cm.
Includes bibliographical references and index.
ISBN 0–312–23151–2 (cloth)
1. World War, 1914–1918—Austria—Propaganda. 2. World War, 1914–1918––Austria. 3. Hungary—History—1867–1918. 4. Austria—Foreign relations––1867–1918. 5. World War, 1914–1918—Public opinion. I. Title.

D639.P7 A93 2000
940.4'887436—dc21

99–059429



This book is printed on paper suitable for recycling and made from fully managed and sustained forest sources.

10 9 8 7 6 5 4 3 2
09 08 07 06 05 04 03 02 01

*For my parents, John and Benita Cornwall*

# Contents

# List of Tables

# List of Illustrations

# List of Maps

# Preface

In his most influential book published in 1927, Harold D. Lasswell, one of the pioneers of the modern study of propaganda, wrote that when the First World War had receded into the past it would be possible to write 'at least a fragmentary history of the international propaganda of the time'.[1] The following work is a contribution to that history. Its purpose is to examine one facet of wartime propaganda: the phenomenon which can be termed 'front propaganda', or the use of propaganda as a weapon of warfare against the enemy. Since Lasswell's study appeared, only a few authors have attempted to assess this modernized weapon of the Great War. The first, Hans Thimme, concentrated on the Western Front in his *Weltkrieg ohne Waffen*. Another, lesser-known, work was by a Pole, Antoni Szuber, and dealt extensively with the Italian Front, the theatre where he had served as a wartime propagandist; however, his study in Polish could only reach a limited audience.[2] Later works, most notably those of George Bruntz, Luciano Tosi, and Michael Sanders and Philip Taylor, continued to emphasize the theme from a western perspective, in the latter cases setting front propaganda in the context of a specifically national wartime development of propaganda (British or Italian).[3] The result has again been to present a fragmented picture of how the weapon was wielded among the belligerents. Indeed, as this study will argue, the effect of these works, even though each has contributed its own piece of the propaganda jigsaw, has been to distort the historiography, building consistently upon long-established myths about western, or more specifically British, superiority in the field of psychological warfare.

This study does not profess to give a complete picture of how front propaganda was exercised during the First World War. My aim is to restore a balance to the historiography, particularly to move away from a British focus, and to do so by investigating the propaganda weapon as wielded by and against the Habsburg Empire. In turn, this serves to open up other facets of the Great War which remain under-researched or often inaccessible to a western audience. Thus, the analysis of front propaganda is concentrated upon the Italian and Eastern Fronts, scenes in any case of the most significant propaganda campaigns of the war (although they are barely mentioned in existing historiography). And because the Habsburg Empire is the focus, either as propagandist or as victim of enemy propaganda, the work naturally explores the strengths and weaknesses of Austria-Hungary during its last war, assessing especially the degree to which its citizens were successfully mobilized on behalf of the Empire or were susceptible to arguments or information which could damage morale and ultimately undermine the Monarchy's viability. In this way, while maintaining front propaganda as the key focal point, the book has a second major purpose of contributing towards the historiography of the collapse of Austria-Hungary.

The project was initially envisaged with a British focus, as a study of wartime British propaganda against the Habsburg Empire, but its concept was gradually moulded into its current shape as a result of the evidence which I discovered in Vienna, Budapest and Zagreb. I owe a special debt to Roy Bridge and Nicholas Pronay of the University of Leeds, who first suggested the research project, provided vital contacts in central Europe, and guided me with enthusiasm and criticism through the early stages: their support has been invaluable. During my research visits to foreign archives, I benefited greatly from lively discussions in Vienna with Lothar Höbelt, Peter Broucek and Steven Beller. In Budapest, my struggle in an environment where the language was wholly foreign to me was significantly eased through the help of Géza Jeszenszky, Márton Farkas and Daniel Szabó. In Zagreb, I was privileged to talk to the late Dragovan Šepić, one of the wise doyens of Croatian history, and also secured untiring assistance from Zvonimir Passek in using the papers of the Yugoslav Committee, and from Damir Zagotta at the Croatian State Archives.

Over the years, many other anonymous individuals have assisted my research in the Viennese Kriegsarchiv, the Hungarian military archives, the library of the Országos Hadtörténeti Múzeum in Budapest, and the Vojenský Historický Archív in Prague. I particularly thank the Kriegsarchiv (Österreichisches Staatsarchiv) in Vienna for permission to reproduce propaganda leaflets from its collection. Since the material in this archive has recently been reordered, some of my references are according to the old system – but are still easy to locate. Where propaganda leaflets are named in this book, the title has been left as in the original (however erroneous the spelling).

In Britain I wish to acknowledge the assistance provided at Churchill College, Cambridge; the House of Lords Record Office; the Brotherton Library, Leeds; and the British Library. I am particularly grateful to Christopher Seton-Watson for many fruitful discussions and for his generosity with access to his father's papers. In mid-1982 I visited the village of Aldbourne in Wiltshire and there discovered, concealed in a chest in an attic, the papers of General Charles Delmé-Radcliffe. I am indebted to his nephew, the late Peter Delmé-Radcliffe, for the use of this material and am only sorry that he did not live to see how the archive of his 'wicked uncle' (as he termed him) added to an assessment of the Italian campaign against Austria-Hungary. Others to whom I owe a debt for shaping my thoughts include Zbyněk Zeman and Norman Stone who read early versions of the manuscript and made valuable comments; Geoffrey Waddington and Frank Magee for their friendship and support in Leeds; the late John Leslie; Chris Bartlett, whose incisive perceptions of the past have constantly enthused me during my years in Scotland; and John Hind, Krzysztof Nawotka and Dieter Kotschick for help in the translation of Romanian and Polish material.

My research was also considerably aided through the hospitality and friendship of certain individuals: the late Eva Nyomárkay and Mr and Mrs Albert Jakab, who warmly welcomed and introduced me to the world of Budapest; Monika Maruska and Erik Roth in Vienna; Radenko Radojčić in Zagreb; Radek Tesař in Prague. Paul Roberts for many years tolerated my joys and anxieties about the project, and accompanied me on visits to the Italian Front: his steady encouragement did much to ensure the book's completion.

Finally, clutching the theory that it is possible to name key historians who are the making of another historian, I mention my mentors, Eric Pankhurst (Stroud), Roy Bridge (Leeds) and Zbyněk Zeman (Oxford), each of whom has taught and enthused me. Dan Healey has been my constant support in the final stages of the book, quietly confident about its completion: to him I am truly grateful. My final thanks are to my parents, John and Benita Cornwall, who provided a model for living. I dedicate the book to them.

JMC
*Dundee*

## Notes

1. Harold D. Lasswell, *Propaganda Technique in World War I* (New York, 1927) p. 12.
2. Hans Thimme, *Weltkrieg ohne Waffen* (Stuttgart and Berlin, 1932); Antoni Szuber, *Walka o Przewagę Duchową. Kampanja Propagandowa Koalicji 1914–1918* (Warsaw, 1933).
3. George Bruntz, *Allied Propaganda and the Collapse of the German Empire in 1918* (Stanford, 1938); Luciano Tosi, *La Propaganda Italiana all'Estero nella Prima Guerra Mondiale. Rivendicazioni Territoriali e Politica delle Nazionalità* (Udine, 1977); Michael Sanders and Philip Taylor, *British Propaganda during the First World War 1914–1918* (London, 1982).

# List of Abbreviations

*[For archive abbreviations see bibliography.]*

| | |
|---|---|
| AK | Armeekommando |
| AOK | Armeeoberkommando (Austro-Hungarian High Command) |
| BH | Bosnia-Hercegovinan |
| CIGS | Chief of Imperial General Staff |
| CPI | Committee on Public Information |
| CS | Comando Supremo (Italian High Command) |
| d. | despatch |
| DMI | Director of Military Intelligence |
| DOHL | German High Command |
| EPD | Enemy Propaganda Department (Crewe House) |
| FAR | Field artillery regiment |
| FAst | Feindespropaganda-Abwehrstelle (Enemy Propaganda Defence Agency) |
| FJB | Feldjägerbataillon |
| FM | Feldmarschall |
| FML | Feldmarschalleutnant |
| GM | Generalmajor |
| GO | Generaloberst |
| Gstbs Abt | Generalstabs Abteilung |
| HFB | Hadifelügyeleti Bizottság (War Surveillance Commission, Budapest) |
| HGK | Heeresgruppekommando |
| HID | Honvéd infantry division |
| HIR | Honvéd infantry regiment |
| HM | Honvéd Ministry |
| Hptm | Hauptmann (Captain) |
| ID | Infantry division |
| IR | Infantry regiment |
| KA | Kriegsarchiv |
| KD | Cavalry division |
| KISA | Isonzo army command |
| KK | Corps command |
| KPQ | Kriegspressequartier (War Press Office) |
| k.u.k. | kaiserlich und könglich |
| KÜA | Kriegsüberwachungsamt (War Surveillance Office, Vienna) |
| Lt | Leutnant / lieutenant |
| MilKmdo | Military command |

| | |
|---|---|
| MK/KM | Militärkanzlei im Kriegsministerium |
| MKSM | Militärkanzlei Seiner Majestät |
| Na. Abt | Nachrichten Abteilung |
| Obst | Oberst (Colonel) |
| Op.Abt | Operations Abteilung |
| OULK | Austrian Official History of the War |
| Pr. | Propaganda |
| pte | private |
| Qu.Abt | Quartier Abteilung |
| SchD | Schützendivision |
| SchR | Schützenregiment |
| t. | telegram |

# 1
# A Theory of Front Propaganda

During the four years of the First World War, both sides gradually introduced an armoury of weapons which had never been seen or even imagined in previous conflicts. Warfare, as one Intelligence officer observed with admiration in 1918, was constantly taking new forms of which neither civilians nor soldiers, nor even generals, were fully aware.[1] Most of the professional military had begun in 1914 with long-held preconceptions about the way that their war would develop. It would be short and sharp as in 1870 and include a major role for the cavalry. Four years later, it was clear that the type of warfare previously conducted had been dramatically re-shaped by the technological developments of the previous half-century, by the need to mobilize all corners of society for an idealistic struggle to the end, and by the lessons steadily learnt on the battlefield about how different techniques or types of weapon could mesh together. Aeroplanes, first used during Italy's war against Turkey in 1911–12, became a regular sight over the trenches; their reconnaissance activity was woven into the fabric of each belligerent's Intelligence network, even if parachutes were still in their infancy and flying was still something to be marvelled at as a dangerous business. The coordination of war from the air with war on the ground was matched by a gradual harmonization of other new types of weaponry with the traditional 'material' of warfare, the infantry: of machine guns; of artillery, which replaced the horse; of chemical weapons; and of front propaganda or psychological warfare.

In many ways, front propaganda was no different from other weapons in the armoury. Through gradual use, it too would secure its own niche and be coordinated with the range of weaponry already available. And like the other types of new weaponry, the sophisticated campaigns of front propaganda which emerged in 1917 were only possible because of the nature of the conflict which had developed: they required as a basic starting-point the technological and educational revolution which had occurred in European society in the decades before the war. Propaganda, however, also differed from other kinds of weaponry in its scope. It employed a whole range of techniques and media for its transmission to the enemy, including the mass distribution of manifestos from the air, 'oral propaganda' in the front line, or a methodology which often overlapped with espionage activities in order to smuggle material into the enemy camp. Its full evolution in the second half of the war reflected in itself a new stage in the Great War, a new type of mobilization by all of the belligerents in an effort to try to win the battle of ideas or human minds which the conflict had increasingly become.

The concept of trying in wartime to persuade the enemy to adopt a particular mindset, or act in a particular way, was not a new one in the early twentieth century. It was as old as the instances of recorded warfare. Herodotus tells how in 480 BC, on the eve of the naval battle of Salamis, the Athenian commander Themistocles tried with some success to get Ionians in the opposing Persian forces to desert by cutting messages into rocks on the seashore.[2] Over 2000 years later during the American wars of independence, American forces tried to secure the surrender of Quebec by shooting into the fortress appeals tied to Indian arrows. By the late twentieth century this front propaganda was continuing. In the Gulf War of 1991, the Allied coalition distributed 30 million leaflets over Iraqi lines.[3] In the Kosovo war of 1999, NATO planes threw out manifestos, urging Serbian soldiers to desert and Belgrade citizens to turn against the regime of Slobodan Milošević.[4] If the propaganda arguments have remained fairly consistent, the techniques employed have grown more sophisticated. In the First World War, it was a considerable feat for Italian aircraft to fly as far as Vienna and distribute manifestos; by the Second World War, British planes were able to fly much further and perform the same task over Nazi-occupied Prague. Over six months in 1918, Italian propagandists on the Italian Front spread 70 million leaflets among the enemy; over six months in 1941, Hitler's war machine would distribute 400 million leaflets on the Eastern Front.[5] Radio broadcasts became a new feature of such campaigns during the ideological struggle with Nazism, and continue to the present day.[6] Yet if later twentieth-century conflicts honed and expanded the use of the propaganda weapon, the conflict of 1914–1918 was a crucial stage in its evolution. It was then that propaganda became systematic, practised and perfected according to what might be termed 'scientific' principles.

Here, at the outset, it is vital to be precise about the type of propaganda which we are going to discuss. 'Propaganda' in its broadest definition might be described as the 'spreading of subversive, debatable or merely novel attitudes', with the objective of persuasion.[7] It can be transmitted through official or unofficial bodies, the work of state organizations or of private individuals. In recent years, the latter 'informal' dimension has increasingly been explored by cultural historians seeking to interpret propaganda in its widest sense as any form of persuasion upon the wartime populace.[8] State-sponsored propaganda was therefore only one element in this mass of competing mental phenomena. Yet it usually secured more resources (and sometimes attention) through its firm association with the political and military hierarchy which was running the war; and its very formality and institutionalization also makes it fairly easy to define and distinguish from other forms of propaganda. In addition, it is worth emphasizing that, as far as wartime Austria-Hungary is concerned, the phenomenon and impact of state propaganda has received little attention from historians. Official propaganda could variously be described as persuasion or mobilization of the population at home, the spread of ideas among neutrals or allies, or the campaigns launched to attack or defend against the enemy. Some historians, Michael Sanders and Philip Taylor for example, have duly tried to encompass all state propaganda in a single analysis.[9] For while it can justifiably be argued that many of those who worked with wartime propaganda envisaged precisely this broad definition of the term, it is equally apparent that different types of propaganda engaged in by a state may be, and often are, interwoven with one another. Thus, to pre-empt what will be discussed later, although the Habsburg Empire initially launched propaganda offensives against its enemies, the enemies responded in kind and the Imperial authorities discovered too late that their own domestic propaganda was inadequate. Any serious study of a wartime propaganda campaign becomes of necessity a study not simply of the nature of its ideas, but also of how they might be circulated, their potential impact among the targeted audience, and their actual impact and results. In other words, in the manner of recent cultural historians, the scope could be widened to include any ideas of any kind which had the potential to uplift or depress the morale of a targeted audience: a very wide scope indeed.

While remaining mindful of this broad definition of propaganda, we will nevertheless do well to heed the advice of those like Ute Daniel who have stressed that any analysis of propaganda has to have fairly precise parameters if it is to be meaningful or manageable.[10] The current study is focused upon 'front propaganda'. Such a term was often employed in the German and Austro-Hungarian armies during the war with a specific definition, meaning the use of propaganda as a military weapon, exercised across the front lines into enemy territory.[11] This usually involved the reciprocal spread of information by the belligerents across the trenches in a written or oral form, but could also be extended to cover literature which was smuggled into an enemy country through other routes, such as the neutral state of Switzerland. The definition therefore is of propaganda against the enemy by *direct* methods and exercised usually as part of a military campaign. It does not include propaganda which might be hostile to the enemy but reached the enemy camp only *indirectly*. Examples of the latter would be those public statements made against the Habsburg Empire by the Western Allies during the war, or news of German atrocities which the West circulated in neutral lands. Both types of information might well eventually reach the Central Powers (Germany and Austria-Hungary) and have some demoralizing impact, but they were part of psychological warfare only in its broadest sense rather than in the shape of 'front propaganda'. As such, they are only mentioned in the current study when they form part of a specifically military campaign of ideas, for it is usually possible to separate the latter and to write about the propaganda campaigns in a concrete and defined sense. Indeed, if this is not done, there is the danger that 'propaganda' will be discussed in the same way as it was by many of the Austro-Hungarian or German elites during and after the war, as a vague term to embrace or excuse all evils, something which was easily exaggerated because it was rarely defined. It is necessary therefore to be clear about the actual machinery of the propaganda campaigns and their potential effectiveness, while at the same time indicating how their influence was often exaggerated and blown into a myth by both sides by the end of the war.

Front propaganda was a feature of the war soon after it started. It is well known that on the Western Front the Germans had begun to drop leaflets over Allied troops by September 1914, and proceeded to produce and distribute the *Gazette des Ardennes* for French soldiers.[12] Less well known is the similar initiative taken by the Russian army on the Eastern Front, which, even if it was more sporadic with less of an immediate follow-up, belies the notion that the Germans were a lone wielder of the weapon in these early months.[13] The idea that the morale of the enemy might be subverted with the written word stemmed rather naturally from the fact that the mass armies at war were more educated than in the past, and that the regimes, in mobilizing their own populations for war, were more conscious of enemy opinions which might also be influenced or discredited. A particular precondition for such an attack with ideas was the level of censorship of news which engulfed all the belligerent states from August 1914. Both sides correctly assumed that the enemy, particularly in the war zone, was trying to keep its troops in quarantine from any ideas harmful to their morale, and this formed an essential basis for all propaganda efforts. At its most mundane, the opposing troops would be told about items of news which their superiors were trying to conceal from them, such as details of a recent enemy exploit or the 'reality' of how well prisoners were treated in the enemy camp. But it was after 1916 that propaganda arguments could become more sophisticated. It was then, with President Woodrow Wilson's appeal to the belligerents in January 1917, that both sides were forced to publicly announce their war aims. This greater 'openness' undoubtedly gave an impetus to the shaping of front propaganda material, even if it also formed a serious area of friction between allies (on either side) if they tried to coordinate their propaganda guidelines too precisely. The first allies to take advantage of the medium were the Central Powers on the Eastern Front. In early 1917, with revolution in the Russian interior and its echoes at the front, they saw for the first time an opportunity in the enemy ranks to stimulate the idea of peace in a coordinated fashion.

A further ingredient which made front propaganda possible was the character of the war which had developed. 'Front propaganda was a child of trench warfare', or at least of the enduring stationary fronts which had quickly emerged in west and east.[14] Since armies were having prolonged contact with the enemy forces, it became more likely that attempts would be made to influence their morale, and more possible to do so than during a fast or moveable campaign. This was undoubtedly one of the reasons why propaganda in the first half of the war was more noticeable on the Western Front, where the belligerents were concentrated for years on the same terrain; a similar trend can be observed on the largely stationary Italian Front from 1915. In contrast, on the Eastern Front, although some material was always distributed by both sides, and regular fraternization occurred at religious festivals (especially Easter), the vast expanse of terrain which was contested and the mobile nature of the war were factors which did much to limit front propaganda until the Central Powers' campaign of 1917. In many ways, therefore, front propaganda emerged naturally from the character of hostilities, assuming a 'mature' form in the East only after March 1917 when sustained fraternization seemed possible and war aims were more developed.

Similarly, it was logical that it was the Intelligence officers of the various armies who were usually the real pioneers in this activity. As the 'eyes' of the army, required to find out as much as possible about the enemy, the Intelligence services became in the course of the war more and more sensitive to the character of the opposing forces and the potential which was there to be demoralized. It was Intelligence officers, for example, who were most closely involved with interrogating prisoners or deserters, thereby sensing the type of information which could usefully be sent over to the enemy in order to encourage further unrest or desertion. Since their primary task was to deal with information, the Intelligence services were at the forefront of those who saw the potential for its dissemination as well, and it seems clear that their perceptions did much to shape the development of propaganda on each of the military fronts. As we will see, Italian Intelligence officers significantly paved the way for a sophisticated propaganda campaign against the Habsburg Empire, and continued to contribute to such activity until the very end. Similarly, British efforts on the Western Front were, until the last months of the war, in the hands of a special section of the War Office under the Director of Special Intelligence, General George Cockerill.[15]

An added dimension to such propaganda – the material smuggled in via neutral states – was also, for both belligerent sides, largely organized by their Intelligence services. Their agents, notably in Switzerland or Holland, often had a dual Intelligence and propaganda role.[16] This was again primarily under military supervision, like the front propaganda specifically carried out in the military theatres. In the latter case, however, it is true that by 1918 for the Allied countries (Britain, France, Italy), journalists or other civilians were being allowed to play a larger role in front propaganda, lending an extra political colour to what had previously been a largely military activity. This in itself was highly significant. It showed the degree of political–military rapprochement, part of a 'secondary state mobilization', which was taking place in the Allied countries from 1917. In contrast, the propaganda of the Central Powers, which had always been exercised by military Intelligence at the front, continued to remain in the same hands, with no civilian or journalistic participation permitted. For Austria-Hungary and Germany, front propaganda would always be a strictly military activity, something which reflected the more delimited military spheres of influence which persisted throughout the war in these empires. This gave the western Allies' front propaganda a certain advantage by 1918, for their campaigns were beginning to rely on a slightly wider range of people to formulate their propaganda material and participate in the organization.

Despite this distinction, we should not exaggerate the primacy of the western Allies in wielding the weapon of front propaganda. What follows will reveal the degree to which the Central Powers played a major role in developing this weapon, and ran at least two crucial propaganda campaigns of the war: on the Eastern and Italian Fronts. For various reasons, neither of these campaigns receive much mention in literature about front propaganda, or propaganda in general, even in the histories published in central Europe. It will be shown that this has caused a significant distortion in the historiography. Until now the standard or accepted version of events has been to place the British firmly at the forefront of any analysis, as pioneers in all aspects of wartime propaganda; in front propaganda too, according to one authority, 'the leading practitioners were the British'.[17] It was they, as 'born propagandists', who were most methodical and active with propaganda in the early years on the Western Front. And from February 1918, when Lord Northcliffe was appointed by Lloyd George as director of a Department of Propaganda in Enemy Countries, the British organization became a notorious model of what could be achieved in attacking the morale of the enemy. Northcliffe's department, based at Crewe House in London, was reputedly responsible in 1918 for organizing and achieving major successes in propaganda campaigns directed against both Austria-Hungary and Germany. According to its own spokesman, 'Crewe House had every reason to be proud of the successes of its work against Austria-Hungary . . . The result was the greatest victory achieved by war propaganda.'[18]

Crewe House's famous role was first questioned in 1944 in the memoirs of General Cockerill, who wrote that it was he who had directed propaganda against Germany for most of the war. In 1979, Michael Balfour proposed that Crewe House needed to be 'demythologized', since its contribution to the collapse of Germany had been vastly exaggerated.[19] When a few years later Sanders and Taylor wrote their influential study of British propaganda, they duly accepted that some adjustment was needed where Germany was concerned, but they continued to suggest that Crewe House could take the credit for leading a successful campaign against the Habsburg Empire.[20] In doing so, they retained a certain amount of the myth about Crewe House which, as we will see, needs to be further deconstructed. They also, by presenting a wholly British perspective of propaganda, contributed themselves to reinforcing the previous historiography which had always overemphasized Britain's primacy. While it might be accepted that British propaganda at home and in neutral countries such as the United States was quite innovative and influential (although this too has recently been queried),[21] in the field of front propaganda the British were no more pioneers than their allies or adversaries. The rest of this book will demonstrate this thesis by presenting an alternative perspective which draws in many of the other belligerent states.

The myth of British primacy in front propaganda, which was fostered after the First World War, owed much to the fact that the British publicized their side of the story while others had their own reasons for remaining silent. Admittedly one of the biggest publicity coups in this regard occurred during the war itself with the public announcement in 1918 of Northcliffe's appointment. Rather than being 'bad tactics', as Harold Lasswell once suggested,[22] the announcement in itself had a demoralizing effect and did more than anything in German and Austro-Hungarian ruling circles to feed their paranoia about 'ubiquitous enemy propaganda'. Their reaction also indicates that Britain's reputation abroad, as a manipulator of public opinion through the press or other channels, was indeed already firmly established. When Austrian MPs first complained about Northcliffe's appointment a week after it happened, they noted how England, from the start of the war, had been influencing world opinion 'with unsurpassed virtuosity and the most unscrupulous methods'.[23] Thus the name of Northcliffe, as a notorious newspaper-tycoon, dramatically focused European attention upon Britain's special role in the use of enemy propaganda. While Northcliffe would personify enemy propaganda to the Central Powers in the last months of the war, the supposed importance of his organization at Crewe House was fully detailed in its immediate aftermath. His deputy Campbell Stuart used a number of official reports in order to write *Secrets of Crewe House: The Story of a Famous Campaign* (which ran into three editions in 1920); at the same time, *The Times History of the War* contained a sizeable chapter on 'British Propaganda in Enemy Countries', claiming that Northcliffe's department had achieved 'devastating results'. Four years later, Northcliffe's faithful lieutenant Henry Wickham Steed published his memoirs, *Through Thirty Years*, which reinforced Crewe House's image as the leading wartime propaganda centre.[24] These three works gained a wide publicity in central Europe, where Steed's memoirs were translated into German, Czech and other languages.

For many German writers in particular, these accounts confirmed an increasing myth that the Central Powers, in losing the war, had been subverted by unchivalrous or underhand methods rather than defeated on the battlefield. The views of Erich Ludendorff and Adolf Hitler were undoubtedly the most influential in this regard. Writing immediately after the war, Ludendorff noted how he had regularly complained in the latter half of the war about Germany's total failure to shape morale or public opinion when compared to the operation of the enemy; Germany had been 'hypnotized by enemy propaganda as a rabbit is by a snake. It was exceptionally clever and conceived on a great scale.' In *Mein Kampf*, Hitler mirrored Ludendorff's views, but perhaps also relied on his own memories of psychological warfare on the Western Front when he wrote that enemy propaganda was 'a real work of genius' in response to which 'there was no counter-propaganda'.[25] But this exaggerated perception was not confined to Germany. It found an exact parallel in the postwar memoirs of the former elite of Austria-Hungary. Enemy or Entente propaganda was mentioned as a particular evil which had conspired with domestic influences to stab the armies of the Central Powers in the back; Northcliffe's organization was usually cited as the leading exponent. Thus, one former Habsburg officer observed that 'Northcliffe's apparatus' had shaken the foundations of the Central Powers in a way impossible with conventional military forces: the Entente had cleverly chosen their moment for launching a psychological offensive.[26] The former Austro-Hungarian Chief of Staff, Franz Conrad von Hötzendorf, concurred but wrote more bitterly. In private notes which were posthumously published, he castigated 'the Jew Northcliffe' for exercising shameless propaganda:

> While we conducted the war according to traditional practices, our enemy did so with all the tricks of modern skulduggery [*Gaunertum*] . . . In a vulgar fashion, the Entente states soiled the chivalrous clothing of their soldiers with the dirty filth of a base and despicable propaganda, which reckoned on the grossest stupidity and depravity of the masses.[27]

While Conrad had nothing but contempt for propaganda, though admitting that Northcliffe had skilfully judged the masses' gullibility, other writers in postwar Austria had a grudging admiration for the performance of 'enemy propaganda'. In their accounts, whether in memoirs or in syntheses about the collapse of Austria-Hungary, they tended to incorporate what was known from the British side as well as occasionally adding knowledge from more personal sources of their own. The phrase 'enemy propaganda' was often used rather vaguely, as in the work of Arz von Straussenburg (Conrad's successor) who wrote of how 'a large-scale enemy propaganda [had] prepared and advanced disintegration in the Empire and at the front'.[28] When front propaganda was mentioned more precisely, as in Edmund von Glaise-Horstenau's important synthesis *Die Katastrophe*, or in the Austrian official history (in a section also written by Glaise), it was usually in the context of an effective campaign organized from Crewe House.[29] The accounts of Stuart, Steed and some others[30] remained therefore prime sources for historical syntheses of the interwar period. In Hungary, for example, they assumed a prominent place when Jenő Pilch discussed propaganda in his three-volume history of wartime Intelligence and espionage.[31] Only rarely did front propaganda as wielded by the Central Powers receive much attention, most notably in the memoirs of Max Ronge, the wartime head of Austrian military Intelligence. His work was rare in dealing at some length with front propaganda against Russia in 1917. But his version of how enemy propaganda was organized still underlined the British dimension, relying on British accounts as well as some exaggerated reports and rumours which had reached him as head of Intelligence.[32]

A different, more accurate or balanced, interpretation of how front propaganda had developed did not emerge for a number of reasons. Firstly, although various memoirs were written in the interwar period which could shed more light on the diverse character of front propaganda, it was always not surprisingly those in the English, French and German languages which gained the widest publicity; these tended to reinforce the myth of western (and especially Anglo-French) primacy. Antoni Szuber's book of 1933 shifted the focus to the Italian Front, but still concentrated on Entente propaganda. And his assessment in Polish was not accessible to most historians anyway; indeed, he was explicitly writing for a Polish audience which he felt to be ignorant of wartime propaganda.[33] Other colourful memoirs, in Slovene by Ljudevit Pivko or in Czech by Vojtěch Hanzal and František Hlaváček, for instance, all of which leant a vital new dimension to the story of propaganda against the Habsburg Empire, were only published in Yugoslavia or Czechoslovakia. Therefore (like Szuber) they fell victim to the new diversity of inter-war Eastern Europe.[34] For the Czechs in particular, and for Slovenes and Serbs in the new Yugoslavia to a lesser degree, their recent exploits in front propaganda against Austria-Hungary were a significant element in their wartime experience. Front propaganda was not a shameful activity to be forgotten about, but something to be celebrated, an integral part of the heroic struggle which had ended in the creation of the Czechoslovak and Yugoslav states. In the 1920s and 1930s the collections of memoirs which emerged in these states reflected this. They showed the influence of war veterans at all levels of society and their desire to remember what had happened. At the same time they were one way in which the new regimes fostered an immediate national consciousness or history for their peoples, building where possible upon the myth of a common wartime sacrifice in which the adventures of front propaganda could not be ignored.[35]

It was a different story for those European countries which ended the war in a dissatisfied or dismembered state. Their critical attitude to wartime propaganda, as something either dishonourable or irrelevant, was a second and particularly influential reason for the Anglo-French bias in the historiography. The example of Italy is particularly instructive. Although the Italian Front had witnessed the most sophisticated campaign of front propaganda during the whole war, it received little attention in Italian literature in the interwar period (or indeed thereafter).[36] Mussolini's Fascist state after 1922 promoted the image of an Italy which had sacrificed all to achieve a heroic victory at the battle of Vittorio Veneto in October 1918, only to be prevented from securing its well-earned territorial prizes by the western peacemakers in Paris and by the new Yugoslavia on the other side of the Adriatic Sea. In this atmosphere, most Italian military writers preferred to ignore an episode of the war which exemplified official Italy's short-lived support for the Slavs of Eastern Europe (including, most embarrassingly, the Yugoslavs). To do otherwise might suggest that the Italian war had been won with less than traditional or honourable methods. When one Italian Intelligence officer, Cesare Finzi, published his memoirs around 1930 they were either pulped immediately or remained an exception to the rule, for they opened a vista which did not accord with the official Italian myth.[37] The latter was clear in the official Italian histories as well as in an account of Italy's war, published in English by the Fascist writer Luigi Villari. Villari gave a straight military description of what had occurred, but still felt it necessary to explain in his introduction that the works of Stuart and Steed, in suggesting that front propaganda had had a role to play, were 'frankly comic': they 'need not be taken seriously'.[38]

As we have noted already, a similar sceptical or ethical approach to wartime propaganda was prevalent among military writers in the defeated nations of Germany, Austria and Hungary. The Austrian official history gave only a brief and dismissive mention to Austria-Hungary's propaganda campaign of 1917 against Russia and completely ignored its subsequent campaign against Italy. The lessons which the Austro-Hungarian military had learnt during the war about how to wield the propaganda weapon were not usually transposed into their postwar writings; even Max Ronge, as an exception, still felt bound to call the 'successful' campaign against Russia a 'nauseating' activity.[39] When wartime propaganda in any of its aspects was discussed in Germany, it was almost always viewed as the special preserve of the enemy, and as a way to understand the catastrophe that had engulfed the Central Powers.[40] In this way, the tone which Ludendorff had set early on and which Hitler had made part of his creed, in simultaneously bemoaning and admiring the skills of British propaganda, was consistently taken up by writers in Nazi Germany. The classic example was Hermann Wanderscheck whose work on *The World War and Propaganda* was almost exclusively a study of 'Britain's campaign' against the Central Powers as described by the Entente propagandists themselves. Northcliffe as usual was given the most prominent place in the discussion since, as Wanderscheck concluded, the press-magnate would 'appear in history perhaps as the most fatal figure of the great world catastrophe'.[41] With the outbreak of the Second World War, the demonization of British propaganda could assume even larger proportions: as an organization which under Northcliffe had directly destroyed the old German Empire and was continuing deviously to spin its web around the whole world.[42]

Despite this trend, which was matched on the British side as well,[43] some works had appeared by this time which attempted a more serious study of propaganda as practised on the Western Front. Both Hans Thimme and the American scholar George Bruntz revealed how from 1915 there had been consistent Entente attempts to undermine the morale of the German armies by distributing propaganda leaflets.[44] Besides the British effort, supervised by Cockerill from March 1915, the French had been particularly active, setting up in August their own Service de la Propagande Aérienne under the control of military Intelligence at the War Ministry. From January 1916, when the French established an overall propaganda agency, the Maison de la Presse, this Service had a closer political liaison but was otherwise a largely military concern until Clemenceau reorganized the French propaganda machinery in 1918. What these analyses showed was that a propaganda war of sorts had been waged on the Western Front from 1915. Yet it was also clear that it had not developed into a fully systematic campaign until the final year of the war (when, for example, the British launched their *Air Post* series of 94 numbered manifestos). Until then, even if Anglo-French propaganda was often more active or imaginative than the front propaganda in other theatres, it may still be described as rather unprofessional and sporadic, without any clear political guidelines or consistent aims.

While Thimme and Bruntz in the 1930s uncovered the machinery of front propaganda in the West, no similar analysis has been attempted of the (arguably) even more significant propaganda campaigns which were carried out on the Eastern and Italian Fronts. A brief summary shows that in 1917 it was the Central Powers who were the first of the belligerents to launch a coordinated campaign of front propaganda: this was against the Russian army. On the basis of this experience in the East, Austria-Hungary turned to wield the same weapon against Italy. And partly as a result of this onslaught, the Italians perfected their own particularly sophisticated campaign to undermine the morale of the Austro-Hungarian troops. The Habsburg Empire therefore was central to three of the major campaigns of front propaganda, experiencing the weapon both as practitioner and victim. Most modern histories of Austria-Hungary in the First World War have duly made mention of part of this experience, even if the tendency has often been to revive the myth of Crewe House's role.[45] Most significantly, Leo Valiani and Luciano Tosi have usefully weakened an overly-British perspective by emphasizing the central Italian dimension to the 'Allied' propaganda campaign against the Empire.[46] Others, such as Manfried Rauchensteiner and József Galántai, have referred in passing to the Eastern campaign in their broad discussions of the Monarchy at war.[47]

By reassessing these perceptions and by bringing much new archival evidence to bear, we can explore and examine for the first time the phenomenon of front propaganda as it was exercised on the Italian and Eastern Fronts. The Italian Front is accorded most attention, as the scene of the most sophisticated 'propaganda duel' of its kind. Through this prism it is also possible to make new judgements about military and civilian morale in Austria-Hungary and the viability of the Empire in its final years. We may be unlikely to share the view of one propaganda enthusiast that enemy propaganda 'played an essential part in bringing about the collapse of Austria-Hungary'.[48] To suggest that propaganda in wartime could have such a grandiose role is undoubtedly misleading. But it will be possible to show that the ideas scattered in front propaganda, whether on the Eastern or Italian Fronts, could indeed act as a catalyst upon existing moods or trends in the war zones and hinterlands. Perhaps more importantly, a close analysis of front propaganda is valuable in its own right because of what it can tell us about the mentality of those who practised it and of those who were the recipients. Besides the many in the Austro-Hungarian Monarchy who scorned or belittled the weapon, there were an increasing number of people who admired or feared or exaggerated its influence: they came to view propaganda as an integral part of the new warfare to which the Habsburg Empire was exposed.

## Notes

1. Ljudevit Pivko, *Informatorji* (Maribor, 1925) p. 38.
2. Herodotus, *The Histories*, translated by Aubrey de Sélincourt (Penguin, 1972) pp. 531–2, 551.
3. Philip M. Taylor, *War and the Media: Propaganda and Persuasion in the Gulf War* (Manchester, 1992) p. 154.
4. *The Guardian*, 17 April 1999, p. 3; 21 May, p. 3; *The Observer*, 2 May 1999, p. 20: 'Hundreds of thousands flee to avoid the pogrom of Milošević. Do not allow your misguided patriotism to be used.' Before the war, the Serbians too had adopted this technique, their helicopters showering leaflets over Albanian refugees which promised them an amnesty if they surrendered their weapons (see *The Guardian*, 7 October 1998, p. 16).
5. Z.A.B. Zeman, *Nazi Propaganda*, 2nd edn (London, Oxford and New York, 1973) p. 160.
6. See, for example, Taylor, *War and the Media*, pp. 151ff for radio propaganda during the Gulf War.

7. Harold D. Lasswell, 'Propaganda', in *Propaganda*, ed. Robert Jackall (New York, 1995) p. 13.
8. See most recently, Aviel Roshwald and Richard Stites (eds), *European Culture in the Great War: The Arts, Entertainment and Propaganda, 1914–1918* (Cambridge, 1999).
9. M.S. Sanders and P.M. Taylor, *British Propaganda in the First World War 1914–1918* (London, 1982). Taylor has since tried to take this even further in his *Munitions of the Mind: A History of Propaganda from the Ancient World to the Present Day*, 2nd edn (Manchester, 1995).
10. Ute Daniel and Wolfram Siemann (eds), *Propaganda. Meinungskampf, Verführung und politische Sinnstiftung 1789–1989* (Frankfurt am Main, 1994) pp. 10, 44.
11. For example, A. von Cramon, *Unser österreich-ungarischer Bundesgenosse im Weltkriege* (Berlin, 1920) p. 135; Edmund von Glaise-Horstenau, *Ein General im Zwielicht*, ed. Peter Broucek, 3 vols (Vienna, 1980–8) I, p. 425.
12. Sanders and Taylor, *British Propaganda*, p. 211.
13. See below Chapter 3, p. 41.
14. Friedrich Felger, 'Frontpropaganda bei Feind und Freund', in *Was wir von Weltkrieg nicht wissen*, ed. Friedrich Felger (Berlin, 1929) p. 498.
15. George Cockerill, *What Fools We Were* (London, 1944) pp. 60ff.
16. See, for example, Wilhelm Ernst, *Die antideutsche Propaganda durch das Schweizer Gebiet im Weltkrieg speziell die Propaganda in Bayern* (Munich, 1933); Peter Schubert, *Die Tätigkeit des k.u.k. Militärattachés in Bern während des Ersten Weltkrieges* (Osnabruck, 1980).
17. Taylor, *Munitions of the Mind*, p. 187. This emphasis continues to be repeated: see Niall Ferguson, *The Pity of War* (London, 1998) p. 225; Roshwald and Stites (eds), *European Culture in the Great War*, p. 350.
18. Campbell Stuart, *Secrets of Crewe House: The Story of a Famous Campaign* (London, 1920) pp. 48–9.
19. Cockerill, *What Fools We Were*, p. 62; Michael Balfour, *Propaganda in War 1939–1945: Organizations, Policies and Publics in Britain and Germany* (London, 1979).
20. Sanders and Taylor, *British Propaganda*, pp. ix, 222ff, 251, 255. The point is repeated in Gary S. Messinger, *British Propaganda and the State in the First World War* (Manchester and New York, 1992), p. 6; and Philip M. Taylor, *British Propaganda in the Twentieth Century: Selling Democracy* (Edinburgh, 1999) pp. 56–8.
21. See the useful discussion in Trevor Wilson, *The Myriad Faces of War: Britain and the Great War, 1914–1918* (Cambridge, 1986), pp. 743–7; Gerald DeGroot, *Blighty: British Society in the Era of the Great War* (London and New York, 1996) p. 180.
22. Harold Lasswell, *Propaganda Technique in World War I* (New York, 1927) p. 15.
23. See Erich Ludendorff (ed.), *Urkunden der Obersten Heeresleitung über ihre Tätigkeit 1916–18* (Berlin, 1922) pp. 284–5.
24. Campbell Stuart, *Secrets of Crewe House: The Story of a Famous Campaign* (London, 1920); *The Times History of the War*, vol. XXI (London, 1920) pp. 325–60; Henry Wickham Steed, *Through Thirty Years 1892–1922: A Personal Narrative*, 2 vols (London, 1924).
25. General Ludendorff, *My War Memories 1914–1918*, 2 vols (London, 1919) I, pp. 361–83; Ludendorff (ed.), *Urkunden der Obersten Heeresleitung*, pp. 280ff; Adolf Hitler, *Mein Kampf*, tr. James Murphy (London, 1939) pp. 156, 164.
26. General Emil Woinovich, 'Feindespropaganda', *Österreichische Wehrzeitung*, 10 June 1921, p. 4. (Woinovich was a former director of the War Archives.) For a less official view of events which assumes that 'Northcliffe propaganda' was effective, see A. Zell, *Warum haben wir den Weltkrieg verloren?* (Klagenfurt, n.d.) p. 80.

27. Conrad von Hötzendorf, *Private Aufzeichnungen. Erste Veröffentlichungen aus den Papieren des k.u.k. Generalstabs-Chefs*, ed. Kurt Peball (Vienna and Munich, 1977) p. 111.
28. Arthur Arz von Straussenburg, *Zur Geschichte des Grossen Krieges 1914–1918* (Vienna, 1924) p. 132. See also, for instance, Count Burián, the wartime foreign minister, whose memoirs mentioned the 'systematic efforts of foreign propaganda': Stephen Burián von Rajecz, *Austria in Dissolution* (London, 1925) pp. 149, 318, 410. And Joseph Redlich's works: *Österreichische Regierung und Verwaltung im Weltkriege* (Vienna, 1925), p. 143; *Emperor Francis Joseph of Austria: a Biography* (New York, 1929) p. 530.
29. Edmund von Glaise-Horstenau, *The Collapse of the Austro-Hungarian Empire* (London and Toronto, 1930) pp. 117ff; Edmund Glaise-Horstenau and Rudolf Kiszling (eds), *Österreich-Ungarns Letzter Krieg 1914–1918*, 7 vols (Vienna, 1930–8) [hereafter OULK], vol. 7: *Das Kriegsjahr 1918*, pp. 18–19.
30. An addition was Hamilton Fyfe, *Northcliffe* (London, 1930).
31. Jenő Pilch, *A hírszerzés és kémkedés története*, 3 vols (Budapest, 1937) III, pp. 139–236: this long chapter is a very able synthesis but the emphasis is almost wholly on the propaganda of the western Allies.
32. Max Ronge, *Kriegs- und Industriespionage. Zwölf Jahre Kundschaftsdienst* (Zurich Leipzig and Vienna, 1930) pp. 268ff, 298ff, 323ff and 340–2 for the organization of enemy propaganda.
33. Antoni Szuber, *Walka o Przewagę Duchową. Kampanja Propagandowa Koaliciji 1914–1918* (Warsaw, 1933) p. ix.
34. Ljudevit Pivko, *Carzano*, 4 vols (Maribor, 1924); Pivko, *Rame ob Ramenu*, 4 vols (Maribor, 1925–8); Vojtěch Hanzal, *Výzvědčíci v Italii a na Slovenskem* (Prague, 1928); Hanzal, *S Výzvědčíky od Švýcarských Ledovců až po Moře Adriatické* (Prague, 1938); František Hlaváček, 'Činnost dra Ed. Beneše za Války v Italii a moje Spolupráce s ním', *Naše Revoluce* XII (Prague, 1936).
35. See, for instance, František Bednařik, *V Boj! Obrázkora Kronika Československého Revolučního Hnutí v Italii 1915–1918* (Prague, 1927); Adolf Zeman (ed.), *Cestami Odboje (Jak žily a kudy táhly Čs. Legie)*, 5 vols (Prague, 1927); Ernst Turk, Josip Jeras and Rajko Paulin (eds), *Dobrovoljci Kladivarji Jugoslavije 1912–1918* (Ljubljana, 1936). The shaping of a national myth was especially strong in Czechoslovakia where a large number of wartime activists (politicians, journalists, and others) published their memoirs alongside the accounts of Czechoslovak legionaries who had fought on the Eastern and Italian Fronts.
36. A point made by Szuber who noted that the Italians had allowed Northcliffe to take the credit: *Walka o Przewagę Duchową*, p. 104.
37. C.P.L. Finzi, *Il Sogno di Carzano* (Bologna, 1926): this work was suppressed; Cesare Pettorelli Lalatta [Finzi], *'I.T.O.' Note di un Capo del Servizio Informazioni d'Armata, 1915–1918* (Milan, 1931; 2nd edn: Milan, 1934).
38. Luigi Villari, *The War on the Italian Front* (London, 1932) p. 3.
39. OULK, VII, pp. 219–21; Ronge, *Kriegs- und Industriespionage*, p. 323.
40. Friedrich Felger was a rare voice on the German side in trying to assess the front propaganda of all the belligerents: 'Frontpropaganda bei Feind und Freund', in *Was wir von Weltkrieg nicht wissen*, ed. Felger (Berlin, 1929) pp. 498–516. Although he still ascribed particular skill to the British (that Northcliffe was head of propaganda on all Entente fronts) and belittled Italy's role, he gave some attention to Germany's work, suggesting that much of it was 'excellent' (p. 512).

41. Hermann Wanderscheck, *Weltkrieg und Propaganda*, 2nd edn (Berlin, 1939), (here p. 237). See also Ludolf Gottschalk von dem Knesebeck, *Die Wahrheit über den Propagandafeldzug und Deutschlands Zusammenbruch* (Munich, 1927).
42. See Gerhard Krause, *Die britische Auslandspropaganda. Organisation, Methoden, Inhalt 1914–1940* (Berlin, 1940) pp. 4, 7; and Gerhard Baumann, *Grundlagen und Praxis der internationalen Propaganda* (Essen, 1941) pp. 151ff. France's propaganda machinery also came in for scrutiny: Matthias Schwabe, *Die französische Auslandspropaganda. Ihre Grundlagen und Voraussetzungen* (Berlin, 1939).
43. For example, John Hargrave, *Words win Wars: Propaganda the Mightiest Weapon of All* (London, 1940).
44. Hans Thimme, *Weltkrieg ohne Waffen* (Stuttgart and Berlin, 1932); George G. Bruntz, *Allied Propaganda and the Collapse of the German Empire in 1918* (Stanford, 1938; reissued: New York, 1972). Admittedly some earlier memoirs had already described France's front propaganda: see Hansi [Jean Jacques Waltz] and Henri Tonnelat, *À Travers les Lignes Ennemies* (Paris, 1922).
45. For example, Z.A.B. Zeman, *The Break-Up of the Habsburg Empire 1914–1918* (Oxford, 1961) pp. 183ff; A.J. May, *The Passing of the Hapsburg Monarchy 1914–1918*, 2 vols (Philadelphia, 1966) II, pp. 604–11.
46. Leo Valiani, *The End of Austria-Hungary* (London, 1973) pp. 227–46; Luciano Tosi, *La Propaganda Italiana all'Estero nella Prima Guerra Mondiale. Rivendicazioni Territoriali e Politica delle Nazionalità* (Udine, 1977).
47. Manfried Rauchensteiner, *Der Tod des Doppeladlers. Österreich-Ungarn und der Erste Weltkrieg* (Graz, 1993) pp. 440ff; József Galántai, *Hungary in the First World War* (Budapest, 1989) pp. 228–231, 272–3. Cf. the absence of any mention in Holger Herwig, *The First World War: Germany and Austria-Hungary 1914–1918* (London, 1997).
48. The conclusion of Colonel Granville Baker: School of Slavonic and East European Studies, R.W. Seton-Watson MSS [hereafter SWP], Draft 'Report on the work of the Department of Propaganda in Enemy Countries', p. 39. This report was compiled by C.S. Kent, Crewe House's financial officer, and was submitted to the British Cabinet in February 1919 as CAB 24/75, GT 6839. Stuart's *Secrets of Crewe House* was largely a shortened version of Kent's report (cf. Philip Taylor, *British Propaganda*, p. 59).

# 2
# Austria-Hungary and the Control of Wartime Morale

In the days after 28 July 1914, when the Habsburg Empire declared war on Serbia, three million men were called to the colours. They represented 11 different nationalities, with their homes in regions of Austria-Hungary which had witnessed bitter national tensions in the prewar period. Yet, there seemed a good deal of truth in the Hungarian Prime Minister's observation on 4 August that 'the atmosphere prevailing in the whole Monarchy is very good'.[1] Whether in Vienna or Budapest, in Prague or Ljubljana, in Innsbruck or Kraków, the publicized image in the principal cities seemed to be the same, of a spontaneous enthusiasm for war against Russia and Serbia, and of troops marching off to the railway stations bedecked in garlands and surrounded by cheering crowds. In 'loyalist' memoirs written after the war this image was naturally sustained. In Vienna, one *kaisertreu* officer recalled how the mayor, Richard Weiskirchner, had suddenly interrupted a music concert in order to make the announcement of general mobilization; it was greeted with brief silence followed by stormy applause and a burst of the national anthem. In Budapest, another observer recalled how a crowd of 20 000 swept through the streets, waving black and yellow (Habsburg) flags, all inspired by 'love of country, the intoxication of the hour, the flame of national instinct'.[2]

Nor was the mood confined to the 'ruling' capitals of Vienna and Budapest. In Prague, notwithstanding a postwar 'consensus' that Czechs had been overwhelmingly opposed to the war from the start, a certain euphoria was also evident and by no means confined to the city's German population. Franz Kafka for one noted in his diary on 6 August how troops were greeted as they marched along *Na Příkopě*: 'Flowers, shouts of hurrah! and *nazdar!*' Only in his next entry did Kafka observe another side to the spectacle as he looked at the soldiers: 'The rigidly silent, astonished, attentive black faces with black eyes.'[3] In each corner of the Empire, the ceremonial of the march to war was being played out by individuals with mixed emotions of excitement and sorrow. The latter was well captured by the artist Oskar Kokoschka in a letter to his mistress:

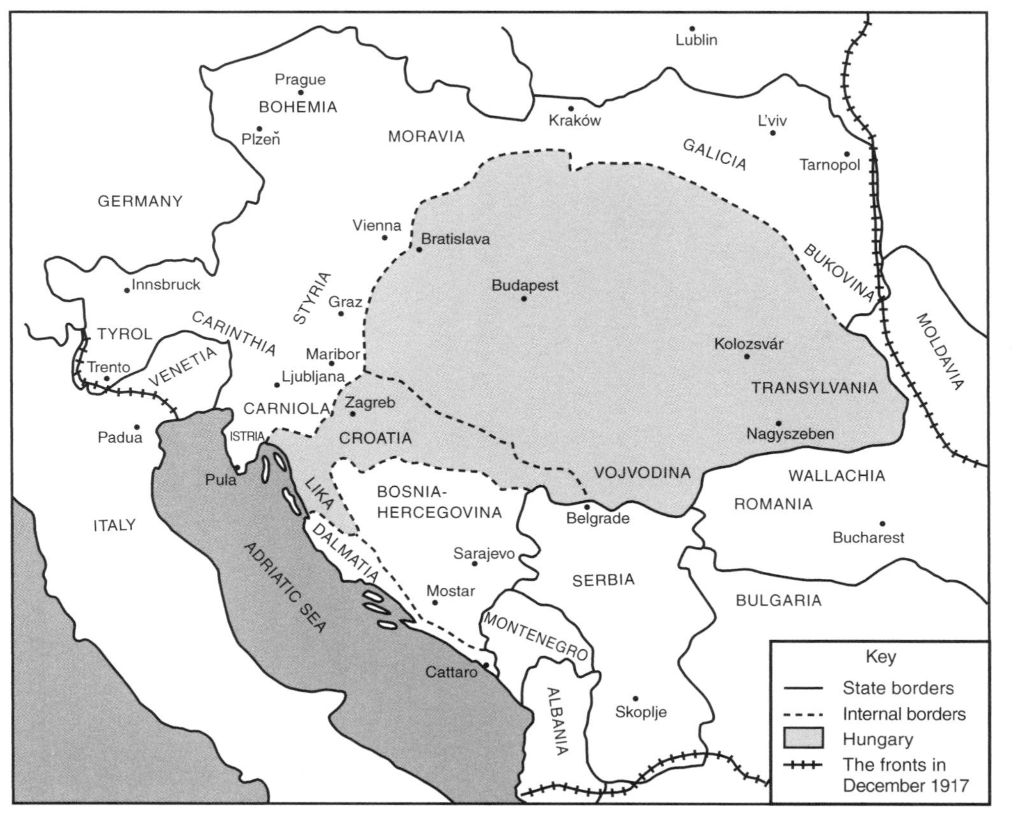


*Map 2.1* Austria-Hungary in the First World War

'Today, in my street [in Vienna], there was a woman who fell on her husband's neck like one demented, because he was having to leave, carrying his few worldly goods in a piece of sacking. Yet the recruits are docile and grateful for a friendly look.'[4]

If the Empire appeared superficially to be united behind a common objective in the summer of 1914, it is an image which needs to be set against the reality of the political and military regimes which were introduced as the war began. These regimes, which had their own distinctive colour in the two halves of the Monarchy (Austria and Hungary), were similar in the way that they immediately adopted a discriminatory policy towards certain nationalities. Such discrimination not only belied the façade of patriotic euphoria, but more importantly, it had a fatal long-term impact: whole sections of the population were treated as 'unreliable' and alienated from the Empire's cause at a very early stage. It would be next to impossible for the authorities to 're-mobilize' these civilians later in the war in a way that was achieved in Britain, France and Italy.

According to legislation which had been prepared in 1912, the political regimes in both Austria and Hungary assumed emergency powers at the start of the war. However, while in Hungary the legislation for the eventuality of war had already been passed by the Budapest Parliament in late 1912, in Austria a wartime regime was imposed in a thoroughly unconstitutional fashion.[5] Since March 1914 the Austrian Parliament or Reichsrat had been adjourned and the Prime Minister, Count Karl Stürgkh, had been ruling by decree (the infamous paragraph 14 of the constitution). On the day of general mobilization, Stürgkh proceeded to pass the whole range of emergency powers by decree, and refused until his death in late 1916 to recall the Reichsrat which constitutionally was supposed to approve any such legislation within a few months. The result was a bureaucratic-military regime in Austria which, until the Reichsrat was reconvened in May 1917, was unaccountable to any forum and could exercise dictatorial powers. Some historians have condoned Stürgkh's decision,[6] on the grounds that he rightly feared that many Reichsrat deputies would not be loyal in a war against Russia. It is also true that many German-Austrian MPs, with an eye to what they themselves might achieve with the goodwill of the Stürgkh regime, were undisturbed by the Reichsrat closure. Nevertheless, the absence of a political forum for non-Germans (since all provincial assemblies were also closed) had fatal consequences when it came to the long-term mobilization of the Austrian population. Perhaps under no other wartime belligerent regime was the abyss between the government and the governed so striking.

Most fatally, the same laws which in Austria gave the political authorities the power arbitrarily to intern dissidents, suspend freedom of speech and association, abolish trial by jury and impose a severe press censorship, also placed substantial power in the hands of the military authorities. The regions of the Empire which in August 1914 became the direct hinterland of the military fronts were designated as 'war zones' where the military authorities had overriding control (although the political regime was not wholly extinguished). At first this meant Bosnia-Hercegovina in the south and Galicia, Bukovina and parts of Moravia in the north-east. But from May 1915, when Italy opened hostilities against the Monarchy, the war zone was extended to cover most crownlands in the south-west of the Empire as well. While this gave branches of the military sweeping powers by mid-1915 over most of Austria, civilians outside the war zone, in Bohemia or 'Austria proper', were also subject to military law for certain types of offence. And military power went further. In late July 1914, with Stürgkh's agreement, the Armeeoberkommando [AOK – Army High Command] was able to create through the package of emergency laws a new body which was to act as a military watch-dog for subversive tendencies, or anything which could be stamped on under the emergency laws as detrimental to the war effort. This Kriegsüberwachungsamt [KÜA – War Surveillance Office] was attached to the War Ministry in Vienna with employees seconded from the various Austrian ministries. It allowed the AOK to interfere directly in what were otherwise non-military spheres of influence in the Austrian hinterland, ordering local military officials to arrest suspect individuals, or the regional censors to suppress 'unpatriotic' news in the press. Because of the secrecy which surrounded its activity, the KÜA's influence has probably been exaggerated, but its very existence was symptomatic of the type of regime which ran Austria for the first three years of the war. It provided the Chief of Staff, Conrad von Hötzendorf, with an extra lever in his struggle to expand the AOK's control in Austria at the expense of Stürgkh's bureaucratic regime. Even if Stürgkh was largely able to counter the AOK's manoeuvres (in Bohemia, for example), the fact remains, as Joseph Redlich observed, that the military dimension to Austria's regime was a logical consequence of Stürgkh's own unconstitutional behaviour.[7] Both would be responsible together for the powerful backlash which would come from the 'oppressed peoples' in the new constitutional circumstances of 1917.

Stürgkh's precept from the beginning was that local authorities should focus everything upon the requirements of the war. When combined with the behaviour of the military leadership in the war zones, this rapidly produced a mood of vigilance bordering on discrimination against certain nationalities of the Empire. Admittedly, in the war zones of Bosnia and Galicia, the military had a difficult path to tread. It was a proven fact that many Serbs in Bosnia and many Ruthenes in eastern Galicia sympathized or were active collaborators with the enemy. Thus, it was not simply on the basis of prewar prejudice, but also due to actual evidence of treason that the military engaged in summary executions of 'unreliable' Serbs and Ruthenes in the first weeks of the war. The real danger lay in the wider implications of this. The military leadership tended towards a blanket assumption that the Monarchy's Serb and Ruthene populations were unreliable as a whole. By September 1914 they had transported out of Bosnia over 1000 political suspects (many of whom were hostages to ensure good Serb behaviour); much of the Bosnian Serb leadership, including 100 clergy and seven delegates of the Bosnian Diet, were among those interned in Bosnia itself.[8] When General Stjepan Sarkotić became governor of Bosnia at the end of the year he found that all was quiet but he was not deceived; sensing that he was 'sitting on a volcano', he resolved to 'prevent any outbreak of lava' by ruling dictatorially, banning any political activity (the Bosnian Diet would not be reconvened), and launching a series of trials of treacherous Serbs.[9]

Similarly in Galicia, the army was so paranoid about civilian links to the enemy that it sent thousands of Ruthenes westward into the hinterland. From Vienna, one influential Austrian politician, Josef Baernreither, noted in his diary that all of the Ruthene peasant population seemed to be treacherous: he had heard of 3000 men imprisoned in L'viv [Lemberg] ready for transportation.[10] It may well have been the case that, as in Bosnia, the scale of executions in Galicia at this time was exaggerated, feeding the rumour-mill of atrocity stories. But it was also a fact that the military regime set a standard of behaviour which could only alienate Ruthenes and Poles from believing that the war was being fought on their behalf. It dealt a blow at the start of the war to any possible unity in the hinterland, while providing a crisis of conscience for many Serbs, Ruthenes or Poles in the armed forces.

As new foreign enemies appeared on the horizon, most notably Italy in 1915, the military behaved in a consistently defensive fashion. Early in the war, the Monarchy's Italians seem to have been given a clean bill of health by the authorities; according to one assessment at least, they were 'by no means suffering from Austrophobia but in most cases strongly dynastic and absolutely loyal'.[11] But from May 1915, as a new front opened in the south-west, the cloud of suspicion fell over Italian soldiers and civilians. While the former would eventually only be employed on the Eastern or Balkan Fronts, 7500 of the latter were transported out of Tyrol to be interned in the interior. With the AOK demanding that irredentism be rooted out, the military in Tyrol itself began to behave indiscriminately, imposing widespread use of the German language which was only likely to antagonize the Italian population and push them further into the irredentist camp.[12]

It could be argued that the military's behaviour was logical in regions bordering the battlefields where security was vital. Yet because of the way that ethnic groups were distributed in the Monarchy, the AOK directly antagonized certain nationalities while privileging others. Moreover, it was a policy mirrored in the Austrian hinterland itself, where it revealed on the one hand the degree of actual national disunity by 1914, and on the other, the way that the authorities poisoned a patriotic atmosphere which could perhaps have been nurtured. Such was the case among the Slovenes. Although in July 1914 Slovene leaders such as Ivan Tavčar and Ivan Šušteršić had made public statements of loyalty, and the AOK always tended to view the Slovenes as reliable military material, the civil and military authorities in the south engaged in the mass arrest of community leaders. In Carinthia and Styria, where Slovenes and Germans particularly rubbed shoulders, there were 910 arrests in the first four months of the war.[13] Justifiably one might emphasize the scale of this, for it was on a par with Dalmatia or Bohemia, two regions where there was far more evidence of openly 'unpatriotic' behaviour. In Dalmatia, the real heartland of Yugoslav agitation before 1914, hundreds were arrested on the outbreak of hostilities, put on a prison-ship at Split, and taken northwards to Maribor to be interned. They included the distinguished Croat politicians, Josip Smodlaka and Ante Tresić-Pavičić, friends of the British historian R.W. Seton-Watson who had done so much in the previous years to alert Europe to the Monarchy's Southern Slav problem (other Yugoslav leaders such as Ante Trumbić and Frano Supilo had escaped to Italy).[14]

Meanwhile in the Czech lands, the KÜA observed after only a few months of war that the mood of the population, initially quite promising, had turned sour. By September, hundreds of wounded soldiers were returning from the East into the Czech communities and painting a quite different picture from that which had been described in the official newspapers. One town councillor concluded in his diary that the war would last a very long time: 'Already the people are grumbling out loud now, although any criticism is strictly forbidden.'[15] By the end of 1914 in Bohemia, 950 people had been arrested for political offences and 32 societies dissolved. As the Russian army advanced into Galicia in the autumn, the evidence had increasingly suggested that many Czechs sympathized with the enemy and had little enthusiasm for the Habsburg cause. Most notably, as we will see later, Czech soldiers in these months quickly acquired a reputation for unreliability to match that of their Serb colleagues. For this reason above all, the military authorities increasingly labelled the Czech nation as suspect. As Emperor Franz Joseph told Stürgkh on 22 November 1914, the behaviour of Czech soldiers could be traced back directly to 'unhealthy political conditions' at home. This supposed link provided the AOK with ample substance to demand repeatedly that the Czech lands as a whole should be militarized. On most levels between 1914 and late 1916, Stürgkh was successful in arguing that the existing emergency laws were adequate to counter any unrest. But if this was something of a minor victory for Austria's political regime in the face of the KÜA, it seems unlikely that ordinary Czechs made much distinction between the bureaucratic and military protagonists who seemed to be in control of their everyday lives. After all, in May 1915 the military gave a clear example of their ability to intervene arbitrarily. They arrested Karel Kramář, the leading Czech politician, put him on trial and sentenced him to death; Kramář thereby gained the status of a martyr, both at home and abroad, one who seemed to personify a Czech idealistic cause which was increasingly at variance with that of the Habsburg elite.[16]

Before turning to assess how the Habsburg authorities tried more positively to harness wartime morale, we need to be aware of the regime which prevailed from 1914 in the Hungarian half of the Empire. In Hungary, in contrast to Austria, Parliament continued in session throughout the war, with all the political parties agreeing to maintain a truce (*Treuga Dei*) as long as the interests of the homeland were in danger. Count István Tisza, the Prime Minister, noted accordingly in one debate in November 1914 that the war had 'given rise to splendid manifestations of unity and mutual love both at home and on the battlefield'.[17] Yet such rhetoric belied deep fissures in Hungarian society which slowly expanded as hostilities continued. Despite the appearance of a representative forum in Budapest, the Parliament was wholly unrepresentative of broad masses of the population. Due to the restrictive franchise it contained no Social Democratic or Radical deputies, while non-Magyar minority nationalities such as the Slovaks and Romanians possessed only 2 per cent of the seats, although they amounted to 40 per cent of the registered electorate.[18] In August 1914 many of these elements might appear to be loyal, with even the Social Democrats agreeing to toe the line in a defensive war against autocratic Russia. By early 1915 a social crisis was already evident. Hungary, like the rest of the Monarchy, did not adjust well to the wartime economy, an immediate result being that the government was forced early on to introduce flour rationing; by June 1915 there were the first major food riots, and Tisza was privately warning that the war could only safely be continued for another eight months. However, Tisza publicly kept silent about any idea of peace and refused to expand his government into a national coalition. The result was that by mid-1916 the façade of any *Treuga Dei* had been shattered: Mihály Károlyi proceeded to leave the Party of Independence and set up his own party, dedicated to peace and a preservation of Hungary's 'true interests'. Although Tisza and the bulk of the Magyar elite would continue to keep hold of Hungary's political strings for the rest of the war, the stage was set for an increasingly conspicuous diversification of Hungarian public opinion in the years 1916–18.

From July 1914, the principal way in which the Magyar regime had maintained a semblance of unity in Hungary was through its own version of emergency legislation. Unity was coerced as much as it was spontaneous. As in Austria, the emergency laws of 1912 invested the civil authorities with special powers of censorship, prohibition and arrest, with the addition of internment by November 1914.[19] The major contrast to Austria was that Tisza's regime, ever protective of Hungary's national sovereignty, excluded the military from exercising such powers on Hungarian soil. The KÜA had no authority in Hungary, nor could the AOK secure those inroads into civilian jurisdiction which were possible in the regions of Austria or Bosnia which became their 'war zones'. The one exception at first was the autonomous region of Croatia. In view of the Serbian army's success against Habsburg forces in August 1914, the eastern part of Croatia had temporarily become a war zone under military jurisdiction. When the Serbians were forced to retreat in September, the military wreaked vengeance upon those local Serb 'collaborators', executing more than 120 and deporting hundreds for resettlement in the Croatian hinterland. If the Croatian civil authorities led by the Governor, Ivan Skerlecz, were furious at the military's arbitrary behaviour, it reflected a deeper tussle in Croatia where the military from the start of the war had been anxious to assert their authority. As in Bosnia and Dalmatia, they had singled out key individuals for detention – in this case, Serb politicians such as the Pribićević brothers and Srdjan Budisavljević – and for the first six months of the war endeavoured to undermine civilian rule even further. Only in June 1915 was it clear that Skerlecz and the politicians had won. The repressive atmosphere was then lightened because the Croatian Diet (Sabor), which had been closed on the eve of war, was allowed to reopen. The existence of this forum would ensure that a certain social stability was introduced in Croatia of a kind which was increasingly lacking elsewhere in the Monarchy (in Austria, for example); the deputies who came together now provided some Croatian legitimization for a continuation of the war. What was also clear, however, from the Sabor's common statement of June 1915, was that the Croatian leaders' support for a Habsburg war was not unconditional. Loyalty to the Habsburg cause was now matched by an open demand for Croat unity within the Empire, an indication that the Croats, like other nationalities, had a dual allegiance to dynasty and nationality which the Habsburg authorities could not afford to ignore if they were to achieve a long-term mobilization of the population.[20]

Many Croatian politicians would maintain an opportunistic stance until the last weeks of the war. They sensed correctly that unless a more favourable option emerged, they were wholly dependent on the Magyar authorities for the continued functioning of the Sabor or any chance of securing Croatia's rights in the future. In contrast, for other nationalities in 'Hungary proper' the choices were more restricted. Under its emergency powers, the Hungarian government had acted speedily, imposing martial law in Serb and Romanian regions, and then extending it to Ruthene communities in the north-east (who by the winter would share the invidious fate of the Serbs of eastern Croatia by falling into a 'war zone' and under temporary military jurisdiction). If in the eyes of the regime, the reputation of Hungary's Serbs and Ruthenes could not be salvaged, its attitude towards the Slovak and Romanian populations was for a time ambiguous. It reflected a dilemma which the authorities faced in many corners of the Empire, whether in the interests of the state it was best to harness or to repress local sentiment. The normal reflex in wartime Hungary might well be to repress anything which did not fit the Magyar chauvinist mood of 1914.

But the government still showed a wariness when it came to Slovak or Romanian sensibilities. Initially, Tisza tolerated some signs of a lively Slovak national consciousness. He only felt the need to suppress it in 1915 when the evidence mounted that some Slovaks were beginning to welcome the idea of Czechoslovak unity (a goal which could only be achieved at the expense of the united Hungarian kingdom).[21]

In the case of the Romanians of Transylvania, however, Tisza's regime trod softly for a much longer period, since from the time of the July crisis in 1914 the Prime Minister had been extremely anxious lest neutral Romania join the war and invade Hungary: nothing should be done to antagonize a potential enemy. Thus, *Romanul*, the newspaper of the Romanian National Party in Transylvania, was allowed to continue for 18 months (albeit under strict censorship); and with a little encouragement, Budapest even secured some patriotic endorsement for the war from certain Romanian religious and political leaders. However, the stance of both sides was to be tested to the full when Romania finally declared war and invaded Transylvania in the summer of 1916. Neither the Transylvanian leaders nor the normally passive Romanian peasantry hesitated to nail their colours to the Romanian mast, fleeing in their droves alongside the Romanian army when it was driven back over the border.[22] The severe Magyar repression which followed for the rest of the war was conclusive evidence that the authorities would no longer bother to cultivate the Romanians of eastern Hungary. They, like the Serbs, Czechs or Italians, now fell decisively into a category marked 'unreliable'. And if this was admittedly due in part to the nationalities' own wartime behaviour, it was equally a result of the deep-seated national inequalities which prevailed in Austria-Hungary. The authorities had not simply failed to resolve the tensions before 1914. Their official attitude in wartime had exacerbated the sense of alienation from any common cause which was felt in many different national communities of the Empire.

As the political regime in Hungary and the bureaucratic-military authorities in Austria tried to sustain the war effort, a significant ingredient in their success was their ability to control the circulation of information in the Monarchy. In a negative sense this meant above all the imposition of a strict censorship of the press under the emergency laws. But censorship also involved what might be termed a positive dimension, namely the efforts of the authorities to foster patriotism through official or unofficial propaganda. Of course, both of these aspects of the struggle to sustain civilian and military morale were common to all the belligerent states. Austria-Hungary was no different from Britain or France or Germany in believing that a strict censorship was vital in wartime. Nor was the Monarchy unaware that patriotism needed to be guided and shaped. If it would be an exaggeration to suggest that an 'immense propaganda apparatus' was erected in the Empire at the start of the war,[23] it would still be true to say that the degree to which the authorities dabbled in patriotic initiatives has been insufficiently analyzed by historians.[24] What is also clear is that in both fields, those of censorship and domestic propaganda, the Habsburg authorities from 1917 were failing to achieve their objectives when compared to their competitors. The British government may well have 'failed abysmally' at managing news during the war, but if so, its ineptness can be viewed as trivial when set alongside the failure in Austria-Hungary.[25] Understanding how and why this was so is important for a number of reasons. First, it provides the general context in which the ideological campaigns of front propaganda were waged by and against the Monarchy in 1917–18. Second, it shows the real dangers from the hinterland which increasingly undermined the morale of the Austro-Hungarian armies. Third, it helps to explain the wider process of national and social disintegration which engulfed the Empire after 1916, particularly the Habsburg authorities' inability to harness or mobilize their peoples for a long war. As we have seen, from early in the war the regimes had helped to alienate whole sections of the population by their discriminatory behaviour. Partly as a result of this, they failed to manage the state of public opinion. In place of any official patriotism which was sufficiently propagated, unpatriotic creeds would be allowed to grow. They could only harm the Empire's war effort because, with nationalist and pacifist agendas, they mobilized whole sections of the community in an opposite direction.

For the first three years of the war the level of press censorship in the Monarchy, especially in Austria, was severe. The KÜA acted as overall supervisor of the press in Austria, while in Budapest a counterpart was established for Hungary in the Hadifelügyeleti Bizottság [HFB – War Surveillance Commission]; the two liaised through a special hotline to try to ensure a coordinated policy of censorship. They each issued directives to regional censor offices, whose job was to scrutinize all newspapers at least three hours before they reached the printing press and score out any items which could damage the Monarchy's war effort. Under this draconian regime with its extremely tight deadlines, some newspapers such as the Bosnian Social Democratic daily, *Glas Slobode*, simply decided to cease publication until a more favourable day.[26] Others were banned in the early months of the war, including for instance all 31 Serb-language newspapers in the Vojvodina.[27] For the rest, journalism became a perpetual game of walking the censorship tightrope, testing what might be permitted while knowing that a 'sword of Damocles' hung over their journals. Jan Hajšman's vivid memoirs, for example, record the fate of his Czech newspaper *Čas* [*Time*] which, after a stream of warnings from the censor, was finally closed down in August 1915 for 'an inadmissible style of writing'.[28]

Yet it would be wrong to suggest that the majority of newspapers were chafing at the bit of censorship. From the beginning, under the force of patriotic spontaneity, a strong degree of self-censorship was apparent. It was in this vein that *Arbeiter-Zeitung*, the Social Democrat newspaper in Vienna, toed the line which had immediately been adopted by loyalist papers such as *Neue Freie Presse*. In Budapest similarly, the radical Hungarian press felt obliged or inclined to adopt a chauvinist tone. In the modernist Radical journal *Nyugat* [*West*], articles appeared enthusing about Hungary's belligerent cause; and even *Népszava*, the Social Democratic organ, observed that although in the future 'we shall again give our opinion frankly and bluntly... all criticism must now fall silent for a time'.[29] Only a few critics were openly prepared to condemn the way that so many writers in Vienna and Budapest had jumped on the patriotic bandwagon. In Vienna, Karl Kraus was something of a lone voice in satirizing how *literati* like Hermann Bahr or Hugo von Hofmannsthal were 'prostituting themselves' in the cause of patriotism.[30] In the Hungarian press, a united façade was even more evident. Mihály Károlyi would note later how 'the press seemed suddenly to have forgotten that there were discriminating people left in the world. Perhaps they were right, for these were so terrorized by public opinion that they were a negligible quantity.'[31]

If from the start the authorities relied on regional censors and on a high degree of patriotism from the German and Magyar press in particular, their major centre for the manipulation of public opinion was in military hands in the shape of the Kriegspressequartier [KPQ – War Press Office]. The KPQ was set up on 28 July 1914 as a sub-section of the AOK, but because of its liaison with journalists was always based at a distance from the AOK headquarters itself. Its role initially was to supervise and control any news about the armed forces or the war effort which was being passed to or written by domestic or foreign journalists. It did so in time-honoured fashion by issuing daily official reports, written by a *Pressereferent*, which could then be embellished for the press by war correspondents who were based at the KPQ.[32] When the journalists chose to write eulogistic articles of their own, the KPQ usually acted as the first point of censorship. Not surprisingly, while some correspondents increasingly felt that their readers deserved to be given a more realistic picture of life at the front (and that this would boost rather than harm domestic morale), much of the readership in the hinterland quickly became inured to the official propaganda which was passed through the sieve of the KPQ. In many newspapers there was little subtlety about the way that the official line was presented, while large blank spaces indicated the unofficial line which had been erased by the censor. According to one Czech journalist, newspaper vendors in Prague consequently called out: 'What is white is the truth – what is black is lies!' One may wonder whether this would actually increase newspaper sales. But it does suggest that the public might be discerning but at the same time curious about both the official and unofficial lines.[33]

The KPQ's role as a censor, as a shaper of the news, logically led on to its emergence as the leading issuer of official propaganda in the Monarchy. This developed gradually, receiving a burst of energy from March 1917 under

Colonel Wilhelm Eisner-Bubna who seems to have hoped that he might eventually set up a Ministry of Information (on British lines) for Austria-Hungary.[34] This was not to be. But the KPQ did grow into an organization employing 880 people and divided into 12 sections. Apart from acting as a military liaison to the press (itself something of a propaganda role), and to the KÜA and HFB for military censorship, it became responsible to a limited extent for stimulating morale at the front. For example, it organized cabaret and film shows for troops in the war zones, ensuring of course that such material was always of an 'uplifting quality' about the Empire and its war. In turn, under its first director, Max von Hoen, the KPQ moved into domestic waters. Most notably, since it was also responsible for war artists and military photography, by 1916 the KPQ was organizing displays of war artists' work in cities of the Monarchy and abroad. Starting in Vienna in October 1915, exhibitions were held in Budapest, Zagreb, Innsbruck and Prague, numbering a total of 26 by May 1917. The aim was to boost civilian morale by linking the civilian to life at the front; as Hoen declared at the opening of an exhibition in Prague in December 1916, the pictures would cultivate an 'inner sensitivity', a 'dialogue between front and hinterland'.[35] It was in the same spirit that the War Ministry in 1916 ordered a 'war exhibition' to be set up in Vienna's Prater park; it eventually included not only war paintings but, for extra bizarre realism, a field given over to barbed wire and trenches.[36]

The Prater event might at least reach a wider audience than the basic art exhibitions organized by the KPQ, for it also included operettas on a war theme and thus tapped more deeply into popular culture. It tried to blend escapism with the reality of war and perhaps managed to avoid the 'official stamp' which hovered over so much KPQ activity. Where the KPQ itself could potentially have the most impact was in film propaganda.[37] Films were one of the most popular and expanding forms of entertainment during the war (the number of cinemas in Prague doubled), offering the KPQ a real opportunity to shape public opinion. As with the press, the KPQ had a monopoly on producing the 'official line' in this medium which usually meant distributing film documentaries which glorified the image of the Habsburg Monarchy and its military exploits. Yet, as with official bulletins to the press, such propaganda had clear limitations. Most fundamentally it presupposed a level of consensus in the conduct of the war which was increasingly at odds with reality; a patriotic film entitled *The Dream of an Austrian Reservist* might play well in Vienna but could be highly problematic in Prague or Ljubljana. Such films also naturally competed, as in the press, with other less controllable material from unofficial sources. However successful the KPQ was in making its films look non-official, the carefully edited footage celebrating *The Battle of the Isonzo* or the latest dynastic event was playing alongside films which were escapist, occasionally nationalistic (Hungary, for example, made its own films), or even originating in enemy countries. The censor might well intervene in the latter case, but the KPQ itself did not have the resources to do more. It increasingly faced competition when trying to perpetuate what Redlich termed 'a spiritually feeble propaganda of victory' among civilians who were war-weary, deeply cynical about authority or any 'Habsburg ideal', and often far more receptive towards nationalistic persuasion in their region of the Empire.[38]

The same weakness was clearly evident in other small-scale attempts by the regime to cultivate patriotism during the war. From the autumn of 1914 the political authorities launched a regular series of campaigns to get the population to subscribe to war bonds so as to finance the war. Accompanied by heroic imagery and much publicity about what the aristocracy were contributing, they were initially successful, the first two campaigns in Austria garnering almost five billion crowns.[39] Yet these were diminishing returns, especially in later years in those parts of the Monarchy where the patriotic Habsburg imagery was anything but seductive; by then, if civilians had any savings left to send to a cause, they were more likely to place them in local or nationalist coffers than risk them in 'Habsburg' war bonds.[40] A similar fate befell any patriotic literature which stemmed from official sources. Some of the political ministries organized this on an ad hoc basis, but it always appears to have been largely German-Austrian or Hungarian in its focus. For example, when a welfare office in the Austrian Ministry of Interior published an almanac in 1916, it contained pictures of the Imperial family and stories or poetry by writers such as Arthur Schnitzler, Rainer Maria Rilke and Stefan Zweig; the purpose set out in the introduction was to 'bear wonderful testimony to the patriotism of our Austrian artists and scholars' so that their thoughts might 'echo in people's hearts'.[41]

The most important attempt, however, to harness Austrian writers to the patriotic cause was made by the military authorities. It was based at the Kriegsarchiv in Vienna [KA – War Archives]. Alongside the KPQ, the KA was the only official centre in the Monarchy consistently devoted to issuing patriotic propaganda, assuming the kind of role which was played by Wellington House in Great Britain. Relying on a long tradition of publishing Austrian military history under its auspices, the KA proceeded to issue heroic accounts of the Galician campaigns of 1915, followed by a series of anthologies such as *Unsere Offiziere* (1915), *Unsere Nordfront* (1916) and *Unsere Kämpfe im Süden* (1917), and from 1917 its own patriotic organ, *Donauland*.[42] The latter has been termed 'the most prestigious journal of Austrian patriotism'.[43] As with the KA's earlier products, it relied heavily on celebrated writers such as Zweig, Bahr and Rilke for its quality and effect. Yet any assessment of such propaganda has to be tempered by a note on its potential audience. The KA material (which had its equivalent in Hungary) was largely restricted to the German-speaking audience of Austria, and its overall product was in military hands, its character bearing a distinctly military stamp. Thus, it was very much a contrast to Britain's

Wellington House whose writers were under civilian control, issuing a range of material which tried to appear non-official. The KA propaganda directly mirrored the outlook of the Monarchy's regime and publicized an image which was at odds with reality; it was particularly unlikely to appeal to 'minority nationalities' like the Czechs or Slovenes.

Since the output of official propaganda was always limited in scope, the Austro-Hungarian authorities were bound to fall back on unofficial propaganda or an unofficial consensus of support for the war.[44] This was then backed up by a tight censorship of news in an attempt to mould public opinion. Ultimately, however, as the authorities were noticeably failing to win the war, they would find it increasingly hard to shape the public mood by propaganda or censorship. What occurred in the Monarchy in the second half of 1916 was the start of a clear breakdown of consensus which, as we have seen, had not been adequately nurtured by the authorities anyway. In Hungary, Károlyi and his supporters broke the 'political truce' and opened up the avenue for political dissent to Tisza's regime. In Austria, where a truce was more a matter of force than acquiescence, the transformation which took place from November 1916 was even more dramatic: with the murder of Stürgkh and the death of Emperor Franz Joseph, public and political pressure mounted for a change in the bureaucratic-military dictatorship. Much of the background to this public unrest was economic. As the enemy blockade began to bite, the Empire's grain production had sharply diminished and also become ever more unevenly divided up among the regions. From mid-1916 a period of real economic exhaustion began to hit the Monarchy, evidenced in May 1916 by the first hunger riots in Vienna itself (where already 54 000 people were attending soup kitchens daily).[45] There was now far less tolerance of a press censorship which stifled the miserable realities. As *Arbeiter-Zeitung* was able to write in June 1916, 'what is publicly said has become a travesty of the innermost feelings of the people and stands in sharpest opposition to secret general opinion ... The crying need of the hour is a thorough overhauling of the censorship.'[46]

During the war this would never happen completely. But in early 1917, censorship in Austria was considerably relaxed as a logical consequence of the constitutional regime which the new Emperor Karl introduced. The result was a press censorship which could still be harsh, but which often differed in the various regions of the Monarchy; in other words it was less 'water-proof' than before, enabling items to appear in one paper which were stifled in another. Of necessity, the censor gradually had to reflect the new constitutional circumstances which prevailed.[47] If in Hungary a similar relaxation occurred after Karl had dismissed Count Tisza in May 1917, it was in Austria that the Emperor's new broom had the most impact. He dramatically reduced the powers of the military, epitomized best when he dismissed Conrad von Hötzendorf as Chief of Staff (sending him to command troops on the Italian Front), and then abolished the special powers which the military had been permitted in the war zones. At the same time, bowing to public pressure and fearful of the revolutionary events in Russia, Karl and his advisers finally decided to recall the Austrian Reichsrat.

In transforming the building on Vienna's Ringstrasse from a hospital back into a Parliament, the new regime seems to have expected that some political consensus might be revived through the deputies who had been banished for so long. On 24 May, the Austrian Prime Minister expressed his hope that the reconvention of the Reichsrat would be a symbol of Austria's inner unity.[48] Indeed, it could be said that this was the ideal time for the authorities to engage in some 'secondary mobilization' of the population, relying perhaps on their political representatives to reinforce the virtue of continuing the war. But was this realistic? Undoubtedly, it was expecting too much of the non-German representatives after almost three years of dictatorship. Many of them had been imprisoned at the outbreak of war, their 'homelands' had been subject to arbitrary military rule, and they were now still faced with an Austrian government which was largely German in outlook. On 30 May, on the opening of the Reichsrat, the Czech, South Slav and Ruthene deputies duly presented radical demands for Czechoslovak, Yugoslav and Ukrainian unity which, though still ostensibly within the Empire, would clearly necessitate its restructuring as a federal state. When the government of Ernst von Seidler refused to discuss any such ideas and clung to the status quo, a secondary mobilization did indeed intensify in Austria, but it was not one on behalf of the Habsburg war effort. Rather, it was characterized by nationalist agitation in the Czech, Slovene and Polish regions which fed off an increasingly war-weary and starving population. In the Czech lands, agitators who had previously worked in secret among the civilians were able to flourish more openly because of the laxer political regime. In the South Slav regions, Slovene leaders took the initiative in leading a grassroots movement on behalf of their 'May Declaration' for Yugoslav unity.[49] In this way, from the summer of 1917, there began that polarization of national and social groupings which would eventually tear the Empire apart: the authorities offered no solution to prevent it. The irony was that in the early years of the war, when a certain consensus was evident, the military authorities had operated ruthlessly and done much to alienate large sections of the population. From 1917, however, when social and nationalist unrest was intensifying, they were relatively powerless to control events in the Austrian hinterland.

Austria-Hungary's military elite would later make much of the fact that Karl's new regime had weakened their powers and opened the floodgates to political chaos. According to Conrad, the AOK had been surrounded by political intriguers who had finally brought it down.[50] In January 1917 its headquarters was moved from Teschen to Baden (near Vienna) and, under a new Chief of Staff,

Arthur Arz von Straussenburg, it became far more a compliant instrument of the Emperor. In fact, as Manfried Rauchensteiner has emphasized, the High Command's power base at Teschen had disintegrated already by the summer of 1916 when the disaster of the Russian break-through against the Austro-Hungarian forces (the Brusilov offensive) was the final blow which forced Conrad to agree to subordinate Austria's leadership of the war to Germany.[51] This in turn had been a steady process of subordination, after the Austrian leadership had led its armies to a series of disasters on the Eastern and Balkan battlefields. And this relatively poor performance not only gave Germany an increasing leverage over its ally. It had disastrous consequences for the quality of manpower at the AOK's disposal.

In Austria-Hungary's first confused campaign against Serbia in 1914, in stifling heat and hostile terrain, the old army had been decimated, losing 600 officers and 22 000 men. By the end of 1914 the number lost on all Austro-Hungarian fronts totalled over a million, a figure then compounded by the devastating Carpathian campaign of early 1915 which resulted in 800 000 casualties; in freezing temperatures one Croat regiment, for example, lost 28 officers and 1800 men through spending one night in the snow.[52] Although these losses could be matched by those from, for instance, the French army in the first weeks of the war, the results for the Monarchy were more devastating because of the army's multinational composition. The manpower shortages resulting from the decimation of the 20–42 age group would never be recovered. In April 1915, military service was duly extended to those aged 18–20; from January 1916, those up to 55 were theoretically liable to be called up. But by this time, with a monthly loss at the front of 224 000 men, the march formations which every month carried reserves to the war zone were no longer covering gaps in the manpower. It meant increased burdens upon existing troops in the front line and a degree of restricted leave which inevitably damaged morale.

This was then exacerbated by the encroaching nationality issue, namely that there were insufficient officers of, for example, Croat nationality to command predominantly Croat regiments with the result that coherence in the command structure was weakened. Moreover, those who had been called up and were now promoted into supposedly reliable positions were ex-civilians. Some of them had strong nationalist sympathies or only a shaky allegiance to the Habsburg cause. Even the Austrian official history felt bound to admit later that at least a quarter of those who went to war in 1914 were not willing, for political reasons, to do their duty to the Emperor.[53] By 1915 the armed forces had already become what István Deák has termed 'civilians in uniform'; rather than being members of a special military caste, they looked at events 'with the same eyes as the nationally awoken urban population'.[54] Their morale would increasingly mirror the mood of the hinterland, where their families were often living in penury, and where after two years of warfare national and social agitation was beginning to escalate.

Although the High Command was only too aware of the interconnection between front and hinterland, it never fully came to terms with the fact that the armed forces were no longer a professional elite. As we will see,[55] until the last year of the war when it finally launched an 'educational programme' in the army, the AOK devoted little thought to the ways in which morale might be boosted in the ranks, preferring instead to rely on simple hierarchical cohesion or on old disciplinary measures. Its normal reaction was also to divert blame for poor morale from the front to the hinterland, and in this regard it was no coincidence that it was the military who thought most about stimulating patriotism in the Empire. Its role here, however, should not be exaggerated. Conrad's normal solution for bad influences among the civilian population was force or further militarization, not propaganda. It is true that in 1915–16 Conrad urged Count Stürgkh to nationalize Austrian primary schools and introduce pre-military training into secondary schools so as to produce 'truly patriotic citizens'.[56] But this appears to have been an isolated example of its kind. That domestic propaganda which the military did sponsor, through the KPQ or the KA, was on a small scale, and reflected an idealized Habsburg patriotism which was consistently at odds with the nationalist diversity of the Empire. The AOK must have sensed this from the start of the war. But its only real solution, in dealing with the gap between its own ideal and the reality which petered through from the hinterland, was to impose its own ideal by force.

It was, of course, possible for the authorities to generalize to some extent about the calibre of various national units. Some nationalities were indeed less committed to the Monarchy's war than others. While acknowledging this fact (the partial product in itself of the elite's behaviour before 1914), it is also clear that the military's discriminatory behaviour towards certain nationalities quickly had the effect of creating stereotypes which rapidly gained credence among many, and seriously undermined any consensus which existed between national groups. While soldiers of Serb or Ruthene nationality had been immediately suspect, from early 1915 it was always the Czechs who had the worst reputation. The mobilization of Czech troops seems to have been faultless, but within a few months on the Eastern Front there were signs that some Czech regiments were of weak morale. On 3 April 1915, when attacked by the Russians, the Czech infantry regiment [IR] 28 laid down its arms and surrendered en masse.[57] Soon afterwards, Czech soldiers of IR36 followed the example. These seem to have been rare events in themselves, but they resounded widely. The subsequent investigation revealed the damaging interaction of front and hinterland, and gave the Czechs a reputation in military circles which they never lost.

What began as stereotypes, often fostered in military circles, had begun by 1917 to become more widely accepted even if they were still simplistic notions and wide of the truth. For one nationality, the stereotype of themselves might become an image to be celebrated as one which they aspired to. For another nationality, the same stereotype was to be publicized as proof of a whole people's 'treachery'; thus by 1917, books about the Czechs' treason in the war were being displayed in the windows of German bookshops in Prague.[58] There was enough truth in these stereotypes for them to gain currency. And consequently they could also form the concrete basis for the arguments of the enemy's propaganda campaign when it was launched against Austria-Hungary in 1918. As for the military authorities, their own perceptions of unreliability were never wholly inaccurate but were often father to the thought. They were always having to juggle a complex number of factors when weighing up the threats to troop morale. Apart from the fundamental dangers of war-weariness and material hardships at the front, they were commanding a chameleon-like force whose colour might change in response both to events in the hinterland and to the nature of the enemy. By late 1916, the Monarchy had already witnessed war on four main fronts: against Serbia, Russia, Italy and Romania. Each of these opponents could occasion a different response from different nationalities; if the Czechs' performance was viewed as more suspect against Russia, the Slovenes and Croats were expected to be more hostile to their predatory neighbour, Italy. Paradoxically, when an enemy was knocked out – Serbia (1916), Romania (1916) or Russia (1917–18) – the effect was not always beneficial. For certain troops then began to question their role, the purpose of the war, and to look forward to a speedy peace.

In 1917, the year when the major campaigns of front propaganda began, the Austro-Hungarian army began to be afflicted by those dangers which would steadily increase thereafter. Although it is notoriously difficult to estimate army morale because of the inbuilt bias of the sources (the perceptions usually of the commanders), some judgements can usefully be made through reference to some major witnesses. In his memoirs, Arz von Straussenburg records how, immediately after succeeding Conrad in February 1917, he ordered the army commands to send in detailed reports about the morale and physical state of the troops. The replies received were generally favourable, with the commanders singling out German, Magyar and Croat regiments for special commendation. At the same time, however, Arz was greatly alarmed at the food crisis now afflicting the Monarchy, and at the quality of the troops who were coming into the war zones; they were not only increasingly undernourished, but – his memoirs hint – were liable to be tainted by the insufficient moral fortitude of the hinterland.[59] Arz's assumptions were basic, matching the general blandness of his memoirs. But their substance was amplified and confirmed by Conrad himself in a report which he wrote from the Italian Front in September 1917.

During the year 1917, the number of desertions to Italy from the Tyrolian region which Conrad now commanded was perceived to have grown dramatically: from 115 in the first six months to a total of 82 for the months of July and August alone. And while in the past the deserters had usually been 'Slavs or Romanians', this was no longer entirely the case. Conrad therefore ordered a thorough investigation, judging that the phenomenon had to have 'apart from nationalist agitation and war-weariness, its own special causes'.[60]

The results, which Conrad dispatched in a short report to the AOK on 15 September, illustrate amply the degree to which the military in the war zone saw events within Austria-Hungary as the major threat to army morale and discipline.[61] General war-weariness or the rigours of life in the front line appeared to be side issues. Above all, the report, based upon the views of corps commanders and their subordinates, put the blame for the rise in desertions upon the amnesty for political prisoners which Emperor Karl had granted in July 1917. Through this, former 'traitors' like Karel Kramář were released and went home to a tumultuous welcome in their home-towns. Apart from the recriminations which followed on all sides, Conrad and other officers were always bitterly opposed to the amnesty because of the bad example it set for military discipline; about a year later, Karl would be told, to his surprise, that since the amnesty desertions had increased by 80 per cent.[62] In his report, Conrad duly highlighted insufficient discipline as a major problem, and pointed to the laxity which seemed to be a feature of the 'new regime'. Most notably, Karl had also decided to abolish two forms of military punishment (tying up and chaining up) which the officers felt to be vital as a means of controlling the ranks. Since the officers would only be left with the option of punishing recalcitrants by placing them in 'labour units', it was a matter over which the AOK would petition Karl energetically in order to have the ban rescinded (which was achieved in early 1918).

For the military, it was a tightening rather than a loosening of discipline which seemed essential because of the low calibre of troops which were reaching the war zone. As Arz had noted earlier in 1917, Conrad in September pointed to the steady influx of 'unreliable elements' from the hinterland, specifying these as men of Serb, Czech, Romanian and Ruthene nationality, who then had to be mixed with 'reliable' German or Magyar troops. Not only, he advised, should this mixing be avoided, since the new recruits were unsettled by serving next to troops speaking a different language, but the assignation of unreliable elements had to stop: 'for otherwise in a short time there will be no units left which we can characterize as *absolutely* reliable'.[63] One officer at the AOK minuted alongside Conrad's words, 'Yes, but where then can we send them?' It had, after all, been normal procedure at least since the behaviour of Czech regiments in 1915 to place known unreliable elements under firm supervision. And especially after the Austro-Hungarian army was reorganized from May 1917, it became standard practice to create nationally-mixed regiments as an extra check upon suspect nationalities.[64] More fundamentally, the military's criteria for judging 'reliability' was highly suspect. It might still be true that Germans, Magyars, Croats, Slovenes and Poles made, on the whole, the most disciplined soldiers. But in 1917, the list of deserters to Italy was beginning to contain more German and Hungarian names – a sign that crude generalizations about reliability could not continue for much longer.

Conrad's report of 15 September was a good summary of the kind of dilemma, if not helplessness, which the military commanders would face for the rest of the war. Having failed to defeat any of their enemies decisively (except little Montenegro in 1916),[65] having tried to run a dictatorship in Austria which antagonized many of the nationalities, the military from 1917 were left at the mercy of a hinterland which was sinking increasingly into an economic and social crisis. Their appeals for discipline or some solution from the political authorities were usually in vain, because the latter were now having to operate in a more constitutional framework and were themselves grasping at straws to sustain the domestic war effort. In attempting to maintain army morale, the army commanders were always trying to keep the troops isolated from poisonous influences, but this was an impossible task for an Empire which was dependent on a 'civilian army' and trying to come to terms with 'total war'. The examples were only too clear in Conrad's report. When he complained that the troops' morale was depressed by their lack of leave, he again blamed the political authorities for exacerbating the problem. It was from the hinterland that there now came newspapers, insufficiently censored, which dwelt too much on thoughts of peace and undermined the men's stamina. It was in the hinterland that those who managed to secure leave were seduced by relatives or nationalist agitators, deserting in the belief that they would be given an amnesty after the war. If Conrad's complaints could well be matched by those of the AOK from the early months of the war when Czech morale in particular was an issue, the threat from the rear now appeared infinitely greater and insoluble. In vain the military would try to keep the troops in the war zones in a kind of quarantine, while seeking to alert the domestic authorities to the danger of allowing too much free expression.

Even if this could be achieved to a limited extent, there were new threats on the horizon which would act as catalysts upon existing troop grievances. Conrad finished his report by mentioning two of them. Firstly, there was the issue of insufficient food supply from the hinterland, which was beginning to result in a regular shortage of rations at the front for men who were often enduring harsh climatic conditions. Secondly, there was the new threat of enemy propaganda leaflets, which were being sent over to the Austro-Hungarian troops to depress their morale. In the following year, both of these threats would escalate. If the food crisis was fundamental in influencing morale in all parts of Austria-Hungary, the phenomenon of front propaganda was one which would interact with existing weaknesses in the Monarchy. It was also an expression of the ideological struggle which the war had become as it entered its fourth year, a struggle which the Austro-Hungarian authorities were increasingly having to wage both internally and externally.

## Notes

1. József Galántai, *Hungary in the First World War* (Budapest, 1989) p. 68.
2. Carl Freiherr von Bardolff, *Soldat im alten Österreich. Errinerungen aus meinem Leben* (Leipzig, 1938) p. 188; Prince Ludwig Windischgrätz, *My Memoirs* (London, 1921) p. 57.
3. Franz Kafka, *The Diaries of Franz Kafka 1910–1923*, ed. Max Brod (Penguin, 1972) p. 301. *Nazdar* is an older Czech form of 'hurrah!' or 'cheers!'
4. Olda Kokoschka and Alfred Marnau (eds), *Oskar Kokoschka Letters 1905–1976* (London, 1992) p. 54.
5. For the following, see particularly Joseph Redlich, *Österreichische Regierung und Verwaltung im Weltkriege* (Vienna, 1925), chapters 2 and 4.
6. See Rauchensteiner, *Der Tod des Doppeladlers*, p. 108.
7. Redlich, *Österreichische Regierung*, p. 137.
8. Rudolf Jeřábek, *Potiorek. General im Schatten von Sarajevo* (Graz, 1991) p. 163.
9. Signe Klein, *Freiherr Sarkotić von Lovćen. Die Zeit seiner Verwaltung in Bosnien-Hercegovina von 1914 bis 1918*, Ph.Diss. (Vienna, 1969) pp. 38–9.
10. Christoph Führ, *Das k.u.k. Armeeoberkommando und die Innenpolitik in Österreich 1914–1917* (Graz, Vienna and Cologne, 1968) pp. 63–4.
11. Undated report of the *Gemeinsamen Zentralnachweisbüro* (which censored correspondence with prisoners of war abroad): Gustav Spann, *Zensur in Österreich während des 1. Weltkrieges 1914–1918*, Ph.Diss. (Vienna, 1972) p. 304 note 712.
12. Luciana Palla, *Il Trentino Orientale e la Grande Guerra* (Trento, 1994) p. 133; and Führ, *Das k.u.k. Armeeoberkommando*, pp. 81ff.
13. Janko Pleterski, 'Koroški Slovenci med Prvo Svetovno Vojno', in Janko Pleterski, Lojze Ude and Tone Zorn (eds), *Koroški Plebiscit. Razprave in Članki* (Ljubljana, 1970) pp. 77–9.
14. Milada Paulová, *Jugoslavenski Odbor* (Zagreb, 1925) pp. 6–9.
15. Václav Pácalt in Jaroměř: Alois Žipek (ed.), *Domov za Války*, 5 vols (Prague, 1929–31) I, p. 295.
16. Führ, *Das k.u.k. Armeeoberkommando*, pp. 30–62.
17. Galántai, *Hungary in the First World War*, p. 70.
18. See Tibor Zsuppán, 'The Hungarian Political Scene', in Mark Cornwall (ed.), *The Last Years of Austria-Hungary*, 2nd edn (Exeter, 2000).
19. For a full analysis, see Galántai, *Hungary in the First World War*, pp. 72ff.
20. See the discussion in Z.A.B. Zeman, *The Break-Up of the Habsburg Empire 1914–1918* (Oxford, 1961) pp. 57–62.
21. Galántai, *Hungary in the First World War*, pp. 98–100.
22. Ibid., pp. 110ff, 146, 263.
23. Cf. Edward Timms, *Karl Kraus. Apocalyptic Satirist. Culture and Catastrophe in Habsburg Vienna* (New Haven and London, 1989) p. 279.

24. My own article, 'News, Rumour and the Control of Information in Austria-Hungary 1914–1918', *History*, vol. 77, No. 249 (1992), is a useful summary of the dilemmas facing the authorities, but it gives insufficient attention to their patriotic efforts.
25. Cf. Gerard DeGroot, *Blighty: British Society in the Era of the Great War* (London and New York, 1996) p. 184. For a useful French comparison to set against the Austro-Hungarian, see Jean-Jacques Becker, *The Great War and the French People* (Leamington Spa, 1993), chapter 2.
26. Vlado Strugar, *Jugoslavenske Socijaldemokratske Stranke 1914–1918* (Zagreb, 1963) p. 121.
27. Andrew Wachtel, 'Culture in the South Slavic Lands 1914–1918', in Roshwald and Stites (eds), *European Culture in the Great War*, p. 194. (This article otherwise pays little attention to the crucial role of the daily press in shaping culture and public opinion.)
28. Jan Hajšman, *Česká Mafie. Vzpomínký na Odboj Doma*, 2nd edn (Prague, 1934) pp. 28ff, 75. See also Vincenc Červinka's experience with the Prague daily *Národní Listy*: 'Persekuce válečná, hlavně tisková', in Žipek (ed.), *Domov za Války*, III, pp. 19ff.
29. Galántai, *Hungary in the First World War*, p. 64. See also Ivan Sanders, 'Hungarian Writers and Literature in World War I', in B. Király and N. Dreisziger (eds), *East Central European Society in World War I* (New York, 1985) pp. 145ff.
30. See Timms, *Karl Kraus*, pp. 285ff. With his focus on Vienna, however, Timms exaggerates the degree to which the whole of Austria-Hungary's press was 'willingly converted into an instrument of propaganda' (p. 281). Niall Ferguson also implies this through his heavy use of Kraus as a vehicle to analyze the press: *The Pity of War*, pp. 239ff.
31. Michael Károlyi, *Memoirs of Michael Károlyi: Faith without Illusion* (London, 1956) p. 60.
32. From 1914–15 the *Pressereferent* (based at the AOK) was Karl Schneller, and from 1915–18, Edmund von Glaise-Horstenau.
33. Hajšman, *Česká Mafie*, p. 31. For the view of one correspondent attached to the KPQ, see Karl Hans Strobl, *Die Weltgeschichte und das Igelhaus: vom Nachmittag des Lebens* (Budweis and Leipzig, 1944) pp. 44ff.
34. Heinrich Benedikt, *Damals im alten Österreich. Erinnerungen* (Vienna and Munich, 1979) p. 352.
35. Hildegund Schmölzer, *Die Propaganda des Kriegspressequartiers im Ersten Weltkrieg 1914–1918*, Ph.Diss. (Vienna, 1965) pp. 17ff. For the organization of the KPQ, see also Klaus Mayer, *Die Organisation des Kriegspressequartiers beim AOK im Ersten Weltkrieg 1914–1918*, Ph.Diss. (Vienna, 1963).
36. Steven Beller, 'The Tragic Carnival: Austrian Culture in the First World War', in Roshwald and Stites (eds), *European Culture in the Great War*, p. 132.
37. See Schmölzer, *Die Propaganda des Kriegspressequartiers*, pp. 26–32; and the essays in Roshwald and Stites (eds), *European Culture*, pp. 132, 173, 184, 202–4.
38. Redlich, *Österreichische Regierung*, p. 124.
39. Rauchensteiner, *Der Tod des Doppeladlers*, pp. 262–3. See the catalogue of posters which accompanied an exhibition held in Gorizia in 1991: Maria Masau Dan and Donatella Porcedda (eds), *L'Arma della Persuasione. Parole ed Immagini di Propaganda nella Grande Guerra* (Gorizia, 1991).
40. As one example, note the situation in Bohemia by 1918 where subscribing to the 8th war loan was totally eclipsed by collections for the 'nationalist cause': Žipek (ed.), *Domov za Války*, V, p. 149.

41. Dr Karl Kobald, Kriegshilfsbüro des k.k. Ministerium des Innerns (ed.), *Kriegsalmanach 1914/1916* (Vienna, 1916) p. 5. Schnitzler's contribution reveals that even those who wished to abstain from such propaganda were often unwittingly caught up in it (cf. Timms, *Karl Kraus*, p. 300).
42. Kurt Peball, 'Literarische Publikationen des Kriegsarchivs im Weltkrieg 1914 bis 1918', *Mitteilungen des Österreichischen Staatsarchivs*, vol. 14 (1961), pp. 240–60. A useful summary is in Peter Broucek, 'Das Kriegspressequartier und die literarischen Gruppen im Kriegsarchiv 1914–1918', in Klaus Almann and Hubert Lengauer (eds), *Österreich und der Große Krieg 1914–1918* (Vienna, 1989) pp. 132–7.
43. Timms, *Karl Kraus*, p. 301.
44. For further examples of this in Austria, see A.J. May, *The Passing of the Hapsburg Monarchy 1914–1918*, 2 vols (Philadelphia, 1966) I, pp. 292–327.
45. There is no space here to detail the economic crisis, but see a standard work: Gustav Gratz and Richard Schüller, *Die wirtschaftliche Zusammenbruch Österreich-Ungarns. Die Tragödie der Erschöpfung* (Vienna, 1930); and for example, Rauchensteiner, *Der Tod des Doppeladlers*, pp. 409ff.
46. May, *The Passing of the Hapsburg Monarchy*, I, p. 308.
47. Cornwall, 'News, Rumour and the Control of Information', pp. 60–1.
48. Felix Höglinger, *Ministerpräsident Heinrich Graf Clam-Martinic* (Graz and Cologne, 1964) p. 179.
49. For the Czechs, see Jan Hajšman's two volumes of memoirs: *Česká Mafie*, pp. 182ff; and *Mafie v Rozmachu. Vzpomínky na Odboj Doma* (Prague, 1933). For the Yugoslavs, see Mark Cornwall, 'The Experience of Yugoslav Agitation in Austria-Hungary 1917–18', in Hugh Cecil and Peter Liddle (eds), *Facing Armageddon: The First World War Experienced* (London, 1996) pp. 656ff.
50. Karl Friedrich Nowak, *Der Weg zur Katastrophe* (Berlin, 1926) p. xliv.
51. Rauchensteiner, *Der Tod des Doppeladlers*, p. 363.
52. Norman Stone, *The Eastern Front 1914–1917* (London, 1974) p. 314 note 16.
53. OULK, I: *Das Kriegsjahr 1914* (Vienna, 1931) p. 44.
54. István Deák, *Beyond Nationalism: A Social and Political History of the Habsburg Officer Corps 1848–1918* (Oxford, 1992) p. 193; and Mate Nikolić's report on the army, cited in Ljudevit Pivko, *Informatorji* (Maribor, 1925) p. 77.
55. See below Chapter 7, pp. 270ff.
56. Mark Cornwall, 'Morale and Patriotism in the Austro-Hungarian Army 1914–1918', in John Horne (ed.), *State, Society and Mobilization in Europe during the First World War* (Cambridge, 1997) p. 180.
57. See Richard Plaschka, 'Zur Vorgeschichte des Überganges von Einheiten des Infanterieregiments Nr.28 an der russischen Front 1915', in *Österreich und Europa. Festgabe für Hugo Hantsch zum 70. Geburtstag* (Vienna, 1965) pp. 455–64.
58. Hajšman, *Mafie v Rozmachu*, p. 230.
59. Arthur Arz von Straussenburg, *Zur Geschichte des Grossen Krieges 1914–1918* (Vienna, 1924) pp. 144–5, 147.
60. Österreichisches Staatsarchiv, Kriegsarchiv Vienna [hereafter KA], AOK, Op.Abt 1917, Op.Nr 44599, Kommando der SW Front to AOK Op.Abt, Op.Nr 17480, 2 September 1917.
61. KA, AOK Op.Abt 1917, Op.Nr 45286, Heeresgruppekommando [HGK] Conrad to AOK Op.Abt, Op.Nr 31165, 15 September 1917.
62. Peter Broucek, 'Aus den Erinnerungen eines Kundschaftoffiziers in Tirol 1914–1918', *Mitteilungen des Österreichischen Staatsarchivs*, vol. 33 (1980), p. 273. For

Conrad's own regular complaints: Nowak, *Der Weg zur Katastrophe*, pp. xxxviii, xlii, xliii.

63. His view was identical to that of other commanders such as Archduke Joseph, who noted in his diary that unreliable elements simply corrupted the good regiments: 'By mixing Hungarians among the "unreliable" troops, these do not become better or more reliable' (Galántai, *Hungary in the First World War*, p. 136).
64. For the restructuring of the army from May 1917, and its mixed benefits, see Richard Plaschka, Horst Haselsteiner and Arnold Suppan, *Innere Front. Militärassistenz, Widerstand und Umsturz in der Donaumonarchie 1918*, 2 vols (Vienna, 1974) I, pp. 33–7.
65. In its conclusion, the Austrian official history noted that all other 'victories' of the Monarchy – over Serbia, Romania or Russia – were partial, since the enemy was able to withdraw and regroup elsewhere: OULK, VII, pp. 823–4.

# 3
# The Experience of Propaganda against Russia

## 3.1 The campaign on the Eastern Front

By 1918 the AOK at Baden was convinced that propaganda, used to undermine the morale of enemy troops, could be a very effective weapon of warfare. This belief owed something to all the belligerents' sporadic dabbling in front propaganda from the beginning of the war. On the Western Front, from September 1914 the Germans were dropping manifestos over enemy lines, eliciting a response from the British and French, even if a full campaign by either side would have to wait until 1918. The Balkan and Italian Fronts too in the early years had witnessed some intermittent front propaganda, in the Italian case of an increasing sophistication under the influence of their army Intelligence officers. The Austrian military's own commitment to the propaganda weapon, however, required time, and above all, months of futile campaigning with traditional armaments before they would even consider employing such an 'unchivalrous' instrument against the enemy. Their outlook changed perceptibly only after the experience of 1917. In that year the Central Powers, Germany and Austria-Hungary, launched the first coordinated propaganda campaign of its kind on any front. They did so on the Eastern Front against the Russians with the purpose of accelerating the Russian army's desire for peace. The campaign was later belittled in the official histories and in memoirs, and historians have continued to underestimate or simply ignore it, thereby focusing attention all the more on the sophisticated Allied propaganda campaigns of 1918.[1] In fact the 1917 campaign helped to make the latter possible and was therefore crucial for all the belligerents. The Central Powers at the time viewed it as a success, judging that their efforts had interacted with events in the Russian hinterland to force an armistice on the Eastern Front. It indicated to them what could now be achieved with the propaganda weapon and they proceeded to wield it in new directions, on the Italian, Balkan and Western Fronts. In turn, the propaganda victory in the East stimulated a response in the

Allied camp: in Lord Northcliffe's words, 'the tragedy of Russia [was] due partly to lack of Allied propaganda to counteract that of the Germans'.[2] In these developments the Eastern campaign was a formative stage for both sides in their conception of psychological warfare, highlighting both the alleged potential of the new propaganda weapon and the need to compete with the enemy in a new field of operations.

Prior to 1917 psychological warfare on the Eastern Front was not unusual. It was the Russians who gave the lead and first made good use of it. The 100 000 manifestos which they scattered as the Russian 'steam-roller' advanced into Galicia in the autumn of 1914 had proclaimed, under the signature of Grand Duke Nicholas, 'liberty' for all peoples of Austria-Hungary.[3] In the following months these leaflets steadily increased in number, 'as if falling from the sky', as one Czech observer noted. While the Russians may have hesitated to issue specific manifestos in the Czech language, their first efforts set an example which was quickly followed: many of their leaflets were soon being copied or forged in the Czech lands of the Monarchy. Moreover, they alarmed the Austrian authorities who stepped up their vigilance against the spread of treasonable ideas, and even sentenced seven people to death in early 1915 for circulating enemy manifestos.[4] The Russians' early perception that the Austrian army's multinational character might be exploited is also clear from other evidence. In August 1914 the Russian Minister of War had agreed to create a Czech unit (*Družina*) specifically to act as propagandists or Intelligence troops among Czechs in the opposing trenches; the *Družina* became the basis for a slow expansion of Czech volunteers in the Russian army.[5]

Yet apart from this limited patrol work, the Russian use of written propaganda in the first years of the war seems to have matched that of their opponents. Namely, it was piecemeal and usually limited to crude appeals about the prisoners and booty captured.[6] Both of the Central Powers were not slow to respond in kind, and occasionally showed some ingenuity. Suggestive letters written by Russian prisoners of war were distributed; and one Austrian leaflet which was scattered widely from the air told Russian soldiers that seven roubles would be paid for every enemy rifle which was surrendered.[7] The Austrians could also themselves play the 'separatist card', announcing, for example, to Russia's Moslems that Turkey had entered the war on the side of the Central Powers.[8] By late 1916 this process had gone a stage further. Balloons were launched from the Austrian trenches, carrying leaflets which communicated the Central Powers' peace offer and their promise to create a postwar independent Poland; it apparently caused a striking increase in the number of Polish deserters from the Russian army.[9]

Between the Germans and Austrians, the key initiative for developing the propaganda weapon from this point appears to have lain with Germany. In view of the paucity of material in the German archives for this period, we are forced to rely heavily on the Austrian records in constructing the 1917 campaign; but they consistently betray the same story of Germany's lead. In July 1916 the German High Command (DOHL) had established a military section at the German Foreign Ministry in order to bring its influence to bear upon Germany's propaganda abroad. Though financed by the Foreign Ministry, this section under Colonel Hans von Häften was from January 1917 directly responsible to the DOHL. It drew up policy for German propaganda in the neutral press, but was also responsible for composing material to be sent to subordinate propaganda offices on the Eastern Front for use against the enemy. In fact Häften soon built up his organization into the major centre for dealing with military aspects of German propaganda abroad.[10]

In Austria-Hungary a tighter coordination of propaganda work abroad and on the Eastern Front occurred only from March 1917. On 15 March the Foreign Ministry at the Ballhausplatz in Vienna, alarmed at the increasingly lively cultural propaganda of the other Great Powers in neutral countries, took the initiative and set up its own 'propaganda section' in the press department of the ministry.[11] Its purpose was to give a greater uniformity and direction to what all acknowledged to have been the 'chaotic conditions' previously prevailing in Austria's cultural and economic propaganda abroad. For the military aspects of such propaganda, the new Chief of the General Staff, General Arz von Straussenburg, welcomed the suggestion of Colonel Eisner-Bubna, the new head of the KPQ, that he should centralize and coordinate military propaganda in neutral countries (especially Switzerland).[12] Thus two centres – at the Foreign Ministry and the KPQ – now cooperated, eliminating previously overlapping activities by many departments, in order to promote Austria-Hungary's image in the neutral and Allied states.

It is not clear whether this reorganization directly influenced the AOK to pay more attention to its propaganda on the Eastern Front. Probably such a change was chiefly due to the Central Powers' sudden awareness of the new opportunities in the East. The event which would galvanize their campaign into action was the fall of the Tsarist regime, and the evidence from the Russian trenches that soldiers were anxious to receive news about the Russian hinterland. By 16 March, on the southern parts of the front, the Austrians were advertising the revolt of the Petrograd garrison and arrest of the Tsarist ministers by means of placards raised above the trenches or leaflets scattered by plane.[13] German military Intelligence was also quick to exploit the obvious deterioration of discipline among the Russian rank and file.[14] For the Germans this was to be only one ingredient in their broader policy of encouraging chaos in the Russian interior with a view to knocking Russia out of the war and achieving a separate peace in the East. Earlier in the war the Austrian High Command had dabbled with the idea of destabilizing Russia by supporting some Russian left-wing agitators. They had, for example, financed Zivin, a Socialist Revolutionary in Switzerland until the summer of 1916, but had then dropped him, possibly because they had expected his work to have a more damaging and immediate impact on the Russian armed forces.[15] Germany had gone a lot further than Austria-Hungary in this type of activity. From 1915 the German Foreign Ministry had been financing Russian revolutionaries; and it was in the aftermath of the March 1917 revolution, with the real prospect of ending war in the East, that Germany's political and military elite agreed to allow the Bolshevik Lenin to travel in the famous 'sealed train' from Switzerland to Petrograd (where he arrived on 16 April).

At the front, it was Russian overtures, especially their increased fraternization across the trenches, which shaped the German response. By late March the Germans were not only making rather clumsy attempts at oral and written propaganda, but also planning to send a special newspaper across the lines to feed the Russian yearning for news.[16] Certainly the Russian commanders in turn stepped up their own use of leaflets against the opposing forces, challenging their enemies' arguments. They urged Austrians of German nationality to revolt against rulers who, in the pocket of the Prussian militarists, were turning the Monarchy into 'an enormous cemetery'.[17] And, in wooden placards erected between the trenches, they advised the enemy to behave 'honourably' and negotiate peace with the new Russian government.[18] It was in this unsettled environment that the Central Powers' campaign was born. The Easter holidays of mid-April were approaching, and the DOHL sensed that the mass fraternization which was bound to occur at that time (as in previous years) would be highly opportune for disseminating some well-organized propaganda. As one German leaflet at this time noted rather casually, 'Germany is ready to make peace, though peace is not necessary for her. She will wait patiently to see if the new and free Russia will start peace negotiations with us in the holy holidays of Christ's resurrection.'[19]

General Max Hoffmann, Chief of Staff of Eastern Command (*Oberost*), was put in charge of this operation. Its express aim was to stimulate the desire for peace among the Russian rank and file and promote chaos so that an armistice would become inevitable.[20] Especially to be targeted were the Russian soldiers' committees which, springing up along the front in previous weeks, were closely tied to the Petrograd Soviet and might be expected to sympathize with its 'Peace Manifesto' of 27 March. Hoffmann drew extensively on Colonel von Häften's organization to gather material for the use of German Intelligence officers during the campaign. The basic arguments to be used were formulated on 9 April by the German Foreign Ministry in a series of propaganda guidelines. Such coordination between the Foreign Ministry and the military, on the broad themes to be used in propaganda at the front, was to become standard practice in the months ahead. In the guidelines of early April it was emphasized that Germany desired peace, but did not need it and, in response to Russian propaganda, would not succumb to any Russian agitation aimed at spreading revolution and shaking the German people from their monarchist loyalty. On the other hand, it was clear that the Russian 'People's Government' needed peace to consolidate their revolution, but was being forced to prolong the war for England's selfish ends. A major theme therefore would be to play on Russia's continued imperialist policy: like the Tsar, the present Russian government was allegedly still a tool of England, something underlined by a notorious pictorial leaflet which implied that the cousins, George V and Nicholas II, had identical influence over Russia's destiny.[21]

While Hoffmann issued these guidelines to the army Intelligence officers, including the Austrian armies within Eastern Command's sphere of influence, on 11 April General Ludendorff communicated the guidelines to the Austro-Hungarian High Command. The AOK thereupon immediately followed the German lead. Already the new head of Austrian military Intelligence, Max Ronge, had assumed overall control of Austrian front propaganda. He placed control of the imminent Eastern campaign in the hands of Captain Pantelija Borovica, head of the Russian section of AOK Intelligence.[22] In the following months, Borovica had the difficult task of supervising Austria's new propaganda machinery on the Eastern Front. Here he would concentrate chiefly upon southern sectors of the front under Archduke Joseph where Habsburg troops predominated. But his job was complicated by the fact that from late 1916 most Austrian armies to the north were directly subordinate to German Eastern Command, something which would place serious obstacles in the way of coordinating an allied campaign which took full account of Austria-Hungary's interests. The potential for the campaign to be weakened by conflicting allied power-centres was abundantly clear from the start.

Gradually, however, from April 1917 'propaganda positions' were set up in each Austro-Hungarian division, consisting of an Intelligence officer, an interpreter and three or four men (*Nachrichtentruppen*), all subordinate to the local army Intelligence section. Their task was to spread propaganda among the enemy forces, including (and again following a German suggestion) *Nedelia*, the Austrian newspaper issued for Russian prisoners of war.[23] At the same time they were expected while on patrol to gather useful intelligence, as well as countering any efforts by Russian troops to make 'counter-propaganda'. The AOK instructed its army commands on how to receive Russian negotiators (with schnapps and tobacco), and for overall guidance in oral propaganda sent them a slightly revised version of the German guidelines. Passages were altered to emphasize Emperor Karl's desire for peace and the 'centuries-old evolution and freedom' enjoyed by all under Habsburg rule.[24]

From the start of the Central Powers' campaign oral propaganda was the priority, especially with the Russian soldiers' committees. By Easter 1917 such contact was already achieved with 107 out of the 214 enemy divisions. The official cease-fire which was then announced produced the expected orgy of fraternization in many sectors as both sides met to exchange gifts and propaganda in no-man's-land.[25] Yet for the Austrians not all results of this exercise were positive. Some Russian negotiators showed themselves equally adept at spreading revolutionary-socialist propaganda among their new 'friends', and in some instances the Russians reactivated their tactic of using Czech troops to entice 'Austrian Czechs' to desert. This produced a few unquantifiable successes in the confused traffic at Easter. Moreover, it was precisely this danger, that propaganda efforts would rebound on Austrian troops and threaten their own discipline, which had made so many Austrian commanders hostile to the campaign from the very beginning. General Alfred Krauss was not alone in being 'extremely unsympathetic to this activity'.[26]

But the damage caused by propaganda was insignificant in comparison to the immediate benefits of the campaign. The AOK and many subordinate commands were clearly impressed with the unofficial cease-fire which descended on the front for many weeks, giving time for reconstruction of positions, saving munition and lives, and eventually allowing six divisions to be transferred to the Italian Front in the following months. They also felt, precisely because the Russians responded in kind, that propaganda was proving itself to be a 'modern fighting weapon' which could not be ignored. The new task after Easter was to expand the initial contacts and work on previously hostile sectors of the front, while limiting any fighting which might galvanize the Russians to resume a more defensive attitude. The AOK and DOHL now agreed that the official cease-fire and mass fraternization would be discontinued, and the Russian soldiers informed that their superiors had seriously 'abused' the period of rest.[27] But meanwhile, German and Austrian Intelligence officers would continue their propaganda, hinting to Russian *parlementaires* that their officers should now be the ones to make some 'peace initiatives'.[28] By late April this policy too was felt to have made some progress, for contact had been established on southern sectors with Russian soldiers either orally or by letter 'almost everywhere', and an unofficial cease-fire still prevailed. Contrary to the pessimistic line taken in the Austrian official history, the Central Powers appear to have been reasonably satisfied with the results obtained.[29]

The beginnings of the campaign were therefore auspicious. But it is clear that by May the Austrians were still not properly organized. It was Germany which was taking the lead, especially on northern sectors of the front where the Habsburg liaison officer with Eastern Command grudgingly observed:

> Our belated campaign not only had to be incorporated into the established German organization, but also to assume a subordinate position. Prussians remained the spokesmen of all negotiations, to the obvious astonishment of the Russians who apparently still did not think our dependence on Germany had gone that far.[30]

This may be a slight exaggeration, reflecting the author's prejudices. But there was some truth in it and in the hint of Austrian tardiness. For example, when in early May Pantelija Borovica first contacted the Intelligence section of the Austrian 2nd Army Command [2AK] he found propaganda work in its infancy and already facing a number of difficulties.[31] Captain Terlecki, deputy-Intelligence officer of the 2AK, revealed that only Eastern Command had sent him instructions on propaganda work; and it was clear that it was the German Intelligence officer at the 2AK who was most prominent in supervising detailed negotiations with Russian *parlementaires* (which were felt to be beyond the remit of simple propaganda personnel). Moreover, even if there had already been some distribution of *Nedelia* and other newspapers in this sector, Borovica was undoubtedly disappointed that very few 'propaganda positions' had actually been set up at the front; only opposite the XVIII corps had traffic with the enemy been possible, partly due to hostilities elsewhere, but partly because the 2AK lacked sufficient Russian-speaking propaganda personnel. It was a situation which Arz and Emperor Karl discovered for themselves on visiting the front at this time.[32] And it caused Arz on 8 May to send a blunt order to all the Austrian army commands: 'our propaganda activity on the Eastern Front has not been at all satisfactory. Our Intelligence officers are evidently doing much less than the Germans.' In future, Arz specified, propaganda positions were to be activated on all Austrian sectors, with a specialized Russian-speaking personnel who would shield their potentially dangerous activities from ordinary Austrian troops: 'I expect a good response to all orders concerning propaganda, [since] this branch of work is now of special importance for the course of events.'[33] As a sign of the new urgency, Borovica himself set off a week later for a brief tour of the Austrian armies under Eastern Command to discuss personally the operation with Austrian and German Intelligence personnel.[34]

For the Austrian leadership the sense of urgency sprang directly from its impatience to conclude a formal armistice in the East. It remained a truism in particular for Count Czernin, the Habsburg Foreign Minister, that the Monarchy could not endure another winter of war. On 12 April 1917, in a notorious memorandum forwarded to Kaiser Wilhelm with Emperor Karl's approval, he had warned: 'If the monarchs of the Central Powers are unable to conclude peace in the next few months, the peoples will do so over their heads, and then the waves of revolution will sweep away everything for which our brothers and sons are still fighting and dying today.' While the German military were adamant that peace in the East must mean German annexation of Russian territory (and even compensation for Russia at Austrian expense), Czernin was quite prepared to make peace for Austria-Hungary on the basis of mutual renunciation of any annexations and reparations.[35] Arz von Straussenburg had come to the same conclusion. On 26 April he agreed with Czernin that the Central Powers ought now to use the existing mood among enemy troops to push for a favourable peace with Russia. Since, Arz argued, 'the impact of informal gossip from trench to trench has exhausted itself', it was time to begin direct talks with the Russian military leadership. Though not at all optimistic about the latter's receptiveness, Arz envisaged more chance of success if the Central Powers put forward concrete terms instead of cloaking their designs with German euphemisms such as 'honourable peace'. Assurances, that the Central Powers would annex no Russian territory, would accept an independent Poland and would 'consider Russia's economic requirements' – these were worth making. For, as Arz concluded: 'If Russia breaks out [*ausspringen*] from the ranks of our enemies, it offers us such great advantages that it really pays to build golden bridges.' With these ideas and the Emperor's backing, he approached the German High Command, proposing that the Central Powers make an official armistice offer to the Russians.[36]

The High Commands were able to agree a new five-point programme, approved by their respective foreign ministries, which was to be used for propaganda at the front and as a preliminary basis for any armistice talks.[37] This programme, suggesting an armistice of three to four weeks, stemmed directly from terms agreed at recent informal Russo-German negotiations in Stockholm; but its innocent reference (point four) to 'frontier rectifications' for Germany in Lithuania and Courland belied the DOHL's vigorous insistence on massive annexation of territory in the East if peace was to be concluded. This fact underlay many of the existing tensions between the two allies.[38] Unlike the Austrians, the DOHL saw no reason for a hasty or compromise peace, sensing that the present course of events could only work to Germany's advantage.[39] As General Ludendorff cryptically informed Arz:

> The internal disintegration of the Russian army will continue even without the high pressure of our propaganda. Time is on our side on the Eastern Front as well. And besides this propaganda channel I expect even greater success through employing copious funds and agents in Petersburg and elsewhere.[40]

What effect these methods were already having is difficult to assess. But the Russian Commander-in-Chief at this very time felt that he knew Ludendorff's objectives, noting in late April that defeatist propaganda in the Russian army 'comes from two sides – from the enemy and from the rear ... and obviously stems from the same source'.[41] At the front, Ludendorff, even though like most commanders initially sceptical of the benefits of propaganda, now expected it would continue to infect the Russian rank and file. But he was dubious about any immediate impact on their officers. He agreed instead to Arz's idea of making an official offer of an armistice to the Russian High Command. If it was rebuffed, as he too felt likely, the incident would at least be grist to the mill of the propaganda campaign in the front line, convincing the Russian soldier even more that it was his leaders who were the obstacles to peace. Yet, such a rebuff was also bound to lead to a scaling down of the Central Powers' propaganda campaign since, as Ludendorff argued (and the Austrians agreed), there was always the danger that too many overtures would be viewed as weakness by the Russians and exploited in their counter-propaganda.[42]

In fact, events in May 1917 developed very much as Ludendorff anticipated. Although the allies' arguments struck many chords among Russian troops in different sectors,[43] the Russian commanders, against all odds, were still managing to keep some lid on the unrest in the ranks. In this they were aided, or at least so the Central Powers always imagined, by Entente advisers whose counter-propaganda, 'conducted with great skill and unscrupulous means' had, so far, 'visibly won the upper-hand on the Eastern Front'.[44] In the middle of May the Germans proceeded to test the water by sending out some officers, armed with the armistice offer, to the Russian 5th army commander General Dragomirov; he immediately exploited the incident for counter-propaganda, publicizing the event as an instance of the enemy's deviousness in trying to weaken the Eastern Front. On 19 May the Germans and Austrians followed up their move along the whole front. Almost 100 *parlementaires* were dispatched across the trenches bearing proposals from Prince Leopold of Bavaria, Commander-in-Chief of the Eastern Front, for a general armistice. The Russian response, however, was still overwhelmingly negative with a number of the emissaries being fired on or arrested as spies.[45]

The DOHL and AOK readily admitted that this direct approach to the Russian commanders had been a complete failure. Yet they had, as we have seen, always viewed it as something of a gamble. It did not mean, as Arz and others would later suggest, that the propaganda campaign as a whole had failed, nor – as the Austrian official history implies with selective quotations – that the Central Powers' 'peace propaganda' was at an end.[46] True, on 29 May Arz informed Czernin that 'the means of the allied armies for continuing peace propaganda in the Russian army are, as recent days have shown, now exhausted'. But he acknowledged the results so far achieved: the Russians had been paralysed at a time of decisive hostilities in the West (the 10th Isonzo battle in Italy and the Nivelle offensive in France) and their infantry were still not capable of launching an offensive for some time.[47] Indeed, as a number of German and Austrian authorities observed, the steady flow of propaganda in May coupled with the armistice offer had served to increase further the gap between the Russian officer and his men. It had caused a rise in fraternization (contact with 70 per cent of Russian or Romanian divisions by the end of the month), and provided fertile ground for future peace initiatives. Most significantly, the 'broad thrust into the enemy front' in mid-May had supplied 'a deep insight into the morale and conditions of the Russian army', something not possible from casual fraternization.[48]

The whole experience therefore had perceptively strengthened the Central Powers' sympathy for the propaganda weapon. Arz, for example, might well feel that large-scale front propaganda should be discontinued, but he admitted that it had performed a service; it should now be carried on on a reduced scale. The aim would be to reach the Russian commanders indirectly through steadily working on the receptive rank and file, and continuing to stress that the Central Powers were ready to make peace.[49] Arz and his deputy, Colonel Alfred von Waldstätten, seem by now to have shared the DOHL's optimism that the Russian army was gradually disintegrating. Their propaganda could slowly gnaw at it, adding to the poison seeping in from the rear, while they themselves concentrated their attention on the other theatres of war.[50]

## 3.2 The 'breaking of Russia'

If the Austrians now felt that they knew something of the propaganda weapon's potential, they had also received extra lessons in the difficulties of allied coordination, both in policy and action. For while the AOK had regularly and calmly discussed the methods and arguments of its propaganda with the Ballhausplatz, the campaign had immediately produced some tension with the German High Command which was much more inclined to send its ideas for propaganda direct to the Eastern army commands. According to Captain Moritz Fleischmann, the Austro-Hungarian liaison officer attached to German *Oberost*, the DOHL was constantly trying to take full control of the propaganda campaign, relegating Austrian personnel to a subservient position and thereby infringing the sovereign rights of the Monarchy. Arz, anxious to be congenial, may have been only slightly irritated, but it certainly ruffled the feathers of Czernin when he learnt of this development. Czernin's main anxiety, however, was about the content of propaganda which the German military were allegedly sending to the Russians. Even though he was well aware of the DOHL's insistence on annexation of Lithuania and Courland, he assumed that the Germans would abide by the propaganda guidelines agreed at the end of April (and reaffirmed in late May).[51] According to these, the Russians would only be told that Germany expected 'frontier rectifications' with regard to these Baltic regions.[52] In early June, however, Czernin learnt from Captain Fleischmann that the DOHL during May had actually ordered Eastern Command to tell the Russians that Germany in any peace settlement would have to annex Lithuania and Courland. If this were true, the Central Powers' agreed propaganda guidelines had been compromised, a prime example of the dangers which could arise when propaganda was not consistent with agreed policy, in this case revealing the German military's hidden agenda. Indeed, Fleischmann argued that Russia's hostile response to the Central Powers' armistice proposal was directly attributable to Germany's unconcealed annexationist goals; the chances of fraternization had diminished and the Russians had been able to publish the armistice offer 'with snide remarks' [*mit abfällige Begleitworten*].[53] Although the veracity of Fleischmann's report was later to be queried, on the basis of his comments Emperor Karl proceeded to write to Kaiser Wilhelm on 7 June, complaining about Germany's behaviour. The Kaiser in reply rejected the accusations, pointing to the steady disintegration of the Russian state as evidence of the process to which German propaganda was continuing to contribute.[54]

At the front, meanwhile, the first task of the Central Powers' more modest campaign was to fend off Russian counter-propaganda in the wake of the armistice offer. The aim above all was to keep up links with the Russian rank and file, while moving onto the offensive and attacking their superiors' 'bellicose' attitude. There would be no more official armistice offers and less talk about what precise terms the Central Powers might offer or demand from the peace; rather the emphasis would rest on their simple readiness for peace in contrast to the Entente or the Russian Provisional Government.[55] Thus from the beginning of June the propaganda went out, by wireless, telegraph as well as written and oral contact, condemning those, like General Dragomirov, who had rejected armistice talks. These commanders and the Petrograd government were, so the argument went, still tied to the Entente and the secret annexationist treaties of the old Tsarist regime. Instead they should be listening to the vibrant mood of peace in their own armed forces; all the more so, as this mirrored the conduct of the Central Powers who since Easter had limited their hostilities, had demonstrated their willingness and their precise terms for peace, but who could, if necessary, fight on and expand their war aims to Russia's detriment.[56]

The AOK might well expect that this message would have some impact amongst the Russian rank and file. For it knew, from increased Russian air and artillery activity, from deserters and from the replacement of enemy units infected with propaganda, that Alexander Kerensky, the new Russian Minister of War, was acceding to Entente wishes and organizing a fresh offensive.[57] This was bound to be a hazardous enterprise for the Russians; the latent discontent in so many Russian units smouldered and became increasingly evident as preparations for the attack gathered pace. It is true that not all appeared black to the Russian leadership. The Petrograd Soviet, for instance, stood firmly behind the offensive as a sign of support for the Revolution; on 10 June it indicated its response to the Central Powers' propaganda, rejecting their calls for any separate peace and naming its own allies as 'the working classes of England and France'. This was something of a rebuff to the Central Powers. Yet they could still draw comfort from the fact that the Soviet was not espousing the Entente's war aims: its reply was testament to the divergent interests which could be exploited in Russia.[58]

Similarly, even if in June many Russian infantry units in eastern Galicia were becoming more hostile to the German-Austrian propagandists, the latter still had many positive advantages.[59] They were working on an army where there were the first signs of mutiny amongst troops being moved up to the front. Moreover, it was at this time that Bolshevik propaganda first began to spread in the front line, especially in sectors in the forefront of the attack; it began to constitute a major unsettling influence thwarting orderly preparations for the offensive. It is important to emphasize that Bolshevik agitation was thoroughly akin to the Central Powers' propaganda. It played on Russia's links to the imperialist Entente, on their 'secret treaties', on the issue of land reform in Russia (a subject which German propaganda had already toyed with) and above all on the futility of the Russian offensive.[60] It was an ideal accompaniment to the Central Powers' campaign. For as one German Intelligence officer wrote later: 'As the Russians' offensive plans became clearer, it was all the more the task of our propaganda to explain the motives of the Russian government, in undertaking an offensive which we had done nothing to provoke, and to ascribe their behaviour to agitation by the Entente.'[61]

This was precisely the line which Pantelija Borovica took in mid-June when seeking to coordinate Austrian propaganda along the front. He advised the 2AK that the build-up of Russian forces opposite the *Heeresgruppe* Böhm-Ermolli offered rich opportunities for propaganda, preferably by balloon behind the Russian lines but also in tandem with neighbouring Austrian armies.[62] And while the allies still took suitable military precautions as the offensive loomed, they were reasonably optimistic about its outcome. Since so many Russian divisions leading the attack were known to be already infected by their propaganda, they could expect that Russian demoralization would quickly become evident during the offensive itself.[63]

In fact, at first the propaganda boot was on the other foot, and worn by Russia. The AOK had always been conscious in these months that the propaganda weapon could easily be used against its own army with devastating results. Indeed, in June 1917 the 2AK was expressly warned by Ronge and Borovica against trying to subvert enemy Ukrainian troops with specifically Ukrainian propaganda, lest this rebound and infect the Monarchy's already suspect Ruthene soldiers.[64] The AOK never showed the same caution when aiming propaganda at Polish troops in the Russian army; and from July, as we will see, the Central Powers were to target special arguments at the Romanian forces opposite the *Heeresgruppe* Mackensen. But generally it was the case that Baden was wary of playing the 'nationality card' in case it caused a backlash in the Habsburg army.

Yet for Austria-Hungary's enemies this could, of course, be a trump card. It was during their last offensive that the Russians decided for the first time to use their Czech volunteer troops as a combatant unit. These Czechs, former prisoners or deserters, had previously only been assigned to Russian units for Intelligence or propaganda purposes. Over 3000 of them were now grouped together in a 'Czechoslovak Brigade' and marched to the front line at Zborov. A British witness praised them as 'grand men with chests like Aldershot gymnastic instructors'.[65] Even so, many of them undoubtedly had mixed feelings about the forthcoming baptism of fire, for they were only too aware of the Russians' low morale. Once in the trenches they saw how the enemy raised red flags and tried to fraternize but, as one Czech described later, they knew how to respond: 'We agreed to send over to them a few "pills" [i.e. shells] which would cure them of their efforts to propagate something which they themselves did not want to hear about.'[66] They also sang Czech national songs with the express purpose of undermining the morale of the Austro-Hungarian 19th infantry division [19 ID] opposite, a unit primarily of Czech nationality.[67] This certainly bore fruit. When on 29 June in sweltering conditions the Russian offensive was finally launched and the Czechoslovak Brigade advanced, it was precisely this division which collapsed and were taken prisoner in their thousands; one of the regiments (IR75 – 82 per cent Czech) lost 2300 men as prisoners.[68] Although Zborov was of temporary military significance, for the land gained was soon retaken by fresh German troops, it had major political importance which justified its subsequent notoriety and place in Czech mythology. For the first time in the war, citizens of the Habsburg Empire had fought in great numbers in an enemy army. It set an example for Czech resistance on the side of the Entente, leading directly to the establishment of a Czechoslovak Legion in Russia, and giving the western Powers clear evidence of how Austria-Hungary's nationalities might be used against the Monarchy to win the war.[69]

The Central Powers too, however, viewed the Galician battle of July 1917 as the 'decisive test' for their propaganda campaign.[70] Until 19 July when they launched a counter-offensive, their Intelligence troops showered the enemy trenches with a range of propaganda material and successfully maintained personal propaganda links. Relying on newly agreed guidelines, the propagandists explained to the Russians why they had to fight yet another battle (for the imperialist Entente) and why any counter-attack would simply be in order to retake Austrian soil.[71] But with a war of movement from July, as the Russians at last retreated out of Habsburg territory (eastern Galicia and Bukovina), the propagandists were being forced to adopt new techniques; oral propaganda, which had been a staple of the campaign's early efforts, was no longer possible. Instead, the scattering of newspapers over the retreating Russian troops became of major significance. This included the newspapers issued for Russian prisoners of war, *Nedelia* and Germany's *Russkii Vestnik*, as well as selected editions of the Viennese socialist daily, *Arbeiter-Zeitung* (ironic, for in 1918 this paper would be used for the same purpose but on the Italian Front against Austrian troops). However, these were not felt to be adequate for the task of sending up-to-date and relevant news to the enemy. Therefore printing presses were set up at the army commands and supplied with material from the Intelligence heads in order to produce daily propaganda papers such as *Obzor* and *Posledniia Izvestiia*. The object was to avoid the unsubtle style used in previous manifestos as well as any overly obtrusive commentary. Rather, the material would speak for itself, providing factual information from the allied or enemy press about the Central Powers' readiness for peace and the chaotic conditions in the Russian interior.[72] It was a technique which the propaganda campaigns of 1918 would perfect.

While the AOK at Baden was becoming more flexible in its propaganda techniques, it was also by the early summer identifying new propaganda targets. Sensitive to the dangerous repercussions of playing the 'nationality card' against the Russians, Baden nevertheless realized the need for specific arguments when turning its new weapon against Romanian forces on the Eastern Front. Romania, after entering the war on the Allied side in August 1916, had been speedily crushed, Wallachia occupied by German troops, and the Romanian army reformed in the 'rump' Romanian state under French supervision.[73] By June 1917 the Central Powers had begun to entice Romanian divisions (chiefly opposite the *Heeresgruppe* Mackensen) with the offer of sending soldiers' letters to their families in Wallachia. They followed this up with assurances of good treatment for deserters and a regular newspaper service, informing the Romanian forces about life in their 'homeland'; it was the same technique currently employed against the Russians, but a richer material was undoubtedly available because of the German control of Bucharest.[74] Only by July did the Austrians envisage more personal contact with Romanian soldiers and for this purpose Baden drew up specific guidelines. The broad theme of these was quite simple. Romania's current misfortune was to be ascribed almost totally to the Entente Powers who, after deceiving King Ferdinand with false promises, had left Romania in the lurch in late 1916; a few months later they were allegedly administering (the rump) Moldavia in a disgraceful manner which 'must deeply offend every patriotic Romanian'. In contrast to the Entente, who were pushing Romania further down the road to destruction, the Central Powers offered Romania peace, a history of excellent prewar economic and cultural ties, and the example of a just and prosperous administration in Wallachia. In view of this, the guidelines urged Romanians to cut loose from the Entente's 'pernicious tentacles' and to follow the example of those thousands of Romanian prisoners who in June had returned to their homeland to lead a quiet life.[75]

While formulating these 'simple truths', Baden could not avoid certain unpleasant realities. Firstly, it was clear from the limited contact across the Romanian trenches that Romanian hostility to Hungary was very strong, possibly strong enough to undermine the effect of all other propaganda arguments.

This persuaded Arz to add to the guidelines a sentence, proposed by Czernin, that 'allegations about the oppression and persecution of Romanians in Hungary belong to the rank of fables', a statement which Czernin supported with the dubious 'evidence' that Romania's cultural renaissance had only been possible in the idyllic free atmosphere of Transylvania.[76] Secondly, in submitting the guidelines for the DOHL's approval, the AOK once again confronted the obstacle of Germany's ambitions in the East. In particular, Ludendorff insisted that the guidelines specify Romania's future effective subordination to the Central Powers, something which Czernin certainly hesitated over before accepting.[77] Whether these 'realities' about Hungary and Germany's ambitions actually inhibited the effect of propaganda against Romanian soldiers is unclear. Possibly many Romanians ('uneducated peasants' in the view of one German Intelligence officer)[78] would be unlikely to appreciate certain nuances within the propaganda. The evidence anyway suggests that in the following months Romanian officers successfully managed to intercept much of the allied propaganda and limited the chances of oral contacts. On the other hand, the propagandists could indeed feel confident of some progress, not least from the fact that after August the number of Romanian deserters to Wallachia began to increase dramatically.[79]

Meanwhile, by mid-August after three weeks' retreat by the Russians out of Austro-Hungarian territory, the AOK was prepared to acknowledge that propaganda had again played an important rôle in the Russian *débâcle*. The evidence from deserters and prisoners (42 000 of them) seemed to suggest its effectiveness in lowering morale. Whole Russian corps were alleged to have become infected, refusing to move into position during the offensive. The Russian XLV corps, for instance, had helped through its passivity to surrender the important city of Tarnopol to German troops. The Russian XL corps, which had been hostile to fraternization in April, had gradually been enticed with rum, cigarettes, newspapers and personal contact and whipped into an 'almost anarchical condition'; at the end of July it allegedly sabotaged Russia's offensive on the Romanian Front by refusing to cooperate.[80] Whatever the truth of these stories, and many similar ones could be cited,[81] their significance lies in their value for the AOK as proof of the propaganda weapon's success. It was in the light of such evidence which had been accumulating since March, that Arz on 10 August praised the propagandists:

> The organs of the propaganda service have undoubtedly made a glorious contribution to the allied troops' successes in Galicia. Through their unflagging activity and efficiency, which so often threatens them with mortal danger or capture, they have sharply diminished enemy morale, rendered valuable service to the Austro-Hungarian leadership, obtained months of rest for our troops and saved them from casualties during this time.[82]

Despite this, the Russian army had not completely collapsed. Many troops, when pushed onto the defensive in late July, had shown surprising resilience to the Central Powers' advance, halting it on the Zbruch river. The counter-offensive was now exhausted, not least because of the usual difficulty of bringing up supplies, especially munition, to troops who had pushed so far forward. Similarly, to the south on the Romanian Front, the enemy had effectively staunched any advance by German-Austrian forces into Moldavia during August. It was not possible in late August, although Austrian propaganda might later suggest otherwise,[83] for the Central Powers to cross the borders and conquer Ukraine and Moldavia. For apart from facing successful Russian-Romanian resistance, the allies already had more pressing demands on their military machines: the AOK was now fully occupied with the 11th Isonzo battle in Italy, while the DOHL's attention varied between the Western Front (the third battle of Ypres) and a desire to advance in the north-east, take Riga (achieved on 3 September) and threaten Petrograd. Both High Commands in fact were prepared by September to put the Eastern Front on the back-burner, treating it primarily as a 'military reservoir' [*Kraftspeicher*] from which to draw off troops for the Western and Italian theatres.[84]

When the fronts in the East had stabilized, however, the Central Powers decided to 'reactivate' their propaganda campaign along the lines pursued since April 1917. The order was obeyed only grudgingly by some commanders who continued to view this activity as a confession of weakness or an invitation to Russian espionage, and certainly a poor alternative to continued offensive action.[85] Pantelija Borovica in turn was quite aware that propaganda would be difficult after a period of hostilities, but he nevertheless urged the Intelligence officers to resume contacts and reactivate the 'newspaper service' from 1 September.[86] In fact the propaganda seeds were now able to fall on ever more fertile ground. Attempts by the Russian High Command to tighten discipline in the wake of the failed offensive were only temporarily successful: they acted like a thin varnish upon soldiers longing for peace, men who increasingly identified those trying to continue the war – whether it be their officers or Kerensky or the Entente – as instruments of a 'counter-revolution' seeking to reverse the achievements of the past six months. The idea that a counter-revolution was being plotted seemed of course a reality when in early September the army's Commander-in-Chief General Kornilov made a clumsy attempt to seize power from the Provisional Government. The 'Kornilov affair' acted as a watershed in revolutionary Russia, pushing the climate of opinion to the left and giving the Bolshevik extremists (in the doldrums since July) a new credibility. They could pose as the real guardians of the 'revolution', offering the utopia of 'peace, bread and land' which Kerensky had been unable to deliver. At the front hundreds of units now began to adopt resolutions calling for peace. The rank and file after the Kornilov affair were not simply becoming more politicized, with a new lease of life for the soldiers' committees as the Austrians suspected, but were falling into a mood wholly receptive to Bolshevik agitation. As one army newspaper editor observed in early October: 'Out of the soldiers' hearts pours forth a whole flood of hatred for the war and all it stands for. The soldiers see the chief culprits as the French, the English and in general the whole bourgeoisie. They forget about the Germans.'[87]

This was precisely the attitude encouraged by enemy propaganda. While the great period of oral propaganda was now passed – on the *Heeresfront* of Archduke Joseph, for example, talks with the Russian XXIV corps were always the exception which proved the rule – the allied campaign now concentrated on sophisticated newspaper propaganda. They filled a gap for Russian soldiers who were poorly supplied with newspapers of their own.[88] The propagandists were able, often very successfully, to monitor mood-swings in opposing Russian units and to feed back to them information which blended hope for the future with despair of the present. On the one hand, they stressed the Central Powers' proven readiness for peace as the real antidote to the chaos prevailing in the Russian interior. On the other, they regularly supplied factual news about the latter and nurtured growing suspicion among the rank and file that it was Kerensky in league with the belligerent Entente who were the main obstacles to stability and a quiet life. As an added dimension to this, these 'warmongers' could be characterized as frustrating or betraying the real aims of Russia's revolution. For example, in one striking cartoon, Kerensky was to be pictured rising in the sky in his own balloon, throwing out ballast marked 'socialism', 'democracy' and 'abolition of the death penalty' so that he could ascend higher; the leaflet implored the Russian leader in the style of a peasant prayer to give up the 'inhumane war' and fulfil what he had promised to the people: peace, bread and land.[89]

All of these themes were evident in draft propaganda guidelines drawn up by the AOK in mid-October for discussion with the DOHL. The core argument was to portray the Entente as the main obstacle to peace. Thus, it was the Entente who had forced Russia to launch a summer offensive, who rejoiced over Kornilov's attempted *putsch*, and who still expected much from Kerensky – in each case because they wanted Russia to stay in the war and serve their rapacious ambitions. It was the Entente who had thwarted the progress of the revolution, particularly the chances of stability and a peace without annexations and reparations. The Central Powers, in contrast, had repeatedly shown that they wanted to end the war, most recently in their decision not to continue their summer counter-attack and in their (very vague) replies to Pope Benedict XV's peace initiative of August 1917. 'These new declarations by the leading statesmen of the Central Powers', asserted the guidelines, 'could find a favourable reception among the majority of the Russian people who are longing for peace.'[90]

Clearly, however, some of these arguments, not least the references to a peace without territorial annexations, were wholly anathema to the DOHL which continued to insist on substantial German expansion in the East.[91] The guidelines which Arz finalized with FM Hindenburg by 20 October were therefore much plainer. The aim was as usual simply 'to advance the desire for peace in the Russian army'. The material was to be spread through newspapers and propaganda speeches rather than by unsubtle manifestos which might alienate the Russians. In content it would develop several themes prominent in the campaign of the past six months, concentrating especially on how the so-called 'revolutionary government' had betrayed the revolution and followed the same path as the Tsarist regime in slandering the Central Powers (despite their readiness for peace) and clinging to the exploitative Entente. In comparison to the AOK draft, the guidelines made hardly any reference to the aims or behaviour of the Central Powers. Instead they sought to encourage grievances against the Provisional Government – for example, its attempts to tighten military discipline – and pointed to the growing misery which would occur if Russia did not make peace.[92]

There was now the prospect of ever greater success with these arguments at the front. For on the eve of the Bolshevik revolution, an official report about the allies' campaign in the month of October judged that the mentality of the Russian rank and file thoroughly matched these ideas. Even if the Russian cavalry remained totally hostile, more Russian divisions were now susceptible to oral contact: of 192 divisions along the whole Russian-Romanian Front (including 57 at some time in reserve), about 50 in October had engaged in some talks with Austrian or German Intelligence officers. And even if the amount of oral contact opposite Austrian troops was undoubtedly meagre, it was balanced by a lively newspaper campaign, enabling the official report to conclude that 'favourable prerequisites' existed for further subversion.[93]

Propaganda according to the new guidelines had barely been sent across the trenches when Lenin and the Bolsheviks moved against the Provisional Government in Petrograd. The Bolshevik revolution of 7 November made peace on the Eastern Front a virtual certainty. For in response to Lenin's immediate appeal to all belligerents for a 'just and democratic peace', the mood of most of the Russian armed forces was quite clear.[94] The fact that most of them now supported the new regime certainly owed something, however hard to gauge, to the efforts of the Central Powers' propaganda campaign which for months had been playing to the Russian rank and file the same tune as the Bolsheviks. As the leader of the campaign on the *Heeresfront* of Archduke Joseph put it:

> The Bolshevik upheaval on 7 November found [Russian] front-line troops prepared for both of the main aims which the new [regime's] programme contained: 'peace and land'. These were the same goals which had been set

by the troops from the beginning of the revolution, but had been ignored by the [Provisional] Government, the same goals which our propaganda had consistently reminded the Russian soldiers about in the past months.[95]

This practice of reinforcing the Bolshevik message, and particularly of pushing the Russian army towards an armistice, was to be the final task of the propaganda offensive. When Ludendorff learnt of the Bolshevik coup d'état he immediately telegraphed Arz and army commands in the East, urging them that the news, 'desirable from our point of view', should be used for propaganda purposes.[96] The Central Powers moved to undermine the lingering stubbornness in some Russian military circles – in the 9th army, for example, as well as at the Russian High Command – by simply repeating Bolshevik propaganda over as wide a terrain as possible. Thus when General Dukhonin, the Russian Commander-in-Chief, refused to obey Bolshevik orders and Lenin then bypassed him on 22 November with a crucial wireless telegram broadcast to all units, ordering them to elect plenipotentiaries for the imminent armistice talks – German military Intelligence picked up the message and immediately relayed it back to all sectors of the front.

The AOK and the DOHL expected after this broadcast that pressure from the Russian rank and file would finally force their commanders to begin peace talks. To add extra inducement, the German-Austrian Intelligence officers were instructed to exploit the existing propitious situation, taking the field in place of any further hostilities. As with much of the propaganda carried out since the failed armistice approach of May 1917, the Intelligence officers were not supposed to dwell on the Central Powers' peace terms which might arouse some resentment. Rather, particularly in the present climate, they were to encourage peace initiatives from the Russians, urging them to be free of England and to follow the government which offered them bread, land, freedom and peace.[97] In other words, the blunt argument of this propaganda was that the Russian army should obey its new regime, a message which was not to be muddled by any talk of Germany's ambitions in the East. When the propagandists set to work, approaching the Russian lines and appealing for authorized representatives to negotiate, they found a favourable response in many sectors which gradually developed into a mass of local cease-fires and regional armistices. A notable success, for example, was in the Russian XI corps (8th army). Its morale was already felt by the Austrians to have been destroyed by their propaganda during the July retreat, and in late November, when the corps again proved responsive, they felt that they were building on this achievement.[98] Certainly the evidence which we possess of the mentality of the XI corps peace delegates seems to prove that German-Austrian Intelligence was finely sensitive to the mood and concerns of many Russian units. For although the XI corps negotiators asked for Germany to publicly renounce all annexationist goals in the

East, they also boldly stated their conviction that 'Present day Russia will never again fight for the interests of the English and French. The government that has given them peace and land will never more be overthrown.'[99]

It was Lenin's direct wireless appeal to the troops (22 November), echoed by German-Austrian Intelligence in this final propaganda thrust, which had persuaded the bulk of the Russian army to back the new regime in demanding peace.[100] While the soldiers could feel that they had brought about the regional armistices, through exercising pressure on their commanders in the name of the new Soviet government, the AOK and the DOHL could equally feel that this development was testament at last to the success of their propaganda campaign. The way was now set for general armistice talks to begin between the belligerents at Brest-Litovsk on 3 December. On that day the Austrians re-echoed Bolshevik statements for the last time: Trotsky's public reply to Czernin, who had agreed to the Bolsheviks' plea for a truce, was duly dispatched over the Russian trenches in leaflet form.[101]

For the Central Powers the eight-month propaganda offensive on the Eastern Front was now at an end. Their objectives for much of the campaign had been the same as the Bolsheviks, to persuade the Russian soldiers to revolt against their leaders; and this harmony of aims seemed to have reached its peak in the weeks after the Bolshevik coup d'état. But from November 1917 onwards, during the months of tortuous peace negotiations at Brest-Litovsk, it was the threat of Bolshevism which was uppermost in minds at the AOK when it thought about propaganda in the East.[102] Earlier in the campaign, as we have seen, the German and Austrian military had feared that their own troops could easily become infected through contact with the propaganda weapon, either from the Russians or even from their own efforts. But it was in November, after Lenin's calls for a general peace, that the AOK and the DOHL took extra precautions. In the final propaganda guidelines, all fraternization or traffic with the Russians (apart from official approaches) was strictly forbidden and one officer was to be appointed in each regiment whose task was to keep ordinary troops at a distance from the propaganda 'meeting-points'.[103] In fact, the German and Austrian Intelligence officers seem to have found it impossible to adhere to this stricture on fraternization and finally had to concede some regulated contact. Similarly, Bolshevik appeals which the Central Powers were exploiting were a two-edged sword. Lenin's 'Decree of Peace' of 8 November, a 'resolution with an enormous propaganda punch' as one Austrian historian describes it, was quickly distributed by Russian planes over Austrian and German troops.[104]

The fact was that the aims of the Central Powers and the Bolsheviks, in using the propaganda weapon, were now beginning to diverge. Both had employed it to create chaos in the Russian trenches, but their second objective was not the same. The Central Powers saw the second and final goal as almost achieved, namely to bring those who controlled Russia to the negotiating table to conclude a separate peace. For the Bolshevik leadership, however, the second goal was to extend the revolution. In the months before November, Lenin had only touched on this broader purpose for propaganda when advocating fraternization at the front.[105] But with the seizure of power, Bolshevik propaganda entered a new phase, being targeted more specifically on Germany and Austria-Hungary with the aim of fomenting revolution there and eventually producing a general 'people's peace'. In keeping with this idea, at first Lenin and the other Bolshevik leaders did not view the peace talks at Brest-Litovsk as an end in themselves. Rather, their negotiators were instructed to spin-out the discussions as long as possible, using them as a public platform for proclaiming the Bolsheviks' subversive messages, while by intense fraternization and distribution of Bolshevik propaganda through the front lines, the supposedly 'imminent' revolution in Germany and Austria-Hungary would be accelerated.[106]

For Austrian military Intelligence it became one of the foremost aims of its 'defensive Intelligence' activity in the winter of 1917–18 to counter this Bolshevik revolutionary threat.[107] Max Ronge, the head of military Intelligence, expected that it would be easy to intercept printed propaganda, even though or perhaps because the armistice agreement of 15 December permitted newspapers to be exchanged and fraternization to occur at a few key points on each sector of the Eastern Front. Yet by early 1918 the slow seeping of Bolshevik material into the Monarchy was to be one factor contributing to the military authorities' near paranoia about ubiquitous 'enemy propaganda'. Where Ronge was more accurate was in assessing the danger of those prisoners of war who would soon be returning from the East to Austria-Hungary; these 'homecomers' were indeed to have a major disruptive impact among the Monarchy's armed forces during 1918.[108] But before that happened the peace talks at Brest-Litovsk had, as the Bolshevik leaders expected, begun to bear some rotten fruit in the Empire, exacerbating war-weariness and nationalist agitation in many corners of the Monarchy. This general impact of peace with Russia, stimulating the hopes of those at home who thought that 'peace is being born there and will come to us',[109] was not something which Austrian military Intelligence could ever properly counter. It was an ironic and indirect result of their own propaganda campaign of 1917.

That the campaign on the Eastern Front had been a success was acknowledged by all those involved in it. One member of an Austrian Intelligence troop unit who had been active in the East boasted later that 'we propagandists worked and broke Russia and forced her to make a separate peace'.[110] It was a myth which, as we will see, quickly gained currency in the West and contributed to the reorganization of the British propaganda machinery in early 1918. The rumours were rife in Allied circles that German propaganda in some form or other had contributed to the Russian upheaval, perhaps even that 'Germany [had] conquered the Eastern front by propaganda'.[111] These claims were viewed as highly exaggerated by the Austrian and German High Commands. But at the time, in late 1917 particularly, they undoubtedly gave their campaign more credit than they were to do after the war when they were less likely to praise their own use of a weapon which, they would allege, their enemy had craftily employed to defeat them. For a start, they were less inclined by late 1917 to view this weapon as 'unfair', a concern of both Emperor Karl and General Ludendorff in the early stages of the campaign.[112] It had been shown that propaganda work was quite a dangerous activity, requiring courageous and dedicated personnel. After all, about 150 of the propagandists active on the *Heeresfront* of Archduke Joseph had been lost in the course of their duties.[113]

The AOK was also well aware that its propaganda would have had little effect without the unstable conditions in the Russian hinterland. Chaos in the interior had been a prerequisite for the Austrians' own propaganda arguments to make an impact. It was in this context that they felt the objectives of their campaign had been achieved. With the aid of the Russian soldiers' committees, the propaganda had managed to widen the gap between the Russian soldier and his officers, fomenting insubordination, damaging the 'Kerensky offensive' of July, and finally forcing the Russian army to sue for an armistice. It would, of course, be argued that the final push in this direction had come from Petrograd after the Bolshevik coup d'état. The Central Powers undoubtedly accepted this. But they also felt, because of the close interrelation between front and hinterland in determining the Russian breakdown, that their own propaganda in converting the soldiers had played its part in the fall of Kerensky and the creation of the Bolshevik revolution. In other words, the Central Powers' propaganda had eventually worked its way back from the front into the hinterland.[114] According to a leading German Intelligence officer, one of the central themes of the campaign, that 'England' should be seen as an imperialist enemy of Russia, had been disseminated in this way; he argued that it was one of the 'most decisive successes' of the campaign that 'Russian public opinion and politics' had been converted to this idea by the Central Powers' propaganda.[115] In plainer language, this was tantamount to arguing that the propaganda campaign had helped to turn Russians against the war and against the Provisional Government. It was only a short step from here to the more exaggerated claim that propaganda had 'broken Russia and forced her to make a separate peace'. The myth was then expanded by rumours of Germany's subversive activities in Petrograd.

For the AOK and the DOHL, however, it was simply sufficient to believe that their propaganda had acted as a significant secondary stimulant upon the Russian armed forces. Whether this was actually the case is, of course, debatable (and requires more research on the Russian side). But this does not detract from the fact that the High Commands had the *perception* that front propaganda had been effective. They were sure that propaganda had proved itself to be a 'modern weapon of warfare', all the more so because of the important by-products and lessons learnt from the campaign.[116] First, as we have seen, their propaganda's alleged success, in demoralizing vast numbers of the enemy and achieving local cease-fires, had enabled vital manpower to be withdrawn to the Italian and Western Fronts, while in the East lives had been saved and resources spared. Second, there were the certain benefits which had accrued to military Intelligence from oral propaganda and regular contact with the Russians. These were concrete results, which could always be measured more accurately than the nebulous effects of propaganda on enemy morale. But besides these gains, it is important also to mention the lessons which the Central Powers had learnt about the use of the weapon. They had secured valuable experience on how to manage front propaganda, coordinating it with infantry and artillery activity, and through trial and error they had adopted and used the most effective material and techniques. For example, it had been found that oral propaganda was the most forceful at the front, but that when literature was used, the Russian soldiers had especially responded to factual newspapers containing news, devoid of comment, about the Russian interior; only a few visual images appear to have been exploited. In each case it had been vital to tune into the Russian mentality, presenting to the soldiers 'objective truths' about the situation, even if the range of such 'truths' was carefully selected according to the interests of the Central Powers.[117]

The bleak Russian conditions at the front and in the hinterland had provided a rich material for this propaganda, but it had still proved necessary to ignore some issues, such as Germany's policy on annexations in the East, concentrating instead on repeating well-worn slogans such as the 'imperialist Entente' or 'betrayal of the revolution'. The issue of German policy in the East was in fact always a potential Achilles' heel in the campaign, since it could not be honestly discussed at the front in view of the allies' continued disagreement over its details. Here too the AOK perhaps learnt a lesson, that front propaganda should always be in harmony with the policies of the Ballhausplatz, for when the propaganda arguments diverged from agreed policy both were usually compromised, either at the time or in the future. A safer alternative therefore might be, as on the Eastern Front, to dwell most heavily on the misery and tensions in the enemy's own camp.

## 3.3 The Serbian campaign

The AOK's clear satisfaction with the results of propaganda against Russia was particularly shown by its immediate use of the weapon on its two other fronts. The first to be targeted was the Macedonian theatre. Here lay the remains of the Serbian army, which in the wake of its defeat in late 1915 had made a dramatic anabasis across the mountains of Albania, leaving its 'homeland' to be occupied by Austria-Hungary as the so-called Militärgeneralgouvernement Serbien [MGG/S]. The Serbian forces, after re-formation on the island of Corfu, had been shipped to Salonika and thence moved up to the front again to constitute part of the Orient army under the French General Sarrail. Their generally low morale, not least because of their diminishing numbers which could only be supplemented by Austrian prisoners of South Slav nationality, was well known to Baden by mid-1917. The AOK also had clear evidence of the Serbians' poor performance during Sarrail's limited offensive in May 1917 when they had lost over a thousand men;[118] and had got wind of a Serbian 'officers' plot' which (though exaggerated by the Serbian Regent to remove dangerous rivals to himself) could appear to Baden as yet another chink in the Serbian armour.[119] All of these weaknesses were highlighted by Arz when on 19 June he wrote to the DOHL suggesting propaganda among the Serbian forces to produce 'desertion and disintegration', for – with a hint to the Russian experience – 'the military and political benefits which can spring from such fruitful activity need no further proofs'.[120]

Arz proposed a two-pronged attack. Firstly, under the direction of Austrian military Intelligence, a number of reliable Serbs would be sent from occupied Serbia [MGG/S] or neutral countries, via Greece, into the rear of the Serbian forces to agitate among their compatriots. Secondly, the main campaign would begin in the front line with propaganda by leaflet, by correspondence to and from occupied Serbia, and orally by establishing a battalion of reliable Croat troops to patrol and proselytize along the whole Serbian sector. Although the forces opposite the Serbians were all German or Bulgarian, collected together under the *Heeresgruppe* of the German General Friedrich von Scholtz, Arz did not hesitate in insisting that Austria-Hungary would take charge of this campaign against its old enemy. He recommended that leadership of front propaganda should fall to the Habsburg liaison officer at the *Heeresgruppe* Scholtz, Major Wilhelm Stipetić:

> Major Stipetić, through his knowledge of southern Slav sentiments [*Volkseele*] and his complete command of the Serbian language is thoroughly suited to control this propaganda and he would be assigned for this purpose two tested Intelligence officers who for years have been working against Serbia.[121]

It was a campaign for which Stipetić would have powerful arguments to hand. Although it would be hard to disguise the past and present reality of life in Serb regions controlled by Austria-Hungary, the propaganda could play on homesickness and war-weariness, not only of Serbs from MGG/S but also of South Slavs formerly in the Habsburg army who had perhaps only joined the Serbian army as a means to desert back into the Monarchy. There was thus an extra knife to twist, sharper than that which the Austrians were using against Romanian soldiers on the Eastern Front.

A week after Arz's letter to the DOHL, he received German approval (and the agreement of the Bulgarian High Command), together with a rider from Ludendorff urging that the propaganda dwell on Serbian homesickness and avoid any discussion of Serbia's political future.[122] It was natural that the AOK had to secure German agreement since the campaign would be launched from the *Heeresgruppe* Scholtz – it was not here a matter of Austrian subservience to German wishes. After all, already by this time and before German approval, the AOK had ordered a half-battalion of Croat troops to move from occupied Montenegro to be placed under Stipetić's direction, while two 'tested Intelligence officers', Zeller and Friedl, had also already arrived at Usküb [Skoplje] to await further orders. The idea at first was that Austrian propagandists would test the water. Stipetić was to establish, from the statements of captured Serbians and from soundings by Zeller and Friedl across the trenches, the state of Serbian morale and the best methods and arguments to use to accelerate desertion. Only if success was assured would the battalion be moved up to the front.

In the meantime, Baden set out certain principles to guide Stipetić for the future campaign. On the basis of the work on the Eastern Front, which was to be daily communicated to Stipetić, traffic with the enemy was to occur only in a narrow zone away from enemy lines; the priority was to encourage desertion by promising freedom and benevolent treatment for all who succumbed to their longing to return home. A crucial role was to be played by the authorities in MGG/S. They were a vital link in the traffic of correspondence; they were also expected to discover pro-Austrian Serbs in the MGG/S for propaganda work at the front, and to compose and supply the necessary literature for the campaign. This material, according to Baden's guidelines, would dwell heavily upon the normality of life in occupied Serbia, illustrating it with a bi-weekly newspaper with photographs and letters, while explaining the dismal failure of the Serbian uprising which had occurred in Bulgarian-held territory earlier in the year. At the same time the propaganda would include, as on the Eastern Front, a message of despair: that the military situation was hopeless for the Serbian army; that they were bleeding on behalf of an Entente which had consistently left Serbia in the lurch; and, as an extra twist, that Serbia's government-in-exile was currently building up an enormous debt in the West which could only result in Serbia's 'complete dependence' on foreign states unless her army broke immediately with the Entente. This latter argument, pregnant with irony, was to be set blatantly alongside the 'attractive photographs' of occupied Serbia.[123]

By August 1917, on the basis of his Intelligence officers' promising reports, Stipetić decided to move the Croat half-battalion (of IR25) into the front line. Having undergone extensive training in propaganda activity, the Croat patrols were assigned to Bulgarian divisions and began to approach the Serbian listening-posts. They were armed with correspondence from occupied Serbia, with copies of *Beogradski Novine* (a Serbian edition of the *Belgrader Nachrichten*), which was the only newspaper permitted in the MGG/S, and with a richly illustrated supplement – *Avallah* – portraying ordinary life in the 'homeland'.[124] The first results in mid-August were not auspicious. Their initial efforts to deposit material, sing Serbian songs and make oral contact, were ostentatiously interrupted by French artillery. But within a few days, the Croat enticements began to bear fruit, causing Max Ronge to judge that 'the spirit of the Serbians seems thoroughly miserable, the moment for launching our propaganda correctly chosen'. It was indeed the letter- and newspaper-traffic which particularly stirred Serbian interests, causing a dozen Serbs to desert after a short period of hostilities in early September.[125] On the other hand, French and Serbian officers seem to have been quite successfully vigilant, even if in their 'counter-propaganda' they were slow to play the 'nationality card' by turning on the Croat patrols and questioning their allegiance to the Habsburgs.[126] More importantly, perhaps, the campaign was weakened by the inadequacy of the Croat half-battalion. Although backed by some regular troops, the patrols were too thinly spread out along a front of 40 kilometres; and efforts by Baden to send reinforcements for this 'promising activity' floundered repeatedly in late 1917 on the Monarchy's manpower crisis, compounded by the shortage of suitable Croat personnel.[127]

It is not easy to follow the progress of the campaign after this initial phase. Major Stipetić's reports have not survived, nor have the relevant documents of Austrian military Intelligence. The campaign, as we have seen, had teething problems which may never have been resolved, and they were certainly exacerbated by tensions between Stipetić and the Bulgarian High Command.[128] Yet recognition of Austria's efforts came in the summer of 1918 from British military Intelligence. It judged that the Serbian army's morale was depressed due to long periods in the trenches, unsympathetic treatment by the French, and anxiety about their relatives in Serbia – 'all accentuated by clever enemy propaganda'.[129] Stipetić himself, similarly, appears to have been reporting back to Baden signs of increasing war-weariness among the Serbians, and how a range of measures were being taken by their officers to boost their morale.[130] During 1918, it is true, he may have been more worried about the state of morale of the Bulgarian army than of the Serbians opposite. Even so, by the end of the war when the Allies broke through on the Balkan Front, Austrian sources agree that their propagandists had managed to persuade a total of nine Serbian officers and 445 men to desert across the trenches, a modest triumph for the campaign. The campaign may also have fulfilled its other aims: in forcing French divisions repeatedly to relieve unreliable Serbian units, while at the same time ensuring a steady flow of useful Intelligence from the trickle of Serbian deserters.[131]

If the results of the Serbian campaign could not compare with those witnessed in the East, the Austrian High Command might still feel that they were proportional to the smaller target. After all, the Balkan Front since 1915 had become something of a 'side-show' for Austria-Hungary while Russia and Italy had remained the principal dangers. From 1917, in any case, the propaganda results there were as nothing compared to what the AOK expected in another theatre. In late 1917 it launched its new weapon against a third target, Italy.

## Notes

1. For example, Charles Roetter, in *The Art of Psychological Warfare 1914–1945* (New York, 1974), suggests that Germany showed particular skill with propaganda against Tsarist Russia, but implies that any efforts in 1917 were a total failure (pp. 74–5).
2. Quoted in Reginald Pound and Geoffrey Harmsworth, *Northcliffe* (London, 1959) p. 593.
3. Leo Valiani, *The End of Austria-Hungary* (London, 1973) pp. 81–2; and Z.A.B. Zeman, *The Break-Up of the Habsburg Empire 1914–1918* (Oxford, 1961) pp. 52–4, 65, who also discusses unofficial Ukrainian propaganda towards Austria's Ruthene population.
4. Jan Hajšman, *Česká Mafie. Vzpomínky na Odboj Doma* (Prague, 1934) pp. 35–6; Christoph Führ, *Das k.u.k. Armeeoberkommando und die Innenpolitik in Österreich 1914–1917* (Graz, Vienna and Cologne, 1968) p. 97.
5. Karel Pichlík, Bohumír Klípa, Jitka Zabloudilova, *Českoslovenští Legionáři (1914–1920)* (Prague, 1996) pp. 27–9, 52–3; Josef Kalvoda, *The Genesis of Czechoslovakia* (New York, 1986) pp. 60ff.
6. Occasionally, even in 1914, the Russians sent longer, more sophisticated appeals: see leaflet, 'Soldaten!/Katonák!', in the leaflet collection of the Országos Hadtörténeti Múzeum, Budapest [hereafter OHM], sz.1497/1–2.
7. J.Y. Simpson, *The Self-Discovery of Russia* (London, 1916) p. 137; Wilhelm Conrad Gomoll, *Im Kampf gegen Russland und Serbien* (Leipzig, 1916) p. 167.
8. Rauchensteiner, *Der Tod des Doppeladlers*, p. 183.
9. Max Ronge, *Kriegs- und Industriespionage. Zwölf Jahre Kundschaftsdienst* (Zurich, Leipzig and Vienna, 1930) pp. 250, 257.
10. Erich Ludendorff, *My War Memories 1914–1918*, 2 vols (London, 1919) I, pp. 380–1; Wilhelm Deist (ed.), *Militär und Innenpolitik im Weltkrieg 1914–1918*, 2 vols (Dusseldorf, 1970), I, pp. lvi-lvii.
11. See Kriegsarchiv Vienna [hereafter KA], Evidenzbüro [EvB] 1917, Faszikel [Fasz.] 5696, Nr 4903: Friedrich Ritter von Wiesner to AOK Nachrichten Abteilung [Na.Abt], 344/5, 13 March 1917; and for reports of the crucial meeting with military representatives on 15 March: KA, AOK Operationsabteilung [Op.Abt] 1917, Karton 111, Nr 39500, report by Captain Edmund Glaise von Horstenau; Nr 39548, report by Colonel Eisner-Bubna to Arz, E.Nr 2243, 19 March 1917.
12. Formerly no less than five bodies had dabbled in this field: (1) the Military Intelligence section of the AOK; (2) the KPQ which supervised military news appearing in the press; (3) the War Ministry's press service; (4) the War Welfare Centre (Kriegsfürsorgeamt); and (5) the notorious KÜA.

13. Alan Wildman, *The End of the Russian Imperial Army: The Old Army and the Soldiers' Revolt (March–April 1917)* [hereafter *The Old Army*] (Princeton, 1980) p. 216.
14. Wildman, *The Old Army*, p. 347: 'this propaganda offensive was blunted by lingering Germanophobia' (all the more since the first German leaflets proposed that the Tsar had actually desired peace but had been overthrown with the help of English intrigue in order to prolong the war).
15. Z.A.B. Zeman (ed.), *Germany and the Revolution in Russia 1915–1918: Documents from the Archives of the German Foreign Ministry* (Oxford, 1958), pp. 18–23. Zivin, who had been sending agents and literature to Russia as well as agitating among Russian prisoners of war in Austria, was taken on to the pay-roll of the German Foreign Ministry from August 1916.
16. KA, Armeeoberkommando [AOK], Op.Abt, Karton 112, Nr 39793, Ludendorff to Cramon, 27 March 1918; Wildman, *The Old Army*, p. 347.
17. See, for example, one Russian leaflet appealing to memories of the German-Austrian disaster 50 years earlier at Königssgrätz: 'Deutsches Volk in Österreich!' (KA, AOK Op.Abt 1917, Karton 117, Nr 41105); and the various examples of Russian propaganda of late March to early April in the reports of the Austrian liaison officer at Eastern Command (KA, AOK Verbindungsoffizier Oberost 1917, Karton 3887, Nrs 3907, 3924, 3976, 3986).
18. See the wooden placard displayed in the Heeresgeschichtliches Museum in Vienna: 'Soldaten der Deutschen und Oesterreichisch-Ungarischen Armee!', which probably dates from this period and also urges the enemy to 'topple their bloody Kaiser'.
19. Alfred Knox, *With the Russian Army, 1914–1917*, 2 vols (London, 1921) II, p. 601.
20. Much of the framework for the description which follows is clearly set out in an extensive report by Hasse, the German Intelligence officer attached to the *Heeresfront* of Archduke Joseph and head of the propaganda campaign on that sector of the front: in KA, 11AK Generalstabsabteilung [Gstbs.Abt.] 1918 Propaganda Berichte, Fasz.448, Pr.2031: 'Zusammenfassender Bericht über die Propagandatätigkeit an der Heeresfront GO Erzherzog Joseph seit Beginn' [hereafter *Zusammenfassender Bericht*], 29 December 1917.
21. KA, AOK Op.Abt 1917, Karton 113, Nr 40043, Ludendorff to Arz, telegram [t.], 11 April 1917, enclosing guidelines; Wildman, *The Old Army*, pp. 348–9; *Zusammenfassender Bericht*, p. 2; Fritz Fischer, *Germany's Aims in the First World War* (London, 1977) p. 379.
22. Ronge, *Kriegs- und Industriespionage*, pp. 269, 275.
23. Indeed, it was one of the first signs of the approaching campaign when on 27 March General Ludendorff informed Arz that *Oberost* was intending to respond to Russian requests for newspapers and send across the trenches *Russkii Vestnik*, the German paper for Russian prisoners of war; Ludendorff suggested that the AOK take similar measures (see KA, AOK Op.Abt 1917, Karton 112, Nr 39793).
24. KA, AOK Op.Abt 1917, Karton 113, Nr 40043, AOK to army commands on the Eastern Front, 11 April 1917.
25. For good examples of the fraternization see Galántai, *Hungary in the First World War*, pp. 228–30, who indicates well the ambivalent attitude of many Austrian commanders but does not place his discussion in the framework of an actual propaganda campaign.
26. Alfred Krauss, *Die Ursachen unserer Niederlage. Erinnerungen und Urteile aus dem Weltkrieg* (Munich, 1920) p. 211; *Zusammenfassender Bericht*, pp. 3, 19; Ronge, *Kriegsspionage*, p. 271. For a summary of the Easter contacts at the front of the *Heeresgruppe* Böhm-Ermolli, see KA, 2nd Army Command [2AK] Na.Abt 1917, Fasz.514, Na Nr 1305.

27. *Zusammenfassender Bericht*, pp. 2–3, 20. For an example of these arguments, see the leaflet 'Soldaty!' in KA, 2AK Na.Abt 1917, Fasz.514, Na Nr 1338.
28. Haus- Hof- und Staatsarchiv, Vienna [hereafter HHStA], Politisches Archiv [PA] I/1050, Liasse 66a, Storck to Czernin, Nr 18802, 20 April 1917.
29. *Zusammenfassender Bericht*, pp. 3–4. See OULK, VI: *Das Kriegsjahr 1917* (Vienna, 1936) p. 100.
30. HHStA, PA I/1050, Liasse 66a, Memorandum by Captain Moritz Fleischmann von Theissbruck, 8 June 1917 (initialled by Count Czernin).
31. The same seems to have been true for the 3AK further south. See, for example, the views of one German Intelligence officer attached to the 3AK: A. Agricola, 'Aus dem Kriegstagebuch eines Nachrichtenoffiziers an der Ostfront', in Wolfgang Foerster (ed.), *Kämpfer an vergessenen Fronten* (Berlin, 1931) p. 516.
32. KA, 2AK Na.Abt 1917, Fasz.514, Nr 1576, 'Hughes' conversations between Borovica and Terlecki, and between Ronge and Terlecki, 3 May 1917.
33. KA, AOK Op.Abt 1917, Karton 116, Nr 40690, Arz to all army commands, 8 May 1917 (draft by Alfred von Waldstätten). Compare the recent views of Rauchensteiner, who very much underestimates Austria-Hungary's own contribution to psychological warfare on the Eastern Front: *Der Tod des Doppeladlers*, p. 442.
34. KA, 2AK Na.Abt 1917, Fasz.514, [unnumbered], Borovica to Na.Abt AOK Baden (Hughes), 15 May 1917.
35. Fischer, *Germany's Aims*, pp. 350–1; Wolfgang Steglich, *Die Friedenspolitik der Mittelmächte 1917–18* (Wiesbaden, 1964) pp. 64–6.
36. HHStA, PA I/1050, Liasse 66a, Arz to Czernin, Op.Nr 247 Geheim, 27 April 1917; OULK, VI, p. 213.
37. The guidelines were as follows: (1) Russia soldiers should demand of their leaders an armistice of 3–4 weeks, (2) the Central Powers would not mix in Russian internal affairs, (3) Russia would get a good deal over the Dardanelles and extra-European questions if it renounced the conquest of Constantinople as an aim, (4) Russia would gain economic support and no war indemnification; but there would be frontier rectifications for Germany in Lithuania and Courland, (5) Poland would become a state. However, the extent to which these guidelines were used in propaganda on the Eastern Front is debatable: see Steglich, *Friedenspolitik*, pp. 100–1 and 443 note 248 for some discussion of this subject.
38. See Fischer, *Germany's Aims*, pp. 370ff for the Erzberger–Kolyshko talks in Stockholm and their repercussions. The clash of views between Czernin and the DOHL is well documented in Steglich, *Friedenspolitik*, pp. 74ff: on 26 April Czernin publicly renounced annexation of Russian territory in his organ the *Fremdenblatt*, but by the end of the month had been brought round to the idea of 'frontier rectifications' for Germany. Similarly, the DOHL had been persuaded to adopt this more innocuous formula for the propaganda guidelines by Zimmermann, the German Secretary of State (p. 83).
39. Their optimism about complete victory was particularly strong at this time: Deist, *Militär und Innenpolitik*, pp. 744–6.
40. HHStA, PA I/1050, Liasse 66a, Arz to Czernin, Op.geh.Nr 260/I, 8 May, enclosing Beilage I: Ludendorff to Arz, Ia.Nr.3107 geh.Op., 6 May 1917. It is not clear which funds or agents Ludendorff is referring to here, but presumably it may be those of the Foreign Ministry whose 'undermining activities' in Russia he would later acknowledge: see Zeman, *Germany and the Revolution in Russia*, p. 71 note 1.

41. Wildman, *The Old Army*, p. 336.
42. HHStA, PA I/1050, Liasse 66a, Arz to Czernin, Op.geh.Nr 260/I, 8 May, enclosing Beilage I: Ludendorff to Arz, Ia Nr 3107 geh.Op., 6 May 1917.
43. See, for example, the response by Russian troops in the far south opposite the *Heeresgruppe* Mackensen: KA, AOK Op.Abt 1917, Karton 116, Nr 40750/I, Verbindungsoffizier beim Oberkommando von Mackensen to AOK Op.Abt, N.res.Nr 213, 9 May 1917.
44. OULK, VI, p. 221.
45. Ronge, *Kriegs- und Industriespionage*, pp. 272–3; Wildman, *The Old Army*, p. 359.
46. Arz von Straussenburg, *Zur Geschichte des Grossen Krieges 1914–1918* (Vienna, 1924) p. 151; *Kampf und Sturz der Kaiserreiche* (Vienna and Leipzig, 1935) p. 76; Wildman, *The Old Army*, p. 360; OULK, VI, pp. 219–21.
47. HHStA, PA I/1050, Liasse 66a, Arz to Czernin, Op.Geh.Nr 290, 29 May 1917. Cf. the words selected for OULK, VI, p. 219.
48. *Zusammenfassender Bericht*, pp. 5–6; Ronge, *Kriegs- und Industriespionage*, p. 273. GM Hans von Seeckt, Chief of the General Staff on the *Heeresfront* of Archduke Joseph, wrote to Arz on 20 May – the day after the Russians had so dramatically spurned an armistice – that the basis for peace with Russia 'has been successfully prepared by our propaganda' since 'to the great dismay of the leading commanders the overwhelming majority of Russian divisions are inclining to trust us': HHStA, PA I/1050, Liasse 66a, Storck to Czernin, Nr 19947, 27 May, enclosing Beilage 1: Seeckt to Arz, Nr 1480, 20 May 1917.
49. HHStA, PA I/1050, Liasse 66a, Arz to Czernin, Op.Geh. Nr 290, 29 May 1917; *Zusammenfassender Bericht*, p. 6.
50. See, for example, HHStA, PA I/1060, Liasse 66a, Waldstätten to Czernin, Op.Geh.Nr 279/1, 16 May 1917, where Waldstätten advises that armistice talks need not be forced since the position of the Central Powers was so favourable. By the end of the month, Arz was rather more concerned that Russia could still recover and launch an offensive.
51. For the revised set of guidelines, see: HHStA, PA I/1050, Liasse 66a, Storck to Czernin, Nr 19907, 26 May 1917; Czernin had pressed for the formula 'frontier rectifications' to be kept against resistance from Ludendorff: Steglich, *Friedenspolitik*, p. 101.
52. Undoubtedly many Russian soldiers interpreted this vague formula as the same as annexation anyway: see KA, AOK Op.Abt 1917, Karton 116, Nr 40750/I.
53. HHStA, PA I/1050, Liasse 66a, Memorandum by Captain Moritz Fleischmann von Theissbruck, 8 June 1917.
54. Steglich, *Friedenspolitik*, pp. 102, 104–5: Steglich questions the degree to which Fleischmann's reports can be believed.
55. See Hoffmann's views, in KA, 2AK Na.Abt 1917, Fasz. 514, Nr 2081, Hoffmann (*Oberost*) to DOHL, *Heeresgruppe* Joseph, etc (Abt 1a Nr 3953/17 geh.), 24 May 1917.
56. See Robert P. Browder and Alexander F. Kerensky (eds), *The Russian Provisional Government 1917. Documents*, 3 vols (Stanford, 1961) II, pp. 1158–9; and the propaganda guidelines and wireless texts in: HHStA, PA I/1050, Liasse 66a, Waldstätten to Czernin, Op.geh.Nr 297/I, 3 June; Op.Geh.Nr 304, 3 June; Arz to Czernin, Op.Geh.Nr 316, 14 June 1917.
57. OULK, VI, pp. 223ff.
58. *Zusammenfassender Bericht*, p. 6; HHStA, PA I/1060, Waldstätten to Czernin, Op.Geh.Nr 304/I, 15 June 1917 (enclosing the Soviet's message, telegraphed to the

Central Powers on 10 June); Browder and Kerensky, *The Russian Provisional Government*, II, pp. 1159–60.

59. See Vladimír Klecanda, *Bitva u Zborova. Vojensko Historická Studie o Bojích Československé Brigády v Haliči Roku 1917* (Prague, 1927) pp. 16, 151 note 17; OULK, VI, p. 226. An upsurge in Russian 'counter-propaganda' seems also to be confirmed in the weekly reports by Hasse, the German Intelligence officer attached to the *Heeresfront* of Archduke Joseph: see KA, 1AK Na.Abt 1917, Fasz.145.
60. Alan Wildman, *The End of the Russian Imperial Army: The Road to Soviet Power and Peace* [hereafter *The Road to Soviet Power*] (Princeton, 1987) pp. 44ff, 73ff.
61. *Zusammenfassender Bericht*, pp. 6–7.
62. KA, 2AK Na.Abt 1917, Fasz.514, Nr 2649, Borovica to Hptm Baier (Hughes), 21 June 1917: enclosing additional propaganda guidelines.
63. See the map in Beilage 12, OULK, VI.
64. KA, 2AK Na.Abt 1917, Fasz.514, Nrs 2546, 2453, 2649: the 2AK had hoped to exploit the Russian 105th Infantry Division [ID] with a band of reliable Ukrainian legionaries.
65. Knox, *With the Russian Army*, II, p. 633.
66. Felix Lánsky, 'Jizerna-Zborov', in Adolf Zeman (ed.), *Cestami Odboje (Jak žily a kudy táhly Čs. Legie), Díl III: Počatky Odboje* [hereafter *Cestami Odboje*], (Prague, 1927) p. 86.
67. See Josef Kohák, 'Ve Zborovskych zákopech', in *Cestami Odboje*, III, pp. 77–8.
68. See the account in OULK, VI, pp. 244–52.
69. See especially Klecanda's comprehensive account, *Bitva u Zborova*, pp. 31ff; Zdeněk Tobolka, *Politické Dějiny Československého Národa od r.1848 až do Dnešní Doby*, 4 vols (Prague, 1932–7) IV, pp. 303ff; and for the later legend, *Zborov, 1917–1937. Památník k Dvacátém Výrocí Bitvy u Zborova. 2. Července 1917* (Prague, 1937).
70. *Zusammenfassender Bericht*, p. 7.
71. See, for example, the leaflet, 'Russkim ofitseram i soldatam!' (in KA, 1AK Na.Abt 1917, Fasz.145); and the new propaganda guidelines issued in late July (which mentioned Lloyd George's speech of 21 July as evidence of Entente imperialism): HHStA, PA I/1050, Liasse 66a, Arz to Czernin, Op.Nr 43294, 26 July 1917, enclosing a copy of Ludendorff to Arz, 1a Nr 4050 geh.Op. [undated].
72. *Zusammenfassender Bericht*, pp. 10–11.
73. For an excellent recent summary, see Keith Hitchens, *Rumania 1866–1947* (Oxford, 1994) pp. 262ff.
74. KA, 1AK Na.Abt 1917, Fasz.145, Nr 2519, 'Feindlage vor Heeresfront Erzherzog Joseph' [by Hasse], 1 June 1917: the *Bukarester Tagblatt* was being distributed.
75. HHStA, PA I/1050, Liasse 66c, 'Frontpropaganda gegenüber der rumänischen Armee, Juli/August 1917': Nr 6322, Arz to Czernin, Op.Geh.Nr 329/I, 4 July 1917, enclosing guidelines.
76. Ibid., Czernin to Esterházy [Hungarian Prime Minister], Z.4018, 16 July 1917.
77. Ibid., Nr 7804, Storck to Baron Mittags (telephone), 4 August 1917, with note by Czernin.
78. KA, 1AK Na.Abt 1917, Fasz.145, Na Nr 3737, 4 August 1917.
79. Ibid., Na Nr 5208: on the *Heeresfront* of Archduke Joseph, the number increased during September from 35 to over one hundred deserters, and many cited 'propaganda' as the reason for desertion (see also HHStA, PA I/834/8796).
80. *Zusammenfassender Bericht*, p. 16. The Austrian official history, while mentioning the demoralization in both of these corps, does not ascribe particular disasters to their behaviour.

81. See Wildman, *The Road to Soviet Power*, pp. 92ff for Russian behaviour during the offensive. He notes (p. 121) that the confusion of these weeks as well as biased sources makes many units' true behaviour, 'the line between myth and reality', hard to establish.
82. Ronge, *Kriegs- und Industriespionage*, p. 299.
83. See, for example, HHStA, PA I/1050, Liasse 66a, Storck to Czernin, Nr 23605, 14 October 1917: Beilage 1, where AOK draft propaganda guidelines suggested that the Central Powers had in August voluntarily declined to advance into 'the richest areas of Russia'.
84. OULK, VI, p. 407.
85. See the opposition expressed by the commander of the *Abschnitt Zloczow* [2AK] in KA, 2AK Na.Abt 1917, Fasz.514, Na Nr 3781, 25 August; and the *Heeresgruppe* Böhm-Ermolli's subsequent reluctance 'at present' to resume propaganda activity (Nr 3785, 29 August 1917).
86. Ibid., Nr 3735, Borovica to 2AK (Hughes), 24 August 1917.
87. Wildman, *The Road to Soviet Power*, p. 240.
88. See the series of reports from the *Heeresfront* of Archduke Joseph (KA, 1AK Na.Abt 1917, Fasz.145) by the German Intelligence officer.
89. Leaflet, 'Posviashchaetsia G-nu Kerenskomu!' (signed 'Austrian Social Democrat') in KA, 1AK Na.Abt 1917, Karton 98.
90. HHStA, PA I/1050, Liasse 66a, Storck to Czernin, Nr 23605, 14 October 1917, enclosing Beilage 1: 'Richtlinien für die russische Propaganda'.
91. See Fischer, *Germany's Aims*, pp. 434ff for the discussions on war aims in October 1917.
92. HHStA, PA I/1050, Liasse 66a, Arz to Czernin, Op.Geh.Nr 413/1, 21 October 1917.
93. KA, AOK Op.Abt 1917, Karton 139, Nr 47427, Chef des Generalstabes des Feldheeres. Abteilung Fremde Heere (Nr 6384a), 9 November 1917, with Anlage: 'Übersicht über die Verhandlungen mit russischen und rumänischen Divisionen im Oktober 1917'. According to this very precise survey, the oral contacts opposite Austrian forces in October were very limited: for the *Heeresgruppe* Böhm-Ermolli there were talks with only one division on one day, while for the *Heeresfront* of Archduke Joseph there were talks at some point with 14 of the 46 divisions opposite (30 per cent).
94. The text of Lenin's peace declaration is printed in Appendix I of John Wheeler-Bennett, *Brest-Litovsk: The Forgotten Peace. March 1918* (London, 1963) pp. 375–8.
95. *Zusammenfassender Bericht*, p. 9.
96. Zeman, *Germany and the Revolution in Russia*, p. 75.
97. HHStA, PA I/1050, Liasse 66a, AOK to Czernin, Op.Geh.435, 23 November 1917. These new propaganda guidelines particularly singled out rumours that Japan would declare war on Russia if the latter made a separate peace; these were to be dismissed by the propagandists as yet more evidence of English lies. Almost identical guidelines were sent to Germany's troops by *Oberost*: KA, 2AK Na.Abt 1917, Fasz.514/5100.
98. *Zusammenfassender Bericht*, p. 17.
99. Wildman, *The Road to Soviet Power*, pp. 386–8.
100. It remains, however, difficult to generalize too far in view of the varied response within the different Russian corps; see for example the mixture of views within the Russian 4th, 9th and 8th armies in early December: KA, 1AK Na.Abt 1917, Fasz.145, Na Nr 7080.

101. Leaflet, 'Vsem!', signed by Trotsky, in KA, 1AK Na.Abt 1917, Karton 98 [appeared 3 December].
102. The Austrians did make a few sporadic attempts at propaganda among the Russians during this period, but were principally vigilant against Bolshevik machinations: see the few examples of Austrian propaganda in January 1918 in KA, VI KK 1918, Fasz.203.
103. Wildman, *The Road to Soviet Power*, p. 384; HHStA, PA I/1050, Liasse 66a, AOK to Czernin, Op.Geh.435, 23 November 1917; OULK, VI, p. 730.
104. Wolfdieter Bihl, *Österreich-Ungarn und die Friedensschlüsse von Brest-Litovsk* (Vienna, Cologne and Graz, 1970) p. 31; Wheeler-Bennett, *Brest-Litovsk*, p. 90.
105. Notably his article in *Pravda* on 11 May 1917: reproduced in Browder and Kerensky, *The Russian Provisional Government*, II, p. 904.
106. See Richard K. Debo, *Revolution and Survival: The Foreign Policy of Soviet Russia 1917–18* (Liverpool, 1979) chapters 1–3; and for a summary of the Bolshevik perspective: Robert Service, *Lenin: a Political Life, Volume 2, Worlds in Collision* (Macmillan, 1991) pp. 293–7.
107. When Max Ronge took over as head of Austro-Hungarian military Intelligence in April 1917 he had totally separated the defensive and offensive activity conducted by the Intelligence Service.
108. Ronge, *Kriegs- und Industriespionage*, pp. 327ff; Bihl, *Österreich-Ungarn*, pp. 33–4.
109. See the views of some Hungarian letter-writers, picked up by the censor in Budapest, about events in Russia in 1917–18 in: Gábor Sándorné, 'Az oroszországi forradalmi mozgalmak visszhangja a magyar dolgozók hadifoglyokhoz írt leveleiben', *Párttörténeti Közlemények*, no. 2 (1958) pp. 136–44.
110. Franz Kreuz to his Italian captors: quoted in Ljudevit Pivko, *Informatorji* [vol. 2 of *Rame ob Ramenu*] (Maribor, 1925) p. 32.
111. See, for example, the comments of a British officer present in Russia in late 1917: E.P. Stebbing, *From Czar to Bolshevik* (London, 1918) p. vi.
112. Ronge, *Kriegs- und Industriespionage*, p. 269.
113. *Zusammenfassender Bericht*, p. 18: ten were killed (including one German officer) and 139 taken prisoner (including 28 Austrian officers and one German officer); a further 13 personnel had been seriously wounded.
114. KA, 11AK Gstbs Abt 1918, Fasz.448, Pr.2030, AOK Op.Nr 766/21: 'Die Propagandaverhältnisse an der russ.Front im Vergleiche zu jenen an der ital.Front' [undated, early February 1918].
115. *Zusammenfassender Bericht*, p. 18.
116. See, for example, the measured comments of Erich Ludendorff: *My War Memories 1914–1918*, I, p. 382.
117. *Zusammenfassender Bericht*, pp. 9–10, 13. The propagandists never seem to have considered how far the Russian troops were literate.
118. See Petar Opačić, 'Solunski Front 1917.godine', in Slavenko Terzić (ed.), *Srbija 1917. Godine. Naučni Skup* (Belgrade, 1988) pp. 144ff: the thousand included a hundred officers dead or incapacitated.
119. This officers' plot led to the subsequent trial and execution (June 1917) of Colonel Dragutin Dimitrijević ('Apis'), former head of Serbian military Intelligence and leading light of the Serbian terrorist group *The Black Hand*.
120. HHStA, PA I/1050, Liasse 66b ('Frontpropaganda gegenüber der serbischen Armee Juli 1917–Sept 1918'): 6208, Arz to GFM Beneckendorf und von Hindenburg, Op.Geh.Nr 319, 19 June 1917.

121. Ibid.
122. Ibid., Ludendorff to Cramon, t.3693 geh.Op., 26 June 1917.
123. Ibid., Arz to General von Scholtz, Na Nr 9316, 29 June; 6270, Storck to Czernin, Nr 20958, 4 July 1917, enclosing 'Richtlinien' for Serbian propaganda material.
124. See Hugo Kerchnawe, 'Die k.u.k. Militärverwaltung in Serbien', in Hugo Kerchnawe (ed.), *Die Militärverwaltung in den von österreichisch-ungarischen Truppen besetzten Gebieten* (Vienna, 1928) pp. 250–3.
125. HHStA, PAI/1050, Liaise 66b, 8939, Storck to Czernin, Nr 22886, 17 September, enclosing report by Max Ronge: 'Serbische Propaganda. Résumé bis 8 September 1917', Na Nr 14289, 9 September 1917.
126. The first signs of this came only in November 1917 when Croat patrols were actually informed that the Serbian army was fighting for the unification of all Serbs, Croats and Slovenes: see the leaflet in ibid., 11314, Storck to Czernin, Nr 24451, 21 November 1917.
127. See KA, AOK Op.Abt 1917, Karton 136, Nr 46279, Arz to Stipetić (t.), 12 October; Nr 46981, AOK to Chef des Ersatzwesens (t.), 3 November 1917.
128. See KA, AOK Op.Abt 1917, Karton 138, Nr 47075. The Bulgarian dimension is an area for future research. In November 1917, a plan by the AOK to launch a further campaign against Greek troops was felt by Ludendorff to be pointless in view of the notoriously bad relationship between Greeks and Bulgarians (see HHStA, PA I/1050, Liasse 66e: 'Frontpropaganda gegenüber griechischen Truppen, Oktober 1917).
129. Public Records Office, London [PRO], War Office [WO] 106/1384, Memorandum on the Serbian situation by MI2(a), 28 June 1918.
130. KA, EvB 1918, Fasz.5756, Nr 23596, MGG/S to AOK (Na.Abt), 30 July 1918: report about the Serbian Intelligence service, p. 43.
131. Ronge, *Kriegs- und Industriespionage*, p. 302; Kerchnawe, 'Die k.u.k. Militärverwaltung', p. 253. Assessing the actual reasons for the Serbian desertions is, of course, far from easy. January 1918 witnessed an unprecedented number of Serbian desertions to the enemy (20), but the Serbian High Command attributed these to 'events in Russia' (see Dragoslav Janković and Bogdan Krizman (eds), *Gradja o Stvaranju Jugoslavenske Države*, 2 vols (Belgrade, 1964) I, document 97, p. 126).

# 4
# Austria-Hungary's Campaign against Italy

## 4.1 The Italian target

The military disaster which overtook the Italians at Caporetto in October 1917 has never been attributed to any great extent to the machinations of 'enemy propaganda'. More conventional 'military' reasons are usually cited in explanation. General Luigi Cadorna, the overbearing and inflexible Chief of Staff of the Italian army, had since May 1915 concentrated almost overwhelmingly on offensive operations against Austria-Hungary on the Giulian front. He had launched 11 major battles on the river Isonzo, 'beating inexorably on the iron doors of the enemy', in the hope that eventually the break-through would come and carry his troops forward to Trieste and Vienna.[1] The result was that the Italians had little experience of defensive warfare except during Austria's Trentino offensive in May 1916; and the deficiencies in Cadorna's defences and disposition of reserves in the weeks before Caporetto showed that few lessons had been learnt. Similarly, Italian tactics had generally not kept pace with those of their allies on the Western Front: the Italians were especially backward in their use of artillery, failing to coordinate artillery fire with infantry operations.

But it was perhaps above all the boldness of the enemy plan and the element of surprise which was crucial to its success in October 1917. In early September, the AOK and the DOHL had resolved for the first time to launch a joint offensive on the Italian Front, choosing for the main thrust the thinly defended sector of Flitsch-Tolmein north of Gorizia.[2] What began as a cautious Austrian design to relieve Italian pressure on the Isonzo became under German influence an ambitious attempt, concentrating on penetrating the valleys, to push the enemy back onto the plains behind the river Tagliamento. The operation, in the words of the Commission which later investigated Caporetto, 'was brilliant, extremely daring and carried out with energy, shrewdness and the use of methods which were new to us'.[3] These included a massive increase in artillery and the employment of phosgene gas for the first time on the Italian Front.

While the German 14th army under General Otto von Below was being constructed in the crucial offensive sector, through the astonishing use of 2400 trains to bring up men and *materiel*, the Central Powers undertook a diversion. German Alpine troops were at first dispatched to the Trentino and in October Emperor Karl inspected the forces there so as to distract Italy's attention; meanwhile, German troops who were clustered in the front line of the 14th army were ordered to wear Austrian caps.[4] These red herrings were partially successful. Cadorna, ever mindful of the near-disaster of May 1916, remained unsure about the significance of movements in the Tyrol, while on the Giulian front weather conditions in October – constant rain and fog – aided the enemy camouflage and hindered Italian air reconnaissance.

Yet it is undisputed that the Italian Comando Supremo [CS] had abundant evidence of Austro-German designs in the weeks before the offensive.[5] On top of steady reports about accumulating forces in the Flitsch-Tolmein region, the Intelligence service knew from Czech and Romanian officer deserters on 20–1 October precise details about the enemy plans and line-up. Where the service failed was not in gathering accurate information, but in sifting and interpreting it correctly. For in contrast to the innovative and imaginative work by some Italian Intelligence officers attached to the individual armies, there existed something of an 'Intelligence muddle' [*guazzabuglio*] at the CS.[6] The Uffizio Situazione, Cadorna's real Intelligence section, showed 'excessive diffidence' in the face of the mounting evidence, preferring to interpret it as a range of impending local attacks. This in turn certainly matched Cadorna's own viewpoint. He found it difficult, especially at a time when the season was so far advanced, to conceive of the enemy launching a major offensive rather than responding to Italy's initiatives, and this despite the opportunities now available to the Central Powers because of the rapid disintegration of the Russian army. It was in a relaxed frame of mind that the Chief of Staff retired to his villa at Vicenza for a fortnight in October 1917, having issued few specific orders to his troops in the case of an enemy attack.[7]

On 24 October the enemy managed to break through all Italian defences and advance, past the village of Caporetto, 20 miles in one day. Cadorna and others immediately ascribed this success and the subsequent disintegration of the Italian 2nd army not to military factors, but to 'defeatist propaganda' which had allegedly been steadily undermining Italian morale. In the view of Brigadier-General Charles Delmé-Radcliffe, influential head of the British Military Mission and fully cognisant of CS thinking, the rout was 'brought about by the deliberate and premeditated action of the troops in dropping their equipment and abandoning their positions under the instigation of... insidious propaganda conducted by pacifists, socialists and enemy agents'.[8] Throwing the blame for low morale onto 'outsiders' like this had been a favourite hobby of Cadorna for years; in the summer of 1917 he had sent four notorious letters to the Italian government of Paolo Boselli, warning it to act rigidly against defeatist forces in the interior which were damaging morale in the war zone.[9]

Certainly it was the case, partly because of the way in which Italy had entered the war in May 1915 (pushed in by a political minority leading an unpoliticized majority of the population), that the country as a whole had never been properly mobilized for the war effort. Its morale and disunited consciousness could usefully be compared to the situation in Austria-Hungary. In November 1916, it is true, Boselli had responded to press criticism and entrusted one of his cabinet ministers, Vittorio Scialoja, with the role of nurturing propaganda at home and abroad. Scialoja seems to have used to good effect a 'Union of Italian teachers' (Unione degli insegnanti italiani per la guerra nazionale) which he had founded himself, but his efforts to raise national morale were always limited by the lack of funding from the Italian Treasury.[10] For many civilians the war was not their war, nor a life and death struggle; even less was it to be labelled the fourth war of the *Risorgimento*. Rather it was an experience which affected them chiefly because of the horrors faced by their loved ones at the front and, by 1917, the economic pinch beginning to affect them at home. Their own war-weariness could not fail to interact with that of their relatives in the war zone. They could be expected to urge their men, that instead of returning from leave, they should join the mass of deserters in the hinterland which one historian has recently estimated at 100 000 on the eve of Caporetto.[11] Thus, as one Italian general remarked later, 'every relative corrupted a relative'.[12] This phenomenon, however, must be kept in proportion. The Commission which investigated Caporetto was admirably careful when assessing the effects of such a vague concept as 'defeatist propaganda'. It characterized defeatism among the troops as a complex mixture of tendencies with diverse origins. It acknowledged that certain events in 1917 outside the war zone probably damaged troop morale. These included news of the disintegration of the Russian army as well as Pope Benedict's peace initiative; but the Commission was far less convinced about the effect of the violent riots which took place in August in Turin, or about the CS claim of widespread socialist subversion in Italy. Despite clear signs that the hinterland was not sufficiently mobilized for war, the Commission came to the conclusion that defeatism in the army could largely be laid at the door of the military authorities themselves, caused by military deficiencies and military errors.[13]

Foremost among military failings was the simple absence of victory. After 30 months of warfare the Italians had made insignificant advances in their front line while sacrificing over 300 000 men. Even the trumpeted conquest of the Bainsizza plateau in August 1917 had been achieved at enormous human expense.[14] The rank and file felt keenly this discrepancy between gain and sacrifice, all the more so as many of them had never come to terms with the idea of Austria-Hungary as a real enemy; by 1917 they were beginning to despair that their task would ever be finished. With this mentality, they increasingly resented their superiors' steady preference for ostentatious offensives. Their resentment was even more deep-seated because of the type of regime which Cadorna was running in the war zone. He insisted on maintaining merciless discipline of a kind which far exceeded that in other belligerent armies. While it has been calculated that one in every dozen Italian soldiers was brought before a military tribunal during the war, the CS also encouraged summary executions for petty disobedience. For example, General Andrea Graziani, later revered as commander of the Czechoslovak Legion, was not unusual in ordering one soldier to be executed on the spot for continuing to smoke a pipe during an inspection.[15] Punishment therefore far exceeded the crime, leaving troops with the feeling that the system of discipline was arbitrary and unjust.

It might also be suggested, at least according to the Commission of inquiry, that Italian soldiers were less responsive to mechanical discipline (allegedly on the German model) and needed a more sensitive approach from their officers.[16] This was a view shared by one British commander: 'The besetting sin of the Italian soldier is vanity – if that bubble is pricked he deflates into a useless pulp, but tell him that you trust him and that he really is a fine fellow and he will fight for you to the death.'[17] Instead of this, the authorities prior to Caporetto had maintained discipline largely by coercion. The Italian soldiers' 'sensitive nature' was even used by some commanders to justify tight control. Thus General Capello, head of the infamous 2nd army, kept his troops in the rear in constant activity on the grounds that 'our soldiers are too southern to be spontaneously or voluntarily active'.

The result of this regime was that the men were often caught between two horrors: on the one hand, the misery of lengthy stays in what they termed the 'slaughter-house' of the trenches, with inadequate food, water or sanitary conditions; on the other, the experience of rigid discipline and meagre recreation when away from the front line. In the 2nd army, according to the Commission, many soldiers returned to the trenches more exhausted than previously.[18] They also had few opportunities to take full leave (perhaps vital to their morale in view of tight Italian family bonds), since the CS viewed the interior as the major source of 'defeatism' and, at most, allotted the men a fortnight every year. This was a gnawing source of discontent and a prime motive behind the Catanzaro mutiny in July 1917. The Italian military authorities, in short, shared the outlook of their Austro-Hungarian contemporaries in being far more concerned about keeping their troops under surveillance, immune from potential dangers, than they were about actively boosting their morale. Before Caporetto there was no consistent system of official propaganda among the troops. In the Italian 1st army, commanded by the enlightened General Pecori-Giraldi, some initiative had been taken to set up special rest homes (*case del soldato*) near the front, where soldiers could go to recuperate; the idea spread and the homes numbered 170 by October 1917. But propaganda in the army as a whole was usually limited to occasional, organized meetings between officers and men.[19] Such 'pep talks' were often counter-productive, either because the themes addressed were alien to the actual experience of life in the trenches, or – more importantly – because the officers or propagandists were held in such low esteem by the rank and file. During the war, as in other armies, the original officer corps had been decimated, but the CS then exacerbated the resulting instability by punishing officers who 'failed' in their duties; for instance, in the space of ten months, 24 corps commanders were dismissed from their posts.[20] The junior officers who were rapidly promoted in their stead lacked the authority which could only come from participating in the horrors of the front. Many remained aloof, failing to nurture their troops' morale through regular contact; others perhaps, were too familiar or lenient in their relations. But their general inexperience was, as Delmé-Radcliffe noted, 'one of the most important causes which adversely affects the morale of the troops'.[21]

Before Caporetto, it was this combination of experiences in the war zone which effectively depressed the morale of the Italian army. If the breakthrough itself was primarily due to enemy tactics and the Italians' misreading of the situation, the rout which followed seems to have owed much to longstanding grievances which had bred a defeatist mentality. A good number of Italian soldiers viewed Caporetto not as a disaster, but as 'the end of a nightmare . . . a condition of collective relief and happiness'.[22] It was this mentality which Austrian front propaganda now sought to exploit.

## 4.2 The launch of an Austrian campaign

The Italian commissioners who investigated Caporetto gave due attention to the nebulous rumours about 'enemy propaganda', but came to no firm conclusions. Although they suggested that enemy agents had indeed been encouraging defeatism in the Italian hinterland, they considered such contacts too 'complex' to investigate, adding only that the number of such agents could not have been very extensive and should not deflect attention away from the essentially military causes of defeatism.[23] With only slightly more substance, the Commission tackled the issue of enemy propaganda at the front itself. They were able to cite a CS circular from 18 June 1916 on the subject of neutralizing Austrian propaganda among the Italian troops.[24] From this document (which incidentally was well known to the AOK as well),[25] it emerges that the Austrians had been using propaganda against Italy for some time, sending over leaflets which exalted Austrian successes or promised good treatment for Italian prisoners of war. Yet, although this activity may have increased in the spring of 1917,[26] the impression remains that these were sporadic efforts left to local officers' initiative which, as on the Eastern Front, lacked any coordination until the AOK embarked on a concrete campaign.

As for the weeks before Caporetto, the Commission suspected correctly that a trickle of 'debilitating propaganda' was reaching some Italian troops on the Giulian front.[27] One Austrian officer, characteristically sceptical of such work, wrote later that neither the Italian officers nor their men had responded: 'in most sectors the results were zero'.[28] But the evidence of one Austrian propagandist, Franz Kreuz, is equally viable. When Kreuz fell into Italian hands in early 1918 he revealed to his captors an unusual story. Before the war, he claimed, he had worked as a waiter in hotels on Lake Garda and, as a linguist, had come to the attention of the AOK. It had sent him to a 'propaganda school' at Dresden and thence to the Russian front where in 1917, he boasted, he had secured the 'highest awards' as a propagandist. In September he had been transferred to the Giulian front and, at Rombon and Čiginj (near Flitsch and Tolmein respectively), began to contact Italians in the weeks before the offensive.[29] There he was operating in a sector which some Italians already described wittily as 'the front of the separate peace' because of its high incidence of fraternization.[30] Besides taking them gifts and assuring them of his friendship, he subtly warned them little by little of the approaching danger: they ought to desert since, 'the German chemists have invented terrible weapons' – gas – and 'no mask will be able to protect you'. His departing words for them were equally striking: 'Goodbye to all of you who will remain alive, goodbye too to those who will not live!'[31] Even allowing for Kreuz's exaggerations, the implication of his account, that gas was used more as a psychological weapon against Italy than as a material weapon, seems to ring true to German military hopes at the time.[32] More importantly, his account is further testimony to the growing appreciation during 1917 of front propaganda as a respectable military occupation. Kreuz himself expressed pride in his work:

> We who execute ideas are also soldiers, just like those others who are dying with a rifle in their hand. I maintain that we are more than soldiers, for our work is more dangerous and requires intelligence and daring bravery to such a degree that one man in every ten thousand is capable.[33]

These words in some ways echo Arz's praise for the propagandists in August 1917. And many at the AOK were, as we have seen, equally appreciative after their experiences on the Eastern Front, now envisaging Italy as the next target. Whether Max Ronge, head of Austrian military Intelligence, had a hand in preparing the new campaign against Italy is not clear. On 12 September he had met his German counterpart at Baden to discuss Intelligence arrangements for the Caporetto offensive, but his memoirs make no mention at all of preparing propaganda in this direction.[34] By October, however, the Austrians were certainly clear about their new target. They felt, from various Intelligence sources, that the situation in Italy could well be such as to provoke a revolution if their autumn offensive was successful. One of their sources for such optimism was 'Bandino', an agent in Berne who had his own contacts in Milan and elsewhere. In early October Bandino painted for the AOK a strikingly bleak picture of Italy. He predicted that peace would come if the Central Powers defeated Italy on the battlefield, occupied Italian territory and simultaneously swamped Italy with leaflets. The manifestos should announce that the Habsburg regime was no longer the same which had oppressed northern Italy in 1848, that it planned no conquests and had no bone to pick with the Italian people, only with their 'false and treacherous government'. Bandino argued that such arguments would find a willing ear among Italy's growing socialist and pacifist movement. Indeed, their agitation, coupled with the clear evidence of military unrest, would 'undoubtedly produce in the last weeks of November a general movement of rebellion' in Italy, leading on to full revolution with Soviets and a general strike on the Russian model.[35]

Bandino's ideas were among those incorporated into the AOK's first guidelines about propaganda against Italy, drawn up in a memorandum on 18 October, a week before the Caporetto offensive. In assessing the prospects for a successful campaign, the memorandum fixed upon the pacifist spirit in Italy and the reports of unrest, all of which suggested that a military setback might result in revolution. But whether or not this occurred, the Austrians still felt that a military defeat would produce an environment to be exploited in their propaganda. They could dwell on the way in which Italy was economically isolated, dependent on imports which were steadily restricted because of the U-boat war; they could emphasize the indifference of Italy's allies, especially England which treated Italy as a 'spineless tool'; and, as in Russia, they could bring home to the Italian population the 'reality' of the Central Powers' success in the war. Apart from this, the AOK guidelines noted the real prospects for propaganda amongst the Italian troops. They were quite accurate in their portrayal of Cadorna's army, an army where discipline was exceptionally harsh, where the men distrusted their junior officers, where desertion was rife (30 000 deserters in Milan alone according to Bandino), and where war-weariness was a natural response to the lack of military achievement: namely, that for every square kilometre conquered, about 5400 Italians had lost their lives. All this material, according to Baden, could be used to advance the will towards peace: 'In conclusion it might still be noted that the [Italian] army with its Romance character will be easier to influence than the Russian. Today's Italians will find it hard to endure a powerful setback. But that is the moment to bring propaganda into action.'[36]

The main campaign therefore was to begin after the offensive had succeeded, in the same way as the Central Powers had resurrected propaganda in the East after their advances in August 1917. However, the AOK had also already decided to use its proven weapon prior to the offensive. Whether its orders encompassed the type of activity engaged in by Franz Kreuz is unclear. But on 15 October Baden had ordered that planes should be used to distribute leaflets over the Italian army, specifying further that the propaganda should be factual so that it would not be possible for unlucky pilots to be court martialled by the Italians.[37] The background to this command was the AOK's own resolution, from earlier in the war (firstly in July 1916), that enemy pilots who were found spreading 'treason' or openly inciting desertion would be court martialled.[38] The AOK's new commitment to this decision was to limit the type of material which could be employed in its campaign against Italy. But it did not stop more indirect subversion. Thus, in October 1917 Austrian planes distributed exact facsimiles of leading Italian newspapers such as *Corriere della Sera* and *Giornale d'Italia*, carrying the 'treasonable' message that revolution had already broken out in Italy.[39] And after the break-through, the fleeing troops were showered with manifestos which Baden had carefully prepared beforehand:

> Italians! With the greatest and seemingly most justified hopes, you marched off twenty-nine months ago to secure a mass of long-range goals against Austria-Hungary. In eleven Isonzo battles and numerous Alpine engagements you have bloodily come to blows, but without even being able to achieve your short-term goals.
>
> The Austro-Hungarian and German troops have now broken through your lines. They fight not against the Italian people, they fight against your perfidious government which wants to wrest from the Monarchy territory which has belonged to the Austro-Hungarian Monarchy for centuries.
>
> The Monarchy has to defend itself against this attack. We want our territory to remain intact. On this basis we are always ready to conclude peace. You could have this peace tomorrow. We are also ready to supply you then with coal and grain of which we have quite enough. Thus your plight would come to an end.
>
> Your government alone is responsible for the tragic war in your country and all the consequences, the losses, the lack of everything: they are preventing peace because they will not give up their mad plans for conquest.[40]

It might be expected that many Italians would agree with these thoughts as they fled back to the river Tagliamento and from there back to the river Piave. In the following weeks, aircraft of the Habsburg navy also scattered thousands of leaflets over the Albanian front and the Italian hinterland.[41] Similarly, the KPQ contributed in its own way by arranging for pacifist material to be smuggled into Italy via neutral Switzerland.[42] Yet despite what seems to have been a consciously concerted Austrian effort, an Italian revolution was not, of course, one of the results of Caporetto. Baden was not too disappointed. As recorded in the October guidelines, the confused atmosphere after any disaster would give ample scope for propaganda. As soon as the Italian Front had stabilized, it would be possible to put the guidelines fully into operation.

The new Italian Front, stationary only by the end of 1917, was to follow roughly the same line until the end of the war. As in the years 1915–17, it still stretched from Switzerland to the Adriatic, and in the mountainous west – the area of the Austrian 10th army [10AK] – it had not been altered by Caporetto. To the east, however, the Central Powers had conquered the whole of Venetia and shortened the front by a third from the river Astico to the sea. In the Trentino, the forces of Conrad von Hötzendorf had pushed forward from the relative comfort of Val Sugana to take up positions on the Asiago plateau; on the plains, the Austro-German armies by 10 November had been brought to a halt at the river Piave. The result was to divide the front neatly into two types of terrain and climate. On the one hand there was the mountainous and Alpine region of south Tyrol, where the 10AK (FM Krobatin) and 11AK (GO Scheuchenstuel) constituted the *Heeresgruppe* Conrad. On the other hand, there was the front along the fast-flowing river Piave. Here in January 1918 a new *Heeresgruppe* of Field Marshal Svetozar Boroević was created, consisting of an Isonzo army (usually abbreviated to KISA, under GO Wurm) and a new 6AK (under Archduke Joseph) to replace German troops who had departed again for the Western Front. Both types of terrain on the new front, the mountains and the river Piave, were to be serious obstacles to oral propaganda, the kind which had proved to be so effective on the Eastern Front.

The campaign which Baden launched on 5 December 1917[43] would prove to be at its most vigorous during the first six months of 1918. In fact, it would last longer than the Russian campaign of 1917, and yet it was destined ultimately to fail. At first, only certain sectors of the front like the 10th army could begin work, for in December on the front of the 11th army hostilities continued. Conrad there finally had some glory, taking the Meletta massif (which he later termed 'my last wartime success')[44] and pushing forward on both sides of the river Brenta to capture both Monte Asolone and Col del Rosso by Christmas. If this and the winter weather postponed the propaganda campaign for the 11AK, the obstacles on the Piave front were to be slightly different. Not only did the barrier of the river require some rethinking of propaganda methods, but the 6AK, when established on the Upper Piave in early January, discovered that their target was missing. Opposite them were newly arrived British and French divisions, whom Baden never considered worth trying to subvert.[45]

Baden gave clear instructions on how the campaign should be organized. In contrast to the Russian campaign where Max Ronge and his Intelligence section had been in overall control, that against Italy was to be supervised until September 1918 by the Operations Section of the AOK.[46] It supplied

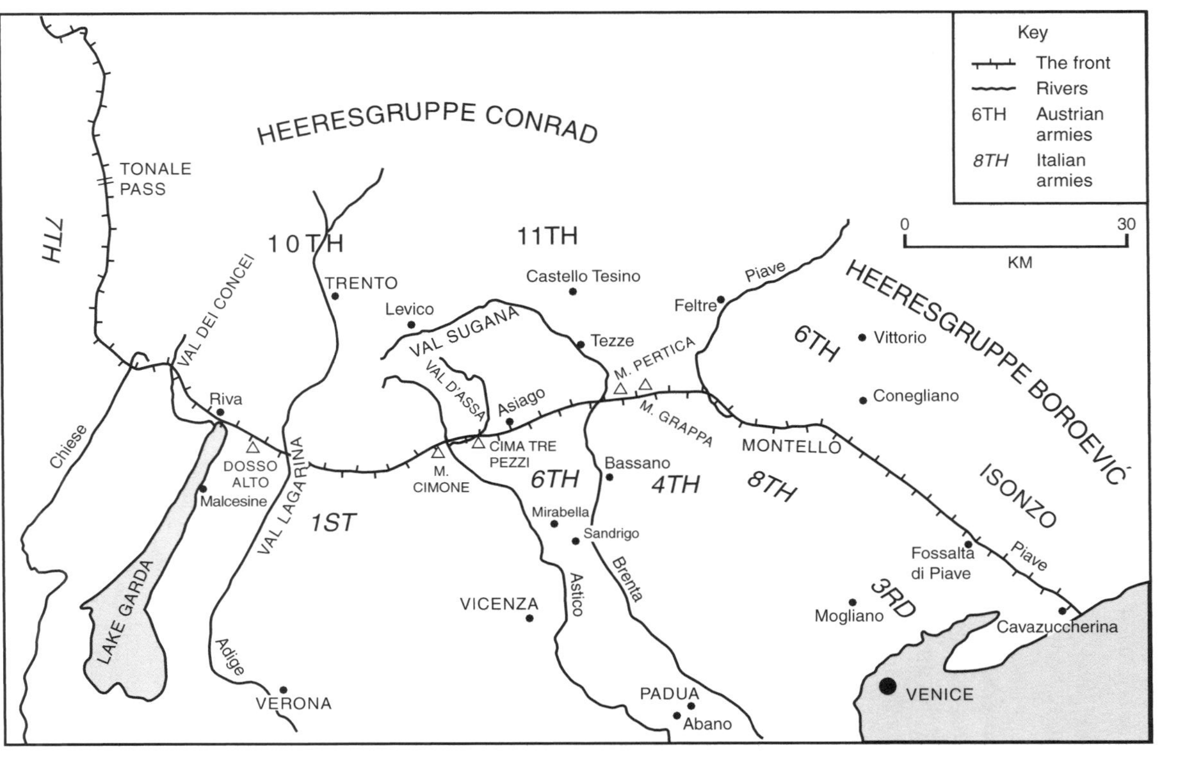


*Map 4.1* The Italian Front in 1918

propaganda guidelines and specified the organizational structure which was inherited from the Eastern Front. But otherwise, perhaps more so than in the East, it allowed considerable flexibility to the propaganda personnel to take their own initiative depending on the type of terrain and the receptiveness of the enemy on each sector of the front. Each of the four armies on the Italian Front appointed a propaganda officer, with overall responsibility for the campaign in his sector on the following lines:

> training and planning, as well as leadership of the propaganda organs, control of propaganda work according to the experiences on the Eastern Front, writing of monthly reports about the state of propaganda activity, composition of propaganda leaflets by using important, contemporary political and military events, replying to enemy counter-propaganda scripts and editing of his own propaganda newspaper.[47]

Subordinate to him, a general staff officer in each army corps had the task of dictating where propaganda was necessary and where the patrols (*Nachrichtentruppen*) should be positioned. The actual propaganda activity was then carried out by a divisional propaganda officer, somebody who had to be 'completely fit for service at the front, completely reliable, eloquent, and if possible a Tyrolian German who at least has a grasp of Italian for official use'.[48] Such personnel were not easy to locate. But by March 1918, after some trials and replacements, 12 of the 14 officers in the 11AK sector were of German-Austrian nationality. A few of these had been involved in propaganda work since September 1917, but for most of them it was a new experience. These officers were assigned one or two interpreters who knew Italian well, and an escort of four to eight reliable and carefully trained *Nachrichtentruppen*, sometimes two units per division, whose job was to protect the officer and assist him in distributing leaflets and confiscating enemy propaganda.[49]

It was clear that because of the terrain the written word would be far more important than on the Eastern Front. The AOK felt that besides leaflets, letters from Italian prisoners could have a major impact if sent back soon after the soldiers' capture. But it was a regular newspaper service which was considered most vital, to provide the Italians with the 'objective news' which they were thought to be lacking. Special care was to be taken to make the propaganda 'true and honest' since, in Baden's view, the Italian soldier had a 'higher intelligence' than the Russian. The result of this directive was that, while polemical manifestos appear to have been most common, the army propaganda officers also produced a variety of newspapers containing factual information about the war; they were designed to appear as objective and normal as possible, even to the extent of including blank spaces to suggest that they had been censored.[50]

For the propaganda officers, however, there would always be the problem of distribution, something which required considerable ingenuity. A common method which quickly developed was to deposit material for collection by enemy troops. KISA created a dozen depositing positions, some on the Piave islands, while the 10th army by January 1918 had 30 posts which it then moved about depending on the Italians' reaction. Even in the Alpine snow around the Tonale pass, three propaganda officers with *Nachrichtentruppen* were soon active, depositing material. One patrol described its work there on the night of 18 January as follows:

> Immediately behind the barrier there was a sentry, smoking a cigarette. The sound of harmonica music and cheerful shouts drifted out of the shelters. At any moment it looked as though the sentry would be bound to see our patrol in full view of him. In spite of this our men wearing snowcoats moved forward, ready to shoot, and crawling to cover the last stretch.

Having deposited their leaflets together with a letter, the head of the patrol called out to the Italians that material had been left which would give them true information about the war. When the Italians replied that the patrol should come over to share in their tobacco and women, the Austrians simply advised them to pick up the manifestos.[51] Elsewhere at the front, the Austrians for a time alerted the enemy to their propaganda by using brightly coloured paper which would show up in the snow,[52] or by erecting large boards which when coated in sulphur were fluorescent at night. By this method the propagandists could also make dramatic announcements, such as 'peace with Russia', with a timeliness which astonished some British troops.[53]

The real inventiveness, however, came where the front was dissected by rivers or gorges, or where enemy hostility prevented any approach. Then megaphones might be used, or the material was thrown over tied to stones or shot over by rifle grenade, mine-thrower or even bow and arrow. In the zone of the XX corps (10AK) a bottle post was begun both on the river Chiese and on Lake Garda, while further north on Monte Scorluzzo small barrels filled with leaflets were rolled down into enemy positions.[54] Under these circumstances, it was even more natural for the Austrians to investigate distribution from the air, a method chiefly employed in the East when no direct contact had been possible; similarly on the Italian Front, Baden always viewed it as a substitute for personal propaganda. In the absence of any long-range propaganda rocket, and since hot-air balloons could be used only sparingly because of their scarcity (propagandists were also advised to test the wind direction), there remained the role of aircraft.[55] From the beginning the AOK had ordered their participation in the campaign, but not without considerable opposition from the airforce whose main fear appears to have been that Italy would execute any pilots engaged in such work. This anxiety was not easily overcome.[56] But, as we will see, when Baden in the late spring wished to step-up its campaign from the air, it was thwarted even more because of the new reality of Allied air superiority on the Italian Front. This, together with the Austrians' inability to pursue oral contacts as fully and effectively as they had in the East, was to prove a fundamental weakness in their propaganda offensive as well as a boon to the enemy's own methods of psychological warfare.

This is not to say that the AOK in the New Year was unrealistic about the task which presented itself. When the euphoria of Caporetto had declined, Baden began to view the Italian target more soberly. Apart from the obstacles of terrain, it was soon apparent that in comparison to the Russian campaign certain crucial ingredients were missing. In the East, domestic turmoil and upheaval had been a vital prerequisite in dissolving military discipline and opening up the field for propaganda to act as a catalyst. In comparison, as Baden noted, 'our propaganda against Italy lacks above all the essential base which it would gain from a political revolution in the interior'. The latter had not occurred, nor by January 1918 was the Italian army disintegrating. But this still opened up a clear field of activity for Austria's front propaganda. First, it would aim to stimulate the grievances of Italy's troops at the front. Second, those troops would be used as the principal medium to take Austria's propaganda into the Italian hinterland (for the Swiss route, operated by the KPQ, was always difficult to keep open); they would hopefully foment instability in Italy which would then, as in Russia, rebound on the front and further undermine the army. In particular, the AOK hoped that if Germany was successful in its spring offensive on the Western Front, the Italians would overwhelmingly demand that peace should be concluded. Advancing this idea was already the key role of Austria's campaign.[57]

Indeed, in the spring of 1918 Austria's propaganda arguments still had great potential. Untainted by German interference, since – as Czernin had emphasized in October – this was to be a strictly Austrian affair, the line of argument had been set out clearly by Baden and the Ballhausplatz in their October guidelines. A major theme of these, and of supplementary guidelines issued in February,[58] was to stress the futility of Italy continuing the war; after all, as many Austrian leaflets showed correctly with explicit maps, Italy had achieved virtually nothing at enormous cost.[59] After Caporetto and the reality of peace on the Eastern Front, it was even less likely that Italy would ever secure its much vaunted goals of Trento and Trieste. Indeed, that such pessimism existed in the Italian interior might be deduced from the rumour that Italian parents whose babies had been christened 'Cadorna' in 1916–17, were now petitioning the Ministry of Justice for a change of name![60] Building on this kind of defeatist mentality, Austrian propaganda could dwell on the high food prices experienced by ordinary Italians, and could quote Italian socialist politicians who readily complained in parliament about widespread misery in Italy's countryside.[61] While this information might reinforce the soldier's concern for his family, he was also encouraged, as on the Eastern Front, to blame his political and military leaders for this state of affairs. The Italian Foreign Minister, Sidney Sonnino, was smeared for his imperialist ambitions against the Monarchy, Cadorna for his ruthless regime, and a 10AK leaflet blatantly lampooned the poet-adventurer Gabriele D'Annunzio (wearing high-heeled shoes) as a 'worthy representative of Italy's maritime power'.[62] The most striking pictorial manifesto of this kind was one composed by the AOK and entitled 'Spaghetti signori!'

Beffa contro beffa.

*Illustration 4.1* 'A Joke against a Joke': Austrian propaganda, lampooning Gabriele D'Annunzio (KA)

*Illustration 4.2* 'Spaghetti Signori!': Austrian propaganda, satirizing the Italians (KA)

It depicted someone who closely resembled the King of Italy being offered spaghetti in the shape of a hangman's noose at a dinner party. Although there are indications that the 11AK commander balked at such material, and the AOK's own guidelines had advised against mocking the Italians, the leaflet was still distributed en masse over enemy troops.[63]

Austria's campaign, however, focused even more on attacking Italy's allies, especially 'England'. Here there was less danger of offending Italian feelings, but ample scope to exploit Entente disunity. Italy was told that it was continuing to fight purely for England's rapacious and selfish dream of conquest. Just as the English had dragged Romania into the war and then left it to fend for itself, so they had behaved with their Italian ally, remaining largely indifferent to Italian war aims. The AOK was quick to pick up Lloyd George's speech of

5 January 1918 to trade unionists which, in defining more precisely what Italy could gain in territory after the war, seemed to be ample proof that 'if necessary Italy's war aims will be abandoned without consideration'.[64] And if England was the source of Italy's raw materials (especially Welsh coal), this was simply increasing Italy's war debts while enabling English and American capitalists to 'grow fat on the blood of the people'.[65] On the other hand, all was not well in England itself. Adopting a technique which was to be copied and perfected in enemy propaganda later in the year, for their newspaper propaganda the Austrians extracted compromising items from the Entente and neutral press. English socialists were quoted as demanding peace and Lloyd George's resignation, while news of arbitrary arrests proved that England's old democracy no longer existed.[66] The *Daily Mail*, meanwhile, provided the 'most delightful' evidence of parsimony in one of London's luxurious hotels. It published a letter from one 'glutton' who was suffering:

> I found myself a week ago in one of the most expensive and elegant hotels in London and from the moment I arrived I was unable to obtain either a piece of beef or a lump of sugar... At lunch there was served a scrap of veal, an egg, a bit of maccaroni and a slice of pudding. For this sumptuous feast one had to pay the best part of five shillings. Dinner consisted of some courses of common fish, the size of a hand. Reading the menu one could fancy oneself at a banquet, but since the *hors d'oeuvre variés* were only, for example, a sardine with a bit of cabbage salad, the *merlan bonnefemme* a plain fish, the *pommes de terre naturels* a single potato, one remained somewhat disillusioned. Evening dress which before the war was de rigueur, has now almost completely disappeared.[67]

If the subtlety of this propaganda may have been lost on many Italian soldiers, the Austrians soon had a far more powerful weapon to hand in discussing events on the Western Front. As they had hoped, the military realities there aided their campaign of ideas in Italy. Apart from the initial German break-through in late March around St Quentin, there was the British retreat (acknowledged even by their own newspapers), and the steady bombardment of Paris which caused a mass exodus to the south while the French Prime Minister, Georges Clemenceau, arrogantly behaved like a 'new Nero' in the midst of disaster[68] – all this seemed to confirm the real strength of Germany and Austria-Hungary. While the Central Powers were easily able to transfer forces from the Eastern Front, the Americans, in contrast, were still failing to make any impact on behalf of the Allies. According to Austrian leaflets, by April 1918 only 200 000 Americans had arrived in Europe and most of these were estimated by the French to be of poor quality.[69] Thus the Entente's much vaunted promise of American help was an illusion. Not only did the Americans prefer to send cereals rather than men to Europe, but the success of the Central Powers' U-boat campaign (a surprisingly popular theme in Austrian propaganda) sounded the knell for Italian hopes of military or economic salvation from across the Atlantic.[70]

Against this disastrous reality in the West, Austria set before the Italians the auspicious reality in the East. In both theatres, events in the spring aided the propaganda campaign. The fact that the Habsburg Empire wanted an end to the war seemed to be confirmed by its behaviour on the Eastern Front where, with its German ally, it was concluding successive peace treaties with Ukraine, Russia and Romania.[71] Naturally, the Italians were not to be informed about the tortuous reality of the peace talks at Brest-Litovsk, nor about the resumption of hostilities against the Bolsheviks in mid-February. Austrian leaflets simply stated that peace was achieved, and they actually pre-empted the peace treaty of 2 March with the Bolsheviks by publicizing Trotsky's premature statement (10 February) that Russia had ceased hostilities and ordered a general demobilization.[72] These favourable developments, particularly the so-called 'Bread Peace' with Ukraine which allegedly would unleash abundant grain supplies for the Monarchy, could be set against the language of western leaders such as Lloyd George who were rejecting peace in order to pursue their dreams of conquest.[73] This accusation was, of course, thoroughly ironic, if not duplicitous. For at Brest-Litovsk one of the major stumbling-blocks to a speedy peace was the German military's continued obsession with annexing large tracts of former Russian territory. The DOHL had reacted furiously when, on Christmas Day 1917, Czernin and the German foreign minister had approved the Bolshevik formula of a peace 'without annexations or indemnities'. Although the Central Powers subsequently argued that what the Bolsheviks termed 'annexation' was in fact a case of 'self-determination' by former provinces of the Russian Empire, all efforts to conclude a peace treaty on this basis came to nothing, in part because the Bolsheviks knew the truth about German designs.

On the Italian Front the Austrians did not have to worry about their ally and could proceed to propagate widely a slogan of 'no annexations or indemnities'. This was calculated to undermine Italy's own annexationist designs upon the Habsburg Monarchy. The notorious Treaty of London, which Italy had signed with the western Allies in order to enter the war in May 1915, had promised the Italians large tracts of Habsburg territory if they won the war. But the slogan also fully matched Count Czernin's own wishes for any general peace settlement; he could be quoted, in a speech of 24 January, announcing his unswerving commitment to such a programme.[74] What this implied for Austria-Hungary's peace settlement with Italy was spelt out in propaganda leaflets which emphasized that the Empire had no territorial designs on Italy and would restore Venetia to the Italians as soon as peace was concluded.[75] Yet apart from this, and regular comments about maintaining the Monarchy's territorial integrity, the Austrians were as cagey about precise peace terms as they had been in the East. For example, the first propaganda guidelines, under Czernin's influence, had expressly forbidden any discussion of the postwar fate of Albania or Asia Minor, stressing that it was above all important to strengthen Italy's will to peace rather than to muddy the waters with talk of peace terms.[76] It was, of course, much safer for the Austrians to make vague and simple statements which would cast the Monarchy in a good light and also leave it more room for manoeuvre in the future. This they could do when discussing their future borders with Italy. For there they had a simple solution, the *status quo ante bellum*, which neatly meshed with the well-known Bolshevik slogan of 'no annexations' but which they had been unable to propagate on the Eastern Front.

If it was natural in the propaganda for the Austrians to dwell on Italy's weaknesses, it was equally natural that they did not dwell on their own. The Central Powers were portrayed as confident and successful, well able to outlast the Entente blockade because of their newly acquired, abundant resources in the East. Most propaganda material which touched on the Monarchy's own domestic turmoil was deemed unsuitable. A rare exception to this rule was when the propagandists felt obliged to explain to Italy the reasons for the widespread strikes which had hit Austria-Hungary in January 1918 largely because of the food crisis. Austria's propaganda denied that the strikes were in any way due to lack of food, attributing them rather to 'purely political demands of the working classes', who had soon recognized the efforts made by 'our beloved Emperor' and his government to conclude peace as soon as possible.[77] Nevertheless, this was a sensitive issue, for simply discussing the Monarchy's domestic affairs would usually place it on the defensive. Not surprisingly, therefore, Baden deemed some of this material too delicate for distribution. This was the fate of one rainbow-coloured manifesto, produced by the 10AK, which described an interview given by Arz von Straussenburg to a correspondent of the Viennese *Arbeiter-Zeitung* on the subject of the January strikes. Although Arz was quoted as emphasizing Vienna's keen commitment to peace, he also mentioned the 'excitement of the population' and the difficulties of achieving peace on the Eastern Front. Perhaps for these reasons, or simply because of his natural aversion to publicity, Arz himself appears to have vetoed the leaflet.[78]

In contrast, what could be described in full for Italy was Austria's allegedly chivalrous treatment of Italian prisoners of war. This, of course, had long been a natural topic for military propaganda used on all the fronts, and Austria was no exception in recounting how prisoners worked an eight-hour day, rested on Sundays and ate the average (supposedly ample) rations of the Austro-Hungarian soldier.[79] What was perhaps unusual about these descriptions was the degree to which they tried to appeal to the Italian soldier's sense of honour in order to raise Austria's reputation in his eyes, either by informing him of heroic Italians who had been decorated by Emperor Karl, or simply by reminding him that Austria-Hungary did not issue appeals for desertion. Whether the Austrians could really justify the latter claim, even at face value, is questionable.[80] And all the more so, since their occupation of Venetia supplied them with a novel, subversive weapon which they certainly did not shy away from employing to undermine Italian discipline. From the start of their campaign, some of the propaganda expressly appealed to the emotions of those Italian soldiers who had left relatives or friends in the occupied zone. As on the Eastern Front, where this method had proved highly useful when the allies had advanced deep into Russian territory, the Italians were urged by leaflet to begin a traffic of correspondence through Austrian lines with their loved ones. One leaflet explained:

> This method of transmitting correspondence affords two great advantages. Firstly, the letters reach their address quicker because they do not have to pass the censor, and thus they travel direct from the sender to the addressee. Secondly, you can write everything frankly. Where the Piave affords no obstacle our patrols will show you spots entitled 'Postal Receiving Centres'. Where the Piave prevents the post being handed in direct, you can throw your correspondence into our trenches in the manner which appears to you most convenient. This method of correspondence shows our desire to be of use to your families behind our lines, who are awaiting news of you with great anxiety.[81]

In fact, the letters would indeed be censored, thereby supplying useful details to Austrian military Intelligence, while the traffic as a whole was bound to stimulate the desire for peace of the Italian soldier. As an additional 'depressant', the Austrians kept him informed about conditions in Venetia through the *Gazzetta del Veneto*, a newspaper which was issued by the KPQ for the Venetian civilian population.[82] Experience would show that such material, besides lowering Italian morale, was equally likely to incite Venetian soldiers to desert from the Italian forces.

## 4.3 The impact of Austria-Hungary's front propaganda

It is clear that the arguments of Austria-Hungary's propaganda in the spring were well matched to the mood of many Italian soldiers who had hoped in vain for peace by the end of 1917.[83] According to one Italian journalist, who was attached to the press office at the CS, Austria's campaign of 'peace and fraternization' was indeed alarming because it seemed to be taking roots in the Italian trenches. Its themes, Italy's failed dream of conquering Trento and Trieste or Italy's fight for Anglo-French interests, were exactly those which suited the rank and file's mentality.[84] This was apparent too to the Austrians from the statements of Italian prisoners and deserters.[85] Most of them were war-weary, some mentioning the impact which peace in the East was having, others the continued bad treatment by their officers. Many were bitter against English and French troops for 'prolonging the war', forcing Italy to continue hostilities. And some certainly deserted in order to reach relatives in occupied Venetia. Those who had received Austrian propaganda said that it was read and circulated eagerly, even if they always had to be careful of their officers' vigilance. A few also mentioned that Italy, because of the propaganda, had had to withdraw some unreliable Alpini troops from the front: an incident, near the river Brenta, which is confirmed by more impartial witnesses.[86] Lastly, a few deserters even suggested that they had crossed the trenches in response to Austrian propaganda.[87]

This type of evidence was enough to convince the AOK that its campaign was worth continuing. Aided by subversive elements in the Italian hinterland, and boosted by news of peace in the East and a German break-through in the West, it seemed quite likely that the combined impact could force Italy to the peace table. Baden quickly acknowledged the positive signs in February 1918:

> The propaganda efforts in January on the south-western front have, especially in the sectors of the 10th and 11th armies, produced very satisfactory results.... The lively exchange of leaflets and letters, and even increasing oral discussions, indicate that the Italians are perhaps more responsive to propaganda than the Russians.[88]

True, there were some obstacles. For most of the 6AK sector no propaganda was possible until April, when British and French troops had been transferred from the Montello hill and replaced by Italian forces; and even then the 6AK was hampered by bad weather and the lack of an effective printing press.[89] KISA, however, despite the obstacle of the Piave, launched itself fully into the campaign. If in February propaganda patrols deposited or sent over 55 000 leaflets (and even some personal contact was temporarily possible in the Piave delta), by March this figure had doubled and was accompanied by a weekly newspaper (*Sprazzi di Luce*). In April, although the high water of the Piave made it impossible to ascertain the effects, manifesto distribution was again stepped up (150 000 leaflets) together with a regular letter-traffic.[90]

But it was on the mountain front in particular that the campaign seemed to be bearing, in Baden's words, 'visible fruits'.[91] There, a certain amount of oral propaganda was possible, something – always most favoured by the AOK because of the Eastern experience – which seemed to be guaranteed proof of Italian receptiveness. In the 10AK zone, where hostilities were scarce, the campaign was perhaps most systematically pursued in these months. In his report for January 1918, the 10AK propaganda officer could observe that

> The general impression is favourable: at any rate, compared to last month there is progress in that our propaganda material has been picked up more frequently and regularly than before, while in several places we have already succeeded in establishing written or brief oral contact with the enemy. Gradually the initial hostile attitude towards our propaganda patrols has ceased.[92]

The story of fraternization on the eastern side of Monte Cimone (near the river Astico and on the edge of the 10AK front) best illustrates the practice and perils of this propaganda work. Cimone-Ost, as the Austrians termed it, became one of the most active positions for oral propaganda in the 10AK sector. Already in mid-January it was clear that the Italian sentries were picking up the deposited material. On 23 January, a member of the divisional *Nachrichtentruppen* managed to abseil down a cliff, exchange Austrian cigarettes for Italian bread and oranges, and learn for the first time that war-weary Italians of the 141st regiment were most eager to read Austrian propaganda. There followed regular visits, with the Austrian patrol being treated to hour-long 'coffee breaks' during which they could encourage and nurture the Italians' ill-feeling towards England and France as well as their evident delight at the news of peace in the East; the Italians further announced that they would spread the Austrian propaganda material in the rear when their sentry position was relieved.[93] In the subsequent weeks even some Italian officers felt disposed to visit the Austrian trenches, have their photographs taken, and discuss their war-weariness and the need for caution when fraternizing.[94] Indeed, danger was ever present. Although the Austrian XIV corps command [KK] had unilaterally forbidden its propaganda personnel to visit enemy trenches, this was disregarded by the propaganda officer on Cimone with the result that on 21 March he and his patrol were surprised and captured by the Italians.[95] Only in late April, after careful preparation with letters and the enticement of cigarettes (the latter by this time a compulsory addition to any propaganda package),[96] could personal contact be resumed. In a conversation on 2 May, Italian sentries complained about the war, swore at their royal family and abused the English and French who were allegedly behaving arrogantly in Italy. If such a response was gratifying for the propagandists, they could still never be quite sure of their target. When a week later, at dawn, three of the *Nachrichtentruppen* visited the Italian positions they did not return.[97] They too had been captured, this time by Italian counter-espionage forces who had deliberately enticed the Austrians in order to ensnare them.[98]

The degree of sustained personal contact on Cimone was unusual. On most sectors of the 10AK front there were intermittent links, but it became much more common for the patrols simply to deposit or scatter material (in a mass which usually greatly exceeded the amount distributed, for example, on the KISA front).[99] Similarly on the 11AK front, the successes of the campaign were mixed, often interrupted by bad weather or an unpredictable Italian reaction. This is evident from the experience of propaganda in the area of the I KK between the rivers Brenta and Piave, especially around Monte Fontana Secca. There, by early February, the 22nd Schützen Division [22SchD] had begun to organize its campaign, appointing a German-Austrian, Lt Franz Weil, as propaganda officer together with a deputy, four interpreters, and some *Nachrichtentruppen*. By March, as in many other divisions, the deputy and three of the interpreters were deemed unsuitable for the work (one could not stand the cold), and had been replaced. The new deputy, Walter de Crinis, a bank official in civilian life, was now put in charge of a second propaganda unit consisting of two of the new interpreters and a patrol of six men.[100] The two units proceeded to operate separately, covering between them a mountainous sector of about three miles. In early February, Weil had managed to approach enemy lines and discover the Italians' desire for peace 'on the basis of the old borders'. But thereafter, since the Italians were reserved, he and his patrol of seven men limited their activity to throwing over leaflets in small packets, observing with satisfaction that they were read and that the announcement of letter-traffic 'was greeted with handclaps'. In the following weeks, however, little progress was made. Either propaganda was impossible because of snowstorms, or the Italians failed to pick up the material, or Weil was shot at when he tried to approach. As the 22SchD commander observed, the Italians were repeatedly abusing propaganda agreements and exhibiting their 'pernicious character'.

Only in early March, when new Alpini troops were in position opposite, could Weil resume oral contact, discovering from his talks that, although the Italians were receptive, they had to be constantly alert in case their officers intervened.[101] Captain Frydman, the officer in charge of 11AK propaganda, passed on this opinion to Baden: 'In general, one can detect that the Italian soldier is thoroughly ready for personal contact and accessible for our propaganda material, but is blocked from such influence by extremely tight supervision.'[102] This indeed seems to have been the main obstacle to Weil's activity until April. Only then, in a short period before the 22SchD was transferred to another front, was he again able to hold regular talks, hand over leaflets and cigarettes, and arrange a mutual cease-fire in his sector.[103] Frydman himself subsequently praised the achievements on this sector of the 11AK front. Through energetic work which had actually been supported fully by the local Austrian commanders, and in spite of enemy counter-measures, the propaganda campaign in the I KK region had produced the best results of the whole army.[104]

As Frydman's comments implied, Austria's campaign was not just obstructed by the nature of the terrain or the hostility of the enemy. It also faced resistance from many within the Austrian army itself. As on the Eastern Front, many commanders and many troops continued to view the campaign as 'unfair', as a dishonourable activity, which might rebound and damage the morale of their own army. Baden and the army propaganda officers acted sharply to counter this impression. Already in February the AOK had advised the 11AK that the divisional propaganda officers needed great tenacity in order to influence the thinking of their commanders, but that the latter would eventually support them when the results became clearer; therefore, the High Command was totally against any weakening of the campaign.[105] In this spirit, Frydman and the other propaganda leaders constantly tried to galvanize their subordinates and perfect their techniques. For example, they organized courses to train propaganda personnel, Frydman ordering that the divisions must exercise great care in choosing officers for his courses at Levico since 'propaganda activity is in every regard on a par with the combat duties of the troops'.[106] The personnel were also encouraged to experiment with different types of distribution (in particular, a long-range propaganda gun was being developed) and report from their local experience with the enemy on how they felt the campaign could best be improved. In view of the dangerous nature of the work, they as well as their troop commanders were warned that it should always be left solely in the hands of the 'professionals', who needed to liaise closely with their divisions in order to avoid surprise through enemy or even Austrian action.

Despite these guidelines, the resistance continued. On 15 May, Frydman called together a meeting of 11th army propaganda officers at Levico to share experiences. He found that although all of them were still optimistic about the campaign, they had one major grievance: the attitude of their own troops. The local commanders, they reported, were often loath to supply a strong enough escort for the propaganda personnel, or supplied Magyar troops or others whom the propaganda officer could not understand. More seriously, the commanders were inclined to keep the propagandists in the dark about enemy positions and sometimes even refused to allow them access to a map of the sector. Because of such a lack of coordination, the propagandists led a precarious existence, exposed not only to enemy fire but also sometimes to the possibility of being fired on by their own troops out of 'pure maliciousness'. Frydman summed up the general feeling:

> Our whole propaganda campaign is characterized as 'unfair' by the troops. The propaganda officers don't find support anywhere. They hang, so to speak, in limbo, are completely disheartened by this, and it is only due to this that so many of them are asking to be relieved from duty.[107]

If many sections of the army were indeed sceptical about the propaganda weapon on the grounds that it was a diversion from 'proper' military activity, some opposed it because it was blatantly irritating the Italians and causing a reaction hostile to the Austrians, either with bullets or with Italian 'counter-propaganda'. However, for those involved in the Austrian campaign, as well as some of the leading military, this Italian reaction was at first viewed very positively. Together with the statements of Italian prisoners and the cases of fraternization, here was 'evidence' that the propaganda was achieving definite results. On some sectors of the front, KISA for example, it was perhaps the only evidence.[108] Frydman's reaction was typical of the propagandists as a whole. Responding on 21 April to propaganda reports from the 11th army front, he noted cautiously that 'although our propaganda activity shows no tangible success because of continuous trench-warfare, various signs indicate that [it] is not without effect on the very responsive and curious Italian soldier'. Frydman pointed to Italian counter-propaganda at the front, the vigilance of Italian officers, but also the increasing nervousness of the Italian press. In particular, the liberal *Corriere della Sera* was clamouring for Italy to respond in kind, arguing that Austria's campaign no longer resembled the 'grotesque' efforts of late 1917: 'Austria has set up a propaganda office against us, just as it did successfully against Russia, and has placed at its disposal the manpower and means which are deemed necessary.'[109] Frydman took these Italian responses as clear proof that propaganda was now an 'essential, modern weapon of warfare' and a most effective complement to traditional arms. The fact that Italy was reacting to Austria's efforts was, he felt, simply further evidence of their effectiveness.[110]

It was a view probably shared by Conrad, Boroević and many at the AOK. From early in the year they had realized that a duel was gradually beginning between their own propaganda and what they always termed the 'counter-propaganda' of the Italians. While prosecuting their own campaign and acting on the offensive, they were increasingly aware of the need also to act defensively and combat enemy propaganda.[111] Yet for the first six months of 1918, Austria's campaign was firmly on the 'offensive foot'; even if the enemy's own efforts began to take up more and more space in their propaganda reports, the Austrians were still confident that their campaign was superior. As one enthusiast noted, 'our propaganda has the advantage over the enemy's of great experience which cannot be vitiated by any counter-measures'.[112] In particular, the AOK began to hope that the real fruits of the campaign would ripen during the military offensive which they were preparing for mid-June. As in Russia in August 1917 or Italy in October, the war of movement would hopefully reveal the true state of enemy demoralization. Therefore, the months prior to the attack were crucial for the campaign, a time to 'use energetically our significant lead and better opportunities'.[113] It meant that if personal contact was impossible, the enemy should still be bombarded with a mass distribution of manifestos so that as many Italians as possible were contacted. By late April the

11AK had ordered all aeroplanes flying over enemy lines and hinterland to throw out what amounted to two-thirds of the 11th army's propaganda material; the pilots were to target troop assembly-points, making sure that the leaflets 'fluttered separately when falling'.[114]

The Habsburg military's continued optimism at this time might be described as reflecting accurately the Central Powers' encouraging position on the Western and Eastern Fronts. The AOK had certainly launched their Italian campaign in an ideal environment, when victory seemed imminent and Italian morale was at its nadir. Yet, as we have seen, the true impact of Austrian propaganda had been very hard to gauge. Although Baden with the Russian experience in mind might pick out the auspicious signs at the front, countervailing currents were always present. The truth was that the Austrians were eventually to be pushed on to the defensive in their use of psychological warfare precisely by those Italian counter-measures which at first they had seen not so much as a threat, but as proof of their own campaign's effectiveness. Italian vigilance had been clear to Baden from the turn of the year. Many of the prisoners who expressed interest in Austrian propaganda also mentioned how eager their officers were to seize the material. For example, in a conversation overheard on the Lower Piave, an Italian officer had instructed his men as follows:

> Early this morning Austrian planes threw out leaflets over our positions. The divisional command orders that absolutely all leaflets be collected and forbids them to be circulated among the men . . . as soon as they are collected, the leaflets are to be surrendered to the regimental command.[115]

Baden also knew that the CS, while promising rewards of money or extra leave for those who submitted propaganda material, was increasingly vigilant about fraternization, ordering on 9 March that anyone found trafficking with the enemy would be shot.[116] This order appears to have had a limited impact.[117] But when combined with the problems of terrain, of vigilance by the Italians and especially their habit of regularly relieving units in order to prevent long-term contact with the Austrians, it meant that a significant barrier was slowly being erected against Austrian attempts to transmit propaganda. Nor could the Austrians be certain whether the Italians who picked up their material were sympathetic or a 'loyal' enemy patrol. By April 1918 it was probably the latter, for from this time most Italians who were captured claimed never to have seen any Austrian propaganda.[118]

From this, one might conclude that Austria's campaign was failing to have an impact largely due to technical obstacles. In fact, it was also the case that the Italians had been positively countering the substance of Austria's arguments and lessening the potential for any break-through. By the spring many Italian soldiers were no longer as receptive as they had been at the time of the Caporetto disaster. As early as 7 January, the British liaison Delmé-Radcliffe had noted that, in contrast to December when the CS had been considering another retreat far beyond the Piave because of Austrian pressure in the mountains, 'there is very little talk about retiring now and not much thinking about it either. The Italian army is hardening and improving every day.'[119]

This was only part of Italy's general regeneration in the aftermath of the disaster. Caporetto, as one contemporary observed, dealt 'a tremendous thrash across the legs of the entire nation' which sprang to its feet.[120] In political terms, it meant the fall of Boselli as Prime Minister, and his replacement by the former Minister of Interior, Vittorio Emanuele Orlando. If Orlando was one of the few people who could hold together a cabinet consisting of such diverse talents as Sonnino (Foreign Minister), Francesco Nitti (Minister of the Treasury) and Leonida Bissolati (minister without portfolio), he was also determined to bring a new unity to Italy's political and military leadership. Backed by Entente pressure, he was able to remove Cadorna, with whom he had regularly clashed in the past, sending him as Italy's delegate to the Supreme War Council at Versailles. Cadorna was replaced as Chief of Staff by General Armando Diaz, with General Pietro Badoglio as his deputy. Both were to be very fortuitous choices. Diaz was a southerner and a long-time acquaintance of Nitti, thereby providing a guarantee of harmony with the government which had been so noticeably lacking under Cadorna. As Visconti Venosta, Diaz's adjutant, told journalists, 'with this man there will be no dangerous independence. State operations will be kept united at all times.'[121] Orlando further ensured this by setting up a War Council which would meet frequently and at least once a month at the front.[122] While Diaz acted as a coordinator, viewing himself very much as the government's military representative, he was balanced by Badoglio, an energetic artillerist from Piedmont who concentrated on military operations at the front. The two therefore were complementary, a happy mixture of southern and northern Italy; or as one Intelligence officer (a northerner!) noted, they represented respectively the heart and brain of the army.[123]

Clear evidence of their fresh outlook was their attitude to troop morale. Although Cadorna's rigid discipline was not relaxed, the new CS, based at Padua, immediately tackled both the material and spiritual side of the army's welfare. The troops' rations were substantially improved (as most Italian prisoners told the Austrians), and leave was extended by half to a total of 25 days per annum. But most significantly, in January 1918 the CS for the first time established a system for propaganda among the Italian forces. Propaganda offices, or Sezioni 'P' as they were known, were created, subordinate to the Intelligence centres of each army. Their task was three-fold. First, to inspect and evaluate troop morale more closely, and counter subversive influences, whether of domestic or enemy origin; this was to be achieved, as before, through censorship of troop correspondence, but also by the vigilance of special police officials supplied by the CS. Second, to organize propaganda lectures for the troops which, in contrast to the past, would be delivered by invalids, veterans or charismatic individuals, and then supported by a wealth of special propaganda newspapers or other material. Third, to ensure that when the men were in the rear they were given every assistance to relax in an expanded number of 'rest homes' so that they returned refreshed to the front.[124]

How the system operated is clear from the memoirs of Tullio Marchetti, head of Intelligence of the 1st army, east of Lake Garda.[125] Already in November 1917, Marchetti had made agreements with local newspapers in order to ensure that the right type of information was reaching the front. With the establishment of Sezione 'P', and guided by instructions from the CS, Marchetti eventually entrusted propaganda to a Florentine lawyer, Gaetano Casoni, who organized lectures, films and theatre for the men. He and his assistants, such as the future military historian Amedeo Tosti, also produced their own trench newspapers – for example, *La Tradotta* and *Signor Sì*.[126] Marchetti, however, went further, installing his own man, Gaetano Cenzato, as editor of the Veronese *L'Arena* so as to guarantee that a supposedly 'non-official' newspaper would be subject completely to his influence without the troops becoming suspicious. As for the 'counter-propaganda' aspects of this work, Marchetti chose Francesco Broccardi who, with 25 agents, circulated in the army sector, observing the troops, reporting on morale, and occasionally countering Austrian propaganda in the front line. This whole system of Italian propaganda may not have diminished the Italian soldier's war-weariness, nor his antipathy to the officers. But it certainly seems to have acted as something of an extra shield, protecting the troops from Austria's campaign. The troops could easily be isolated from Austria's propaganda and fed a careful diet of optimistic material instead. In its effectiveness this was also, as we will see, a contrast to the AOK's own propaganda efforts among its own troops. Not only was that work begun several months after the Italians', thereby falling behind in the battle of 'defensive propaganda', but it lacked many of the key elements – such as the control of newspapers – of the Italian system.

A final element which strengthened Italy's morale in confronting Austria's campaign was military assistance from its allies. In late 1917, 11 British and French divisions had hurried to Italy, and the news was published widely in order to boost morale. Generally, as British memoirs recall, the new forces were received with enthusiasm by the native population, viewed more as evidence of allied solidarity at this critical moment than as prolongers of the war.[127] It seems likely that this opinion was also shared by many Italian soldiers, thereby weakening one of the key arguments of Austrian propaganda, that 'England' was purely selfish and would leave Italy in the lurch in order to pursue its own interests. True, some Italian prisoners would grumble about their allies to the Austrians, and the latter in their propaganda would be quick to exploit the news in March that six of the Entente divisions were departing again for the Western Front. Yet, on the whole, it was a mistake for the AOK to expect that in Italy they could exploit allied divisions in exactly the same way as in Russia; for in contrast to the Eastern Front, Entente forces were at least actively engaged in fighting alongside their ally in the Italian theatre.

On the whole, allied cooperation in Italy ran remarkably smoothly, in spite of a rather patronizing attitude by the new arrivals. The commander of the French forces, General Fayolle, was quick to observe that the Italians were 'imperfectly trained in the methods of present day warfare',[128] a comment which ignored Italy's remarkable advances both in mountain warfare and in Intelligence work. Lord Cavan too, who in March would take over the control of British forces from General Plumer, felt on his arrival that 'the happy-go-lucky, childish spirit seems still to pervade everybody, much talk, little action'; in the following 12 months he was to be constantly critical of the Italian military's 'frothy enthusiasm' but lack of 'thoroughness' – 'the greatest of their short comings'.[129] However, the British in particular were concerned not to offend their hosts, but to encourage them by example. When for instance Cavan visited the perilously unguarded top of Mantua cathedral, he felt obliged to appear fearless so that Italy's faith in British courage would not be diminished.[130] More seriously, the British quickly established training schools in order to instruct the Italians in techniques of defence (something which Cavan considered a major cause of Caporetto), and when they moved to the front on the Montello in late November they organized their sector 'as a model with the object of showing the Italians how few men it is necessary to keep in the front-line'.[131] If the Italians were rather slow to adopt the new training techniques, the Entente example of constantly harrying the enemy at the front was more promising. Partly in response to a successful French attack on Monte Tomba in late December which captured 1500 prisoners, and to frequent British raids, the CS was stirred to a more offensive approach, illustrated in late January by their forces attacking and recapturing Monte di Val Bella and Col del Rosso.

In the air battles over Venetia as well, the British made a substantial impact. Their cooperation from late 1917 enabled the Italians to achieve a superiority in the air which both reinvigorated their morale and limited the methods which the Austrians might use in their propaganda campaign. When British squadrons of the Royal Flying Corps arrived in Italy after Caporetto, they had found their ally on the defensive in the face of a 'confident and aggressive' Austrian airforce, supported by several German squadrons.[132] At the turn of the year, enemy planes repeatedly bombed the CS headquarters at Padua, something which Delmé-Radcliffe for one considered 'rather a nuisance' for it necessitated long hours of refuge in the cellars at night.[133] Eventually, the damage inflicted and the strain of the raids (General Plumer narrowly escaped injury), forced the CS to leave the town and settle nearby at Abano.[134] By February, however, the British by means of constantly offensive operations had begun to dominate the air, producing what captured Austrian aviators termed a 'regular calamity' for their airforce: 'The British and Italian scouts have been inflicting terrible losses on us. Not a day passes without the funerals of two or three of our comrades...Our aviation has never passed through a more trying period'. As for the skill of the British pilots:

> They are perfect marvels of dare-devilry; a few days ago they broke the windows of army headquarters at S.Vito al Tagliamento with machine-gun fire! They come down to a few metres off the ground, fire on troops on the march with machine guns and then make off, right under our very noses, in the most maddening manner. We should never have believed, coming from Romania, that in Italy we could possibly be so inferior. Here we are absolutely crushed.[135]

While the average daily British toll was eight enemy aircraft and two balloons, they themselves lost only 47 planes during their 12 months in Italy.[136] The Austrians, it is true, were never to be totally excluded from crossing Italian lines. In late February, for example, they successfully bombed Venice while at the same time dropping red leaflets which warned that this was a reprisal for the bombing of Innsbruck.[137] But they had speedily recognized their enemy's new superiority in the air.[138] It meant that they could never fully engage in aerial propaganda, notably when – from April 1918 – they began to realize its advantages for mass distribution prior to their June offensive. In turn, it gave the Italians a significant extra weapon in their own propaganda armoury; it also increased their confidence in the spring that they could stand firm against any further Austrian attacks.

On 11 April, Delmé-Radcliffe could report to the War Office: 'the presence of the British and French troops in Italy during the last five months has been of inestimable value to the Italian army, which has profited to a great extent by the example and by observing the British and French methods of training and fighting'. With this, added to the shock of Caporetto, 'it is correct to say that the morale in the country and in the army is better than it has ever been before'. Nevertheless, Delmé-Radcliffe did not underestimate the continued dangers for the morale of the Italian soldier, including war-weariness, domestic pacifism, irritation at junior officers and 'shirkers' from military service, and not least, a particularly energetic Austrian propaganda campaign:

> On the front, the enemy has created an elaborate propaganda organization, through which he endeavours by leaflets, by communication by voice, by

fraternization, etc, etc, to demoralise the Italian troops. The enemy also uses other subtle means for this object. He recently caused it to be known that all the Italian prisoners whose homes were in the occupied territory would be given three months' liberty in which to cultivate their fields....The distribution of the leaflets does not appear to produce any result. On the other hand, some fraternization at one or two quiet points of the front has taken place. A few men have been induced to desert and the proper tension and watchfulness have been a little relaxed here and there on the 'live and let live' principle. An improvement is taking place in this respect and strong measures are being taken to suppress tendencies of this kind.

Delmé-Radcliffe concluded that, when compared to the autumn, the morale of 20 per cent of the Italian army had indeed improved, but for 70 per cent it was in a state of equilibrium and for 10 per cent it was actually worse.[139] Admittedly, he was writing at a time when the Germans were making headway on the Western Front and the outcome of the war was not particularly auspicious for Italy. But his comments still suggest that, despite CS efforts, there was enough 'weak material' in the Italian forces to justify the AOK's continued optimism in employing the propaganda weapon. The Austrians expected that Italian morale, already lowered by Caporetto and events on the Eastern and Western Fronts, would reveal its true, depressing character during Austria-Hungary's next military offensive. And their judgement, that Italian morale was a fluctuating barometer, highly dependent on military success or failure, was equally shared by the British. As Lord Cavan noted in late March, 'I consider the Italians to be in a state of equilibrium – by which I mean that a success – even a small one, will act as a great incentive to high "morale" – but a failure would unduly depress them'.[140]

Later in the year some Austrian propagandists, notably of the 11AK, would feel that Austria-Hungary had been too slow in bringing a full propaganda offensive to bear immediately after Caporetto. Then, they argued, Italian morale had been at its nadir and more results might have been expected.[141] Such a view appears rather anachronistic. In December 1917 Conrad's military operations had continued in the mountains, and the AOK had certainly never envisaged giving propaganda precedence when traditional military methods might still reap more success. In the spring, when the propaganda campaign was fully launched, it still had considerable potential to help weaken Italian morale since its arguments, dwelling on war-weariness and Italian weakness, were largely based on fact. As long as this continued, the campaign might be quite effective. On the other hand, Italy in early 1918 was not identical to Russia in 1917. The AOK had realized this to a certain extent, noting the absence of any revolution in the hinterland, the absence of revolutionary committees at the front, and therefore the extra obstacles to disseminating ideas. Yet Baden was still perhaps too inclined to adopt propaganda arguments and techniques from the Eastern Front, assuming that they could be employed equally effectively in Italy. In argument they dwelt heavily on 'English selfishness' (largely ignoring the issue of 'land for the peasants' which might have been exploited); in technique they were far too inclined, in spite of the terrain, to concentrate on personal contact across the trenches and to neglect, early in the campaign, a mass distribution of material from the air.

Indeed, it was especially the nature of the Austrians' 'propaganda machinery' in the Italian environment which hampered their campaign: the material was simply not reaching the Italians. When the latter began their own campaign, they were able to bombard the Austrian trenches with aerial propaganda on a scale far in excess of Austria's efforts. The Austrians could not compete with this, partly because they were concentrating anyway on 'trench propaganda', but also because by February 1918 they were no longer masters of the skies in the Italian theatre. Furthermore, although the AOK had realized that its campaign would have to try to influence each individual Italian soldier (since no revolutionary committees existed to spread the ideas),[142] the limited 'trench-propaganda' was highly unlikely to achieve this result, all the more so as it could easily be obstructed by vigilant Italian officers in the front line. The CS counter-measures, advanced enthusiastically by Diaz and Badoglio, seem to have acted as a fairly reliable shield, preventing the soldiers from experiencing Austria's propaganda at a time when they were most susceptible.

In turn, the CS counter-measures were not wholly defensive. It was partly as an offensive response to Austria's campaign that the new CS would launch its own battle of ideas against the Austro-Hungarian army. While inadvertently adopting many of Austria's own techniques and arguments, the Italian campaign would strike further, by attempting to exploit nationalist tensions within the Habsburg forces. It was naturally a threat which the AOK had been fully conscious of during its Russian campaign, especially in the later stages, but only in the final year of war would the menace fully materialize. As the head of Conrad's Intelligence staff warned Baden in February 1918, 'the danger that systematic propaganda activity will produce a similar outcome to that in Russia exists *for our men far more* than for the Italians'.[143] Many of the Austrian military undoubtedly shared this view. But until the early summer they still felt that their own campaign required more attention than the enemy's. In the propaganda duel on the Italian Front, the Austrians preferred to concentrate on the offensive, spreading their own ideas, rather than using their energy defensively, to combat Italian propaganda and protect their own forces. Only by July 1918 did the AOK realize that it had lost the duel. By then it was also clear that the Austro-Hungarian forces were inadequately equipped to resist the propaganda weapon which was wielded by the enemy.

## Notes

1. Cesare Pettorelli Lalatta [Finzi], *Note Informazioni di un Capo del Servizio Informazioni d'Armata (1915–1918)*, 2nd edn (Milan, 1934) p. 141.
2. OULK, VI, pp. 493ff for the preparations: this sector was singled out by the AOK in July as the ideal base from which to attack.
3. *Relazione della Commissione d'Inchiesta. Dall'Isonzo al Piave, 24 Ottobre–9 Novembre 1917* [hereafter *Relazione*], 2 vols (Rome, 1919), II: *Le Cause e la Responsabilità degli Avvenimenti*, p. 552.
4. OULK, VI, pp. 511, 520.
5. See *Relazione*, I: *Cenno Schematico degli Avvenimenti*, pp. 8ff; and II, pp. 43ff, for a discussion of the available Intelligence.
6. The words of Tullio Marchetti, *Ventotto Anni nel Servizio Informazioni Militari* (Trento, 1960) p. 246. See also the discussion of Odoardo Marchetti (who had just become head of Italian military Intelligence): *Il Servizio Informazioni dell'Esercito Italiano nella Grande Guerra* (Rome, 1937) pp. 175ff.
7. Giorgio Candeloro, *Storia dell'Italia Moderna*, vol. 8, 4th edn (Milan, 1993) pp. 184–5; *Relazione*, II, p. 48.
8. PRO, Cabinet minutes [CAB] 23/4, W.C.260, 30 October 1917. The British ambassador in Rome, Sir Rennell Rodd (an arch-rival of Delmé-Radcliffe) gained the same impression: 'What has happened was not so much a military defeat as a refusal to fight – something like a strike on the part of the 4th army corps of the 2nd army . . . they had been undermined by the socialist and clerical peace propaganda. They had also no doubt received communications and promises from the enemy. They were "fed up" with the monotony of existence and contemplated another winter of it with dread' (House of Lords Record Office [HLRO], Lloyd George MSS, F/56/1/56, Rodd to Lloyd George, 4 November 1917).
9. *Relazione*, II, pp. 506ff.
10. Luciano Tosi, *La Propaganda Italiana all'Estero nella Prima Guerra Mondiale. Rivendicazioni Territoriali e Politica delle Nazionalità* (Udine, 1977) pp. 80–7.
11. Giovanna Procacci, *Soldati e Prigionieri Italiani nella Grande Guerra* (Rome, 1993) p. 63.
12. *Relazione*, II, p. 453 note 1.
13. Ibid., pp. 454ff and 519ff.
14. According to the British official history, the Italians lost 40 000 dead, 108 000 wounded and 18 000 prisoners, while the Austrians lost 10 000 dead, more than 45 000 wounded and about 30 000 missing: J.E. Edmonds and H.R. Davies, *Official History of the War. Military Operations Italy 1915–1919* (London, 1949) p. 38.
15. Procacci, *Soldati e Prigionieri*, pp. 25, 51 note 75.
16. *Relazione*, II, p. 381.
17. Churchill College Cambridge [CCC], Cavan MSS, 1/3, Memoirs: 'Recollections hazy but happy', part I, p. 36.
18. *Relazione*, II, pp. 375–9; Procacci, *Soldati e Prigionieri*, pp. 78ff.
19. Tullio Marchetti, *Ventotto Anni*, pp. 297–8. See *Relazione*, II, pp. 381ff, for a full discussion of propaganda among the Italian troops.
20. OULK, VI, p. 561.
21. PRO, WO 106/814, 'Morale of the Italian army': report by Delmé-Radcliffe, 11 April 1918.
22. Procacci, *Soldati e Prigionieri*, pp. 64–5.
23. *Relazione*, II, pp. 502–3, 527.

24. Ibid., pp. 503–4.
25. See KA, 11AK Gstbs Abt 1918, Fasz.448, Pr.2030, AOK Op Nr 766/21: 'Die Propagandaverhältnisse an der russ.Front im Vergleiche zu jenen an der ital.Front' [early February 1918].
26. Finzi, '*I.T.O.*', pp. 137, 140: Finzi, however, suggests that the manifestos had little effect.
27. See *Relazione*, II, pp. 485, 552.
28. F. von Lembruch, quoted in Amedeo Tosti, *Come ci vide l'Austria Imperiale. Dall'Ultimatum alla Serbia a Villa Giusti* (Milan, 1930) p. 211.
29. Ljudevit Pivko, *Informatorji* (Maribor, 1925) pp. 31–3.
30. Rino Alessi, *Dall'Isonzo al Piave. Lettere Clandestine di un Corrispondente di Guerra*, ed. Arnoldo Mondadori (Milan, 1966) p. 136.
31. Pivko, *Informatorji*, pp. 33–6.
32. See Tosti, *Come ci vide l'Austria*, p. 210 note, quoting the German general, Krafft von Dellmensingen.
33. Pivko, *Informatorji*, p. 39.
34. See Ronge, *Kriegs- und Industriespionage*, p. 311.
35. HHStA, PA XL/199, Military attaché in Berne to AOK Na.Abt (Res.No 5111), 9 October 1917.
36. HHStA, PA I/1050, Liasse 66d, 'Frontpropaganda gegenüber der italienischen Armee Juli–Dezember 1917', Waldstätten to Czernin, Op.Nr 450/286 geh., 22 October 1917, enclosing Beilage 2: 'Richtlinien für die Propaganda gegen Italien'.
37. KA, HGK Conrad 1918, Fasz.66, Na Nr 400a/95, HGK Conrad to 10AK, 10 March 1918.
38. KA, 11AK Gstbs Abt 1918, Fasz.275, 12–10/4, 11AK Gstbs Abt to HGK Conrad, Op.Nr 2058, 13 April 1918.
39. HLRO, Lloyd George MSS, F/56/1/56, Sir Rennell Rodd to Balfour, pte, 7 November 1917; Richard Challener (ed.), *United States Military Intelligence 1917–1927* (New York and London, 1978), II, weekly summary, 8 December 1917.
40. HHStA, PA I/1050, Liasse 66d, Waldstätten to Czernin, 22 October 1917, Beilage 1. Most of this leaflet was identical to a text suggested by Czernin (drafted by Friedrich von Wiesner) a few days earlier; but significantly, the AOK omitted the sentence, 'we don't demand an inch of Italian territory from you' (see ibid., Czernin to AOK, Nr 5537 geheim, 19 October).
41. KA, 11AK Gstbs Abt 1918, Fasz.448, Pr.2014, Flottenkommando (Admiral Njegovan) to AOK, Res.Nr 539/Op., 25 January 1918: texts of the leaflets were sent by radio or Hughes telegram to the naval stations at Trieste and Sebenico where they were printed. Some of the leaflets were thrown onto the Italian coast in bottles by torpedo units, but most were distributed by air, 12 flights taking place between 31 October and 20 December. For example, on 16 November, two seaplanes from Pula threw 20 000 leaflets over Ravenna and Rimini; on 28 November the same occurred with 13 000 leaflets over Sinigallia during a reconnaissance of the area from Ancona to Rimini.
42. See Hildegund Schmölzer, *Die Propaganda des Kriegspressequartiers im Ersten Weltkrieg 1914–1918*, Ph.Diss. (Vienna, 1965) pp. 73ff, for the KPQ's moves to indirectly influence Italian morale.
43. Hadtörténeti Intézet és Levéltár, Budapest [hereafter HIL], 6AK Gstbs Abt 1918, Fasz.83, Op.Nr 118/Ev., 6AK to corps and divisions, 9 February 1918.
44. Oskar Regele, *Feldmarschall Conrad. Auftrag und Erfüllung 1906–1918* (Vienna and Munich, 1955) p. 398.

45. KA, AOK Op.Abt 1918 'I Gruppe', Fasz.586, Op.Nr 766/34, AOK to Conrad, Boroević, etc., 10 February 1918.
46. KA, 11AK Gstbs Abt 1918, Fasz.448, Pr.2005, AOK to Kmdo SW front, HGK Conrad, Boroević, XIX corps, Flottenkmdo, Op.Nr 450/684, 5 January 1918: Waldstätten here set out what should be included in the monthly propaganda reports to the AOK.
47. KA, 11AK Gstbs Abt 1918, Fasz.448, zu Pr.2002, 'Organisation der Propagandatätigkeit bei der 11.Armee', 19 January.
48. Ibid.
49. Ibid., Pr.2082, 11AK to corps, 4 March, Beilage 1 Verzeichnis; Pr.2003, 'Dolmetschverzeichnis': most of the interpreters appointed in the 11AK sector were of Italian, German or Slovene nationality.
50. Ibid., Pr.2030. See newspapers (usually four-sided) such as *Novità Mondiali*, *L'Astico* and *Il Risveglio della Pace*: KA, 11AK Gstbs Abt 1918, Karton 768.
51. KA, HGK Conrad 1918, Fasz.66, Na Nr 400a/19, 10AK to Conrad, Op.Nr 1022/7 Prop, 23 January 1918.
52. However, colourful leaflets were soon forbidden as it was felt that they would be too easily noticed by Italian officers and confiscated.
53. Imperial War Museum, London [IWM], diary of Captain L.I.L. Ferguson, entry for 14 February: 'it was not till two days later did we hear Russia had signed a separate peace. To this day we wonder how the blighters got that notice up.'
54. See, for example, KA, HGK Conrad 1918, Fasz.66, Na Nr 400a/25, 10AK to Conrad, 28 January 1918.
55. KA, 11AK Gstbs Abt 1918, Fasz.449, Pr.2168, 11AK to corps, 21 April 1918.
56. See KA, HGK Conrad 1918, Fasz.66, Na Nr 400a/95, Conrad to 10AK, 10 March 1918; HIL, KISA Gstbs Abt 1918, Fasz.77, Op.Nr 6023/1, 16 May 1918: 'the pilots' nervousness about throwing out leaflets has still not been overcome'.
57. KA, 11AK Gstbs Abt 1918, Pr.2030, AOK Op.Nr 766/21: 'Die Propagandaverhältnisse an der russ. Front im Vergleiche zu jenen an der ital. Front'.
58. KA, HGK Conrad 1918, Fasz.66, Na Nr 400a/59, AOK to Conrad, Boroević etc, Op.Nr 766/34, 12 February: enclosing 'Richtlinien für die Propaganda'.
59. See, for example, KA, HGK Conrad 1918, Fasz.66, Na Nr 400a/255: leaflets, 'I sogni imperialistici del Governo Italiano!', 'La guerra d'Italia', 'I sogni imperialistici del governo inglese, dei Sonnino e complici'; and KA, 11AK Gstbs Abt 1918, Fasz.448, Pr.2004/2: 'Italia nella guerra mondiale'; Pr.2004/29: 'Le perdite dell'Italia!'
60. KA, HGK Conrad 1918, Fasz.66, Na Nr 400a/292: *Notiziette*, 13 April 1918.
61. KA, 11AK Gstbs Abt 1918, Fasz.448, Pr.2004/20: 'Soldati squarciati, imboscati decorati...' (speech of Maffi on 19 February); HGK Conrad 1918, Fasz.66, Na Nr 400a/292: *Notiziette*, 9 April 1918.
62. KA, HGK Conrad 1918, Fasz.66, Na Nr 400a/236, 10AK to Conrad, Op.4092/9, 5 May 1918, enclosing leaflet 'Beffa contro beffa'.
63. KA, 11AK Gstbs Abt 1918, Fasz.449, Pr.2230, AOK to 11AK, Op.Nr 766/134, 18 May 1918, enclosing leaflet 'Spaghetti signori!' (with minute by GO Scheuchenstuel).
64. See, for example, KA, HGK Conrad 1918, Fasz.66, Na Nr 400a/59; 11AK Gstbs Abt 1918, Fasz.448, Pr.2004/1: 'Italiani!', Pr.2004/26: 'Aiutateci!'
65. Ibid., Pr.2004/21: 'Chi pagherà le spese di guerra?'; Pr.2004/32: 'L'Italia sfruttata dall'Inghilterra e dall'America!'
66. KA, HGK Conrad 1918, Fasz.66, Na Nr 400a/292: *Notiziette*, 25 April 1918; KA, 10AK 1918, Fasz.418, leaflet: 'L'Inghilterra comincia a ravverdersi!'

67. KA, HGK Conrad 1918, Fasz.66, Na Nr 400a/292: *Notiziette*, 18 April 1918.
68. See KA, 11AK Gstbs Abt 1918, Fasz.448, Pr.2004/12: 'La grandiosa offensiva germanica in Francia'; Pr.2004/15: 'Due armata inglesi completamente sconfitte'; Pr.2004/18: 'La potente offensive germanica in Francia'; Pr.2004/35: 'Offensiva germanica'. The war correspondent Philip Gibbs was quoted at least twice in Austrian propaganda, explaining the horrors experienced by British troops (HGK Conrad, Fasz.66, Na Nr 400a/292, *Notiziette*, 20 and 23 April 1918); the same newspapers repeatedly told of panic in Paris.
69. KA, 10AK 1918, Fasz.418, leaflet: 'Illusioni che sfumano!'; HGK Conrad 1918, Fasz.66, Na Nr 400a/292, *Notiziette*, 6 April and 23 April 1918.
70. KA, 10AK 1918, Fasz.418, leaflet: 'I disastrosi effeti della Guerra'; 11AK 1918, Fasz.448, Pr.2004/27: 'Comunicati dell'Ammiragliato Inglese sulla Guerra dei sottomarini' (the British Admiralty confessed that eight million tons of shipping had been lost since the start of the U-boat war); HGK Conrad 1918, Fasz.66, Na Nr 400a/292, *Notiziette*, 11 April 1918: the *Daily Telegraph* and *Le Matin* disputed the effects of the U-boat war, the former admitting that it had been a disaster for the Entente.
71. KA, 11AK Gstbs Abt 1918, Fasz.448, Pr.2004/6: 'La pace con la Russia conchiusa!'; Pr.2004/7: 'Pace coll'Ucraina'; Pr.2004/9: 'I preliminari di pace colla Romania firmati'.
72. See Pr.2004/6. In oral propaganda too the actual peace treaty was anticipated by the propagandists by a month.
73. See Pr.2004/5: 'Italiani!'; and Pr.2004/7.
74. KA, 11AK Gstbs Abt 1918, Fasz.448, Pr.2025, KISA to 11AK, Na Nr 320/6, 1 February 1918: 'Novità del giorno'.
75. Ibid., Pr.2004/5: 'Italiani!'; Pr.2004/30: '4 Domande': 'Non è meglio fringuel in man che tordo in frasca?'
76. HHStA, PA I/1050, Liasse 66d, Czernin to AOK (Nr 5537 geheim), 19 October 1917.
77. PRO, FO 371/3228, Rodd to Balfour, despatch [d.] 94, 14 March 1918.
78. KA, 11AK Gstbs Abt 1918, Fasz.448, leaflet in Pr.2004: 'Il Capo dello Stato Maggiore Austro-Ungarico sullo sciopero terminato'.
79. Pr.2004/10: 'Soldati Italiani!' Cf. the reality, described in Procacci, *Soldati e Prigionieri*, pp. 240ff.
80. Pr.2004/0: 'Soldati Italiani!'; 10AK, Fasz.418: 'Soldati italiani!', telling of the chivalrous treatment accorded to one Italian officer. Rino Alessi records that there were some Austrian leaflets 'in a Bolshevik style' which urged the Italians to follow the Russian example, revolt and desert: Alessi, *Dall'Isonzo al Piave*, p. 211.
81. PRO, FO 371/3228, Rodd to Balfour, d.94, 14 March 1918, enclosure no.1. See also, KA, 11AK Gstbs Abt 1918, Fasz.448, Pr.2004/3, 'Soldati Italiani!', appealing to Italians to make contact by letter.
82. KA, HGK Conrad 1918, Fasz.66, Na Nr 400a/60, AOK to Conrad, Boroević, Op.Nr 766/37, 15 February 1918. Other small brochures were distributed, showing with photographs how well the Venetian population was treated: see 'Die Wahrheit im Bilde' (in Pr.2004) which was probably produced by the AOK at the suggestion of the 11AK (Pr.2008), and was widely propagated.
83. See Procacci, *Soldati e Prigionieri*, pp. 101ff for a recent survey of Italian morale.
84. Alessi, *Dall'Isonzo al Piave*, pp. 211, 220–1.
85. See the prisoner and deserter statements in KA, 11AK Gstbs Abt 1918, Fasz.442, Na Nrs 8–1827.

86. Ibid., Na Nrs 385 and 401: the latter is the statement of an Alpini officer and three men who deserted when on patrol on Monte Solarolo, detailing contact with Austrian propaganda in this sector. See also Delmé-Radcliffe's comments, of how 'it was even found necessary to transfer some of the Alpini battalions from the Brenta-Piave sector to the eastern side of the Lake Garda so as to [stop] temptation to desert' (PRO, WO 106/814, 11 April 1918).
87. An early example of this: KA, HGK Conrad Evid.Gruppe 1918, Fasz.56, Na Nr 700/31, 10AK to Conrad, t.Op.Nr 695/2, 6 January 1918.
88. KA, AOK Op.Abt 1918, Fasz.586, AOK to Boroević, Conrad, the armies, etc., Op.Nr 766/34, 10 February 1918.
89. Before April, the 6AK only attempted some propaganda in the sector of the XV corps (later part of the 11AK): see KA, 11AK Op.Abt, Fasz.444, Na Nr 529, 6AK to Boroević, Op.Nr 360/Ev., 28 March 1918, Beilage 5; Fasz. 445, Na Nr 716, 6AK to Boroević, Op.Nr 540/Ev., 30 April 1918, Beilage 10.
90. KA, 11AK Op.Abt, Fasz.444, Na Nr 428 (Beilage 8); Fasz.445, Na Nr 609 (Beilage 8); Fasz.445, Na Nr 756 (Beilage 11).
91. Ibid., Fasz.445, Na Nr 735, AOK to 11AK, Op.Nr 766/122, 8 May 1918.
92. KA, HGK Conrad 1918, Fasz.66, Na Nr 400a/25, 10AK to Conrad, Op.Nr 1128/2 Prop., 28 January 1918.
93. KA, 11AK Op.Abt 1918, Fasz.444, Na Nr 427: 10AK propaganda report, February 1918.
94. KA, HGK Conrad 1918, Fasz.66, Na Nr 400a/97, 10AK to Conrad, Op.Nr 1983/5, 7 March 1918: enclosing photographs of the meetings on Cimone-Ost.
95. KA, 11AK Op.Abt, Fasz.444, Na Nr 595, Beilage 1: 10AK propaganda report, March 1918. Prior to this the propaganda officer, Jerkowitz, had been demonstratively speaking to at least 20 Italians during his visits to their trenches.
96. See, for example, the 10AK cigarette orders for the month of April: 1500 'better cigarettes' were required in order to resume contacts on Cimone (KA, HGK Conrad, Fasz.66, Na Nr 400a/136, 10AK to Conrad, t.Op.Nr 2450/5, 3 April 1918).
97. KA, HGK Conrad 1918, Fasz.66, Na Nrs 400a/262, 264, 334.
98. This seems to be the incident described by Tullio Marchetti in his memoirs: *Ventotto Anni*, p. 303.
99. In terms of the leaflets produced by the 10AK, the following number were distributed on the 10AK front: January – 442 000 copies; February – 357 000; March – 367 000; April – 144 000 (the number was limited by bad weather). These figures seem to be inclusive of 10AK propaganda newspapers, but exclude material sent in from other armies, the HGK or the AOK.
100. KA, 11AK Gstbs Abt 1918, Fasz.448, Pr.2002, 2039, 2132.
101. Ibid., Fasz.448, Pr.2058, IKK to 11AK, Op.Nr 60/13, 14 February 1918; Fasz.449, Pr.2109, 22SchD Kmdo (GM Rudolf Müller) to 11AK, Op.Nr 73/10, 15 March 1918.
102. Ibid., Pr.2120, 11AK Propaganda report for March 1918.
103. Ibid., Pr.2160, I KK to 11AK, Na Nr 101/7, 14 April 1918.
104. Ibid., Pr.2168, 11AK (Frydman) to the four corps, 21 April 1918.
105. Ibid., Fasz.448, Pr.2015/1, Conrad to 11AK, Na Nr 400a/34, 18 February 1918.
106. Ibid., Pr.2047, 11AK to I, III, VI and XXVI corps, 11 February 1918. For example, the 10AK held such meetings on 4 February and 23 March; the 11AK on 24–6 January and 26 February (at Levico); the 6AK on 23 March (at Vittorio).
107. Ibid., Pr.2200: minutes of meeting at Levico, 15 May 1918.

108. See KA, 11AK Op.Abt 1918, Fasz.445, Na Nr 609, KISA Monatsbericht über den Feind, Op.Nr 5400, Beilage 8 [March 1918].
109. 'E noi?', *Corriere della Sera*, 14 March 1918.
110. KA, 11AK Gstbs Abt 1918, Fasz.449, Pr.2168, 11AK to I, III, VI, XXVI corps, 21 April 1918.
111. For the respective views of Conrad and Boroević, see KA, 11AK Op.Abt 1918, Fasz.444, Na Nr 427, Conrad to 11AK, Na Nr 8650/14, 8 March 1918: propaganda report; and ibid., Na Nr 593, Boroević to 11AK, Op.Nr 300/847, 13 April 1918.
112. KA, 11AK Gstbs Abt, Fasz.449, Pr.2168.
113. Ibid., Pr.2171, AOK (Waldstätten) to Conrad, Boroević and armies, Op.Nr 766/96, 18 April 1918.
114. Ibid., Pr.2168, 11AK to Koluft, 21 April 1918.
115. KA, 11AK Op.Abt 1918, Fasz.445, Na Nr 609, KISA monthly report: Beilage 8, Op.Nr 5060/21, propaganda report for March 1918.
116. Ibid., Fasz.444, Na Nr 593, Boroević to 11AK, Op.Nr 300/847, 13 April. For the rewards offered: KA, 11AK Gstbs Abt 1918, Fasz.448, Pr.2078, IKK to 11AK, Na Nr 50/18, 26 February 1918.
117. At least according to the 10AK: KA, 11AK, Fasz.445, Na Nr 706, 10AK propaganda report for April 1918. Therefore the CS on 20 May felt obliged to repeat the warning: Procacci, *Soldati e Prigionieri*, p. 146 note 230.
118. See the prisoner statements in KA, 11AK Gstbs Abt 1918, Fasz.442.
119. IWM, Sir Henry Wilson MSS, [File] 22/2, Delmé-Radcliffe to Wilson, 7 January 1918.
120. Marchetti, *Ventotto Anni*, p. 282.
121. Alessi, *Dall'Isonzo al Piave*, p. 166.
122. Alberto Monticone, *Nitti e la Grande Guerra (1914–1918)* (Milan, 1961) pp. 263–4. Monticone's work details the close contact between Diaz and Nitti during 1918.
123. Marchetti, *Ventotto Anni*, p. 281.
124. Finzi, '*I.T.O.*', p. 219. There is now a substantial Italian literature on efforts to raise army and civilian morale: see, for example, N. Della Volpe, *Esercito e Propaganda nella Grande Guerra* (Rome, 1989); A. Fava, *Fronte Interno. Propaganda e Mobilitazione Civile nell'Italia della Grande Guerra* (Rome, 1988); M. Simonetti, 'Il Servizio "P" al Fronte', *Riforma della Scuola* (August–September 1968).
125. Marchetti, *Ventotto Anni*, pp. 298–306.
126. On this subject generally, see Mario Isnenghi, *Giornali di Trincea 1915–1918* (Turin, 1977).
127. One of the most important British memoirs is that of Norman Gladden, *Across the Piave: A Personal Account of the British Forces in Italy, 1917–1919* (London, 1971); but see also IWM, diary of L.I.L. Ferguson (entry, 16 December 1917), and memoirs of V.G. Ricketts.
128. Edmonds and Davies, *Military Operations Italy*, p. 145.
129. PRO, WO 79/67, Cavan MSS, Appendix F, Cavan to CIGS, 10 November 1917; WO 106/852, Cavan to CIGS, 25 May 1918.
130. CCC, Cavan MSS, 1/3, Memoirs, part 1, pp. 3–4.
131. PRO, WO 106/799, British expeditionary force in Italy. Summary of events from 5 November–31 December, by C.H. Harrington [6 January 1918], pp. 6, 14.
132. PRO, AIR 1/2127/207/80, Summary of the Royal Air Force in Italy, November 1917–November 1918; H.A. Jones, *The War in the Air* (Oxford, 1937) VI, pp. 274ff.
133. IWM, Delmé-Radcliffe MSS [hereafter DRP], diary, entries for 4 and 5 January; IWM, Wilson MSS, 22/2, Delmé-Radcliffe to Wilson, 7 January 1918.

134. PRO, WO 106/799, Summary of events by C.H. Harrington, p. 16; CCC, Cavan MSS, memoirs, 1/3, p. 7.
135. PRO, WO 157/634, Daily Intelligence Summary [DIS], no. 93 (from French and Italian sources), 5 March 1918. The confession of these Austrian pilots was well known: see Ugo Ojetti, *Lettere alla Moglie 1915–1919*, ed. Fernanda Ojetti (Florence, 1964) p. 490.
136. Captain Wedgwood Benn, *In the Side Shows* (London, 1919) p. 221; PRO, AIR 1/2127/207/80, Summary.
137. PRO, AIR 1/2282/209/73/2, H.C. Swan (British vice-consul at Venice) to J.H. Townsey (consul at Milan), 28 February 1918. In reply a flight of Italian seaplanes bombed Pula and distributed leaflets with the words 'reprisal for Venice': Luigi Villari, *The War on the Italian Front* (London, 1932) p. 193.
138. See, for example, KA, HGK Conrad Evid.Gruppe, Fasz.57, Na Nr 5500/32, KISA Monatsbericht, Na Nr 422, January 1918; KA, 11AK Op.Abt 1918, Fasz.444, Na Nr 400, 6AK to HGK Boroević, Op.Nr 207/Ev, 26 February 1918.
139. PRO, WO 106/814, Delmé-Radcliffe report on the morale of the Italian army, 11 April 1918. Suggestions here on how morale might be raised owed much to the ideas of the editor of *Il Popolo d'Italia*, Benito Mussolini, who Radcliffe had met in Milan on 21 March to discuss this very issue: see DRP, Mussolini to Delmé-Radcliffe, 26 March; and entry in Delmé-Radcliffe's diary for 21 March (describing Mussolini as a 'most interesting and able man').
140. IWM, Wilson MSS, 28A/1A, Cavan to Wilson, 24 March 1918. For a similar view at this time, see G.M. Trevelyan, *Scenes from Italy's War* (London, 1919) p. 207.
141. KA, 11AK Gstbs Abt 1918, Fasz.449, Pr.2200: notes by Frydman for speech in Levico, 15 May 1918.
142. Ibid., Fasz.448, Pr.2030, AOK Op.Nr 766/21, 'Die Propagandaverhältnisse an der russ. Front im Vergleiche zu jenen an der ital. Front'.
143. KA, HGK Conrad 1918, Fasz.66, Na Nr 400a/34, minutes by Captain Erich Rodler.

# 5
# The Seeds of Italy's Campaign

## 5.1 Obstacles to effective propaganda

When the new Italian Comando Supremo began a propaganda campaign against Austria-Hungary in the spring of 1918, it was acting partly in response to Austria's own campaign, partly in response to the shock of Caporetto. The CS realized increasingly that scruples ought to be set aside and weapons of any kind might justifiably be employed against a dangerous enemy. The propaganda weapon, in Italy's hands, had an explosive quality precisely because it could exploit Austria-Hungary's nationalist tensions, either through manifestos or through propaganda patrols. In the latter case, the Austro-Hungarian forces would eventually be faced with patrols composed of Czech or Yugoslav volunteers, men who had deserted or been captured by the Italians and then returned to the front to influence or subvert their former comrades. As the events at Zborov in June 1917 had shown, the very presence of such units, as propaganda patrols or even as combatants, could have a devastating effect.

Yet Italy's ability to make a success of front propaganda by fully pursuing the 'nationality principle' in the front line, had been and always would be hampered by deep-seated political qualms. In essence, Italy's adoption of what became known as 'nationality politics' (*politica delle nazionalità*) was always obstructed by its foreign minister, Sidney Sonnino. On the Eastern Front, the Central Powers' campaign had, arguably, been weakened because the DOHL had a secret annexationist agenda which had to be excluded from propaganda; in other words, propaganda was not wholly squared with policy. In Italy's case the same was true, but here it was always the Yugoslav question which was the Achilles' heel of the Italian campaign. Italy had entered the war in May 1915 after signing the Treaty of London with the Triple Entente, a treaty which promised the Italians not only the prime irredentist goals of Trento and Trieste, but also all of Istria and northern Dalmatia. By including these southern Slav regions, the Treaty of London clashed head-on with Yugoslav aspirations and those who espoused them: firstly, the Serbian government (in its Niš declaration of war aims of December 1914), and secondly, the Yugoslav Committee of southern Slav émigrés from the Habsburg lands. Since the London treaty was Italy's only international bargaining counter for a future peace conference, the Consulta (the Italian foreign ministry) rigidly refused to repudiate it or weaken it by actions which might have positive Yugoslav implications. On this point, as on so many others, Sonnino's 'mind was as narrow as his forehead, his will as obstinate as his chin'.[1] Furthermore, his commitment to Italian supremacy in the Adriatic did not mean that he favoured or envisaged the dissolution of the Habsburg Empire. On the contrary, Sonnino felt that Austria-Hungary's destruction could bring Italy some unsavoury neighbours: Russia on the Adriatic and Germany on the Brenner Pass. It was far better therefore if the Empire, despite various territorial amputations to Italy, survived into the postwar world. Thus it was that, at the very moment, 25 October 1917, when the Austrians and Germans were advancing from Caporetto, Sonnino was to be found proclaiming to the Italian Parliament that 'neither the dismemberment of enemy states nor the changing of other peoples' domestic arrangements figure in our war aims'.[2] A speech like this – which quickly found its way into the Viennese press – could only undermine the image of Italy as a supporter of Austria-Hungary's 'oppressed nationalities'. If such views continued to be officially voiced, they would, when coupled with the Treaty of London, effectively sabotage any front propaganda built on the nationality principle. In particular, enemy Croat and Slovene soldiers, already alarmed at Italy's nationalist aspirations in the Adriatic, might simply have their prejudices and hostility reinforced in the sure knowledge that, behind all the propaganda, the Italians had a secret agenda.

Until the summer of 1917, there had been few public figures in Italy who openly questioned Sonnino's point of view. The most notable exceptions from 1915 were Leonida Bissolati, reformist-socialist politician (and later minister without portfolio in the Boselli and Orlando governments), and his friend Professor Gaetano Salvemini, historian and editor of the Rome weekly, *L'Unità*. Both had been influenced, among others, by Cesare Battisti, a former socialist deputy to the Austrian Reichsrat, who in September 1914 had been the first Italian to state publicly that Austria-Hungary should be liquidated. In the spring of 1915, Bissolati and Salvemini both came round to the idea that Italy should intervene in the war and invoke the nationality principle to destroy Austria, while claiming only ethnically Italian territory. Musing on the alternative of Sonnino's policy, Salvemini, an historian of the Triple Alliance, vividly expressed his conviction 'that the nationalists' Adriatic programme is disgraceful and *ruinous*, and must serve simply as a trampoline to achieving Austria's salvation and Italy's return to eating German vomit again'.[3]

If in 1915 these views carried little weight, not least because of vigilant Italian censorship of anything which deviated from the nationalist line, by late 1916

Bissolati in particular was in a stronger position. Having entered Paolo Boselli's cabinet, he unleashed a press polemic when in September he suggested that he had joined the government partly in order to encourage an Italian–Yugoslav agreement. A month later at Cremona, speaking in honour of Battisti who had been captured and executed by the Austrians, he became the first 'Entente' statesman to propose publicly that Austria's destruction should be a war aim ('the hydraheaded monster must be slain'). These statements greatly encouraged Czech and Yugoslav émigrés, but they were always dampened by the official Sonnino line. On 5 December 1916, when Boselli suggested in Parliament that Yugoslav propaganda was largely the work of the enemy, he was still able to carry most of the deputies with him.[4]

It was the case, as we will see, that some of the Italian military were already out of step with Sonnino with respect to the nationality principle and were ploughing their own furrow. But the Consulta, through its negative attitude to the Austro-Hungarian émigré movements, was able for a long time to obstruct the émigrés' effective participation in Italy's war. It did so by ignoring their organizations and refusing to recognize Austrian prisoners in Italy as anything other than enemy prisoners of war. Naturally, out of the best-organized émigré movements in the West – the Czechs and the Yugoslavs – it was the Yugoslavs who had the steepest path to tread in Italy. Since most South Slav émigrés who had fled from Austria to Italy in the first months of the war hailed from Dalmatia or Istria, lands coveted by Italy in the Treaty of London, it was not surprising that official Italy was extremely wary and questioned their integrity. Indeed, under pressure from hostile public opinion, the émigrés in April 1915 were forced to leave Rome for Paris where they officially founded the Yugoslav Committee (*Jugoslavenski Odbor*) under the presidency of the dry Dalmatian lawyer, Ante Trumbić; not until April 1918 would they be allowed any official representative in Italy. Their struggle for recognition during the war, moreover, was further complicated by their relations with the Serbian government of Nikola Pašić. This was clear from the beginning. When in early 1915 Trumbić had pressed Pašić to found a special Adriatic legion on Serbian soil, composed of southern Slav volunteers from the Habsburg lands, he received no response, a sign already that Pašić's agenda for Serbian expansion up to the Adriatic did not envisage competition with any other 'Yugoslav' body.[5]

In this way, the Yugoslav Committee, caught in the cross-fire between Italian and Serbian suspicions, was doubly obstructed in its quest for Entente recognition as the official representative of Austria-Hungary's South Slavs. It could also hardly expect to be allowed access to men of southern Slav nationality in Italy's prison camps.[6] After a few years of war these numbered at least 20 000 men and officers (about 16 per cent of Italy's prisoners), who were usually mixed up with prisoners of other nationalities, since only deserters were separated and dispatched to a special camp at Bibbiena. The Italian authorities would only release Austrian prisoners who were ethnically Italian and could prove their 'political reliability'. In all other cases, Sonnino took a very firm line. His standard argument, repeated until the end of the war, was that it was against international law (the Hague Convention of 1907) for prisoners of war to be used for 'military purposes' against their former army, and that to do so would provoke reprisals by the Austrians against Italian prisoners. A more substantial reason, of course, was Sonnino's aversion to undermining the Habsburg Empire by rewarding 'treasonable conduct' and, most importantly, his refusal to countenance any Yugoslav recognition which might undermine the Treaty of London. He would never allow southern Slav prisoners to be organized into combatant units as in Russia.[7]

Sonnino's priorities were revealed, and the whole issue was complicated, when from early 1916 the Serbian government, now on Corfu, began to petition Rome to release 'Yugoslav' prisoners and permit them to join the depleted Serbian forces in the Macedonian theatre. If some of these Yugoslavs had reached Italy's prison camps via the Italian Front, many others, about 8000, were ex-prisoners of the Serbians who had been evacuated to Italy from Albania after the Central Powers occupied Serbia in the winter of 1915–16. In June, Pašić approached Sonnino, cunningly linking his request for Yugoslav prisoners to Italy's own desire to acquire ethnically Italian prisoners from Russia; in turn, the French and Russian military and their governments made repeated requests on Serbia's behalf. But Sonnino, constantly alluding to the 'moral' and 'international' implications, would only agree to release individual prisoners at regular intervals. Not even this properly materialized. Although the Entente governments, for example at their Petrograd conference in February 1917, might press Italy to permit Serbian recruiting in the prison camps so as to strengthen the Serbian army in morale and numbers, the Italians were deaf to all such requests. By June 1917 only 140 prisoners had been released and sent to Salonika. All of them were Serbs from Bosnia or Vojvodina: in other words, none were prisoners whose origin lay in territory upon which Italy had pretensions. Sonnino in any case far preferred to retain all prisoners in Italy and use them to Italy's own advantage, even as 'labour units' in the war zone although this could well be interpreted as work for 'military purposes'. As a result, by the time of Caporetto, Serbia had made little progress. Conscious that the Italians might now be more receptive, Pašić when in Paris in November 1917 felt bound to petition the allies once again, reminding them how

> at this moment when the Central Powers are using all possible methods to strengthen themselves, both by recruiting in occupied territory and stimulating anarchical parties in enemy lands, it would be a mistake for the Entente powers not to make good use of all those elements who are willing to help us fight against the Central Powers.

A few weeks later in Rome, Pašić personally gave a memorandum to Sonnino which summed up the benefits of freeing Yugoslav prisoners: 'Liberating them would certainly influence many Austrian soldiers of Slav nationalities to surrender on first contact with the Italian army, as soon as they were assured that Italy would permit them to fight against their eternal enemy.'[8] Sonnino in reply brought up the old argument of Austrian reprisals, and then proceeded to ignore the Serbian requests.

Since the Consulta opposed all moves which hinted at Yugoslav recognition of any kind, it was only the Czech émigrés who were able to forge a path in Italy during 1917. Thereby they pushed the Italians towards 'nationality politics' and benefited the Yugoslav cause in the long run. In January 1917, when the Entente had made their first statement of war aims to the American President, they had, due to Sonnino's sensitivity, omitted any mention of the Yugoslavs; but for the first time they had raised the Czechoslovak cause as an international issue by proposing to liberate the 'Czecho-Slovaks from foreign domination'. The inclusion of this phrase was a personal success for Edvard Beneš, secretary of the Czechoslovak National Council based in Paris. Having persistently urged the Quai d'Orsay in this direction, he only discovered that he had been successful on 10 January when he was on a train, approaching Rome for the first time in his life; it was, as he noted later, 'a marvellous introduction to the eternal city'.[9] Beneš's main official Italian contact before this time had been Nicola Brancaccio, head of Italian military Intelligence in Paris. Brancaccio had taken a personal interest in the Czech cause after talking to Beneš's Slovak colleague, Milan Štefánik, in the winter of 1915 and he had subsequently, as we will see, facilitated some preliminary Czech propaganda on the Italian Front.[10] By the summer of 1916, Beneš was feeding to Brancaccio intelligence from his *Mafie* contacts in Bohemia; and Brancaccio in turn appears to have been a prime mover, urging Beneš to visit Italy and advance the Czech cause there in a way already evident in France and Russia.

Before this visit, Czech agitation in Italy had largely been in the hands of a few Czech individuals who had escaped internment: Oskar Brázda, a painter, who had been first to inform the Czech National Council about Italy; Bohumír Chytil, who had translated Lützow's short history of Bohemia into Italian; but especially Karel Veselý, director of a sugar refinery, who had lived in the country for many years and was foremost in trying to publicize the Czechs in the Italian press. The Italian response was commensurably small but growing. Apart from Salvemini and his intellectual circle, the Czech cause was gradually able to arouse interest even among some fervent anti-Yugoslav nationalists such as Sonnino's nephew, Colonna di Cesarò, who in April 1916 had suggested to Parliament that an independent Bohemia was vital as a barrier to German expansion.[11] As for the government, even Sonnino, despite the implications, had felt able to express privately some sympathy to Štefánik when he passed through Rome in mid-1916; while Leonida Bissolati, on entering the cabinet, had found a real ally in the person of the leading republican Ubaldo Comandini, a minister without portfolio but entrusted with keeping an eye on Austria's activities abroad. In the summer of 1916, Comandini's secretary, Gino Scarpa, had met Beneš in Paris and then arranged greater access for Veselý to the Italian press.[12] Publicity at this time was everything, for the Czech cause in Italy had no official recognition. Czech and Slovak prisoners of war remained mixed with other Austrian prisoners in diverse locations, their efforts to contact the émigré leadership usually thwarted by vigilant camp commanders or the Italian censor.[13]

In January 1917 when Beneš arrived in Rome at the invitation of Comandini's ministry, he was able to capitalize on the Entente's statement of war aims.[14] He established, through Comandini's good offices (and with the approval of the Consulta), a Czech press bureau which would have direct links to the government and be run by Karel Veselý. One of Veselý's prime tasks would still be publicity, for example, publishing and distributing copies of Lützow's history as well as an Italian version of Beneš's own book, *Détruisez l'Autriche* (translated by Veselý himself as *La Boemia contro l'Austria-Ungheria*). But the bureau would gain valuable support from a new network of contacts. Beneš had not only made some tentative approaches to the Consulta (visiting Giacomo De Martino, its general secretary); he had sought out some of Salvemini's circle, for example the liberal economist Antonio De Viti de Marco, a co-editor of *L'Unità*, and the writer Umberto Zanotti-Bianco, who in 1918 would be closely involved with front propaganda. With Scarpa's help, Beneš also founded an 'Italian Committee for Czechoslovak Independence', and even gingerly courted the nationalist propaganda group, *Dante Alighieri*, trying to persuade them that hostility to the Habsburgs should mean friendship towards the Yugoslavs. Beneš returned to Paris, bubbling with optimism that he had been received in Italy like the representative of an independent nation.[15] Certainly, his visit was to prove a watershed in Italy's official stance towards Austria-Hungary. Most importantly, perhaps, as far as future front propaganda was concerned, Beneš had secured guarantees that Czech and Slovak prisoners of war would be separated and could be contacted and visited by the Czech émigrés. It was at this very time that a group of Czech prisoners, headed by a deserter Jan Čapek, spontaneously created a 'Czech volunteer corps' in the southern camp of Santa Maria Capua Vetere. Their numbers swelled from 200 to 450 by the end of April, by which time they had been visited by Miroslav Plesinger-Božinov, head of the Czech bureau in Switzerland. Finally, in July 1917 the Italians began to concentrate them and other 'Czechoslovak' prisoners in a new camp at Padula near Salerno.[16]

When Beneš returned to Italy in late August 1917 he found that the public mood had significantly changed. One of the most prominent converts by this time to the nationality principle was Senator Luigi Albertini, editor of Italy's most influential newspaper, the *Corriere della Sera*. Whereas in late 1916 the *Corriere della Sera* could be described as 'Slavophobe' by Salvemini,[17] by the following summer it was at the forefront of those who were urging Italy to rethink its attitude towards the nationalities of the Habsburg Empire. Albertini was increasingly aware that unless Italy changed its policy, it might not emerge with any gains or influence after the war. This was a danger because of a number of developments. In January 1917, the Entente powers had signalled their growing commitment to 'nationality politics'; in March, the United States, which had not signed the Treaty of London, had entered the war; and in July, the Yugoslav Committee and the Serbian government in a 'Corfu Declaration' had at last expressed outward solidarity by calling for an independent Yugoslav state. For all of these reasons, Sonnino's foreign policy seemed far less secure. Albertini, from his editorial position, was fully conscious of Italy's 'imperialist' image abroad, its low-standing in the eyes of the western Allies, and this undoubtedly did much to persuade him that Italy could not be allowed to fall too far out of step with them. Indeed, one Italian historian has even suggested that Albertini's conversion to the nationality principle was not sincere, but 'only a convenient expression exhibited to throw smoke in the eyes of the Allies'.[18] In fact, Albertini's behaviour was as much practical as tactical. Although he would never share Salvemini's ideological commitment to the Czechs or Yugoslavs, he realized, partly as a logical consequence of Sonnino's isolation, that Italy must moderate its aspirations and renounce Dalmatia if it was to emerge from the war with any influence. Since Entente policy seemed to be moving in the direction of Austria-Hungary's destruction, it was vital for Italy to be a key player among the ruins of the Monarchy.[19] At the same time, Albertini was naturally aware that with the stone of 'nationality politics' one could kill two birds: as well as restoring Italy's reputation and influence, the weapon could in itself produce the Monarchy's ruin and Italy's victory in the war.

In his outlook, Albertini was fully on the wavelength of colleagues who wrote for the *Corriere della Sera* such as G.A. Borgese and Ugo Ojetti, both of whom would play a prominent role in the propaganda campaign of 1918. Indeed, Albertini's views were shaped to some extent by Professor Borgese. Borgese was a well-known writer and critic, a specialist on Germany (having spent two years there before the war) and a national-liberal who had for a long time wished Italy to assume an influential and moral stance in the struggle against the Central Powers.[20] From the outbreak of hostilities he had been assigned first to the CS to analyze the foreign press, and then to the Ministry of the Navy with the purpose of strengthening their propaganda service in allied countries. It was in this capacity that Borgese in early 1917 visited France and discovered there Italy's lamentable reputation and the prevalence of 'Austrophilia'. He was then sent to the Balkans and, after observing the degree of French influence there, he returned with the conviction that Italy, in order to reassert its control in the future, must make a special agreement with Serbia. On the strength of these reports (and possibly Albertini's influence), in June 1917 Borgese was assigned a more specific mission in neutral Switzerland. This appears to have been largely on the orders of Colonel Garruccio, the head of Italian military Intelligence, who was based at Rome and was increasingly dabbling in the political sphere.[21] The task for Borgese, and his assistant Gaetano Paternò (a former legation secretary in Montenegro, who by this time was attached to the CS), was to investigate the truth about the Yugoslav émigrés. In Borgese's words, they aimed to discover

> whether the queer word 'Yugoslavia', never heard before, had any meaning at all or was merely an Austrian trick contrived to ensnare public opinion and to lure the western Powers into a separate peace with Austria, thus cheating Italy of the promised rewards.[22]

There took place, at the Serbian press bureau in Geneva in late July, three meetings with Serbian émigrés and members of the Yugoslav Committee. Since Switzerland was a hot-bed of intrigue and espionage, the visit and its purpose was soon well-known to the Austrians, for Borgese inadvertently discussed it with an Austrian agent.[23] To the émigrés, Borgese explained that he represented a new current in Italy which desired to remove Italian–Yugoslav conflict and find a basis for agreement. The South Slavs answered that the Italians must show by their deeds that they were not imperialist and not hostile to a Yugoslav state. In particular, as Julije Gazzari (an exile from Dalmatia) stressed, 'national freedom' for Dalmatia was vital: if Italy made this clear, 'Yugoslavs' in the Austrian forces would cease to show such resistance to the Italians.[24] Borgese and Paternò returned to Italy and drew up a lengthy report, for the eyes of the political and military authorities, emphasizing the genuineness of the Yugoslav cause. They recommended that Italy should set up a press office in Switzerland in order to be better informed about the Yugoslav question. But most importantly, they urged Italy to renounce Dalmatia and become the centre for Yugoslav agitation, directing such powerful ideas at southern Slav regiments in the Austro-Hungarian forces.[25] For Borgese, this change of direction was the means by which Italy would secure its rightful place of 'primacy and leadership' in postwar Europe, a contrast to the more idealistic Salvemini who, Borgese claimed, was still living in the smaller, vanished world of Giuseppe Mazzini. Although the report was 'highly praised' by Garruccio, it was, in Borgese's words, 'deeply buried' by more influential figures (probably Sonnino).[26] But many of its ideas were to be adopted by Orlando after Caporetto. For Albertini, moreover, it appears to have finally confirmed the direction which he was taking, convincing him that some accommodation with the Yugoslavs would eventually be essential.[27]

For all Italians it was naturally the Yugoslav issue which would remain the most sensitive element of 'nationality politics'. While some of them were nearer to Salvemini's perception and some to Sonnino's, some like Albertini and Borgese adopted a practical stance which roughly fell between the two. Only with the shock of Caporetto would they all, ostensibly at least, begin to converge and move more determinedly towards the idea of an Italian–Yugoslav agreement, papering over some substantial cracks with the chief purpose of securing victory on the battlefield. In the meantime, in the late summer of 1917, it was on the Czechoslovak issue that there could be more consensus; thereby the door to the other nationalities could be steadily opened. For this purpose, Karel Veselý's press bureau had been notably effective in Italy. In mid-June 1917, Veselý had dispatched a thousand questionnaires to prominent public figures who had previously been sent Beneš's book; he received almost unanimously positive replies, including one from a newspaper editor, Benito Mussolini, affirming that Czechoslovakia must indeed be an independent state in order to guarantee European peace in the future.[28] An even more zealous advocate was Nicola Brancaccio in Paris. In late June he confided to his diary his regrets that Italy might be lagging behind its allies in supporting the Czechs: 'At this moment', he wrote, 'by encouraging the Czech cause we will have an extra instrument with which to shatter Austria' and one which could be an economic asset to Italy in the future.[29] The Czech émigrés were now able to exploit these Italian hopes and fears, particularly at this time the fear, which Brancaccio clearly shared with Albertini, that Italy's allies were making all the running when it came to Austria-Hungary. After all, the French had just negotiated with Beneš the creation of a Czech Legion, while the Russians had not only made Zborov possible but had agreed to dispatch 30 000 Czech volunteers to the Western Front. It was these arguments which the Italian military could put before Sonnino, persuading him eventually to invite Beneš for a personal interview in Rome.

The idea that military pressure played some part in influencing Sonnino seems clearer when we note that it was Colonel Garruccio who on 6 September escorted Beneš to the Consulta. Beneš on this visit, contrary to Leo Valiani's account, was to get much of what he desired.[30] Sonnino agreed to recognize the National Council as the highest representative of the Czechoslovak cause and to free Czech and Slovak civilians from internment. He was, as is clear from his behaviour, anxious above all to secure some control of events and reassert Italy's influence, particularly with regard to the Yugoslav issue. Thus, he emphasized to Beneš, Italy had a special interest in the Czech cause; thus also, he was prepared publicly to send his best wishes when on 30 September the 'Italian Committee for Czechoslovak Independence' organized a huge reception in Beneš's honour. Beneš, however, while acknowledging Sonnino's worth as 'one of the strongest personalities of the war', was soon to understand that platonic speeches were one thing, concrete decisions another.[31] Sonnino especially remained equivocal on the subject of Czech prisoners of war, citing as usual the Hague Convention, and blatantly opposing Beneš's wish that they be sent to the Western Front, for this would strengthen French influence in the whole business. The only possibility was that a Czech Legion might ('if a suitable way was found') be organized on Italian soil.

On 5 October, after lengthy negotiations at the Consulta and the Ministry of War, where he boldly insisted that the Czechs had already sabotaged the Habsburg army's effectiveness, Beneš received the final Italian proposal in his room at Rome's Grand Hotel.[32] It was a memorandum which was highly disappointing for someone as optimistic as Beneš. Although signed by Giardino (Minister of War), its 'extremely twisted style' indicated the pervasive influence on the one hand of Sonnino, and on the other of General Paolo Spingardi, who headed the War Ministry's prisoner of war commission and was highly sensitive to his own powers and influence. While agreeing to free Czech and Slovak prisoners and form them into units, the Italians proposed first, only to employ them as labour units in the rear of the front and second, to continue their legal status as prisoners rather than liberated members of a Czechoslovak army. The danger was that Sonnino had gone as far as he would, and might even try to reverse these concessions in the future.[33]

Nevertheless, Beneš's initial shock was quickly tempered when Bissolati, Comandini and others advised him that this was only the beginning. As the Marchese della Torretta, a friend in Spingardi's commission, observed, the memorandum was a 'strait-jacket' but one in which the Czechs were able to move their arms so that it could eventually be torn off![34] Beneš, therefore, after registering his objections to certain aspects of the note, returned to Paris feeling that 'the situation is not *all* I wished, but there has been a great improvement'.[35] He had reorganized the Czech office in Rome, leaving it now in the capable hands of an officer-deserter, František Hlaváček, with specific instructions to propagate the Czech cause, stimulate the morale of Czech prisoners, but to stall if Italy tried to form them into labour units. In fact, events were to show that neither the Czech émigrés nor the Consulta could control the use of Czech soldiers when they were in the war zone. Both sides, for their own reasons, wished to limit this employment – Sonnino, as a matter of principle, Beneš, in order to avoid half-measures and ensure that Italy created a Czechoslovak army fully under the National Council's control. These political reservations were always likely to take second place when it came to Italian military requirements. Some of the Italian military had for a long time had an interest in furthering the nationality principle, oblivious of political repercussions and purely for military ends. Sonnino might try to block this trend, the Czech and Yugoslav émigrés might try to harness it. But after Caporetto, military considerations were the priority when Italy weighed up the benefits of 'nationality politics'.

## 5.2 The role of Italian military Intelligence

Among the Italian military, it was rather naturally the Intelligence officers who became the chief missionaries for using propaganda to divide and depress the nationalities of the opposing army. Since the Intelligence Service, the 'eye of the army at war',[36] was trying to gather as much information as possible about the enemy, it was usually most keenly aware of the enemy's weaknesses and the opportunities to exploit them. The network of contacts and channels which wartime military Intelligence developed in order to pick up useful information, could equally be used to distribute poisonous ideas. Thus it was that Austria's propaganda campaigns against Russia and Italy were largely entrusted to Intelligence personnel, men who were quick to publicize the importance of the new weapon to the surprise of some of their more conservative commanders. The Italian army, as we will see, possessed even more energetic and imaginative Intelligence officers, individuals whose significance has escaped discussion in the historiography of the Great War. They were to become committed to the nationality principle partly from experiencing at first-hand the nature of the Austro-Hungarian army. But their beliefs were reinforced, especially in one case, by a longstanding interest in Italian irredentism in the Trentino [southern Tyrol] and a subsequent appreciation of Czech, Polish or even Yugoslav aspirations.

Until 1918 at least, Italian military Intelligence was a thoroughly uncoordinated business. This stemmed in part from the way in which the Service was organized from May 1915. Ufficio I, the Intelligence centre attached to the Italian General Staff in Rome, had done little during the months of Italy's neutrality to prepare for wartime activity apart from establishing seven Intelligence centres (*centri staccati*) on the northern frontier. Most of these on the outbreak of war became the Intelligence offices of the respective Italian armies (from October 1916 termed Uffici I.T.O. – Informazioni Truppe Operanti). Ufficio I, meanwhile, moved to Udine to act as the CS's Intelligence centre. There resulted a lack of real coordination. At Udine, Ufficio I became largely a receptor for information from a wide range of different sources, while the actual sifting and analysis of Intelligence for the High Command was jealously assumed by the Ufficio Situazione di Guerra. But apart from the tensions caused by this division of labour, the chief obstacle to centralized control was the independent activity of the army Intelligence offices. Their officers were directly responsible to the individual army commands and as such, as one authority notes, were from the start 'uprooted from the main trunk' of the

Intelligence Service; their branch, highly luxuriant though it became, was never fully grafted back onto the main stem.[37] Although they had to dispatch regular reports to Udine and attend weekly meetings with the head of military Intelligence, some of the more independently minded Intelligence officers quickly questioned the competence of CS Intelligence and what they viewed as its indiscriminate gathering of information from suspect sources. It was a point graphically underlined in early 1916, when CS Intelligence (notably the Ufficio Situazione) refused to believe the warnings of an approaching Austrian offensive in the Trentino provided by the 1st army Intelligence officers, leaving the latter thoroughly disillusioned.[38]

It is not an exaggeration to say that Tullio Marchetti and Cesare Finzi, the two leading Intelligence officers of the lst army, were the men who did most to further the nationality principle among the Italian military. Although other Intelligence heads (particularly Attilio Vigevano of the 4th army) were similarly involved in such activity from the beginning of the war, it was Marchetti and Finzi who were the most resourceful and ingenious. They built up an Intelligence network of contacts and controls which by 1918 was not only the equal of British and French military Intelligence, but which provided a basic foundation upon which to construct Italy's propaganda offensive against Austria-Hungary.

For Tullio Marchetti, in particular, the idea of undermining the enemy through exploiting nationalist tensions was a logical sequel to his own irredentist background. A native of the Austrian Trentino (from Bolbeno, near Tione), Marchetti had already, in the 1890s as an Alpini officer, dabbled in amateur Intelligence activity, keeping in touch with acquaintances in the western Trentino. From 1902 he was officially employed by Ufficio I and expanded his network of agents, by regularly taking official leave in Bolbeno and also by visiting other parts of the Tyrol through clandestine journeys via Switzerland. Unlike some of his less cautious brethren (the eccentric Giuseppe Colpi, for example), Marchetti managed to escape discovery by the Austrians and by 1915 was to be found at Milan creating an Intelligence centre for the prospective lst army.[39] When on the eve of war *centri staccati* were established in Brescia and Verona, Marchetti took over the former and filled it with many of his old 'Trentini' agents (now refugees) – veterans such as Damiano Cis and Arturo Castelli. When in May 1915 the *centri* at Brescia and Verona were grouped together as part of lst army Intelligence, Marchetti retained his organization at Brescia while Cesare Finzi (in August) assumed control of the centre at Verona.

For Marchetti it was an axiom from his pre-war experience that military Intelligence in the front line had to be balanced by information-gathering *in profundità*: in the rear of the enemy forces. Although his own network in the Tyrol had largely disintegrated into a flood of refugees, Marchetti by May 1915 had repositioned three 'pawns' of his own foreign service: Baron Silvio a Prato at Zurich, Giovanni Giovannazzi at Zernetz on the Austrian–Swiss border, and the fearless Luisa Zeni at the key railway junction of Innsbruck. By September all had been exposed and fled to Italy (Giovannazzi vainly trying to fool the Swiss authorities by swallowing his invisible ink as if it were medicine).[40] Marchetti therefore started again, this time more successfully. By the summer Ufficio I had established its own CS Intelligence centre in Berne, but Marchetti was always highly sceptical of its competence, describing it once as 'stunted with rickets';[41] it made him all the more determined to preserve his own 'foreign empire'. In mid-September he dispatched to Zurich, as a replacement for Baron a Prato (who had first fled to France), four 'Trentini' who had already distinguished themselves: Artemio Ramponi, Clemente Albertini, and Luigi Grandi and Luigi Granello (both former professors in Trieste, the latter especially knowledgeable about Austria's domestic affairs). Working undercover, as supposed employees of a timber merchant, their job was to scrutinize the Austro-Hungarian press, particularly Tyrolian papers; to make new contacts with Austrian citizens who could be useful for espionage; and to strengthen ties with Czech, Polish or Yugoslav émigré groups whom Marchetti was already assessing as valuable instruments for the future.[42] His 'Swiss centre', using the CS Intelligence office at Berne as something of a shield, was to remain largely inviolate until 1918, and some of the agents then continued to act as valuable lynchpins in Italy's new propaganda campaign.

Marchetti, however, always had an additional string to his bow through being able to re-establish some agents in Austria itself. Through the contacts of Mario Mengoni, a former hotelier on Lake Garda, Marchetti acquired a nucleus of reliable informers. One was a greengrocer who travelled regularly between Zurich and the Tyrol and hid information in pellets in the base of his pipe. Another was a Swiss industrialist who visited Besenello every so often to inspect a silk factory (and anything else on the way).[43] But the key agent was Mansueto Zanon, an Italian soldier in the Austrian army at Innsbruck who could observe all troops movements on railways into the Tyrol, while also at times having access to high-level military discussions at Bolzano [Bozen]. With the aid of a Czech friend who worked on the Austrian railways, Zanon was able to supply timely and accurate information to Mengoni in Switzerland, the methods of communication becoming ever more eccentric, from writing in invisible ink to concealing thin strips of paper within candles or cough sweets.[44] This notwithstanding, Zanon remained until the very end of the war Marchetti's special confidant, an agent who on many occasions made reliable predictions about Austrian intentions, not least about the ill-fated Trentino offensive of May 1916. Marchetti himself would later express his feelings of 'reverence and admiration' for Zanon, his 'best informer'. And it was undoubtedly largely due to the latter's reports that one British Intelligence chief, on arriving in Italy in late 1917, singled out 1st army Intelligence for particular commendation: '[It] had long before organized a special local service which extended its activities throughout the southern Tyrol with such success that the Intelligence of this army was always well supplied with information pertaining to this portion of the theatre.'[45]

Marchetti's foreign network was proof to some extent of how middle-class Italian irredentist sentiment in the Trentino could be effectively exploited and harnessed to undermine the Habsburg Empire. At the front too, from the first months of the war, 'Trentini' were employed by military Intelligence to analyze the enemy situation opposite, or – in the case of Cesare Battisti himself in 1916 – to produce detailed maps and reports about the terrain and military defences of the southern Tyrol.[46] In the 1st army, which again appears to have been the most inventive in its techniques, front-line Intelligence fell into the hands of Cesare Pettorelli Finzi (since Marchetti preferred to stay in Brescia and concentrate on his espionage network). It became the ideal partnership, with Marchetti and Finzi acting as a control upon each other's sources of information. Finzi had at first been drafted into the Intelligence office at Verona as an interpreter. He was a former military attaché in Budapest, spoke German and Hungarian and was married to a Slav. Despite a prejudice against Croats, who had allegedly maltreated his grandfather during Radetsky's campaign in 1849, his perception of the enemy forces far exceeded in sophistication that of many compatriots who tended to group all their opponents together as 'Austrians'.[47] When he took over the Verona office in August 1915, Finzi still seems to have rated highly the tradition and experience of the Habsburg forces, backed by a 'state organism [with] foundations which appear to be very solid, despite so many races, so many languages, the different mentalities, the divergent aspirations'.[48]

It was only perhaps in early 1916 that Finzi adjusted his horizons, realizing that Italian Intelligence must in its essence begin to reflect the mosaic qualities of the Austro-Hungarian army. For in the months prior to Austria's Trentino offensive, many more deserters, 'startled birds' at the onset of a whirlwind as Finzi describes them, began to cross to the Italian lines. And these, besides the usual 'Trentini', were chiefly of Czech nationality, including some Czech reserve officers who clearly lacked the type of imperial loyalty ingrained in the psyche of the old career officers.[49] Finzi had been collecting prisoners and deserters together at Verona's Procolo fortress, a building which ironically had been built by the Austrians in the 1840s as a safeguard against Italian rebels. He now began to use three intelligent Czech officer-deserters as 'pigeons' (spies) within the fortress to weed out information from incoming prisoners.[50] It was a technique which was to be adopted by other Intelligence heads, was peculiar to the Italian army, and was subsequently viewed somewhat critically by British military Intelligence who felt that it produced information which was 'detached and fragmentary in its character'.[51] It meant, however, that Slav deserters from the Austrian army were increasingly employed for Intelligence purposes which had formerly been restricted to Italians or 'Trentini'. By 1917, on the basis of their success, Finzi was extending his techniques, dividing up prisoners in the Procolo fortress according to nationality and slipping into their 'cages' reliable Czech agents, who posed as fellow-prisoners and 'squeezed and sucked, as from a lemon, everything which the prisoners could have seen' or experienced.[52] It was a short step from here to employing Czech deserters in other fields: to intercept enemy telephone conversations, to interpret or compose Intelligence reports, or even to engage in some propaganda work to influence the morale of their former compatriots. In very exceptional circumstances, these tasks might even be allotted to Slavs of other nationalities; by the early summer Finzi was using one Croat deserter-officer, Mate Nikolić from southern Dalmatia, in 1st army Intelligence.

While Finzi and Marchetti acted as torch-bearers, notably in their trust of Czech deserters, their outlook was in part an understandable derivative from regular contact with the enemy. From 1916, Italian military Intelligence was certainly aware that among the enemy forces, it was soldiers of Czech nationality who were sometimes more likely to be an unreliable element. This was clear from some notable officer desertions on the Tyrolian front, but it was also the case in the Giulian sector, on the river Isonzo. There, the Intelligence officers were perhaps less enlightened than in the lst army, but at least by the summer of 1916 the Italians were beginning to use some Czech officer deserters as interpreters or informers before sending them off to the prison camps. For example, Václav Pán aided 2nd army Intelligence for two months, while Jaromír Vondráček, a company commander who deserted in mid-August, brought over plans of his sector which enabled the Italians to attack and seize a key point; he was employed at 3rd army Intelligence for three months before being dispatched to the officer-deserter camp at Bibbiena.[53]

But it was the reserve officer František Hlaváček, a deserter who later played a leading role in establishing the Czech Legion in Italy, who was the most glittering prize for Italian Intelligence on the Isonzo.[54] As a civilian, Hlaváček had worked for the Prague chamber of commerce, had travelled extensively abroad and had a number of contacts in Italy (his wife's cousin was the painter Oskar Brázda). After settling his domestic affairs when on leave in Prague in July 1916, he managed on 11 August to desert to the Italians at Salcano during the battle for Gorizia, giving them valuable information about enemy artillery. More importantly, he brought with him detailed plans for an offensive in a crucial sector (of Auzza-Descla), which might enable Italy to capture the Bainsizza plateau. Although encountering much scepticism and suspicion, Hlaváček was interviewed by some sympathetic Intelligence officers (including Giuseppe Lazzarini, a friend of Bissolati) and as a result was eventually able to expound his views to the CS at Udine. This did not prevent his dispatch to the camp at

Bibbiena in October. But in April 1917, possibly at the insistence of General Pietro Badoglio, chief of staff of the 2nd army, Hlaváček was recalled to the latter's headquarters at Cormons and ordered to elaborate his plan in minute detail.

According to Czech sources, although the plan was never fully put into practice but remained in May a local operation, that in itself achieved remarkable success because of the response in the Austrian camp. At Bodrez-Loga on the northern edge of the Bainsizza plateau, almost a whole battalion of Czechs declined to fight and deserted to the Italians. If such behaviour was not a normal occurrence, despite the few legendary cases on the Eastern Front, on the Italian Front it undoubtedly set a precedent for possible Czech behaviour, while among the Italian military it 'made Pauls out of some of the Sauls'. When Hlaváček subsequently met Major Dupont, the head of 2nd army Intelligence, and General Capello, the 2nd army commander, he was given a much warmer reception (Capello going so far as to shake his hand) and was able to exploit his new leverage. While the Italians were now envisaging a full Bainsizza offensive, Hlaváček became the first Czech prisoner to be liberated in Italy. He was allowed to travel to Rome to work briefly in Veselý's bureau, before returning in August to Cormons where in Italian uniform he interrogated prisoners and helped Dupont to construct a comprehensive picture of the Austrian line-up. This activity for the Italians in the summer of 1917 was to earn him the military cross. In turn, Hlaváček had himself significantly advanced the Czech cause, spreading Czech literature in military circles, making valuable new contacts for the future (not least Dupont and Badoglio), and indicating by his own example how the Italian army might adopt the nationality principle for military advantage. His extensive and growing influence would later earn him a quip from Czech legionaries, that 'God in heaven is the first God, but Hlaváček the second God'.[55]

It was through using Czech deserters in this way that Italian military Intelligence also began to employ them for the purposes of propaganda. Front propaganda was a task naturally assigned to the Intelligence officers since they were increasingly aware that by spreading manifestos they could provoke more desertions, and thereby gain more information about the enemy. Gradually, they would also realize the need for these manifestos to be trimmed to suit the mood and character of the Austro-Hungarian forces, but a sophisticated operation would only begin in the last year of the war. It seems to have been in June 1916, in the wake of Austria's Trentino offensive, that the Italians first took up the propaganda weapon to any degree. A few months earlier at Easter some manifestos had been distributed which gave basic information about 'Entente successes',[56] but the CS otherwise appears to have hesitated because of Austrian threats that enemy pilots who spread treasonable leaflets would be executed.[57] However, after the failed offensive, when the Austrians had still spread leaflets glorifying their 'successes', 1st army Intelligence in revenge sent back brightly coloured manifestos which depicted the Austrian attack as a broken bottle and also proceeded to revel in Austria's retreat in the East during the Brusilov offensive.[58] These efforts were continued in August when the Italian capture of Gorizia was broadcast to the enemy, together with news of Russian advances in the Caucasus, Anglo-French advances on the Somme and the resurrection of the Serbian army in the Balkans.[59]

Most of the leaflets at this time and in the following year contained a text in several languages, translated (often badly) by deserters, and they were not usually tailored specifically towards any particular nationality. They aimed to illustrate above all, firstly the strength and secondly the justice of the Entente cause, countering Austrian 'lies' and exploiting any negative turn in the fortunes of the Central Powers. In March 1917, for instance, leaflets informed the Austrians that although the Tsar had abdicated, the Russian army was regenerating itself (supposedly under Grand Duke Nicholas);[60] by April, the leaflets told of the entry into the war of South America and the United States, with President Wilson determined to crush the 'hereditary enemy' with all available forces.[61] As a result, the Central Powers were now portrayed as the enemies of 'all cultured peoples'. The propaganda at this time was not averse from openly attacking the 'over-ambitious German Kaiser' who had 'shocked the whole world by his most atrocious methods of warfare' and was now seeking to pull the chains ever tighter around the peoples of Austria-Hungary.[62] Thus Italian front propaganda was beginning to contain a distinctly moral note, even though Italy's own professed morality (that it was fighting a 'holy national war') was hardly one which would appeal to all Austro-Hungarian soldiers.[63]

Yet the nationality principle slowly began to creep into some manifestos. The first signs of it were the result of a specific initiative by the Czech émigré organization in Paris. In late 1915, when the Slovak aviator and astronomer Milan Štefánik had got to know Nicola Brancaccio, he had alerted him to the possibility of some Czech propaganda on the Italian Front. Štefánik then composed a preliminary manifesto which, although highly emotional and rather repetitive, had already been distributed over Austrian lines by the turn of the year.[64] The CS was immediately impressed, reporting to Brancaccio that among Austrian prisoners (and even among Russian POWs working in the Austrian rear lines) the impact had been 'great'; the CS duly requested more texts which would be printed in Italy with Štefánik's autograph.[65] Instead of this, Brancaccio organized a direct approach. Štefánik, a pilot in the French army, was allowed to visit the Italian war zone where he met leading military figures and personally threw out leaflets from his plane over the Austrian trenches. These manifestos made Štefánik a marked man in Austria-Hungary[66] since their text, although signed by the 'Czechoslovak Foreign Committee', clearly revealed the Slovak's own personal role:

Slavs! Czechs!

The Germans and Magyars have declared war on the whole world, for they want to dominate all nations and specifically to make slaves of us Slavs in order to have somebody to work for them. Our Russian brother and our friends, France and England to whom Italy has allied itself, want to crush this pride and conceit.

The glint of their victories can be seen on the horizon. In the east our Russian brothers have halted the Germans and trounced the Turks, in the south the Serbian army with the help of France and Italy has once again entered the fight and the intimidated Bulgarians are quaking in the face of its speedy retaliation, in the west at Verdun the French have struck the Germans a mortal blow. The days of the Slavs' enemies are numbered. The victories of the Russians, England, France, Italy, Serbia, Belgium and Portugal, who have united in this conflict with the Germans and Magyars, signify the liberation of oppressed peoples, and especially the creation of an independent Czechoslovak state and unification for the Yugoslavs.

You who are honourable of spirit and have Slav blood in your veins, should remember that it is your sacred duty to use every circumstance to weaken those whom you currently serve. Give yourselves up to the Italian army at the first opportunity, just as whole Czech regiments have already done, voluntarily and enthusiastically, when the Magyars and Germans sent them against Serbians, Russians and the French. All those who surrendered were received with open arms. Thousands of them, instead of hospitality, asked for a sabre and a rifle and turned against the murderers of the Czechoslovak people.

For don't forget that the same Magyars and Germans who push you forward are torturing our national leaders at home, ravaging our cottages, shooting and hanging old people, women and children, confiscating the estates of patriots. Do all of you who are Slavs wish to sacrifice your lives for a contemptible band of criminals who have set as their goal the extermination of our whole nation? For those of you who continue to fight after this announcement, may the dishonour and curse of the nation lie on you. Victory over the Germans and Magyars is certain, and by resisting you are only prolonging your own suffering.

This message is sent to you by the leaders of the Czechoslovak nation, especially Professors Masaryk and Dürich.[67] But Lieutenant Dr Milan Štefánik has himself come from France to Italy and over your trenches in order to deliver it to you from his aeroplane. Remember brothers, at these great historical moments, your national duty, your Czechoslovak homeland, and our dear people.[68]

This manifesto, containing the type of vivid language which would be so evident in the propaganda of 1918, was, in the words of one authority, 'the first significant and successful step in Italy on behalf of the Czechoslovak foreign resistance'.[69] The Czech émigrés followed it up during the summer of 1916 by presenting Brancaccio with thousands more leaflets which they hoped could be distributed.[70]

By this time some of the army Intelligence officers were themselves coming separately to the same conclusion, following a train of thought which derived naturally from their own experiences as much as from any knowledge of Štefánik's initiative. As we have seen, from June 1916 the Italians began to increase their distribution of manifestos. While most of these dwelt on Italian or Russian victories, there were some 'rare birds' (as Marchetti and Finzi termed themselves) who now realized that it was the 'latent racial malady' which Italy should be exploiting. As Marchetti was to write so incisively: 'the decay had still not infected the [Austrian] army which, through secular traditions, through the cementing symbol of the person of the old sovereign, through its iron discipline, was still solid and healthy, materially, morally and politically'.[71] Yet he had noticed the 'first insidious cracks' in the old imperial building. 1st army Intelligence now became a pioneer in propaganda work, proposing to the CS on 1 August 1916 that propaganda should be intensified and concentrated especially on provoking unrest among the various races. In Finzi's words, they were 'seeking to make the sense of nationality resonate, to throw out the seeds of what could be future discord'. Finzi himself was convinced that this path should be followed because of his experiences in interrogating prisoners of various nationalities, and also from discovering that deserters showed such interest in propaganda leaflets, often carrying them as 'passports' for good treatment in Italy.[72] Indeed, most of the 'national' leaflets which Finzi prepared in the next 12 months were probably simple appeals to desert, sometimes with a special twist to entice a particular nationality. Many seem to have dwelt on the comfortable life enjoyed by all Austrian prisoners in Italy, but even in these unsophisticated messages the Czechs might be reminded that Russia was Italy's ally, the Romanians and Croats about the Magyar threat, and the Poles about conditions in Galicia.[73]

By the early summer of 1917, although the manifestos continued to be in a rather stilted language and full of spelling mistakes, one could sense a more radical tinge which increasingly matched Štefánik's early efforts. Czechs were informed about their compatriots fighting in the Russian ranks, Poles about the 'rebellion' against the Central Powers by Józef Piłsudski's Polish legion.[74] The influence of the Czechoslovak National Council was evident again both in new versions of Štefánik's original leaflet and in more optimistic proclamations signed by the Czech émigré leadership.[75] Its role, in supplying a more political-nationalist dimension to Czech propaganda, was undoubtedly facilitated on the Isonzo front through the employment of František Hlaváček by military Intelligence. By the summer of 1917 at least, he was pressing the Italians to scatter new Czech proclamations over the Isonzo, since his interrogation of prisoners had convinced him that it would produce many desertions. While the 'less politically conscious' Czechs would be satisfied with assurances about food, he emphasized that it was vital to supply the 'politically more educated elements' with 'more extensive instruction', not sparing on the length of the manifestos since these men were keen to read about the 'world situation'. Hlaváček was among those arguing for a more sophisticated form of front propaganda, tuned more precisely to the mentality of various enemy soldiers, and disseminated more carefully (for example, by night) so that it reached the hands of its target audience.[76]

It is clear that this idea of making Italy's propaganda more politicized was gaining ground for it was evident in the content of some manifestos. A few announced that the Entente had promised freedom to the Czechoslovaks, or even that a new, major Entente war aim was freedom for all the peoples of Austria-Hungary and Germany.[77] By allowing these statements to pass (and significantly, none except Štefánik's leaflet spoke of Yugoslav unification), the Italian Intelligence officers showed that they were already unconcerned if their front propaganda exaggerated the realities of the situation. They were more concerned about the positive effect of the propaganda. For by mid-1917, many in the wider Italian Intelligence network sensed that 'nationality politics' could be Italy's salvation: witness the opinions of Brancaccio or of Colonel Garruccio, head of military Intelligence in Rome, who by this time was vainly urging the government to establish a Czechoslovak legion and was also instrumental in preparing Borgese's Yugoslav mission to Switzerland.[78] At the front, and particularly in the lst army, the Intelligence officers were even more sensitive to these issues, and their practice in propaganda was almost always ahead of Italian official policy. Marchetti's view was that the nationalist virus, stimulated by propaganda, required a period of long incubation before it could penetrate the Austro-Hungarian armed forces.[79] But events in the summer of 1917 seemed to prove to lst army Intelligence that the virus was already fast achieving the desired effect, infecting large numbers of enemy 'cells' and finding willing hosts among certain nationalities.

## 5.3 The dream of Carzano[80]

On 10 July 1917, an Italian aeroplane flew over the front of the Austrian 18ID, just north of Val Sugana, and scattered propaganda leaflets. Austrian troops in the 'Carzano sector' marvelled at the skill of the pilot: such a feat was still highly unusual. When some of the leaflets had been brought in, they were examined by officers of the 5th battalion of the Bosnian-Hercegovinan regiment Nr 1 [V/BHIR1]. They were amused at the awkwardly composed texts, one of which in Polish described the fate of Piłsudski's Polish legion, while another

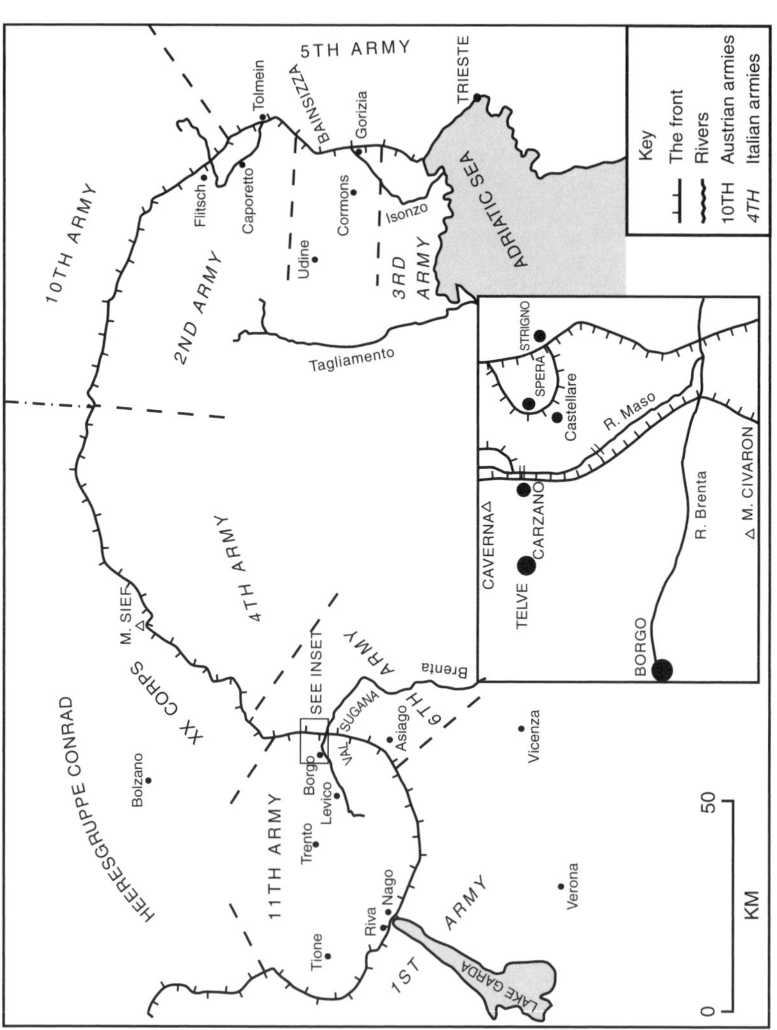


*Map 5.1* The Italian Front in 1917

simply compared the abundant Italian rations with the so-called 'barbed wire' (Austrian slang) which the Austrians themselves received as food. One of the officers, Ljudevit Pivko, who was temporarily in charge of the battalion, resolved that patrols should go out to recover the rest of the leaflets from no-man's-land.[81]

This was the beginning of regular Austro-Italian contacts between Pivko and Finzi, forming the basis for the Carzano plot, one of the most notorious attempts of the whole war to betray positions to the enemy. The daring exploit was the brainchild of Pivko, a Slovene reserve officer, who had carefully recruited about 70 fellow-conspirators, chiefly Czech officers and Bosnian Serbs from the ranks. His plans, if they had succeeded on the night of 17–18 September, would have opened up the roads into northern Tyrol with possibly devastating results for Austria-Hungary; certainly, as Pivko intended, it might have sabotaged the Central Powers' Caporetto offensive. Instead, on the crucial evening the Italians hesitated to act and the plotters had to flee to Italy. Yet this did not signify total failure. Far from being a complete fiasco,[82] the episode had major consequences for Italian warfare. It acted, in Pivko's words, 'like an invisible force which suddenly flowed up from the depths of a sandy desert and... produced new vegetation far and wide'.[83] In particular, it persuaded Italian military Intelligence even more that they should exploit nationalism in the opposing forces. And by 1918 it provided a new basis for doing so in the form of Czech and Yugoslav propaganda patrols, organized by Pivko in Italy.

The Carzano plot also substantially reinforced the Austrian High Command's fear that a nationalist poison was slowly spreading within the armed forces. Ljudevit Pivko himself was striking proof of the degree to which an officer could conceal his true nature from his superiors; and, as an unreliable Slovene, he undermined even more the AOK's former categorization of their troops into 'reliable' and 'unreliable' nationalities. Pivko's own anti-Habsburg convictions had matured before the war. In civilian life, as the post-Carzano Austrian investigation discovered, he had been headteacher at a teacher-training college in Maribor, a town of mixed population on the sensitive German–Slovene language border; but at the same time he was a leading personality in the local Slovene Sokol (gymnastics) organization. Indeed, according to one police agent, Pivko had been obsessed with the Slovene problem, a Serbophile fanatic who in 1912 had observed that in any Austro-Serbian war the Slovenes could not be relied on by the Monarchy. After searching his house at Maribor, police found a book written by Pivko himself: a 'History of the Slovenes', which dwelt heavily upon the oppression of the Slavs but ended optimistically with the view that the Slovenes would soon compete independently among the peoples of Europe.[84]

Pivko's own colourful memoirs,[85] which seem to be highly accurate when checked against Austrian and Italian sources, suggest that from the start of the war he was thinking of ways to betray the Monarchy. Already, when posted to the Balkan Front in 1914, he had tried to desert with 20 men to Montenegro, but instead had been wounded and gained an Austrian decoration for his 'bravery'. It was just the first of such risks which Pivko turned to his advantage, gathering a reputation for reliability as the most decorated officer of his battalion by the summer of 1917. After a period of leave in early 1915, when he witnessed at first hand the wartime authoritarian rule in Maribor and in Prague, Pivko seems to have felt that instead of simply deserting to the enemy he should stay and organize 'revolutionary work' against Austria at the front. His overall goal was still Slovene rather than Yugoslav: 'the destruction of Austria and the freedom of my nation, which can only be achieved by the destruction of Austria!'[86] In this ideal, he gradually found consensus among some younger Slav reserve officers of the battalion, chiefly Czechs like Karel Mlejnek, Josef Kohoutek and Karel Pajger, but occasionally Bosnian Serbs such as Sime Čačić and Cvijo Djurić. The burgeoning group, many of whom were with him during Austria's conquest of Montenegro in the winter of 1915–16, were, in Pivko's words, 'amphibians': they fought in the Austrian army but at the same time they rejoiced at Austria's defeats.[87]

By August 1916, when Pivko's battalion (V/BHIR1) had been transferred to Corvara in northern Tyrol, it had to engage in hostilities with the Italians on Monte Sief. At the same time Pivko, as commander of the 4th company, made his first secret contact with Italy. He managed to arrange for two Russian prisoners to desert across the lines, taking with them documents (signed under his code-name Ivan Vidović Pavlin) about his small group of agitators and about the Austrian positions which had been regularly reconnoitred by his patrols. By this time Pivko could rely for his cause on about 50 Bosnian Serbs of his own company, men who felt personally committed to their charismatic commander and seem to have been instinctively more receptive to his views than their fellow-Bosnian Moslems. His own reliability in his superiors' eyes had only been strengthened by his personal heroism on Monte Sief, with the result that he gained more access to official documents at the brigade level.[88] It was knowledge and experience which he built upon when the battalion in late 1916 was moved to the sector of the 18ID near the village of Carzano.

In the new position there was not only the advantage for Pivko's plotters of the Italians lying in close proximity. The position also defended key routes of access to the Austrian rear, through Val Sugana to Trento, and along a new road being built in early 1917 through the Calamento valley to link Borgo with Ora and hence Bolzano. Any Italian break-through could therefore have far-reaching consequences. Pivko immediately set out to place his conspirators at the disposal of the Italian CS, attempting already in January 1917 to cross with his plans to the Italian lines. He failed due to the snow, and then went on leave for the last time. Six months later he was in a much stronger position. A German officer in Levico, who was a friend, provided him with precise information about 11AK troop movements; his plotters were able to reconnoitre the entire region, including the road to Ora which had now been completed; and he himself was even temporarily placed in charge of the whole battalion. It was thus that in early July 1917 Pivko resolved to send Karel Mlejnek, an honest if rather naïve individual, on a mission to the Italian lst army command. Under cover of searching for enemy propaganda leaflets, Mlejnek would take to the Italians a letter from 'Lt Pavlin'. It informed them that Yugoslav and Czech rebels of the battalion were now at Italy's disposal, eager as 'allies of the Entente' to give them the military advantage before the forthcoming Austrian offensive on the Isonzo; Italy should prepare a surprise thrust in the Sugana valley, for there the plotters could sabotage Austrian defences and act as guides for the Italian advance. On the evening of 11 July, Mlejnek crossed the short no-man's-land of apple trees to the Italian lines, equipped with the letter and a package of detailed maps and plans. The Italians were asked to fire two grenades over Carzano to acknowledge that they had received the package, and to return Mlejnek to Carzano with a reply as to how 'Pavlin' himself could meet the Italians.[89]

The two main accounts of how the plot developed in the following months, by Pivko and Finzi, differ slightly in their timing of events, but they converge on all major points. Finzi was clearly intrigued at the precise details which Mlejnek's package contained although, it seems, he did not understand why 'Pavlin' should be doing this. Mlejnek was probably taken down to Vicenza to meet Finzi[90] and was then returned to the Austrian lines, his long absence converted into an 'heroic incident' by Pivko which his superiors would only question much later. Finzi meanwhile ordered the signals to be given, and met Pivko at Strigno for the first time on the night of 21 July; it was to be the first of eight such encounters. Finzi at this initial meeting was rapidly inclined to trust Pivko: when Pivko insisted that the war would destroy Austria (and that the sooner it occurred 'the sooner we Slavs will achieve the fulfilment of our national ideals'), Finzi simply replied, 'that is the theory which guides my work as well'. Both men undoubtedly exaggerated for the other their own importance at this time. Finzi seems to have suggested that he had already been in touch with the CS, while Pivko asserted that his men were now Finzi's 'foremost guard in such a vital and dangerous position, like no other Italian guard'. But the two departed enthusiastically expectant about their future contacts, Finzi instructing Pivko to expand the number of plotters and send him as much information as possible about the Val Sugana sector.[91]

Finzi would later suggest that at this meeting his own Italian prejudices against the Slovenes and Croats had evaporated. In fact, at their second meeting on the night of 26 July the logical clash of their nationalist standpoints was quickly revealed. When Pivko tried to suggest that all Slavs in the Monarchy were revolutionary, Finzi countered with the evidence of the recent May Declaration by Austria's South Slav leaders in the Reichsrat, according to which they desired unification but still under the Habsburg sceptre. Finzi was clearly sceptical about Pivko's attempts to excuse the declaration. Nor did he feel that the Corfu Declaration between Serbia and the Yugoslav Committee (of which Pivko was still ignorant until this time) was an accurate reflection of a similar Yugoslav unity inside Austria-Hungary. Indeed, such declarations, according to Finzi, were of 'academic significance' since they took no account of military realities or the views of the Great Powers. Pivko rightly sensed in Finzi's language his commitment to Italian aspirations as laid down in the Treaty of London, something which would always remain a sensitive point in their relationship. Equally, it is clear that at this time Finzi was thoroughly realistic in evaluating the situation: in correctly suspecting that most 'Yugoslavs' of the Monarchy were not united or even revolutionary, and in pointing to the absence of any Entente commitments to the Yugoslav cause. The upshot of this early discussion in any case was that, in their subsequent dealings, Finzi and Pivko were usually able to subsume the sensitive territorial issue, concentrating instead on their common zest to destroy Austria-Hungary in the military field.[92] The real strength of Italy's campaign with front propaganda would depend on maintaining such a common purpose despite the otherwise divergent interests.

In the following weeks Pivko energetically stepped up his preparations. His plotters, whose number steadily expanded, were assigned specific reconnaissance tasks. About half of them sent in details from the rear. For example, Pivko posted a Czech officer, Jiří Maštálka[93] whose father had been imprisoned for treason, to Trento to assess troop movements; a Slovene named Gobec sent in reports on the basis of extensive travelling, since he was responsible for inspecting the telephone and telegraphic network of the sector; another Czech, Antonín Stránský, was recruited in a bakery at Novaledo, on the main road along the Val Sugana.[94] The rest of the conspirators remained in the front line, drawing maps, hoarding munition and dismantling defences in order to facilitate an Italian invasion. During August, Pivko ensured that many of the key plotters went on leave for the last time and gave some of them extra tasks. František Jirsa, a late recruit and commander of the battalion machine-gun company, took a special message of reassurance to Pivko's wife in Bohemia. Josef Kohoutek was assigned a more political role, for Pivko not only entrusted him with a letter about the Corfu Declaration for a Slovene contact, but also urged him to meet leading Czech politicians if possible.[95] (It is not clear if this occurred, but it perhaps indicates Pivko's sensitivity to Finzi's criticism of the absence of revolutionary signs in the hinterland.) Meanwhile during August, Pivko was able to betray to the Italians the details of three local Austrian raids, two of which he effectively sabotaged. And more importantly, he relayed to Finzi a steady stream of information about all aspects of the Val Sugana sector as well as of the Trentino as a whole, including all official communications from the 11AK and some even from the AOK at Baden. In light of this, Pivko would later assert that during the First World War no belligerent was so precisely informed about the strengths and intentions of an opponent as were the Italians about the Austrians in the Sugana valley in the summer of 1917.[96]

Finzi's memoirs lend weight to this contention: that by early September, on the basis of Italian Intelligence at least, 'Trento was already virtually ours'.[97] On one starry night Finzi even donned Austrian uniform and was escorted around the Carzano sector by Pivko, who indicated where the electric wires would be cut, where an extra bridge could be constructed over the river Maso, and where the Italians would be able to advance unnoticed by Austrian artillery.[98] Yet Finzi's enthusiasm for the enterprise was not shared by his superiors, and events would prove that Intelligence alone would not guarantee success. Despite his confident assurances to Pivko, Finzi had found the CS initially sceptical when he visited Udine on 4 August, since all eyes were turned upon the imminent Bainsizza offensive. Only after a month, when the offensive on the Giulian front had ground to a halt, was Finzi able to gain access to Cadorna and convince him, particularly in view of the weak Austrian occupation of the Trentino, that the Carzano plot ought to be exploited for more than Intelligence purposes. And even then, when details of the attack were finalized (7 September), Finzi was again to be disillusioned. The 6th army commander, General Etna, who had already shown scepticism, put forward a very cumbersome plan of action which contrasted markedly with the meticulous and rapid operation proposed by Ljudevit Pivko himself. Nor did it bode well that the officer chosen by Cadorna to command the enterprise, Brigadier Attilio Zincone, had never performed such a task before; in short, as Finzi wrote acidly, 'he did not have the makings of a *condottiero*'.[99]

For the Carzano plotters, any delay in the operation could be fatal. Even before the agreement with Cadorna, Finzi seems to have told Pivko that the attack would be on 13 September. Pivko was then undoubtedly alarmed when he learnt on 4 September that action would be in 15–20 days, since by this time there were increasing signs that his battalion might soon be transferred to another sector or front.[100] Such delay also heightened the risk of discovery or betrayal. Pivko, as the temporary commander of the battalion, had been able to disguise his movements by unilaterally 'taking patrols into no-man's-land', and he could be sure that his superior officers were at least in Telve or further afield. Through an arrangement with the Italians, he had also tried to ensure that their artillery fired whenever there loomed an official Austrian inspection of the sector, so that the tour would be cancelled. But this was not a foolproof procedure, and Pivko's position was weaker from 7 September when a Magyar, Major Lakom, officially assumed command of the battalion at Telve and proceeded to tour the sector. Moreover, Pivko had to be constantly vigilant as the potential enemy was always in his midst. Alongside the 70 or so conspirators who had been recruited by early September, it is significant that there remained a mass of 'Austrians' including some prominent officers (Knott, Ertl, the Bosnian Moslem Trampa, and the battalion doctor Turold) to whom the plot could never be divulged. Pivko might occasionally test one of these officers' convictions,[101] but was increasingly wary about recruiting too widely. At Finzi's suggestion, it was agreed that on the fatal night those of the battalion who were not party to the plot would be drugged. Finzi arranged for the army chemists at Turin to produce bottles of brandy laced with opium, as well as extra doses of the drug in powder form for use in the battalion kitchens. As Pivko observed, 'he who is not with us, let him sleep'.[102]

The plot, however, almost began to unravel before such drugging was possible. Like the Italians, Pivko seems to have been unnecessarily paranoid about the 'skill' of Austrian espionage in Italy. But it was a far simpler indiscretion which endangered the whole conspiracy. In his enthusiasm for new recruits, Karel Mlejnek had divulged elements of the plot (his own visit to Vicenza, the imminent Italian invasion and the use of opium) to an old Czech acquaintance, Urban, who had just started to work in the officers' mess kitchen at Telve. On 11 September Urban, after wrestling with his conscience, betrayed these details to the divisional command, which ordered that Mlejnek and Alojz Lahvička (who had also confided in Urban) should be arrested and that an investigation should be undertaken by Auditor Klima. Pivko's own dramatic account of this eleventh-hour betrayal[103] corroborates what the later Austrian inquiry suspected: namely, that he had time to brief Mlejnek and Lahvička about how to behave before Klima. While they pleaded total ignorance and portrayed Urban as a stupid and cowardly individual, Pivko himself when questioned was able to play on his own excellent reputation to discredit Urban's 'fantasies'. As the Austrian inquiry noted later:

> Naturally this highly intelligent, ingenious criminal understood precisely how to leave his accomplices spotless. Pivko was looked upon as the best officer in the battalion. It was therefore not at all easy to bring such charges against an officer who was so decorated and described with such distinction.[104]

Klima therefore dropped all charges against the accused, enabling Pivko, who had prepared for an armed rebellion if the judgement had been unfavourable, to return to his comrades in the front line. Well might the conspirators feel, notwithstanding, that a volcano was beginning to stir under their feet.[105] On the very next day Pivko was called to Levico to represent the battalion at an inspection by Emperor Karl, an occasion on which, ironically, the monarch accompanied by both Arz and Conrad praised Pivko, brushed aside the recent shadow over his reputation, and proceeded to promote him to 11AK headquarters. Pivko fancifully informed the Italians that if they attacked immediately they might capture the Emperor, 'news which would send a buzz [*bi preletela*] through Europe and overseas and probably mean the end of the war'.[106] More realistically, it was now vital in view of the betrayal and Pivko's imminent transfer that the Carzano plan was executed as soon as possible. On handing over the brandy and opium to the plotters, Finzi fixed 17 September as the probable night and arranged that the code-word for the attack would be 'Como-Cadorna'.

All the evidence suggests that on the crucial night, Ljudevit Pivko and his *Carzanci* were as coordinated as was feasibly possible, given the boundaries of secrecy.[107] Much of the battalion was drugged in the early evening, with the cook of the 3rd company giving the men a double-dose of opium for good measure. The electricity through the wires in no-man's-land was cut at the appropriate time, as were all telephone links with neighbouring sectors. The key plotters were in place to act as guides for the 12 columns of Italian troops which were initially expected. The key sentry positions were largely in 'reliable' hands; Pivko made sure, for example, that Sime Čačić replaced Lieutenant Knott in command of the vital guard at Castellare, a point which Pivko's battalion commander had always viewed as the sector's Achilles' heel which needed to be reinforced.[108]

But in contrast, there was to be a distinct absence of coordination on the Italian side, revealing in particular an abyss between Finzi's efficient Intelligence and Zincone's clumsy operations. Most damaging was the fact that, unbeknown to the plotters, Italian 'winter time' had been introduced on 15 September, so that the Italian advance was an hour behind the time which Pivko expected. This, when added to Italian delays and the fact that 'the foremost Italians crept like snails', meant that the tight schedule was quickly in arrears. By 2 a.m. only 30 Italians had crossed both front lines and a bridge over the Maso to reach Carzano; by 4 a.m. it was still only 200, and the alarm had long been sounded by 'Austrians' who had recovered from their drugging.[109] These delays were exacerbated by Italian suspicions and caution in the face of the enemy. For in contrast to Finzi, many of the Italian officers had not been carefully instructed and still made no distinction between the opposing 'Austrians'. Finzi's increasing commitment to disaffected Austrians was clear during the operation, when he was prepared to employ several Austrian Slav deserters (including Novy and Nikolić) in trustworthy roles of liaison between the Italians and *Carzanci*.[110] But other Italian officers who slowly advanced with their columns on the route from Strigno towards Carzano could not betray their mistrust. It was as a result of this that Mlejnek (as a guide of the 9th column) was wounded by his own Italians, while even Pivko was 'arrested' for a time by the wary commander of the 5th column.[111] As dawn came, Zincone finally lost his nerve and ordered a retreat. He himself had already contributed to the *débâcle* by diverting the later columns onto a route which was both narrow and slow of transit so that many failed even to reach Spera.[112] True, some troops had advanced to seize the battalion command at Telve, so that the first of three phases of the operation had been completed. But this was not enough. Only five of the 12 columns had reached their allotted destinations, and two critical high-points, Caverna to the north and Civaron to the south, remained untouched, leaving Italians crossing the Maso exposed to Austrian guns in daylight.

So it was that, largely due to Italian hesitation, the Carzano operation was abruptly terminated. Instead of becoming what Finzi would later call a prospective 'Austrian Caporetto',[113] it became an episode for the Austrians to scorn. Only much later would Austrian commentators feel able to talk about Pivko as a 'psychological phenomenon'.[114] For the Italians, meanwhile, it was a story to conceal. As a result of an inquiry ordered by Cadorna, both Etna and Zincone were relieved of their posts, but the episode remained secret. Even in 1926 when Finzi's account was published in Bologna, it was confiscated by the Fascist censor as an incident unworthy of remembrance.

Nevertheless, the dream of Carzano was not at an end. During the last year of hostilities it was to have far-reaching repercussions for the way in which warfare was conducted on the Italian Front, supplying a major basis for a new type of front propaganda. While Pivko and his key accomplices were escorted, disillusioned and nervous, to Verona to be housed in the Procolo fortress, Cadorna still hoped to exploit Austrian confusion in Val Sugana. He personally ordered Finzi to re-establish contact with those many conspirators who had been abandoned on the Austrian side, as a prelude to a second Carzano operation. Finzi duly sent two of his own Czech agents over the front, who reported back that while the Trentino was still weakly garrisoned, the Austrians were now investigating the conspiracy. Other intelligence from Marchetti's network seemed to suggest that reinforcements were moving into southern Tyrol, but Finzi dismissed this as a diversion to conceal an Austrian build-up on the Isonzo.[115] He himself turned to Ljudevit Pivko to draw up a new Carzano project on the basis of his detailed knowledge, and also requested from Pivko some volunteers who would immediately try to contact their old battalion at Carzano. In the end, the dozen Bosnian Serbs and Slovenes who travelled back to Strigno on 2 October discovered on their first night that the battalion had been dissolved. The CS then resolved to cancel a second Carzano, all the more so because of alarming signs on the Isonzo. While Pivko was left largely ignorant of the reasons (his memoirs record that 'they told us many things in reply'), the short post-Carzano episode was still highly significant. For the first time, volunteers from the *Carzanci* had been allowed to don Italian uniform (with the initial 'J' – *Jugoslavo* – on their caps) in order to work for Italian Intelligence in the front line.[116]

This did not mean that Pivko and his dozen officers were now committed to such activities. Most of them hoped to take advantage of a guarantee which Finzi had given them in August, supposedly allowing them freedom if they were forced to flee to Italy. Some hoped to join the Czech Legion in France, others to travel to Salonika and the Serbian army: few were enthusiastic about returning to the Italian Front. Pivko himself shared these doubts, not least because of the experience of Carzano, and his anxiety increased during his first weeks in Verona. He sensed that few Italians shared Finzi's enlightened viewpoint; the average Italian thought vaguely of the war as a struggle for Italian unity, categorizing all the enemy as 'Austrians' and using 'Croat' as a term 'synonymous with cruelty and barbarism'. It was, he felt, 'appalling' that 'Italy, who had been at war with Austria for three years already, did not see the necessity of scattering among the nationalities elementary ideas about the lands and peoples who wished to be free of the Austrian yoke'. Even if the Czechoslovak movement seemed to have a few Italian adherents and a new office in Rome in the hands of František Hlaváček, the atmosphere hardly appeared conducive to winning similar support for Pivko's Yugoslav ideal, something which the Yugoslav Committee itself seemed to acknowledge through its total boycott of the country.[117]

Such arguments were challenged by Finzi, who told Pivko in mid-October that it was precisely Italy where the Yugoslav movement needed to win friends and where 'a propitious area for propaganda' now existed. Although Finzi did not suggest that he himself had abandoned Italy's nationalist claims, he firmly acknowledged that his horizons were widening as a result of Carzano:

> It is a fact that you altered the opinion of the Slavs in me and in every head who worked with you in the last few months and knew your work... Your honest propaganda should now concentrate directly on Italy with the aim of convincing the Italian public about the justice of your aspirations and the need to solve the Yugoslav problem.

If for Finzi it was the military benefits which remained the priority in his thinking, his language also suggests that he was in tune with publicists such as Luigi Albertini or G.A. Borgese who were newly converted to 'nationality politics': namely, that this was a weapon which had to be embraced in order to win the war. Additionally, while Finzi spoke to Pivko about 'new wars of liberation', on behalf of Slavs as well as Italians, he knew that the Slavs within the Monarchy were not yet revolutionary, as Pivko pretended, and so posed no threat to Italian aspirations. Pivko continued to suspect Finzi's ambivalence, but he was nevertheless persuaded by the Intelligence head's eloquence, the challenge he offered and the probable absence of any alternative. There seemed to be three useful and inter-locking roles which the *Carzanci* might fulfil in Italy: a military role, as volunteers at the front against Austrian oppression; a 'moral' role, by demonstrating Slav unity and their belief in an Entente victory; and a political role, by working to convince Italian public opinion that Austria's Slavs were ready to form their own states. Each of these roles might directly or indirectly inflict damaging propaganda against the morale of the Habsburg Empire.[118]

On 16 October, after sending a report on his decision to the Yugoslav Committee in London, Pivko began with the aid of Finzi's officials in Verona to train a unit which would carry out propaganda and Intelligence work on the 1st army front. Numbering less than 20 men at this stage, the unit was to be divided into groups, each of which would be fed by and liaise (via Italian Intelligence personnel) with the nearest battalion command; otherwise it would act independently and receive orders direct from lst army Intelligence at Vicenza. Their specific task, apart from gathering information by intercepting enemy telephone conversations, was to contact former comrades, teach them the 'realities' of their position and incite them to have the moral courage to desert. 'In that way', Pivko noted, 'we begin to decompose the solidarity of the Austrian army, [for] with propaganda the Germans and Austrians smashed the Russian army: they discovered in "fraternization" a new weapon, one which will be even more dangerous when we turn it against them on the Austrian front.'[119]

The unit's baptism of fire was on the front from Asiago north to Monte Zebio, whither it was transported on 26 October and divided into three groups. Most of the individuals were former *Carzanci* (Kohoutek, Mlejnek, Veselko-Sedlecký) who only weeks before had been agitating on the other side of the trenches. During the next ten days, while the Italians were retreating across the Venetian plains after Caporetto, the unit's main achievement appears to have been to use an eavesdropping apparatus on Monte Zebio from which Finzi allegedly received 'important and diverse telephone dispatches as never before'. If this was so, their propaganda work of singing and calling out while camouflaged in the undergrowth seems to have been less rewarding. Pivko's account, while portraying the enemy as overwhelmingly hostile, still concludes that the unit achieved 'fine success' and caused 16 'Yugoslavs' to desert.[120] Yet of those whom he names, at least nine had deserted over a month earlier, and none are to be found in the full list of Pivko's volunteers as one might expect of 'Yugoslavs' who responded to idealist propaganda.[121] Any success in any case was cut short because on 7 November the Italians were forced to retreat on this front as well, and Pivko's volunteers returned to Verona.

Yet if Pivko was inclined to exaggerate his unit's achievements, it was indeed the case that its short stay in the front line had already earned it some publicity in Italian military circles. In the following five months, when the volunteers were assigned no further propaganda work and the Italians were largely on the defensive, Pivko's main priority was to acquire for his unit a greater respectability and so prepare the ground for the establishment of a Slav legion. For this purpose, the volunteers in Verona were regularly drilled and trained in the art of future Intelligence and propaganda duties. From January 1918 they acquired in the person of Lieutenant Stane Vidmar, a famous Slovene Sokol leader from Ljubljana who had just deserted, an enthusiastic teacher who even included regular singing lessons in his Sokol training syllabus.[122] In the meantime, Finzi was gradually incorporating the volunteers into the Intelligence network. Pivko was asked by Marchetti's office to peruse the Monarchy's Slav newspapers which arrived via Switzerland, to clarify news items, and draw up reports relating them to military developments.[123] A handful of the volunteers, led by Finzi's confidant Mate Nikolić, were also employed from the autumn in the mysterious Dolfin villa at Rosà near Bassano. This building was not simply a key centre for Intelligence analysis, but housed the most recent Austrian prisoners who were thus immediately available for interrogation with the aid of Slav volunteers, after they had been sifted at the Procolo fortress.[124] Already by January 1918, the impression which Pivko's volunteers were making in the lst army zone was enough to draw from František Hlaváček the remark: 'I see that in Italy the ice is broken.'[125]

Although Pivko had tried to establish contact with Edvard Beneš during the Carzano episode, it was only in early January that the Czechoslovak National Council in the person of Hlaváček showed an interest. As we will see, Hlaváček since his appointment to the Rome office in September had successfully cultivated friends in governmental and journalistic circles. When he then visited Pivko's volunteers at Verona on 6 January, he was impressed at the progress made in military circles, for he could contrast it with his own former experience in the war zone as well as his current frustrations in the hinterland. He urged Pivko to obtain permission from lst army command to expand the small unit, and particularly to include more Czechs for, since the Czechoslovak cause was making more headway than the Yugoslav, it would be accorded more publicity, but in turn this could only react favourably on the Yugoslav question.[126] Pivko took Hlaváček's advice and, with Finzi's permission, he began to recruit for his *reparto czeco-jugoslavo* among recently deserted Austrian Slavs. Since Carzano there had been few additions to the group, for Finzi was still testing the water. Because of Italian prejudice, he had advised the volunteers to present themselves as American Slavs to inquisitive Italians and to avoid any indication of their 'Austrian' origin. Pivko himself was naturally aware that the Italians had to be cautious, and that care also had to govern his own choice of recruits:

> Our task, especially the task of propaganda in enemy trenches, demanded intelligent and in every respect reliable and self-sacrificing volunteers. Therefore, we chose carefully so as to preserve our expanding unit at a level qualitatively close to that of the original *Carzanci*.[127]

Although among the 18 new 'Yugoslav' volunteers, there might be some who glowed with 'a lively desire to enter the fight against the Austrian oppressor', these were usually Bosnian Serbs or those who had been active in the prewar Sokol clubs. Many of the Croat or Slovene prisoners who passed through Verona or the Dolfin villa were found to be 'hardened Austrians', while others simply had no wish to continue any military role.[128] They were all sent off to prison camps in the south, while the 'Yugoslavs' and 53 new 'Czechoslovaks' donned Italian uniform (with Slav cockades and red, white and blue colours on the collars) and began a vigorous training under Stane Vidmar in the Procolo fortress.

For Finzi and Marchetti, as we will see, this expansion was one element in their overall campaign to exploit Austria's nationalist tensions in the months after Caporetto. Since lst army Intelligence needed CS permission to employ Slav volunteers more systematically as patrols in the front line, on 17 January Finzi wrote a memorandum on the subject and dispatched it to the new CS headquarters at Abano. In it he claimed bluntly that most subject peoples of Austria-Hungary were 'nationalist' and anti-Austrian, and that therefore the presence of Slav patrols on the Italian side would provoke widespread desertion and considerable embarrassment for the enemy AOK. Since, Finzi admitted, many of the Italian lower commands were still diffident, it would be necessary to present the patrols as special allied units. But he pointed to the experience of Carzano as evidence of what might be achieved with a committed group of ex-Austrians, who could be moved around the front, fully at the disposal of the Intelligence service.[129] It was Pivko's unit which was the natural forerunner and model for such activity. In early February, the CS approved Finzi's request for 'Czech propaganda patrols'.[130] On 25 March 1918, Finzi was able to inform Pivko that Abano wished to establish Slav units for propaganda and Intelligence work in every Italian army.

In the intervening period, Pivko's novices had required extensive training in Verona until 21 March when the whole unit was transferred to a new headquarters, an open camp at Tugurio near Sandrigo. This was in keeping with a general reorganization of Italian forces through which a new 6th army was being created (to include British and French divisions); Pivko's unit moved in order to remain subordinate to Finzi who became the head of 6th army Intelligence at Breganze. Four days after its arrival, the unit, with the mountains looming in the background, staged an impressive gymnastic and cultural display on the plain for the benefit of French and Italian officers. Among those present were the Intelligence heads of the neighbouring 4th and 8th armies, Vigevano and Dupont, who received an education in what they too might achieve with Slav deserters. For the volunteers the formal, public display signalled something of an initiation in the war zone, for the next day they were driven northwards into the mountains for their first experiment in front propaganda.[131]

According to Pivko, it was with the express purpose of countering Austria's propaganda that his unit was sent to the front at Stoccareddo, north of Col d'Echele (see Map 4). During March in this sector, *Nachrichtentruppen* of the Austrian 26 Schützendivision [26SchD] had been particularly active, depositing material about peace in the East and the German offensive in the West, and claiming for itself 'generally favourable results'.[132] The Italians in turn may have been alarmed at some desertions to the enemy in this area and speculated incorrectly that Austrian propaganda was responsible.[133] If so, their suspicions about enemy intentions were perhaps confirmed when in mid-March they captured near Val Frenzella a member of the opposing Austrian propaganda team. This individual was Franz Kreuz, who gradually revealed all to Mate Nikolić when he was slipped into his prison cell as an Italian 'pigeon'. Besides supplying illuminating details about Austria's propaganda work on the Eastern and Isonzo fronts in 1917, Kreuz claimed that around the river Brenta Austria was engaged in vigorous propaganda specifically in order to prepare for a forthcoming and decisive offensive with its main thrust on the mountain front: 'We are learning to use again the methods with which we were successful against the Russians and at Caporetto in order to open some doors for the army.'[134] If Pivko's unit was now despatched to close this particular door, it also had a definite offensive role to play. Finzi undoubtedly felt that the predominantly Czech 26SchD was itself ripe for demoralization, for earlier in the month there had been a steady trickle of Czech desertions to Italy from Schützenregiment 9 [SchR9]. The troops' dire material position at a high altitude was probably enough to cause these, cut off as they were in the snow with wholly inadequate shelter.[135] But the Austrian 11AK still speculated that 'Italian propaganda' might have played a part, for one of those involved was known to have trafficked with the enemy before desertion and Italian aeroplanes had on several occasions distributed manifestos over the sector. Clearly it was an area which seemed to offer both sides the prospect of some propaganda coup.[136]

For a fortnight from 28 March Pivko's unit was active opposite the Austrian positions, singing Czech songs such as *Hej Slované* and *Kde domov můj*, hoisting bread on bayonets, and proclaiming the liberationist message that they were soldiers of the 'free state of Bohemia'. Besides calling out, they threw or shot over hand-written and printed manifestos, sometimes using newly invented rockets (*razzi manifestini*) which could store leaflets and travel up to 500 metres:

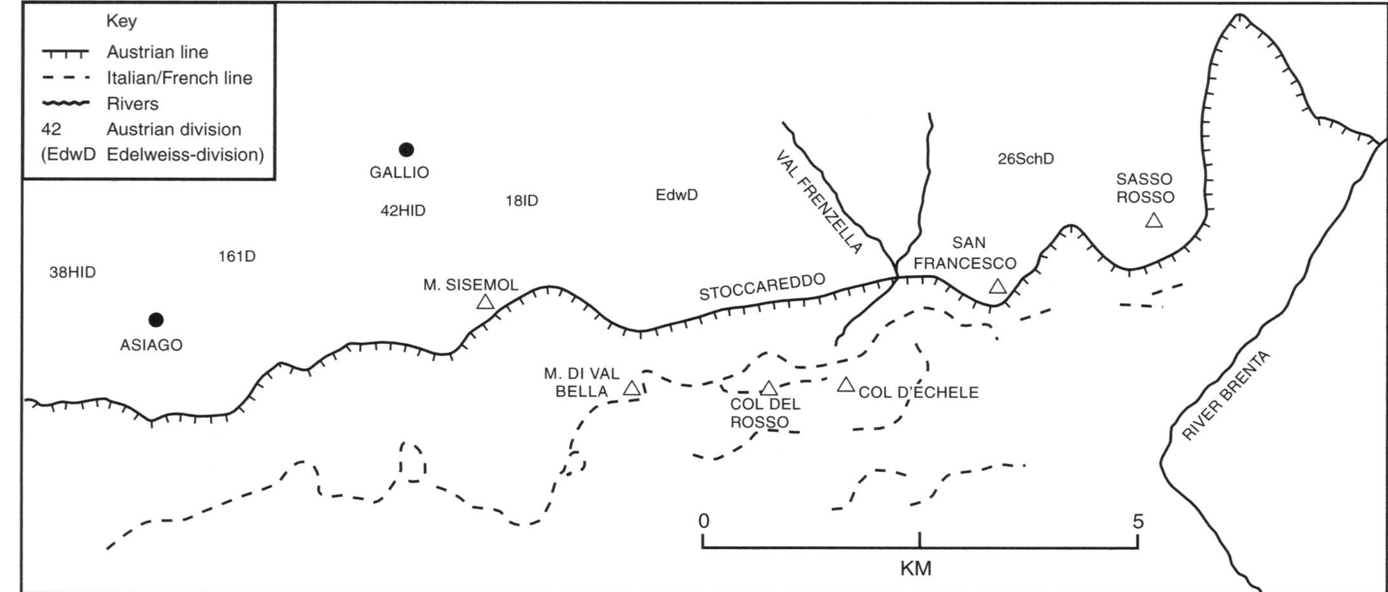


*Map 5.2* The Front east of Asiago (June 1918)

> Czech officers and soldiers! Do you know who throws you these appeals? We are Czech volunteer officers and soldiers who have begun to fight for your freedom. Come out of the trenches and come across to us so that your German and Hungarian officers don't see you. Just think how happy we will be when we can welcome and embrace you here in Italy.
>
> Tell your comrades too that we are on this part of the front, so that they too can come over with confidence to us. Italy and the other Allies are with us; they are helping us to victory.[137]

Pivko claimed later that this activity had completely thwarted Austrian propaganda in the sector, but this was only partially true. On Col del Rosso, where there were French troops, the *Nachrichtentruppen* did temporarily halt their propaganda excursions, for Czech calls that the French would soon be relieved by Slavs made the 26SchD uncertain about the nationality of their opponents. Elsewhere, however, the efforts of Pivko's unit seem chiefly to have stimulated a propaganda duel. The Austrians continued to scatter their material regularly, employing new rifle grenades, opening a new propaganda post at Stoccareddo (overhanging the Italian positions) and even concluding in mid-April that their work was having 'very favourable results' in some places.[138]

Pivko's other major claim about his unit's success must also be treated with reserve in view of Austrian evidence. He suggests that through turning the Austrians' 'weapons against them, they had to withdraw SchR12 from the line'. In fact, it is clear that, although rumours abounded in the regiment itself that it would have to be exchanged, this did not occur; it was simply reinforced with more reliable elements and remained in position until after Austria's June offensive. Pivko's claim should therefore be taken as grandiloquence in front of the local Italian commander.[139] But where, apart from this, the Czech propaganda may well have had a noticeable impact was in the lingering impression it left on the opposing Czech garrison. One Czech deserted and mumbled, before dying of his wounds, that the whole garrison at Stoccareddo was ready to follow. This was not, however, what Finzi desired. Instead of encouraging a mass desertion which the Austrians might be able to hush-up, Finzi wished the Czechs for the moment to stay on the Austrian side and spread more widely the demoralizing propagandist message which they had heard. It is impossible to determine the results of this strategy. All that can be said is that the impact of Pivko's unit was undoubtedly tempered at this time by an experience which Austrian propagandists had themselves had to suffer in recent months, namely their own forces' mistrust of the propaganda weapon. In this particular case, it was the French troops on Col del Rosso who, with the view that 'a Boche is a Boche', proceeded to direct flanking fire on anything which moved out of the enemy trenches (including the unfortunate Czech).[140] While Pivko was in despair at French behaviour, Finzi was able immediately to contact the new commander of the 6th army – the 'energetic, capable and tactful' General Montuori[141] – and secure an order on 4 April that troops ought to be careful when firing so as not to disturb valuable propaganda activity or place propaganda patrols at risk.[142]

This early problem of Allied coordination does not appear to have been noticed by the Austrian divisional commander, Brigadier Klein. And Klein's later report for his superiors also, rather typically, gave no indication that Czech propaganda had made any impact on his own men or besmirched the reputation of his division:

> At the end of March and in the first half of April, it was confirmed fairly certainly through frequent observation that on Col del Rosso there were Czech propaganda troops which, now here, now there, sang Czech songs from the Italian trenches opposite our outposts, and attempted to entice our men with shouts. This seems to have caused quarrels with the Italians, because our side always opened fire under which, naturally, the Italian posts had to suffer and not the well-hidden propaganda troops.[143]

From 10 April nothing more was heard. Rain was interrupting the propaganda, and Pivko's unit after inspection by General Montuori was returned to Tugurio for a rest.

The Stoccareddo events are a useful example of how difficult it is to unravel the influence of propaganda at the front. Often the rumours of what happened were even more important than the actual reality. We can perhaps safely judge that at this time the work of Pivko's unit was having a greater impact on Italians than on the enemy. The incidents at Stoccareddo seem to have increased local Italian officers' trust of propaganda, and were soon to be reported in the Italian national press.[144] Even the Prime Minister, Orlando, on visiting the war zone in early April seems to have been alerted by Finzi to the significance of Stoccareddo as a concrete example of the benefits of 'nationality politics'.[145] In this way, the *Carzanci*'s original role in Italy's war had considerably expanded. In the summer of 1917 they had suddenly offered to the Italians a singular opportunity to strike at the enemy. At the same time, they had strengthened a growing belief among the influential leaders of 1st army Intelligence that the nationalist virus was spreading in the Austro-Hungarian forces and that Italy might provide a catalyst in that process. It was after Caporetto that the wider Intelligence service, the new CS, and Italy's journalists and politicians all began to move in this direction, sensing the benefits which might accrue from picking up and wielding the nationalist weapon. Pivko's expanding unit contributed to the new mentality by its very presence in the Italian war zone, by posing as a pioneer for the employment of Slav volunteers and therefore as a precursor for a properly constituted Czechoslovak or Yugoslav legion. According to Pivko's memoirs, both Finzi and Hlaváček had predicted that his unit could play an influential role 'and get Italy on his side'. And to some extent by the late spring they had been proved right.[146]

## 5.4 The propaganda duel

The propaganda contest which took place in microcosm at Stoccareddo reflected the propaganda duel which was developing on all parts of the Italian Front from the turn of the year. For the new CS of Diaz and Badoglio, an increase in propaganda distribution over the enemy was very much a response to Austria's own campaign in the wake of Caporetto. It was a defensive reaction and therefore, not surprisingly, many of Italy's early leaflets were concerned with countering Austrian arguments. However, as we have seen, Italy's campaign was also rooted in the Italian military's growing appreciation of this weapon, and particularly the lessons which military Intelligence had learnt at Carzano and thereafter. The Intelligence officers, especially Tullio Marchetti, who was an old acquaintance of Diaz, found a more receptive ear at the new CS when they paid their weekly visits to Abano. If they were already demonstrating their own commitment to 'nationality politics' by unilaterally making more use of Slav volunteers, they now pressed for Italy to establish a Czechoslovak legion in order further to undermine enemy morale. In fact, Marchetti and Finzi were pushing at an opening door. After Caporetto, in the new atmosphere of resistance and a commitment to victory in political and journalistic circles, it was far more feasible for the Czech (and later the Yugoslav) cause to make rapid headway in Italy. As the country under Orlando's government seemed, ostensibly at least, to be adopting nationality politics, so a firmer and more genuine base was created for adopting such a stance in Italy's propaganda at the front. In the spring, Orlando himself would be brought, by Luigi Albertini in particular, to understand the military advantages of this new course. And it was thus that in March 1918 the Prime Minister directly intervened with the CS to coordinate a proper campaign of propaganda against the enemy.

On 11 January, Diaz had ordered leaflet distribution to be intensified as a response to Austria's campaign.[147] For the Italians this tended to mean distribution from the air. While the Austrians' campaign had been characterized from the start by 'trench propaganda' and an ingenious range of methods to disperse material, such techniques were rarely used by Italy in the spring. Only occasionally did the Austrians encounter Italian patrols on their own model, as on the Lower Piave in March when the cries opposite ranged from 'We have much good wine and bread!' to 'Ukraine has forced you to make peace!'; by this time, the Italians were occasionally experimenting with wooden mine shells and rockets of the kind used by Pivko's unit.[148]

If Italy propagated chiefly from the air it would probably produce unquantifiable results and certainly limit any precise targeting of enemy nationalities. But on the other hand, the air would soon be a zone dominated by the Allies and evacuated by the Austrians. It also enabled the Italians to send uplifting propaganda to those Italian citizens who had been left behind in Venetia and the Trentino when the Central Powers invaded. They were quickly reminded in manifestos scattered over Feltre, Vittorio and other large towns that mother Italy was not abandoning her dearest sons; she knew all about the suffering which they endured at the hands of the occupier: 'your scream of pain has reached us, has pierced our heart, has tortured our soul'.[149] They should 'scornfully oppose everything which the enemy says or does to diminish [their] confidence or power of resistance', for 'the moment of victory and liberation cannot be far off'.[150] These were appeals which the Austrian occupiers tried to suppress, both by announcing severe measures against anyone concealing the brightly coloured leaflets and by feeding the Italian population with their own 'truths' in the shape of the official *Gazzetta del Veneto* (the work of the KPQ). In the words of a poster which was affixed in all public places:

> The army command regularly informs the public about the war situation. It puts up our own and the Italian war reports in all the larger towns where there are military commands, and allows the *Gazzetta del Veneto* to be sold publicly. Thus, nothing is concealed and anyone who reads the reports can construct a picture of the situation on the front which most interests them. Nevertheless, it is the case that some malevolent individuals dare to circulate intentionally false news about the war – fantastic news about the success of Italian arms – which tends to arouse hopes which can never become reality.[151]

Despite a threat of military discipline, the local population maintained a passive resistance to their occupiers and seem to have been stimulated by the Italian appeals. One imprudent woman, Elvezia Erveso, who lived near Conegliano, even went so far as to express publicly her joy that according to manifestos the Italians would return in 20 days; she boldly told the authorities that this was indeed her wish – and was promptly arrested and imprisoned for spreading lies.[152] Her conviction was probably representative of many others whom the occupiers alienated immediately through their mass confiscation of food and property. The *Gazzetta del Veneto*, even if it might have some impact when sent over to Italian soldiers in the enemy trenches, could never overcome in Venetia what one Austrian observer termed the 'horrific memory and feeling of hatred and enmity' which the occupation engendered. Nor of course would the Austrians find it easy as the year progressed to fill the *Gazzetta* with news which favoured the Central Powers.[153] Italy could always play on these realities, with a steady flood of manifestos and later even with its own falsified *Gazzetta del Veneto*.[154] So, the contest for the minds of those in the occupied territories was always weighted in Italy's favour.

The same was not true, at first, for Italy's campaign at the front. Here in January 1918 the initiative lay with the Austrians, with the Italians on the defensive, exerting much effort in countering Austrian arguments about the desirability of peace or the rosy prospects of the Central Powers. There were no Italian military successes to match the conquest of the Bainsizza plateau the previous summer, the last major coup to be trumpeted in Italian leaflets.[155] Italy's new material might often contain an 'offensive' note, but it was only really noticeable from March 1918 in tune with the Italian army's growing confidence. Similarly, it was at that time that the manifestos began to exploit the nationality principle more demonstratively, by channelling ideas to particular nationalities instead of, as in 1917, usually issuing translations of the same text. As in the past, however, the breadth of material in these months still reflected the lack of clear guidelines and the decentralization of Italy's propaganda campaign among the Intelligence offices. Likewise, the quality of material varied from crude to sophisticated depending on the outlook of the local propagandist.[156]

Responding to Austrian approaches, some Italian manifestos simply offered a rebuff, dismissing the enemy's 'polite offers' of establishing correspondence links with relatives in the occupied territories.[157] But most material proceeded to challenge Austria's main contention that Italy after the events of late 1917 should conclude peace. For instead of arousing defeatism or even revolution, Caporetto had produced a *union sacrée* of all classes and parties and 'generated in full force the cooperation of France, England, Italy and America', determined to fight on to the bitter end.[158] The Allies did not want a peace without victory, and certainly not the kind of peace which the Central Powers had imposed on Russia. That peace in any case had not really materialized – the peace with Ukraine was a 'comedy' – and the main cause was Germany's voracious appetite.[159] It was perhaps the major theme in this Italian material (and a parallel to Austrian propaganda's persistent attack on Italy's allies) to question why Austria-Hungary was continuing the war for the interests of Prussian militarism. The Germans were alternatively portrayed as the old 'Prussians of Sadowa', as the barbarians who 'leapt like wolves on the defenceless Russian population', or simply as the personification of death; the manifestos emphasized that peace could never come if Austria-Hungary continued at Germany's side.[160] Peace would only come if Austria's soldiers turned away from barbarism and revolted or deserted to Italy. Here it was occasionally implied that the Entente had a monopoly on Christian morality: it was they who had entered Jerusalem in December 1917 and 'liberated the holy tomb from its centuries-old desecration'.[161] At times, the Italian propaganda was even less subtle, comparing

Italian unification to the Holy Trinity,[162] or – in one widely distributed leaflet – making wildly immodest assertions:

> Austrian soldiers . . . do you know what it means to be Christians? Come to Italy to learn, to Italy who created the civilization of the world, to Italy who made you Christians and whose venerable sanctuaries you now seek to destroy with shells. Don't ask those who lead you and piously attend Holy Mass, but do not live with Christ . . .
>
> Do you know now why Italians entered the war and why they are resisting you? They are fighting and resisting you because your gracious government prevented them from living freely among other nations, because it stopped them breathing, just like today German imperialism prevents you from accepting the proposals of Lloyd George and Wilson, and enslaves you to a megalomania which treats the civilized peoples of Europe, and begins to treat you, like negroes. . . . Do you understand at last, after the recent examples which come out of Russia, where there is civilization and where barbarism, and who are the real enemies of European peace?[163]

This was the kind of material which would be singled out as unsuitable by those who later helped to coordinate Italy's campaign.[164] Nor were the Austrians themselves impressed. It is possible to follow their opinions in the monthly reports which each Austrian army propaganda officer composed, since these always contained a section on 'enemy counter-propaganda'. In the spring of 1918 the reports were overwhelmingly scathing about Italy's manifestos, assessing them as badly translated, unconvincing and amateurish. As the 10AK propaganda officer noted in his summary for March, 'the leaflets, with their hollow phrases and clumsy language, at least when it comes to texts in German and Hungarian, show little understanding for the average outlook and psyche of our soldiers'. He was unsure whether the Italian efforts signified an organized campaign, and suspected correctly that such organization was emerging but was as yet in its infancy.[165] Certainly there were danger signs in certain manifestos, in hints of propaganda patrols, in the demands of the Italian press, that Italy was about to play the 'national card'. Already in February, FM Boroević warned that Austria-Hungary had to be vigilant since it was clear that the Italians, supported by their allies, now believed that they had a new means to hand with which to paralyze the Austrian army and stir up a Slav rebellion in the Monarchy.[166] The only consolation was that Austria's own propaganda campaign still seemed to be far superior.

It would be wrong, however, to consider Italy's efforts in the spring as wholly unpromising. They formed a crucial basis for the coordinated campaign which began in April 1918. Many of the Italian propagandists were beginning to assess their opponent in an increasingly sophisticated manner, exploiting any small signs of unrest in the Empire and targeting specific nationalities with new messages of hope or despair. Admittedly, some of the propaganda only edged in this direction. In early February a revolt occurred on ships of the Austro-Hungarian navy at Cattaro, and three sailors – a Croat and two Poles – escaped to the Italian coast by seaplane. There they were received with suspicion and were imprisoned, but not before they had put their signatures to manifestos which announced their marvellous reception, 'a brilliant testimony to the noble civilization and humanism of the Italian people'.[167] In a range of Slav leaflets, but also by wireless telegram, their plea that others should revolt and follow their example was spread by Italian naval Intelligence over the Adriatic coast and was even intercepted by a British steamship which took it to be Austrian propaganda.[168]

In the Italian front line, propaganda which exploited enemy unrest in this way was pursued rather more subtly. There, Intelligence officers like Finzi were weighing up what might appeal to different nationalities but also what might entice the rank and file and the officers respectively. On the one hand, the leaflets might gnaw at basic instincts by comparing the rations or the family allowance for soldiers in Italy and Austria-Hungary; Slav soldiers were targeted as 'you are the only real victims of the Germans and Hungarians'.[169] On the other, the Slav officers were told to revolt against their German and Austrian masters, and were provided with examples to follow. In a novel development which would later be standard practice, the fiery speeches which some Czech and Polish MPs were now delivering in the Austrian Reichsrat were quoted directly from the Austrian press. One manifesto recalled the Czech MP Isidor Zahradník's notorious words of 6 February that treason was only committed by those who sinned against their own nation. It concluded that for Czech soldiers: 'your parliamentary delegates are telling you that it is your duty to fight against Austria, and not for the Austria which exploits you, limits your rights and wildly persecutes your brothers'.[170] Thus, in a few leaflets directed to the so-called 'oppressed nationalities' it was already possible for the Italians to play on signs of unease in the Monarchy, evidence which they chiefly acquired from the enemy press or from their Intelligence sources.

By March some propagandists, Finzi included, further extended the scope by aiming at Magyar troops. In a series of cleverly composed and accurately translated leaflets, the Hungarians were chiefly reminded that they were not fighting for their own interests. Instead of using the war to pursue Hungarian independence in the tradition of 1848 (of Kossuth, Petőfi and the Arad martyrs), Hungarians had been betrayed by Count Tisza, the servant of the Viennese camarilla, who with his 'cronies' had tied them into Prussian service and bled them white.[171] The result was that Hungarians were continuing to die in their thousands on fronts far from home at a time when Russia was no longer a threat to Hungary's borders, and when there was serious unrest and famine in every town and village (a rare reference was made to the January strike in Budapest).[172] These Italian arguments were a small foretaste of those which would be used in later months. They not only emphasized Hungary's historic traditions, but also tried to undermine the standing of Hungary's ruling elite personified by István Tisza. In other words, they accurately mirrored the social and political debate which was steadily sharpening in the Hungarian half of the Monarchy.

For Hungarian soldiers, Italian propaganda could only be optimistic in vaguely offering them a future of peace, 'independence' and, in the short term, a better life if they deserted to Italy. For other nationalities the propaganda sometimes offered slightly more, by suggesting a clearer Italian commitment to their aspirations. Although the manifestos at this time rarely gave evidence from the Austrian hinterland to suggest that a Slav rebellion or even agitation was feasible, the implication of some leaflets was that it was indeed imminent and that Italy was now actively working to support these nationalist goals. This message was particularly directed at the Czechs. When told, for example, about the hopeless U-boat campaign of the Central Powers, Czech soldiers were also informed that they were now recognized as 'allies of the Entente' who should not continue to serve in 'an army of pirates' or against their own people.[173] In other leaflets, Italy's own commitment was even clearer. One singular manifesto which reported the 'Epiphany Declaration' of Czech Reichsrat deputies (6 January), went on to claim that Italy

> is waging war for the liberation of your people from German-Magyar slavery. The Italian nation wants to be united in one free country, and it demands the same right for you, for the Poles, the Romanians, the Ruthenes and the Yugoslavs. With all these nations the Italian people want to live in a firm and friendly harmony, defending their free existence against blood-sucking pan-Germanism . . .
>
> The Italian government and parliament have recently repeatedly proclaimed as a war aim the liberation of oppressed nationalities. Therefore the Italian nation is the ally of your country and you should not fight against it!

By concluding that the Allies had recognized the Czechoslovak National Council as the official representative of an independent Czechoslovak state, this propaganda was fast outpacing the reality of official Italian policy.[174] But the Italian Intelligence officers had few scruples on this score, and occasionally this even applied to the very sensitive issue of establishing a Yugoslav state. Already in January 1918 one leaflet, which appears to have originated in Finzi's office, specifically asked Slovene soldiers whether they knew that all the Allies including Italy were fighting to create a 'Great Independent Yugoslav state'.[175]

One might imagine that these words stemmed from the pen of Ljudevit Pivko himself. As yet, however, they appear to have been an isolated example, just as in the spring the use of the nationality principle in general was not commonplace in the propaganda. Some of the Intelligence offices were beginning to adopt it, and were suggesting some radical techniques for the future. But the overriding theme of the material in these months remained one of despair. It particularly emphasized Austria-Hungary's hopeless link to Prussian militarism, while occasionally hinting that the Allies had some special concern for the welfare of the Monarchy's nationalities.

It was the progress made by the Czech cause in Italy which added some substance to this gradually novel direction in front propaganda. While some Intelligence officers were pioneers for the nationality principle, they could in the months after Caporetto find many more receptive ears in both military and political circles. Above all, their ideas were now complemented by the vigorous activity of the Czechs' official representative in Rome, František Hlaváček. Hlaváček played perhaps a crucial role in these months by establishing a network of influential military and political friends who would advocate the creation of a Czechoslovak legion on Italian soil. His publicity work made it much easier for Milan Štefánik when he arrived in Italy in late February to begin talks on this subject with the CS and the government. In the military sphere, Hlaváček already had useful contacts from his period working at the front, including Tullio Marchetti who in December 1917 had communicated his warm wishes 'for the complete success of the noble Czech cause'.[176]

In early January, through the influence of military Intelligence in Rome, Hlaváček was once again called to the war zone by the new CS in order specifically to help the Intelligence offices to organize 'trench propaganda' against the enemy. It was a tour with important repercussions. Hlaváček became aware for the first time of Finzi's work among the *Carzanci*, and urged its expansion. In turn he seems to have stimulated the interest of the other Intelligence officers in using Czech prisoners more effectively. It seems clear that the Intelligence heads of the 3rd and 7th armies, Smaniotto and Vecchiarelli, remained rather suspicious of establishing patrols; Ercole Smaniotto at first preferred to confine the Czechs to limited Intelligence tasks, while Vecchiarelli appears to have been a difficult character who was suspicious about Czech reliability.[177] But in the person of the head of 4th army Intelligence, Attilio Vigevano, Hlaváček gained a reliable ally on the Finzi–Marchetti model. Vigevano not only promised to employ his existing Czech propaganda scouts in more strictly military roles, but also began to petition Diaz and Badoglio to make some firm decisions which would accelerate the creation of a Czechoslovak legion.[178]

It was naturally the legion which Hlaváček viewed as the military priority. Although pleasantly surprised at Pivko's largely Czech unit and the Italian military's growing commitment to using Czechs in propaganda and Intelligence work, he could not officially sanction such behaviour on behalf of the National Council since it was completely outside the latter's control. For the moment it simply had to be cautiously welcomed as one step forward.[179] Hlaváček certainly envisaged the ultimate prize, which he might secure from his journey into the war zone, as CS agreement to an independent Czechoslovak army. As he had noted to a French politician before his departure, such a force would 'accelerate the agitation and definite destruction of Austria':

> It is not just a question of the immediate impact which they would have in combat, but more the immense moral impact which their appearance at the front would produce upon Czech soldiers and other oppressed nationalities in the Austrian army.[180]

In fact Hlaváček found the CS, notably General Diaz, still rather wary about making any open commitment to the nationality principle in the form of a legion. Instead therefore it was left to Finzi and Marchetti (and Vigevano) to exercise pressure on Abano on his behalf. Finzi did so in the form of two memoranda: the first (as mentioned earlier) requested official sanction for Slav propaganda patrols, while the second stated unequivocally that Italy should now recognize a Czechoslovak state, since it was 'necessary to create the moral issue which in the eyes of the [Czech] officers justifies and glorifies their own desertion'.[181]

Marchetti followed these petitions with a memorandum carefully drawn up in close consultation with Hlaváček and delivered to the CS in early February.[182] In it he argued persuasively for a Czechoslovak legion on Italian soil. He pointed first to the example set by the French, who on 19 December had formally established such an army on the Western Front (a move which the Czech émigrés certainly expected to snowball in Italy), since on a front directly opposite Austria-Hungary a similar force could have 'ruinous effects'. It was vital at this stage of the war that Italy turn to exploit the weak point – nationalism – in the enemy forces. Specifically, it could do so by supporting the Czechs, an 'intelligent, home-loving, energetic, courageous, disciplined and instinctively anti-German people', who had already demonstrated these qualities in numerous military ventures including the Carzano episode. By employing 15–20 000 Czech prisoners as 'volunteer-propagandists' at the front, the CS would significantly exacerbate the prevailing crisis of morale in the enemy forces, but also contribute external pressure to match what Marchetti portrayed as a prevailing domestic Czech struggle for independence. He ended by brushing aside Sonnino's qualms about international law and Austrian reprisals, and emphasized for Diaz the degree to which the prejudice of Italian officers towards the Czechs was fast disappearing.

By suggesting that Czech troops should be employed in the front line, Marchetti's memorandum contained certain hidden implications. In October 1917, the Italian Ministry of War had only conceded to Edvard Beneš that Czech and Slovak prisoners might be freed from the camps and formed into labour units in the rear of the front. Since in this situation they would technically remain prisoners, and the National Council would lack any official jurisdiction, Beneš had told Hlaváček to vacillate over the issue of forming labour units until the Czechs could be assured more control over their own affairs. Hlaváček duly adopted this stance, but he had a very difficult path to negotiate in his dealings with General Spingardi who supervised Italy's prisoners of war. On the one hand, he pestered Spingardi to concentrate all Czech and Slovak prisoners in the camp at Padula and allow himself and other National Council representatives to visit the prisoners and boost their morale. Spingardi, ever mindful of his own sphere of influence, certainly dragged his feet on these matters, but at times was perhaps quite realistic when, for example, he explained to Hlaváček the problems of separating 'Slovak elements' from Hungarian prisoners.[183] On the other hand, Hlaváček did not want the Italians to be so efficient in organizing Czech and Slovak prisoners that they would begin to dispatch labour units of these prisoners into the war zone.

Yet by the New Year this was clearly the wish of the CS who were, as yet, more concerned to utilize Czech prisoners to build secondary defence lines in case of a further Italian retreat, than to employ them in any psychological offensive against the Austrians. Thus on 10 February, after his promising tour of the war zone, Hlaváček was suddenly summoned by Spingardi who told him that the CS now demanded Czech labour units to build defensive lines. If the units were not immediately dispatched, Spingardi pompously argued, the National Council's agreement of October would be invalid and the thousand or so Czech prisoners would be sent off anyway but in ethnically mixed units. Faced with this ultimatum Hlaváček was bound to concede, his only solace being the assurance of some Italian friends (including Bissolati and the new head of military Intelligence, Odoardo Marchetti) that the labour units would not now be an end in themselves, but a step towards a Czechoslovak legion. Hlaváček duly sent instructions to the Padula camp. At the same time he finally persuaded Beneš to send Milan Štefánik to Italy to take control and steer the Czech cause through this critical period.[184]

It was to be Štefánik who from February to April laboriously negotiated with Orlando, Sonnino and the CS to establish a Czechoslovak legion on Italian soil: 'the greatest success of his political activity', as Beneš observes in his memoirs.[185] Yet of the Czechs it was Hlaváček, bitterly irritated by Štefánik's own independent style when he arrived in Italy, who had prepared the propitious environment. In the Italian army Hlaváček had played his part in stimulating interest in the Czech cause, and by March was not only organizing labour units at the Padula camp but also choosing suitable volunteers for Intelligence work in the 2nd (soon to be 8th) and 3rd armies. Meanwhile, the memorandum which he had helped Tullio Marchetti to compose had been widely circulated among leading military and political figures including Orlando himself.

Indeed, from the autumn and particularly after Caporetto, Hlaváček's broader propaganda assignment had been energetically to target key individuals among Italy's political and journalistic elite, successfully convincing substantial sections of them that the nationality principle, embodied in the reliable Czech cause, was a straw for Italy to grasp in the shadow of defeat.[186] If he could naturally rely on those like Bissolati, Salvemini and Albertini, the number of new converts to the cause mounted steadily with the creation in December of the Fascio della Difesa Nazionale, a broad grouping of politicians and publicists committed to Italian victory. By the end of the year most of the Italian Senate were in favour of a Czechoslovak army, their vote on this issue only being deferred due to Sonnino's intervention. But it was precisely at this point that the *Corriere* group around Albertini reinforced Hlaváček's efforts. Their own number was significantly strengthened in the person of Giovanni Amendola, the paper's Rome correspondent, who for some months had been persistently cultivated by Hlaváček to the extent that in late December he pressed Albertini to launch a campaign for a Czechoslovak legion in the columns of the *Corriere*.[187] While this began in January, the *Corriere* group ensured that the Czech issue gained extra publicity by placing it on the agenda of two major gatherings in Milan: at a meeting on the 19th of Lombard deputies (whom Hlaváček addressed) and, more importantly, at a Fascio congress attended by 150 politicians at the Scala in early February when the Czechoslovak cause was publicly supported.

The message from these gatherings in favour of the nationality principle placed renewed pressure on Orlando who was already swinging in the same direction. The Prime Minister had been won over to 'nationality politics' after visiting London in late January (in the wake of worrying speeches by Lloyd George and Woodrow Wilson which both seemed to query whether the Treaty of London would ever be implemented). By 8 March, when he visited the war zone, Orlando had decided to establish a legion, convinced all the more through talking at the CS to Tullio Marchetti and the other Intelligence officers.[188] Thus Milan Štefánik had influential backers among the military and the cabinet. The arguments which he used, many of which were supplied by Hlaváček, were finally enough to win over Diaz, who had been a major sceptic, while Orlando himself seems to have persuaded an obstinate Sonnino.[189] Perhaps, as Hlaváček suggests in his memoirs, it was simply Štefánik's own arrogance or impetuosity when dealing with the Italians which prevented a speedier conclusion of the negotiations.[190] But if the agreement between Orlando and the National Council was only signed on 21 April, this had not delayed the increasing dispatch of Czech volunteers from the camps into the war zone. The CS, besides demanding labour units, had also, as we have seen, decided by late March to establish Slav units for propaganda and Intelligence work in every Italian army. On 27 March, Hlaváček once again visited the *Carzanci* and gave them the good news that 500 Czech volunteers were on their way to the war zone to join each of the armies. They would perform similar work to the *Carzanci*, but also form part of a forthcoming Czechoslovak army.[191]

The Italian press, notably *Corriere della Sera*, *Secolo* and Benito Mussolini's *Popolo d'Italia*, had played a leading role in the creation of the Czechoslovak Legion.[192] At the same time in the spring, the *Corriere* in particular had appealed repeatedly for Italy to coordinate and launch a fully effective propaganda campaign against Austria-Hungary at the front. For the *Corriere* group around Luigi Albertini, such an appeal derived logically from what many of them envisaged as the main purpose of nationality politics, to stir up unrest in the enemy camp. However, the articles published in the *Corriere* show that one of Albertini's major concerns was that Italy should provide efficient counter-propaganda to challenge Austria's own 'effective' campaign. In early February, the newspaper turned its attention to the latter and pressed the CS to wield the propaganda weapon more intensively in a 'victorious counter-offensive' which might include using Austrian parliamentary speeches in order to inform enemy soldiers about the realities of life in the Monarchy.[193] A few weeks later, the paper emphasized that the Austrians had already employed propaganda to good effect against Russia and Serbia, and Italy must now follow the same course, agitating with new nationalist arguments at the front so that eventually the propaganda would seep back and poison the Austro-Hungarian interior as well.[194] Here, in Albertini's argument, there was an interesting parallel with the contemporary thinking of Austrian propagandists who in their campaigns against Russia and Italy had always envisaged that agitation at the front would slowly penetrate to the rear and provoke revolution.

A final spur to Albertini's pleas in the *Corriere* for an efficient Italian campaign came from Great Britain. As we will see, it was in London under the influence of the foreign editor of *The Times*, Henry Wickham Steed, that a vital element in Italy's *politica delle nazionalità* was being forged: agreement with the Yugoslavs. It was undoubtedly from his contact with Steed that Guglielmo Emanuel, the *Corriere* correspondent in London, wrote to Albertini on 10 February urging him to use his authority to have a propaganda organization created at the CS. It should consist of a large group of experts who would lauch a uniform, unceasing and massive 'moral bombardment' of the Austrian trenches with Yugoslav and other manifestos. When on 13 February the British established a propaganda centre of their own under the newspaper tycoon Lord Northcliffe, Emanuel repeated his request to Albertini with a suggestion that his boss might place himself at the head of a similar body, as the 'Italian Northcliffe'.[195] Albertini did not pursue the idea, but in the *Corriere*'s columns he could present the new British organization as extra evidence of the importance of front propaganda, something over which the Central Powers had formerly had a monopoly. Italy could not now afford to renounce a weapon which in its hands, with its arguments, could be so effective. Italy must follow the Austrian and British examples, establish its own 'propaganda organism' and place it in the hands of 'capable people', aided by representatives of the Austrian oppressed nationalities.[196]

It would be wrong to suggest that the *Corriere*, in advancing such arguments, was a lone voice in Italian official circles. Many in the war zone, for example journalists such as Rino Alessi of *Secolo* who were clustered around the press office in Padua, felt that the Italian trenches were being daily flooded with enemy manifestos and warned that Italy should organize counter-propaganda, perhaps in the shape of a special committee which would compose appeals to the Slavs of the Monarchy.[197] These ideas were also, of course, familiar to Italian Intelligence officers whose own efforts were hardly as archaic as the Italian press implied. For example, in late January Finzi had ended one memorandum to the CS (advocating a Czechoslovak state) with the suggestion that a 'permanent committee for agitation in enemy countries' should be set up at the Supreme War Council.[198] By mid-February there was talk at the CS that an 'office for enemy propaganda and Intelligence' would be set up at Abano under Ercole Smaniotto, the head of 3rd army Intelligence.[199] But real progress on the *Corriere*'s lines came from outside the war zone and owed much to Albertini's personal influence with Orlando and the close contacts of both men with the new CS of Diaz and Badoglio. If Orlando was one of the most recent converts to nationality politics and its benefits, he had shown much earlier that he valued the use of propaganda and the control of information. One of his first moves on becoming Prime Minister after Caporetto had been to appoint as Under-Secretary for propaganda and the press, Romeo Gallenga Stuart, a politician whose national-liberal outlook matched that of Amendola or Borgese and who now became a key link between Albertini and the Prime Minister.[200]

On 8 March at the CS, Albertini and Orlando met a mutual friend, the art-critic and former *Corriere* journalist, Ugo Ojetti. Ojetti had been responsible during the Caporetto retreat for moving Italian art treasures from Venetia and the war zone back into the hinterland. But more importantly, he had been employed for many years as a writer in the CS press office and was an adherent of nationality politics: he was the kind of trusted and 'capable person' whom Albertini sought.[201] Already on 23 February, immediately in the wake of Northcliffe's appointment, Albertini had written to tell Ojetti that Orlando approved the idea of Ojetti heading an Italian propaganda office at the front. Ojetti in reply told Albertini of Smaniotto's prospective appointment, but hinted that 'if one should command me to remain here and *control* propaganda here I will obey'.[202] Otherwise, Ojetti was keen to leave the regimented atmosphere of Abano (he had hoped to use his writing talents more freely in a posting to the 6th army) and, evidently hearing nothing from Albertini, he accepted on 2 March Smaniotto's offer that he become head of air Intelligence for the 3rd army. At the meeting in Abano a week later Orlando finally asked Ojetti if he would organize what was described as 'playing the big card', propaganda against the enemy.[203] Ojetti at first declined, giving as his reasons the enormity of the task and the certain opposition of the CS; presumably, he did not feel that Diaz would sanction such civilian interference in the military sphere. Orlando, however, was able to assure him that any objections at Abano could be overcome, and that the post would carry a degree of responsibility and freedom commensurate with Ojetti's wishes. Ojetti spent the next fortnight in expectation that Orlando would officially request his appointment from Diaz: the delay was in fact due to the very resistance which Ojetti had suspected.[204]

In the meantime, on 19 March at Mogliano (3rd army headquarters), Smaniotto himself entrusted Ojetti with the task of organizing propaganda against the enemy from the Lower Piave front. The move appears to have been Smaniotto's response to a general CS order of 9 March – during Orlando's visit – that leaflet propaganda should be intensified. It is also probably evidence that 3rd army Intelligence had not been as diligent as the lst (Finzi) when it came to propaganda, something of which Ojetti was soon aware.[205] He readily accepted the post, feeling in particular that if he had to assume the larger role proposed by Orlando it would be a useful apprenticeship. He found in any case the job of writing manifestos very appealing and immediately set to work, reading enemy proclamations, prisoners' statements and extracts from the press, visiting Venice to find the necessary printing types for the languages of the Monarchy, and even requesting his wife to set aside the *Baedeker* on Austria-Hungary.[206] His work was saluted by Gaetano Salvemini who enthused about the need now for a proper enemy propaganda office whose staff, including Slav representatives, would write and issue a 'daily shower of manifestos': 'I feel that in this way we could obtain substantial results.'[207] Others felt the same. As Ojetti had hoped, his appointment at the 3rd army was short-lived. On 21 March Orlando asked Diaz to place Ojetti directly at his (Orlando's) disposal since, he argued, the new propaganda post would not have an expressly military character. The next day the CS received an official telegram from Orlando 'requesting' that Ojetti be appointed 'Royal Commissioner for propaganda to the enemy'.[208]

The fact that Italy's propaganda campaign was being coordinated in this way shows the relationship of Orlando's government to Diaz's Comando Supremo, a degree of political influence unthinkable under General Cadorna. Ugo Ojetti's appointment was made politically, and the campaign was thus signalled from the start as a joint political–military effort, an expression indeed of the Italian *union sacrée* which had emerged so quickly after Caporetto. Italy's propaganda campaign in 1918 therefore differed noticeably in character from the campaigns of Austria-Hungary in 1917–18. They remained strictly in military hands, although acquiring some guidelines from the Foreign Ministry in Vienna, and they failed to draw on any degree of political or public consensus from the interior of the Monarchy. While Austria's campaign on the Italian Front was a logical extension of success with psychological warfare in the East, Italy's campaign had more diverse roots.

Prior to Caporetto there had been a number of influential figures in Italian political and military circles who were working separately to undermine Austria-Hungary by exploiting nationalist unrest. The politicians and journalists who clustered around Bissolati, Salvemini and Albertini embraced nationality politics as a way to pursue Italy's historic nationalist mission (and acquire postwar influence for Italy) while at the same time destroying Italy's historic enemy. In turn, enlightened individuals in military Intelligence such as Tullio Marchetti and Cesare Finzi were from 1916 increasingly dabbling in nationality politics for its strictly military rewards; they observed the reality of the opposing forces and became pioneers in propaganda techniques, with episodes such as Carzano spurring them on to new experiments. Between them and the political-publicist circles there flitted representatives in particular of the Czech émigrés who by late 1917, through the leverage of their potential military contribution, were helping to draw the two strands together. Caporetto then did more than anything else to strengthen and unite these advocates of the nationality principle. The fact that they began to focus much of their attention upon a campaign of front propaganda against the enemy was a natural and immediate way in which to put the principle into practice. Indeed, for many Italians, including Orlando, it was a major reason for adopting the principle. Yet the moves to pull together the threads of Italy's front propaganda were perhaps above all a response to Austria-Hungary's own propaganda campaign in the spring. The *Corriere della Sera* had signalled this (with some exaggeration) as a 'moral offensive' which was 'in full swing, becoming ever more active, succeeding more and more, and constantly employing new methods'.[209]

The evidence suggests that the new CS still remained slow to respond in these months and was not as enlightened as some historiography has suggested. But by March combined political and military pressure persuaded Diaz to order an increase both in manifesto distribution and in Slav propaganda patrols. By late March Ojetti's precise role in front propaganda still remained undefined and he proceeded to sulk in Rome, waiting for instructions from Orlando.[210] The very nature of his appointment was clearly likely to arouse some friction in conducting propaganda in the front line in view of the Intelligence officers' independent experience in the field. Equally, Ojetti sensed a challenge from British 'experts' since Britain seemed already to be taking a lead in coordinating an Allied propaganda offensive against the Habsburg Empire.

## Notes

1. G.A. Borgese, *Goliath: the March of Fascism* (London, 1938) p. 133.
2. Luigi Albertini, *Venti Anni di Vita Politica. Parte Seconda: L'Italia nella Guerra Mondiale*, 3 vols (Bologna, 1953) III, p. 235.
3. Gaetano Salvemini, *Carteggio 1914–1920*, ed. Enzo Tagliacozzo (Rome and Bari, 1984) p. 304: Salvemini to Ugo Ojetti, 24 April 1917.
4. Dragovan Šepić, *Italija, Saveznici i Jugoslavensko Pitanje 1914–1918* (Zagreb, 1970) pp. 63ff, 177; Leo Valiani, *The End of Austria-Hungary* (London, 1973) pp. 95ff, 143ff.
5. Milada Paulová, *Jugoslavenski Odbor* (Zagreb, 1925) pp. 34–40, 72–3.
6. The following is based largely on Bogumil Hrabak, *Jugosloveni Zarobljenci u Italiji i njihovo Dobrovoljačko Pitanje 1915–1918* (Novi Sad, 1980), chapters 2–6; and Nikola Popović (ed.), *Jugoslovenski Dobrovoljci 1914/1918. Zbornik Dokumenata* (Belgrade, 1980) no. 218, pp. 341–5: summary of the volunteer question by the Serbian foreign ministry, 10 March 1918.
7. For this development, see Ivo Banac, 'South Slav Prisoners of War in Revolutionary Russia', in S.R. Williamson and P. Pastor (eds), *Essays on World War I: Origins and Prisoners of War* (New York, 1983) pp. 119–48.
8. Popović, *Jugoslovenski Dobrovoljci*, pp. 346–7.
9. Edvard Beneš, *Světová Válka a naše Revoluce. Vzpomínky a Úvahy z Bojů za Svobodu Národa*, 3 vols (Prague, 1927) I, p. 263. (The French, and especially the English, translations are abridged and also contain inaccuracies.)
10. Nicola Brancaccio, *In Francia durante la Guerra* (Milan, 1926) p. 24.
11. Vojtěch Hanzal, *S Výzvědčíky od Švýcarských Ledovců až po Moře Adriatické* (Prague, 1938) pp. 27–8.
12. Beneš, *Světová Válka*, I, p. 253.
13. Therefore, some prisoners resorted to ingenious methods to smuggle letters out. František Hlaváček, from the camp at Polle, hid a letter for his wife's cousin, Oskar Brázda, in a consignment of eggs: see Hlaváček, 'Činnost dra Ed. Beneše za Války v Italii a moje Spolupráce s ním', *Naše Revoluce* XII (Prague, 1936) p. 15.
14. See Beneš, *Světová Válka*, I, pp. 262–76.
15. Vojenský Historický Archív, Prague [Archive of Military History, hereafter VHA], Sychrava MSS, Krabice 2, Sychrava diary, entry for 5 February 1917.
16. Hanzal, *S Výzvědčíky*, pp. 45ff.
17. Salvemini, *Carteggio 1914–1920*, p. 283.
18. Luciano Tosi, *La Propaganda Italiana all'Estero nella Prima Guerra Mondiale* (Udine, 1977) p. 123. Cf. Valiani's discussion of Albertini's motives (*The End of Austria-Hungary*, pp. 221–4 and p. 417 note 93): Albertini later wrote that he had been strongly influenced by Cadorna who opposed Italian possession of Dalmatia.
19. See Šepić's discussion: *Italija, Saveznici*, pp. 216–17.

20. See the excellent discussion of his activities in Luciano Tosi, 'Giuseppe Antonio Borgese e la Prima Guerra Mondiale (1914–1918)', *Storia Contemporanea*, IV/2 (June 1973) pp. 263ff.
21. See Hlaváček, 'Činnost dra Ed. Beneše', p. 32 note 22: Milada Paulová in the 1920s (*Jugoslavenski Odbor*, p. 406) was unable to discover the person who ordered this mission, but Borgese himself later told Hlaváček that Garruccio was the real initiator. Valiani's account (*The End of Austria-Hungary*, p. 224) appears confused since Gallenga Stuart at this time had not been appointed Under-secretary for Propaganda.
22. Borgese, *Goliath*, p. 135.
23. HHStA, PA I/771 (Generalia XII), Musulin to Czernin, Nr 125/P–F, 10 August 1917. On the basis of this agent's information, Musulin (the Austrian minister in Berne) asked Czernin whether a trustworthy Croat politician could be sent to meet Borgese when he returned again to Switzerland, so as to convince him that Austria-Hungary's South Slavs wanted unity only within the framework of the Monarchy. While this agent appears to have been reliable, another – codenamed 'M' and clearly a Serbian – was not: he reported that Luigi Albertini had accompanied Borgese (see KA, EvB 1917, Fasz.5699/14976).
24. See the undated report on these talks by the head of the Serbian press bureau, Božidar Marković: Arhiv Hrvatske, Zagreb [hereafter AHZ], Julije Gazzari MSS (798/8), 'Referat o konferencijama s Italijanima Profesorom Borgese i Markizom Paterno'. The Italians had been instructed by the CS to find out particularly the views of Gazzari, a member of the Yugoslav Committee in Switzerland; as Borgese discovered, there was a certain difference in the priorities of the Serbians and the 'Yugoslavs'.
25. The report, 'La Questione Adriatica', was later published in G. Amendola, G.A. Borgese, U. Ojetti, A. Torre, *Il Patto di Roma* (Rome, 1919). See Tosi, 'Giuseppe Antonio Borgese', pp. 283–6 for an analysis.
26. Borgese, *Goliath*, pp. 132, 136; Paulová, *Jugoslavenski Odbor*, p. 408.
27. Tosi, 'Giuseppe Antonio Borgese', p. 286.
28. Hlaváček, 'Činnost dra Ed. Beneše', pp. 29–30.
29. Brancaccio, *In Francia durante la Guerra*, pp. 111–12: here he was referring to Italy receiving coal supplies from Bohemia after the war.
30. Valiani, *The End of Austria-Hungary*, p. 173. See Beneš's own account: *Světová Válka*, I, pp. 380ff.
31. Beneš, *Světová Válka*, I, pp. 382, 394.
32. See the arguments presented by Beneš: VHA, Fond ČSNR, Čs. Vojsko v Italii, 'Dossier sur la question tchécoslovaque' [October 1917].
33. Hlaváček, 'Činnost dra Ed. Beneše', pp. 39–40.
34. Ibid., p. 42.
35. Hugh and Christopher Seton-Watson, *The Making of a New Europe: R.W. Seton-Watson and the Last Years of Austria-Hungary* (London, 1981) p. 238.
36. Tullio Marchetti, *Ventotto Anni nel Servizio Informazioni Militari* (Trento, 1960) p. 170.
37. Odoardo Marchetti, *Il Servizio Informazioni dell'Esercito Italiano nella Grande Guerra* (Rome, 1937) p. 205.
38. See the extensive discussion in Marchetti, *Ventotto Anni*, chapters 10–12.
39. See Tullio Marchetti, *Luci nel Buio. Trentino Sconosciuto 1872–1915* (Trento, 1934).
40. Marchetti, *Ventotto Anni*, pp. 69–76.
41. Ibid., p. 208. The CS Berne office, besides propagating Italian views in the Swiss-German press, sent information to a special counter-espionage centre at Milan (later known as Sezione M) which relayed it to Udine.

42. Ibid., pp. 116, 120–5.
43. Ibid., pp. 133–5.
44. Ibid., pp. 125–31. Ljudevit Pivko, when at one of the 1st army Intelligence offices, heard how an agent from Franzensfeste took his reports to a chemist in Innsbruck who then concealed them in cough sweets and 'exported' them to Zurich: Pivko, *Zeleni Odred* (Maribor, 1925) pp. 78–9.
45. PRO, WO 106/1550, Report on the Intelligence Service in Italy by [Brigadier-General] C.H. Mitchell, 30 April 1919, pp. 108–9.
46. Marchetti, *Ventotto Anni*, pp. 144–6.
47. Ljudevit Pivko, *Naši Dobrovoljci u Italiji* (Maribor, 1924) p. 18.
48. Cesare Pettorelli Lalatta [Finzi], *'I.T.O.' Note di un Capo del Servizio Informazioni d'Armata (1915–1918)* (Milan, 1934) p. 66.
49. Ibid., pp. 47, 67–8.
50. Of these three Czech pioneers, two – Ryant and Doležel – had deserted in June 1915 (Jan Ryant having been entrusted by Austrian military Intelligence with sabotaging an electricity centre in Valcamonica); the third, Novy, deserted in March 1916. At Procolo, Finzi entrusted overall supervision to Francesco Baradello, an officer whom he discovered at the front and who knew most languages of the Habsburg Empire.
51. PRO, WO 106/1550, report by C.H. Mitchell, 30 April 1919, pp. 27–8.
52. Finzi, *'I.T.O.'*, pp. 128–9, 144. However, it was a sign of Italian uncertainty about even these 'reliable' Czech agents that they were themselves watched secretly by trustworthy Italians in order to ensure maximum security (p. 130).
53. Hanzal, *S Výzvědčíky*, pp. 70–2. Hanzal's work is a valuable summary of the research carried out between the wars on the subject of the Czech movement on the Italian Front.
54. For the following see: Hanzal, *S Výzvědčíky*, pp. 72–84; and Hlaváček, 'Činnost dra Ed. Beneše', pp. 12–13, 16–18, 31.
55. KA, 11AK Gstbs Abt 1918, Fasz.442, Na Nr 1725, 10AK to 11AK, Op. Nr 8167/6 Feind, 2 October 1918: statement of a (recaptured) Slovak, Martin Badinka.
56. See the leaflet collection of the Országos Hadtörténeti Múzeum, Budapest [Museum of Military History – hereafter OHM]. Leaflets in Hungarian, German and Italian: 'Magyarország és Ausztria katonáihoz!' (OHM, sz.1476/2, 1576, 1549), which largely described the Entente advances on all fronts (including the Russian capture of Trebisond on 17 April 1916). At this time, Italian soldiers on the Isonzo were also throwing over hand-written letters which reported events of the war and urged the Austrians to desert: see KA, AOK Na.Abt 1917, Karton 3601, Na Nr 3463.
57. Odoardo Marchetti, *Il Servizio Informazioni*, p. 93.
58. Tullio Marchetti, *Ventotto Anni*, p. 210. For leaflets on these themes, see OHM, sz.79.72.1: 'Az osztrák parancsrokság nem szól nektek a saját balsorsáról' [July 1916]; and KA, EvB 1917, Fasz.5696/4255: leaflet in Croat, 'Talijani tieraju . . . ', dated 24 June 1916 (and discovered on a soldier in hospital the following January).
59. See leaflet in Slovene in VHA, Fond Czechoslovak National Council [ČSNR]-Paříž, 'Italian propaganda leaflets from the Italian Front 1915–1918': 'Vojakom Avstrijskega Cesarstva in Ogrskega Kraljestva!' And for a positive Slovene reaction to this leaflet: Franc Grafenauer, 'Od Gorice do Soluna', in Ernest Turk, Josip Jeras and Rajko Paulin (eds), *Dobrovoljci Kladivarji Jugoslavije 1912–1918* (Ljubljana, 1936) p. 683.
60. Leaflet [seven languages], 'Vojíni rakousko-uherské armady!' (in KA, AOK Na.Abt 1917, Na Nr 4745).

61. Ibid.: leaflets [both multilingual], 'Soldati dell Impero d'Austria e del Regno d'Ungheria!' and 'Soldaten der österreichisch-ungarischen Armee!' The latter countered the Austrian charge that US entry into the war was simply a 'colossal speculation' by American capitalists. The former is also in the aerial leaflet collection of IWM, 3(45), File 44.
62. HIL, Propaganda Anyag, Fasz.4516, BI 4/20, leaflet [in four languages], 'Soldaten des österreichischungarischen Heeres!' [inscribed, 13 February 1917].
63. The bulk of Italy's propaganda continued to be very simple, telling, for example, of Anglo-French booty in the Nivelle offensive: leaflet [in six languages], 'Za vrieme zadnje ofenzive zarobile su siedinjene francuzko-englezke vojske' (in KA, AOK Na.Abt 1917, Fasz.5699/13390).
64. See VHA, Fond ČSNR-Paříž, leaflet [dated 1915 with a note that it is the 'first Czechoslovak revolutionary leaflet'], 'Čeští vojíni! Synové českých matek!'
65. VHA, Fond ČSNR-Štefánik, Karton 1, 34/2/1, Brancaccio to Štefánik, 9 January 1916.
66. KA, EvB 1917, Fasz.5696/6318, AOK Na.Abt to KÜA, 17 April 1917. This lengthy report about Štefánik mentions his propaganda flight in 1916 and the fact that the manifesto had been found repeatedly on the Italian Front.
67. Josef Dürich, a Czech Agrarian politician, was a Czech émigré particularly active in Russia who later fell out with Masaryk.
68. Leaflet, 'Slované! Čechové!' (KA, EvB 1918, Fasz.5759/28207); also reproduced in Hanzal, *S Vývědčíky*, pp. 25–6.
69. Ibid., p. 27.
70. Brancaccio, *In Francia durante la Guerra*, pp. 24, 32. Whether these manifestos reached their destination is unclear, but one example seems to be the leaflet, 'Češi, Slované! Drazí bratři!', signed by Beneš and Štefánik, which especially stressed that Karel Kramář had been condemned to death (KA, EvB 1918, Fasz.5759/28207).
71. Marchetti, *Ventotto Anni*, p. 211.
72. Finzi, *'I.T.O.'*, pp. 116–19, 140.
73. For examples of such leaflets: OHM, sz.7923, 'Soldaţi Români!' [five languages, different texts]; KA, EvB 1917, Fasz.5699/15709, 'Hrvatski vojnici! Vaši častinici lažu...' [five languages, different texts]; OHM, sz.3379, 'Soldaten des österreichisch-ungarischen Armee!' [seven languages, same text with pictures of prisoners in Italy].
74. KA, EvB 1917, Fasz.5699/12516, 'Čeští důstojníci a vojíni!' [dated June 1917]; Ljudevit Pivko, *Jablane med Frontama* (Maribor, 1924) p. 8.
75. Leaflet of Štefánik type [issued in Czech and Croat]: 'Proglas. Slavjani!' (KA, AOK Op. Abt 1917, AOK Op. Nr 44522; copies also in KA, EvB 1918, Fasz. 5759/28207, and IWM, 3(45) Italian leaflets, File 42). Masaryk, Štefánik, Beneš leaflet: 'Čechové! Slováci! Draží bratří!' (KA, EvB 1917, Fasz.5699/16935).
76. VHA, Fond ČSNR-Řím (Hlaváček), 36/9/4, undated memorandum [mid-1917]: 'Hlaváčkův návrh na proklamace k rak.uher. vojákům'. See also Hanzal, *S Výzvědčíky*, pp. 82–3.
77. Leaflet [in five languages]: 'Hrvatski vojnici!' telling of Russia's readiness to free all Slav peoples (HIL, 'Propaganda Anyag', Fasz. 5018); and the leaflets already cited in KA, EvB 1917, Fasz.5699/12516 and 16935.
78. Luciano Tosi, *La Propaganda Italiana*, pp. 126–7.
79. Marchetti, *Ventotto Anni*, p. 243.
80. The title of Finzi's account, *Il Sogno di Carzano* (Bologna, 1926).
81. Pivko, *Jablane med Frontama*, pp. 6–8.

82. Cf. Ronge, *Kriegs- und Industriespionage*, p. 310. The Austrian official history similarly dismisses the incident in a paragraph: OULK, VI, pp. 509–10.
83. Ljudevit Pivko, *Seme* (Maribor, 1924) p. 6.
84. KA, EvB 1917, Fasz.5700, Nr 19230: documents concerning the police investigation in Maribor (October 1917).
85. The eight volumes have recently been republished together in independent Slovenia: see Ljudevit Pivko, *Proti Avstriji 1914–1918* (Maribor, 1991).
86. Pivko, *Seme*, pp. 20ff, 58–60, 65.
87. Ibid., p. 21.
88. Ibid., pp. 76–107.
89. Ibid., pp. 110–28.
90. Finzi, *Il Sogno di Carzano*, pp. 12ff. Finzi's account makes no mention of Pivko's precise letter about Slav grievances, nor about meeting Mlejnek (who told Pivko that Finzi had tried to bribe him in Vicenza).
91. Ibid., pp. 21–6; Pivko, *Jablane med Frontama*, pp. 37–43.
92. Ibid., pp. 52–8; Finzi, *Il Sogno di Carzano*, pp. 36–8.
93. Later, before the 11AK court on 15 October, Maštálka would feign total ignorance of the plot, pleading in particular that Pivko and his Czech officers had usually spoken in German which he could not understand: see KA, EvB 1917, Fasz. 5700, Nr 17701/I, 'Protokoll über die Aussage des Fhr. Georg Maštálka'.
94. Pivko, *Jablane med Frontama*, pp. 81–3, 110–11.
95. Ibid., pp. 74, 107–8.
96. Pivko, *Naši Dobrovoljci u Italiji* (Maribor, 1924) p. 20.
97. Finzi, '*I.T.O.*', p. 158.
98. Pivko, *Jablane med Frontama*, pp. 118–20; Finzi, *Il Sogno di Carzano*, pp. 65–9. Pivko dates this tour to the night of 10 September, while Finzi gives 25 August.
99. Finzi, *Il Sogno di Carzano*, pp. 49, 70, 73–7, 90–6. Pivko's detailed plan is published in ibid., document 9, pp. 174–88, while for the final Italian plan, and Finzi's criticisms, see document 10, pp. 189–94.
100. Ibid., p. 85; Pivko, *Jablane med Frontama*, pp. 87, 115.
101. For example, when he tested the views of a Polish officer Hardy and faced a rebuff: ibid., pp. 99–100. This minor incident is worth recording as it was corroborated in the battalion commander's later report: see KA, EvB 1917, Fasz.5700, Nr 17701, report by Obstlt Emil Vidale, 26 September 1917.
102. Pivko, *Jablane med Frontama*, p. 88.
103. Pivko, *Vulkanska Tla* (Maribor, 1924) pp. 21–62.
104. KA, EvB 1917, Fasz.5700, Nr 17701, Vidale report, 26 September 1917.
105. The words of František Jirsa: *Vulkanska Tla*, p. 65.
106. Ibid., pp. 76–92; and for Finzi's viewpoint: *Il Sogno di Carzano*, p. 99.
107. For much of the following, see Pivko's account, *Carzanska Noč* (Maribor, 1924).
108. Ibid., pp. 20–1. Obstlt Vidale reiterated this point in his later report (KA, EvB 1917, Fasz.5700/17701) written after he had returned from leave in Vienna.
109. Pivko, *Carzanska Noč*, pp. 42–50, 64.
110. Finzi, *Il Sogno di Carzano*, pp. 80–2, 100. During the summer, about 80 'agents' (chiefly Italian, but also including some ex-Russian prisoners who had escaped from Austria) had been trained at the Procolo fortress in Verona for use in the Carzano attack. In August, Finzi had also used two Romanian deserters to contact former comrades in Val Posina, and appears to have had a Polish agent operating in Val Lagarina (p. 55).
111. Pivko, *Carzanska Noč*, pp. 56ff, 90–1.

112. Finzi, *Il Sogno di Carzano*, pp. 127–30.
113. Ibid., p. 10.
114. See 'Der Verrat von Carzano', *Österreichische Wehrzeitung*, Folge 43, 23 October 1925, p. 2. It reports a well-attended lecture in Vienna by a Major Josef Seifert, who had served among German-Austrian troops at Carzano.
115. Finzi, *Il Sogno di Carzano*, pp. 141–3; Finzi, *'I.T.O.'*, pp. 163–4; Marchetti, *Ventotto Anni*, p. 265.
116. Ljudevit Pivko, *Zeleni Odred* (Maribor, 1925) pp. 20–2.
117. Ibid, pp. 23–9; Pivko, *Naši Dobrovoljci u Italiji*, p. 34.
118. Pivko, *Zeleni Odred*, pp. 28–38; p. 94 for Pivko's continued uncertainty about his patron's motives. Pivko would later report to the Yugoslav Committee that he had been particularly influenced in October 1917 by the advance of the Czech cause in Italy, for all of his *Carzanci* officers were Czechs and he felt 'after a solution of the Czech question the turn of the Yugoslav question would come sooner or later': see Arhiv Jugoslavenske Akademije Znanosti i Umjetnosti, Zagreb [hereafter AJA], Yugoslav Committee Archive [JO], 60A/X/1, Pivko report of 21 August 1918.
119. Pivko, *Zeleni Odred*, pp. 39–40.
120. Ibid., pp. 41–60.
121. This is clear from KA, EvB 1918, Fasz.5746, Nr 9089, Beute no 38 'Austrian deserters' [captured Italian interrogation statements of deserters]; and Pivko, *Naši Dobrovoljci u Italiji*, pp. 52–64. Finzi too suggests a slight rebuff (*'I.T.O.'*, p. 165).
122. Pivko, *Zeleni Odred*, pp. 97–9, 104–8.
123. Ibid., pp. 68–9.
124. Ibid., p. 77. The Dolfin villa was similarly used during the Second World War, and still retains its forbidding atmosphere.
125. Ibid., p. 87.
126. Ibid., pp. 85ff; and for Pivko's attempt to contact Beneš: *Jablane med Frontama*, pp. 47–8, 58.
127. Pivko, *Zeleni Odred*, p. 100. Pivko was at first only allowed to recruit from deserters, but from 28 January from prisoners too (Hanzal, *S Výzvědčíky*, p. 237).
128. Pivko, *Zeleni Odred*, pp. 99–102.
129. Finzi, *'I.T.O.'*, pp. 176–9.
130. Marchetti, *Ventotto Anni*, p. 290.
131. Pivko, *Zeleni Odred*, pp. 109–10; Marchetti, *Ventotto Anni*, p. 311.
132. Ljudevit Pivko, *Informatorji* (Maribor, 1925) p. 59. The 26SchD propaganda work is recorded in KA, 11AK Gstbs Abt 1918, Fasz.449, Pr.2124 and 2135, but the 'favourable results' seem to consist chiefly of seeing Italians pick up the deposited leaflets.
133. On 16 March, two Italians deserted to the enemy near Sasso Rosso, claiming that they were war-weary and had relatives in occupied Venetia. They in fact told their captors that they had not read any Austrian propaganda, but said that such material was eagerly read by their comrades; the Austrians made them compose a letter which was then thrown over to the Italians. (KA, 11AK Gstbs Abt 1918, Fasz.442, Na Nr 476, Überläufungsaussagen, 20 March 1918).
134. Pivko, *Informatorji*, pp. 39–40. Kreuz's version of his own role is slightly suspect since he does not appear in the Austrian records as a member of the 26SchD *Nachrichtentruppen*; but his 'confession' to Nikolić still provided a valuable insight into Austria's use of propaganda, and Nikolić drew up reports for Italian Intelligence on this basis. Having pretended to be a deserter, Kreuz was finally executed at Sandrigo by a Czech legionary.

135. HIL, M.Kir.42 Honvéd Gyaloghadosztály [42HID records], Fasz.1661, Op. Nr 4404. For the known desertions (which included four Germans): Fasz.1661, Op. Nrs 4404, 4406; Fasz.1662, Op. Nrs 4413, 4414.
136. KA, 11AK Gstbs Abt 1918, Fasz.449, Pr.2120, 11AK Propaganda report for March 1918; Fasz.272, 4–6/1–2, 26SchD (GM Klein) to VI KK, Na Nr 269/2, 5 March 1918.
137. Pivko, *Zeleni Odred*, p. 118 and note; Finzi, '*I.T.O.*', pp. 212–13. For 26SchD reports on this propaganda: HIL, 42HID 1918, Fasz.1663, Op. Nrs 4505–10, 4513: Slovene and Polish songs were also heard.
138. KA, 11AK, Fasz.449, Pr.2163, 26SchD to VI KK, Na Nr 488, 8 April; Pr.2164, 26SchD to VI KK, Na 525, 16 April 1918: these reports list in detail the mass of material distributed and effectively suggest this as proof of 'success'.
139. Pivko, *Informatorji*, p. 59; for the SchR12's position: KA, 11AK 1918 Op. Akt., Fasz.269, 1–17/15–18/8 Op. Nr 2608/18, 26SchD to VI KK, Op. Nr 172/5, 21 June 1918.
140. Pivko, *Zeleni Odred*, pp. 119–20; Finzi, '*I.T.O.*', p. 213.
141. PRO, WO 106/852, Cavan to CIGS, 28 April 1918. Pivko also noted Montuori's enlightened knowledge of foreign peoples: 'a rare bird among Italian officers' (*Informatorji*, p. 7).
142. Finzi, '*I.T.O.*', p. 215.
143. KA, 11AK Gstbs Abt, Fasz.264, Op. Nr 1400/15, 26SchD [GM Klein] to VI KK, Na Nr 573 [monthly report], 24 April 1918.
144. See the article by Achille Benedetti, 'Gli Czechi–Slovacchi al fronte italiano' in *Giornale d'Italia*, 3 May 1918. Austrian Intelligence noticed it (KA, EvB 1918, Fasz.5752/16221), just as the KPQ had picked up an earlier article, on 9 April, by Benedetti in the same paper about Austrian propaganda efforts (KA, FAst 1918, Fasz.5994, Res.109).
145. Pivko, *Naši Dobrovoljci u Italiji*, p. 36; *Zeleni Odred*, p. 128; Hanzal, *S Výzvědčíky*, p. 240 (who also confirms a largely hostile Austrian reaction).
146. Pivko, *Zeleni Odred*, pp. 31, 96.
147. Luciano Tosi, *La Propaganda Italiana*, p. 185.
148. KA, 11AK Op. Abt 1918, Fasz.445, Na Nr 609, KISA Beilage 8: Report on propaganda activity for March 1918.
149. Leaflets: 'Fratelli italiani! Sappiamo che il nemico . . .' (KA, EvB 1918, Fasz. 5758/26661; other copies in OHM sz.82141–3), and 'Italiani! Non è più il saluto delle ore della fortuna' (KA, 6AK 1918, Fasz.15, Abwehr-Stelle, Aw.Nr 317).
150. Leaflets: 'Agli Italiani delle terre invase' (KA, 11AK, Fasz.451, File 'Unerledigt 1918 11AK Feindespropaganda'), and 'Fratelli, noi sappiamo quello che soffrite!' (KA, 6AK 1918, Fasz.15, Aw.Nr 617).
151. KA, 6AK 1918, Fasz.15, Aw.Nr 504, 6AK Abwehr-Stelle to subordinate commands, 5 March 1918, enclosing proclamation in German, Hungarian and Italian: 'An die Bevölkerung des besetzten Gebietes!'
152. Ibid., Aw.Nr 793, 20 March 1918.
153. See the vivid reports on the occupied areas sent to Count Czernin from his representative at HGK Boroević: HHStA, PA I/1050, Liasse 67. On 28 March, for example, Ippen reported on the mass seizure of bed-linen: 'I will only mention in passing the issue of how this will morally affect the native population. Our occupation [of Venetia] bears so heavily upon the population that we should not indulge in any illusion that we might gain sympathy here. Nevertheless, the mentioned requisitioning will simply cause us to be hated.'

154. Marchetti, *Ventotto Anni*, p. 208. See Chapter 8 (p. 361) for further examples of this propaganda in the Italian language.
155. Leaflets [each in six languages] detailing the gains in land, booty and prisoners: 'Vojini rakousko-uherske armady! Ve velké ofensíve...' (HIL, 'Propaganda Anyag', Fasz.4516, BI 4/20); 'Vojini rakousko-uherske armady! Vitestvi Itálu na Isonzu jest velkolépé' (OHM, sz.1480/2).
156. It is also clear that some material originated in governmental ministries. For example, Ubaldo Comandini, now responsible for domestic propaganda in Italy, also liaised with the CS in the spring to send manifestos for distribution over the lines. See Comandini's letter to František Hlaváček of 7 March, inviting the latter to help in this work: Archív Národního Muzea, Prague [hereafter ANM], František Hlaváček MSS, Karton II/i.
157. Leaflets: 'Oesterreicher! Wir können Eure Höfligkeit [*sic*] nicht brauchen' [six languages] (in OHM, sz.1481/2; version in German/Italian in OHM, sz.1548); 'Österreicher!!' (in KA, 11AK, Fasz.448, Pr.2043).
158. Leaflet [German/Slovene]: 'Soldaten! In Deutschland und noch mehr in Oesterreich...' (in OHM, sz.1562/1; KA, EvB, Fasz.5744/4538; copy in Czech/Italian in EvB, Fasz.5748/10657); 'Oesterrichische und Ungarische Soldaten!' (in KA, 11AK 1918, Fasz.452).
159. Leaflet [six languages]: 'Vojnici austro-ugarski! Nezasitni niemacki zahtievi...' (in KA, EvB 1918, Fasz.5748/10657, 5751/15384); leaflet [seven languages]: 'Soldati Austro Ungarici! Ecco il vostro errore!' (in KA, EvB, Fasz.5744/4538).
160. See, for example, the series of pictorial manifestos depicting Austrian subservience to Prussian militarism: 'Habt ihr noch nicht verstanden...?' (KA, EvB, Fasz.5753/18306), 'Österreich-Ungarische Soldaten!!' (HIL, Fasz.4515, BI-4) and 'Richt dich auf Bruder' (HIL, Fasz.4516, BI 4/51). Also: leaflet [six languages], 'Vojnici austro-ugarski! Branite se od germanstva' (in OHM, sz.1484); and leaflet [six languages]: 'Mi'r činiti jest jeden účet' (KA, 11AK, Fasz.451/I; HIL, Fasz.4515, BI-4).
161. 'Christen, Eine aus englischen, italienischen und französischen Kräften bestehende Armee...' [six languages] (HIL, Fasz.4515, BI-4).
162. Leaflet in German (which might stem from pre-1918): 'Die unzetrennbare Dreifaltigkeit macht das unzetrennbare Vaterland geltend' (HIL, Fasz.4516, BI 4/20).
163. 'Austrijski vojnici, želite vi mir?' [six languages]: numerous copies distributed in March 1918 (in OHM, sz.1459, 1478; KA, EvB, Fasz.5747/8782; KA, 11AK Gsts Abt, Fasz.449, Pr.2106).
164. Notably Henry Wickham Steed who quoted this leaflet. See British Library [BL], Northcliffe MSS, vol. XI, Add.Mss 62163, report by Steed on the British Mission for propaganda in Austria-Hungary, 30 April 1918.
165. KA, 11AK 1918, Fasz.444, Na Nr 595, Beilage 1: 10AK propaganda report for March. See also KISA's report for March (ibid., Fasz.445, Na Nr 609); and the 11AK report for February (Fasz.448, Pr.2075).
166. KA, 11AK 1918, Fasz.444, Na Nr 447, HGK FM von Boroević, February monthly report.
167. Three types of leaflet which used the sailors' signatures were produced [separate texts, in Croat, Polish, Czech but also German]: (1) 'Kamarádi! Jsme zdejšími poměry velmi mile překvapeni' – dated 25 February (KA, EvB, Fasz.5751/14707; OHM, sz.1446/1); (2) 'Soudruzi vojáci a namořníci!' – dated 1 March (KA, EvB, 5749/12437); (3) 'Polacy! Główny komitet marynarzy...' – dated 6 March (KA, EvB, 5749/12437). In April, a fourth leaflet signed by the sailors told of a failed Austrian

naval exploit (see 'Mornari!' in KA, EvB, 5751/15172). The sailors' actual miserable experience in Italy is recalled in Anton Sesan's account, published in Dragoslav Janković and Bogdan Krizman (eds), *Gradja o Stvaranju Jugoslavenske Države*, 2 vols (Belgrade, 1964) I, no. 149, pp. 198–201.

168. PRO, FO 371/3228, Rodd to Balfour, d.94, 14 March 1918. The messages were picked up by all armies on the Italian Front as well: for example, KA, HGK Conrad 1918, Fasz.66, Na Nr 400a/66.
169. Leaflet in Croat/Czech and in Slovene/Polish: 'Vojnici! Vaša vlada Vam pripovjeda puno stvari o nas Italijanih...' (KA, 11AK 1918, Fasz.451, 'Flugzettel III'), quoted in Finzi, '*I.T.O.*', pp. 193–4. A more simple comparison of rations was the subject of a multilingual leaflet: 'Austro-ugarski vojnici! Dnevni obrok...', dated 12 March (OHM, sz.1226).
170. Leaflet, 'Vojáci Československtí!' (KA, EvB 1918, Fasz.5744/4538). It paraphrased Zahradník's speech in the Reichsrat: *Stenographische Protokolle über die Sitzungen des Hauses der Abgeordneten des Österreichischen Reichsrates* (Vienna, 1918) XXII Session, vol. III, 58.Sitzung, 6 Feb.1918, pp. 3049–50. The same technique was used with a speech by the Polish deputy Głombinski: leaflet 'Żołnierze Polacy!' (OHM, sz.1456).
171. Leaflet, 'Magyarok! Evszázadok óta küzd...' (OHM, sz.1489; KA, EvB, Fasz.5748/10658): 'Long live the revolution of '48 and the memories of its glorious heroes!'
172. Leaflets: 'Magyar bakák!' (OHM, sz.1230/1); 'Magyarok! Az Egyesült Államok óriási...' (OHM, sz.7927); 'Magyar katonák! Németország világuralmi...' (KA, 6AK 1918, Fasz.15/1153); 'Magyar katonák! Az oroszok forradalmat csináltak...' (KA, EvB, Fasz.5748/10655).
173. Leaflet, 'Vojáci československé národnosti!', found on the mountain front in late March (KA, 11AK 1918, Fasz.448, Pr.2043).
174. Leaflet, 'Soudruzi vojáci národnosti československácke!', dated 6 March and signed by the 'Central Committee of Oppressed Nationalities in Rome' (KA, EvB 1918, Fasz.5758/26661).
175. Leaflet in Slovene, 'Slovenski Vojaki!', distributed by Italian planes on 26 January (KA, EvB 1918, Fasz.5744/4538).
176. ANM, Hlaváček MSS, Karton II/ii, Marchetti to Hlaváček, 2 December 1917. (Already in late September Marchetti had congratulated Hlaváček for his services in the war zone.)
177. For Smaniotto, see Hanzal, *S Výzvědčíky od Švýcarských Ledovců*, pp. 97–8. For one view of Vecchiarelli see: Marchetti, *Ventotto Anni*, p. 292, but also ANM, Hlaváček MSS, Karton II/ii, Vecchiarelli to Troiani, 13 February 1918.
178. ANM, Hlaváček MSS, Karton II/ii, Vigevano to Hlaváček, 3 February 1918.
179. See Hlaváček's report to Beneš of 26 January in ibid., Karton IV/c (also reproduced in Hlaváček, 'Činnost dra Ed. Beneše', pp. 65–9).
180. ANM, Hlaváček MSS, Karton II/i, Hlaváček to Franklin-Bouillon, 4 January 1918.
181. Finzi, '*I.T.O*', pp. 176–82.
182. The memorandum is reproduced in Beneš, *Světová Válka*, III, document 100, pp. 313–17; and in Hanzal, *S Výzvědčíky*, pp. 104–5.
183. ANM, Hlaváček MSS, Karton II/i, Spingardi to Hlaváček, N.49218, 14 December 1917; Spingardi here agreed to transfer to Padula from other camps 119 prisoners whom Hlaváček had listed for him.
184. Hlaváček, 'Činnost dra Ed. Beneše', pp. 275–80.
185. Beneš, *Světová Válka*, II, p. 55.

186. For the following, see the accounts in Milada Paulová, *Jugoslavenski Odbor* (Zagreb, 1925) pp. 413ff; Hlaváček, 'Činnost dra Ed. Beneše', pp. 55ff. The real breadth of Hlaváček's activity is evident in VHA, Fond ČSNR-Řím, Karton 5/3 and 5/4.
187. ANM, Hlaváček MSS, Karton IV/c, Hlaváček to Beneš, 30 December 1917.
188. Ugo Ojetti, *Lettere alla Moglie 1915–1919*, ed. Fernanda Ojetti (Florence, 1964) p. 498; Leonida Bissolati, *Diario di Guerra*, ed. G.Einaudi (Turin, 1935) p. 104.
189. On 8 March, Diaz was still opposed (Bissolati, *Diario*, p. 103), and he was felt by the Czechs to be a sceptic until late June 1918: see the notes by Lev Sychrava in VHA, Fond ČSNR-Štefánik, Karton 3/4, 35/5/3. Orlando told Olindo Malagodi on 20 March that he had gradually persuaded Sonnino to agree: Olindo Malagodi, *Conversazioni della Guerra 1914–1919*, ed. Bruno Vigezzi, 2 vols (Milan and Naples, 1960), II, p. 305.
190. For Hlaváček's embittered view of Štefánik's negotiations ('He wanted to appear like a meteor'), see Hlaváček, 'Činnost dra Ed. Beneše', pp. 282–90; see also Hanzal, *S Výzvědčíky*, pp. 111ff, who notes the dearth of written evidence about Štefánik's talks.
191. AHZ, Dobrovoljački Arhiv, II/2, Stane Vidmar to Ljudevit Pivko, 4 April 1918; Pivko, *Zeleni Odred*, pp. 121–2.
192. Luigi Albertini, *Venti Anni di Vita Politica*, III, pp. 247ff.
193. *Corriere della Sera*, 5 and 6 February 1918. On the 6th the paper was responding to a reader's letter which advocated using as front propaganda a speech by the Dalmatian politician Ante Tresić-Pavičić (on 19 October in the Austrian Reichsrat) which had condemned atrocities against the South Slav population. It is clear that the *Corriere* followed up this idea, and in April 1918 some copies of the speech (a 71-page booklet in Croat, Czech and German) were distributed by Italian propagandists in the front line. See booklet, 'Jugoslaveni', in HIL, Fasz.4515, BI-4; and Umberto Zanotti-Bianco, *Carteggio 1906–1918*, ed. V. Carinci (Rome and Bari, 1987) p. 604. See also below pp. 193, 294.
194. Albertini, *Venti Anni*, III, p. 249.
195. Luigi Albertini, *Epistolario 1911–1926*, ed. Ottavio Barie, 3 vols (Verona, 1968) II, pp. 894, 899.
196. 'Azioni necessarie ed esitazioni funeste', *Corriere della Sera*, 21 February; and 'E noi?', *Corriere della Sera*, 14 March 1918.
197. Rino Alessi, *Dall'Isonzo al Piave. Lettere Clandestine di un Corrispondente di Guerra*, ed. Arnoldo Mondadori (Milan, 1966) pp. 207–8, 213–14.
198. Finzi, '*I.T.O.*', p. 182.
199. Ojetti, *Lettere alla Moglie*, p. 476.
200. See Tosi, *La Propaganda Italiana*, pp. 152–4.
201. Ibid., p. 186; Ojetti, *Lettere*, pp. 419ff. As a writer Ojetti in February 1916 had been responsible for boosting Cadorna's low reputation in the press, while after Caporetto he had drafted for Orlando the royal proclamation issued to the Italian public.
202. Valiani, *The End of Austria-Hungary*, p. 434 note 236; Albertini, *Epistolario*, II, p. 903.
203. Ojetti, *Lettere*, pp. 491, 498–9. At this time, Ojetti also discussed propaganda at length with Giovanni Amendola and with the poet-adventurer (and later propagandist) Gabriele D'Annunzio.
204. Albertini, *Epistolario*, II, p. 913.
205. KA, AOK Feindespropaganda-Abwehrstelle [FAst] 1918, Fasz.5994, Res.89, AOK to FAst, Op. Nr 766/107, 10 May, 'II Richtlinien für die Propagandatätigkeit'.
206. Ojetti, *Lettere*, pp. 500–2.

207. Salvemini, *Carteggio 1914–1920*, pp. 369–70: Salvemini to Ojetti, 23 March 1918.
208. Ojetti, *Lettere*, p. 504; Tosi, *La Propaganda Italiana*, p. 234 note 109.
209. 'Prima che sia troppo tardi', *Corriere della Sera*, 21 March 1918.
210. Albertini, *Epistolario*, II, p. 924.

# 6
# Italy's Campaign against Austria-Hungary

## 6.1 The British contribution

The fully coordinated propaganda offensive which was launched on the Italian Front in April 1918 would always remain a largely Italian enterprise. Since the end of the First World War, most literature written about this 'Allied campaign' has tended to highlight Great Britain's supposedly predominant role, often suggesting that the British, through Lord Northcliffe's Enemy Propaganda Department at Crewe House, initiated or even controlled the campaign. Harold Lasswell in his seminal work asserted that 'it was the British who did most of the propaganda of dissolution against Austro-Hungarian armies'.[1] Such an emphasis is misleading but not surprising. Northcliffe's very public appointment was itself a propaganda coup since his name aroused alarm in the Central Powers to a degree which Luigi Albertini could never emulate, even if he had followed Northcliffe's example. Northcliffe's organization, moreover, was the most publicized of its kind and therefore became a clear focal point in 1918 for those in the Habsburg Empire who became paranoid about the machinations of 'enemy propaganda'.

As we have seen in Chapter 1, this reputation gained ground after the war when two members of Northcliffe's 'team', Sir Campbell Stuart and Henry Wickham Steed, published accounts which emphasized the role of Crewe House.[2] From Vienna the former AOK staff officer Edmund von Glaise-Horstenau, in reviewing Stuart's work, commented, 'we can no longer ignore the fact that besides [President Woodrow] Wilson, Northcliffe and his Austrian reporter Steed were the destroyers of the Danube Empire'.[3] In his later works Glaise adopted a more moderate tone, but he still accorded Northcliffe's initiative a definite weight when he mentioned the propaganda campaign on the Italian Front.[4] Subsequently, historians have usually used Crewe House as the starting-point for their discussions, most recently adding valuable substance to understanding the campaign from a British perspective.[5] Italian scholars have also pursued the Italian dimension, but to a surprisingly limited extent.[6] What has been lacking has been a full and balanced analysis of the most sophisticated wartime campaign of front propaganda, by pulling together the various strands – Italian, Austrian, British, etc. – of which it was composed. The British role seen in this overall context was essentially twofold. Firstly, it was to bring Italy and the Yugoslavs to some agreement which could be used as a partial basis for effective propaganda at the front; secondly, it provided, in the shape of Crewe House and its personnel, a centre which helped to coordinate the Italian campaign in April 1918 and subsequently gave some inspiration to the Italian propagandists.

Prior to the creation of the Enemy Propaganda Department (EPD) in February 1918 there had been little official British propaganda specifically directed at undermining the Habsburg Empire. Indeed, propaganda against the Central Powers as a whole had been on a small scale, organized by two separate centres which were both linked to British military Intelligence. In early 1916, possibly in response to an increase in German propaganda on the Western Front, a new section MI7(b) was set up at the War Office under the Director of Special Intelligence, General George Cockerill. Its purpose was to carry on a 'paper war' against Germany on the Western Front, and it continued to do so under Cockerill's supervision until the summer of 1918.[7] A separate initiative was taken by Austin Guest, an official who worked at Wellington House, the War Propaganda Bureau which had been established in September 1914 to counter Germany's 'propaganda' and educate public opinion abroad. Guest's remit was Holland and Germany, and by 1916 he had discovered ways of smuggling literature into enemy countries via Holland and Switzerland.[8]

Both Cockerill and Guest concentrated their efforts upon Germany, Britain's foremost enemy; and in both cases the work could be described more as a continuous routine than as a campaign of the kind launched by the Central Powers against Russia in 1917. Guest's efforts, however, impinged on Austria-Hungary. It is clear that some of his Intelligence contacts in Switzerland were using similar channels to Tullio Marchetti's Intelligence network or those of the Czech underground organization (the *Mafie*) in order to smuggle subversive material into the Empire. One of Guest's contacts was an official, Deneke, who worked under cover of the British consulate in Zurich. Another centre was Geneva where the two vice-consuls, Middleton Edwards and Hugh Whittall, were both working for British military Intelligence and had interlocking duties of collecting information and organizing propaganda in Switzerland and in enemy countries.[9] By influencing the Swiss press, the propagandists could expect that their views might eventually peter into Austria or be taken up by some enemy newspapers. However, the principal route for Guest's network seems to have been direct. According to a 'propaganda map' drawn up by the British Department of Information (into which the War Propaganda Bureau was incorporated in February 1917), propaganda into Austria-Hungary and Germany in 1917 consisted chiefly of the 'secret distribution of pamphlets'. John Buchan, the director of the Department of Information, was only prepared to set down limited evidence on paper about Guest's activity:

> The branch of the Department which deals with propaganda in enemy countries has from the beginning worked in closest connection with the various branches of the Military Intelligence concerned with the same subject.... The subject is complicated and details must necessarily be kept secret. It may be said generally that suitable propaganda literature is specially printed in miniature for the purpose, and through various channels a large amount of skilfully disguised material is conveyed to enemy readers.[10]

The network was similarly praised by Henry Wickham Steed who learnt about it from Guest on 7 March 1918. In Steed's words, parts of the organization were excellent 'and one of his Swiss channels might be used by us to get our stuff into Austria. But his work hitherto has been of a mild "poison gas" type...our methods will have to be mainly of the "high explosive" type.'[11]

From the beginning of the war, Henry Wickham Steed himself had been engaged in unofficial propaganda (in the broadest sense of the word), designed indirectly to undermine and destroy the Habsburg Empire. As *The Times* correspondent in Vienna from 1902 to 1913 and as foreign editor in London from 1913, Steed had come to believe by the outbreak of war that Austria-Hungary should not survive. He began to campaign for a radical transformation of the Eastern European map, including independent Yugoslav and Czechoslovak states, as an essential condition of any lasting peace. While he was infected by his employer Lord Northcliffe's obsession with winning the war, he regularly emphasized the Habsburg dimension to an Allied victory: 'the position of Austria-Hungary as the most vulnerable point in the enemy combination'.[12] He was joined in his campaign by the historian and Eastern European expert R.W. Seton-Watson, who in the decade before 1914 had probably travelled more widely than any other British scholar in the Monarchy and the Balkans. Having initially decided upon a 'programme of amputation of the Monarchy' in order to create a Southern Slav state, Seton-Watson by the autumn of 1914, after talks with the Czech émigré leader Tomáš Masaryk, was also converted to the idea of an independent Czechoslovakia. The creation of such a state would inevitably mean the death of the Empire. Seton-Watson and Steed acted from the start as confidants for Yugoslav and Czech émigrés such as Supilo, Trumbić and Masaryk, and as intermediaries through whom they might try to influence British official circles. At the same time they actively publicized their vision, especially for a Yugoslav state, and worked in an ever more coordinated fashion from late 1916 through the foundation both of a Serbian Society of Great

Britain and a weekly journal, *The New Europe*. Most of their propaganda in the early years concentrated on boosting the reputation of Austria's adversaries rather than damaging the Monarchy directly. However, by December 1916, with the belligerents beginning to compete over war aims, Seton-Watson felt it necessary to state bluntly in the pages of *The New Europe* that the logic of Britain's promises to its allies was that Austria-Hungary was to be destroyed.[13]

In the field of front propaganda it was Steed who had the wider experience of the two publicists. According to his memoirs, Steed had advised Masaryk as early as September 1914 that those Czechs who wished to desert on the Eastern Front should sing nationalist songs such as *Hej Slované* in order to cross safely into the Russian lines. Steed rather typically credits himself with some successes from this advice, but the episode still illustrates that he was conscious from early in the war that Habsburg army morale might be undermined and, as a journalist by profession, sensed the potential of spreading ideas across the front lines. In June 1916 Steed accompanied Northcliffe on a trip to the Italian Front; he learnt of Štefánik's recent propaganda flight over the Austrian trenches and also heard about a 'Yugoslav' officer who had deserted to Italy in order to betray Austrian positions around Gorizia.[14] Both Steed and Seton-Watson felt that such occurrences, and their wider dream of a Yugoslav state, had been seriously obstructed when the Entente promised Italy Yugoslav regions in the Treaty of London. The effect had been to 'galvanize Austria-Hungary into new life' since southern Slav regiments had acquired a reason to fight against Italy in order to protect their homeland.[15] Certainly from May 1915 the Habsburg military were able to use 'Italian imperialism' as a useful propaganda stick among the Croat and Slovene regiments. It therefore became one of the priorities for Steed and Seton-Watson to foster some Italian–Yugoslav compromise or understanding. The chief aim was to give credence in Allied circles to the idea of a viable Yugoslav state, but a secondary consideration was that Italian–Yugoslav solidarity would then proceed to weaken the Habsburg enemy.

Although Steed seems to have become more optimistic after his visit to Italy, when he had talked to Bissolati and Albertini, it was not until a year later that he and Seton-Watson sensed that change was really in the air. Both on the Yugoslav and the Italian side there seemed to be signs of a willingness to compromise. Among the Yugoslavs, Steed and Seton-Watson played their part in persuading the head of the Yugoslav Committee, Ante Trumbić, to visit the Serbian government on Corfu in order to negotiate a joint declaration of Yugoslav solidarity (July 1917). Steed would later claim that the Corfu Declaration had had serious results for enemy morale, 'stimulating a movement among the southern Slav troops of Austria-Hungary in favour of unity and consequently of defection from the Habsburgs'.[16] This seems highly unlikely (witness Pivko's own ignorance of the pact), but in the following months it suited Steed as an argument in order to encourage some Italian–Yugoslav agreement. Italy, he wrote, 'must understand that the hardest blow she could hit Austria [*sic*] would be to be able to announce an agreement with the Southern Slavs as the basis for her whole programme of liberating the Hapsburg peoples'; this would counteract the effect of the 'wretched "pound of flesh" Convention [the Treaty of London]'. By August 1917, Steed was encouraged by Albertini's conversion and the stance of the *Corriere della Sera*; and also by talking in London to Italian politicians such as Romeo Gallenga Stuart (soon to be Italian Under-Secretary for Propaganda).[17] Gallenga too was a convert to the idea of an Italian–Yugoslav deal in order to destroy Austria and strengthen Italy's postwar influence.[18] Steed sensed correctly that influential Italians were now moving towards his own standpoint. At the same time, he could know from Seton-Watson that the voices of discontent and war-weariness in the Habsburg Empire were mounting.[19] Thus, his growing perception that a psychological offensive could be launched against the Empire was dependent on changing circumstances in the Italian and enemy camps.

However, it required the jolt of Caporetto for further progress to be made. If Austria-Hungary won the war, neither the Italian or Yugoslav dream would be realized; hence the need for them to combine efforts on the basis of the nationality principle. The Czechs under Hlaváček were able to exploit Italian fears in Italy itself. The Yugoslav Committee, however, had less adept leaders than the Czechs and were naturally hampered by the sensitivity of their cause in Italy. It was therefore Steed in London who took the initiative to pull Italy and the Yugoslavs together, thereby laying a basis for that vital cooperation if Italian propaganda against the enemy was to be truly effective. Significantly, it was the Italian military whom Steed approached first on 5 December, suggesting that General Mola, the military attaché in London, should begin talks with the Yugoslav Committee; Mola easily secured the approval of his superiors in Italy. A week later Steed persuaded a nervous Trumbić that the Italians were amenable to the idea of some agreement since they 'understand that the Convention [the London treaty] is a mistake which rebounds on them'.[20] Steed then arranged two meetings between Trumbić and Mola at his house, attended also by Seton-Watson, Emanuel and some members of the Yugoslav Committee.[21] From the start Steed emphasized that because of the Allies' critical situation a general Italian–Yugoslav agreement was vital which could be used as the basis for a 'political offensive' against the Habsburg Monarchy. Pointing to the 'results' already of the Corfu Pact (which had supposedly even influenced FM Boroević),[22] Steed added that 'by this means the Austro-Hungarian "home front" might be broken and the defeat of Germany hastened'.

The idea naturally appealed to Mola and his superiors. Trumbić, however, following his instincts as an experienced lawyer, wanted any Italian–Yugoslav agreement to bind Italy as closely as possible to the Corfu Declaration; above all, Italy had to renounce the Treaty of London. This was a sticking-point (and would remain so for the rest of the war), for whereas Trumbić wished for something tangible, Steed and the Italian military simply wanted a vague agreement for propaganda purposes. Nevertheless, out of the meetings there emerged a preliminary compromise which gave some satisfaction to both sides. Trumbić and Mola confirmed that Austria-Hungary was to be dismembered and new frontiers created according to strategic interests and the principle of nationality. For Trumbić this statement in itself was a considerable step forward, since Mola, acting 'privately' but clearly with some official military backing, had conceded that Italian claims to Dalmatia might be modified and the Treaty of London revised. For the Italian military a first step had been taken towards what Mola termed 'a force of moral cooperation to use as a weapon of war against the enemy'. The next move was to negotiate 'a public declaration which affirms the full agreement between Italy and Yugoslavia'.[23]

In early January 1918, the speeches made by Lloyd George and Woodrow Wilson (his 'Fourteen Points') pushed the Italians and Yugoslavs further in this direction. Both speeches contained passages which effectively denied that the Treaty of London would be implemented or that the United States or Britain favoured Austria's dissolution. Both Italian and Yugoslav aspirations seemed under threat, and both parties became convinced that their best course lay in making some public declaration of their common interests. Trumbić remained justifiably cautious about treating with the Italians since, in his own words, 'everything is still in embryo and... we are treading on ice'.[24] But he was now encouraged to maintain an Allied spotlight on the Yugoslav cause, not least by his representative in Paris, Ivo de Giulli. At the end of January De Giulli, who was himself stimulated by regular contact with other émigrés in the French capital, urged Trumbić that 'now the psychological moment is favourable for us, but when people begin to forget the Italian defeat, and if they should have some success no matter where... the situation could be more favourable for them'.[25] Trumbić also felt pressure to act because he could expect no initiative from the Serbian government-in-exile. Pašić at this time made what Trumbić considered to be a feeble protest at the Allied speeches, and he also opposed a suggestion that Serbia convene a 'Yugoslav assembly' to proclaim the Corfu Declaration. Since Pašić was clearly prepared to sacrifice Trumbić and his fellow Croats and Serbs as long as Serbia secured Bosnia-Hercegovina as war booty, the Yugoslav Committee decided to take the lead and seek recognition for their full Yugoslav cause through agreement with Italy.[26]

Among Italians the Allied speeches encouraged many to feel that the line advocated by the *Corriere della Sera* was the best means to victory, since it would provide sympathy for Italy among the enemy's oppressed peoples and among Italy's own allies. In late January Orlando himself visited London to seek an explanation from Lloyd George about the terms of his speech; he was told that the full Treaty of London could never be implemented even in the case of complete victory. Steed and Mola (who continued on behalf of the Italian military to encourage Steed to intensify an anti-Austrian campaign)[27] persuaded Orlando to meet Trumbić. Trumbić on this occasion emphasized that the Treaty of London was the only obstacle to Italian–Yugoslav cooperation, cooperation which would supposedly stir the Slav nationalities into destroying Austria from within. He came away from the meeting believing correctly that Orlando was 'flexible' [*gibak*] and anxious not to hinder an agreement.[28] In fact the visit to London had convinced Orlando not that Italy should renounce the London treaty, but merely that it was expedient for Italy to wear the mask of 'nationality politics' for the purpose of propaganda among the Allies and against the enemy on the Italian Front. He hinted as much to Steed when he said that Italy resembled someone who had made a calculation, found that it did not add up, and was forced to alter the arithmetic: Orlando did not suggest that the final total would be any different.[29]

Orlando's public 'conversion', which through Steed's prompting he announced at the opening of the Italian Parliament on 12 February,[30] was sufficient for those grouped around the *Corriere della Sera*. For Albertini and his colleagues, who from January were engaged in a campaign in the newspaper's columns for Italian cooperation with the Czechs and Yugoslavs, it was not only vital that Italy should adopt the nationality principle. Even more urgent perhaps was the publicizing of the new course so that Italy could claim the leadership of the oppressed peoples of Austria-Hungary. This was the thinking behind the idea of staging a 'Congress of Oppressed Nationalities' in Rome. The idea originated with G.A. Borgese and matched the lessons he had learnt from his visit to Switzerland the previous summer. On 10 January, Borgese had written a memorandum for Albertini in which he proposed that a congress be held in order to influence President Wilson over the Austrian question, and also to place Italy 'at the head of the Habsburg peoples'.[31] The idea was seized upon by Amendola and Albertini and sold to members of the Fascio della Difesa Nazionale in early February after their grand assembly at Milan. Although the French in turn had been toying with organizing 'leagues' of the oppressed nationalities in Paris, they were reluctantly persuaded that Rome should be the setting for the first of a series of congresses.[32] On 15 February, Albertini proceeded with Orlando's approval to set up an Italian executive committee, whose purpose was to organize a Rome Congress. Much to Salvemini's disgust it included nationalist members of the Fascio such as Barzilai and Di Cesarò, an indication of Albertini's own more flexible interpretation of 'nationality politics'.[33] It was now the *Corriere* grouping, working through this committee, which pursued the initiative taken by Steed after Caporetto. Albertini proposed to send one of the committee, Andrea Torre (former Rome correspondent of the *Corriere*), to London to make a 'general agreement' with Trumbić which would then be proclaimed at the Rome

Congress.[34] The aim of both Albertini and Steed was the same, to maintain the momentum in order to pursue propaganda which would damage the Habsburg Empire. As Steed noted, 'the matter now most urgent [is] to agree upon general principles rather than to discuss details'.[35]

Under Steed's auspices the Torre–Trumbić agreement was finally signed on 7 March. It consisted of two parts. The first made general statements about the right of the oppressed nationalities to fight 'against the common oppressor for their entire liberation so as to attain complete national unity in free and united states'. The second applied to relations between Italy and 'Jugoslavia', affirming that the national unity and independence of both countries was a vital interest to both, and that territorial disputes would be settled on the basis of nationality, self-determination and 'in such a manner as not to infringe vital interests of the two nations'.[36] Trumbić was not fully satisfied with these vague terms for, in the words of a colleague, he did not 'believe in the sincerity of the Italians in which these naïve English believe'; after all, the Treaty of London was not renounced, nor was the Corfu Declaration mentioned, nor was the Italian government officially bound by the agreement since Torre was only the representative of an ad hoc committee. However, Trumbić had to weigh the dangers of obstinacy. He was conscious that agreement would not simply improve the standing of his Committee; it would also create 'a good mood among the oppressed nations – especially the South Slavs – and would have favourable results in the Austrian ranks on the Italian Front'.[37] He was only too aware of Italy's priorities and realized what Torre had managed to secure for Italy: a general declaration which could be used for propaganda purposes both at the Rome Congress and in a psychological offensive at the front.

It could be argued that this Italian–Yugoslav basis was essential if Italy was to launch an effective campaign against Austria-Hungary with the nationality principle as the leading argument. In the same way, Austria-Hungary's propaganda campaign seemed effective in the spring because it was playing on the reality of Italy's low morale and the apparent strength of the Central Powers on all fronts. The weakness of the propaganda campaigns came when their arguments diverged too far from reality. In the Italian case this danger would always exist because even though Italy's official circles seemed to be embracing the Yugoslavs, they refused to abandon the Treaty of London; Orlando kept Sonnino in office because he himself was trying to keep both irons in the fire. It remained to be seen if this ambiguous policy would have detrimental effects on the practice of front propaganda. In fact, what seemed to be evidence of sudden Italian–Yugoslav solidarity, beginning with the Torre–Trumbić agreement, might be sufficient for the purposes of the propagandists who only required broad and not detailed arguments in their campaign. It was in producing this framework that Steed had played a major role. He had been instrumental in bringing 'official Italy' into contact with the Yugoslav émigrés even if the final success had depended as much on Albertini and the *Corriere* grouping. At the same time, the British were becoming more directly associated with the idea of a propaganda offensive because of their creation of a Department of Propaganda in Enemy Countries. The launch of the EPD did not launch Italy's campaign since, as we have seen, a certain amount had already been achieved in that direction by the Italians themselves. Rather, the EPD served as a stimulus to greater coordination of an existing campaign.

On 13 February Lloyd George had persuaded Lord Northcliffe, the proprietor of *The Times*, to accept the post of director of the EPD. The precise origin of the EPD is not quite clear. Certainly it stemmed in part from Lloyd George's general reorganization of British propaganda in January 1918, according to which John Buchan's Department of Information was abolished and replaced by a Ministry of Information under Lord Beaverbrook.[38] But the evidence suggests that the idea of a separate EPD was chiefly a response to what the British perceived as the Central Powers' 'successful' use of front propaganda in late 1917. The key successes were taken to be the events in Russia and at Caporetto, and these, together with the disaster of Passchendaele on the Western Front, convinced many that the enemy needed to be answered in kind. On 16 November Northcliffe himself, having returned from heading the British War Mission in the United States, had published an open letter to Lloyd George in *The Times*. In it he discussed one of his favourite themes, the insidious nature of German propaganda: 'we have had the tragedy of Russia, due partly to lack of Allied propaganda to counteract that of the Germans. We have the tragedy of Italy largely due to the same enemy propaganda.'[39] Later, Northcliffe claimed that he had been asked to become director by those who had 'seen the effective propaganda of Germany among our former Russian and present Italian Allies'.[40] By the turn of the year Lloyd George was fully aware of the influence ascribed to enemy propaganda, for example by British military and diplomatic representatives in Italy, and may have weighed this factor when trying to find suitably energetic people to direct British propaganda.[41]

However, the precise idea of a separate EPD may have originated with Sir William Tyrell of the Foreign Office who thought of it particularly as an instrument for propagating Allied war aims, such as Wilson's Fourteen Points, in Europe and thereby weakening the enemy's pervasive influence. Northcliffe was the logical choice as director because of his clear obsession with the subject, and perhaps also because Lloyd George wished to muzzle him as a critic of governmental policy.[42] It was partly because of this danger that Northcliffe was rather reluctant to accept. He was undoubtedly attracted, however, by the lure of running his own independent department, subject only to the Prime Minister, and was then urged to accept by Steed. Steed clearly saw in the EPD a means to pursue his own maturing plan of a political offensive against Austria-Hungary. Having urged the Italians for some months that they should seize the moment, he was now provided with a legitimate platform for his own actions in the shape of the EPD. Indeed, since Northcliffe was unwell for most of 1918 (though still an interested and influential figurehead), it was to be Steed who dominated the organization from the start. It enabled him to exert greater influence on British governmental policy than had been feasible as foreign editor of *The Times*, and at the same time it further enhanced his standing among the Italians. Perhaps the EPD's first triumph in mid-February was in Italy, where news of its creation was successfully used by Albertini and others to reinforce their argument for a coordinated propaganda offensive.

In the previous weeks Steed had repeatedly urged the Italian government to adjust its policies by proclaiming the nationality principle, thereby seizing the 'moral leadership of the Alliance in Europe'.[43] With the creation of the EPD Steed could pressure the British government to move in the same direction. Although he was undoubtedly sincere in his belief that effective propaganda needed to be based on clear guidelines which were fully in harmony with governmental policy, he now turned this connection on its head: since the British were committed to propaganda against the enemy they must clarify their policy and commit themselves openly to the destruction of Austria-Hungary. Steed and Seton-Watson were aware that the government in recent months had continued to make overtures to Austria about a separate peace, but through the EPD they moved to sabotage any further contacts.[44] Northcliffe was easily persuaded by Steed that Crewe House, where the EPD was to be based, should concentrate its efforts first upon 'smashing Austria-Hungary'. Steed's rather shaky logic for this was that after the Russian and Italian disasters only Austria's and not Germany's morale could be seriously damaged. He thereupon drew up a memorandum for Northcliffe on EPD policy for presentation to the Foreign Office.

The document was closely based on a more detailed study by Seton-Watson and, when sent, it contained a short introduction in which Northcliffe mentioned his own personal concern to publicize in Austria news of American strength. It then set out two possible but distinct options for British policy.[45] Option (a) was for the Allies to work for a separate peace with Emperor Karl, a policy which had been tried and found to be impossible chiefly because of Germany's influence. Option (b), which the memorandum favoured, was that the Allies 'try to break the power of Austria-Hungary as the weakest link in the chain of enemy states, by supporting and encouraging all anti-German and pro-Ally peoples and tendencies'. Since the Foreign Office at this time was still pursuing links to Vienna – 'anxious that the door remain ajar'[46] – in replying to the memorandum on 26 February, the Foreign Secretary observed that the two policies outlined were not mutually exclusive, since by encouraging the anti-German elements one would be inducing the Emperor to make a separate peace and modify the constitution of his empire. The British government, to

Steed's irritation, was still not prepared to give absolute precedence to policy (b). Thus, when the War Cabinet met to discuss the issue on 5 March it agreed to policy (b), but added the condition that 'no promises should be made to the subject races in Austria which we could not redeem: for example we must not promise them complete independence if the best we could get was autonomy'. Steed advised Northcliffe, who had attended the cabinet meeting, that this restriction was not really an obstacle to progress. After all, the cabinet meeting had otherwise approved the EPD's task, instructing Northcliffe to contact the General Staff so that the British military in Italy could be used to distribute propaganda over the Austrian lines.[47]

From Steed's point of view, the EPD campaign against Austria-Hungary inevitably meant an Allied rather than a British campaign. In terms of propaganda policy and practice, he realized that it would require close liaison with the Italians but also the French and Americans. From early March, Crewe House began to acquire a key coordinating role among the Allied propaganda organizations. However, it is clear that the real root of this coordination lay in Italian hands. In December 1917, Gallenga Stuart, as Orlando's Under-Secretary for Propaganda, had begun to sound out the British and French about closer cooperation between their propaganda organizations; this was not a surprising move since one of Gallenga's key tasks was to improve Italy's reputation among the Allies and for this purpose he had himself made an investigative trip to Britain the previous summer.[48] In early February, when Italy had begun to canvass the idea of a Congress of Oppressed Nationalities, Gallenga journeyed to Paris partly in order to pre-empt French efforts and convince the Austrian émigrés that the congress should be staged in Rome. An equally important reason for his visit, however, was to convene a first inter-Allied propaganda conference.

It met in Paris on 6–8 March under the chairmanship of the French foreign minister. Italy's delegation was headed by Gallenga and Borgese (who was now working for Gallenga's ministry); France's by Henri Franklin-Bouillon, chair of the foreign committee of the French chamber, who was the chief French politician to champion the oppressed nationalities; and Britain's by John Buchan, whom Gallenga wanted to attend because of his experience with propaganda.[49] After discussions on various aspects of coordination, the delegations on the last day examined propaganda against the enemy, the British pointing to Northcliffe's organization and its decision to target Austria-Hungary. Indeed, Steed had already decided to convene a meeting of Allied representatives to discuss this very subject, and Buchan was able to issue an invitation to those present to proceed to London a week later. The idea may again have originated first with Gallenga or Franklin-Bouillon, both of whom Northcliffe may have met soon after his appointment. But the Italian and French delegations seem also to have deferred naturally to Crewe House over this aspect of propaganda, partly because of Steed's key role in the Torre–Trumbić talks, and even more perhaps because the EPD was the only organization specifically geared to such work. Both the Italian and French propaganda organizations lacked such a clear-cut character at this time.[50]

The second conference, which met at Crewe House on 14 March, was something of a sequel to the Paris gathering in that those present, including Gallenga and Franklin-Bouillon, reaffirmed their commitment to united action in the field of enemy propaganda.[51] They decided to set up a small committee representing Britain (Steed), France (Henri Moysset) and Italy (Borgese) which would meet regularly in Paris 'in order that we might ascertain exactly what each country was doing and not duplicate the work of one another'. In fact, this initial idea of Allied coordination was to prove still-born. More significant was Gallenga's proposal, which the conference approved, that Steed should now travel to Italy to help coordinate Allied propaganda against Austria-Hungary. It seems clear that Gallenga here acted on his own initiative, ignorant of the important move which had just been made by Orlando to coordinate Italy's campaign under Ugo Ojetti. Steed's Allied mission would for this reason inevitably cause some friction with those like Ojetti who felt that the campaign had already been placed in their own Italian hands. Even so, Gallenga's initiative shows the sudden impact which Steed and the new EPD had made upon Italian thinking from February 1918. The British painted a picture of a propaganda offensive on a wider canvas than the Italians had hitherto envisaged. The Italians felt bound to accept this Allied help even if they still thought of the painting largely in Italian colours.

## 6.2 Steed's coordinating mission

Early on the morning of 19 March Steed left London on a military train bound for Italy. His month-long mission, which he had himself envisaged in some form even before Gallenga's specific proposal, had a dual purpose: to organize propaganda at the front and to help arrange and participate in the Rome Congress, the 'first great act of inter-Allied propaganda'.[52] In both cases British efforts would begin to dovetail with already established Italian initiatives. At first, however, it was Allied disunity rather than unity which Steed encountered. With Gallenga's approval he had chosen Seton-Watson to accompany him to work in Rome while he was busy at the front, only to be told by Northcliffe on the 18th that this was impossible. Sonnino had protested to the British Foreign Office that Seton-Watson's presence in Italy would be regarded as provocative due to his hostility to the Treaty of London. Sonnino in fact was probably as irritated with Gallenga as with the British, for the Under-Secretary had sanctioned Steed's mission without reference to the Consulta, and his independent ministry, subject only to Orlando, was increasingly viewed by Sonnino as a threat to his control of Italian foreign policy. However, Sonnino's move, the first of what Steed portrayed at the time and in his memoirs as a series of mysterious intrigues to prevent 'effective propaganda' against Austria-Hungary, failed to have the desired effect. Thanks to Northcliffe's influence Seton-Watson was able to follow Steed across the Channel on 23 March.[53]

Steed meanwhile had arrived in Paris on the 20th accompanied by Guglielmo Emanuel and by Lieutenant-Colonel Bernard Granville Baker. The latter had been recommended as a military member of the mission by General Macdonagh, Director of Military Intelligence. Baker had had considerable experience of central and Eastern Europe before the war, for he had been educated partly at the military academy at Dresden and then after service in Burma had secured for most of the 1890s a commission in the 9th Royal Prussian Hussars. As a cavalry officer he had enjoyed the convivial environment and admired the German work ethic, but at the same time had felt at first hand the harsh discipline and rigid hierarchy of the German army. He had proceeded in late 1914 to write a colourful but surprisingly balanced account of his experience as 'an infinitesimally small cog-wheel in the mechanism of the mightiest machine of destruction that the world has yet produced', his conclusion being that Prussianism had to be eradicated because of its pernicious influence upon the German peoples.[54] Baker gave no sign in this work that he felt similarly about the Habsburgs. By 1914 he had made several visits to Austria-Hungary and the Balkans, on Intelligence missions for the War Office as well as on holiday, but appears to have had nothing but praise for Emperor Franz Joseph and his 'constitutional government'. Only later perhaps would Baker conclude that the 'Teuton–Slav conflict', which he had portrayed as imminent in 1913, had eventually been fought out in the Habsburg Empire with Prussianism slowly gaining influence as the war progressed.[55] During the war he himself served with distinction on the Western Front (being mentioned in despatches in May 1917), and after being invalided out because of wounds and trench fever, he was chosen to join the EPD in early March 1918, attending the second Allied propaganda conference. He was undoubtedly intrigued by this chance to experiment with new weapons of warfare: in one of his books he had noted that 'the true soldier is interested in everything that pertains to his craft... the psychology of the situation is a fierce desire to outshine the enemy in technical skill'.[56] Baker would bring to his new role in Italy, as British representative in an Allied propaganda campaign, a diligent commitment. But his specifically military outlook would also lead him at times to clash with those Italians whom he viewed as inefficient or inattentive to Allied concerns.

Steed's mission was unable to leave Paris until the evening of 23 March, partly due to French suspicions about Baker's suitability (because of his German links), and partly due to confusion in the French capital caused by the start of

Germany's spring offensive.[57] Steed used the delay to pay some important visits. He met Colonel Zopff, head of French propaganda on the Western Front, who arranged for a French engineer, Captain Naud, assisted by a Lieutenant Moreau, to join the mission in order to demonstrate in Italy the rifle grenades which they had invented specifically for leaflet distribution. The fact that this was thought necessary indicates that the British and French were ignorant of the devices which the Italian Intelligence officers were already using. Steed also saw Franklin-Bouillon, Beneš and General Giardino, the Italian representative at Versailles, who telegraphed ahead to the CS urging support for the mission. He then attended a special meeting of Yugoslav, Czech, Romanian and Polish émigrés at which a preliminary propaganda manifesto for Austrian troops was drafted. Most important, however, was Steed's encounter with Clemenceau at which the Prime Minister granted the mission official French support of the kind it had already secured from the British governmental and military authorities. Under the impact of the German offensive as well as Steed's forceful assurances that his task was to begin propaganda and 'forestall an Austrian offensive against Italy', Clemenceau gave his blessing, all the more so as he himself believed that an Austrian attack was scheduled for 10 April.

This idea was widely circulated among the Allies and had even been used by Northcliffe to sell the EPD's campaign to the British government.[58] But it was completely false. The AOK had only despatched orders for a new offensive in late March, the transportation of forces from other fronts would begin on 8 April and the date of attack was initially set for 20 May. Yet on 24 March the CS warned the British commander, Lord Cavan, that the enemy would probably attack on 10 April.[59] The anxiety appears to have been caused partly by false Intelligence or by its interpretation. The CS, which had been expecting a major Austrian offensive for some months, was convinced that an attack was imminent in tandem with Germany's attack in the West, and therefore they readily misinterpreted Austrian troop movements in southern Tyrol. At the same time it seems clear that Tullio Marchetti's network, particularly Mansueto Zanon in Innsbruck, had on this occasion picked up inaccurate details about an attack in mid-April.[60] But such rumours were also convenient at this time for Diaz, who was anxious that the Allies should not further reduce their forces in Italy in order to strengthen the Western Front. On 17 March, he had pleaded with the British CIGS not to transfer any more divisions, giving as his alleged reason the fact that 'the Central Empires are preparing to make their principal effort against Italy'. A few days later in Turin, Sir Henry Rawlinson noted in his diary how he had 'sat for two hours hearing Diaz['s] very exaggerated statements of the dangers of the situation on the Italian Front'.[61] The same arguments were grist to the mill of Steed and the propagandists since they underlined the urgency of their mission; indeed, the information about an

April offensive was to be viewed as authentic by the EPD long after April had passed. Thus was born the myth, perpetuated by Crewe House, that Allied propaganda in early April had forced the Austrians to postpone their offensive. In reality this first 'success' of the coordinated campaign at the front was based on a false if understandable premise.[62]

On reaching Milan on 25 March, Steed was advised by Luigi Albertini to gain Orlando's express approval for the mission so as to prevent the CS putting up any further resistance to the idea. The party therefore divided: Steed and Emanuel travelling to Rome, while Baker, Naud and Moreau proceeded direct to Padua where on the evening of the 26th they were met by Delmé-Radcliffe, head of the British Military Mission. Radcliffe had been ordered by the War Office to support Steed's mission and had probably met Northcliffe in London earlier in the month; his first move on meeting his new guests was to send them off to see Ercole Smaniotto, the head of 3rd army Intelligence at Mogliano.[63] Radcliffe was to prove an enthusiastic supporter of the propaganda offensive. Already convinced that insidious enemy propaganda had played its part in the rout at Caporetto, he observed on returning to the Italian Front in mid-March that 'the enemy is making some propaganda efforts and daily sends over leaflets which are fired in shells from guns and howitzers or trench mortar-bombs and dropped by aeroplanes'. It was at this time that Radcliffe discussed Italian morale with Benito Mussolini, and shortly afterwards talked on the same subject to Marchetti, Finzi and Smaniotto, meetings at which the idea of front propaganda must also have been on the agenda.[64]

Radcliffe seems to have been sincerely intrigued by the prospect of supporting the oppressed nationalities. Like Granville Baker, he had been partly brought up in Germany, had served in the colonies, and acquired a broader perspective than many on the nature of the World War. In mid-1917, after the Corfu Declaration, he had told Finzi that the Treaty of London would have to be revised; a year later Lord Cavan observed that 'his enthusiasm and belief in the Czech and Jugoslav propaganda business is extraordinary'.[65] At the same time Radcliffe was undoubtedly attracted by the idea of playing a central role in any Allied organization on the Italian Front. Since his appointment as head of the Mission in May 1915, he had built up a formidable array of contacts, including King Victor Emmanuel himself, to the extent that one newcomer to the theatre in 1918 commented: 'Delmé-Radcliffe is quite a personality, he speaks Italian, is well-known to [the King and Diaz], is energetic and has brains. Consequently they look to him in all military matters.'[66] The negative side to this was that Radcliffe (whose father-in-law was the royal surgeon Sir Frederick Treves) had an exaggerated idea of his own sphere of influence and made many enemies quickly. One member of the Yugoslav Committee, while gratified at Radcliffe's interest in propaganda, learnt on arriving in Padua that 'he is not a serious man and nobody can endure him'.[67] *The Times* correspondent in Rome went much further, commenting in August 1917 that Radcliffe's unpopularity was thoroughly deserved since he was 'entirely lacking in manners', 'actively rude' and had 'the most arrogant manner possible with officers of inferior rank':

> Wherever he has been he has acquired an abiding unpopularity. I know that many soldiers of position at home and elsewhere are thankful that he has been 'shunted' to Italy... He goes beyond his duty as our representative and suggests that he is really God Almighty and Sir Douglas Haig rolled into one tremendous personality. He is a man of tremendous energy and boundless energy but of markedly limited intelligence. He is an *arriviste* and has not known how to disguise it.[68]

The War Office, however, gave more weight to Radcliffe's contacts and experience than his evident vanity and self-importance. Thus he remained at his post and from March 1918 was to be a valuable asset to Steed's mission and those involved in the propaganda campaign.

While in Rome Steed could be satisfied from talks at the Consulta that Sonnino and his colleagues were becoming more flexible. Through Gallenga, Steed gained access to Orlando who, together with Francesco Nitti (Minister of the Treasury and significant because of his close links to Diaz), gave letters of recommendation for Steed's role as coordinator of an Allied propaganda organization at the front. Orlando's support for Steed's 'good and useful work' signified his conversion to Gallenga's idea of accelerating the amount of Allied cooperation in the field of propaganda instead of simply coordinating Italian efforts at the front. A week earlier when he had appointed Ugo Ojetti as 'Royal Commissioner for propaganda to the enemy', the latter idea had been foremost in Orlando's mind through the encouragement of Albertini. Since then Ojetti had been waiting impatiently in Rome, frustrated at Orlando's neglect of him in favour of Steed whom Ojetti considered a usurper. An additional irritant for Ojetti was Gallenga, who on returning from London and Paris proceeded to claim for himself overall control of Italian propaganda against the enemy, proposing that Ojetti should act as a liaison officer with the CS but as a subordinate within Gallenga's ministry. Ojetti's consequent disgust at the 'eunuchs' in the government, who were allowing Allied interference in the control of Italian propaganda, resulted in his writing to Orlando at the end of the month declining the post which he had been offered.[69] His experiences during March go far to explain Ojetti's sensitivity and 'Italian-centred' outlook when he later took charge of the Allied propaganda campaign. His appointment had been a specifically Italian initiative which then seemed to have been superseded through British interference.

When Steed arrived in Padua on 29 March, Delmé-Radcliffe immediately introduced him to the Italian Intelligence heads.[70] 'Some of them', Steed acknowledged in his private report for Crewe House, 'had already done good work on the lines now contemplated, but it had hitherto lacked coordination and the support of the Italian and Allied Governments and Higher Commands.' While this point was correct, Steed omitted it from his memoirs where he presents a highly dramatic account of his own role as coordinator of the campaign: it is a version which requires adjustment. The key coordination meeting was chaired by General Badoglio at Abano on the 30th, and attended, among others, by Radcliffe, the members of Steed's mission and the six Intelligence heads who were accustomed anyway to meet every Saturday at the CS. Cesare Finzi's own short and equally partisan account of the discussion places Steed's role in a new light. When Steed explained the general purpose of his mission, Finzi could not contain his impatience at the fact that the Allied leaders still seemed to be 'infants' in their use of propaganda 'while we are already adults'. He spoke passionately for an hour about Italy's use of the weapon since 1916, to which Steed apparently answered: 'thank you for the courteous lesson – I note with pleasure that you are already ahead of us'.[71]

Steed's mission, however, now acted as a catalyst upon the mood prevailing at the CS. Badoglio in particular was anxious to intensify propaganda, partly with an eye on what he viewed as an imminent enemy offensive. He therefore proposed an increase in the manufacture of Italian propaganda rockets (from 500 to 4000 per day) and, pending the reorganization of a printing works at Venice which had been requisitioned by the military, he ordered that the printing works of the various armies should proceed 'at full pressure' to produce propaganda material. The Intelligence officers were told to submit within 24 hours draft leaflets in the languages of the troops opposite their respective fronts. As for the content of these manifestos, Steed was able to present as an example the draft proclamation which had been written a week earlier by the émigrés in Paris. But Finzi and Marchetti took the initiative as well. They came forward with the suggestion that Austrian troop organization could be disrupted in a month if the Allied governments authorized proclamations of independence by the various national émigré committees. Such an idea was, as we have seen, fully in accord with the two key Intelligence officers' thinking since the New Year; there is no reason to believe that they needed any prompting by Steed, or that they were acting contrary to what they perceived as the Italian government's inclinations.[72] After all, while Sonnino's views were well-known, Orlando himself had visited the war zone in early March and clarified for the Intelligence officers his own conversion to nationality politics. For Finzi and Marchetti, the idea of proclamations of independence was simply an extra tool with which to paralyze the enemy; they had not shied away from issuing such manifestos for some months without governmental approval. For Steed, their suggestion had greater potential: it was another means by which he could press the Allied governments to make a stronger policy commitment to the oppressed nationalities, with the argument attached that only then would they reap the full benefit of the propaganda campaign. In particular, Steed saw it as a way to overturn the restriction which had been placed on Northcliffe by the British Cabinet on 5 March. He therefore urged the Intelligence officers to proceed and draw up suitable manifestos, while he himself would seek to lift the British restriction. Steed here was working with a broader, political agenda in mind than Finzi or Marchetti whose primary concern was simply how best to undermine the enemy.

The discussions on 30 March significantly advanced preparations for what was intended as an inter-Allied propaganda campaign. They owed much of their success to the common enthusiasm of those present. Even Delmé-Radcliffe, who lunched that day with Finzi and Smaniotto, decided himself to compose a manifesto for enemy troops.[73] As for the Intelligence officers, if at first they were sceptical about Steed's mission, they seem to have quickly acknowledged his role as a belated Allied coordinator. Equally, their initial scepticism about Captain Naud's rifle grenades (which had a limited range)[74] seems to have softened in the face of arguments about the weapons' greater reliability compared to rockets: the conference agreed to order 20 000 such grenades immediately and a further 300 000 from the French Ministry of Armaments for future use on the Italian Front. Finzi's own optimism about the turn of events after Steed's visit is most clearly revealed in a letter which he wrote on 1 April to Ljudevit Pivko, then engaged in propaganda work at Stoccareddo:

> I have a lot of good news to communicate to you.
> 1. England has agreed to my thesis: Austria will be dismembered. From today onwards you can tell the Czechs, Yugoslavs, Romanians, Poles, (a) that we will consider subjects of those nationalities as free citizens and friends of the Entente; (b) that prisoners of those nationalities in Italy will be freed; (c) that recruitment for a Czech army will be permitted.
> 2. It is very probable that the Czech and Yugoslav revolutionary committees will be invited to proclaim the independence of their peoples. The Entente governments will recognize their independence.
> 3. On 8 April there will take place in Rome a conference of representatives of all the oppressed nations. It would be desirable if you too participated.[75]

Pivko's volunteers might be forgiven for thinking that Finzi's message was an April fool's hoax, for surely things had not moved so fast in Italy? In fact, the letter indicates the degree to which Finzi was now enthused to make the fullest use of the nationality principle in front propaganda, even if on this occasion he was (as usual) pre-empting the Allies' degree of commitment as well as taking many of Steed's assurances at face value. But as he wrote later, he was convinced by this time that propaganda could have the same impact on the Austrian forces as shell bombardment, 'shaking the moral forces of this Empire which, despite so many apparent cracks, seemed set on such bases of granite that no hurricane could shake it'.[76]

Soon after the coordinating meeting, Steed went to visit the headquarters of the British and French forces which were both grouped under the new Italian 6th army. He found Lord Cavan at Lonedo, installed in an old and half-dismantled Italian château, and they discussed the propaganda weapon. Cavan expressed an interest – he had invited Steed to visit – since, as he noted on one occasion:

> There is nothing the soldier loves more than to be consulted in a matter of cunning. It is inherent in the British race to try and be a little bit more clever than the other fellow. A man would rather tell you that he got 10 to 1 about a horse that started as a 4 to 1 chance – although beaten – than that he backed a 6 to 4 on winner.

At the same time Cavan's outlook was thoroughly traditional. On the Italian Front, since his arrival after Caporetto, he had begun to value what he perceived as the 'sportsmanlike conduct', the 'chivalrous warfare', conducted by friend and foe; and in this spirit he tended to believe, like many of his contemporaries on both sides, that propaganda was an 'unfair' activity. Since on his own admission he was a simple 'soldier and fox-hunter' who was ignorant of politics, he would never quite understand Delmé-Radcliffe's enthusiasm for propaganda but preferred always to trust in traditional weapons of warfare.[77] Nor was he enlightened about the character of the Austrian enemy. According to Steed, who tried to explain to him the enemy 'tribes' by reference to tribes on the Indian north-west frontier, Cavan even spoke about 'Yugoslovaks' and 'Czechoslavs'; indeed, his ignorance continued long after the war when he still thought of the Habsburg army as 'composed of four nations'.[78] Steed could feel happier when he spoke to Cavan's chief Intelligence officer (the Irish Canadian C.H. Mitchell), who had of necessity been liaising closely with Finzi and meeting the kind of problems which had long been encountered by Italian Intelligence when monitoring the Austrian forces.

It is clear, however, that Steed himself was rather naïve when assessing the enemy army. For example, he presupposed that it would be entirely possible to target certain enemy troops with manifestos in their own particular language. On 1 April he returned to Abano and found out to his delight from Italian Intelligence that certain divisions opposing the British and French were chiefly Slovene, Romanian or Croat. This information was not strictly correct.[79] Nor, because of the increasingly mixed composition of all Austrian divisions and regiments since early 1917, would it ever be possible, as Steed suggested, to target the nationalities with any great accuracy. When material was distributed from the air, mistakes were bound to be frequent and unavoidable, with many leaflets missing their target altogether.[80] Nevertheless, the idea that there were easy targets, susceptible to skilful propaganda, was quickly exploited by Steed. On 2 April, when he telegraphed Northcliffe with the request for Allied approval of proclamations of independence, he could mention this fact as well as the British and French military's eagerness to begin propaganda with 'high explosive methods'. Since Germany's offensive was in full swing on the Western Front, both London and Paris were now prepared to agree to the types of propaganda manifestos which had been suggested originally by the Italian Intelligence officers. By the time that Steed went to Rome a few days later, he received British and French consent to the rather vague idea that they approved of such proclamations. Sonnino was also prepared to adhere to such a vague formula, though he balked still at using the word 'recognition' in the manifestos because of its Yugoslav implications. As usual these political scruples would be largely ignored by the military propagandists at the front. Steed might now instruct the CS to begin immediate distribution of the new leaflets, but the political permission which he had secured was largely academic. It never limited the propagandists' arguments; it simply stamped a firmer Allied seal of approval upon a campaign which employed the nationality principle.[81]

By 8 April, 15 million new manifestos, printed on the various army presses, were ready for distribution. They had been composed at the Intelligence offices, with the aid of Slav volunteers such as Stane Vidmar and his men at Tugurio who had been informed that 1200 aeroplanes would scatter them over the enemy.[82] Many of the short texts continued with familiar but topical themes of despair: the food crisis of the Central Powers, their failure to impose peace upon Bolshevik Russia, and the disaster of Germany's latest offensive in the West when 40 German divisions had been annihilated in six days, necessitating (allegedly) the despatch of Austro-Hungarian troops to the Western Front.[83] Alongside this gloomy picture there was growing emphasis upon government repression and nationalist agitation within the Empire itself, themes which would be commonplace in the following months. The leaflets suggested (with no evidence) that rebellion had erupted in the Czech lands, while in the south of the Monarchy the authorities were struggling vainly to suppress nationalism and had (an accurate statement) placed three towns in the Lika region under siege.[84] More concretely, they could quote on the one hand a speech made in the Austrian Reichsrat by a Dalmatian politician, Ante Tresić-Pavičić, about the brutalities suffered by the Croat population; and on the other, the famous and rather timely speech of Count Czernin on 2 April who had declared those peoples who demanded national rights to be 'enemies of Austria-Hungary' and had termed 'the Czech patriot Masaryk a despicable wretch!'.[85]

Such information was now in sharp contrast to the message contained in the most important of the new leaflets, those which confidently proclaimed Italy's support for the freedom of the 'oppressed nationalities' and their right to form independent states. In line with Finzi's note to Pivko, and regardless of Sonnino's ban on certain phrases, the propaganda informed Slav and Romanian soldiers that Italy had recognized their right to unite in independent states, and had agreed with the émigré leaders that prisoners or deserters of those nationalities would be treated like Italian soldiers. Although these were half-truths, there was some substance to back them up. The Czechs could be told that Italy had now recognized the Czecho-Slovak army, 'fighting by our side under the glorious flag of the ancient independent kingdom of Bohemia'.[86] The Yugoslavs were assured, rather less convincingly, that

> There will be a southern Slav state! All Serbs, Croats and Slovenes will be free and happy under one flag and one government. International agreements have now crowned the irresistible movement which your political leaders and your women have organized in your homeland. The Serbian Prime Minister Pašić, when he opened the Skupština [Parliament] on Corfu, announced that Italy like the other [western] Powers is in agreement with Serbia over the formation of a Yugoslav state.[87]

This, of course, was not true, for Orlando's government would never commit itself in this direction. But this type of leaflet matched the priorities of the propagandists who simply wanted a broad, Yugoslav statement to send across the trenches. Whether such a Yugoslav statement also matched the mentality of Serb, Croat and Slovene soldiers opposite was, as we will see, more questionable: it would always be an extra pitfall in the effectiveness of Italy's southern Slav propaganda.

Although the manifestos had been hurriedly produced by 8 April, the full 'offensive' was not yet launched as some historians have suggested. In his private report, though not in his memoirs, Steed admitted that bad weather in early April hampered the propaganda campaign for almost a fortnight and prevented distribution.[88] Consequently, any claims by Steed that the campaign quickly forced the enemy to replace Slav troops opposite the Italian 6th army with Magyar soldiers (let alone that it was responsible for thwarting an Austrian offensive) must be discounted. What is clear is that the Italian military thought that an exchange of troops had taken place, not because of the new leaflet campaign but because of Pivko's efforts at Stoccareddo. This, as we have seen, is in itself questionable. But that it was believed on the Italian side is evident from a rare leaflet in Hungarian which was thrown over in that sector by an Italian patrol on 21 April. It explained to the 'Hungarians opposite' why they had had to relieve the Czechs and then reminded them of Italy's common struggle of 1848 with Hungary against the Austrians. (Why, with the Russian threat removed, were the Magyars not at home with their families rather than 'here on the snowy mountains, hungry, without bread and half-frozen!'?)[89] Here again, the rumour of success with the propaganda weapon was as important as the actual reality in stimulating new efforts. The CS, partly because of the 'proof' in early April that front propaganda was effective, was increasingly optimistic about the new weapon. All the more so, because at this time the French were urging Diaz to launch some attack in order to relieve pressure on the Western Front. The CS might point to psychological warfare as a temporary substitute for what it feared would be costly operations if they used Italian troops with shaky morale. The Serbian liaison officer at Abano, Major Filip Hristić, summed up the prevailing mood: while propaganda had previously been organized irregularly with insufficiently defined principles, the Intelligence officers were now better prepared and much was expected of the inter-Allied propaganda commission which had been coordinated on Steed's initiative.[90] The basic arguments for the imminent campaign had also been enhanced by the Rome Congress of Oppressed Nationalities.

Preparations for the Rome Congress had accelerated in the weeks after the signing of the Torre–Trumbić agreement in London. Since then Borgese, Amendola and Torre had submitted the agreement to the émigrés in Paris for approval and slight modification, and had persuaded the Poles to attend the Congress even though Germany and not Austria was their principal enemy. All of the 'oppressed nationalities' were to be represented except the Ruthenes (Ukrainians): Polish–Ukrainian rivalry over Galicia made any Ruthene presence anathema to the Poles and would later seriously limit the amount of propaganda material which could be directed at Ruthene soldiers on the Italian Front. Roman Dmowski's Polish National Committee, however, sent representatives for the three partitioned regions of Poland, while the Yugoslav delegation, though containing no Slovenes, had been authorized to represent them and also included 12 deputies from the Serbian Parliament. For the future 'Czechoslovakia' there came, apart from Beneš, Štefánik and Hlaváček, Antonín Papírník who was about to relieve Hlaváček of the Rome office,[91] and Jan Šeba who had been sent by Masaryk to organize the Czech army in Italy. For the Romanians, who until October 1918 possessed no émigré organization comparable to the councils of the other nationalities, there came delegates representing both the Romanian Parliament and their compatriots in Transylvania. Steed and Seton-Watson were unofficial representatives for Britain; Franklin-Bouillon, Étienne Fournol and the socialist Albert Thomas for France, and the historian Nelson Gay for the United States. But it was the Italian delegation which proved to be most impressive. It contained men from all shades of the Italian political spectrum, from Salvemini, De Viti De Marco and Ojetti who favoured a detailed agreement with the Yugoslavs, to nationalist members of the Fascio such as Barzilai and Di Cesarò. All were now uneasily united in believing that a public manifestation of Italy's new policy would provide material for propaganda against the enemy and accelerate Italy's path to victory. Not all, however, shared by any means the émigré delegates' hope that the Congress would additionally pave the way for Allied recognition of independence for the peoples of the Habsburg Monarchy. The comment of one Italian nationalist, who witnessed the arrival of the émigré delegates at Rome station on 7 April, reveals the reality behind the unity which the Congress was about to proclaim: '"As long as the war lasts... we'll utilize these people; when the war is over and victory is ours, we'll _____ them". Thus saying he raised one of his arms in the obscene gesture which was not yet the Roman salute.'[92]

However, for the purpose of propaganda against Austria-Hungary the gathering in the Campidoglio on the Capitoline Hill on 8–10 April proved to be a remarkable success.[93] For the first time representatives from the oppressed nationalities and the Allies had come together to proclaim publicly, by endorsing the Torre–Trumbić agreement as the 'Pact of Rome', the need to form a united front to dissolve the Habsburg Empire and build new states on its ruins. Apart from the unanimous approval of these joint resolutions, which included the Italo-Yugoslav clauses, individual delegates publicly explained their national causes. Trumbić in particular received acclaim with a 'tactful and impressive speech', emphasizing that 'the main preoccupation of us all is to secure victory over the common enemy'.[94] While this was what the Fascio delegates especially wanted to hear, the Slavs and Romanians were themselves pleasantly surprised by the response of 'official Italy'. True, no member of the Italian government attended the proceedings, but Sonnino, while refusing to abandon the Treaty of London, permitted Steed to announce to the assembled that the whole Italian government, without exception, was 'in hearty sympathy with the aims of the Congress and desire the success of its efforts'. The good effect on the national delegates was reinforced on 11 April when their leaders were warmly welcomed by Orlando. He accepted the Congress's resolutions with the observation that 'the history of Italy, now completed, is simply your history now awaiting completion'. Assuring Steed that this acceptance could be taken as Italian official sanction of the nationalities' declarations of independence, Orlando told him to carry out propaganda on these lines.[95]

No less sensational than the public pronouncements of the Congress were the private discussions on 9 April of three committees dealing with future propaganda and policy. Their substance remained confidential but was in fact the meat on the bones of the Pact of Rome.[96] The first committee was the most significant in that it discussed what had so far been organized against the Central Powers, especially on the Italian Front. Steed and Franklin-Bouillon explained the Allies' plan and Steed's mission. This was firmly commended by the committee with a final resolution that the émigrés should be able to fully participate in the campaign at the front, where propaganda would proclaim the Allied governments' full support for their aspirations. The second committee considered the plight of those members of the oppressed nationalities who were prisoners of war, resolving to do everything possible to free them, and to give special attention to Romanian prisoners (since the Czech and Yugoslav causes had already gained some advantages). The third committee dealt with future publicity in Allied lands, proposing to hold another Congress in Paris as soon as possible, and recommending that representatives of the Allies and the nationalities should form a 'permanent committee' in each Allied capital; the permanent committee which was formed in Rome under Andrea Torre had the specific task of furthering the principles of the Pact of Rome and the resolutions of the first and second committees. Much of this future organization would remain on paper only, but at the time the émigré leaders could view the future with real optimism. As Trumbić noted later, the Congress had provided a platform from which they could proclaim their message to both enemies and allies. It had also laid down 'a path to follow on the basis of common action' which the émigrés hoped would soon lead to Allied diplomatic recognition of their national organizations.[97]

On 14 April Steed arrived back at the front with Seton-Watson and Emanuel. Delmé-Radcliffe noted in his diary, 'they had a conference with Badoglio in the afternoon. Czech, Jugo-Slav propaganda arrangements going well.' Steed's mission had returned to the war zone in order to make the final arrangements for the 'Central Inter-allied Propaganda Commission' (hereafter referred to as the Padua Commission). This body, which was to be based in Padua itself within easy reach of the CS at Abano, had been decided upon in principle at the coordinating meeting of 30 March. At that time Steed had, according to Granville Baker, insisted that Italians should be preponderant on the Commission since its efforts would be directed from the Italian Front against Italy's immediate enemies. The Commission was to form part of a 'Press and Propaganda Office' presided over by a Colonel Grossi and his deputy, Colonel Domenico Siciliani (head of Intelligence at the CS), with an Italian clerical staff and Allied representatives. Baker was to represent Britain and also serve as Northcliffe's envoy; an Alsatian, Major Gruss, was delegated by the French Military Mission; and Ugo Ojetti was to act as the Italian 'liaison officer'. All three had just attended the Rome Congress and mingled with members of the oppressed nationalities.[98]

Ojetti's appointment in the capacity of liaison officer reflected a typical compromise by Orlando between the ambitions of Gallenga and Ojetti, both of whom now expected to be given the leading role in supervising propaganda against the enemy. Ojetti was hardly satisfied with Gallenga's idea that, while serving as a liaison between the Prime Minister and the CS, he should carry out his propaganda work as a member of Gallenga's ministry. The result was that while Gallenga in theory was left in overall charge of 'Italian propaganda', Orlando singled out Ojetti for a special role. He was appointed on 11 April as

Orlando's political representative or liaison officer on the Padua Commission with the task of coordinating the propaganda offensive with the political designs of the government. This meant that Ojetti was directly subordinate to Orlando (not Gallenga), and in the wake of the Prime Minister's show of support after the Rome Congress, he was also specifically entrusted with supervising Italy's relations in the war zone with the émigré national councils, their volunteer forces and their prisoners of war. It was a role which left Ojetti with a great deal of potential influence, and slightly worried Diaz because of the degree of political interference in 'military matters'.[99]

It is clear from a recently published letter that Ojetti intended to take full advantage of his personal 'investiture' by Orlando (as he termed it). He was prepared to pay lip-service to Gallenga's position as head of Italian propaganda, but intended himself to oversee any aspects of that work which might constitute propaganda against the enemy.[100] From the start he saw himself as the key personality in the Padua Commission, rather than as an Italian representative on an Allied body, and his own perception quickly became reality because when the Commission began work its nominated heads faded into the background. Both Baker and Ojetti agreed that Colonel Grossi, though a pleasant individual, had no competence in propaganda work; he soon handed over his presidency to Siciliani who was himself more interested in his Intelligence duties than in psychological warfare. As a result it was Ojetti who became unofficial leader of the Commission, subject to Orlando and the CS, and the lynchpin of what was a military and political propaganda campaign. Although it is clear that Steed realized that Ojetti's role would be crucial, the ambiguities of Ojetti's position allowed him to impose his own independent, Italian stamp upon the campaign in a way which he had envisaged when first approached by Orlando. Because of this, the degree to which it was an Allied enterprise would soon be sharply called into question.

Before leaving for Paris on 16 April Steed and Seton-Watson had another conference with the Intelligence heads and then took leave of Diaz who 'thanked them warmly for the excellent work of the mission'. It had been decided on 30 March that representatives of the oppressed nationalities would form part of the Commission to act as translators and 'political supervisors' of the manifestos, a notion which had been confirmed in the first committee of the Rome Congress. On the eve of his departure, therefore, Steed urged Gallenga to send Polish and Czech representatives to Padua, and pressed Trumbić to visit the front together with 'an intelligent Yugoslav officer'.[101] When passing through Milan, Steed wrote again to Trumbić on notepaper of the *Corriere della Sera*, advising him on his arrival at the front to contact Radcliffe, Siciliani and the Intelligence heads, particularly Tullio Marchetti since he already had some Yugoslav officers working for him and was 'exceptionally well-informed about everything'. Ojetti was to arrive from Rome on the 17th 'to take everything in hand' and, Steed concluded, although it would take some time to organize the work, 'the mood of everybody is excellent'.[102]

Steed himself was in buoyant mood as he travelled back to England via Paris. At a luncheon at Versailles on the 20th his optimism was well observed by one British officer bound for Italy: 'Various people were present including a man called Steed, a Propaganda man. He never ceased talking. Interesting, but I should say inaccurate and he talks too much. If his advice is followed the war should soon be over!'[103] If Steed's confidence owed much to the success of the Rome Congress and arrangements at the front, it also stemmed from his sincere though mistaken belief that the new propaganda had already forced the enemy to postpone their offensive and withdraw unreliable troops from opposite the Italian 6th army sector. In Paris, on the last stage of his mission, and later with the British government, Steed made much of this 'evidence' when pressing the Allies to make a more definite commitment towards the oppressed nationalities so that the proven success of the propaganda weapon could continue. For example, when visiting Versailles with Beneš on 22 April, he enumerated for the British military the benefits which would accrue. The Austrian offensive could be prevented altogether and within the Habsburg Empire, especially Bohemia, rebellious elements could be pushed into open revolt: 'It is only because the wobbling policy of the Allies in titivating for peace with Austria and in supporting the Austrian Empire has made their [the Czechs'] position uncertain, that they have not been able to do more.'

Steed argued that it was now essential in using the propaganda weapon, as with any military campaign, for the authorities to have a clear plan or policy so that propaganda could be 'directed into the best channels to attain the objects desired'.[104] As usual he was pressing for Allied policy to keep up with the more radical propaganda agenda. Yet so far, Allied commitment to emancipating the subject races and destroying Austria-Hungary had been minimal, evident only by implication. Even in early April during Germany's spring offensive the British and French governments had merely agreed, on Steed's prompting, to the idea that proclamations of independence could form part of the propaganda offensive on the Italian Front. Orlando had gone slightly further by publicly endorsing the resolutions of the Rome Congress, but Sonnino blocked a more substantial commitment and no broader Allied support for the event was forthcoming.[105] It was now a principal task of both Steed and the émigrés to sustain governmental interest and particularly, with the propaganda campaign and the Czechoslovak volunteer forces as their bargaining counters, to press for a joint Allied declaration recognizing the independence of Austria-Hungary's nationalities. While Steed and Seton-Watson returned to London on 26 April, such an idea was being avidly discussed in Paris by émigré representatives under the guidance of Albert Thomas' 'Socialist Committee of Understanding between the Oppressed Nationalities'. The agitators had been enlivened by socializing and exchanging ideas in Rome: they were optimistic, spurred on by each other. As Ivo de Giulli wrote to Trumbić:

> All who have returned from Rome are satisfied with the success of the Congress and how things are going.... Thomas is wholly of the opinion that the government declarations must follow as quickly as possible, and that we must forge while the iron is hot. Clemenceau is said to be in favour. Steed also thinks that we mustn't delay. Only Franklin-Bouillon would like to wait for the [Paris] Congress, but he has his own reasons for that. At any rate, the preliminary work must begin right now and as fast as possible.[106]

For the British propagandists, the emissaries of the EPD, their key contribution to the Italian propaganda campaign had now been completed. The main role of Steed's mission had been to synthesize at a crucial moment the various Italian military and political strands which were in favour of a broad propaganda offensive: the result was the Padua Commission. From this point, Britain's role in the campaign reverted to being chiefly indirect rather than direct. The campaign would never be run from Crewe House, nor could any successes which it might have in the future be ascribed to the EPD, except to the extent that it was Steed who had helped to coordinate its organization at Padua. During the eight months of its existence in 1918, the EPD can best be characterized as an umbrella organization which served as a cover for a wide range of activities associated with influencing enemy morale or undermining the stability of the Central Powers. In some of these activities Crewe House had more control than others. Indeed, it was one of the real 'secrets' of Crewe House that the EPD's publicized image, in 1918 and afterwards, did not match the realities. The image was of a tightly run organization, while the reality was a very loosely coordinated body. The image was that it was Lord Northcliffe's vehicle to undermine the enemy. The reality was that Northcliffe was only nominally in charge, ill and absent from Crewe House until August, his directorship passing chiefly to his deputy, Campbell Stuart, who, together with Steed, Seton-Watson and other key individuals like Austin Guest, dealt with the everyday decisions of the organization.

To oversee the general direction of the EPD's work, Northcliffe appointed a number of prominent publicists and politicians to an advisory committee. It was destined to meet 14 times before the end of the war, chiefly to hear and endorse reports from the various sections of Crewe House.[107] Of these sections, it was the Austro-Hungarian branch under Steed and Seton-Watson which was undoubtedly the most active and which in the postwar period gained most publicity. But in terms of direct influence upon front propaganda it was probably the 'German section' of Crewe House which had the most impact in the last months of the war. The section was at first directed by

H.G. Wells, who meticulously elaborated the type of propaganda which should be directed against Germany, and then by the journalist Hamilton Fyfe; by August 1918 it had taken over most of the propaganda work hitherto done by MI7(b) of the War Office and was composing and printing its own material for despatch to France. Its particularly intensive activity from August rapidly attracted the German military's attention and appears to have far exceeded anything practised by the French on the Western Front.[108] In contrast, Crewe House's 'Bulgarian section' did little and was prepared to leave most work to the French on the Macedonian front; plans to send a former British consul in Sofia (Captain W.B. Heard) to Salonika in a similar vein to Steed's mission to Italy were never realized.[109] As for propaganda against Turkey, Crewe House was even less involved. From July 1918 the work was left to an American journalist in Beaverbrook's Ministry of Information who worked through British Intelligence contacts in Switzerland and the Aegean to scatter manifestos over the Turkish mainland.[110]

After the war it was to be the 'Austrian campaign' of the EPD which gained most attention. In *Secrets of Crewe House*, Campbell Stuart went so far as to observe that 'the conception of the whole propaganda campaign – its policy, its scope, its application', had been formulated by the Austro-Hungarian section. Just as this was a gross exaggeration which belittled Italy's major initiatives, so it was incorrect to suggest that the campaign from April 1918 was directed from London by Steed and Seton-Watson.[111] Although they received regular reports from Baker and Delmé-Radcliffe and instructed Baker accordingly, they had no direct involvement in the Italian campaign of the kind eventually exercised by the EPD's German section on the Western Front. Instead, the Austrian section of the EPD, synonymous with the persons of Steed and Seton-Watson, was a department which provided them with an official status from which in the summer months they persistently tried to modify Allied policy towards the Habsburg Monarchy. With their base at Crewe House, they employed as a secretary for their activities a former employee of the censor department, Dorothy Cocking. She, like Granville Baker, was a sympathetic and informed recruit: until February 1918, she had been interned at Raabs in an Austrian prison camp, and her parents (her father was allegedly 'well-informed on Austrian military affairs') still remained there in miserable conditions.[112] With her industriousness and personal commitment at their disposal, Steed and Seton-Watson contributed to the propaganda offensive against Austria chiefly in an indirect manner, by agitating successfully among the Allied governments and thereby providing new arguments for the campaign on the Italian Front. Just as their role in early 1918 had been one of coordinating Allied use of the propaganda weapon, so it continued to be so until the end of the war. The EPD retained its prestige as a propaganda centre among the Allies. But the actual propaganda offensive against Austria was based elsewhere, centred for its preparation and execution in northern Italy in the hands of the Padua Commission.

## 6.3 The Padua Commission

In the thinking of the Italian High Command at this time, the propaganda weapon was viewed chiefly as a kind of pre-emptive strike at the enemy. In late March, Diaz and Badoglio had responded warmly to Steed's mission since they were convinced that an Austrian offensive was imminent, and were persuaded by the Intelligence officers and political pressure to believe that intensive propaganda might sabotage the enemy's plans in advance. When the offensive did not occur (and the propagandists already claimed some credit for the 'postponement'), the CS did not alter its view of the task which had been entrusted to propaganda. Military Intelligence continued to suggest, especially from late April, that the Austrians would soon attack. With this uncertainty, the CS preferred to wait on events: completing the reorganization of Italian forces which Badoglio had supervised since the spring, making occasional raids into enemy lines, but not launching any larger strike which the enemy might exploit. In Badoglio's words, 'we have to keep hold of all our cards and play them without any hesitation'.[113] This was frustrating for the French who wanted some relief from German pressure in the West, and also for Lord Cavan who was expecting until late May that his forces would be allowed to make a local thrust on the Asiago plateau in order to boost British troop morale. When the CS called off Cavan's operation, because of clear evidence of the impending Austrian attack, Cavan reported to London with some irritation: 'If the big Asiago offensive is not to take place, I am sure that better results will be obtained by a series of vigorous but short armed blows than by trusting to propaganda and intrigue amongst disaffected men.'[114] This was not the view of Badoglio who clearly envisaged the new weapon as part and parcel of Italian strategy. Although in June the CS conceded the need for some small attacks, it continued to expect significant results from playing the propaganda card. Hopefully, the work of the new Padua Commission together with increasing activity by Slav propaganda patrols would rapidly bear fruit, helping to weaken the impending Austrian attack, but also paving the way for a major Italian armed response when the time was right.

The first meeting of the Padua Commission was held on the afternoon of 18 April at 1, Corso del Popolo, where the CS had set aside 15 rooms for the Commission's work. Chaired by Siciliani, the meeting was attended by Ojetti, Baker, Gruss and also a number of visitors invited by Baker: Hristić (Serbian liaison officer to the CS), Trumbić and two other members of the Yugoslav Committee, Dinko Trinajstić and Julije Gazzari, who were to direct the Committee's newly opened branch in Rome. According to Baker, the Italians resented this Yugoslav presence and 'thus gave the first indication of the conduct they intended to adopt towards the representatives of the oppressed races for whose liberation such perfervid perorations had resounded from the Roman Capital'.[115] While this may have been true for Siciliani, who later proved to be a 'Sonnino man', it was not the case for Ojetti, who summarized his conversation with Trumbić on this occasion as being 'practical, clear, detailed: in agreement on everything'. But Ojetti was already irritated by Baker's attitude. At the meeting, Siciliani emphasized bluntly that the Commission was going to be purely under Italian control with the British and French representatives acting only as advisers. Baker, however, had already shown initiative in inviting the Yugoslavs, and then had proceeded to sit through the meeting in silence, remarking only (as Ojetti scornfully noted) that he knew how to paint in watercolour.[116] The tension between Ojetti and Baker, stemming from the different ways in which they viewed each other's role on the Commission, was already clear. The seeds of serious friction had been sown.

While Ojetti industriously set about organizing 'his office', the Italian military resumed the distribution of manifestos over the enemy. Since the weather improved in late April, it was finally possible to scatter from the air the leaflets which had been composed at the Intelligence offices. At the same time the army presses now produced new material which reflected more precisely Italy's commitment to nationality politics, recalling the Rome Congress and its resolutions[117] or presenting personal messages from the head of the Yugoslav Committee. These leaflets, which Steed had urged Trumbić to compose, included one in which Trumbić told Yugoslav soldiers about his long and 'very satisfactory' chat with General Diaz at the front:

> There will come a day when you too will know what they talked about.[118] You will be convinced of how Dr. Trumbić with the Yugoslav Committee cares about the happiness of our nation. They are moved to tears when they think how close they are to you, yet cannot embrace you because your enemy has you in his grasp. Don't lose hope. The sun will rise before our door as well. The day will dawn when you will be free from the Kraut [*švapskih*] and Magyar barons and counts who oppress our people. Long live the united and liberated homeland of the Serbs, Croats and Slovenes![119]

When such material, usually printed on brightly coloured paper, was spread over the Austrian positions and southern Dalmatia, it made an immediate impact on the enemy. In early May, Conrad von Hötzendorf himself was already alarmed at the idea in many manifestos that Italy was releasing her Slav prisoners, since (if true) it was 'an extremely dangerous form of propaganda which might have a demoralizing effect on the men of Slav nationality and lead to desertions on a larger scale'.[120] From this evidence alone it is clear that the new type of front propaganda which Italy launched from late April had an immediate potential to shock the Austrian commanders to an extent lacking in previous efforts. Admittedly, many of the claims made in the manifestos were stretching the truth, both about Italy's commitment to the nationalities and about the degree of unrest in Austria-Hungary. The Padua Commission's manifestos would build on both of these main themes with a far larger amount of information, but also by providing material which was based more precisely on fact than on rumour. To some extent, this naturally reflected the reality of the deteriorating situation in the Monarchy which the Commission could exploit. One of the strengths of the new propaganda issued from Padua would be to utilize accurate news items from the Empire which the Habsburg authorities were trying to conceal from the soldiers. In particular, the latter would be constantly reminded that nationalist agitation in the Monarchy was keeping pace with the efforts of the émigrés and the Allies: there was little point in continuing to fight if compatriots on both sides of the front were united and no longer believed in the Empire's viability.

The Commission's main source of information about events in Austria-Hungary was to be an Italian Press Bureau – Agenzia Italiana della Stampa – which was set up in early May in Berne in Switzerland. Subject to Gallenga's ministry, and financed by it, the bureau was to be directed by Borgese who in the previous months had headed Gallenga's news and information office as well as playing a major role in the success of the Rome Congress. It had been one of Borgese's recommendations after his important mission to southern Slav émigrés in Switzerland in July 1917, that Italy should establish a press bureau there in order to be better informed about the Yugoslav question. Ten months later the purpose of the bureau was defined more widely and practically, since it formed a key element in Italy's propaganda offensive. It had a dual task: of maintaining regular contact with Slav émigrés in Switzerland, while at the same time feeding to Padua and Rome intelligence from these contacts and information which had been extracted from Austro-Hungarian newspapers. Indeed, Borgese's bureau utilized some of the channels and personnel which formed part of Marchetti's Intelligence network. One of those who joined the bureau, Luigi Granello, had long been an agent of Marchetti and from late 1917 had been working under cover from the press office of the Italian legation in Berne. He, like most of Borgese's recruits to the new bureau, for example the socialist MP Francesco Arcà, were adherents of nationality politics, for the bureau was to carry out work in line with Borgese's thinking about Italy's wartime and postwar mission, and therefore at odds with the views of Sonnino or the Consulta's own official representatives in Switzerland.[121] In late May, Seton-Watson visited Switzerland on a mission from Crewe House to help coordinate the work of enemy propaganda and Allied Intelligence agencies. He was impressed by Borgese's bureau which he found employing 'expert readers for the press of each subject race of Austria-Hungary', sending daily bulletins to Ojetti in Padua and Gallenga in Rome.[122] In the months ahead it was to become the most important information centre for the Padua Commission, supplying them also with long weekly digests of the enemy press which could not be speedily secured except via the route of neutral Switzerland.

Austrian military Intelligence knew something about Borgese's bureau. By July it was reliably informed by the Austrian consul in Lugano that Gallenga had sent Borgese, 'a famous Goethe specialist' and *Corriere* correspondent, to Berne where he had rented an office at 28, Obere Dufonstraße and recruited a large number of helpers including Granello, Filippo Sacchi and Ernesto Vercesi. However, although an Austrian agent code-named 'Milan' was in touch with Granello, Austrian sources were only partially correct about the bureau's precise purpose, assuming that its task was simply to intensify the amount of Italian propaganda in Switzerland.[123] Evidence for this was the fact that since Borgese's appearance 'the Italians have begun to carry out a very busy agitation among the Slav nationalities of Austria-Hungary' resident in Switzerland.[124]

Borgese was indeed in constant contact with the émigré bureaux, most notably the Serbian press bureau of Božidar Marković and the Czechoslovak press bureau in Geneva. And in late May Seton-Watson, as part of his co-ordinating mission, introduced him to the chief British propagandists in the country, Deneke and Edwards. These were all gatherers of Intelligence as well as being agitators and propagandists against Austria-Hungary. For example, the Czechoslovak press bureau run by Štefan Osuský acted as a link between the Czechoslovak National Council in Paris and the underground *Mafie* organization in Bohemia, smuggling instructions to the latter while accumulating information about conditions in the Monarchy for the use of the Czech movement abroad or Allied Intelligence. The staff were also involved in translating articles from the Austrian press though, as the Austrian censor position on the Swiss border observed in an extensive report about Czech agitators in Switzerland, 'what kind of articles they are and why they are translated is not clear: probably it's for use as political propaganda'.[125] This was indeed the case. The Czech émigrés' diligent research and Intelligence sources were now at the disposal of Borgese's new bureau which could communicate timely information to Padua for use as propaganda against the enemy.

Besides the bureau, Ojetti would rely for raw news material on Allied military Intelligence, particularly the Italian network. Already on 20 April he noted with satisfaction that Marchetti and Finzi 'were in agreement on everything', holding 'clear and Italian political views'; in the following months he would regularly attend the Intelligence heads' weekly Saturday meetings at Abano.[126] When it came to actually composing the Commission's leaflets, much would be carried out by the Italians themselves, and all manifestos had to have Italian translations so that Ojetti could preserve (as directed by Orlando) the 'necessary political control'. It was partly to act as translators that delegates from the oppressed nationalities were assigned to the Commission. But their participation, symbolic in itself of Italy's commitment to their cause, was all the more vital since it was thought that they would inject the correct tone and choose the most pertinent themes for the manifestos. As Steed had emphasized on 30 March, 'only representatives of the oppressed races were fully qualified to speak to their co-nationals on the burning subjects of the time'.[127] Both they and Ojetti wrote manifestos, for translation into or out of the Italian language. Both also sought to establish better contact in the war zone with volunteers and prisoners of the subject races. If for the émigré councils this was a natural obsession, in Ojetti's case such links were yet another source of propaganda material. He also viewed them as part of that overall coordination of 'nationality politics' at the front with which Orlando had personally entrusted him.

By 8 May the main national delegates had arrived in Padua. Most seem to have been chosen by their émigré compatriots for their breadth of experience or their knowledge of the Italian Front; some had a striking independence of character. However, the first to appear was an Italian, Benedetto de Luca, who was to represent Romanian interests. Although he had been a 'Romanian' delegate to the Rome Congress and was a former correspondent of the *Corriere della Sera* in Bucharest, De Luca's appointment was fully indicative of the

*Illustration 6.1* The Padua Commission in June 1918. *From left*: (D'Arturo), Ojetti, Lasić, Cotruş, Kujundžić, Jambrišak, (Bissolati), Zamorski, De Luca, Rybka, (Allamandola: Bissolati's secretary), (unknown), Szuber (Szuber, *Walka o Przegawę Duchową*, Warsaw, 1933)

disorganized Romanian émigré community. Ojetti was effectively able to pick his own Romanian delegates for the Commission, gradually supplanting De Luca with Cotruş, a Transylvanian volunteer-prisoner, and thereby keeping a firm grip on Romanian propaganda.[128]

Polish propaganda was to be far more autonomous, in the hands of Jan Zamorski (and his assistant Antoni Szuber). Before the war Zamorski had been a teacher in Tarnopol, a rural agitator in Galicia, and an MP for the Polish People's Party in the Reichsrat in Vienna. In November 1914 he had been temporarily arrested by the Austrian authorities on a charge of treason. He had been called up a year later and then traumatically captured on the Italian Front and placed in a prison camp. Easily recognisable from his bald head and 'thick, brown, very neglected beard', he was, according to Italian military Intelligence, 'a vigorous champion of Polish independence'. Indeed, he had made the leading speech for the Poles at the Rome Congress and it was a sign of his alleged notoriety that he was allowed to undersign personally many of Padua's Polish manifestos.[129]

A substantially quieter individual was the 'Czechoslovak' delegate, Josef Rybka. Steed had clearly envisaged František Hlaváček as the natural Czech representative because of his long experience in Italy, but Hlaváček's tense relationship with Štefánik prevented it. Instead it was Rybka, a former teacher from Louny west of Prague, who was extracted from an Italian prison camp and sent to Padua. Although he seems to have come to the fore through agitating for the Czech cause in the camps, Rybka was older and less vociferous than others on the Commission and also seems to have had far less contact with his national council than, for example, the Yugoslav delegates. The Czech leaders seem to have left him to his own devices, while knowing that their cause was being propagated vigorously anyway by their newly established Legion on the Italian Front.[130]

It was to be the Yugoslav delegates with whom Ojetti would work most carefully, since their cause was the most sensitive in the propaganda offensive and Ojetti was himself also personally committed to Italo-Yugoslav fraternity. The three delegates seem to have been deliberately chosen by Trumbić in order to represent the broad Yugoslav wartime experience. Dr Milivoj Jambrišak was a Croat dentist from Zagreb who had been taken prisoner on the Eastern Front and then 'with humour and Olympian coolness' had helped to organize Yugoslav volunteers in Odessa.[131] On the strength of this he had, in December 1916, been co-opted on to the Yugoslav Committee, and by 1918 was its representative in France among the volunteers arriving from America and among Yugoslav prisoners in the French prison camps.[132] His comrade on the Commission was Bogoljub Kujundžić, a Serb from Livno in western Bosnia who, like Jambrišak, had been captured by the Russians and would similarly prove to be a cool-headed and loyal ambassador for Trumbić, convinced in his own words that there could no peace 'as long as the monster exists which is called Austria'.[133] In June they were joined by a Slovene, Dr Stojan Lasić, who appears to have been an American volunteer discovered by Jambrišak, and who continued to wear a distinctive military uniform until the latter persuaded Trumbić that he was suitable for permanent membership of the Commission.[134] The 'three satellites', as Finzi mockingly termed them,[135] reported regularly to Trumbić and it was perhaps as much due to this discipline as to the sensitivity of their cause that their activity soon became the most publicized of the national delegates in the war zone.

On 18 April Ojetti had immediately taken control of the Commission. He recruited as an assistant Giuseppe Donati, a journalist and close friend of Salvemini, and secured Umberto Zanotti-Bianco, who was recovering from a war-wound in Rome, as his personal liaison with Gallenga and other ministries in the capital. Together with Donati, whom he rapidly grew to admire, Ojetti simply ignored Baker and Gruss and associated instead with the national delegates, meeting them every evening for a business discussion, but also taking their meals together at which they exchanged their wealth of ideas and wartime experiences.

Some time after arriving in Padua, Jambrišak set down on paper the aims of the Commission as he understood them from Ojetti:

> The purpose of the work is to carry out propaganda among Austrian soldiers (of the oppressed races), to encourage them to be friendly to Italy and also to weaken their military constitution...The work is planned in *two directions*: first at the front itself, to get in touch with Austrian patrols, to swamp them with manifestos and agitate among them in a pacifist and nationalist direction, and to spread hatred and mistrust of the Austrian military authorities. For that purpose we will throw leaflets into the Austrian trenches with the aid of special apparatuses. *In the second direction*, to pay attention to the rear of the Austrian front, especially the Istrian and Dalmatian coast.[136]

For Ojetti in the early weeks there were two major tasks to solve: the printing and the distribution of propaganda. At first he thought of having the material printed in Rome, but finally resolved upon using the Istituto Veneto d'Arti Grafiche which had been transferred after Caporetto from Venice to Reggio Emilia. The army bought it for the Commission, and Ojetti, who was particularly concerned not to copy the typographical mistakes of earlier leaflets, set about ensuring that the press secured from Turin the exact printing types for all languages of the Monarchy.[137] Distribution was to be a longer-lasting headache. It was expected that much material would simply be sent to the Intelligence offices and distributed by propaganda patrols such as Pivko's. Although the patrols might use rockets, Badoglio and the Intelligence heads agreed that the Naud grenades recommended by Steed were inadequate for the range required on many sectors of the Italian Front.

Yet it was air which was to be the vital medium for propagation. Ojetti, as mentioned, wished not only to swamp the enemy war zone with manifestos, but to distribute tons of material over the Istrian and Dalmatian coast and if possible to target particular towns with specific messages. As was the case in Austria when the Austrian propagandists hoped for support from their airmen, so in Italy in mid-1918 the idea of scattering propaganda was met with resistance by some of the military authorities. After some frustrating weeks, Ojetti finally had to use Orlando's influence in order to persuade the CS to designate one *Caproni* per army for propaganda purposes. Even then a range of obstacles persisted. It was not long before some Italians began to object to the Yugoslav material which they were supposed to distribute. In particular, although Ojetti thought he had arranged with the naval authorities to use their seaplanes to spread material over the Dalmatian coast, on 11 June he was told at Abano that Admiral Thaon di Revel – a supporter of Sonnino – refused to do so since the leaflets bore the names of Trumbić and Trinajstić, 'well known adversaries of Italy'.[138] It was one struggle which Ojetti would never fully master. Some consolation came from the fact that the 87th squadron, created in February to carry out bombing raids deep in the Austrian hinterland, agreed to take material on two major propaganda raids over Ljubljana and Zagreb. As we will see, these expeditions in June had a notable impact upon the 'enemy' population and caused a stir in the Austrian press.

Despite these problems of distribution, the front propaganda campaign of the Padua Commission was destined to be the most extensive and sophisticated of its kind during the whole war. From 15 May until early November 1918, the printing works at Reggio Emilia issued 643 brightly coloured manifestos, totalling about 60 million copies, and 80 newssheets, totalling almost two million copies.[139] This was about three times the amount of propaganda which the British were distributing on the Western Front over the same period.[140] Almost all of Padua's leaflets were numbered consecutively (see Appendix), the final manifesto being number 492,[141] and most were directed specifically at one nationality in the enemy forces. Of this material it is possible to calculate that the amount in Slav or Romance languages accounted for 80 per cent (48 million copies) of the total, while the Commission, initially reluctant to appeal to German-Austrian or Magyar soldiers, gradually increased its output in those languages during the summer, ending with a total of 46 German texts (four-and-a-half million copies) and 112 Hungarian texts (nine-and-a-half million). In contrast, Yugoslav material, for example, numbered 136 texts (over 13 million copies) and 20 editions of the single-sheet newspaper *Jugoslavia*: about 30 per cent of Padua's total propaganda.[142]

In terms of material, the Commission from the start envisaged a weekly newspaper as one of its main types of propaganda, both for use over the enemy lines and among prisoners in the Italian camps. It would, as Ojetti told Kujundžić on his arrival, be 'purely journalistic, a short and popular exposition of current affairs... [which] would only tell the truth and not be propaganda for its own sake'.[143] In fact, of course, 'The Truth', as Ojetti at first intended to call the paper, could be elastically interpreted. The newssheets which finally emerged, written in four languages under the titles *Jugoslavia*, *Československá Samostatnost*, *Polak* and *Neamul Românesc*, differed little from the ordinary manifestos except in the amount of information that they contained; they tended to be a mixture of imaginative writing by the national delegates and short items of news from the enemy press. However, the chief emphasis was certainly on providing supposedly impartial information of interest to a particular nationality. The idea for this may have partly derived from the kind of newssheets which were being used in Austria's own campaign against Italy, but it also indicates the Italians' correct perception that the enemy authorities were desperately trying to isolate their troops from poisonous information; after all, the CS after Caporetto was trying to do exactly the same thing. Alongside the newssheets, ordinary manifestos could be blunter, more emotional and would presumably have a greater appeal among the less educated. And as a third type of propaganda, Ojetti was keen to go further in this emotional direction, using national flags, symbols, anniversaries or religious imagery in order to arouse the soldiers' curiosity. For example, pictures of the Black Madonna of Czestochowa would be sent to Poles, leaflets about the anniversary of Jan Hus's death to Czechs, and each leaflet might be headed with appropriate national pictorial symbols.[144] The material would therefore supply topical items of news, but would usually accompany them with images or ideas which played on deep-seated national or personal sentiments.

In the short period before Austria launched its offensive on 15 June 1918, the Commission produced and distributed about 13 million copies of 84 different leaflets. Much of the material contrasted news about the Allies' strength with the Central Powers' desperate position. In particular, while Germany was failing to break through on the Western Front, the United States was galvanizing itself for action. Padua was especially quick to publicize President Wilson's speech in New York on 19 May in which he had underlined America's determination to fight with all its resources towards victory.[145] But the new ingredient, when compared to the former propaganda of Italian military Intelligence, was that Italy was now shown to be clearly committed to the nationality principle and this fact mirrored precisely the national aspirations in the Monarchy itself: the manifestos aimed to give as much attention as possible to the 'reality' of national polarization within Austria-Hungary.

In the material directed at 'Yugoslav' soldiers and civilians, most was in Serbo-Croat in the predominant štokavian dialect and in the Latin alphabet. Only in July would Cyrillic lettering (with which Serbs were most familiar) creep into the manifestos,[146] and leaflets in Slovene were not issued until Lasić had arrived at Padua. It was therefore the Croats who were targeted at first in an effort to dispel their fears about Italy. It was also undoubtedly the case that Jambrišak and his colleagues wished to emphasize uniformity in the propaganda, minimizing any differences which existed among the Yugoslav peoples. For example, he was against distributing religious imagery, for in contrast to its use with the Poles or Czechs, he felt 'it would have a damaging effect on our nation'.[147] Nor would any propaganda be aimed for the present at Moslems from Bosnia since they were viewed as unyielding or indifferent. As the Bosnian Serb Kujundžić told an inquisitive Granville Baker: 'although there are a few exceptions, they generally lack a national consciousness and are like religious fanatics with a liking for Turkey'. Only when there were more Moslems in Italian captivity might they be trained to act as Yugoslav pioneers in Bosnia.[148]

Indeed, Jambrišak and Kujundžić faced a fundamental dilemma. They were proclaiming a Yugoslav message to soldiers or civilians who rarely shared such an all-embracing ideal in 1918. But this could not stop the propagandists implying that the ideas of their manifestos were equally attractive or applicable to all the southern Slavs – Serbs, Croats and Slovenes. For example, they would often refer to legendary figures such as Matija Gubec or Bishop Strossmayer, who came from totally different periods of the southern Slav historical experience, but were grouped together as examples of heroes in the common fight for freedom. One of the first Yugoslav leaflets had a specifically Croat historic theme.[149] It told of a celebration organized in Rome on 30 April to commemorate the 'martyrdom' in 1681 of the Croatian rebels Zrinjski and Frankopan: 'two of the most outstanding representatives of our fight for justice and freedom' who had 'died because they loved too much those whom Austria hated so terribly'. Although the leaflet suggested that such a commemoration could not occur in Austria, the reality was that Zagreb on the same day had been decked in black and witnessed large demonstrations. The Rome events described in the leaflet therefore had a potential resonance among Croats, and all the more so because on 11 May a radical Zagreb newspaper proceeded to report them in full together with an uncensored version of the speech which Ante Trumbić had delivered.[150] It was a notable example of how some of Italy's radical propaganda could mirror precisely the mentality of radical agitators in Austria-Hungary.

The crucial element in the Rome commemoration (and the leaflet) was, of course, that Italians had hosted it. From the start, Padua's Yugoslav material emphasized that Italy was fighting for the Yugoslav cause. Evidence for this was the Rome Congress; the presence in Italy of Yugoslav Committee delegates who were working with Italians in Rome and at the CS; and the supposedly good treatment which Italy was meting out to Yugoslav prisoners. It only then seemed a slight exaggeration to suggest that 'all of Italy's land, sea and air forms of communication are at our disposal'![151] Trumbić himself, who in May was visiting the Serbian High Command on the Salonika Front, could be quoted to sum up the new spirited mood:

> The future of a great Yugoslav state is much more certain now than ten months ago [the time of the Corfu Declaration]. For this revolution for the better one must thank especially the attitude of Italy. As evidence of that, it is enough to mention that when I was in Rome I was received in all circles not as an ordinary Yugoslav delegate but as the representative of a friendly country, indeed an independent country. I am convinced that the Italian people really are amicably disposed towards the Yugoslavs and that that friendship will grow ever deeper and more affectionate. Italy's greatest political thinkers completely understand the need for friendship between us and the Italians. They are sure that free and united Yugoslavs will be the strongest defence against Germany breaking through to the Adriatic sea.[152]

Such benevolence by Italy could be directly contrasted in the manifestos with the attitude of the Habsburg authorities. It was at this very time that they were beginning to debate the future of their southern Slav lands, faced as they were with a home-grown Yugoslav movement, the so-called 'declaration movement'. This had originated in Slovene regions in August 1917 and was slowly spreading southwards under the leadership of Monsignor Anton Korošec.[153] Padua duly secured some news about the growing polarization in the Monarchy over this issue. On 3 May 1918, the Austrian Prime Minister assured German-Austrian MPs that if there was any southern Slav unity under the Habsburg sceptre it would never include Slovene territory since to do so would separate Austria from the Adriatic. On 25 May the Emperor himself went further by telling a German deputation from the Slovene lands that he opposed a united Slovenia under any circumstances. Padua commented: 'The German-Magyar government gives the Germans the right to oppress the Slovene fatherland'.[154]

Further proof that this was true was supplied in one of Padua's first manifestos in Slovene which quoted at length an article from the radical Ljubljana daily *Slovenec*. The article refuted German claims that the Slovene peasantry would have a miserable existence in any Yugoslav state. On the contrary, while at present it was Germans who dominated the Slovene economy and educational system, in Yugoslavia the ordinary Slovene would gain security: 'every Slovene peasant would be protected by law and would not be subject to the monstrous orders which the foreigner imposes on him simply to exploit him'.[155] Alongside this manifesto of ideas, Padua was also able to give a few hints of the declaration movement on the ground: how a mass of Slovene parishes were adhering to the

Yugoslav cause, how food riots had taken place in late April in Ljubljana, and how there were mass rallies at which oaths for unity and independence were being sworn.[156] If the news which Padua secured on this subject was still rather sketchy, it was generally accurate and was a useful foil to negative items about German-Magyar oppression. The extent of the latter was often exaggerated and described in colourful, if not violent, language:

> When twenty-four thousand Magyars have been sent to Zagreb, Sušak, Karlovac, Rijeka and other towns of Croatia, when these murderers kill our fathers and brothers, and rape our daughters and wives – at this time you ought to support those who bring you freedom and unity. What are you still waiting for? Are we going to be servants of a foreign country for ever? Doesn't the blood stir in your veins? Have you lost your sight and are blind? Can't you hear the groans of your fathers as they are hung, the scream of your weak ones and the howl of your slaughtered and violated mothers and brides? Hear them once and avenge them.[157]

Padua's first manifestos in the Czech, Polish and Romanian languages followed the same pattern as the Yugoslav. They emphasized on the one hand the national polarization in the Monarchy, and on the other the extent to which the Allies, particularly Italy, were demonstrably committed to the nationality principle. Evidence for these themes was especially plentiful for Czech propaganda. The Czech material, although always labelled as 'Czecoslovacco', contained nothing in the Slovak language: it was written in Czech by Rybka, with Czech news and sentiments, and thereby the fiction was propagated (far more than in the Yugoslav case) that there existed one Czechoslovak nationality. In the first edition of Padua's Czech newspaper, *Československá Samostatnost* (deliberately given the same name as the official organ of the National Council in Paris), Czechs were 'reminded' of how they had all taken a moral stance against the Habsburgs from the beginning of the war. After a long period of passive resistance in the Czech towns and countryside, the people from mid-1917 had begun to speak out: witness the speeches in the Reichsrat on 30 May 1917, the Epiphany Declaration of 6 January 1918, and more recently the response made by Czech MPs to Count Czernin's untactful attacks on Masaryk and the 'treacherous' Czech nation.[158] Padua in this period certainly had much material to hand because of contemporary dramatic events in Prague, not least, as we will see, the demonstrations in mid-May on the 50th anniversary of the founding of the Czech National Theatre. The Czechs, like the Slovenes, could also be given ample 'proof' of the economic realities at home where the state continued to make requisitions while their families were starving.[159] In this environment of German oppression, the manifestos proclaimed that the Czechs at home were now determined to create their own independent Czechoslovak state, ever mindful of their glorious history and the need to avenge their subjugation by the Habsburgs at the Battle of the White Mountain (1620).

Meanwhile, Padua had strong proof to support its argument that Italy supported this Czech mission. While in the Yugoslav material no evidence could be provided of Yugoslav troops on the Italian Front (only on the Salonika Front),[160] the creation of a Czechoslovak Legion in Italy was the most prominent and natural theme in Padua's Czech propaganda. Many of the early manifestos were signed by Štefánik or by 'volunteers of the Czechoslovak army' and announced that Italians and Czechs were now shedding their blood for the same cause and would welcome deserters into their ranks.[161] One long piece, an emotional article by Hlaváček, was reproduced to describe the atmosphere in the war zone where Czech soldiers wandered happily through Italy's romantic medieval towns, mingling with an admiring native population.[162] But the most notable event for the Czech cause in Italy took place on 24 May. At a solemn ceremony in Rome, on the third anniversary of Italy's entry into the war, 'brothers' of the 34th Czechoslovak regiment were handed their colours in the presence of Orlando, Sonnino, Bissolati and the ambassadors of the Allied powers. Padua provided a fervent and rather verbose commentary, declaring it to be a baptism for the new state, with Orlando acting as the godfather:

> For years to come, as long as the bright sun of freedom shines on us, [the brothers] will tell their friends and children about this day of euphoria and fraternity between two peoples. One of them great, free, so exalted by culture and the past that it has always stood in the forefront of humanity; the other, reckoned to be modest, subjugated, desiring freedom so that it too could exercise all its typical racial attributes in order to further develop a humanitarian civilization and culture. For after all, it is full sympathy, respect, sincere fraternization which has vitalized everything which was said and done on the soil of the eternal city.

After speeches by Štefánik and General Graziani, Italian commander of the Legion, the Czech national anthem was played and the troops marched off to the Campidoglio. The propagandists, possibly Ojetti himself, penned some concluding words: 'In these marvellous days the eyes of Czechs are melting with joy. In Austria our brothers and friends are executed, but here in a foreign country, they overwhelm us with demonstrations of love and friendship.'[163]

While the Legion in itself seemed to be proof of Italy's commitment to the Czech cause, Padua could never quite suggest that Italy was actually fighting to create an independent Czechoslovakia. Here Polish propaganda had a slight advantage. For on 3 June in their Versailles Declaration, the Allies gave a new pledge, singling out the creation of a united and independent Poland as 'one of the conditions of a solid and just peace'. Jan Zamorski, whose signature regularly accompanied the early Polish manifestos, commented that Polish soldiers had a choice between this freedom which was guaranteed by an Allied victory and the slavery which would continue after a Prussian-Austrian victory: 'I demand of you as a brother and compatriot, as an MP and chairman of the Christian People's Party, as a Pole and true son of the fatherland, throw away your Austrian weapons and surrender, all of you, to the Italians.'[164]

In a subsequent leaflet Zamorski suggested, falsely as far as one can tell, that 217 Poles had indeed succumbed to his invitation and crossed the trenches.[165] The reality was that, in contrast to Czech exploits in the Italian war zone, Zamorski had no comparable examples to relate in his material; there was as yet no sign of a Polish legion, and only Tullio Marchetti had recruited a dozen Polish volunteers as patrols on the lst army front. Zamorski therefore made the most of limited evidence. He recalled the historic examples of Polish heroes who had formed legions in Italy: Adam Mickiewicz and Henryk Dąbrowski (who fortuitously had died 100 years before on 6 June 1818).[166] And when on 9 June one of Marchetti's Polish volunteers was killed in the front line, Zamorski, after accompanying Ojetti, Rybka and Kujundžić to the funeral, wrote a manifesto which contrasted the dead volunteer's ideals with those of the Austrian, possibly Polish, 'slave' who had fired the fatal bullet.[167]

But perhaps the strongest arguments in Zamorski's propaganda came from enemy sources, emphasizing a message of despair to be contrasted with the hope which the Allies were offering. In his key speech at the Rome Congress, Zamorski had stated that Germany was the main opponent of the Poles who had to be defeated.[168] In his propaganda it was regularly the German or Prussian threat which he highlighted. Padua's first Polish manifesto told of a legendary exploit which Poles ought to emulate. It recalled how at the battle of Grunwald (1410) the valiant Władysław Jagiełło with Polish, Lithuanian and Russian armies had defeated the Teutonic Knights and freed Poland from the Germans; 500 years later, statues to Jagiełło and his cousin Witold had been unveiled in Kraków, and now the people made daily pilgrimages to the monument, lighting candles and offering prayers that a second Grunwald might be unleashed on the Germans. Yet, the leaflet stressed, the 'Teutonic reptile' was the same whether in Berlin or Vienna.[169] It was the same German who forbade anniversary celebrations for Dąbrowski in Posen; who sent troops to Palestine to help the pagan Turk retake the Holy Places (a matter naturally dear to every Catholic Pole); or who fired on women and children in the streets of Kraków.

When Poles thought of the Habsburg Empire, Zamorski warned, they ought to remember their starving families in Galicia, or the 'treason' committed by the Austrians earlier in the year when they had announced the partition of the province in return for their worthless 'Bread-Peace' with the Ukraine.[170] Especially, they ought to remember the subsequent course of events: how

General Haller and his Polish legionaries had revolted and deserted en masse to the Russians, leaving 117 legionaries to be dispatched to a 'German court' and the rest to be sent back to the front line as 'German excrement'. Many of Zamorski's leaflets specifically targeted those former Polish legionaries who had been transferred to the Italian Front, reminding them of their comrades' dismal fate (even suggesting incorrectly that Haller under German pressure had committed suicide) and demonstrating that 'there is no place for Polish soldiers in the Austrian ranks'.[171] If the Poles had historic models in Jagiełło and Dąbrowski, they had some modern models in Haller or even in Austria's Polish MPs who, after 50 years' loyalty to the Habsburgs, had moved into opposition in the Reichsrat.[172] The example to emulate was clear. It was perhaps, however, an example which insufficient Polish soldiers had followed before June 1918. Hence Zamorski's persistent calls for desertion (far more than in the propaganda to other nationalities); hence too the message of one manifesto, that it was only really Poles, Germans and Magyars who were holding the Habsburg Empire together.[173]

Padua's Romanian propaganda could not match this range of arguments. Certainly it suffered because the Romanian delegates, De Luca and Cotruş, were more firmly under Ojetti's control; and he soon started to use Cotruş to write leaflets in Hungarian instead. But Padua also simply lacked sufficient evidence about Romanian agitation at home or abroad. To show Allied sympathy, the manifestos reported Romanian participation in the Rome Congress and especially the work of two émigrés from Romania who were active in Italy: Gheorghe Mironescu (a future Romanian Prime Minister) who was visiting Romanian prisoners of war, and Simeon Mîndrescu who was leading negotiations with the Italian government on behalf of the 'Society of Romanians from Transylvania, Banat and Bukovina'.[174] But the propaganda could contain no evidence of actual unrest among the Romanians of Austria-Hungary. It often resorted to reproducing disquieting news about other parts of the Empire in order to fill up the columns of the Romanian newssheet, *Neamul Românesc*. This accurately reflected the reality of Romanian political passivity in the Monarchy until after the Central Powers had signed the Peace of Bucharest with Romania (7 May), for from late 1916 the Magyar authorities had effectively stifled any Transylvanian agitation and left Padua little substance to work with. The best that Padua could achieve was to condemn the peace, and instruct Romanian soldiers in florid language about how the Central Powers were exploiting the riches of the Romanian kingdom:

> The ancient forests which cover the Carpathians, the oil-wells which are inexhaustible, the rich fields of the plains which lie in Wallachia – all have been handed over to the control of Hungarians and Germans! The grain of Romanian producers is being bought at a price which serves simply to

> subsidize the greedy and implacable oppressors of the nation! Thus for a long time Romania has been strangled by the Germans, Hungarians and Bulgarians! For God's sake! This shame must be washed clean! Italy, France, England and America have pledged it! . . . Brother Romanians! Your fate is now in your own hands! As rescuers of your brothers on the Danube, go and complete their salvation![175]

This was probably a vain plea since most Romanian soldiers, at least according to British military Intelligence, had little interest in the idea of a greater Romanian state. It was probably more productive for Padua simply to appeal to anxiety about Hungarian oppression in Transylvania or about the futility of Romanians fighting any longer for 'Prussians and Magyars'. Thus, in one vivid proclamation, Traian Vuia (a famous Transylvanian scientist who headed a National Committee of Romanian émigrés established in Paris on 30 April), urged Romanians to 'rise up against your exploiters and hasten the time of their defeat which will be your salvation from the two calamities, war and the Hungarian yoke', for with Allied help the future was bright: 'like a putrid body, riddled with an unpleasant disease, Austria is about to decompose'.[176]

If Padua at this time could target its arguments better towards some nationalities than others, there were two events occurring in the Monarchy in May 1918 which above all served to confirm the theme of national polarization which was at the very heart of the propaganda. Their supra-national significance made them suitable as a subject in leaflets addressed to all elements in the opposing army. The first event was Emperor Karl's 'Canossa' or journey of repentance to the German GHQ at Spa following revelations that he had been secretly involved in peace negotiations with the West (the notorious 'Sixtus Affair'). On 12 May, the two Kaisers signed an agreement which included a *Waffenbund,* binding together the German and Austro-Hungarian military machines more closely than ever before. Although the agreement was actually dependent on a solution of the Polish question, and was not a new '25-year alliance' as Italian propaganda maintained, its terms certainly suggested a future empire of *Mitteleuropa.* In that light they were triumphantly interpreted by the Austro-German press, the *Neue Freie Presse* extolling them as a victory of Germans over Slavs, while the *Frankfurter Zeitung* noted calmly that 'with the new alliance Austria-Hungary ceases to be an independent state and becomes a region of the German Empire'. In quoting these views, Padua could instruct Yugoslavs and other 'oppressed' that Karl's behaviour at Spa removed the last vestige of any obligation towards a state or dynasty which had sold itself to the German Reich.[177]

Padua also proceeded to write in the same vein in the few German and Hungarian manifestos which were issued prior to the June offensive. German-Austrian soldiers were told (inaccurately) that in the wake of the Spa treaty the brutal General Max Hoffmann who had enforced the *Diktat* of Brest-Litovsk in the East was now about to take over and prussianize the Austrian army: 'Austrians' should begin to think about the fate which befell the citizens of Bavaria and Württemberg![178] As for Magyar soldiers, they could be sent some propaganda when Ojetti had found a Hungarian translator. In the first such leaflets, Padua quoted the views of the German and Magyar press about the *Waffenbund*, and notably those of the outspoken head of the 'Independence Party', Count Mihály Károlyi; on 15 May he had railed against Germany's expansionist aims, German responsibility for the war, as well as his own discovery of a plot by German Intelligence to discredit him.[179] The Magyars could also be given, as in Finzi's progressive leaflets a few months earlier, some historical figures of their own to emulate (Rákóczi and Kossuth). They were now advised to revolt against their subjection to Germany in line with the old Hungarian saying, 'the German is a scoundrel and the Devil take him!'[180] It was the start of an increasingly sophisticated campaign directed at Hungarian soldiers, a scheme which Ojetti could only fully implement from June when Cotruş had joined the Commission.

Against the Spa agreement and its message of germanization, Padua could set a second major event which occurred in May. It too seemed of relevance to all nationalities, but in this case there seemed to be a hopeful message, that the peoples of the Monarchy were indeed taking up the 'liberationist struggle' which the Allies were trying to encourage. The celebration in Prague from 16–18 May of the 50th anniversary of the Czech National Theatre was presented in Padua's propaganda as a direct echo of the Rome Congress a month earlier. There was some truth in this. Partly as a result of suggestions from the Czech émigrés, the organizers of the theatre anniversary turned the event into a mass demonstration by domestic representatives of the 'oppressed peoples' of the Monarchy. Czech and Slovak politicians and literati such as Karel Kramář, Alois Jirásek and Pavel Hviezdoslav were joined by prominent Slovene, Italian and Polish delegates who openly proclaimed self-determination and unity in the face of German-Magyar injustices.[181] In the words of one Yugoslav manifesto, 'that which the representatives of those peoples spoke in the Campidoglio, these delegates affirmed in Prague: "only on the ruins of Austria is our freedom and unity possible"'.[182] The Czech events thus had a supra-national significance, matching that of the Rome Congress. Padua could not only give a particular nationalist slant to each description presented to the individual nationalities, but could even quote a German journalist who himself emphasized the Prague–Rome connection when writing that the Prague Congress had 'an international and world historical significance'.[183] As for the specifically Czech dimension to the events, Padua's propaganda exploited it fully. The second edition of *Československá Samostatnost* was dominated by references to the new historic connection between Rome and Prague, two cities which had formerly had no links due to unhappy Czech memories of the Vatican. Suddenly in the wake of the Rome Congress the link was made by the Prague celebrations which, 'like a flash of lightening in front of an amazed foreign audience, lit up the darkness which had been engulfing Austria'.

The way in which this propaganda was prepared and presented to Czech soldiers is an interesting example of Italy's newly integrated propaganda machinery at work. After the Prague events, the Austrian authorities had suppressed editions of the Czech daily, *Národní Listy*, which had carried full texts of the speeches of Kramář and others. However, Luigi Granello at the Berne bureau managed to secure copies of these editions from the Czech community in Switzerland and passed them on to his former Intelligence head, Tullio Marchetti. Marchetti thereupon composed and printed for Ojetti an account of the speeches and accompanied them with the front page of the last (censored) edition of the newspaper. As manifesto number 66 it was a powerful image, which Marchetti later claimed to have reaped some success, and it was one which was firmly based on the reality of what had occurred in Prague.[184] But it was also always presented by Padua alongside a misleading and exaggerated account of how the Austrians had actually reacted. The leaflets asserted that the authorities had used grapeshot and gallows so that 'our blood has begun to flow in the streets of Prague and masses of innocent of people are lying in the prisons'. In fact, the demonstrations had passed off relatively peacefully. There was no bloodshed or use of troops, even though alarming rumours were circulating in Vienna about what had actually happened.[185]

Padua's early propaganda set the tone for the language and imagery of its later material. The language was usually literary and emotional, and at times florid or violent. The appeal tended to be 'personal' with a distinct characteristic of supplying historic examples and making each nationality conscious of the sweep of their heroic destiny. While the four main oppressed peoples – the Czechs, Poles, Yugoslavs and Romanians – were the chief targets, Ojetti had already discovered that the material which he could use against the four was very uneven. The Czechs undoubtedly supplied the strongest case and the Romanians the weakest. Perhaps rather surprisingly, however, it tended to be news items about disruptive events in Austria-Hungary which so far provided the best propaganda arguments; items about Italy's or the Allies' increasing solidarity with the nationalities were less prominent in the material, and rarely suggested any real commitment to their independence. This uneven balance accurately reflected the fact that, as Padua began its campaign, nationalist agitation was fortuitously taking a more radical direction in the Monarchy, whilst in Italy the momentum of the Rome Congress was not being maintained as the national émigrés had expected. The natural danger was that this discrepancy might undermine Padua's campaign altogether (just as the Austrians' own propaganda efforts were coming increasingly unstuck through their inability to present a strong and stable picture of themselves to Italy). Not surprisingly, therefore, the Padua Commission in its first months of operation was increasingly scarred by tensions which directly arose from creeping doubts about Italy's real commitment to the spirit of the Rome Congress.

It was not until June 1918 that these doubts and suspicions were fully confirmed. In the weeks after the Congress there were regular signs of Allied goodwill, and the émigrés could feel that their Allied friends and sympathizers were at least managing to extract extra promises from Paris and London. In Paris from late April, the national councils under the guidance of Thomas, Franklin-Bouillon and others were working on separate declarations which could be amalgamated into a general Allied statement and proclaimed at a second Congress to be held in the French capital. The work proceeded slowly. In the first place, the Yugoslavs under Ivo de Giulli were often completely out of touch with Trumbić (who was away on the Salonika Front for most of May), and did not feel able to act without his authoritative presence or at least adequate instructions. Secondly, Franklin-Bouillon and Étienne Fournol seem to have stalled for a time, possibly because they were especially keen for the Paris Congress (postponed repeatedly) to be the scene for any Allied declaration, and so regain for France that role of champion of the oppressed which it had lost to Italy. In the event, the émigrés and the French did manage to present a statement of their conclusions to the Quai d'Orsay by the end of May. They thereupon hoped that the Allies would negotiate a declaration of recognition to be proclaimed in early June at Versailles.[186]

Meanwhile, the members and associates of the EPD were trying to push the British and American governments in the same direction. Immediately after the Italian–Czech convention had been signed on 21 April, recognizing a Czechoslovak Legion on Italian soil, Štefánik returned to the front and urged both Delmé-Radcliffe and Granville Baker that the British should approve a similar convention. Radcliffe enthusiastically telegraphed to his superiors that such a move would 'be valuable for propaganda purposes'. Baker went much further in his report for Crewe House, emphasizing, with an eye to Czech military feats in Russia, that 'the recognition of a Czecho-Slovak state' would make 'a considerable impression in Austria-Hungary' and that he himself should be appointed military attaché to the new Czechoslovak army.[187] Baker, Radcliffe and Štefánik also pressed their views on the new American Military Mission in Italy with the result that its chief telegraphed to the US ambassador in Rome: 'British mission here attaches great importance to the United States recognizing the Czech-Slav movement and recommends that the action . . . be taken if possible within the next few weeks.'[188]

This pressure, together with further entreaties from the US envoys in Italy and Switzerland that their government should make some declaration of sympathy for the subject races and forget about trying to detach Austria from

Germany, eventually contributed to the US Secretary of State, Robert Lansing, declaring on 29 May that the United States had followed the Rome Congress 'with great interest... and that the nationalistic aspirations of the Czecho-Slovaks and Jugo-Slavs for freedom have the earnest sympathy of this Government'. Even so, such language was more important for its effect on the Allies and on further diplomatic moves than for its use by the Padua Commission. Ojetti clearly viewed it as too weak to merit more than a passing reference in his manifestos, and concentrated instead on the strident speech which Wilson had just delivered in New York.[189]

It was when the EPD flirted directly with the British government that statements were forthcoming of a kind most useful to the Padua Commission. On 10 May, Steed introduced Beneš to Balfour and Robert Cecil at the Foreign Office. Although Beneš, in common with the other émigrés after the Congress, was now publicly committed to securing an Allied declaration which would benefit all of the oppressed nationalities, he privately had qualms about adopting this approach in view of both Allied and émigré disunity.[190] Beneš's realistic priority was to secure full Allied recognition for the Czechoslovak army, arguing that the French and Italian agreements were tantamount to recognition that the National Council was the supreme organ of the Czech movement in Allied countries. In his dealings with the Foreign Office Beneš went so far as to belittle the role of the other peoples of the Monarchy, alleging that the Czechs had 'caused the military disasters of Austria' or that

> the Czecho-Slovaks have done much more harm to Austria-Hungary than other nations in revolt... A manifestation of sympathy to our cause would enormously increase the internal confusion in Austria-Hungary and would considerably strengthen the force of resistance of the Czecho-Slovaks which would hasten the internal collapse of Austria-Hungary.[191]

It was Beneš's single-mindedness which secured from Balfour on 3 June a letter recognizing the Czech army, but also (a significant advance on the French and Italian position) acknowledging the Czechoslovak National Council as the supreme organ of the Czechoslovak movement in the Allied countries. In Padua's Czech propaganda, however, it was British recognition of the Czech Legion which was viewed as the higher priority.[192]

For the EPD the advance secured by the Czechs, though gratifying, was never divorced from the need for a common Allied statement towards all the émigré organizations. Thus when Delmé-Radcliffe visited London in mid-May, a memorandum which Crewe House helped him to compose for the Foreign and War Offices laid equal emphasis upon recognition of the Czechoslovak and Yugoslav causes. Both movements could lead to 'the complete paralysis in the immediate future of the Austrian military machine', all the more so since (the document boldly asserted) it was now entirely possible to coordinate them fully with Czech and Yugoslav agitation within the Austrian ranks. What was vital, therefore, was for the British, French and American governments to recognize publicly the independence of the Czechoslovak and Yugoslav nations with their émigré committees as provisional governments. Former experience with the propaganda weapon was then emphasized: 'This would be the most efficient form of propaganda and would constitute a straightforward means of achieving in Austria results similar to those which Germany achieved in Russia by foul means.'[193] While such language flowed naturally from the mouth of Crewe House, it is clear that Delmé-Radcliffe himself was personally committed, and increasingly active, in trumpeting the use of the new weapon on the Italian Front, not least perhaps because of the opportunity to play a pivotal role in the campaign. A number of observers noticed Radcliffe's 'extreme optimism regarding disaffection among the Czechs'.[194]

It was as a direct result of the Radcliffe-EPD memorandum that the British Foreign Office's policy towards Austria-Hungary was finally clarified. On his return journey to Italy, Radcliffe, interpreting his own brief rather widely and with characteristic indiscretion, showed the document to Clemenceau who then asked London if these were now the views of the British government. In reply Cecil telegraphed on 21 May:

> We feel that policy of trying to detach Austria from Germany must be abandoned as both inopportune and impracticable. Recent meeting of Emperors has obviously led to bonds between two Empires being tightened. We think that best plan is to give all possible support to oppressed nationalities in Austria in their struggle against German-Magyar domination.[195]

The following day Cecil spoke in the same spirit at a banquet at the Mansion House to celebrate the third anniversary of Italy's entry into the war. The speech, discussed with Steed beforehand, contained the first public approval by the British government of the Rome Congress and Italy's new course towards the oppressed nationalities; 'we are', Cecil added, 'anxious to see all these peoples in the enjoyment of full liberty and independence'.[196] Steed, while commenting mischeviously in *The Times*'s leading article that it now remained for the Allies to give 'prompt and concrete expression to their common policy', was able to inform the EPD committee at Crewe House that the speech 'had had an excellent effect in Italy and among the subject races of Austria-Hungary': it was 'being vigorously used for propaganda among the enemy troops'.[197]

Certainly at the Padua Commission, Britain's statement delighted the Yugoslav representatives in particular. According to Milivoj Jambrišak, Cecil's speech was 'balm to his spirit as he was getting very anxious about the delay in making such a pronouncement in England'.[198] Bogoljub Kujundžić too confirmed for

Delmé-Radcliffe that the speech had made a 'remarkable impression': it was 'formal confirmation that England believes in carrying things through to the end'. At the same time, however, Kujundžić was healthily suspicious of Cecil's view that the main issue was not the dismemberment of the Monarchy but the liberation of its oppressed peoples, for that could be taken to mean autonomy rather than independence. Such a prospect the Bosnian Serb would not contemplate: 'It was not for nothing that I left home and family and went over to the other side. Freedom and Austria are incompatible. Austria denies freedom just as freedom denies Austria.' In this regard, he added cryptically, the British were still 'afraid of snakes of the trees and lizards'.[199]

Even so, Cecil's speech suggested to the Yugoslavs that Britain was inclining towards France's patronage of the oppressed nationalities, and that they could expect a radical declaration at the next meeting of Allied leaders at Versailles.[200] As for the Italians' attitude, the Yugoslav émigrés did not now envisage that they would prove an obstacle to such progress. Indeed, even Ante Trumbić was rather naïvely optimistic about the 'revolution' which had taken place in Italy. His private thoughts fully matched the propaganda statements which in April had been scattered over the front in his name, implying that all Italians accepted the idea of a united Yugoslav state. As he wrote to De Giulli on 2 May:

> The old atmosphere of mistrust is dispelled and a new atmosphere of trust is being created... Italian public opinion is opening its eyes and only now is realizing that the Yugoslav Committee is Italy's friend, for the very reason that it is fighting for the independence of its own nation and for its freedom from Austria-Hungary.[201]

Italian official pronouncements in late May sustained this picture. On 24 May in Rome at the anniversary celebrations, Orlando in the presence of Sonnino announced for the first time that Italy, in fighting for Trento and Trieste, was 'fighting in the same way for Warsaw, Prague and Zagreb. In that lies our victory, that we do not carry on a war of egotism, but a war for all those who are oppressed, who suffer the same as our unliberated brothers suffer.'[202]

Leonida Bissolati added his voice, confirming that Italy had made war 'for the liberation of the Yugoslavs, Czechs and all oppressed nationalities of Austria-Hungary'. Two days later in Milan he announced how, with the Allies and especially Italy committed to Czech and Yugoslav independence and Austria's destruction, 'the war has entered into the fullness of its meaning and has acquired that powerful rhythm which makes of it not a war for nationalist interests but for the moral and juridical revival of the world and of nations'.[203]

At Padua, Kujundžić rejoiced over this language. Even if (as a Serb) he noted that Orlando might have mentioned Serbia as well, he described Bissolati's Milan speech as 'exceptional as a medium for our propaganda' and it was duly employed in manifesto 45. Furthermore, when at the end of May Gaetano Salvemini paid one of his periodic visits to the front to deliver some morale-boosting lectures to the troops, Italy's commitment to the principles of the Rome Congress seemed again to be assured. On 2 June at a public meeting in Padua, Salvemini gave a speech which, Kujundžić reported to Trumbić,

> was unambiguous, very liberal and also mentioned us. After viewing the London Pact as a piece of paper which embodies the imperialism of the Entente, but especially of Italy, he criticized Sonnino for his political short-sightedness and political obsoleteness. It was best exemplified by this pact of his, because all his political cunning was embodied in it as to whether Italy would get one piece of Austria, more or less. The Capitol agreement upset his policy because the new Italy understands differently the problem of war as well as the problem of the nation.

The speech was received 'with uncommon enthusiasm', and afterwards Salvemini's wife asked Kujundžić to write a few lines for her as a memento, summing up his impression. Kujundžić obliged: 'Your husband spoke not like an Italian but like a Yugoslav. Hence I am extremely grateful to him.'[204]

Yet these hopeful signs were to be dashed the next day. The émigrés and their friends in London and Paris had failed to appreciate Sonnino's continued influence and his underlying hostility to Italy's new course. Although tolerating the Rome Congress, and even approving of the Padua Commission to the extent that 'whatever tends to create disaster in Austria-Hungary and weaken her military power is advantageous', Sonnino still considered Italy's objectives to be the defeat, not the dismemberment, of the Monarchy.[205] In contrast to Orlando, who was prepared ostensibly to embrace both camps, Sonnino never believed that Italy's true interests could be served by espousing the Yugoslav dimension of nationality politics, since this would inevitably undermine the London treaty and could produce a Yugoslav state as a serious rival to Italy on the Adriatic. At Versailles on 3 June, Sonnino insisted that the Yugoslavs did not merit the same recognition as the Czechs for, he claimed, 5 or at most 10 per cent of Yugoslavs desired independence while the other 90 or 95 per cent simply wanted autonomy within Austria-Hungary.[206] Faced with this argument, which Orlando felt obliged to support, the British and French were forced to agree to an Allied declaration which, while endorsing the creation of a Polish state, did no more than sympathize on the lines of Lansing's statement with the aspirations of the Yugoslavs and Czechoslovaks. Replying to protests from the EPD about this, Balfour observed that the 'frigid isolation' of the Polish declaration would not diminish its propaganda value.[207] This was true. As we have seen, Zamorski quickly employed it in several manifestos for Polish soldiers, and did so partly through prompting from the EPD which at the same time was telling Delmé-Radcliffe to calm the nerves of the Yugoslavs in Padua.[208] Nothing, however, could alter the general weakness of the Versailles Declaration, which both the CS and most of the national delegates at Padua felt could only do harm if published. Consequently, it was given little space in their Czech, Yugoslav or Romanian propaganda.[209] For the supporters of the subject races the hopes, cherished since the Rome Congress, of a joint Allied statement recognizing the nationalities as allies had been abruptly shattered. And the sincerity of Italy's adherence to nationality politics was now called sharply into question.

It was to be a constant feature of the six-month propaganda campaign against Austria-Hungary that those involved, directly at Padua or indirectly at Crewe House, felt that their efforts were being compromised by Italy's duplicitous behaviour towards the Yugoslavs. They argued, with perhaps questionable logic, that a solid Italian commitment to a Yugoslav state would reap chaos among the southern Slav regiments of the Austrian army: this implied that there was a receptive 'Yugoslav mentality' in the trenches opposite which could be exploited. The propagandists were undoubtedly more accurate in general terms. For when Italy vacillated over the Yugoslav issue, any Allied policy of destroying the Monarchy and forming new states could not be stated unambiguously in Padua's propaganda. This certainly weakened the potential of Padua's arguments. Official Italy's attitude also had a corrosive effect within the Padua Commission itself. Many soon began to wonder whether Ojetti and other Italian propagandists were themselves sincerely committed to nationality politics or whether they simply viewed it as a means to victory.

For Ugo Ojetti the commitment was sincere. On 14 May, for example, at a reception in Padua for the national delegates given by the wealthy and influential Contessa Papafava, he had made a speech comparing the Yugoslavs to heroes like Mazzini, working for their country's freedom while in exile.[210] But it was his general approach to the campaign which undermined the confidence of the other propagandists. From the start he had a patronizing view of the national delegates – 'my *balcanici*', as he termed them – believing that their role on the Commission should be to act as translators of manifestos prepared and vetted by a thoroughly Italian organization under his own control. According to Gallenga Stuart (who admittedly had some reason to malign him), Ojetti was indeed pro-Yugoslav but 'unfortunately he was egotistical and anxious to run the whole propaganda committee on his own inexperienced and ignorant lines'.[211] This could not fail to influence harmony in the Commission. Baker and Gruss had immediately found themselves relegated to being mere 'advisers', with little access to the national delegates since Ojetti, on his own admission, felt that they were only to be consulted 'when it is profitable to ask for their advice or when it is opportune to display to them the results of our work'.[212] Gruss quickly retired into the background, the French Military Mission rather irritated at Italy's understandable decision not to employ the Naud propaganda grenades. Baker, however, interpreted his brief with a breadth similar to Ojetti's, and would fight hard to maintain his place as 'the British representative' on an Allied Commission.

The national delegates also soon objected to Ojetti's strict control over work which they felt themselves to be engaged in on behalf of their national committees. Jambrišak, only three weeks after arriving in Padua, reported in disillusioned tones to the Yugoslav Committee: 'The work is obstructed by the impracticability and slowness of the Italians' and 'because they wish to conduct both military propaganda and propaganda for themselves and their aims, two concepts which cannot be linked together'. He had come to Padua

> with the greatest desire and ambition, firstly to work for the propaganda project, and secondly to make good and friendly mutual relations with Italians with whom I came into contact. I wanted to convince them about our profound belief that our relations must be based upon present realities and not on past historic traditions.

Italians, however, Jambrišak diagnosed, had closed their eyes to the present: 'in no way can they understand that one cannot defeat modern guns with Dante, Michelangelo and others. They are in love with the past and they live with the conviction that the Italy of the past is the same as today's Italy.' In character, they were 'people made up of a wide range of intelligent, witty and passionate traits, which never form a harmonious unity'. Rather, it made them unstable, so that 'they want everything at the same time: for example, at the same moment both to support the Croats and Slovenes, and to popularize and realize Sonnino's *Patto di Londra*'. Ojetti was, in this sense, 'a true representative of Italian society' with views which were 'never anything definite, clear or determined'.[213]

Ironically, Ojetti himself felt much the same about the Yugoslavs. As a close associate of Salvemini he had attended, before and after the Rome Congress, meetings between Salvemini, Trumbić, Trinajstić, Steed, Bissolati and others, at which Salvemini had urged Trumbić to define more precisely the future Italian–Yugoslav border and renounce Istria to Italy in return for Italy's renunciation of Dalmatia. Trumbić, however, had refused to commit himself, partly it seems because of the effect this would have on Slovenes and Croats of his own Committee (including the Istrian Trinajstić), partly because Austrian propaganda might then be able to continue exploiting fears of Italian imperialism among Slovenes and Croats of the Monarchy.[214] Ojetti declined to concede this latter argument and reproached Trumbić for taking a blinkered Yugoslav stance. If the Yugoslavs were sincere about the Pact of Rome, then they ought to be more open and prepared to make a detailed agreement with the Salvemini group, rather than with Torre who had 'signified nothing'; until this was done, the Treaty of London would have to be retained by Italy as 'a means of insurance at the future peace conference'.[215]

Ojetti's own pragmatic stance towards the Yugoslav question was further revealed in mid-May in an incident which again led him to question the Yugoslavs' dedication to what they believed in. On 12 May, in Sonnino's mouthpiece, the *Giornale d'Italia*, a journalist, Franco Caburi, wrote an article alleging that Anton Korošec's agitation in the Yugoslav regions of the Monarchy was being carried out with the full connivance and support of the Viennese authorities. Ojetti pressed the Yugoslav delegates for a public refutation of the assertion, even though it had been agreed at the Rome Congress that polemics within the Allied camp should be avoided. Jambrišak and Kujundžić for their part objected, explaining that they were prepared for such attacks as a matter of course, that they wished to avoid polemics, and that in any case they could not act without the approval of Trumbić and the Yugoslav Committee.[216] Ironically, the upshot was that Ojetti's own motives became suspect among the émigrés. Although he was actually urging the Yugoslavs to clear themselves, the rumour emerged in Switzerland that he was part of the problem. When Seton-Watson visited Switzerland at this time, he reported back to Steed the news 'that Ojetti is being influenced by Caburi and others in direction of suspecting Yugo-Slav clergy of Austrophilism. Borgese had written him stiffly.'[217]

The accusation had arisen because the EPD, like the Yugoslav delegates, failed to detect the difference between Ojetti's wish to control propaganda as a purely Italian concern, and the fact that an effective campaign was already being obstructed by other Italian 'influences'. Baker and the Yugoslavs considered Ojetti himself to be the main culprit for this. But it is clear from Ojetti's letters to his wife and Albertini that he had his own frustrations. Although he was backed by Orlando, with whom he was in regular contact, and Badoglio, who was increasingly confident about the new weapon, he faced obstacles in 'Sonnino-men': notably, his nominal superior, General Siciliani, who wished manifestos to promise only autonomy and not independence; and, as we have seen, the naval chief who balked at distributing Yugoslav material over Dalmatia.[218] In view of this, it was perhaps not surprising that Ojetti was uneasy about the idea of propagating the Corfu Declaration in his Yugoslav material.[219]

The EPD viewed such Italian censorship in itself as a fundamental evil. By June, after complaints from Jambrišak in particular about the way the Commission was functioning, Crewe House was telling Delmé-Radcliffe that it was

> indispensable that the representatives of the nationalities to the Central Inter-Allied Commission should be consulted and asked to draw up appeals to the Austro-Hungarian troops of their own race in the form and with the arguments which they consider most likely to be effective.

Radcliffe, who was already consoling the delegates after the weak Versailles Declaration, immediately contacted Bissolati, Siciliani and Badoglio, urging them to remedy these grievances. On 10 June he assured Northcliffe that the delegates would indeed be allowed to draft their own material.[220] These moves did something to dispel the tension. Jambrišak, who in early June had departed for Rome to see Trumbić, feeling that Italians were 'fickle and disloyal... mad and megalomaniacs', calmed down on his return: 'Relations here are now much better than before my departure for Rome. Both the tone and the work have significantly changed for the better (General Radcliffe!).'[221] He proceeded to buy three bottles of champagne for his colleagues. It was a sign of sorts that a more stable marriage might be emerging in the Padua Commission. A few weeks earlier Zamorski had commented that the national delegates were still on honeymoon with the Italians in Padua, meaning not that it was a blissful experience but rather that the relationship was gradually maturing.[222] In fact, it had proved to be a rocky start for a number of reasons. Yet Ojetti had still managed to lay a firm basis for an intense and sophisticated campaign against the Austrians in the weeks before their June offensive.

## 6.4 Trench propaganda

Alongside the political-military propaganda centre under Ojetti, there developed during these months a network of 'trench propaganda' which was wholly in military hands. It evolved from the example set by Cesare Finzi in the 6th army sector and benefited substantially from the changes in Italy in April 1918, particularly the creation of a Czechoslovak Legion. 'From May onwards', as Ljudevit Pivko notes in his memoirs, 'the whole front from Switzerland to the sea was equipped with mobile Czechoslovak reconnaissance units.'[223] As we have seen, it was in late March (before Steed's visit) that the CS had decided to create Slav propaganda patrols in every Italian army on the Pivko model. The ideal source for recruitment was felt to be reliable Czechoslovak prisoners who had been concentrated for months at Padula near Salerno. By April, trains containing hundreds of volunteers were beginning to leave the camp, bound for the war zone and the separate Italian armies. For some of the army Intelligence officers these would be a largely new phenomenon, for others – Finzi and Marchetti – they were a welcome supplement to existing Slav resources. In late May, after the creation of the Legion, its commander, General Graziani, decided to reinforce each army's Czech unit, and divided up between them the 2nd battalion of the 31st regiment (which had been training with the rest of the Legion in Perugia). From the Italian point of view, this move was undoubtedly desirable because evidence was mounting of an imminent Austrian offensive which a mass of propaganda troops might investigate and disrupt. For the existing Czech propaganda units, it was a move which gave them some added security. As 'islands in an Italian sea', isolated from each other and subordinate to the individual Intelligence offices, they were now – nominally at least – all grouped together as the II/31st regiment and each unit proceeded to take an oath to the Czechoslovak National Council.[224]

In the weeks before the Austrian offensive the task for the Czech propaganda units was identical. They were to creep into the front line, gather information for the Intelligence offices, and make propaganda which might lower enemy morale and perhaps even provoke some desertions in advance of the forthcoming battle. Their psychological role thus in many ways matched that of the Padua Commission, but for the Italians it was more tangible and direct. The effectiveness of the patrols depended on a variety of circumstances, most of which were shared by their Austrian counterparts: there was the difficult terrain; the basic receptiveness of enemy units to propaganda; and lastly, the degree of support which the patrols could expect from their own (Italian) military.

All of these variables are apparent in the trench propaganda conducted by Czech units of the 3rd, 8th and 4th Italian armies. In these three easterly sectors, which ran from the river Brenta to the sea, the Intelligence officers had until April chiefly used Slav volunteers for strictly Intelligence purposes. However, the Intelligence heads (Smaniotto, Dupont and Vigevano respectively) were naturally aware of the 1st army's experiences, and in early April it was to their sectors that the first Czech trains from the Padula camp were directed. In these months trench propaganda in this zone was to be most effective in the 3rd army, and this can serve as a detailed example of the patrols at work. In the 4th army sector, dominated by Monte Grappa, the only initiative of note was in mid-May when Vigevano sent his Czechs out to Monte Pertica; there they made contact with Czech regiments opposite, secured a few desertions, and certainly forced the Austrians to exchange some of their front-line troops.[225] In the 8th army sector there were more active patrols, concentrated on the river islands south of the Montello; they sang Czech songs as well as securing valuable information for Dupont, not least from one garrulous Czech deserter.[226] The negative aspect to 8th army propaganda was that Dupont left the patrols out on the front when the Austrians finally attacked. This suggests a serious lapse in his own Intelligence network, and it resulted in 35 captured scouts, 25 of whom were publicly executed by the Austrians.

In contrast, Czech efforts on the 3rd army front achieved more tangible successes, decisively confirming for both Italians and Austrians the real potential of the propaganda weapon. Although Ercole Smaniotto had initially been sceptical though curious about employing Slav volunteers in this manner, his reservation had been largely overcome in late March when he met members of Steed's mission and attended the CS coordinating meeting.[227] When soon afterwards 107 Czech volunteers arrived at Mogliano, Smaniotto still questioned them seriously, but proceeded to send them out to Cavazuccherina on the Lower Piave to entice Czech troops of IR21 opposite. It was quickly apparent that the 'enemy' was receptive. Austrian and Czech accounts agree that as a result of the patrols' work, luring with food and friendly conversation, about a dozen Czechs were persuaded to desert. Indeed, the Italians speedily exploited such demoralization and secured over 20 prisoners during two raids into enemy lines. KISA's April report on these events might well list with confidence the counter-measures which had been taken, but it ignored one other significant result, namely that at least one company of IR21 had had to be withdrawn to the rear and disciplined.[228] From the deserters, moreover, the Italians learnt some colourful details. Czechs in the regiment had apparently turned violently on a German captain who had tried to punish the 'fraternizers'. The story was sent on to Padua where Ojetti published it as manifesto 37, detailing how the Czechs under investigation in the rear had refused to betray their comrades: 'in the face of such unanimous and manly behaviour the German-Magyar murderers had to give in'.[229] The incident was a prime example of how the Italians were already learning to coordinate their trench and aerial propaganda, feeding back as manifestos to the Austrians news of unsettling incidents which had actually been provoked by their own effective trench propaganda.

Since Smaniotto was also impressed by the work of his Czech units, the 3rd army patrols in May were moved north to Fossalta di Piave with the new task of discovering the character of the forces opposite. Here they encountered the 12ID, which was predominantly Polish but also contained a sizeable Czech element. In this sector there had been some limited propaganda by both sides in March and April. But the few KISA records which have survived show that Italian efforts dramatically increased in May. From 6 May the 12ID began to receive a steady stream of manifestos shot over by rocket; from 19 May the division was reporting regular Czech calls for desertion: 'fear not, we are your brothers, we will not fire on you!'[230] One patrol finally made direct contact with IR56 and with a Czech lieutenant Karel Stinný, who indicated that he would desert with all of his men if they could be helped across the Piave. This was no easy task in view of the river's fast current. After frustrating attempts with boats on consecutive nights, Stinný and four of his men were finally hoisted by a pulley system across the river. Further desertions were halted by Austrian fire. But, as Vojtěch Hanzal noted, Stinný's desertion was 'one of the greatest successes of the Czechoslovaks' Intelligence activity'. Hanzal left it for future historians to assess how crucial was Stinný's betrayal of the forthcoming Austrian offensive; the idea is pursued below in Chapter 7.[231] At this point what can be confirmed is that the Stinný case became a *cause célèbre* both in Austrian and Italian circles, a notorious example of Czech treachery or sacrifice. Perhaps especially because Stinný composed a leaflet 'to all Slavs' which was sent across the front, the incident was well known to Austrian Intelligence;[232] and in the wake of Austria's June disaster, it was taken up by the Hungarian press as typifying general Czech perfidiousness.

In Italy meanwhile, the Czech patrols of the 3rd army received fulsome praise both in their own sector and further afield from the lips of Graziani himself.[233] They could feel that they had proved their effectiveness and benefited the wider Czech cause, even if, as in the other armies, their experience of working with Italians was not without friction. It was in fact still an uneasy partnership. Smaniotto had undoubtedly smoothed the ground by appointing as their Italian liaison Moses Kobylinskij, a Russian Jew with a formidably bear-like appearance, who had been attached for some time to 3rd army Intelligence and was a Czech enthusiast.[234] In mid-May, 3rd army command had also ordered its subordinates to lend full support to the propaganda patrols, emphasizing that their self-sacrificing exploits were already 'sending deep confusion into the hearts of enemy units'.[235] Nevertheless, the evidence of one Czech officer of the unit, who visited the Padua Commission, shows that a new relationship with the Italians could not be made overnight. As Lt Kouba explained:

> There are a mass of things which so irritate us about these people that, if I was not committed to this cause, I would either commit suicide or go back [to the prison camp]. In a very real sense they exploit us. Every day they send us out to the most dangerous positions and make themselves heroes on our backs. Every day we hear from the officers 'compliments' that we are traitors, that we've come because we are starving, that we've come to prolong the war, etc. One officer told me openly that a position near Capo Sile was not under bombardment when we weren't there. If we start a conversation with our people on the other side, they call us traitors, yelling to us to come back or they will fire. That has actually happened several times and as a result we protested energetically that we would not tolerate it any longer. But the most deplorable incident occurred a few days ago when five of our deserters were killed by the Italians at the moment when they wanted to swim across the Piave.[236]

Pivko's unit had, of course, faced just the same dangers on the mountain front in the preceding months. Pivko's own frustration at Italian suspicions would never completely disappear. Yet it was the case that in the lst and 6th army sectors, under the influence of an Intelligence service which had already employed Slav patrols, the wave of new Czech recruits was received more benignly by local Italians. On 14 April, a mass transport of 450 Czechs with 15 officers arrived in Verona, destined to serve as propaganda troops on the mountainous front from the Swiss border to the Brenta. Marchetti was careful to prepare for their reception both among the military and the civilian population. He drafted for the lst army command a letter to each army corps, ordering them to banish their prejudices about employing Slav volunteers.[237] Since the Czechs were to be trained initially in the Procolo fortress, he also publicized their presence in Verona itself so as to persuade a possibly unsympathetic civilian population. A week after the volunteers' arrival, the ladies of Verona organized a special celebration in the Teatro Filarmònico at which the Czechs were presented with their colours. After eulogies spoken by Graziani, Hlaváček and Stane Vidmar, the national anthems were sung and a blanket of carnations and lilacs was scattered over the volunteers.[238]

If such a *union sacrée* amply matched Marchetti's wishes, it concealed at this time some anxiety on the part of those training the Czechs about their actual calibre or suitability. It had soon become apparent that some of them, after several years in captivity, were reluctant to submit to authority: they either resisted any hierarchy *per se*, or objected to former Habsburg officers retaining the same ranking in the Legion. When Vidmar, who was in charge of training, was presented with a petition on this subject, he exclaimed that it was 'Bolshevism'. Josef Kohoutek (one of the original *Carzanci*), who had been seconded with others from Tugurio to aid Vidmar, agreed. He reported to Pivko on 26 April that a certain 'socialist corruption' was evident among the recruits who had clearly been spoilt during their sojourn in captivity.[239] Although this 'rebellion' quickly subsided, the leading Slav officers were naturally sensitive about any signs of indiscipline which might tarnish their reputation among the Italians. Pivko, for example, would always assert that all of the recruits were volunteers and idealists. When in May a few Czechs in the 1st army sector got drunk and started praising Austria, they were immediately dismissed and returned to the prison camps.[240] It was vital that widespread Italian suspicion about the volunteers should cease; for, as we will see, it was an Achilles' heel which in August 1918 the Austrians would skilfully try to attack.

By May the 450 new volunteers had been divided up and dispatched to the 7th, lst and 6th armies, the number allocated to each army depending on the number requested by the local Intelligence office. In the following weeks propaganda patrols were most active on the 1st and 6th army sectors. If this owed much to the groundwork laid by Marchetti and Finzi in comparison to the relative scepticism of Vecchiarelli in the 7th army (who initially requested only a dozen Czechs), it also reflected the hazardous Alpine terrain of the 7th army sector. Over much of it warfare was conducted in glacial conditions in mountains which were five times the height of those to which the Czechs were accustomed in their homeland.[241] Vojtěch Hanzal, the Czech officer in command of the 7th army units, was specifically chosen because he had formerly carried out reconnaissance work in the mountains from the other side – for Austrian Intelligence. He proceeded in early June to send some units up to the Tonale pass to agitate in anticipation of an Austrian attack. Otherwise their main work was in more congenial terrain in Val dei Concei (west of Lake Garda) where they reconnoitred enemy positions, marked out the Austrian lines for the first time, and deposited a listening apparatus.[242]

In the lst army sector, substantially more could be achieved in these crucial weeks prior to the Austrian offensive. By June, Tullio Marchetti's units were operating at five points in the front line, their role as usual being to investigate sectors where Czech troops were suspected opposite, to make propaganda, and to demoralize the enemy in advance of a local Italian attack. The latter objective was achieved on Monte Corno, a long-contested point where Cesare Battisti had been captured in 1916; those Czechs who were taken prisoner after the Italian capture of Corno (13 May) confirmed that they had been deeply affected by the Czech songs opposite.[243] Elsewhere the volunteers were experimenting with propaganda rockets. For example, in the sector between Val Lagarina and Lake Garda, where Austrian electric wire was a major obstacle, a Czech unit under Karel Čižek agitated vigorously and shot over leaflets.

Austrian records indicate that the Austrians in May were wholly aware of this upsurge in Czech propaganda patrols and usually suspected the sectors which the Italians were targeting. In early May the 11AK came to know from the Swiss press about the creation of a Czechoslovak Legion in Italy. On 7 May it sent out orders (later fully approved by the AOK) which set a price of 300 Kronen on the head of each captured legionary. Czech patrols were to be fired upon immediately, and the shell fire was to be followed by a special manifesto addressed to Italians which described the legionaries as 'delinquents' and 'rascals' who by their presence on the Italian side were violating international law and dishonouring the customary rules of warfare.[244] It was just one of the Austrian means used to combat the new danger, a method which was still part and parcel of their own propaganda offensive against Italy.

The Austrians in these weeks were similarly conscious of lively propaganda emanating from the Italian 6th army, an area which provides us with a detailed example of trench propaganda in the mountains. The 6th army, with Finzi as the Intelligence head, remained the zone of Pivko's units (even though his men usually operated only in the east under Italian control, since British and French divisions were present in the west). Finzi was steadily incorporating Czech and Yugoslav volunteers into his Intelligence service, keeping two of them (Mate Nikolić and Božidar Pajk) permanently at his headquarters at Mirabella, while giving others new tasks such as eavesdropping on enemy telephone conversations on the Asiago plateau.[245] In line with the CS's own priorities, Pivko's units were soon leaving Tugurio and ascending the steep slopes to the front line in order to engage in specific front propaganda. Once again, the units which General Ferrari of the XX corps command requested on 30 April were to be directed at the 26SchD which was believed to have positioned Czechs in the front line. This section of the front, moreover, was still considered by the

Austrians as an area very receptive to their own propaganda, an area in other words where Italian soldiers continued to gather the Austrian manifestos and warn the Austrians when Italian officers were approaching.[246] Ferrari undoubtedly perceived that Pivko's unit could again serve several purposes; first, by encouraging desertions and gathering Intelligence, and second, by countering the considerable Austrian propaganda offensive which continued until mid-June in this particular sector. As a sideline, it might be hoped that Pivko's officers would mix with Italians at the front and educate them to withstand the promises and threats contained in Austrian leaflets.[247]

It was usual for Pivko himself to examine any new terrain in which his units would be operating, but the zone of the XX corps must have been reasonably familiar to him. Most of those under his control were now not former Czech or Yugoslav *Carzanci*. They were either part of his allotment from the 450 Czechs who had arrived from the Padula camp, or (from late May) they were members of the II/31st regiment which had been training at Perugia and then divided up by Graziani.[248] Already on 4 May three units from Tugurio, of 15 men each, arrived at XX corps HQ and were sent on to the front-line *Bersaglieri* battalions, positioned around the Frenzella gorge and Croce San Francesco. A fortnight later, two more units took up position on Sasso Rosso, while at the end of the month Finzi assigned three predominantly Czech squads to Monte di Val Bella, Col del Rosso and Col d'Echele to the west.[249] The volunteers were relieved about every fortnight but they led an uncomfortable and strenuous existence. In late May Eduard Klímek, who had assumed control of the patrol on San Francesco, reported to Pivko that his men were tired and that he had broken his spectacles:

> I am blind, completely useless [*siromak*]. Send me spectacles... and underwear for the men. We are ragged and dirty. I fear infectious diseases because it is getting hotter. Every day there is a lot of propaganda, partly among the Italians but even more among the Austrians with lively incidents and experiences.

As in the past the patrols' work continued to be complicated by the Italians themselves, some of whom ignored official orders and, in tune with Austria's own propaganda leaflets, blamed the Czech patrols for attracting enemy fire to their positions.

Certainly Pivko's volunteers seem to have paid rather dearly for the results they achieved. When they first arrived at the front, some contact had been possible with Czechs opposite. At San Francesco, for example, when the unit threw over bread and spoke enticingly about the 'Masaryk legionaries', an elderly Czech corporal replied. He mentioned with amusement the 300 Kronen reward which had been placed on a legionary's head, and went on to suggest that his company could send correspondence from Czech legionaries back to Bohemia. But he hesitated when asked about desertion. A week later in the same position, the Czechs opposite had disappeared to be replaced by German-Austrian *Sturmtruppen* and a hostile reception. Pivko correctly observed, 'the Austrian command was undoubtedly informed of our presence and so fights usually took place instead of conversation'. For the patrols there were, of course, grave dangers in 'flirting' with an enemy regiment. When Klímek took over on San Francesco he managed to converse with a German-Austrian opposite, but was unsure of how to entice him; finally he concluded that such propaganda was too precarious to be continued and his patrol took the man prisoner.[250] Any satisfaction which the Czech patrols might have about provoking a swift Austrian reaction, such as an exchange of unreliable troops, was tempered by the fact that their Czech target was no longer visible.[251]

Nor was it clear that Pivko's units were winning the propaganda duel in the 6th army sector. On the contrary, the distribution of manifestos by Austrian *Nachrichtentruppen* was continued vigorously and even increased in some positions. In the first week of June, for example, over 2000 pieces of propaganda were thrown or deposited by the Austrians on both Sasso Rosso and San Francesco respectively.[252] The very presence of Pivko's units, and their role in stiffening Italian resolve, may well have forced the Austrians to cease their propaganda in some positions such as Col del Rosso and the western slopes of Sasso Rosso. But against this has to be set the fact that the patrols during May had suffered six casualties, four of them fatal, as the price for only seven Austrian deserters.[253] Where Pivko's units were undoubtedly more successful was, as on the other army fronts, in supplying Italian Intelligence with timely information about the imminent enemy offensive.[254] As for front propaganda, the best conclusion is perhaps to measure its effect not by individual incidents but in its broader and long-term impact: namely that at this critical point when the Austro-Hungarian army was about to attack, its soldiers were conscious of a new Czech presence in the Italian ranks. Even if few Czechs had openly responded to the calls of the patrols, many in the Austrian trenches had been stirred and were left, in the words of an official Austrian report, to act as 'yeast' for future agitation.[255]

The Czechs remained one of Italy's strongest cards to play in terms of trench propaganda. They were the most advanced in their military organization in Italy; they did not carry the same sensitive 'political baggage' as Poles, Romanians or (especially) the Yugoslavs; and the Intelligence service knew from long experience that Czechs in the Austrian ranks always supplied a steady trickle of deserters and were often the most receptive to enticement. Yet it was logical that the CS would soon seek to incorporate other nationalities into their psychological offensive. In the case of Polish or Romanian soldiers, it proved to be a slow process. If this was partly because neither had an émigré organization in Italy to match that of the Czechs, it was also because Poles and Romanians were far more reluctant to volunteer for re-employment on the Italian Front. From the autumn of 1917 Polish prisoners had been concentrated together in camps, the officers at Santa Maria Capua Vetere near Naples. Delegates of the Polish National Committee, including Antoni Szuber, had been allowed access to them for cultural purposes. The Czechs' advance then ensured that new horizons opened up. In April 1918, for instance, Marchetti chose a dozen volunters from Santa Maria and, adding them to a few in Verona, formed a propaganda unit for the lst army; it seems to have served valiantly in the following months.[256] Other Intelligence offices did the same (notably the 4th army), so that by the end of the war 180 Polish volunteers were active at the front. However, the process never expanded beyond this unilateral Italian recruitment, because Zamorski and the Polish National Committee laid down political conditions before they would sanction full military cooperation. It was a stance, as we will see, which matched that of the Yugoslav Committee. And since it was only in late October that Polish officials appeared in Padua to try to build a legion, Polish trench propaganda always remained a sporadic activity.[257]

In the case of Romanian prisoners there were similar obstacles, but it appears that the Intelligence service was able to make more use of them, not least because after the Czechs they tended to form the largest number of deserters. As with the Czechoslovak cause, Romanian émigrés who were pressing for a Romanian volunteer force to be created out of the prison camps had powerful Italian political backing. In the wake of the Rome Congress, Gallenga's ministry began to finance a Romanian committee under Simeon Mîndrescu as well as a Comitato Italiano pro Romeni led by Maria Rygier which advocated a legion on Italian soil.[258] At the same time Gheorghe Mironescu, together with Benedetto de Luca (the 'Romanian' delegate to the Padua Commission), had been allowed to visit Romanian prisoners at Monte Cassino, and waxed lyrical about their desire to shed their blood for the Allied cause.[259] As a result, by 7 May most Romanian officers were collected together at Cittaducale while 3600 soldiers were transported to two camps in the war zone.[260] There they were finally under CS jurisdiction and could be recruited more easily for Intelligence or propaganda tasks. In the lst army, for example, Marchetti formed a small Romanian patrol which seems to have secured some deserters from the largely Romanian IR50.[261] The other Intelligence officers seem to have followed suit sporadically, and in the June battles the CS even permitted Romanian troops to be used in combat. The creation of a legion took longer since there was firstly the issue of how far Mîndrescu's committee could represent the voice of Transylvanian Romanians, and secondly the very real reluctance of Romanian prisoners to enter a body which would fight for the ideal of a united Romania. Although a legion was finally proclaimed in October 1918, the evidence suggests that Transylvanian Romanians were always viewed by the Italian military as an uncertain tool in their propaganda campaign.[262] Their occasional use in trench propaganda simply complemented the relative weakness of argument in Padua's Romanian manifestos.

It might be considered even more of a risk to employ Yugoslav prisoners in the Italian army. Could Croat or Slovene soldiers be trusted, but perhaps more importantly, would not their enrolment imply that Italy was committed to an independent Yugoslav state which claimed 'Italian' territory on the Adriatic? In fact, southern Slav patrols were destined to increase in number as the summer approached, thereby illustrating that the CS was largely prepared to set aside political scruples. Diaz and Badoglio were now keen to exploit the Yugoslav issue for its propaganda benefits, even though at the same time the political Italian–Yugoslav relationship remained unsettled and always threatened to undermine the efficacy of such propaganda. After the Rome Congress, the Yugoslav Committee expected that 'Yugoslav' prisoners in Italy would be treated like their Czechoslovak counterparts: they would be separated from other nationalities, delegates of the Committee or the Serbian army would visit them and urge them to volunteer for service, and those who responded would be allowed to join the Serbian army as members of a Yugoslav legion on the Salonika or Italian Front.

In early May, after pressure from Trumbić, about 200 Yugoslav officers were collected together in a camp at Nocera Umbra Bagni. At the same time 11 600 Yugoslav soldiers were moved to six camps in the war zone where the CS planned to use them as labour units.[263] On 18 May Dinko Trinajstić informed the Committee offices in London and Paris:

> Concerning the prisoners, we have been promised so far that they will be selected and concentrated, with men and officers separated. The men will be temporarily employed for work in the rear zones until the government here decides to admit them into the fighting ranks, since at present there are practical obstacles to that. We have about 20 000 prisoners and about 12 000 of them have just been collected together. As soon as we acquire the register promised to us, we will visit them and make contact with them.[264]

This register, however, was not to be forthcoming. Although a week later the Italians permitted Trinajstić, Gazzari and Stane Vidmar to visit Nocera Umbra (where they discovered a majority of officers eager to enter the Serbian army), neither the Yugoslav Committee nor Serbian official representatives were allowed to begin agitating for volunteers in the other camps.[265] Partly this reflected the desire of both Sonnino and the CS that Yugoslav prisoners should be employed only on the Italian Front, but it also highlighted Sonnino's and Spingardi's objection to the creation of a Yugoslav legion which would include Slovene and Croat volunteers, in other words prisoners who might originate in regions assigned to Italy in the Treaty of London. Not surprisingly, by early June Jambrišak still felt that little progress had really been made: 'Spingardi could not help Austria better if he were an Austrian general.'[266] In fact, some advance was on the cards but it was not of a kind which the Yugoslav Committee could sanction.

Since large groups of Yugoslav prisoners had been moved into the war zone, they were subject to the CS which duly began to exploit them. On 25 May, Nikolić and Pajk had hurried to Tugurio from 6th army Intelligence to exclaim that 'Italy had changed'. For the first time, the CS was going to allow recruitment for special Yugoslav units similar to Pivko's small group in the 6th army sector. Badoglio's telegram, issued that day to the army commands, announced that 'Serbo-Croat elements' from Austrian prisoners employed in the war zone were to be selected for propaganda duties in the Italian army; the army commands should send delegates to the 'labour defence offices' at Goito or Badia Polesine to choose suitable volunteers.[267] Finzi and Marchetti naturally selected Pivko as their recruiting officer for the 6th and 1st armies. Pivko in turn, feeling that his new task was the first stage towards a Yugoslav legion, chose as recruiters to accompany him two of his officers, one a Slovene and one a Croat, together with eight men as representatives of the 'Yugoslav regions'.[268] Working from bases south of Lake Garda, Pivko and his men visited nine *centurie* (labour units) in the last days of May and chose 200 Yugoslav volunteers.[269]

What he found was a striking indication of the actual reality of 'Yugoslav awareness' behind the enthusiastic claims of the Yugoslav Committee. Although Pivko himself spoke to all the prisoners and assured them that Austria-Hungary was finished, that King Petar of Serbia would be ruler of Yugoslavia, and that those who volunteered would be part of a Yugoslav national army in Italy, the response was undoubtedly weaker than he anticipated. From one *centuria* of 387 men, only 15 volunteered; from another of 113 men, only 30 were found to be 'nationally mature'; and in four of the *centurie* he found only a shadow of Yugoslav national awareness. Most of the Slovenes and Croats in particular remained 'Austrian' at heart or were simply not prepared to jeopardize their lives for some new cause. Pivko might have expected this since a few weeks earlier Vidmar had visited a Yugoslav camp to the south and discovered that most Slovenes were indifferent while the Croats and Moslems were openly hostile to his overtures.[270]

It was the Serbs who always formed the predominant element among volunteers. They were certainly most attracted by the chance of being transported to the Salonika Front to serve in the Serbian forces. Pivko proceeded to criticize some Serbs who ignored the wider Yugoslav cause and refused to volunteer unless they were sent immediately to the Serbian national army; in view of the Italian government's attitude, he knew that such hopes were unrealistic. However, he dangled a carrot in front of them, suggesting that they should become 'revolutionaries' for the new cause and would then, when liberated, have the chance of links with both the Serbian government and the Yugoslav Committee. Rather than waiting for a favourable decision from Spingardi or Sonnino, which could mean waiting for ever, the Serbs should take advantage of the CS's progressive attitude, and prove their commitment by deeds at the front. Pivko added, rather optimistically, that although he and the hierarchy of the Yugoslav Committee were agreed that Yugoslav troops should remain on the Italian Front, the CS would indeed concede if the Committee decided to transfer the volunteers to Salonika. However, in this case Pivko's 'carrot' was not attractive enough and was rejected by a mass of Serbs (from the Banat) who were only prepared to volunteer in order to fight for 'Greater Serbia'. The simple fact was that the Yugoslav cause was not a reality for many South Slav prisoners in Italy. Consequently the Italians were quite justified in their suspicions or uncertainties; indeed, doubts on the Serb or Croat side were matched by some from Italians who seemed most committed to Pivko's cause. Even Tullio Marchetti admitted later in his memoirs that he had excluded Slovenes from the Venezia Giulian region from those whom Pivko had recruited: for their enrolment could have caused embarrassment in view of Italy's territorial aspirations in 'Slovenia'.[271]

Pivko sent the 200 recruits to Verona where they were issued with Italian uniforms and began a fortnight's training course which included Intelligence work, rifle drill and gymnastics. Then on the eve of the Austrian offensive they were divided, half joining the volunteers at Tugurio while half remained near Verona as a new *Reparto Posina* in the lst army sector. Despite this division, Pivko himself retained considerable control of the Yugoslav units in both the 1st and 6th armies since both were supplied with officers from Tugurio. From mid-June a Slovene officer, Oton Kovačić, who had deserted at Tonale and knew Pivko from his days in Maribor, was assigned to organize a Yugoslav reconnaissance unit for the 7th army sector.[272] Thus Pivko's overall supervision of Yugoslav trench propaganda incorporated all army sectors from Switzerland to the river Brenta.

Where Pivko had far less control was in the sectors between the Brenta and the sea. This was largely due to the way in which trench propaganda had evolved at a different pace in the eastern sectors over the previous months. Badoglio, moreover, had instructed the 3rd, 4th and 8th armies to send representatives for Yugoslav recruitment to a different labour office (at Badia Polesine) so that they acted with little reference to Tugurio, something which Pivko appears to have resented.[273] Vigevano of the 4th army was able to recruit 100 Yugoslav volunteers, most of them Serbs but none of them officers; an attempt to recruit directly from the camp of officers at Nocera Umbra failed since they insisted on being used only as members of the Serbian army.[274] Smaniotto's Intelligence office appears at first to have gained only 28 recruits for the 3rd army: 17 Serbs (chiefly Bosnians), eight Croats and three Slovenes, most of whom had been prisoners for several years.[275] As for the 8th army, their Intelligence office had made use for some weeks of a Dalmatian Croat, Nikola de Marchi, who in April had been individually summoned to the war zone to help compose propaganda leaflets. In June, the 8th army command sent De Marchi westwards to the labour units where he recruited 100 volunteers, chiefly Serbs, who were then dressed in Italian uniform with red, white and blue Yugoslav collar insignia and put through some intensive training.[276]

Although Italian military Intelligence retained control of all these volunteers, trench propaganda was not totally divorced from the work of the Padua Commission. Ojetti and other members of the commission, including the national delegates, had from the start viewed it as part of their remit to liaise with actual or potential volunteers from among deserters or prisoners. Thus Ojetti and Baker had been quick to visit Tugurio. Ojetti thought Pivko 'the highest and purest example of someone who hates Austria and loves Italy that I have encountered among Slavs in four years of warfare'. Baker was amazed at the quality of military Intelligence in the 6th army sector where Major Finzi had created the 'model bureau'.[277] A certain uneven liaison developed between the Intelligence network and Padua, so that the former occasionally supplied material for manifestos while the latter sent some of its manifestos for direct distribution by patrols in the front line.

One area offering particular potential for friction was the political status of the volunteers. In the Czech case all had been resolved since, as we have seen, from May all volunteers were part of the Legion and took an oath to the Czechoslovak National Council. In the Yugoslav and Polish cases, the matter was unresolved and it was their delegates at Padua who assumed the task of following in the Czech footsteps, demanding that Italy treat their volunteers as soldiers of a future Yugoslav or Polish state. This inevitably meant that the Yugoslav Committee was not happy with Pivko's extensive activity. Trumbić himself had not had time in April to visit Tugurio, but knew about Pivko, Vidmar and Nikolić, noting down that 'all three were good for propaganda' and that 'Pivko is a man of great moral ascendency over people'.[278] But when the first exchange of letters, the first real contact, took place between the Committee and Tugurio, Jambrišak on 10 May replied to a letter from Vidmar in a rather lofty tone which indicated clearly the Committee's priorities on the volunteer issue:

> Certainly we contemplate your cooperation as soon as we begin to form our unit here in Italy. Remain for now in contact with the Czech unit because

> there you can give useful help. It is good that you develop your talents with them because they too need good organizers for the army and their tendencies are the same as ours. As far as Professor Dr Pivko and the remaining Slovenes are concerned who wish to assist in our work, please tell them that we are thinking about their cooperation too and that they will be informed at the proper time. We are indebted to you and Dr Pivko for your serious and energetic work.[279]

While Jambrišak and Kujundžić were in favour of retaining Yugoslav units on the Italian Front, they felt that the existing situation, where volunteers wore Italian uniform and technically remained prisoners, was compromising the Committee's efforts to found a Yugoslav legion. Rather, the new units should wear Serbian uniform and take an oath to King Petar. Although the Committee's office in Rome explained this to Vidmar when he visited the capital in May, he and Pivko were already irritated by the Committee's indifference to their work.[280] They were inclined to maintain some independence, something which was, of course, fully shared by Intelligence officers like Finzi who did not want political interference in a military sphere which seemed to be working effectively; Finzi commented dryly that Pivko had far more authority than Trumbić in the war zone.[281] The Yugoslav Committee, however, was gradually extending its leverage. Its members helped to persuade volunteer-officers at Nocera Umbra not to agree to be sent to the front unless they went as officers of the Serbian army. And in the war zone itself, the Committee for a time retained a loyal follower at the 8th army in the person of Nikola de Marchi. From the start of his 'enrolment', De Marchi had been in touch with the Committee and would do nothing without reference to Jambrišak and Kujundžić at Padua. Since they regularly advised him to move cautiously until the volunteer question was properly solved, De Marchi faced increasing tensions in his relations with the Intelligence office of the 8th army. Major Dupont was, not surprisingly, irritated at De Marchi's divided loyalties and began to rely on two other Yugoslav officers who were more of the 'Pivko persuasion' and would carry out Italian orders without reservation. When De Marchi realized that he was being elbowed out and the Committee ignored, he simply resigned and returned to Nocera Umbra.[282] It was another taste of the actual reality behind Italy's public commitment to the Yugoslav cause, and it foreshadowed a steady battle over the volunteer issue during the summer.

It was clear during these first months of Italy's propaganda campaign that the Yugoslav issue could bedevil its efficiency. In both trench propaganda and the work of the Padua Commission, it was already apparent that there were major problems in presenting the Yugoslav cause to the enemy. The Yugoslav ideal, which some like Pivko or even Ojetti sought to propagate, was indeed just that, an ideal. It was often at variance with the reality of *kaisertreu* Croats and

Slovenes, or Serbs who wished only to fight for a Greater Serbia. On this basis, it was no easy task to construct a common Yugoslav propaganda. Such difficulties were then compounded because of the attitude of official Italy. The Italian government might profess a 'nationality policy', but in the Yugoslav case was highly reluctant to make specific commitments, to create a Yugoslav legion, or to accept fully the theory of 'Yugoslavism'. They were, in short, wary of drawing logical conclusions from the grand celebrations of the Rome Congress. Thereby, as the propagandists always argued, the Italians were weakening the very essence of their own propaganda campaign, based as it was on the slogans of liberation and national unity. It remained to be seen how long this paradoxical state of affairs could continue. Already by June 1918, cracks had appeared in the façade which Orlando had erected at the Rome Congress. But even more serious cracks seemed to be appearing in the enemy stronghold. The Comando Supremo was confident that when the Austrians launched their long-awaited offensive, the first fruits of their coordinated psychological campaign would fully materialize.

## Notes

1. Harold D. Lasswell, *Propaganda Technique in World War I* (London, 1927) p. 200.
2. Sir Campbell Stuart, *Secrets of Crewe House: The Story of a Famous Campaign* (London, 1920); Henry Wickham Steed, *Through Thirty Years 1892–1922: A Personal Narrative*, 2 vols (London, 1924).
3. *Österreichische Wehrzeitung* (Vienna), 8 April 1921, Folge 13, p. 3.
4. Edmund von Glaise-Horstenau, *The Collapse of the Austro-Hungarian Empire* (London, 1930) pp. 119–23, 162; [Glaise-Horstenau in], OULK, VII, pp. 18–19.
5. Hugh and Christopher Seton-Watson, *The Making of a New Europe: R.W. Seton-Watson and the Last Years of Austria-Hungary* (London, 1981); M.L. Sanders and P.M. Taylor, *British Propaganda during the First World War 1914–1918* (London, 1982).
6. For example, Piero Melograni, *Storia Politica della Grande Guerra 1915–1918* (Bari, 1972) pp. 521ff; Leo Valiani, *The End of Austria-Hungary* (London, 1973) pp. 221ff; Luciano Tosi, *La Propaganda Italiana all'Estero nella Prima Guerra Mondiale* (Udine, 1977) chapter 4.
7. IWM, Sir Campbell Stuart MSS: manuscript, 'Propaganda by War Office during the Great War'; George Cockerill, *What Fools We Were* (London, 1944) pp. 60ff. According to Cockerill, the DSI had actually begun such propaganda in March 1915, and the efforts were then tightened up a year later.
8. Sanders and Taylor, *British Propaganda*, pp. 216–17. Guest was formerly a clerk in the National Insurance Commission, whose premises were taken over by the War Propaganda Bureau in 1914; he has left no papers of his wartime activities and was killed by a V-2 in 1944 (I am grateful to his son-in-law, Dr W.L. Weinstein, for this information).
9. SWP, 'Report on work in Switzerland' by R.W. Seton-Watson, pp. 1–4.

10. PRO, FO 395/235, Department of Information, report by Buchan, 1 December 1917 (enclosing maps); ibid., 'Inquiry into the content and efficiency of Propaganda' by Robert Donald, 14 December: Appendix I, Buchan's comments in reply, 21 December 1917.
11. BL, Northcliffe MSS, vol. XCIV, Add.Mss 62246, Steed to Northcliffe, 7 March 1918.
12. Steed, *Through Thirty Years*, II, pp. 33, 53, 118. For a summary of Steed's most notable journal articles, see Peter Schuster, *Henry Wickham Steed und die Habsburgermonarchie* (Vienna, Cologne and Graz, 1970) pp. 168ff.
13. Seton-Watsons, *The Making of a New Europe*, pp. 102, 111, 191.
14. Steed, *Through Thirty Years*, II, pp. 42–5, 101–6. Note also Steed's efforts ('a useful bit of Allied propaganda') to depress the morale of an Austrian diplomat whom he met on a train in Switzerland: pp. 108ff.
15. Ibid., p. 66; Hugh and Christopher Seton-Watson *et al.* (eds), *R.W. Seton-Watson and the Yugoslavs: Correspondence 1906–1941* [hereafter *Seton Correspondence*], 2 vols (London and Zagreb, 1976) I (*1906–1918*), pp. 213, 279.
16. Steed, *Through Thirty Years*, II, pp. 169–70; Albertini, *Epistolario*, II, p. 1054. Steed's claim is accepted uncritically by Sanders and Taylor, *British Propaganda*, p. 225.
17. *The Times* Archive, London [hereafter TTA], Steed MSS, Steed to W.K. McClure (correspondent in Rome), 26 June, 14 August, 2 October 1917.
18. Luciano Tosi, 'Romeo A. Gallenga Stuart e la propaganda di guerra all'estero (1917–1918)', *Storia Contemporanea*, II (1971) pp. 529–30: he communicated these views to Orlando on 13 August.
19. See Seton-Watson's views, based on an examination of the enemy press in his work from May 1917 for the Intelligence Bureau of the Department of Information: Seton-Watsons, *The Making of a New Europe*, pp. 214–15, 228.
20. AJA, JO 19/15, notes by Trumbić: 'Conversation with Steed at his invitation', 11 December 1917. Steed's prime initiative in the whole affair is clear from these notes, but he played it down in his memoirs. Mola had been told to proceed by his friend the Minister of War, General Alfieri, and presumably had also informed his actual superiors at the CS.
21. The following discussion uses the three accounts of the meetings: those of Emanuel (Albertini, *Epistolario*, II, pp. 1054–61); Trumbić, used here in the slightly edited form which Trumbić sent to Steed on 13 February (AJA, JO 19/39; full version in JO 136/2/4); and Steed, which partially drew on Trumbić's account (*Through Thirty Years*, II, pp. 169–79).
22. According to Emanuel's notes (Albertini, *Epistolario*, II, p. 866), it was possible that Boroević favoured Yugoslav unity. The idea stemmed from Boroević's own remarks to a Croat politician (Franjo Barac) in Zagreb which were passed on to Trumbić. If Boroević was sincere, the evidence suggests that, like many 'Croats' (Boroević was a Croatian Serb), he felt dual loyalties to Croatia and to the Habsburgs: see Ivan Meštrović, *Uspomene na Političke Ljude i Dogadjaje* (Zagreb, 1969) pp. 86–7.
23. Albertini, *Epistolario*, II, p. 1060.
24. Janković and Krizman (eds), *Gradja o Stvaranju Jugoslavenske Države*, I, no. 72, p. 96.
25. AJA, JO 27/91, De Giulli to Trumbić, 28 January 1918 (reporting a long discussion with Edvard Beneš).
26. Paulová, *Jugoslavenski Odbor*, pp. 386–402.
27. See Tosi, *La Propaganda Italiana*, p. 172.
28. Janković and Krizman (eds), *Gradja*, I, no. 69, p. 90: Trumbić to De Giulli, 6 February; Šepić, *Italija, Saveznici i Jugoslavensko Pitanje*, pp. 266–7.

29. See Emanuel's fairly optimistic report to Albertini about Orlando's desire to 'cross the Rubicon': Albertini, *Epistolario*, II, pp. 875ff.
30. AJA, JO 19/18, Trumbić notes on meeting with Steed, 14 February 1918.
31. Albertini, *Epistolario*, II, pp. 849–50; Tosi, 'Giuseppe Antonio Borgese e la Prima Guerra Mondiale (1914–1918)', *Storia Contemporanea*, IV/2 (1973) pp. 288–90.
32. Šepić, *Italija, Saveznici i Jugoslavensko Pitanje*, p. 265. The evidence suggests that the Italians were spurred on to organize because the French wished to take the lead. But Valiani is incorrect to suggest that the idea of a congress occurred simultaneously to Beneš in Paris (see Valiani, *The End of Austria-Hungary*, p. 231; Beneš, *Světová Válka*, II, p. 42)
33. Salvemini, *Carteggio 1914–1920*, pp. 355–6: Salvemini complained that the nationalists planned to use the Slavs against Austria and then 'throw them away like a squeezed lemon'.
34. Albertini, *Venti Anni di Vita Politica*, III, pp. 266–7. Valiani's whole account of this development (pp. 230–7 with excessive notes) is detailed and rather unreadable; for refreshing clarity, see Seton-Watsons, *The Making of a New Europe*, pp. 247ff and Šepić, *Italija*, pp. 261–8, 285–91.
35. TTA, Steed MSS, Steed to McClure, 20 February 1918.
36. Text in *Seton Correspondence*, I, p. 384; Steed, *Through Thirty Years*, II, pp. 183–5; Šepić, *Italija*, pp. 292–6.
37. Janković and Krizman (eds), *Gradja*, I, no. 90, pp. 114–16: Trumbić to De Giulli, 5 March 1918; Šepić, *Italija*, p. 295.
38. See Sanders and Taylor, *British Propaganda*, pp. 70ff.
39. Quoted in Reginald Pound and Geoffrey Harmsworth, *Northcliffe* (London, 1959) p. 593.
40. TTA, Northcliffe MSS, Memorandum by Northcliffe, 28 February 1918.
41. See especially the reports from Sir Rennell Rodd in HLRO, Lloyd George MSS (F/56/1/56 and /57) and those from Sir Edward Carson on 5 December about the 'insidious' network of German propaganda in Italy and elsewhere (F/6/2/50 and /51). German propaganda was later to be blamed for Caporetto by *The Times History of the War*: vol. XXI (London, 1920) p. 327.
42. Henry Wickham Steed, *The Fifth Arm* (London, 1940) p. 14; Sanders and Taylor, *British Propaganda*, p. 90.
43. After speaking to Orlando, Steed, on Orlando's advice, had written a long letter to Sonnino on 29 January recommending Italian agreement with the Yugoslavs and setting out all the military and political arguments (Steed, *Through Thirty Years*, II, pp. 182–3; the full text given to Trumbić is in AJA, JO 9/8). See also Steed's remarks about *il primato morale* in TTA, Steed MSS, letters to McClure of 8 and 19 February 1918.
44. British policy towards the Habsburg Empire has been fully examined in K.J. Calder, *Britain and the Origins of the New Europe 1914–1918* (Cambridge, 1976); and (a less satisfactory work) Wilfried Fest, *Peace or Partition: The Habsburg Monarchy and British Policy 1914–1918* (London, 1978).
45. For this and what follows, see Steed, *Through Thirty Years*, II, pp. 186–91; Seton-Watsons, *The Making of a New Europe*, pp. 259–60; Stuart, *Secrets of Crewe House*, pp. 28–36. Seton-Watson's undated memorandum, 'Austria-Hungary', is in SWP; see also his views on policy and propaganda expressed in July and December 1917: May, *The Passing of the Hapsburg Monarchy*, II, p. 605; *Seton Correspondence*, I, pp. 308–9.

46. PRO, FO 371/3133, Balfour to Rumbold, t.300, 2 March 1918.
47. PRO, CAB 23/5, War Cabinet meeting 359, 5 March.
48. For Gallenga's new organization, see Tosi, *La Propaganda Italiana*, pp. 155ff; for his visit to London in August 1917, pp. 134–6. Sanders and Taylor suggest (*British Propaganda*, p. 230) that Gallenga had already approached the French in July 1917 with a plan for propaganda cooperation.
49. See PRO, FO 170/1145, Algar Thorold to Buchan, 26 February 1918.
50. Tosi, *La Propaganda Italiana*, pp. 177–9 for the Paris conference; BL, Northcliffe MSS, vol. X, Add.Mss 62162, lst meeting of the Committee for Propaganda in Enemy Countries, 14 May 1918.
51. Steed, *Through Thirty Years*, II, pp. 191–6; PRO, FO 371/3474, C.J. Phillips to FO, 19 March 1918. Tosi's dating of this conference (*La Propaganda*, p. 182) is incorrect.
52. In early March, Steed was already planning a visit to France, Italy and Switzerland: TTA, Steed MSS, Steed to Sir Ronald Graham, 11 March.
53. Seton-Watsons, *The Making of a New Europe*, p. 261. For the Sonnino–Gallenga rivalry, see Tosi, *La Propaganda Italiana*, pp. 191ff.
54. See [B. Granville Baker], *The German Army from Within by a British Officer who has Served in it* (London, 1914) pp. 25, 27, 46, 173, 187.
55. B. Granville Baker, *The Danube with Pen and Pencil* (London, 1913) pp. 88, 90; Baker, *The Passing of the Turkish Empire in Europe* (London, 1913) p. 12; Baker, *Old Cavalry Stations* (London, 1934) p. 39.
56. Baker, *The German Army from Within*, p. 186.
57. Much of the following draws on Steed's lengthy 'Report on the British Mission for Propaganda in Austria-Hungary', 30 April 1918 [hereafter *Steed Report*] in BL, Northcliffe MSS, vol. XI, Add.Mss 62163, Steed to Northcliffe, 30 April 1918; and Steed, *Through Thirty Years*, II, pp. 198ff.
58. Steed, *Through Thirty Years*, II, p. 190: Northcliffe's letter to Balfour, 28 March.
59. IWM, Wilson MSS, File 28A/1A, Cavan to Wilson, 24 March 1918.
60. Marchetti, *Ventotto Anni nel Servizio Informazioni Militari*, pp. 344–8; Alessi, *Dall'Isonzo al Piave*, pp. 209–10, 225–8.
61. IWM, Wilson MSS, File 16/4, Diaz to Wilson, 17 March; CCC, Rawlinson MSS, RWLN 1/9.
62. BL, Northcliffe MSS, vol. X, Add.Mss 62162, Minutes of the 6th EPD Committee meeting, 9 July 1918; Stuart, *Secrets of Crewe House*, p. 40; Steed, *Through Thirty Years*, p. 206; Lasswell, *Propaganda Technique*, pp. 29, 215. Cf. the Austrian view: Glaise-Horstenau, *The Collapse of the Austro-Hungarian Empire*, p. 121; Ronge, *Kriegs- und Industriespionage*, p. 361.
63. IWM, DRP, Radcliffe diary, entries for 26 and 27 March 1918. Since Northcliffe had been told at the cabinet meeting on 5 March to see Radcliffe, if the meeting occurred it must have been on 7 or 8 March when the latter made no entries in his diary (he left for Italy on the 9th).
64. IWM, Wilson MSS, 22/3, Delmé-Radcliffe to Wilson, 17 March 1918; DRP diary, entries for 21–3 March.
65. Finzi, *Il Sogno di Carzano*, p. 39; IWM, Wilson MSS, 28A/16, Cavan to Wilson, 24 May 1918.
66. IWM, L.A.E. Price-Davies MSS, 77/78/3, letter to wife, 1 May 1918. In similar vein, Sir Samuel Hoare (head of British Intelligence in Rome, 1917–19) wrote to Radcliffe on leaving Italy: 'Upon many occasions your advice has been of the greatest value to me whilst your unrivalled knowledge of modern Italy has time after time been the

means of assisting my work' (DRP, File 'Personal Letters In', Hoare to Radcliffe, 1 January 191[9]).

67. AJA, JO 28/63, Bogoljub Kujundžić to Ante Trumbić, 4 June 1918.
68. TTA, W.K. McClure MSS, McClure to Bonar Law, 10 August 1917. This opinion and other details about Radcliffe's character and career were confirmed by Radcliffe's nephew, the late Peter Delmé-Radcliffe (interview at Aldbourne, Wiltshire, 12 July 1982) to whom I owe a special debt for his help and hospitality.
69. Albertini, *Epistolario*, II, pp. 924–5; Tosi, *La Propaganda Italiana*, pp. 186 and 234 note 110.
70. For the following, see *Steed Report*, and Steed, *Through Thirty Years*, II, pp. 204–8.
71. Finzi, '*I.T.O.*', pp. 248–9.
72. Cf. Z.A.B. Zeman's ideas: *The Break-Up of the Habsburg Empire 1914–1918*, pp. 190–1 (repeated by Fest, *Peace or Partition*, p. 219 note 36).
73. DRP, diary entries for 30 March and 6 April (by which time his leaflet had been printed and distributed; it has not proved possible to identify the leaflet).
74. See Finzi, '*I.T.O.*', p. 249.
75. Pivko, *Zeleni Odred* (Maribor, 1925) p. 121.
76. Finzi, '*I.T.O.*', p. 246.
77. CCC, Cavan MSS, 1/3, Part I: 'The Guards' Division, Lord Kitchener's intentions regarding it', p. 18; 'Italy', p. 9.
78. Ibid., 'Some Notes on the Battle of Vittorio Veneto and after', p. 37.
79. The divisions identified for Steed seem to have been the 6ID (25 per cent Slovene in fact, while Steed thought it to be 40 per cent), the 38HID (50 per cent Romanian, but 85 per cent on Steed's information) and the predominantly Croat 42HID.
80. Norman Gladden recalls how British troops inadvertently received Slav leaflets meant for the enemy: *Across the Piave: A Personal Account of the British Forces in Italy, 1917–1919* (London, 1971) p. 107.
81. PRO, FO 371/3134, Delmé-Radcliffe to DMI, t.10266, 2 April; Northcliffe to Steed, tel, 4 April 1918. Steed's memoirs exaggerate greatly not only the speed with which he acted and secured Allied approval, but also the significance of such approval for the campaign at the front.
82. AHZ, Dobrovoljački Arhiv II/2, Vidmar to Pivko, 4 April 1918. The texts in English of many of these leaflets are in the *Steed Report.*
83. Leaflets [all in German, Hungarian, Czech, Croat]: 'Österreichisch-ungarische Soldaten! In eurem Lande und in Deutschland...' (OHM sz.5661); 'Oesterreichisch-ungarische Soldaten! Russland empört sich gegen den ihm aufgedrungenden Frieden...' (KA, EvB 1918, 5744/4538); 'Österreichisch-ungarische Soldaten! Die deutsche Offensive...' (ibid.; OHM sz.1467); 'Österreichisch-ungarische Soldaten! Ganze Truppen-Divisionen...' (OHM sz.1474/1).
84. Leaflet [Slovene/Polish and Czech/Croat]: 'Slovani! Čehi in Jugoslovani vstajajo...' (KA, EvB 5754/21352: confiscated from a soldier in Bosnia; KA, 11AK, Fasz.449, Pr.2195). The various themes of despair were also all combined in one leaflet [in five languages]: 'An alle Soldaten des oesterreichischen Heeres. Die grosse oesterreichisch-deustche Offensive...' (KA EvB 5752/17003; 5753/18306; OHM sz.1472).
85. For Tresić-Pavičić, see above Chapter 5 note 193 and the leaflet in Croat, 'Okrutnost Austrije-Ugarske protiv hrvata' which seems to have been printed in Milan through Albertini's influence (KA, EvB 5758/26661); for Czernin, the leaflet in Croat/Polish/Czech: 'Slavenski vojnici! Koji vjerujete u autonomiju vaših naroda...'(OHM sz.1330, 1416).

86. For example, see leaflets: 'Všem vojínům česko-slovácké národnosti!' [Czech/Croat/Polish] (KA, EvB 5750/13431); 'Vojnici Slaveni! Iza čestitog sporazuma talijanskog naroda...' [Croat/Czech] (OHM sz.1632; KA EvB 5751/14886); 'Soldaţi Români! Voi sunteti totdeauna consideraţi ca fraţi noştri...' (KA, HGK Conrad, Fasz.66 Na Nr 400a/307; HIL, Fasz.4517); 'Všem Slovanům! Armáda československá...' [Czech, Croat, Slovene, Polish: different print types] (KA, 11AK, Fasz.451, Files I & II; OHM sz.1413/2, 1420/1, 82.13.2; VHA, Fond ČSNR-Paříž).
87. Leaflet: 'Jugoslovenski vojnici! Jugoslavenska država će biti!' [Croat, Czech, Slovene: separate issues] (KA, EvB 5758/26661; 11AK 1918, Fasz.451, File I; OHM sz.1245, 79.84.1).
88. The Austrian records confirm this. Cf. Sanders and Taylor, *British Propaganda*, p. 227; Zeman, *The Break-Up*, pp. 191–2; and Melograni, *Storia Politica*, p. 524.
89. KA, 11AK Gstbs Abt 1918, Fasz.448, Pr. 2043, translation of Hungarian leaflet found by the 27ID (which was in line next to the 26SchD and contained two predominantly Magyar regiments).
90. Janković and Krizman (eds), *Gradja*, I, no. 145, pp. 188–9: Hristić to Serbian High Command, 25 April 1918.
91. Concerning the reasons for Hlaváček's transfer to Paris, Beneš undoubtedly considered him to have been effective but too independent in his behaviour in Italy. It was also the case that his relations with Štefánik had been very tense since the latter's arrival in Italy. But, perhaps crucially, Beneš soon discovered that Hlaváček had accepted payment from the Italian military for his work for them in the summer of 1917. This was felt to be inexcusable (see Hlaváček's attempt to explain his behaviour to Beneš and Štefánik in Paris on 16 June 1918: ANM, Hlaváček MSS, Karton IV/c).
92. Borgese, *Goliath: The March of Fascism*, p. 138.
93. See Seton-Watsons, *The Making of a New Europe*, pp. 265ff.
94. AJA, JO 19/19, 'Discours de M.Trumbić au Congrès des Nationalités opprimées tenu à Rome'; PRO, FO 371/3135, Rodd to Balfour, d.128, 10 April 1918.
95. *The New Europe*, no. 81, 2 May 1918: 'The Roman Congress of Oppressed Nationalities'; *Steed Report*.
96. For the following, the most detailed account is Beneš, *Světová Válka*, II, pp. 107–10. Paulová, *Jugoslavenski Odbor*, pp. 440–1 is useful but slightly inaccurate. The resolutions of the three committees are preserved in AJA, JO 19/40.
97. AJA, JO 76/9, typed statement by Trumbić in 1919.
98. SWP, Draft 'Report on the work of the Department of Propaganda in Enemy Countries', compiled by C.S. Kent, Crewe House's financial officer [hereafter *Draft EPD Report*], p. 34; *Steed Report*.
99. Tosi, *La Propaganda Italiana*, pp. 234–5, notes 110 and 114; Ojetti, *Lettere alla Moglie*, p. 506.
100. Umberto Zanotti-Bianco, *Carteggio 1906–1918*, ed. V.Carinci (Rome and Bari, 1987) pp. 614–17: Ojetti to Zanotti-Bianco, 16 April 1918.
101. PRO, FO 170/1145, Steed to Gallenga Stuart, 15 April; AJA, JO 9/2(2), Steed to Trumbić, 15 April 1918. (Both sent by Delmé-Radcliffe via the British embassy in Rome.)
102. AJA, JO 9/1(2), Steed to Trumbić, 17 April 1918.
103. IWM, Price-Davies MSS, 77/78/3, letter to wife, 20 April. Major-General L.A.E. Price-Davies had been appointed liaison officer between the War Office and British forces in Italy.

104. Two memoranda drawn up by Lt-Colonel Stanhope after meeting Steed and Beneš: PRO, CAB 24/50, GT 4414, 'The Czecho-Slovak movement'; PRO, AIR 1/2296/209/77/20, SWC 184, 'Notes on Propaganda in time of war', 28 April 1918 (copy also in HLRO, Beaverbrook MSS, BBK E/3/33).
105. Sidney Sonnino, *Diario 1916–1922*, 3 vols (Bari, 1972), III, pp. 265–6.
106. AJA, JO 27/188, De Giulli to Trumbić, 24 April 1918.
107. The minutes of the 14 meetings are in BL, Northcliffe MSS, vol.X, Add.Mss 62162 – all except the seventh meeting on 23 July.
108. The propaganda campaign on the Western Front remains to be fully researched and analyzed; from August 1918 at least, the British manifestos were numbered in a similar way to those of the Padua Commission. For the present, apart from the older assessments by Thimme and Bruntz, see Sanders and Taylor, *British Propaganda*, pp. 208ff, 235ff, and Cockerill (*What Fools We Were*) who claims that the success of propaganda against Germany was largely due to MI7(b). The Northcliffe papers contain Fyfe's reports to the advisory committee and detailed memoranda by Wells.
109. Documents in PRO, FO 371/3474.
110. See HLRO, Beaverbrook MSS, BBK E/3/11, E/3/34, E/3/44.
111. Stuart, *Secrets of Crewe House*, pp. 48–9. It is an idea repeated since: for example, Sanders and Taylor, *British Propaganda*, pp. 229, 245.
112. PRO, FO 383/359 (69566/2162), Dorothy Cocking to Owen Monk, 19 April 1918. After the war she translated Gheorghe Mironescu's *Le Problème du Banat* (Paris, 1919) from French into English.
113. Alessi, *Dall'Isonzo al Piave*, p. 236.
114. PRO, WO 106/852, Cavan to CIGS, 10 June 1918. On 10 May Cavan had written (ibid.) that the CS expected 'great results from the Czech propaganda'.
115. SWP, *Draft EPD Report*, pp. 34–5.
116. Ojetti, *Lettere alla Moglie*, pp. 505–6.
117. Leaflet in Croat and Czech, 'Vojnici Slaveni i Rumunji' which detailed the Congress resolutions (KA, HGK Conrad, Fasz.66, Na Nr 400a/290).
118. There is no record of what they did discuss on 18 April, but Austrian Intelligence imagined quite plausibly that it concerned the use of Yugoslav volunteers in the Italian lines: see KA, EvB 1918, Fasz.5754/19617.
119. Leaflet in Croat only: 'Jugosloveni: Srbi, Hrvati i Slovenci! Izaslanstvo . . . ' (KA, EvB 1918, Fasz.5754/20417, 5758/26661; OHM sz.1431). The draft of this and other leaflets composed by Trumbić are in AJA, JO 35/155–6.
120. KA, 11AK Op. Abt 1918, Fasz.445, Na Nr 725, Conrad to 11AK, Na Nr 1414/I, 5 May 1918 (enclosing translations of some of Italy's April leaflets).
121. See Tosi, 'Giuseppe Antonio Borgese', pp. 293–4; Tosi, 'Romeo A. Gallenga Stuart', p. 533. Arcà had been a member of the executive committee planning the Rome Congress. Granello had helped to improve links to the Serb émigré community in Switzerland in late 1917, from which had emerged an Italian 'Committee for Propaganda for Italo-Yugoslav Understanding', of which Salvemini was the most prominent member (see Paulová, *Jugoslavenski Odbor*, pp. 437–9).
122. SWP, 'Report on work in Switzerland', p. 7. For fuller details of the mission, see Seton-Watsons, *The Making of a New Europe*, pp. 284–7.
123. KA, EvB 1918, Fasz.5754, Nr 21247, Military attaché in Berne to EvB, V.Nr 3262/18, 11 July, Beilage 3 and 9; KA, Feindespropaganda-Abwehrstelle 1918, Fasz.5994, Res.163, AOK Na Nr 13094, 11 June 1918: one source suggested that Borgese's

bureau would be modelled on that of the French organized by Emil Haguenin in Berne.

124. KA, EvB 1918, Fasz.5756, Nr 23481, Military attaché in Berne to EvB, V.Nr 3870, 2 August 1918.
125. KA, Zensurstelle Feldkirch, Fasz.5952, E-Stelle tschechische Gruppe (Res.Nr 5663N), 'Wahrnehmungen über tschechische Spionage- und Nachrichtenorganisation in der Schweiz bezw. im feindlichen Auslande', [late] July 1918.
126. Ojetti, *Lettere alla Moglie,* p. 507.
127. SWP, *Draft EPD Report,* p. 34.
128. Antoni Szuber, *Walka o Przewagę Duchową. Kampanja Propagandowa Koalicji 1914–1918* (Warsaw, 1933), p. 155; Ojetti, *Lettere,* p. 512; AJA, JO 19/109.
129. KA, Militärkanzlei Seiner Majestät 1918 [MKSM], 59–1/7, AOK to MKSM, EvB Nr 3881, 26 February 1918, enclosing captured report of Italian Intelligence about an interrogation of Zamorski in November 1916. (Copies also in KA, EvB, Fasz.5743/3881, and HHStA, PA I/1069, Nr 2571.) See also Zanotti-Bianco, *Carteggio,* p. 617 note 3.
130. Only one letter by Rybka to the National Council has been discovered (on the subject of Czech prisoners of war): VHA, Fond ČSNR-Štefánik, Karton 1, 34/2/14, Rybka to Štefánik, 12 July 1918. But see KA, 11AK 1918, Fasz.442/1674, for a scrap of information discovered by Austrian Intelligence about him; Antonín Papírník, *U Národní Řady v Římě,* in *Naše Revoluce* XII (Prague, 1936) p. 396; and Josef Logaj, *Československé Legie v Italii* (Prague, 1922) p. 32.
131. Ante Mandić, *Fragmenti za Historiju Ujedinjenja* (Zagreb, 1956) p. 48.
132. AJA, JO 35/250, Jambrišak to Trumbić, 18 March 1918.
133. AJA, JO 19/121, Trumbić to Siciliani, 26 April [draft]; JO 19/119, Kujundžić to Trumbić, 7 June 1918.
134. AJA, JO 19/117, De Giulli to Trumbić, 6 June; JO 19/117, Trumbić to Jambrišak, 21 June 1918. Trumbić's almost indecipherable notes in JO 46/14 mention that Lasić had a brother in Cleveland, Ohio.
135. Finzi, '*I.T.O.*', p. 260.
136. AJA, JO 19/109, Jambrišak to Trumbić, 22 May 1918.
137. Zanotti-Bianco, *Carteggio,* pp. 617–18; Ojetti, *Lettere,* pp. 510, 515, 537.
138. Ibid., pp. 513, 519–21, 524, 536; Zanotti-Bianco, *Carteggio,* p. 620.
139. AJA, JO 28/48(1), 'Pregled rada, manifesti sul nemico'; JO 28/48(2), 'Giornali sul nemico'. Szuber gives 73 million as the final total produced: *Walka o Przewagę Duchową,* p. 156. Ojetti's own figures do not seem to be accurate; particularly his claim that 112 newspapers were produced does not correspond to the number found in the archives in Vienna and elsewhere: see Ojetti, *La Propaganda sul Nemico,* in G. Amendola *et al., Il Patto di Roma* (Rome, 1919) p. 134.
140. Stuart, *Secrets of Crewe House,* p. 93. It might also be estimated to be twice the amount which the French were distributing in the West: from December 1917 to August 1918, the French had distributed 25 million leaflets (see PRO, CAB 24/61, G.T.5492, p. 10).
141. Manifesto 492: 'Das Ende!' (in VHA, Fond ČSNR-Paříž). Ojetti's total of 723 leaflets must either result from counting separately those leaflets which bore the same text and number but in different languages, or must include those leaflets without number which continued to be issued at times by the Intelligence offices.
142. AJA, JO 28/48(3), (4) and (5). This was almost exactly the same as the amount directed at Poles: Szuber, *Walka o Przewagę Duchową,* p. 147.

143. AJA, JO 19/123, Kujundžić to Trumbić, 1 May 1918.
144. Ibid.; Ojetti, *Lettere*, pp. 509, 521; Zanotti-Bianco, *Carteggio*, pp. 618, 624. Ojetti's idea of symbols to head each leaflet did not materialize, but for his use of Hussite imagery see manifesto 131: 'Necht' Vás posílí pohled na velkého mučednika – M.JANA HUSA!' (KA, Flugzettel Sammlung). See below, pp. 355–6.
145. Manifesto 33, *Jugoslavia* no. 2, 6 June 1918 (copies in AJA, JO 19/66; KA, EvB, Fasz.5758/26661). This item was also discussed in Padua's Czech, Polish and Romanian newssheets. For an example of the Germans' weakness, including their abandonment of submarine warfare, versus American strength, see manifesto 18, 'Bitka na zapadnom frontu!' (KA, EvB, Fasz.5752/16897; AJA, JO 19/110b).
146. First in manifesto 135 (*Jugoslavija* no. 6) although Cyrillic types were available earlier since they were used in Ukrainian leaflets.
147. AJA, JO 19/109, Jambrišak to Trumbić, 22 May 1918.
148. AJA, JO 19/123, Kujundžić to Trumbić, 1 May 1918. It was significant that when Pivko recruited 'Yugoslavs' for his units, there were only five Moslems among the 943 volunteers (Pivko, *Naši Dobrovoljci u Italiji*, p. 41).
149. Manifesto [unnumbered but probably no. 1]: 'Hrvati, Srbi i Slovenci!' (KA, FAst, Fasz.5996, Res.486/28). It was the first leaflet composed by the Yugoslav delegates (see AJA, JO 19/123).
150. *Glas Slovenaca Hrvata i Srba*, broj 90, 11 May 1918. For the events in Zagreb, see the military commander's report in KA, EvB, Fasz.5750/13281, Beilage 4.
151. Manifesto 16, 'Hrvati, Srbi i Slovenci!' (KA, EvB, Fasz.5754/21105) which publicized the names of Trinajstić, Gazzari, Jambrišak and Kujundžić. See below, p. 266.
152. Manifesto 33, *Jugoslavia* no. 2. Trumbić's words were paraphrased from an interview to *The Times* (24 May, p. 5).
153. For a recent detailed study of this movement, see Mark Cornwall, 'The Experience of Yugoslav Agitation in Austria-Hungary 1917–1918', in Hugh Cecil and Peter Liddle (eds), *Facing Armageddon: The First World War Experienced* (London, 1996) pp. 656–76.
154. Manifesto 4, 'Srbi, Hrvati i Slovenci' (AJA, JO 19/110a). Emperor Karl's speech was mentioned in manifesto 74, *Jugoslavija* no. 4 (AJA, JO 19/66; KA, EvB, Fasz.5758/26661). For the context of the speeches, see Lojze Ude, 'Deklaracijsko gibanje na Slovenskem', in *Naučni Skup u Povodu 50-Godišnjice Raspada Austro-Ugarske Monarhije i Stvaranja Jugoslavenske Države* (Zagreb, 1969) p. 155.
155. Manifesto 50, 'Srbi, Hrvati i Slovenci!' (OHM sz.1333). The economic benefits of Yugoslav unity were also the subject of manifesto 38 [Slovene], 'Gospodarska važnost jugoslovanske deklaracije', with manifesto 39 being a summary in Serbo-Croat on the reverse (AJA, JO 19/100; IWM, leaflet collection, 3(45)/39; KA, 11AK Gstbs Abt 1918, Fasz.448, Pr.2000).
156. Manifesto 57, 'Srbi, Hrvati i Slovenci' (OHM sz.1448) about a rally at Sveti Vid on 31 May; manifesto 19, *Jugoslavia* no. 1 (KA, EvB, Fasz.5758/26661; AJA, JO 35/160); manifesto 33; and especially, manifesto 85, 'Jugoslovenski pokret' (VHA), which detailed a number of plebiscites in Carinthia.
157. Manifesto 29, 'Hrvati, Srbi i Slovenci!' (AJA, JO 111/4, 19/78, 19/79: coupled with manifestos 32, 30 and 31 respectively on the reverse; no. 29 is also in OHM sz.1243, 1259; IWM, 3(45)/39).
158. Manifesto 21, *Československá Samostatnost* no. 1 (KA, EvB, Fasz.5758/26661; AJA, JO 35/160; IWM, 3(45)/39).
159. Manifesto 11, 'Krajané Čechoslováci!' (KA, EvB, Fasz.5744/4538), dated 12 May 1918.

160. See manifesto 33, *Jugoslavia* no. 2.
161. For example, manifesto 9, 'Drazi bratři Čechoslováci!' (KA, EvB, Fasz.5744/4538; IWM, 3(45)/39); manifesto 30, 'Čechové a Slováci!' (OHM sz.1243, 1244; AJA, JO 19/76); manifesto 48, 'Bratři! Češi! Slováci!' (AJA, JO 19/84).
162. Manifesto 67, 'Z 13. čísla Československé Samostatnosti' (OHM sz.1460). Hlaváček's article was reproduced from the Paris edition of *Československá Samostatnost.*
163. Manifesto 34, *Československá Samostatnost* no. 2 (KA, EvB, 5758/26661; AJA, JO 19/66). See also the pictorial leaflet showing the presentation of the flag to Graziani: 'Čechoslováci' (KA, FAst, Fasz.5995/432).
164. Manifesto 61, 'Polacy!' (KA, 11AK, Fasz.451, File 'Flugzettel I'; AJA, JO 111/4; IWM, 3(45)/39). The declaration was also discussed by Zamorski in manifesto 76, *Polak* no. 4, issued from late June (KA, EvB, Fasz.5758/26661; OHM sz.3507; AJA, JO 19/66).
165. Manifesto 62, 'Bracia żołnierze!' (KA, EvB, Fasz.5744/4538).
166. Manifesto 43, 'Żołnierze-Polacy, Legioniści!' (KA, EvB, Fasz.5744/4538; AJA, JO 111/4); manifesto 51, 'Polacy!' (KA, Flugzettel Sammlung).
167. Manifesto 65, 'Polacy!' (OHM, sz.1449: copies on blue and bright pink paper). See Ojetti, *Lettere alla Moglie*, p. 535.
168. Beneš, *Světová Válka*, II, p. 109.
169. Manifesto 2, 'Polacy!' (KA, Flugzettel Sammlung).
170. See manifestos 43 and 51; manifesto 44, *Polak* no. 3 (KA, EvB, Fasz.5758/26661) which commented on events in Palestine; manifesto 10, 'Polacy!' (KA, EvB, Fasz.5744/4538) which told of Polish socialists complaining to Seidler about famine in Galicia.
171. Manifesto 12, 'Legioniści polscy!' (AJA, JO 111/4); manifesto 42, 'Legioniści polscy!' (IWM, 3(45)/39; KA, EvB, Fasz.5744/4538).
172. Manifesto 23, *Polak* no. 1 (KA, EvB, Fasz.5758/26661; AJA, JO 35/160); manifesto 82, 'Polacy z pod zaboru austryackiego w opozycyi...' (KA, 11AK, Fasz.451, File 'Flugzettel I').
173. Manifesto 58, 'Polacy!' (KA, EvB, 5761/31651).
174. Manifesto 22, *Neamul Românesc* no. 1 (KA, EvB, Fasz.5758/26661; AJA, JO 35/160; IWM 3(45)/39). For the work of Romanian émigrés in 1918, see I. Gheorghiu and C. Nuţu, 'The Activity for the Union carried out abroad', in Miron Constantinescu and Ştefan Pascu (eds), *Unification of the Romanian National State: The Union of Transylvania with Old Romania* (Bucharest, 1971) chapter 5.
175. Manifesto 6, 'Mândre catane Române!' (AJA, JO 19/70).
176. Manifesto 54, 'Mândre catane române!' (OHM sz.7926, 1265; KA, EvB, Fasz.5758/16661, 5744/4538).
177. Manifesto 17, 'Jugosloveni! Draga braćo Srbi, Hrvati i Slovenci!' (KA, EvB, Fasz.5756/22782 and 5752/16897/6). The *Waffenbund* also featured in manifesto 45, *Jugoslavia* no. 3 (AJA, JO 19/66; KA, EvB, Fasz.5758/26661); manifesto 49, *Československá Samostatnost* no. 3 (ibid.); manifesto 46, *Neamul Românesc* no. 3 (ibid.); manifesto 35, *Polak* no. 2 (ibid.); manifesto 51, 'Polacy!'. The Polish leaflets dated the Spa agreement incorrectly as 10 May.
178. Manifesto 55, 'Oesterrichische Soldaten!' (KA, EvB, Fasz.5758/26661; IWM File 3(45)/39). The imminent arrival of Hoffmann was also a subject in manifesto 56, 'Srbi, Hrvati i Slovenci!' (AJA, JO 19/99); manifesto 52, 'Bratři Češi a Slováci!' (AJA, JO 19/87); manifesto 54 in Romanian; and manifesto 53, 'Polacy!' (OHM, sz.7926, AJA 19/87).

179. Manifesto 41, 'Magyar Katonák!' (OHM sz.802491, 3389; HIL, Fasz.4517 'Propaganda Anyag'; also partly reproduced in Stuart, *Secrets of Crewe House*, between pp. 176–7). The intrigues of German Intelligence are discussed at length in Károlyi's *Gegen eine ganze Welt. Mein Kampf um den Frieden* (Munich, 1924). For Ojetti's problems: *Lettere alla Moglie*, p. 522.
180. 'Mégis hunczut a német, hogy a fene enné meg!'. See manifesto 89, 'Miért harcoltok ti?' (OHM sz.5663) for the historical references.
181. Šepić, *Italija, Saveznici i Jugoslavensko Pitanje*, pp. 313ff. As in Rome, Ruthene delegates were not present because of Polish opposition. And it is worth noting, as another similarity, that the Prague meeting also had some specific practical and military repercussions in that it was agreed in Prague to set up a revolutionary committee whose first task would be to organize a revolt among the naval forces in Šibenik.
182. Manifesto 26, 'Srbi, Hrvati i Slovenci!' (OHM sz.1447; AJA, JO 19/80).
183. Manifesto 68, 'Österreichischer Begriff von Hochverrat' (quoting a lengthy article from *Die Freie Zeitung* of 29 May: KA, EvB, Fasz.5758/26661; IWM 3(45/39)). For various interpretations of the events, see, for example, manifesto 35, *Polak* no. 2; manifesto 57, 'Srbi, Hrvati i Slovenci!' (OHM sz.1448); and manifesto 36, *Neamul Românesc* no. 2 (AJA, JO 19/66) which was significantly unable to quote any speech by the Romanian delegate, Professor Juraj Stacu of Charles University.
184. Marchetti, *Ventotto Anni*, p. 337. Manifesto 66, 'Národní Listy rakouskou vládou zastaveny' (KA, EvB, Fasz.5758/26661).
185. See manifestos 26 and 28 (Croat and Polish respectively); and the blunt tone of manifesto 27, 'Bratři Čechoslováci!' (KA, EvB 5758/26661; AJA, JO 111/4): 'our people are beginning to revolt in their own motherland too... they know that they have to pay for freedom with blood'.
186. See De Giulli's impatient letters to Trumbić in AJA, JO 27/188 (24 April), 27/77 (4 May), 27/71 (29 May).
187. PRO, FO 371/3135, Radcliffe to CIGS, t.10318, 24 April; Baker to Northcliffe, no. 452/8, 30 April 1918, p. 2. Radcliffe was already fully aware of Štefánik's views after meeting him twice in Rome on 19 April: DRP, Radcliffe diary.
188. *Papers relating to the Foreign Relations of the United States 1918*. [FRUS] *Supplement 1. The World War*, I (Washington, 1933) pp. 799–802.
189. Padua did not, as Dragan Živojinović suggests, 'play the declaration for all it was worth' (*America, Italy and the Birth of Yugoslavia 1917–1919* (New York, 1972) p. 147). The speech was only mentioned in manifestos 45 and 74 (*Jugoslavia*, nos. 3 and 4), and in July for the Czechs in manifesto 113, *Československá Samostatnost* no. 5 (KA, 11AK, Fasz.451, File 'Flugzettel I').
190. Beneš, *Světová Válka*, II, pp. 111–12.
191. PRO, FO 371/3135, Beneš to Balfour, 10 and 11 May 1918; Beneš discusses the talks in *Světová Válka*, II, pp. 205–11.
192. Manifesto 80, 'Československé vojsko uznáno anglickou vládou' (KA, 11AK, Fasz.451, 'Flugzettel I'), issued after the June offensive, and manifesto 113.
193. PRO, FO 371/3135, Delmé-Radcliffe to Cecil, 19 May 1918, enclosing 'Notes on the possible effects of the Czecho-Slovak and Yugo-Slav movement on the military situation... '
194. IWM, Wilson MSS, 32A/8, Price-Davies to Wilson, 30 April 1918. On 10 May at Versailles, Radcliffe had given British military representatives 'a surprising impression of the rocky state of the Austrian army' (PRO, WO 106/593).

195. PRO, FO 371/3135, Cecil to Derby, t.1012, 21 May 1918. Seton-Watsons, *The Making of a New Europe*, p. 278.
196. 'Lord Robert Cecil and the Rome Congress', *The New Europe*, 30 May 1918.
197. BL, Northcliffe MSS, vol. X, Add.Mss 62162, minutes of the 2nd EPD Committee meeting, 27 May; *The Times*, 23 May 1918, p. 7.
198. IWM, Wilson MSS, Delmé-Radcliffe to Wilson, 26 May 1918.
199. AJA, JO 19/119, Kujundžić to Trumbić, 7 June 1918 (discussing a talk on 28 May with Radcliffe, who was at this time continuing to sound out all parties about the chances of a joint Allied statement).
200. AJA, JO 27/71, De Giulli to Trumbić, 29 May 1918.
201. Quoted in Šepić, *Italija, Saveznici i Jugoslavensko Pitanje*, p. 318.
202. Manifesto 45, *Jugoslavia* no. 3. Significantly, the Italian press left out the mention of Zagreb, an omission pounced on by Kujundžić (AJA, JO 28/63, JO 19/119), but manifesto 45 included it. Orlando's speech was also used in the equivalent Czech, Polish and Romanian newssheets.
203. *The Times*, 29 May 1918, p. 5. The full speech is printed in Bissolati, *Diario di Guerra* (Turin, 1935) pp. 114–20.
204. AJA, JO 19/118, Kujundžić to Trumbić, 9 June 1918. See also the report of the Questore Padova in: Archivio Stato di Padova, Gabinetto Prefettura, 242, Cat XVI/1, Questore to Prefetto Padova, N.1154, 3 June 1918.
205. FRUS 1918, *Supplement 1*, I, p. 802.
206. Ibid., pp. 805–6; Sonnino, *Diario 1916–1922*, III, pp. 265–6. See also Paulová, *Jugoslavenski Odbor*, pp. 458–9; and BL, Northcliffe MSS, vol. X, Add.Mss 62162, Minutes of the 4th EPD Committee meeting, 11 June 1918.
207. PRO, FO 800/212, Northcliffe to Balfour, 6 June (drafted by Steed); FO 800/329, Balfour to Northcliffe, 8 June 1918.
208. PRO, FO 371/3474, DMI to Radcliffe, t.59793, 8 June (from Northcliffe); Radcliffe to DMI (for Northcliffe), t.10443, 10 June. The Czechs were to be compensated by additional statements, including the publication of Balfour's letter to Beneš (of 3 June); the Romanians gained nothing.
209. See, for example, manifesto 81, 'Unutrašnje prilike u Austriji' (KA, 11AK, Fasz.451, File 'Flugzettel I').
210. AJA, JO 28/42, Kujundžić to Trumbić, 20 May 1918.
211. PRO, WO 106/817, Delmé-Radcliffe to DMO, no. SBM 249, 'Very Confidential', 2 August 1918.
212. Ojetti, *La Propaganda sul Nemico*, p. 125.
213. AJA, JO 19/109, Jambrišak to Trumbić, 22 May 1918.
214. Šepić, *Italija, Saveznici*, pp. 304–6. Salvemini's record of these talks is in *Seton Correspondence*, I, pp. 321–7.
215. AJA, JO 19/109, Jambrišak to Trumbić, 22 May; JO 28/42, Kujundžić to Trumbić, 20 May 1918. Ojetti's views were very much those expressed by Salvemini and De Viti de Marco.
216. AJA, JO 28/42, Kujundžić to Trumbić, 20 May 1918.
217. PRO, FO 371/3474, Rumbold to FO, t.860, 30 May 1918. Note Seton-Watson's attack on the Caburi article in *The New Europe*, no. 88, 20 June 1918.
218. On Siciliani, see Ojetti, *Lettere alla Moglie*, pp. 523ff; on Badoglio, see Albertini, *Epistolario*, II, p. 936.
219. AJA, JO 19/116, Jambrišak to Trumbić, 18 June 1918.

220. PRO, FO 371/3474, DMI to Radcliffe, t.59793, 8 June; Radcliffe to DMI, t.10440 and 10441, 9 June, t.10443, 10 June.
221. AJA, JO 35/252, Jambrišak to Banjanin, 7 June; JO 19/116, Jambrišak to Trumbić, 18 June 1918.
222. AJA, JO 28/42, Kujundžić to Trumbić, 20 May 1918; Ojetti, *Lettere alla Moglie*, p. 537.
223. Pivko, *Informatorji* (Maribor, 1925) p. 69.
224. Useful data about the state of the Czechoslovak Legion at this time is contained in Jan Šeba's reports to Štefánik. In early June he had numbered the Czechs involved in Intelligence work at the front at 1200, and he then travelled to the war zone to supervise the taking of the oath. See VHA, Fond ČSNR-Štefánik, Karton 1.
225. Hanzal, *S Výzvědčíky od Švýcarských Ledovců až po Moře Adriatické* (Prague, 1938) pp. 259–63; and KA, 11AK Gstbs Abt 1918, Fasz.449, Pr.2333 (captured order of Vigevano, 4 May). For Austrian concern about the Czech patrols on Monte Pertica, see KA, EvB, Fasz.5758/27418.
226. Hanzal, *S Výzvědčíky*, pp. 279–84. For some Austrian evidence, see KA, 11AK Gstbs Abt, Fasz.446, Ev.Nr 841 (6AK report); and for the significance of Rudolf Paprskař's desertion, see below Chapter 7, p. 302.
227. See Smaniotto's letter to Hlaváček of 18 February (ANM, Hlaváček MSS, Karton II/i); and DRP diary: apart from attending the meeting on 30 March, Smaniotto met Granville Baker (27th) and Delmé-Radcliffe (23rd/28th) on separate occasions.
228. Hanzal, *S Výzvědčíky*, pp. 305–9; KA, 11AK Op.Abt 1918, Fasz.445, Na.Nr 756, KISA Op.5800, monthly report, Beilage 11 (10 May).
229. Manifesto 37 [Polish and Croat], 'Polacy!' (OHM, sz.1445/1).
230. HIL, KISA Gstbs Abt 1918, Fasz.77, Op.Nrs 5927 ('Propaganda activity increases daily', 6 May); 5970, 6061 (the leaflets on this occasion were all burnt by the rocket), 6085, 6110, 6139, 6151, 6184, 6379 (calls on 4 June).
231. Hanzal, *S Výzvědčíky*, pp. 310–12. See below pp. 301–2.
232. Manifesto (in Czech/Polish, signed by Stinný), 'Všem Slovanům rak.uherské Armády!', in KA, EvB 1918, Fasz.5744/4538; and IWM, aerial leaflets, 3(45)/44. See Ronge, *Kriegs- und Industriespionage*, p. 364.
233. Hanzal, *S Výzvědčíky*, pp. 312–14.
234. Ibid., pp. 97, 305. Before the war, Kobylinskij had been a professor of psychiatry at Genoa University and knew several east European languages.
235. KA, EvB, Fasz.5752/18742: captured order of 3rd army command (Lt General Fabbri), dated 14 May 1918. Fabbri noted that some Czechs had deserted to Italy, while some had remained behind to ferment rebellion in the Austrian ranks.
236. AJA, JO 19/118, Kujundžić to Trumbić, 9 June 1918.
237. Marchetti, *Ventotto Anni*, p. 311; Pivko, *Zeleni Odred*, p. 126.
238. Hanzal, *S Výzvědčíky*, pp. 133–4; Pivko, *Informatorji*, p. 68. Marchetti had felt it necessary to secure governmental permission for publicity among the Veronese, and it was Steed who wrote to Gallenga on his behalf: see PRO, FO 170/1145, p. 102: Delmé-Radcliffe to Rodd, t.10298, 15 April enclosing Steed's request.
239. Hanzal, *S Výzvědčíky*, p. 132; Pivko, *Informatorji*, p. 68.
240. Hanzal, *S Výzvědčíky*, pp. 198–9.
241. For a vivid study of warfare in this remote region, see Luciano Viazzi, *I Diavoli dell'Adamello. La Guerra a Quota Tremila 1915–1918* (Milan, 1981).
242. For details, see Hanzal, *S Výzvědčíky*, pp. 140–5.
243. Ibid., pp. 200–1.

244. KA, 11AK Gstbs Abt 1918, Fasz.449, Pr.2205, 11AK (Frydman) to corps, 7 May 1918; Fasz.448, Pr.2004/24: manifesto, 'Ufficiali e soldati italiani!'
245. Pivko, *Informatorji*, p. 74.
246. KA, 11AK 1918, Fasz.449, Pr.2183, VI KK to 11AK, Na Nr 423/8, 25 April 1918. For continued Austrian propaganda efforts until the June offensive, see Pr.2213, 2232, 2251, 2278, 2292.
247. Pivko, *Val Bella* (Maribor, 1928) pp. 53–4.
248. Of the '450' from Padula, five officers and 183 men left Verona for Tugurio on 2 May; on 21 May, Tugurio received a further four officers and 110 men as its allotment from the II/31st regiment.
249. Pivko, *Informatorji*, pp. 90, 93–4; *Val Bella*, pp. 6ff.
250. Pivko, *Informatorji*, pp. 91–4.
251. In some sectors, such as the Frenzella gorge (where a unit under Karel Pajger was operating), the Austrians seem to have been overwhelmingly hostile from the beginning (see the 26SchD report contained in HIL, 42HID 1918, Fasz.1666, Op.t.126/4, 6 May). The 26SchD continued in June to record the efforts of Czech propaganda patrols but always implied that the efforts had been repulsed (see 26SchD propaganda reports under note 246 above).
252. KA, 11AK 1918, Fasz.449, Pr.2278, 2292: these reports give in detail the material which was distributed by the 26 SchD *Nachrichtentruppen*.
253. Pivko, *Informatorji*, p. 93. One of the deserters from SchR9 on San Francesco was Anton Barek, who might be identified as the elderly Czech corporal who had engaged the patrol in conversation: see HIL, 42HID, Fasz.1667, 26SchD to 42HID, t.Op.Nr 135/6, 16 May 1918.
254. See below Chapter 7, p. 302.
255. Report of the KPQ of 27 July 1918, as quoted in Pivko, *Val Bella*, p. 71.
256. Marchetti, *Ventotto Anni*, pp. 317–18; Ojetti, *Lettere alla Moglie*, mentions two Polish officers who were killed during their propaganda work: pp. 535, 556.
257. Szuber, *Walka o Przewagę Duchową*, pp. 158–62; Albertini, *Epistolario*, II, no. 867, p. 977; Ojetti, *Lettere alla Moglie*, pp. 528, 618. The AOK knew that Italy was having problems over Polish recruitment: see KA, AOK Op.Abt 1918, Fasz.370, Nr.109614, military attaché in Berne to AOK, Res.Nr 829/M, 17 July 1918.
258. Luciano Tosi, *La Propaganda Italiana*, p. 237 note 134. The Austrians had intermittent news about Rygier's committee but thought he was a woman (see KA, EvB, Fasz.5761/32389).
259. G.G. Mironescu, *Aperçus sur la Question Roumaine* (Paris, 1919) pp. 114–17; see also George Moroïanu, *Les Luttes des Roumains Transylvains pour la Liberté et l'Opinion Européene* (Paris, 1933) pp. 209–11.
260. AJA, JO 59/2(2): 2000 at Cavatzere, 1600 at Mantua.
261. Marchetti, *Ventotto Anni*, pp. 316–17 who claims that the Austrians had to withdraw IR50 from the line.
262. Thus Orlando later told Delmé-Radcliffe that Transylvanian Romanians and Ruthenes could not be trusted and often would not submit to Mîndrescu's authority: IWM, Wilson MSS, 22/18, Radcliffe to Wilson, 12 September 1918. For the creation of the legion, see Ion Ardeleanu, 'Romanian Combatants in Italy during World War I', in B. Király and N. Dreisziger (eds), *East Central European Society in World War I* (New York, 1985) pp. 547–51. The evidence which reached the Austrian authorities similarly suggested that Italy faced problems with recruitment, even if in October the Italian press naturally reported how Mîndrescu and Rygier

were rapturously received by the new Romanian legionaries before their departure for the front (*Giornale d'Italia*, 9 October, contained in KA, EvB, Fasz.5761/32389).

263. See Franc Grafenauer, 'Od Gorlice do Soluna', in E.Turk, J.Jeras, and R.Paulin (eds), *Dobrovoljci Kladivarji Jugoslavije 1912–1918* (Ljubljana, 1936) pp. 689ff. For the six camps, see AJA, JO 59/2(2), Trinajstić to Jambrišak, 20 May 1918.
264. AJA, JO 35/224, Trinajstić to JO London/Paris, 18 May 1918.
265. Pivko, *Informatorji*, p. 102; AJA, JO 59/4, Trumbić notes on talk with Pašić, 31 May; AJA, JO 35/127(a), JO Rome office to Vigevano, 30 May 1918. The visits to Nocera Umbra were mentioned in manifestos 18 and 33, while manifesto 16 ('Hrvati, Srbi i Slovenci!') claimed that 'our prisoners in Italy are totally separated... and we are allowed to visit them if we wish' [!]. See p. 266.
266. AJA, JO 35/252, Jambrišak to Banjanin, 7 June 1918.
267. Pivko, *Val Bella*, pp. 7–8.
268. The two officers were Hugo Plhak, who had joined Pivko's unit earlier in the year; and Mirko Belošević, who had only just deserted on the Asiago plateau and therefore might be presented as living proof of a new commitment by Croats from the Austrian ranks.
269. For the following see Pivko, *Val Bella*, pp. 28–40.
270. See Pivko, *Informatorji*, pp. 102–3, for Vidmar's visit to the camp at Avezzano where he collected the names of 305 Serb volunteers.
271. Marchetti, *Ventotto Anni*, p. 318.
272. Pivko, *Informatorji*, pp. 114–15; *Val Bella*, p. 47.
273. Pivko, *Naši Dobrovoljci u Italiji*, p. 40.
274. AJA, JO 28/50, 'Zapovjedništvo 4e Armate, Ured informacija, Popis vojnika Jugoslavenske čete'; AJA, JO 35/129, Officers at Nocera Umbra to Lt Pindemonte (Vigevano's envoy), 31 May 1918; Janko Poljak, 'Nocera Umbra in majniška deklaracija', in *Dobrovoljci Kladivarji Jugoslavije*, p. 702.
275. AJA, JO 28/52, 'Jedinačni spisak odela Eksploratora 3e Armije'.
276. AJA, JO 28/170, statement by Nikola de Marchi; JO 28/51, VIII Armata (table of volunteers).
277. Ojetti, *La Propaganda sul Nemico*, p. 123; Pivko, *Informatorji*, p. 70.
278. AJA, JO 35/156, Trumbić notes [undated].
279. Pivko, *Informatorji*, pp. 72–3.
280. AJA, JO 19/186, Trumbić notes (May/June 1918); Pivko, *Val Bella*, p. 75.
281. Finzi, '*I.T.O.*', p. 229.
282. See statement of Nikola de Marchi in AJA, JO 28/170. De Marchi referred to his fellow-officer Zdravko Wiegele as a 'shameless soldier volunteer' since he totally complied with Italian wishes.

# 7
# Austria-Hungary on the Defensive

## 7.1 The perception of enemy propaganda

From the time of the Rome Congress, according to Edmund von Glaise-Horstenau, 'an especially dangerous and brilliantly organized campaign of propaganda threatened the morale of the Austro-Hungarian armies'.[1] To understand how the Austro-Hungarian authorities came to perceive 'enemy propaganda' as a pervasive force, it is important to appreciate the context in which they were operating. Having witnessed the collapse of Russia's army, stimulated in part by their own effective propaganda, the Austrian military leaders by the spring of 1918 were vigilant, bracing themselves for the onslaught of Bolshevik propaganda from the East. This coincided with the most serious internal crisis to engulf the Monarchy for the whole war. In mid-January, mass strikes due to the food crisis and expectation of peace began in Vienna, and spread simultaneously to Trieste, Kraków, Budapest and all other major urban centres.[2] By February the strike encompassed 34 000 miners in the coalfields of Moravia-Silesia; mass Polish demonstrations erupted in Galicia as a result of the Monarchy's peace with Ukraine; and, most alarming for the AOK, the naval forces in the gulf of Cattaro revolted. It was a time when the Emperor was pleading with his foreign minister to make a speedy peace at Brest-Litovsk with the Bolsheviks, as the alternative seemed to be an imminent revolution. He himself, having fled out of Vienna with his family, contemplated for a while a 'ministry of generals', an effective dictatorship or *Staatstreich*. Even if this idea proved abortive (not least because the military themselves now shied away from it), the widespread unrest, which the authorities were only just able to master, was bound to make them take stock at this eleventh hour.

When assessing the degree of social disruption, the regime naturally tended to make comparisons with what had just occurred in Russia. Arz von Straussenburg warned that a social-revolutionary movement was visible in the Monarchy, stimulated from the East, and it was vital that it did not enter the armed forces and produce the kind of chaos witnessed in Russia.[3] Others, the Minister of War, Stöger-Steiner, and the Hungarian Minister of the Interior, for example, saw dangerous parallels in the seditious socialist leaflets which had been circulating in Budapest.[4] There and elsewhere, the *Flugblatt* (propaganda leaflet) was increasingly accorded a special sinister mystique by the authorities. Its presence could be tied in with what Austrian military Intelligence thought it knew about the Bolsheviks' plans. The Bolsheviks had allegedly set aside two million roubles for socialist propaganda, which would be smuggled into the Central Powers from neutral states or via returning prisoners of war.[5] By February, the revolutionary material which had been discovered in the Monarchy's cities seemed indeed to be matched by an increasing amount of Bolshevik propaganda which was seeping through the Russian border.[6] For Austria-Hungary's military and political leaders, therefore, the domestic crisis of early 1918 was immediately associated in their minds with enemy subversion. 'Propaganda', moreover, was treated reverentially precisely because the Austrians had already used it and appreciated what it could do.

While the threat from the East seemed the most tangible, there were signs that the western Powers were devising a strategy too. Austrian Intelligence was aware of an article in *The Times* of 10 January, probably included by Wickham Steed, according to which copies of President Wilson's 'Fourteen Points' were to be distributed over enemy lines 'translated in all Austrian Slav languages and circulated by every possible means in Austria-Hungary'. That this was no idle threat was confirmed for Baden a few weeks later when such leaflets were discovered on the Italian Front.[7] But there was also evidence of a more deep-seated intrigue. A month before the British publicly announced Lord Northcliffe's appointment, Baden had received some substantial news from a 'reliable Entente source' on the 'Italian border'. According to this, on New Year's Eve a special Allied propaganda committee had been constituted in Washington. Its membership included Northcliffe (in fact in London by this time), Lord Reading, Senator Stone, and many editors of the American press; its purpose was to organize revolution in Germany and the other enemy states. Trained agents, who had been recruited in the West, were to be sent out from 'stations' in neutral countries into the Central Powers to foment revolutionary ideas and spread subversive material. The whole operation would be financed by America. It was a report which Max Ronge continued to believe, and included in his memoirs. There is no evidence that the information was accurate, but it fitted the AOK's concept of an Empire which in its last year was facing an ideological onslaught from both East and West.[8] The standard line, in memoirs and in Austrian military reports from the spring, was that the enemy had turned to the use of propaganda because they had been unable to defeat the Central Powers with conventional weapons. Although this argument might equally be applied to Austria's own propaganda campaigns, it was consistently repeated and lent a kind of moral authority to the 'respectable' war which the Monarchy was waging.[9]

When Lord Northcliffe was appointed as 'Director of Propaganda in Enemy Countries', the Austrians were given a concrete western opponent to match that of Bolshevism in the East. It was the first public admission by the western Allies that they were organizing a propaganda campaign, and with this absolute proof in mind, the Habsburg authorities would increasingly place subversion of all kinds at the door of ubiquitous 'Northcliffe propaganda'. In July 1918, the editor of the *Reichspost*, Friedrich Funder, would tell a rally of Catholics in Vienna: 'we know that Lord Northcliffe has been entrusted with so-called "domestic propaganda" in enemy lands and that millions of the English treasury have been placed at his disposal'.[10] Northcliffe from the start was assumed to be the key figure in the Allies' campaign, not surprisingly in view of the absence of any other information. The loyal Budapest daily *Pester Lloyd* was the first to pick up Reuter's announcement of the appointment on 18 February, and published the next day on its front page a vivid description of the man who came to personify enemy propaganda for the Central Powers. It revealed how ten years before, at an exhibition in Berlin of the Hungarian painter Philip de Laszló, the German Kaiser had been fascinated by a portrait of Northcliffe. Questioning the artist closely, the Kaiser had shown 'astonishing vision': 'it was obvious to him that Harmsworth was destined to play a fatal role in contemporary history'. And indeed, after 'diabolical advancement' Northcliffe had contributed crucially to pushing Sir Edward Grey into war in August 1914. Today the peer of the realm

> has control over the most influential and widespread newspapers of the island empire, is more or less the dictator of public opinion of the British people, a man at whose hint generals and ministers vanish from the scene, a kind of mortal weather god who has it in his hand to let governments walk in the sun-light of popularity or to unleash murderous hurricanes against them.

*Pester Lloyd* presumed that Northcliffe's chief task was to divide the Monarchy from its German ally, and assured its readers that such intrigues would never succeed.[11] Nevertheless, the appointment caused some alarm in loyal political circles. On 7 March the Austrian Prime Minister, Baron Ernst von Seidler, had to assure Christian Social deputies in the Reichsrat that the government was not only fully aware of the danger, but was actively combatting it: 'In the interest of success I cannot at present communicate any details. I can however say this much, that the organization which we have set up against enemy influences is working very earnestly and also with good results.'[12]

If Seidler's words had any meaning, the organization to which he was referring must have been the Intelligence Service, for no other special organization had been created by this time. Immediately after the Reuter announcement, Ronge had ordered the Evidenzbüro, his 'collecting centre' for Intelligence in Vienna, to draw up a report. The report, a few days later, made the same kind of comments as *Pester Lloyd* about 'the infamous press king', and surmised that Northcliffe's appointment signified that the press was to play a major role in the enemy propaganda campaign. He, however, would be one of a trio, since it was known that Lord Beaverbrook had been appointed 'Propaganda Minister' [actually Minister of Information] while the newspaper editor, Robert Donald, was said to be 'director of propaganda in neutral countries'.[13] With these facts as an initial basis, Austrian Intelligence in the following months tried to piece together a clearer picture, assuming increasingly that Britain and America were the leaders in the psychological offensive.

On 5 April, Ronge summed up what was known so far about 'Anglo-American Propaganda'.[14] Since the enemy had failed to defeat the Central Powers from without by conventional weapons (force of arms or blockade), they had taken up the weapon of insidious propaganda from within. From small beginnings the enemy campaign, which was organized especially through the press, had grown into 'a centralized system which encompassed the whole earth: we are faced today with a new enemy whose dangerousness we are still unable to assess'. The evidence now suggested that earlier in the year propaganda centres had been established in London, Paris and Rome for the purpose of spreading literature in central Europe. As far as Northcliffe and Austria-Hungary were concerned, the key distribution point seemed to be Switzerland. From there the press baron planned to send Dutch, Swedish and Spanish agents, dressed as businessmen, to agitate in the Monarchy, encourage pacifism and thereby indirectly force Germany to end the war as well. American agents were similarly agitating in neutral Holland and Switzerland, and it seemed true to say that Allied influence over the neutral press would be 'the most important tool' in the campaign. Ronge's report was not wholly inaccurate. It was indeed part of the EPD's remit to spread material into the Monarchy via Switzerland, though little is known about this. Ronge even tried to sketch out the structure of Britain's new propaganda machinery. However, Austrian Intelligence was always led astray by concentrating too much on Northcliffe and the press, and too little upon evidence which was emerging from the Italian Front.

Admittedly, in another report a month later, the Austrians showed that they were soon able to guess more accurately about Allied propaganda coordination.[15] Information was now available to show France's, and particularly Italy's role in the offensive. Earlier, little had been known about French propaganda except that Clemenceau himself might have been responsible (Ronge had vainly approached Berlin on the subject). But by May it was correctly assumed that Henri Franklin-Bouillon was playing a key role, coordinating meetings in Paris between Italians[16] and the Czech and Yugoslav Committees, and participating in propaganda conferences in Paris and London in the middle of March. Austrian Intelligence knew about these crucial meetings because they had briefly been mentioned in the Allied press. Most significant seemed to be the presence of the Italian Under-Secretary for Propaganda, Romeo Gallenga Stuart. According to the *Giornale d'Italia*, the day after the London conference the American 'Luncheon Club' had hosted a breakfast, attended by Gallenga, Northcliffe, Beaverbrook and Franklin-Bouillon. Gallenga had made an impassioned speech, appealing to America to discover the new Italy just as Columbus had once discovered America, and to recognize Italy's idealistic commitment to the war. The Austrian Intelligence report concluded that at this meeting of minds in London, the Allies had made some important resolutions and decided to divide up between themselves the tasks of enemy propaganda. The Italians, it seemed, had been assigned the chief role of conducting the propaganda campaign against Austria-Hungary. They would concentrate upon strengthening links in four directions, with Yugoslavs, Czechs, Poles and socialists of the Monarchy: 'In all these directions in Italy at the moment, there is a striking and in many cases novel activity which has come to the fore in political discussions in public, in the Parliament and the press, and is winning ever more converts.' The Italians were building upon solid agreements made with the four groupings and, the report suggested, they could find a very willing ear, especially among socialists in the Empire. If Austrian Intelligence officers were particularly alert to socialist subversion because of the unrest earlier in the year, it would soon become clear to them that Italy's priority lay with fomenting nationalist agitation. Most notably there was the evidence of the Rome Congress which was well publicized in the Monarchy by the Austro-Hungarian press itself. In Yugoslav regions, for example, newspapers of all political persuasions were able to reproduce accounts from the Swiss press, one describing it as 'A propaganda meeting financed by Northcliffe' while another commented that the Italians were trying to 'divide the skin of a bear which is still alive'.[17]

If by the early summer concrete signs of enemy propaganda were only too evident on the Italian Front, the Habsburg authorities would always treat 'enemy propaganda' as something more nebulous and ubiquitous. From the premise that it was 'an organized system encompassing the whole world', enemy propaganda easily became a 'catch-all' phrase for any poisons infecting the Monarchy, an evil which seemed to have links to every facet of nationalist or social unrest. Northcliffe still continued to be seen as the real mastermind or soul behind the campaign, the man who with American support and millions of pounds at his disposal was steadily building up centres in the neutral states from which to infiltrate the Central Powers and unleash a revolution.[18] The link to mounting unrest in the Monarchy was easily made. In July, for example, at a meeting between Ronge and a group of Intelligence officers to discuss the 'Czechoslovak movement', those present naturally assumed some connection:

> Newspaper reports about the careful preparation and large-scale execution of the Allies' propaganda service are innumerable. The whole network of the organization which Lord Northcliffe has called into being lies before us. Agents report just as frequently about details of the campaign being prepared against us and our allies. The agitation in the Monarchy is said to be prepared in Switzerland.... [While Czechs abroad are in league with this campaign], we can see in our fatherland the effects, which we ascribe to a large extent to enemy propaganda. But unfortunately we still do not know about the threads which lead from the known causes to the clear effects. The meshes of the network have for the most part not been uncovered.[19]

The idea that Northcliffe had spun a large web across the Monarchy called for extreme vigilance on the part of the already hard-pressed security forces. However, they could rarely be given specific data about the nature of enemy propaganda. They were simply informed that the Entente, in league with domestic and foreign nationalist agitators, had created various organizations to destroy the Monarchy by means of agents, leaflets and sabotage, but that more precise details of the 'network' were unknown.[20] This often resulted in Intelligence agents or military commands indulging in wild speculation about the supposed detection of 'enemy propaganda'. A few examples will suffice. When in July 1918 wireless links were cut between Pula and neutral Spain, an Austrian agent in Spain assumed that it was the work of 'Entente propaganda'.[21] Meanwhile, Entente agents were regularly reported to be entering the Monarchy from Switzerland, although they were rarely discovered. If there was a grain of truth in this particular idea, it was highly improbable that the same phenomenon could be detected also on the Monarchy's eastern borders. There, for instance, 'Entente agitation and propaganda' was said to be especially lively between Moldavia and Transylvania, while from a centre in Moscow Entente agents were allegedly entering Galicia as Ukrainian 'homecomers', equipped for some reason with Spanish passports.[22] In these cases any underhand methods of the enemy might be labelled as 'Entente propaganda'.

Another tendency was to blame enemy propaganda for many aspects of the domestic unrest which was engulfing the Empire. In May, when a revolt occurred in a Slovene regiment in Judenburg, the court martial proceedings concluded:

> It can certainly be said with regard to the influence of national political factors, that the Yugoslav parties and, in the broadest sense, also the revolutionary campaign of the Entente and therefore the English propaganda ministry played some role, although there is no immediate evidence available for this.[23]

In the same way, when ugly rumours circulated about the Emperor and his wife in July, there were always those who placed the blame on the 'lie factory' which the Entente was constructing in the Empire. The Foreign Minister, Count Burián, publicly reminded the Austrian and Hungarian Prime Ministers that there was 'actually a Minister for Propaganda in England':

> Our enemies are endeavouring by means of the propaganda offensive to cripple us internally and make us defenceless... Enemy propaganda is not content with endeavouring to stir our peoples up against each other. It has not even shrunk from fostering suspicion between the peoples of the Monarchy and the hereditary dynasty by the dissemination of monstrous and contemptible slanders.[24]

Thus 'enemy propaganda' by the summer at least had become a convenient label for many anonymous evils. At times it was a term used loosely to describe Entente machinations, the supposition being that the enemy by 1918 had actively infiltrated the Empire and was in direct contact with nationalist agitators within. But the very vagueness of the term was also exploited by the authorities to justify their own predicament. If some were indeed paranoid and felt encircled, others had in 'enemy propaganda' an ideal bogey which could be blamed, both during the war and thereafter, for domestic unrest and a whole host of errors which were to lead to the final collapse. As a Swiss newspaper commented scornfully:

> If the Austrian army suffers a defeat on the Piave because of the incompetence of its generals, if the peoples of the Monarchy want to emphasize their century-old demands, if the population of Bohemia despairs because of hunger, if the imperial couple is disliked, this is all blamed on the influence of Northcliffe's propaganda.[25]

Until the end of the war, Austrian Intelligence gained little new information about the real organization of enemy propaganda. As we have seen, they had some accurate suspicions: about Allied attempts at coordination, about Borgese's office in Switzerland; and in the summer they learnt correctly that French propaganda had been reorganized under a French diplomat, Klobukowski. But through an indiscriminate accumulation of fact and fiction there were also some striking errors. At one point, when asked to supply details about England's propaganda organization, the military attaché at The Hague replied that it was led by Lord Beaverbrook [Max Aitken] under whom were serving Northcliffe, Robert Donald and 'Sir M. Aitken (a Canadian)'.[26] The impression is that Ronge's Intelligence service, though highly competent in gathering detailed reports from all corners of the Monarchy as well as abroad, was always overloaded with information. It could accumulate data effectively, but it was weak in the area of sifting and analyzing, and often neglected to build upon knowledge from previous reports. Perhaps this was quite understandable in view of the vast territory which it was trying to monitor, not to mention the accelerating course of events which might well be observed but increasingly could not be acted upon.

It would be wrong, however, to suggest that the Austrians' view of enemy propaganda was wholly speculative or based on unsubstantiated reports. From the theatre where the main campaign was actually being waged, the Italian Front, there was indeed material evidence available. It was not only increasingly sophisticated, but was slowly finding its way into the interior of the Monarchy, thereby giving some substance to the paranoia mentioned above. In the spring months, Austria's military commanders in the south-west had been well aware from the Italian press that their enemy was about to launch 'counter-propaganda'; they began to monitor the signs of an emerging Czechoslovak Legion as well as an upsurge in leaflet distribution. Not surprisingly, it was from late April that the commanders began to register a striking increase both in enemy patrols and manifestos. One division over a month found 5000 leaflets of 30 different types,[27] while the number collected and sent to higher authorities by the lst corps command doubled from 11 813 in May to 20 624 in June. It is a measure of the perceived danger that such precise figures exist at all.[28] There was also a clear change in content and language in comparison to the badly translated and amateurish manifestos issued in the spring; they were now increasingly orientated towards the Slav nationalities in skilfully phrased language. As the 10AK noted in its propaganda report for June:

> For the first time the Italians have thrown out a kind of propaganda-newspaper in several languages: Czech, Polish, Croat and Romanian. The leaflets, of which those in the same language are numbered consecutively, are grammatically and stylistically accurate, sometimes very suggestively composed, and betray an intimate knowledge of the views and emotions of the individual Slav peoples of the Monarchy. This proves that Italian counter-propaganda is now directed by clever experts from one or more centres, with Austro-Hungarian deserters at their disposal.[29]

The alarm which this provoked in the war zone was equalled whenever one of the manifestos was discovered in the interior. This could occur through direct or indirect means, but the impact was the same, suggesting that insidious enemy propaganda was managing to send a range of couriers into the heart of the Empire. In the south of the Monarchy for instance, General Sarkotić, who governed Bosnia-Hercegovina and Dalmatia, was always convinced that Yugoslav agitation in 'his' territory was a largely external phenomenon, fomented by the Entente. He had offered this as a prime reason for mutinies at Cattaro and Mostar in February; and when Italian planes proceeded to shower Dalmatia with leaflets from the Cattaro ring-leaders it simply confirmed for him that a foreign stimulus was 'revolutionizing the Balkans'.[30] In June, much more of a stir was caused when planes of the Italian 87th squadron made propaganda flights over both Ljubljana and Zagreb. Carefully instructed by Ugo Ojetti, the pilots flew low over the cities and distributed three types of leaflet in Croat, two of which were 'signed' by Ante Trumbić. In one of them, Trumbić addressed the civilians as 'Yugoslavs!' and assured them that

> **Our cause is going very well.** If anything should happen which you cannot at first properly understand, you can be absolutely sure that our cause is a vital question for all our allies. We are now on the best of terms with Italy. All the Allies have completely given up the idea that Austria can reorganize and separate itself from Germany. **All are convinced that Austria cannot exist after the war... The behaviour of Emperor Karl removes the last vestige of any obligation towards the state and dynasty, and imposes an absolute and unconditional duty on you to fight against such a solution of our question...**
>
> Everyone must do all they can so that we achieve our freedom and unity ... **FIGHT FEARLESSLY AND ACTIVELY WITH ALL YOUR MIGHT AGAINST 'MITTELEUROPE' TO RESURRECT A FREE 'YUGOSLAVIA'.**[31]

In another leaflet he gave proof of Italian sincerity by naming Jambrišak, Kujundžić and other members of the Yugoslav Committee who were now permanently stationed in Italy.[32] The propaganda flights drew together a curious audience below who waved handkerchiefs at the pilots while they in turn took photographs of the distribution. The flights also drew a sharp response from the local press and acted as something of a touchstone for loyalty to the Habsburgs. One Zagreb daily newspaper mischeviously observed that the aeroplanes had been 'neither German nor enemy'.[33]

By this time domestic Yugoslav agitation was fast falling outside the control of the authorities in Slovene and Croat regions of the Monarchy. The Slovene clerical leader, Monsignor Anton Korošec, was touring southern Slav areas and speaking to mass-rallies in favour of Yugoslav unity and independence, much to the exasperation of his rival Ivan Šušteršić who was head of the Carniolan provincial Diet and fiercely pro-Habsburg. After the propaganda flight over Ljubljana, Šušteršić's mouthpiece, *Resnica*, launched a virulent attack upon Trumbić; it claimed that he was appealing to Slovenes 'just like Dr Korošec' and that the Allies had to be hard up if they needed his help during the Austrian offensive. The paper then turned upon Jambrišak, Kujundžić and others whose names had been publicized:

## Hrvati, Srbi i Slovenci!

Materijalno i moralno jedinstvo Sila Sporazuma, nije nikada bilo jače i coršće kao danas. To jedinstvo ne može niko više da razbije, jer je osnovano na borbi: **života ili smrti.** J mi, kao članovi toga jedinstva, došli smo na istoriski Kampidolio, sa kojega je, svečano proglašeno narodima:

**VAMA SLOBODA, A SMRT UGNIETACU VASEM I NASEM.**

To je osnovna misao ovoga sporazuma, koga njemačko-magjarski faktori hoće da potcijene, jer ga se boje, jer je on odlučan, samrtni udarac njihovom nasilju. Njegovu važnost umanjuju time, što tvrde, da njega ni jedna Sila Sporazuma priznala nije, a i u samoj Italiji, da je neprijateljski primljen.

**Mi vam odgovaramo jedino faktima:**

1). *U Rimskom Odboru, sastvljenom od Izaslanika Italie i izaslanika potlačenih narodnosti Austro-Ugarske, sede i dva člana* **Jugoslovenskog Odbora:** *D.r TRINAJSTIĆ iz Istre i adv. GAZARI iz Šibenika;*

2). *Pri Vrhovnoj Komandi Italijanske Vojske nalaze se dva Izaslanika Iugoslovenskog Odbora: D.r JAMBRISAK iz Zagreba i Bogoljub KUJUNGITCH iz Livna;*

3). *Zarobljenici naši u Italiji, potpuno su odijeljeni; sa njima se naročito dobro postupa i nama je dozvoljeno, da ih kad hoćemo posjetimo:*

4). *Sva suvozemna, morska i vazdušna komunikcaciona srestva Italie, stoje nam na raspoloženju, i po jednome od njih i ovaj manifest šaljemo vam, sa našim srdačnim pozdzavom:*

**Do vigjenja u slobodnoj i ujedinjenoj Jugoslaviji.**

**D.r ANTE TRUMBIĆ**
presjednik Jugoslovenskog komiteta.

Manifesto N. 16 (Jugoslavo)

*Illustration 7.1* Manifesto 16: Trumbić announces to Zagreb and Ljubljana that Italian–Yugoslav relations are excellent (KA)

These then are the traitors who bear the guilt for so much spilt blood! Dr Trumbić gives us proof in his manifestos of who it is who is prolonging the war for us and on whom the Entente are relying in the last resort. Since they cannot defeat us militarily they hope to be saved by Dr Trumbić and his Yugoslavs. Dr Trumbić is barred for all time from returning home; only with Allied troops can he set foot in his homeland again. But there is little chance of that happening and therefore he is trying to involve as many unfortunate associates as possible in his fate. He has however opened our people's eyes to such agitation.[34]

To re-emphasize this stance, on 19 June Šušteršić persuaded the small Carniolan provincial council (the executive organ of the Diet which had not met during the war) to ordain that regional parish councils should publicly condemn Trumbić's behaviour. Korošec in turn told the editor of *Slovenec*, his radical mouthpiece, to instruct parish councils through its columns either to ignore Šušteršić's order, or to stand resolutely by the May Declaration of 1917 which by now euphemistically implied a commitment to Yugoslav independence, the same ideal as Trumbić's. As a result the parish councils at first ignored Šušteršić. Then, when on 3 July the Carniolan council issued a second circular, the 164 parish councils who replied expressed their disapproval of Trumbić's propaganda, but also proceeded to reaffirm the May Declaration, thereby subtly invalidating their own disapproval.[35] The parish councils' defiance was backed up the mayor of Ljubljana, Ivan Tavčar, who announced that Šušteršić's order was a violation of local government autonomy in Carniola.[36] Šušteršić's stance had therefore backfired, revealing the weakness of his own position while lending increased publicity to the fact that Allied propaganda was actually in tune with Korošec's native movement. It was just one example of how Italy's campaign was beginning to act as a catalyst upon unrest in the Monarchy. The propagandists themselves were delighted with what they knew of the response, Steed noting that 'we have at least this proof that our propaganda has had the effect of angering the enemy'.[37] It gave them confidence to aim at propaganda targets further afield, such as Vienna itself.

By the summer months in any case Padua's manifestos, so evident in the war zone, were penetrating into the interior by indirect means which the propagandists could hardly imagine. Soldiers on leave, or hospital patients, were taking home manifestos which they were supposed to have surrendered in the war zone. The leaflets began to turn up not only in Innsbruck and Graz, or in regions near to Zagreb or Ljubljana, but also as far afield as St Pölten, Bratislava, Turnov in northern Bohemia, and even Kraków and Lublin.[38] This might seem an academic point, but for the authorities it was not. Each discovery was treated with reverence, necessitating a scrupulous investigation and the eventual dispatch of the leaflet to Ronge's Evidenzbüro in Vienna. For example, in mid-September in Kolozsvár a Lieutenant Erwin Ridley came across three soldiers who were surreptitiously reading one of Padua's newssheets; it had, he was told, been smuggled into Transylvania by one of them from the war zone. The three men subsequently disappeared, whereupon the local battalion commander, lambasting Ridley for not having arrested them on the spot, ordered an immediate examination of all the battalion's correspondence and all the soldiers' belongings.[39] Such a procedure was not unusual whenever a single manifesto was uncovered in the hinterland, whether it stemmed from Italian or Bolshevik or Polish revolutionary sources. In each case, the security forces were reminded, it was their duty to root out what Arz termed the 'dangerous mischief' of smuggled leaflets by meticulous enquiries.[40] This sometimes assumed absurd proportions. On 10 June, for instance, a hospital in southern Bohemia sent to the military command at Prague two Czech leaflets which had been discovered on a patient who had been transported from the Italian Front. A lengthy investigation and correspondence ensued which lasted over two months. The authorities tracked the guilty patient down from Vienna to Sarajevo to Dalmatia, only to discover that he had simply been curious and, as a Croat, had not been able to make much sense of the dangerous manifestos.[41]

It cannot be denied that the military were doing all they could to root out the evidence of 'enemy propaganda'. Ronge himself on one occasion observed that *Flugschriften* might be the prime danger in this regard. Only later would he write that leaflets had simply been a symptom of what was fundamentally wrong in the Monarchy; the real disease, the deeper affliction, had needed serious treatment but had been left unattended by the government.[42] He might have added that leaflets or any other form of 'enemy propaganda', viewed as so pervasive by the authorities in 1918, could only cause harm if they had a diseased environment in which to flourish.

## 7.2 The Feindespropaganda-Abwehrstelle

It was a consistent complaint by the Austro-Hungarian military in the last year of war that, while they were doing all they could to eliminate enemy propaganda, the political authorities in the Empire were failing to match their efforts. Subversive ideas were being left unchecked to circulate in the hinterland. How could the military protect the armed forces at the front if their morale was constantly under threat from contact with social and political unrest in the interior? This was not, of course, a new consideration: the military had blamed domestic conditions for the notorious Czech desertions of 1915, and in the summer of 1917 Conrad had concluded that lax discipline on the Italian Front was directly caused by lax discipline or inefficiency in the hinterland. What was new in 1918 was the degree of social and nationalist agitation and the fact that the domestic authorities seemed increasingly powerless to control it. Stimulated by the food crisis and war-weariness, a 'secondary mobilization' was now taking place among broad swathes of the population. It was not, however, the kind of resuscitation witnessed in Italy after Caporetto. In Austria-Hungary, rather than being a movement to support the Empire at a time of crisis, it had a diverse nationalist, pacifist and social agenda: it was essentially a 'counter-mobilization'. The Habsburg military could note with alarm that this movement in the interior increasingly echoed the work of ubiquitous 'enemy propaganda' stemming from outside the frontiers. In this situation the armed forces seemed to be placed in a vice, between two aspects of the same merging phenomenon. The AOK had the impossible task not simply of keeping the troops immune from subversive ideas, but of sustaining and strengthening their commitment to the Habsburg state during a fourth year of total war.

From January 1918 it was in the context of all the perceived dangers, from home and abroad, that the AOK took counter-measures to try to tighten discipline and protect troop morale. At the front precautions against desertion were increased. The men were reminded that all deserters would be court martialled, their property would be confiscated, state benefits to their families would be halted, and they could expect no amnesty after the war. As further deterrents to insubordination, Arz managed to persuade the Emperor to reinstate those punishments he had abolished in mid-1917, while persistent offenders would henceforth be grouped into 'disciplinary units' for three months and used for hard labour near the front line.[43] Hand-in-hand with these guidelines, the officers were to be vigilant in seeking out all dangers associated with 'enemy propaganda'. Because of evidence that subversive leaflets were being circulated in the hinterland, the AOK ordered a reorganization for the whole Empire of the *ambulante Reisekontrollen*, the military personnel whose duty was to inspect travellers and maintain discipline on the railways. On 10 March the same fears led Baden to order a sudden search of all soldiers' belongings in the war zones. The result was largely negative at this time, but as Arz reminded his subordinates on 27 May, this left no room for complacency. Since 'Northcliffe Propaganda' and 'social-revolutionary agitation' were at work, the troops should be observed constantly and inconspicuously; their luggage should be searched if they were going on leave, they should be reminded that it was a treasonable offence to be in possession of any propaganda leaflets, and if any 'treason' was uncovered there should be an immediate and sudden examination of the unit's effects.[44]

If many of these orders were chiefly applicable to the Italian Front, where over two-thirds of the army were now stationed, in the East the AOK was making special arrangements for dealing with an influx of Bolshevik propaganda through the dissolving Eastern Front. There it was not so much a question of smuggled leaflets, but a question of how to treat the thousands of ex-prisoners, so-called 'homecomers', who, in the wake of the Treaty of Brest-Litovsk, were flooding back into the Monarchy. Already in early 1917 Austrian military Intelligence had decided that instead of receiving a jubilant welcome, all homecomers would have to undergo a strict examination to assess their behaviour in Russian captivity and ensure that they had not been tainted by Bolshevism or other poisons. Thus, from early 1918 they were coldly 'processed' by the Austrian authorities, kept in 53 special camps under miserable conditions, and even when judged 'reliable' were usually conceded only a few weeks leave before having to rejoin units at the front. By June 1918 over 500 000 had entered the Monarchy and almost 2000 had been dispatched again to the front. Max Ronge would judge later that the apparatus established to deal with the homecomers had been a 'too widely meshed sieve' to counter Bolshevism (particularly since the necessary Intelligence personnel were lacking). In fact, it was the very nature of the apparatus which bred much of the homecomers' disillusionment with a homeland where they were 'treated just like cattle'. Many proceeded to desert when on leave. Others who rejoined their units constituted small insubordinate cores which were largely responsible for six major rebellions in the hinterland in May 1918.[45] It was a prime example of what could happen if the authorities were insensitive to the outlook of 'demobilized' soldiers. By putting the emphasis on discipline and security, rather than any positive educational or human agenda, the very dangers which Baden most feared were brought to life and multiplied.

Yet Austria-Hungary's military leaders were certainly aware that simple defensive measures were not likely to provide adequate protection from enemy propaganda. As the Minister of War had noted in a letter sent to all military commands in early February, the Russian army had disintegrated precisely because in late 1917 its 'educational organs' had been insufficiently equipped to withstand revolutionary propaganda.[46] In other words, sharp vigilance and discipline had to be accompanied by well-organized 'patriotic instruction' (*Vaterländischer Unterricht*) on behalf of the Habsburg cause. Until 1918, although the KPQ had made some small efforts, it was chiefly the military pastorate in the Austro-Hungarian army who had undertaken this task. Some military chaplains undoubtedly made no impact amid the horrors of the trenches (they merit no mention in Ljudevit Pivko's memoirs for instance). A few may well have resembled the disreputable Otto Katz, the coarse and drunken padre in Jaroslav Hašek's novel *The Good Soldier Švejk*, who was based on a real individual. But others were certainly viewed as a valuable asset by the military hierarchy because of their frequent visits to the trenches, sharing the troops' hopes and fears, and awakening 'their sense of duty toward the monarch and the fatherland with appropriate lessons'.[47]

At first the AOK simply envisaged an intensification of such work by the immediate officer commanding each unit. Through informal conversation he would enquire into a man's background and private life, 'in order to gain insight into the psyche, mentality and level of intelligence of his subordinates, to encourage the man's trust in the officer [and at the same time] discover the destructive elements, socialists, anti-militarists, etc., among his subordinates and paralyze their damaging influence upon the other men'. The soldiers would be reminded of their military oath, taught about the true causes of the war (how Italy, the Monarchy's 30-year ally, had stabbed it in the back) and instructed in a way to bolster *Staatsgedanken*, or ideas of state loyalty: how after success on the Eastern Front the Empire could feel very optimistic about the future, determined to continue fighting until an honourable peace was concluded.

While many of these forthright ideas were the same as those contained in Austria's propaganda against the Italian army, the officers were told that that was a distinctly separate activity, the prerogative of the *Nachrichtentruppen*, who alone were responsible for trying to influence the enemy.[48]

As support for the new 'instruction' in the Austrian ranks, the KPQ moved to step up its own activity. In February 1918, a special 'Front propaganda section' was created at the KPQ under Lt-Colonel Arthur von Zoglauer who began to organize patriotic lectures in the war zone. In addition, the KPQ was to be responsible for producing a weekly journal with articles on topical subjects. The first editions appeared on 7 March, entitled *Heimat* in German and *Üzenet* in Hungarian, and a very limited number were dispatched to the Italian Front to be presented to troops as a 'privately published' newspaper. From the start there were hints of the difficulties to come. While the German and Hungarian editions were easily produced, it proved impossible to find writers or typesetters for journals in the other languages of the Monarchy; as a result Croat and Slovene editions, though planned, were never to see the light of day. Then there was the issue of content. In the third edition of *Heimat*, for example, a long piece extolled the virtues of being an Austrian, claiming that Austrians with their traditions of empire, racial mixture and *Gemütlichkeit*, were called upon to rescue the soul of Europe.[49] Ideally, such a piece would simply be reproduced in any Hungarian or Czech editions, but to do so was problematic because of the increasingly heterogeneous outlook of the armed forces. The AOK was faced with the dilemma of wishing to propagate a united Austrian patriotic message while realizing that, if it was to be successful, each nationality would also require a different slant to match its own viewpoint. This fundamental issue was resolved unsatisfactorily, again because (ironic in a multinational empire), the personnel could not be found to act as editors or writers for different national editions. The AOK might want uniformity with a 'national twist' in some articles. Instead the Czech edition, *Domov*, had to remain as a simple translation of *Heimat*, something which was hardly likely to endear itself to the most sceptical nationality in the Monarchy.[50] Not surprisingly, none of the journals gained many individual subscribers so that, by the autumn of 1918, Baden would decide to send hundreds of free copies out to military positions. It is important to note that, in contrast to other belligerent armies, the 'news vacuum' at the front does not appear to have been filled by unofficial 'trench newspapers' composed at a grass-roots level. Rather it was the Empire's nationalist press, backed up by Italy's manifestos, which could fill the gap for those who wanted 'real news', propagating information in a far more enticing way than anything the Austrian authorities could offer.[51]

The High Command's moves, however, were only the start for a programme of patriotic instruction which it envisaged on a far grander scale. On 14 March, Arz announced the creation of a special organization to control education in the armed forces. It seems most likely that he was encouraged to do so by the example of Germany, where patriotic instruction had already begun in the summer of 1917. The AOK always seem to have believed that Germany's apparatus was functioning excellently, and it accordingly took Germany as something of a model for Austria-Hungary, sending a representative to Berlin in June 1918 to consult more closely.[52] In fact, as we will see, patriotic instruction in the Monarchy would be a strictly military affair, and ironically far less of a 'political offensive' than was possible in the military-run German Reich.[53] But if Germany was one model in the spring of 1918, the Monarchy had another model in Italy where, in the wake of Caporetto and in the face of Austrian propaganda, a galvanizing of forces was known to be taking place. In the words of the KPQ report for January, 'no country demonstrates like Italy how modern warfare can even offset defeat and how national consciousness can be regenerated by the power of propaganda'.[54] Here indeed the two enemies were taking note of each other's skill with offensive and defensive 'propaganda'. On the Italian side there were loud calls for Italy to follow the example of Austria's offensive campaign, while among the Austrian commanders it was Italy's defensive educational measures which were being particularly noted and recommended.[55]

Similarly, from the Eastern Front, too, the AOK heard voices which pressed for *Vaterländischer Unterricht*. Especially influential may have been a personal letter from Dušan Petrović, chief of staff of the 54SchD, to a friend at the AOK. Writing from Ukraine, from the new 'peaceful front' as he called it, Petrović drew attention to continued Russian attempts to fraternize with Austrians and the rising number of Austrian desertions. He enclosed an order from his own commander, which called for more pastoral care and patriotic instruction in the ranks, and he himself pressed the AOK to respond with some kind of 'obligatory patriotic instruction' so that the men could be moulded by more than blind obedience to discipline.[56] The precise outcome of Petrović's plea is not known, but one direct result was that he was appointed as deputy-head of the AOK's organization for patriotic instruction. The new organization thus was springing to life because the Russians had set a woeful example, while the Germans and Italians were already suggesting that new measures were required to protect the armed forces during a fourth year of war.

When on 14 March the organization was announced (to the military authorities, not publicly), the reasons which Arz gave for the new body reflected clearly the AOK's perception and prioritization of tangible dangers. First, it was needed to combat those elements, buoyed by war-weariness, which were threatening Austria-Hungary politically and socially from within. Second, it would counter Bolshevism, which despite its frightening characteristics could still be tempting to the masses. Third, it would fight 'propaganda stemming from the enemy' since 'Northcliffe's appointment as English "Propaganda minister" shows most clearly what hopes our enemy sets in its publicity work'.[57] The three inter-linked dangers were encapsulated in the title of the new organization, the 'Enemy Propaganda Defence Agency' [FAst – Feindespropaganda-Abwehrstelle]. This suggested, in tune with AOK thinking or at least with what the ranks *needed* to think, that the danger was essentially foreign, alien to both army and Empire, even if certain subversive agents within might be in league with 'enemy propagandists'.

The head of the FAst was to be an invalid who worked at the War Archives, Egon Freiherr von Waldstätten (brother of the deputy Chief of Staff). On 20 March, at the FAst inaugural meeting at the War Ministry, Waldstätten set out for other military authorities the AOK's plans for patriotic instruction. The first task was, along the lines of Germany's example, to organize teacher-training courses for propaganda officers. Separate courses would be run in Vienna and Budapest (the latter in July to cater for Hungarian Honvéd units), and those who passed through them would then act as FA instructors amongst military units in the field or hinterland so that a vast FA network would evolve throughout the Monarchy. Already at this meeting there were those who pointed out possible problems. Zoglauer, the head of the KPQ's new 'Front propaganda section', spoke pessimistically already about his own experience in organizing lectures at the front. It had proved very difficult to condense the material, since 'a lecture could not last longer than 30 minutes, or with slides 45 minutes, without tiring the audience'. Zoglauer's fellow KPQ delegate, Colonel Reich, broached a more intractable problem, that of unity of ideas in the curriculum. He observed, however, that it was unity of 'spirit' rather than 'form' which was vital in the education: the correct tone would still have to be found for each nationality while at the same time ensuring a general unity of purpose. Although it appears that those present shared Reich's optimism that this balance could be achieved, it was to be a major dilemma which the FAst would never master successfully.[58]

In the following weeks Waldstätten began to pester the military authorities with a range of issues which seemed to be within his new jurisdiction. He made suggestions to Baden about how officers should behave at the front. He warned the War Ministry about subversives in the interior: subversive newspapers, but also agitators like the satirist Karl Kraus who, at a recent public meeting in Vienna, in the presence of soldiers, had criticized Germany's use of gas on the Western Front, referring to the 'chlorious' [*chlorreichen*] rather than 'glorious' offensive.[59] But Waldstätten and his deputy Petrović were, of course, above all concerned at this time with establishing their new machinery. It would be centred upon an office in the KA (Stiftgasse 2, Vienna), reflecting that institution's modest role in domestic propaganda since the start of the war. To the FAst were appointed about a dozen staff. They included most notably Professor Ernst Keil, the founder of the satirical journal *Die Muskete*, who had good political and academic connections and came to head the 'propaganda and political' section of the FAst, responsible for producing FA propaganda. Another key individual was Roderich Gooß, a Hungarian citizen and former employee in the State Archives who would take charge of the FAst's 'historical-constitutional' section, dealing especially with FA content and keeping Waldstätten aware of Hungarian sensitivities. As a whole the FAst was to be directly subject to Arz (with Edmund von Glaise-Horstenau as the liaison), had the Operations and Intelligence sections of the AOK at its disposal, and would cooperate closely with the KPQ to finance and print its propaganda material.

By the end of April more flesh had been put on the FA bones. On 26 April all army commands were issued with guidelines about 'patriotic instruction and defence against enemy propaganda'.[60] These specified that the FAst in Vienna would be the coordinating centre, producing propaganda material and training education officers; in turn, each army command should appoint an education chief (*Unterrichtsreferent*) and each division an education officer (*Unterrichtsoffizier*), so that a hierarchical network would be created. The FA education, while paying attention to protecting the troops from damaging influences through vigilance and censorship, was also to be distinctly positive in outlook. Conducted with the active support of all officers, it was to lay particular emphasis upon *Staatsgedanken* or ideas which would stimulate loyalty to the Empire. The soldiers were to be reminded of the 'freedom and equality' which all citizens of the Empire supposedly enjoyed, and of the advantages of living in a large state ruled by the Habsburg dynasty. These rather vague concepts were meant as a substitute for dealing with the whole subject of nationalist politics in the Monarchy. Arz himself had observed that 'only love of the dynasty and mutual respect for all nationalities' was necessary or desirable in the armed forces, a notion which might have been applicable before 1914 but was highly questionable in the 'civilian army' of 1918.[61]

Indeed, at the FA inaugural meeting the idea of excluding politics from patriotic instruction had been challenged. It had been clear that the Minister of War, Stöger-Steiner, wanted Bolshevism tackled head-on, and Colonel Reich too, in his exposition on national individuality, more than implied that FA education could not be divorced from national politics. A compromise was reached, largely it seems by default through lack of discussion, that the dangers of socialism or national irredentism might be taught to the troops, but this should never develop into a fully politicized discussion on the domestic politics of the Monarchy. This was perhaps necessary and understandable since the Habsburg authorities had, for example, no clear ideas or solutions for the Czech or South Slav questions which would be acceptable for public consumption. But it meant that the FAst position was weakened from the outset since it had to ignore the widespread evidence of domestic agitation, a topic which enemy propaganda was quite prepared to discuss and exploit. Not surprisingly, some of the FA lecturers in Vienna were to find it very difficult to deal with the issues of Italian or Romanian irredentism without also touching on the Monarchy's nationality problems.[62] The FA tried to fill this serious omission with guidelines which simply encouraged a soldier's sense of duty, discipline and order: that desertion was a disgrace with serious consequences, that indiscipline and laziness had produced the great defeats of the Russian and Italian armies in 1917, that Austria-Hungary must not be allowed to fall into chaos like Russia. The tone had to be optimistic, showing that it was not just a duty but also worthwhile to hold out for victory since the Monarchy was morally superior (Britain was the real cause of the war, Italy was the traitor) and could look forward with confidence to a favourable outcome before the United States affected the balance of forces. Here were general sentiments of a kind which Austria was already propagating against Italy in early 1918. But they would increasingly have a hollow ring both in the Italian and Austrian trenches, not least because the real and increasingly obvious character of the Habsburg organism had to remain a taboo subject in Austrian propaganda.

By the time of Austria-Hungary's ill-fated Piave offensive of June 1918, two FA training courses had been held in Vienna and about 150 *Unterrichtsoffiziere* had passed through them. While the first course was primarily for (34) officers from the fronts and occupied territories, 80 per cent of the 118 officers on the second course stemmed from units in the hinterland where FA was to be organized in each military district in the same way as in the war zone. The numerous lectures held every morning during the fortnight of each course reflected the themes suggested in the AOK guidelines. Thus Karl Werkmann, head of the imperial press office, discussed 'the dynasty and the war' with the purpose, as he assured Waldstätten, of 'destroying the rather widely-held belief that members of the imperial house do not participate in the duties and suffering of this war to the same degree as other citizens of the Monarchy'.[63] Then there were lectures on the real nature of the war and the need to stand firm: 'Austria-Hungary's strength in the World War' (by Glaise-Horstenau), 'The World War up to now' (by Petrović), 'Why are we fighting?', 'How to personally see it through' (by the later Hungarian right-radical Prime Minister Gyula Gömbös). Enemy propaganda was presented in context: by the Austrian historian, Hans Übersberger, on 'The Russian revolution'; by Max Weber on 'Socialism'; and by others on 'The organization of enemy propaganda in the hinterland', 'The military significance of enemy propaganda' and 'Italian and Romanian irredenta' (the latter by Roderich Gooß). Turning to optimistic plans for the future, notable academics were brought in to lecture on 'Care for war invalids' (Rudolf Peerz) and 'Industrial and social reconstruction after the war' (Friedrich Hertz). Others gave instruction on the nature of the press, on film propaganda, or even on 'war and the woman' (Margarete Roller). Many of these lectures were eventually issued as brochures for the benefit of FA personnel, and they were regularly supplemented by the KPQ with new themes ranging from the 'The war aims of England' (47 colour slides) to 'The holy egoism of the Italians' or even 'The significance of fertilizer in modern agriculture' (26 slides).[64]

It was with these aids at their fingertips, and from July with a regular information 'package' from the FAst known as the *Vaterländische Bildungsarbeit*, that the education chiefs and officers proceeded to their work in the armed forces (including the navy). Having passed through the first information course in mid-May, for example, Captain Ljubomir Jemrić returned to Belgrade and held his own education course there in late June for officers and padres of military units in occupied Serbia. His lectures mirrored precisely what he had been taught in Vienna, but occasionally added local 'colour' such as tips on how to explain the recent mutiny at Kragujevac where 44 soldiers had been sentenced to death.[65] In the same way, the *Unterrichtsreferent* for Kraków military district, having attended the second information course in early June, established a series of courses and lectures in western Galicia. Special attention was paid to the presence of homecomers in the region, and also to railway stations as 'danger spots' since it was there that those on leave arrived from the Italian Front bearing enemy propaganda leaflets.[66]

On the Italian Front itself the same trickling-down of FA activity began slowly to occur in June. On the Upper Piave, for instance, Captain Franz Zeidner, the diligent *Unterrichtsreferent* for the II corps, began to send detailed reports to the FAst. After returning from Vienna, he had held a three-day course for selected education officers who had then started to teach at divisional level and had been well-received despite the very mixed composition of the units. 'The men *want* to be educated', he gushed, 'and in this way we will anticipate the enemy!' Calling for the FAst to send out more material, especially light and witty leaflets, he observed that patriotic instruction clearly had a willing audience, but could not be left to the padres who tended to be 'indolent' or 'Bolshevik', inclined to condemn all of the belligerents equally.[67]

Similarly optimistic was the *Unterrichtsoffizier* of the predominantly Croat 42HID, situated on the Asiago plateau. Lt Juraj Šušnjak was a former history teacher, who after instruction from his corps 'education chief' began FA work in the division on 1 June, precisely at a time when a string of officer desertions to the enemy were under investigation. On 12 June he discussed with his selected regimental counterparts the guidelines for their work which included, besides the usual themes, an explanation of Italy's alleged friendliness towards the South Slavs, the nature of Italy's aspirations to Croatian territory, and hence the 'reality' behind the claims of enemy manifestos. The Austrian military, Conrad's Intelligence section, for example, had recommended many months before that the Italians' true face should be exposed for Slav troops, to show that they had not actually renounced their designs on Croat and Slovene territory; now such arguments were to be put directly to the soldiers.[68] According to

Šušnjak, both men and officers immediately showed a keen interest in the new patriotic instruction: 'The men were very receptive to the plain-speaking explanation and grasped the complete futility of enemy propaganda, especially as regards the Yugoslav question.' Although, as we will see, recent desertions suggested the exact opposite, Šušnjak stated confidently that 'enemy propaganda has had absolutely no success among field units of the division'. He painted for the FAst a surprisingly rosy picture of the troops on the eve of the June offensive, of men eager to fight against their hereditary enemy. If all treasonable agitation in the hinterland could be suppressed and the Monarchy's political problems quickly solved, he opined, all harmful influences would indeed be removed from the army![69]

Despite such wild optimism the FAst leaders themselves were aware from the start that there were fundamental obstacles to their work. Not least was the very small budget they were allotted. When in April Waldstätten asked the AOK for unlimited credit and a monthly allowance for the FAst of 2000 Kronen, his request was refused on the grounds that the work had to be funded out of the KPQ budget and consequently 'the utmost thrift' was necessary. As a result the FAst was unable to match the scope of its remit. It could not meet the increasing demands for propaganda literature, for example, from Sarkotić in Bosnia when he requested 18 500 copies of reading material for soldiers travelling on the railways (a response in itself to the FAst urging all military commands to spread patriotic literature in trains and stations). Nor could it even pay for the full subsistence of those who attended the courses in Vienna, leaving a sour taste indeed in the mouths of participants. By July, Waldstätten was complaining to the AOK that FA incorporation in the KPQ budget was an unsatisfactory arrangement; he began to approach the military ministries directly for a credit advance for propaganda purposes.[70]

A second practical problem, which affected all military fields by 1918, was that of manpower and the lack of suitable personnel for the FA network. It was not just a case of too few translators for *Heimat* (the KPQ, for example, had no translators for the Slovak or Romanian languages!).[71] It also manifested itself in a dearth of suitable instructors. Some of those who attended the second information course in Vienna were felt by the FAst to be too old or far too young.[72] Baden might specify that 'only men experienced in war, inspired with ideal energy and capable of expressing their views in eloquent language, were suited to educate and convey really effective propaganda into the ranks'. But in practice it was impossible to match this criterion. Indeed, the situation was exacerbated when the AOK added that due to a lack of officers, only those who were incapable of active service (like Waldstätten himself) should be employed as *Unterrichtsoffiziere*. The inevitable tendency was either to choose individuals from the lower officer ranks who lacked sufficient experience, or (against AOK orders) to appoint individuals who were already occupied with a military command but were expected to take on additional FA duties.[73]

Such a case was Major Richard Gablenz, a battalion commander in the 48ID on Monte Pertica in the Italian mountains. On 1 July he wrote a private letter to Waldstätten, complaining about the double burden of work. He also summed up well the views of many when he set out the impossible environment in which patriotic instruction was supposed to operate:

> It is high time to begin this work if it's generally going to have any success. For the bow has been drawn very tightly. Every glance in the newspapers informs officers and NCOs about the political confusion [of the hinterland]. Press reports and newspapers talk of the ever growing Czecho-Slovak armies. I myself am based with my battalion on Monte Pertica, where we've been officially notified to expect that men of the Czecho-Slovak brigade will dress in Austrian uniforms and attack our positions – doing this when half of our regiment is itself Czech. I won't go into the miserable state of our position except to supply some buzz words: 8° centigrade, heat and light forbidden, no water, ice-cold food, no caves, no shelter etc. – repeated desertions, countless Italian propaganda leaflets, but no press reports of our own.[74]

In a few sentences Gablenz described the formidable uphill task which faced the FA network. It was only being created after a full four years of warfare. And it immediately came face to face with two major internal enemies which had to be removed if patriotic instruction was to have any impact. First was the Monarchy's food crisis, which consistently undermined the spirit of soldiers already enduring severe conditions in the war zone. Second was the radicalization of domestic politics in the hinterland, which for the FAst seemed to be most dangerously expressed in the circulation of wild ideas through the radical nationalist press. Both threats helped to give Padua's manifestos their real bite, both were to prove insurmountable, nibbling away at the morale which commanders were trying to sustain. The military as usual were inclined to blame the hinterland for these evils, from which the 'ordinary soldier' in the war zone could not be protected, and over which they themselves had far less influence than earlier in the war.

Of the two, it was hunger which was the most dangerous threat to army morale in the last year of war, 'a valuable ally for enemy propaganda'.[75] General Ottokar Landwehr, who had been appointed by the Emperor in February 1917 to coordinate the Monarchy's food supplies, was trying valiantly to juggle a range of options, but none of them were really secure. This is clear from a brief survey of the food crisis. As far as the armed forces were concerned, they could expect to acquire all grain surpluses from occupied Serbia and Poland, as well as a percentage of the Romanian harvest (although this had to be regularly renegotiated with Germany). But the bulk of army supplies still had to come from domestic sources: from Hungary. In the last months of 1917 the crisis had deepened. Due to a disastrous summer harvest in Hungary, compounded by hoarding of grain in the countryside, the supply of flour waggons to the troops was slowing down. Count Hadik, the obstinate Hungarian food minister, might assure the Empire's Common Ministerial Council that it was a priority to feed the army, but his promise to Landwehr that Hungary would supply 200 waggons of flour per day to the armed forces could not be matched in practice.[76] By the turn of the year the AOK was concluding that the armed forces were 'living from hand to mouth': they needed 219 flour waggons daily to supply them with adequate rations but only an average of 112 waggons was available.[77]

Therefore, in the spring Landwehr put his faith in two new initiatives. Firstly, he persuaded the Hungarian leadership to implement requisitioning in the countryside, a move which seemed more promising as Hadik had been replaced by the energetic and empire-orientated Prince Ludwig Windischgrätz. In February, field units in Hungary and Croatia proceeded into the country, notwithstanding the AOK's anxieties about placing troops in such close contact with civilians. In April the action was stepped up, but a month later Windischgrätz was still unable to give Landwehr a very positive picture.[78] Secondly, Landwehr looked with the whole of the Monarchy expectantly to the East where the peace with Ukraine in February was championed as a *Brotfriede*, a 'Bread Peace' which would surely solve the whole of the Monarchy's grain crisis. In fact, although under the peace terms the Ukrainians agreed to supply Austria-Hungary with a million tons of grain, and Habsburg troops advanced into the region ostensibly to bring 'peace and security' to its population, the chaotic situation in the East prevented the import of more than 46 000 tons before the end of the war.[79] The average grain imports for March were only seven waggons a day, for April only 15 (and the army needed 219 daily). If the Ukrainian native population was reluctant to surrender or sell its produce to the Austrian and German occupiers, it was also the case that the food which the troops collected there was barely able to cover their own requirements.[80] There was even talk of the Monarchy having to export flour to Ukraine to feed the occupying forces.[81] The celebrated *Brotfriede* produced neither the bread, nor the complete cessation of hostilities in the East which had been expected and which was propagated so vigorously in FA propaganda. For Landwehr, struggling to tide over the army and the Austrian half of the Empire for another month, drastic measures were unavoidable and could only be taken at the expense of an unresponsive German ally. In late April he made the bold move of confiscating over 2000 waggons of Romanian grain which were bound for Berlin.[82] But the pay-off from this was more serious. On 18 May, the Monarchy felt obliged to conclude a new economic agreement with Germany, according to which it would receive regular supplies of grain from Ukraine on condition that full economic control there was placed in German hands. It was just one more indication of how far Austria-Hungary's survival could be determined in Berlin. The Habsburg authorities from mid-1918 were repeatedly having to travel northwards to petition their ally, all the more so as, despite Germany's promises, material aid from Ukraine and elsewhere always continued to fall far short of what was agreed on paper. By the middle of June, grain waggons from the East had dried up completely.[83]

This persistent pattern of erratic supply was mirrored on the Italian Front throughout the period of Italy's propaganda onslaught. The Austrian commanders in 1918 would obsessively note the divergence between theory and reality in food supplies from the hinterland. Not that all had seemed hopeless in late 1917. After Caporetto, with the conquest of the fertile Venetian plains, it had (as Landwehr hoped) been possible for two months to feed the Austrian troops under Archduke Eugen exclusively from Venetian produce. But already by the turn of the year the narrow strip of land between the mountains and the sea was being milked dry. As Archduke Eugen wrote to General Sarkotić,

> Economically the situation here is less pleasing. The food situation is at the moment worse than critical since, from the start of the offensive, I have fed the three armies under my command exclusively from the occupied territory. Supplies from the hinterland are irregular and scarce. Almost no tobacco, which the troops find hard to bear, but they do still get every day half a litre of wine [the full ration] which is plentifully available in this region. Bread is bad and only half the ration.[84]

In subsequent months Austrian troops on the plains would continue to benefit from some local vegetable and meat provisions, as well as having the chance to requisition in neighbouring Trieste and Istria.[85] For flour supplies, however, their position was to differ little from troops in the mountains in that they relied exclusively on what Landwehr could conjure up at home and abroad. Given the crisis in the hinterland, the AOK began to order a reduction in the bread ration. But in January 1918, the Isonzo army command (KISA) was unable to distribute even half of this reduced ration, since flour supplies that month were only sufficient to cover eight days, not 31. It was not long before KISA troops in reserve were living exclusively on potatoes, having given up their bread rations to those in the front line.[86] As for the latter, a unit like the 10ID, located next to the sea, was quickly reduced to a chronic state in its new position. Inadequate shelter (a major issue for troops on the plains) was compounded by damp conditions: the fact that the men were often wet-through, standing in water and lacking any change of clothing so that cases of illness abounded. As the weather improved this would change; water pumps would also be an asset in the Piave delta. But as bronchial catarrh diminished, cases of malaria would soar, and still nothing would be able to relieve the pangs of hunger.[87]

On 17 February, FM Boroević duly telegraphed Arz to warn that the food crisis in his armies (the Isonzo and 6th armies) was beginning to undermine discipline at the front.[88] A week later he spoke out more bluntly:

> Even if in the end the occupied Italian territory is bled dry by totally disregarding the needs of the civilian population and completely neglecting cultivation, any improvement in army supplies would only be secured for a few days...If [after this] supplies from the hinterland remain the same, there will be a rapid decline in the physical powers of the fighting troops and a dwindling of their morale, already much lowered in the past few weeks due to insufficient food. As a result one will have to say that the innumerable sacrifices of life and property have been in the end in vain.

Boroević had no patience with what he considered plain incompetence by the Monarchy's political authorities:

> The troops are no longer moved by incessant empty phrases, that the hinterland is starving or that one must hold out, especially as it is known that in the Monarchy there are still extensive regions with unexhausted food supplies, and because the men are sure that the provisions for German troops are far better. The troops will endure no more experiments, they must be adequately supplied to be able to live and fight. I therefore beg again most urgently for vigorous measures to overcome the present food crisis as quickly as possible.[89]

These words were naturally heeded by the AOK, but when the High Command was not powerless it usually felt obliged to give priority in supplies to the even worse predicament of troops in the mountains. The upshot was that in May, just a few weeks before the crucial June offensive, Boroević's armies could not be given increased rations in preparation for the attack. Boroević himself warned Baden that he could not take the responsibility for beginning an offensive with undernourished men; he vainly petitioned his superiors to postpone the attack until they were strong enough.[90]

In the mountains the story had been similar but worse. There, as is shown below in a case study of one Croat division, the food crisis was exacerbated by complicated supply lines through treacherous terrain. When in January Conrad von Hötzendorf had ordered his armies to reduce the daily bread ration for front-line troops from 700 to 500 grams, Krobatin of the 10AK had already felt bound to go further, reducing the ration to 350 grams because of severe flour arrears (only increased, in theory, in late March).[91] The result was clear in a number of censored letters from the trenches which Krobatin forwarded to Baden, questioning as he did so how far his officers would really be able to offset the effect of enemy propaganda if the ranks were so weakened by hunger. In one of the letters, a Polish corporal described his daily diet as follows:

> Early in the morning half a litre of coffee which is pure water, only browner and warmer. At midday a piece of meat as big as an egg and half a litre of pure water with about three leaves of boiled cabbage which would be very good if one could only get more of it. Apart from this nothing. In the evening half a litre of coffee and a piece of bread, as big as we used to give to the beggars; it would be tolerable if it wasn't made of maize. This piece of bread has to suffice for the whole day... This is no life, it is torture. In these mountains your feet go numb, you move in the darkness, you collapse, rest, then get up and go ever onward. The cabbage which you give the cow to eat I would like to eat up with my eyes. No one will be able to recognize me any more, since my hands, feet and face have become skinny and weak.[92]

For the 11AK, which was in the spring still engaged in some fighting, Count Scheuchenstuel similarly warned his superiors of the consequences:

> Because of the inferior quality of meat, the small fat ration of six grams and the lack of vegetables which can only be substituted by flour, the present measure of 500 grams is already the minimum which a man should get under the existing fighting and climatic conditions in order just to survive... Any reduction of the bread ration seems to me very risky because bread is the most indispensable foodstuff and our men cannot be fully compensated with meat.

Although Baden proceeded to order a rise in the meat ration to offset the bread reduction, the measure which was set was usually academic anyway.[93] Like Boroević, Conrad proceeded to blame the hinterland, judging that the situation could 'only be saved if the central authorities quickly seize the opportunity to overpower all those groups who appear to have made questions of provision a political issue'.[94] He was presumably referring to the Hungarians but, as we have seen, not even vigorous requisitioning in the Hungarian countryside was a solution. Shortly before the Monarchy's June offensive, the 11AK considered that its food situation had never been so bad. Like the commanders on the plains, it warned that 'under such circumstances, to prepare for the approaching offensive is completely out of the question'.[95] The divisions might not be starving, but they were always undernourished, and the final raising of the bread ration on 8 June, a week before the attack, was as usual a theoretical rather than feasible order. Conditions in the 18ID, a division stationed on the Asiago plateau, exemplify how a persistent food and material crisis was then compounded by problems of transport and terrain. Writing only two days before the offensive, Brigadier Julius Vidalé noted that food and munitions had to be brought to the front line at night by a road under constant enemy fire; because of a dearth of horses, the men themselves had to act as carriers of supplies and so were considerably weakened. Vidalé, like so many of his fellow divisional commanders, concluded at this time that the spirit of his troops (chiefly German, Magyar and Slovene) remained excellent; but he cautioned his superiors to consider what effect divisional conditions might have on the success of the imminent offensive.[96] In the words of the Austrian official history, it was 'with completely undernourished troops that the Austro-Hungarian army embarked upon its fatal battle'.[97]

The FAst had been aware from the beginning that the food situation had to be tackled. One of Waldstätten's first moves upon his appointment had been to write to Arz reminding him that during the 'temporary' food crisis it was important to calm the men and ensure that the officers' mess had exactly the same rations.[98] A month later, in his introductory lecture to the first FA information course, Waldstätten – evidently now better informed – readily acknowledged that FA would be hampered because of food shortages: 'A man with an empty stomach', he observed, 'is less receptive to the most attractive language.' However, he remained hopeful: 'If everyone knows what is at stake, then they will be more easily and more decisively prepared to see it through, even in the hinterland.'[99] The implication was that propaganda emanating from the FAst and its network would be able to seize any initiative from enemy propaganda. After all, in contrast to the latter, which presumably faced basic obstacles of distribution and reception, FA work could be regular, methodical and undertaken in immediate proximity to its audience.

The reality unfortunately was that the war zone was never a vacuum in which the FAst and the Padua Commission could duel with their ideas on equal terms. Poisonous ideas were also reaching the troops from the hinterland, or were infecting those soldiers who managed to secure leave and then witnessed the national agitation and social misery in their homeland. It was almost impossible to keep the armies on the Italian Front in quarantine from such reality, all the more so as the troops' links to their families and home environment always provided them with a sense of security and well-being, an essential prop to good morale. But building such a quarantine was exactly what the AOK attempted to do. Since in the second half of the war the military no longer possessed the power to directly intervene and suppress radical politics in the hinterland, the alternative was to try to obstruct the means of communication of radical ideas, enforcing censorship so that patriotic instruction would be able to operate more easily.

The clearest example of this was in the AOK's attitude to the domestic press. As we saw in Chapter 2, the flow of information in the Monarchy had been eased when in 1917 Emperor Karl had restored some constitutional rule in Austria. The guidelines for censoring the press in both Austria and Hungary might for some time remain the same, but in practice the watchful eye of the Reichsrat in Vienna ensured a laxer or more erratic wielding of the censor's pencil in different corners of the Empire. Due to complaints in the Reichsrat the KÜA was dissolved in September 1917 (even if its duties were simply inherited by a commission in the War Ministry). Similarly, parliamentary pressure in October forced the Austrian government to agree to limit press censorship of political matters, in theory at least, to removing items which were contrary to pre-war penal statutes.[100] The result was to produce a level of censorship in the press which was far more attuned to the restless political and social mood which was sweeping the Empire from the summer of 1917. For the AOK this was alarming. Of the two types of news which they felt affected their interests, 'strictly military' and 'other' (which could undermine morale), it would still be possible to control the former through the KPQ's official war reports. 'Other' categories of information, however, were unmanageable. They were liable to fall outside the AOK's remit since they might be deemed a political preserve, even if the military could justifiably argue that all items of news indirectly concerned their conduct of the war effort.[101]

In early 1918 the AOK was brought face to face with this dilemma. By then, the phenomenon which Conrad had attacked in September 1917, of newspapers writing too expansively about an end to the war, had grown hydra-headed in tune with the mood of the hinterland. On 15 February, Arz proceeded to complain to government ministers about the domestic press. Instead of behaving in a way designed to calm troops at the front, many newspapers were regularly attacking Germany, writing impartially about the Entente's 'honourable' offers of peace, and commenting gloomily about the Monarchy's food crisis and widespread social unrest. Arz demanded not simply tighter censorship for the rest of the war, but consciously uplifting articles in the press so as to boost military morale. Replying to this, however, Count Toggenburg (the Austrian Minister of the Interior) set out for the AOK the constitutional parameters within which the censor was having to operate. With regard for instance to the often sensational speeches which were delivered in the Reichsrat:

> Because of existing constitutional provisions it is not possible to keep these events secret from the public. The so-called parliamentary censor, whose legal basis is rather dubious anyway, can only act against the most blatant cases. Consequently the newspapers have to be permitted a somewhat wider latitude than before.

Arz's only consolation was to note that Toggenburg had issued new censor rules, clamping down on criticisms of the war leadership or the food crisis in Austria. Otherwise, the Ministry of the Interior advised that the best way forward would be to put subtle (not draconian) pressure on newspaper editors, while the AOK might consider banning unsuitable newspapers from the war zone.[102]

Effectively, Arz was being told that the radical political agitation, which was emerging fast within Austria's constitutional structure, could not be silenced by the censor. In the following months this was something all the more galling, since the military noted how enemy propaganda was steadily beginning to use the domestic press in order to publicize everything negative about events in the Monarchy. It was certainly a prime source for Padua's manifestos, with news items secured via Borgese's bureau in Berne and transmitted to Ojetti; it was also exploited, or so the AOK always imagined, by 'English propaganda', which was presumed to be working indirectly through the Swiss press in order to proclaim the Monarchy's imminent dissolution.[103] When on 26 April a meeting was held at the AOK to discuss 'offensive' and 'defensive' propaganda at the front, a prime consideration in the latter case was the subject of the press. The minutes of the discussion recorded how 'our newspapers, especially the Slav, are the most effective means of propaganda supporting the enemy; there is no Italian concoction [*Machwerk*] which can come anywhere near that of these newspapers in providing such good service to the enemy'. The fact that censorship in Austria-Hungary completely lacked direction, and that the government was 'agonizingly weak' – this all combined to make the press 'the first and foremost enemy of our fatherland'. One solution, it was suggested, would be to ensure that the men in the trenches always received timely 'official' news about events in the hinterland before the arrival of any newspapers.[104] Another was to badger the domestic authorities with a tirade of complaints.

From the middle of May, the AOK began to circulate to the main political and military centres a daily selection of extracts from the press which it deemed treasonable. They illustrate well the character of certain newspapers in mid-1918 as well as revealing Baden's sensitive outlook. Most of the extracts were from Czech, southern Slav or socialist journals, and most described or implied either the brutality of the German-Austrian authorities or the goal of national liberation for the oppressed peoples of the Monarchy.[105] Thus, one Slovene paper (*Straža*) recalled German tyranny in Austria in the early years of the war, but hinted that the persecution would not last much longer. The socialist *Arbeiter-Zeitung* condemned the authorities' brutality in Prague during the celebrations for the National Theatre, concluding that Austria, like England with the Irish, would finally have to grant home rule. The radical Yugoslav paper *Glas Slovenaca Hrvata i Srba* was unabashed in claiming that the struggle in the south of the Monarchy would end with the victory of 'democracy over German-military rape'. And several Czech papers could be quoted, calling for

Czech unification on the basis of the right to self-determination. The AOK exclaimed, with reason, that much of the language being used – 'self-determination', 'persecution', 'demands of oppressed peoples' – was synonymous with the vocabulary of enemy propaganda. But all of the AOK protests could only make small inroads into curbing this explosion of radical ideas. Unless the chief culprits could be banned (like the Czech *Národní Listy*) or heavily censored, the military were forced to fall back on defensive tactics.

Just before the June offensive, Arz took up Toggenburg's suggestion and announced the creation of an 'index' of newspapers which henceforth would be prohibited in the war zone. They included the socialist *Arbeiter-Zeitung*, *Arbeiterwille* and *Népszava*, and 'extreme' nationalist organs such as *Slovenec*, *Glas Slovenaca Hrvata i Srba*, *Lidové Noviny*, *Venkov* and *Kurjer Lwowski*.[106] Increasingly over the summer months it would be clear that these were indeed some of the chief newspapers which Italian propaganda was exploiting for its own ends. Moreover, since the AOK index continued and was steadily updated, Padua's manifestos gained an added importance in the final months of the war in that they were trying to break through the artificial quarantine of the war zone.[107] Yet the index alone could never be a substitute for censoring or closing down radical newspapers and the sources which fed them in the hinterland. There they continued to circulate in the midst of nationalist-social agitation which the authorities could not control and which any troops passing through to the war zones were bound to experience.

Patriotic instruction in the armed forces was thus consistently disrupted by the disintegration of authority in the hinterland. The flow of radical ideas in the press (and even the *Neue Freie Presse* was not above reproach from military quarters)[108] was merely a symptom of the fact that national-social movements in all corners of the Empire were now mobilizing with agenda which ran counter to the basic precepts of the FAst. Either the domestic authorities had to suppress these movements by force, or they needed to counter them positively with their own political solutions coupled perhaps with a coordinated 'secondary mobilization' of the population on behalf of the Habsburg cause. Neither course was feasible in the circumstances of 1918. Suppressing radical agitation might be attempted, but was always limited by manpower resources and by the constitutional regime in Austria. Thus, for example, Anton Korošec's notorious journeys and rallies in the south of the Empire on behalf of Yugoslav unity could not be prevented.[109]

As for organizing any movement to promote *Staatsgedanken* throughout Austria-Hungary, it might have been possible earlier in the war when there was tighter central control in the Monarchy and more evidence of public consensus behind the war effort. But even then, as we have seen, the authorities had only made superficial efforts, or had acted in ways which often served to undermine public morale. In 1918 it was simply too late and never attempted anyway. In short, patriotic instruction was to be limited to the armed forces. The FAst, while having a strictly military remit, was occasionally reminded that similar work was vital yet absent in the hinterland. Such a suggestion came from civilian FA lecturers like Rudolf Peerz, who in his own words had been active in 'state propaganda' for the Austrian Ministry of Interior for some years (in what context is not clear).[110] Similar proposals were made from units at the front and in the hinterland.[111] They included, again with an eye on Northcliffe's 'Propaganda Ministry', the idea of setting up in the Monarchy an 'Imperial Society' which would be deliberately non-official so as to attract personalities from all nationalities and walks of life with the purpose of promoting propaganda on behalf of the Monarchy.[112] On paper it was a fine idea, evidently first formulated before the war; in practice, in the Monarchy's rapidly disjointed social and political environment of 1917–18, it had no future whatsoever. Indeed, none of the proposals could be taken up. The FA instructors therefore had to go about their business in the knowledge that outside the war zone or the military barracks their pupils would always be prey to subversive ideas. Well might they observe that 'enemy propaganda' in its domestic guise was far more dangerous than anything stemming direct from foreign territory.

## 7.3 The case of the 42nd Honvéd Infantry Division

By a close examination of one military unit, we can better understand how Italy's propaganda campaign began to act as a catalyst upon these other threats to morale which originated either in the Austro-Hungarian hinterland or in the war zone itself. Assessing troop morale is not easy. While grass-roots sources from the Austro-Hungarian trenches are difficult to find, local commanders rarely gave detailed reports to their superiors unless specifically ordered to do so on the eve of battle or after some disaster had occurred in a particular unit. Then there is the issue of the reports' reliability. Since officers had a responsibility to maintain and nurture morale, a disquieting report would inevitably reflect badly upon their own abilities. Furthermore, the evidence of a conspiracy like Ljudevit Pivko's indicates how far it was possible to conceal the real mood or outlook among the lower ranks. As a case study, the story of the 42nd Honvéd Division (42HID) is instructive. As a predominantly Croat unit which was recruited in Croatia, it was usually considered by the military authorities to be composed of loyal, reliable elements. Yet in the final weeks of the war it was to be one of the first divisions on the Italian Front to rebel, thereby setting off a string of mutinies in other units in the war zone.[113] Its reliability in 1918 had been increasingly shaken by the material and ideological crisis of the hinterland. Partly for this reason a number of detailed reports about the division were composed and found their way to the AOK. And these, together with the surviving divisional records in the Hungarian War Archives, allow us to draw certain interesting conclusions about the ways in which threats to morale could interact.

The 42HID had begun the war in 1914 in the Balkans, when a striking percentage of Serbs from its regiments had deserted.[114] Thereafter it served chiefly on the Eastern Front, participating in the brutal Carpathian campaign of early 1915 and witnessing, after the liberation of eastern Galicia in 1917, the dramatic collapse of the Russian forces. In January 1918, when it had been announced that the division was to be one of those transferred to the Italian Front due to imminent peace in the East, its chief of staff reported that its overall morale remained 'excellent'. Fifty per cent of the unit had actually served in the battles of 1914, while 25 per cent had been at the colours in peacetime; their health and discipline remained good, with most individuals 'battle-tested and reliable'. The only perceived weaknesses were the division's inexperience with gas and mass artillery fire (as practised by the Italians), and particularly a crisis in manpower. As the only division recruited in Croatia which had the status of *Domobran* or 'home guard', the 42HID was unique in being entitled to use Serbo-Croat as its language of command, thereby necessitating a steady supply of Croat-speaking officers. That had been a problem even in peacetime, but it was all the more so after wartime losses. By 1918 the division was 50 per cent below the prescribed number of officers.[115] The divisional commander, Brigadier Michael Mihaljević, rather typically blamed the military authorities in Croatia for this situation, alleging that they were retaining Croat officers in comfortable positions at home rather than dispatching them to the front. At the same time, perhaps more accurately, he bemoaned the degree to which soldiers on leave were deserting and joining notorious deserter-bands in the countryside, in part at least because of insufficient vigilance on the part of the Croatian authorities.[116] In each case the result was to diminish manpower in the division, something which would steadily undermine its overall capability until the end of the war.

Still, Mihaljević expected that the troops would perform enthusiastically when transferred to the south-western front. On the eve of their departure from the East, he painted for them a vivid picture of the role which 'His Majesty' had asked them to perform against a new villain, Italy:

> Our perfidious ally,[117] cunning neighbour, who yearns for the regions of our homeland, for those Croatian baptismal hills which defend our Adriatic sea from the continent. There, where through the centuries Croatian heroic songs have echoed; where the Croat mother has given birth to most sons of our nation; where the scarlet sunrise, dark red dawn of all Croats has been reflected in the blue waves of the sea; where a shining future is blossoming and awaits: there our perfidious ally wants to propagate his own dirty seed

> and deal a deadly blow to our people. This enemy, the Italian, unswervingly waits for our avenging Croatian hatred.

The *Domobrani* would have a chance to show themselves worthy sons of their ancestors, proclaiming in their spirit: 'We too with God have faithfully done our duty to king, homeland and golden freedom!!!'[118] This 'freedom', this historic tradition which Mihaljević was evoking, was the alternative to that which Padua would appeal to in its manifestos. Italy's front propaganda would remind Croat soldiers of seventeenth-century martyrs such as Zrinjski and Frankopan, of broken Habsburg promises, of the Hungarian 'yoke', and of a 'freedom' which was yet to come. Mihaljević was reminding the same soldiers of how their ancestral 'frontiersmen' had fought with Marshal Radetsky in 1848 against the Italians, of their age-old loyalty to the Habsburgs, and of a 'freedom' which Italy was now threatening. Both messages had strong elements of truth, reflecting as they did the ambiguous historic tradition in Croatia as well as the dual loyalty which many Croat soldiers continued to possess in 1918, both to their nationality and to their Habsburg monarch. One might suggest that, in contrast to the Czechs or even Slovenes, such dual loyalty had a certain resilience among Croat soldiers which Padua would find very hard to penetrate with its message of a Yugoslav utopia.

Yet in material terms the 42HID was as open to attack as any other unit in the army. Its physical resilience would be worn away on the Italian Front.[119] Not only was marching up to the Asiago plateau in February 1918 something of an ordeal in itself, but the division was dismayed to find immediately on its arrival how critical were the routes of supply to positions at the front and in reserve. There were only two supply lines to the division. The first was a winding road, 34 kilometres in length and crossing three mountain ridges, which was impassable when snow fell heavily in early March. The second was a light cable-car or *teleferiche*, which for some time (until a second *teleferiche* was opened in April) was the only means to bring food, munitions or any technical material to the division. Although many Italian mountain divisions faced similar supply hazards, their lines were always nearer to the plains than the Austrians, their food resources always more plentiful. For the 42HID, the reduced food ration could not be fully issued, and two-thirds of the division began to live on snow-water due to a chronic water deficiency in the sector; shelters were also inadequate and, in terms of basic clothing, 90 per cent of the troops were soon wearing rags instead of underwear. Not surprisingly, the health of the division sharply deteriorated. In March 1918, 909 men fell ill while 107 were wounded; in April, 1003 reported sick while 73 were wounded, many having to be transported over treacherous terrain to be treated.

In the front line the misery was further compounded by the fact that the enemy was blatantly superior in artillery fire and in control of the air. While from the start the 42nd's infantry was steadily run down by an incessant bombardment (all calls for extra munition being ignored or hindered by the bad supply lines), the division in May began to be aware of the enemy's propaganda offensive in the shape of a mass leaflet distribution by plane. Already in March they had noticed some leaflets, and then become aware of the stronger efforts which Pivko's unit was making against the neighbouring 26SchD. By May the enemy was swarming over their own sector with 39 planes seen on one day alone. In response, the divisional *Nachrichtentruppen* stepped up their own propaganda efforts, depositing material for the Italians in no-man's-land and approaching the enemy lines to fraternize, something which had not previously been attempted because of the distance involved. However, the Italians were overwhelmingly hostile, and since the rest of the troops opposite were French and not an appropriate target, the 42HID was at an immediate disadvantage in the propaganda duel.[120] In this field, as in so many others, the division was already on the defensive.

It was against this disturbing background that a notorious event occurred, the desertion of four individuals to the enemy. In the previous years, and until May 1918, desertions from the division seem to have been relatively rare; in the last four months of 1917 on the Eastern Front, for instance, 17 individuals are known to have deserted.[121] In the late evening of 12 May 1918, Lt Mirko Weiss-Belošević and his batman Stanko Paprić, together with a propaganda officer, Luka Kostrenčić (all Croats from HIR26), and Vitěslav Štětina, a Czech one-year volunteer of HIR25, crept across the lines to the French trenches near Monte Sisemol. The desertions had been planned for weeks if not months beforehand, and much of their background can be pieced together from Pivko's memoirs and the later Austrian enquiry. Mirko Belošević was a Jew from Zagreb whose impeccable Yugoslav credentials seem clear from the fact that he immediately joined Ljudevit Pivko's Yugoslav unit, and was chosen by Pivko as a recruiter of other volunteers during Pivko's tour of the camps in late May.[122] According to what Belošević told Pivko, he had fraternized with Russian soldiers in 1917 and planned to desert to them if it had not been for the Bolshevik Revolution; then on leave in Zagreb, he had spread Yugoslav literature among Jewish students who were beginning to incline in a radical direction.[123] When the 42HID was moved to the Italian Front, Belošević in April was sent on a four-week training course of the 42nd *Sturmbatallion*, part of the division's traditional practice to steadily drill as many troops as possible in *Sturm* duties.[124] There in the rear at Castello Tesino (just to the east of Carzano) Belošević had begun to think more clearly about agitation within the division, stimulated by like-minded officers such as Štětina, Dejan Popović and Božidar Zvonarević. Together, they formed a secret club known as the 'cadet party' with a certain Mile Buzadžić as its leader.

It was a sign undoubtedly of how far 'Yugoslav thinking' had progressed in the army and hinterland in the past six months, that the cadet party, while secretly plotting their own desertions, felt able to be far more open than the *Carzanci* about their radical gospel. They issued a lithographed newspaper, *Jugoslaven*, which they read out to their men during training, they collected money for a Slovene national theatre in Ljubljana, and they even publicly displayed red and blue Yugoslav insignia in their caps and urged others to do so in order to distinguish Yugoslavs from other nationalities. The wearing of these colours was an idea 'exported' from the hinterland. There the authorities were beginning to notice their adoption by some soldiers in Slovenia and Dalmatia, and in a letter to Štětina from Zagreb (which arrived after his desertion), his Croat fiancée had praised the plotters' efforts to 'gain a following for this new Yugoslav badge at the front as well'. While at Castello Tesino, Štětina had cut up a Croat tricolour flag into strips (concealing the white sections to make them distinctly 'Yugoslav') and persuaded some men on the *Sturm* course to wear them as a badge. Although some 'loyal' officers noticed them and ordered their removal, few seem to have been aware of their real significance and no investigation was undertaken. Later, a witness would tell the 42HID military court that Belošević while at Castello Tesino had been 'an enthusiastic Yugoslav and condemned the war'. Another, who shared his quarters at the front, would testify that Belošević and his batman had both returned to their regiment wearing Yugoslav insignia. But no witnesses had felt at the time that it was a matter to report to their superiors. As with the *Carzanci*, but even more so, indifference or perhaps even a conspiracy of silence appears to have reigned among many of the officers, enabling the plotters to plan and act undetected.[125]

For Belošević and Štětina, their plot to desert was aided considerably by involving in their scheme a like-minded propaganda officer, Luka Kostrenčić. Kostrenčić had probably been assigned to the 42HID *Nachrichtentruppen* because he knew German and Italian well. Born in Crikvenica on the north Adriatic coast, he had attended naval academy, and from 1916 until early 1918 had been employed in the HIR26 reserve at Karlovac, examining Austrians who had been recaptured in Serbia as well as other politically suspect elements from south-west Croatia.[126] Whether it was at that time or earlier that he became a secret Yugoslav is unclear; his upbringing in a Croatian coastal town might suggest Yugoslav inclinations. But neither in Karlovac nor at the front does his reliability appear to have been questioned. The positions he held, most notably in propaganda work against Italy, immediately implied that he was trusted. Indeed, when in May 1918 one of the divisional propaganda officers went on leave it was Kostrenčić who temporarily replaced him.[127] Probably only at that time, under Belošević's influence, did Kostrenčić decide to desert to the enemy for in the previous few months he would have had a number of opportunities to do so. On the evening of 12 May he was able to disguise himself and the three others as a propaganda patrol, going out into no-man's-land to deposit newspapers. By telephone he told regimental command of his intention, an essential move since rules about entering no-man's-land had been tightened a few months earlier to prevent desertions, and any stray individuals would be shot on sight.[128] The four deserters gave different excuses to their comrades as to why they would be absent from their quarters that night. They met at Belošević's quarters, dressed in front of Belošević's unsuspecting room-mate, and then proceeded outside. On the way they were noticed by a sentry, but he let them pass having received from Kostrenčić the pass-word 'ensign of hunters'. The sentry did not (as required) demand written proof, nor did he question why the group might be depositing propaganda in front of French rather than Italian positions. They disappeared into the darkness, and crossed the short 150 metre stretch to the enemy.[129]

The group proved to be of considerable value to Italy. They imparted detailed information about Austrian positions so that 'the 83rd Brigade [42 HID] was fired upon immediately after their desertion, and enemy planes which previously had not flown over Tesino did so already at 7 a.m. on 13 May'.[130] Kostrenčić in particular could betray many secrets about the organization of Austrian propaganda, confirming that the Austrians had faith in that weapon after its success against Russia; and he illustrated with a selection of military orders the degree to which, after a preparatory attack on Italian morale with propaganda, an Italian collapse in the forthcoming offensive was firmly expected. The deserters confessed that many Slav officers also shared that optimism, but they insisted that a younger generation was slowly rising, 'ripening into a secret revolutionary movement'.[131] Belošević, 'ardent in his hatred of the Habsburgs' as a British report noted, even claimed that most of the officers at battalion headquarters sympathized with the Yugoslav idea or 'at all events rather unwillingly concealed their sympathies and inclinations'.[132] As we will see, evidence on the Austrian side implied as much, and the divisional authorities came close to admitting it. Italian Intelligence in any case was convinced, and decided to exploit the situation with the aid of the new deserters.

All agreed to join Pivko's unit, and Kostrenčić was soon commandeered by Finzi because of his special experience. All proceeded to compose manifestos at 6th army Intelligence for duplication and distribution over the enemy. In the following weeks Italian planes spread leaflets, mostly in Croat and signed by the deserters, over the whole 11th army front.[133] These echoed the line of the Padua Commission, assuring their 'Yugoslav brothers' about the marvellous environment in Italy: 'The Italians and Yugoslavs are in complete agreement and the Italians receive us and accept us as allies and brothers. Everyone who comes here is sorry that he did not come before, for here hunger and misery, fear and slavery, are unknown.'[134] Then they appealed to a heroic epic tradition which embraced the 'Yugoslav nation'. Yugoslav soldiers ought to be fighting for liberty rather than for their sworn enemies: 'Dare the nation of Petar Svačić, Zrinjski, Frankopan and Kvaternik fight on the side of Krauts and Magyars? Dare the nation of Miloš Obilić, Marko Kraljević, Majka Jugović and Kosovo field fight on the side of the Turks?'[135] To do so was to forge the shackles of slavery for the Yugoslav people, to aid oppressors who were already tyrannizing those at home, in their goal of exterminating the Slav race and establishing themselves on the Adriatic. Rather than waiting 'to become corpses or invalids' in the approaching offensive, Yugoslavs should desert to those who were fighting for civilization, who had unlimited resources with which to crush German militarism:

> The war will be ruthlessly continued until that magnificent moment when the idea of freedom and justice celebrates victory over medieval barbarism and the sun of freedom shines on the human race. On the ruins of Austria two new Slav buildings of freedom will be reconstructed, a Yugoslav and a Czechoslovak state. Brothers, it is in your hands to accelerate that great moment, to help to create what we have been dreaming about for centuries, to end the time of suffering for our people . . . The hinterland in Austria is undermined, it needs only a spark and the old cracked sepulchre called Austria will explode into the air. Make that spark! Men at the front, take up your arms, come to us, to become free men as another final blow to Austria![136]

Despite this self-publicity from the deserters, and their obvious betrayal of information in the crucial weeks before the offensive, the 42HID was remarkably negligent about investigating the incident or tightening security. As a result, two weeks later, four more members of the cadet party were quite easily able to desert to Italy: ensigns Dejan Popović, Luka Kereković and Božidar Zvonarević, together with one-year volunteer private Franjo Svetec, all from HIR27. Their desertion in the Val Bella sector was not only a direct sequel to the first group's, but was stimulated by the latter's propaganda back across the trenches. The divisional enquiry revealed that Popović, Zvonarević and Svetec had all associated with Belošević in Castello Tesino and worn Yugoslav colours. Popović, whose cousin Milica was engaged to Vitěslav Štětina, was well-known, at least among his associates in the regiment, as a rather violent 'political hothead' who was often to be found discussing Yugoslav, or rather Great Serb, ideas with junior officers in the mess. According to the regimental command, he seemed to be the ring-leader of the four deserters and had probably won over Zvonarević to his cause while on the *Sturm* course. Zvonarević allegedly was a 'notorious drunkard', lazy and irresponsible (and his behaviour in Italy would also leave something to be desired).[137]

As for Kereković, retained as an adjutant in the 3rd battalion although the regiment noted in hindsight that he had lacked the necessary sense of duty, his political leanings could only be ascertained from one fact. On the day of his desertion he had suppressed a piece of enemy propaganda which he had found, a leaflet telling of a parliamentary speech by Ante Tresić-Pavičić about atrocities against Croats. More certain proof of Kereković's state of mind came from a comment he had made to a fellow officer after finding one of the leaflets signed by Belošević: 'these scum of HIR26 are now sitting comfortably in a café in Rome while I get myself killed here by enemy grenades and can't get any leave'. Having not associated with the 'cadet party' at its birth, it seems likely that Kereković joined the plotters chiefly because he had not been on leave for 15 months; but his was still a significant desertion as he knew a lot about the divisional defences.[138] Franjo Svetec, on the other hand, seemed more obviously committed to radical politics. Among his personal effects were found fragments of a book about the anarchist Bakunin, and he was known when on the *Sturm* course to have worn Yugoslav colours and recommended them to a friend in Zagreb on the grounds that there was not enough political agitation in the hinterland. Like his fellow-deserters, Svetec was also probably spurred on to act by the example set by the first group of the cadet party and by their signed manifestos which proved that they had safely reached enemy lines. On departure, Svetec left behind a note for his company commander saying that he was 'following in the steps of Lt Belošević, ensign Kostrenčić and volunteer Štětina, because my life is dearer to me than glory'.[139]

The way in which the second group deserted was also remarkably similar to the first. On the evening of 26 May, Popović, Zvonarević and Kereković met for a game of cards without arousing any suspicion. Then they went out with Svetec, who was often on sentry duty and knew the terrain, and posed as an 'officers' patrol' in no-man's-land near Val Bella. In the darkness they were challenged by a sentry, but were easily allowed to continue, crawled under the wires, and escaped into Italian lines. It was around this very spot that one of Pivko's patrols was about to begin trench propaganda, and although the deserters do not seem to have been enticed by anything more than enemy manifestos, they would all be destined when in Italy to join Pivko's Yugoslav unit.[140]

Only after these desertions did the 42HID begin to take precautionary measures. But their inadequacy is clear from the fact that just a fortnight later another patrol, of seven men from HIR28, was able to go missing (and later turned up in Pivko's unit).[141] Divisional precautions meanwhile had included halting all propaganda against Italy in the sector, thereby curbing unnecessary patrols, but also leaving the field wide open to the enemy propagandists.[142] Since the second group of deserters was thought to have betrayed vital details about the sector and the imminent offensive (something immediately borne out by the direction of enemy artillery fire after 26 May), the 42nd command also considered radical changes in the layout of their forces, including withdrawing HIR27 from the front altogether.[143] But above all, the divisional picture was to be clarified at this time by a thorough investigation into the reason for both sets of desertions. In the reports which emerged from the enquiry, it was generally agreed that the deserters had been infected in some way by Yugoslav agitation, but it was less clear how large a role it had played. As the divisional court proceedings observed, the second group of deserters were 'all youths of about 20 years of age, and one cannot say that they have a serious understanding of politics or real life in general'. Less idealistic motives seemed 'clear' from the message which Svetec had left behind, from Kereković's frustration about leave, from Kostrenčić's supposed 'timidity', and from the fact that Popović owed his batman 300 Kronen.[144]

All this supported a divisional consensus that it was cowardice which was the leading motive, something which the regimental commanders were keen to highlight while insisting that there were no other signs of political agitation or unreliability in their units. The desertions were portrayed as unique incidents which occurred even among the most reliable troops and would in no way tarnish the glorious reputation of the 42HID. In particular, all were agreed that among the rank and file there was no sympathy whatsoever. 'The behaviour of the men is exemplary', wrote the HIR27 commander; 'they unanimously condemn the deserters' treacherous conduct and threaten that if they are caught they will be lynched.'[145] For the men, the main source of discontent remained, as revealed in postal censorship during May, their material conditions and particularly the food crisis. They were not likely to be receptive to Yugoslav propaganda since, as FML Soretić the new divisional commander explained, 'our men, mostly peasants, stick to tradition and are rooted too firmly in their native soil to be susceptible to these ideas'. He warned, however, that if propaganda was cleverly disguised, it might well constitute a danger to the ordinary soldier.[146] Indeed, one disguise might be for the enemy propagandists to dwell on social unrest in the hinterland, for the men were naturally always anxious about their families and property. In 1917–18, cases of absence without leave were soaring from even the most reliable divisions. For example, in a 'loyal' Croat division like the 36ID, the court martial records abound with such cases, often caused because the men on leave discovered a miserable home environment and were persuaded to remain there by insistent family members.[147]

If these basic threats to morale were only hinted at in the 42HID enquiry, the specific danger of Yugoslav agitation among the officer corps was firmly acknowledged. The regimental commanders might emphasize that the desertions were an exception, that the officer corps was generally reliable, but at the same time they could not deny that younger reserve officers who were joining the division were sympathetic to the Yugoslav message. It did not mean that they were necessarily disloyal to the Emperor. A dual loyalty seemed to persist for many Croats, of loyalty both to the Emperor and to southern Slav unity. But from this duality there was a strong possibility of Habsburg patriotism being slowly eroded by more radical nationalism reaching the army from front and rear. The HIR27 commander presented the problem very clearly. He divided the younger officers into two categories, those who had completed their training before the war or in its early years, who were reliable and patriotic; and those whose training fell after 1916, who were politically infected, listless and untrustworthy. The blame for the latter could be set squarely at the door of the hinterland where the authorities lacked political direction, where the political vacuum was filled by Yugoslav agitators, and where the press was full of sensational and disruptive news. The result was that 'infected' young officers like Popović were, after training, being sent out to the division without any record being communicated of their past misdemeanours.[148] Summarizing these views, the divisional and corps commanders also blamed the hinterland for most ills, particularly using the opportunity to complain once again about the dearth of older, experienced Croat officers in the division. Such men, they alleged, were being allowed to remain in comfortable positions in the hinterland instead of taking their turn at the front. It left a bitter taste in the mouths of officers in the front line, but it also weakened morale in the officer corps as a whole, because older individuals would naturally act as a stabilizing influence upon the younger ones and steer them on a straight patriotic path.[149]

The front-line commanders expected that if this single issue could be resolved, by dispatching to the 42HID a good number of older reliable officers, most of the existing threats to morale would disappear at an instant. In fact it was a fallacy to suggest that a surplus of Croat officers existed in Croatia. The reserve which was available there was tightly stretched. Nor could many of the other front-line troubles blamed on 'the hinterland' be easily resolved by the military commanders in Croatia. When in July the 42HID invited the chief of staff of the VI Honvéd military district (Zagreb) to make a report on the whole issue of divisional manpower and its relationship with the Croatian hinterland, Lt-Colonel Nádasdy's conclusions put the 42HID complaints in clear perspective.[150] Nádasdy readily confirmed that the number of older active officers in the division was far too small, while younger reserve officers were fast losing their former balance of 'dual allegiance' and inclining to Yugoslavism due to nationalist agitation in the hinterland. However, Nádasdy then described in detail why Croatia could no longer meet the twin divisional requirements of supplying sufficient, but also reliable, officer reserves. The number of officers there was steadily shrinking since, apart from acting as a reserve for Croatian divisions, the district also had to supply Serbo-Croat-speaking officers for most Bosnian units and for the administration of occupied Serbia and Montenegro. The result was a dearth of officer material in Croatia itself, which had a direct impact on the ability of the authorities to exercise an efficient administration, not least to round up the growing number of deserters in the countryside. According to Nádasdy, a good 70 per cent of military administrative staff were now women, while those officers in place (and 116 were vitally lacking) were in crucially necessary posts rather than in 'comfortable positions' as the 42HID insinuated. The prospect therefore of meeting the 42HID demands was not bright for a combination of reasons. Nádasdy, estimating that a reserve of only 8000 men was available for the division for the rest of the year, recommended that the whole system of managing manpower in the Monarchy would need to be transformed if 'patchwork measures' [*Flickerei*] were not to continue.

A few months later patchwork measures were indeed continuing. Although the 42HID benefited in September 1918 when a regiment (HIR33) was dissolved and assigned to it, the issue of human resources remained fundamental to the division's morale. In late September FML Soretić continued to view a manpower crisis as imminent since the number of those deserting when on leave (60 per cent in one regiment) was spiralling. He could not prohibit leave altogether as he felt it might directly cause mass desertion. He could only call for action in Croatia itself, warning of the immense dangers now constituted by 'the sinking state of affairs at the front combined with an armed hinterland which mocks the authorities'.[151] It was a call of despair, but it could not gain a hearing in the recruitment ground of Croatia where perhaps 9000 deserters from the 42HID reserves were now at large.[152] Soretić's military superiors simply noted that some reorganization of the 42HID might be possible at the end of the year.

What the 42nd commanders had long viewed as the most serious threat to morale, the absence of reliable officers, persisted therefore until the end of the war. The division could not be supplied with many new officers, and the cohesion of the existing officer corps was steadily weakening as chaos took hold in Croatia and the environment of the war zone deteriorated. The military had, of course, exacerbated this state of affairs through launching a final offensive against Italy in June 1918. Just as the 11th army lost over 1000 officers and 44 000 men in this enterprise, so the 42HID suffered proportionally (Table 7.1). The division's material crisis, its inferior position in artillery and in the air, its slightly crumbling hierarchical cohesion – all these weaknesses were exposed in June in the way that the division collapsed after an initially impressive performance against French positions.[153] As with so many other Austro-Hungarian units, the 42HID troops had been fired up to perform well

*Table 7.1* Diminishing Strength of the 42HID (1918)[154]

| *Unit* | *30 January* | | *1 May* | | *28 June* | |
|---|---|---|---|---|---|---|
| | *Officers* | *Men* | *Officers* | *Men* | *Officers* | *Men* |
| HIR25 | 53 | 1912 | 50 | 1461 | 38 | 1125 |
| HIR26 | 56 | 2119 | 56 | 2070 | 27 | 860 |
| HIR27 | 44 | 2015 | 54 | 2260 | 30 | 1137 |
| HIR28 | 70 | 2006 | 80 | 2072 | 41 | 938 |

by the promise of rich booty. But after a few days they had over 4000 casualties and were 'completely exhausted'.[155] On 24 June they were withdrawn to the rear, Soretić specifying that failure in the long-awaited offensive was the main reason for 'the deep depression' which pervaded the whole division. It was, in his view, no longer the physically and morally efficient instrument which had arrived earlier in the year to fight the hereditary enemy; it had suffered from poor supplies, from inferior weaponry and seeping Yugoslav agitation. None of these evils would be removed in the following months, and all would contribute in their way to sabotaging Soretić's overall solution for curing the division's 'deep depression'. In his words: 'Only a major, sensational [military] success will be able to give the optimists among the officers the upper hand and carry the men securely along with them.'[156]

The previously untold story of the 42HID is all the more valuable because its nickname 'Devil's Division' (*Vražija Divizija*) always symbolized a reputation for fiery reliability. In 1918, its effectiveness as a military unit was being eroded by the same threats which had long-undermined far less reliable Czech or Romanian divisions. All units in the army were now subject to a range of similar pressures. Their morale was lowered by a perpetual crisis in material and human resources, and this was compounded for each nationality (in varying degrees) by the ideological struggle which was being waged in the hinterland. Developments in the 42HID illustrate how educated soldiers in particular might be affected by nationalist agitation from their home-region, and how Italy's front propaganda might then act as a small catalyst upon nationalist phenomena in the war zone which the Austrian military were desperate to eliminate.

While the division's FA officer could portray his pupils' outlook in glowing colours, a different picture of the division had emerged from the May desertions and the troops' rapid exhaustion during the June offensive. It was a picture which made any productive FA work among the troops highly questionable. If in the summer months the division lapsed into what Soretić termed a 'critical passivity', there were also alarming hints of what was beneath the surface (and these must remain hints in the absence of any detailed reports). In late July, for example, about a dozen men who were on a training course in the rear refused, due to their poor rations, to obey orders which were given by a commanding officer who could not speak Croatian.[157] It was a minor incident, but it is probably significant in view of the division's later history. On 22 October, two days before the final Italian offensive began, regiments of the 42HID (HIR 25/26) in the rear were some of the first Austro-Hungarian units to revolt against their commanders. Most of the mutineers were rounded up by a reliable *Sturmbatallion* without bloodshed, but they had still set a public example for others. Soretić judged a few days later that the rest of his division in the front line was now unreliable as well. More importantly, the 42nd's challenge to Habsburg authority had been enough to set off a string of mutinies in the war zone.[158] In this way, the collapse of the 42HID's dual allegiance was finally complete.

## 7.4 Austria loses the propaganda duel

Both the Allies and the Austrians had expected that the Monarchy's summer offensive would be decisive in revealing the effectiveness of their respective propaganda campaigns. This was indeed the case, and it was Austria-Hungary whose illusions were shattered. As with the experience of the 42HID, the June offensive had the effect of clarifying the reality behind the Austrian commanders' assumptions. The AOK was forced to accept that its campaign was already inferior and had been largely unsuccessful when compared to the Italians'. While the Austrians had single-handedly had an opportunity to wield the propaganda weapon with some vigour in the spring, the subsequent propaganda duel, especially from April 1918 onwards, had been weighted more and more heavily in Italy's favour.

The Allied propagandists were the first to claim success for their own efforts in the months before the June offensive. Steadily from April, Henry Wickham Steed had been using a myth, that propaganda had already forced the enemy to postpone his offensive, as a bargaining chip in Allied circles. He proceeded in late May to tell the EPD committee in London that the campaign of leaflets and trench propaganda had influenced the morale of 'a considerable proportion of the Austro-Hungarian forces'.[159] It was a vague claim, yet one which those at Padua undoubtedly supported on the basis of more specific 'evidence'. Jambrišak, for example, professed to be able to see visible effects of the Rome Congress: 'deserters come in greater numbers, and all are motivated by having heard that an [Italo-Yugoslav] agreement has been reached'.[160] Ojetti enthusiastically concurred, writing to his wife on 9 June that 'all deserters are arriving with leaflets in their hands... [saying] that our manifestos have a great effect because they tell the truth and tally with the few newspapers which come from the interior to the lines'.[161]

In assessing such evidence and the real impact of Italy's campaign in these months, certain facts cannot be denied. As we have seen, the bogey of enemy propaganda was certainly alarming the Austrian authorities and forcing them to take counter-measures. The threat was perceived as something vague and ubiquitous, but it also had a specific Italian shape in manifestos and trench propaganda which seemed ever more cleverly attuned to each nationality's outlook. At the front, there was indeed clear evidence that Czech propaganda patrols, especially on the river Piave, were making a mark, securing some desertions from their efforts or at least winning over disgruntled soldiers who then remained in the Austrian trenches to act as 'yeast' for future fermentation. The case of the 42HID also indicates how by May 1918 Italy's efforts were playing a subtle role in contributing to the material and ideological crisis which was undermining troop morale in all quarters. One can suggest that Italy's campaign was acting most effectively as a catalyst upon the thinking of educated reserve officers, men like Belošević and Kostrenčić who were following in the steps of Hlaváček and Pivko from earlier in the war. But less effectively could the campaign influence the less-educated rank and file. After all, in terms of the impact of Padua's manifestos, a crucial basic obstacle (and one which never seems to have occurred to the Allied propagandists) was the issue of literacy. Literacy figures from British military sources (Table 7.2), even if not wholly accurate, raise a question-mark over how many soldiers could actually read Padua's leaflets, all the more so as the language of the leaflet would have to match its recipient's own language proficiency. Nor did the manifestos contain the number of pictorial images which Ojetti had first envisaged, and which might have done something to offset the literacy problem. From this premise it seems difficult to believe that large numbers of men deserted to Italy in direct response to Padua's often rather subtle arguments. In contrast, the work of propaganda patrols in the front line might be considered far more dangerous. The Austrian commanders always viewed it as such, since the very presence of the patrols introduced new confusion into the purpose of the war which the Empire was fighting.

A question too must hang over the Allied propagandists' claims that their early successes were directly reflected in an increase in the rate of enemy desertions. Steed wrote in his memoirs that in May 1918 'hundreds' of Czechs and Yugoslavs had sought refuge in Italy, bringing Allied leaflets with them as a passport to a better future.[162] The reality was undoubtedly more modest. It is true that, as before any offensive, desertions to the enemy were increasing and

*Table 7.2* Percentage of literate males, aged 16–50, in Austria, Hungary and Bosnia-Hercegovina[163]

| *Nationality* | *Austria* | *Hungary* | *Bosnia* |
|---|---|---|---|
| Ruthene | 28 | 25 | – |
| Polish | 60 | – | – |
| Czech | 97 | – | – |
| Slovak | – | 75 | – |
| Romanian | – | 45 | – |
| Italian | 88 | – | – |
| Slovene | 84 | – | – |
| Serb | 35 | 45 | 18 |
| Croat | 50 | 50 | 25 |
| German | 97 | 75 | – |
| Magyar | – | 78 | – |
| Moslem | – | – | 12 |

*Table 7.3* Desertions to the Italian 4th Army, 15 May–14 June 1918[164]

| *Reason for Desertion* | *Nationality** | | | | | | | | | *Total* |
|---|---|---|---|---|---|---|---|---|---|---|
| | *Cz* | *I* | *B* | *S-C* | *R* | *U* | *P* | *G* | *M* | |
| Nationalism | | 4 | | | | | | | | 4 |
| Join Cz. Legion[+] | 1 | | | | | | | | | 1 |
| Join Serb Legion | | | 1 | 1 | | | | | | 2 |
| Propaganda[+] | | | 1 | | | | | | | 1 |
| War-weariness | | | 1 | | | 1 | | | | 2 |
| Fear | | | 1 | | | | | | 2 | 3 |
| Ill-treatment | | | | | 1 | 1 | | | | 2 |
| Hatred of Austrians | 1 | | | 2 | | 1 | | | | 4 |
| Hunger | 1 | | 15 | 1 | 1 | 1 | 1 | 3 | 1 | 24 |
| TOTAL | 3 | 4 | 19 | 4 | 2 | 4 | 1 | 3 | 3 | 43 |

*Notes*:
* Cz (Czech), I (Italian), B (Bosnians: it is unclear whether Moslems are specifically meant), S-C (Serbs and Croats together), R (Romanian), U (Ukrainian; Ruthene), P (Polish), G (German), M (Magyar).
[+] On the 7th army front during the same period it is known that six Czechs gave joining the Legion as their reason for desertion, while two Czechs specified 'enemy manifestos'.

occurring in the Czech case with a certain regularity. Yet, of 25 officers and 990 men who went missing from the *Heeresgruppe* Conrad during May, only five officers and 145 men were definitely known to have deserted to Italy.[165] Of these, it seems reasonable to suppose that the number who deserted in direct response to Allied propaganda was relatively small; 'baser' motives were in the forefront of most soldiers' minds. It was also in the deserters' interest to tell the Italians that they had acted due to some high-minded ideal. But we know from Italian 4th army records (Table 7.3) that most deserters in that sector gave 'hunger' as their chief motivation, not 'enemy propaganda' or a desire to join the Czechoslovak Legion. The tendency seems clear, even if for any individual desertion there could be a mixture of reasons, among which the appeal made by an enemy manifesto might be an added stimulus and a guarantee of safe-conduct across the lines.

For the British propagandists at Crewe House, the success of 'their' campaign at this stage was measurable in another form as well. Allegedly, the deserters who were stimulated by Allied propaganda had betrayed vital information to the Italians on the eve of the Austrian offensive.[166] This claim too requires qualification. And it enables us to take up Vojtěch Hanzal's challenge to future historians of assessing how far these desertions were crucial for Italian Intelligence in June 1918.[167] In the days and weeks before the Austrian attack, the work of the Czech propaganda patrols was certainly helping to clarify the picture for the Intelligence network; they gained precise details about the trend and timing of the offensive. The desertion of Karel Stinný on the 3rd army front in late May appears to have been a real prize, for he knew convincing facts about the attack across the Piave which made the Italians decide not to proceed with a local offensive on the Asiago plateau.[168] Stinný's disclosures were supported a few days later by Rudolf Paprskař who was enticed to desert by 8th army patrols and spoke openly about an imminent offensive across the river to the Montello hill.[169] Pivko's units also played their part in honing the accuracy of Intelligence data. From listening devices and a stream of desertions, Finzi could feel the 'nimbus of the offensive' gathering on the mountain front as well. On 9 June he knew that the enemy had delivered reserve rations to the troops. On 13 June the 6th army bulletin duly announced that attack was imminent. On 14 June Pivko's scouts learnt at three separate points that it would begin at 3 a.m. the next morning, a fact confirmed by deserters in other sectors.[170] As a result of such precise Intelligence the Italians were not at all surprised by the offensive, and could pre-empt it in the mountains with a heavy bombardment from midnight; Lord Cavan noted, 'the Austrian attack on our positions began to the expected minute'.[171] Thus there is reliable evidence to suggest that Italian Intelligence was substantially enhanced by the work of Czech propaganda troops prior to the offensive. Italian commanders like Giardino (4th army) sincerely believed this, concluding that such precise data had done much to sabotage the Austrian attack.[172]

It should be emphasized, however, how far the Italians since the spring had suspected the main trend of Austrian plans. They were not solely reliant upon enemy desertions for such clues. Just before the offensive, Finzi could boast to Pivko that he knew everything happening in the Austrian war zone thanks to the Intelligence network's finely tuned efficiency.[173] It had gathered information from agents like Mansueto Zanon at Innsbruck, from reconnaissance flights over enemy territory, from eavesdropping on Austrian wireless activity, and from the very large number of prisoners taken prior to the offensive (870 for example during Austria's diversionary Tonale attack on 13 June). Alongside these sources, which included the valuable work of Czech propaganda troops, the role of individual deserters could be a useful check but was unlikely to be decisive. It is a point, surprisingly, with which Max Ronge after the war agreed. Rather than blame Slav deserters for the *débâcle* in June 1918, he wrote dispassionately: 'Failures should not always be linked together with treachery even though one likes to make treason responsible.' He himself was more inclined to point to Austrian errors in the front line, including the failure to conceal their wireless chatter from the Italians.[174]

Yet Ronge too therefore was implying that the outcome of the June offensive was decisively affected by the fact that Italy knew exact data about its timing and orientation. A more fundamental reason for the failure would seem to be that the operation was 'a rather bungled affair even before it started'.[175] Memoirs and the official Austrian inquiry of December 1918 confirm that the

Austrian forces were undernourished and insufficiently equipped for a major onslaught, Boroević and others pleading only a few days before the attack that it ought to be postponed. Peter Fiala's work has revealed also the degree to which the AOK and leading Austrian commanders were themselves completely at odds over the exact character of the operation. The result was that Austrian forces were spread evenly along the whole front, with no overwhelming point of concentration which might have aided a break-through. These deficiencies in planning were fully acknowledged by Rudolf Kiszling in the Austrian official history (volume seven, published in 1938).[176]

But in 1918, in the wake of the offensive, such an interpretation was naturally not forthcoming. Conrad von Hötzendorf served as a scapegoat for the failure and was dismissed as commander of the Tyrolian front by the Emperor. Otherwise the AOK proclaimed that the offensive had been vital in forestalling an Italian move, and had been most excellently prepared. It put the blame for defeat on Slav deserters, singling out for publicity in the Austrian press the cases of Stinný and Paprskař.[177] While this deflected from the AOK the storm of abuse which had arisen in the Austrian and Hungarian parliaments, it also attracted the attention of the Allied propagandists. They could seize upon it as further proof of their own success.[178] In this way, the two sides became unlikely allies in exaggerating the power of the propaganda weapon.

For the Padua Commission, events which occurred during the offensive had further contributed to the growing myth of their success in Italy. After the battle General Diaz himself received members of the Commission and thanked them for their efforts to which, he allegedly remarked, the victory 'was in considerable measure attributable'.[179] Even if such language may actually be that of Wickham Steed, it seems clear that the CS was truly impressed by the large number of deserters and prisoners secured during the offensive. Just before the attack, Badoglio had been anxious to see the real effects of the propaganda campaign, since he already presumed it to have gained some useful Intelligence and even to have forced the enemy to postpone their operation from April to June.[180] After some days of the battle there were indeed signs that Padua's leaflets had got through to the enemy. Ojetti asserted that almost all prisoners had read them and exclaimed to his wife, 'my thirty million manifestos have achieved miracles!'[181] The reality as usual was more modest: we know that 200 Romanians who were captured on the Montello hill had never heard of Allied propaganda. But there seems no reason to doubt Ojetti's claim that on one day 800 leaflets had been found upon 350 prisoners. Jambrišak had a similar experience when he visited Yugoslav prisoners and discovered that most of them possessed leaflets, including some which had been distributed a few weeks earlier over Ljubljana.[182] The most that can be inferred from this is that Italy's manifestos may have helped some soldiers to feel that surrender during the offensive was a viable option. Some of the leaflets which they clutched may have been those issued specially on the eve of offensive by Italian Intelligence precisely in order to assure them that they could pass safely into Italian lines.[183] Padua believed that this had happened. It seemed to be proven by the large number of prisoners taken – almost 22 000 from mid-June to mid-July – and the fact that 6000 of these were of 'Yugoslav' nationality.

Thus most of the propagandists' claims had some degree of truth, even if they tended to make unsubstantiated links between their campaign and any sign of national unrest in the enemy war zone. One link which did exist was in the field of sabotage behind enemy lines. Crewe House suggested that Czechs had been responsible for blowing up munition dumps in the rear during the offensive.[184] The limited information which can be put together on this subject confirms that Italian Intelligence began in early June to use Czech and Croat deserters as agents behind enemy lines. It was a new way to employ disaffected Slavs against the enemy, and one which Marchetti in particular would perfect over the summer months. In early June, both Finzi and Marchetti began to train a small number of reliable individuals for these risky ventures, but whereas Marchetti's group got no further than training, some of Finzi's saboteurs were sent into enemy territory before the June offensive.[185]

A first attempt was made by two Czechs, Karel Mlejnek (one of Pivko's colleagues) and Artur Žák, but it was unsuccessful because of vigilant Austrian sentries. Equipped with explosives, poison and forged documents, the two agents were supposed to have crossed the lines in the Brenta valley and proceeded into Val Sugana to destroy munition dumps. In their place Pivko chose a young Croat, Florijan Babec, who on 13 June posed as an escaped prisoner and successfully arrived in the Austrian positions at Asiago. His task was to carry out the sabotage and then to proceed to Croatia where he would hand over to 'nationalist deserters' a coded report which was concealed in his prayer book. Whether he succeeded is unknown.[186] It is more likely that those who succeeded and from whom Crewe House took the credit were a third group of Finzi's agents. Eight of them were sent over at the same time as Babec (indeed Babec may have been part of their group) with the purpose of destroying targets identified by Finzi. In the next ten days, Italian Intelligence recorded two incidents of munition deposits exploding in the rear, one on 22 June at Tezze which involved 160 000 shells. On 3 July two of the agents crept back across the front line into British positions. They reported their adventure, how they had made their way to the rear, challenged only once by a guard who had accepted the validity of their documents. Once in Val Sugana they had planted their bombs at Tezze and then proceeded westwards to Levico where they counted a dozen aeroplanes. Some of them had then decided, as Finzi had suggested, to stay behind and try to reach their families, while two agents returned back to the Asiago plateau and after waiting three nights in the undergrowth managed to pass across no-man's-land to the British trenches.[187]

This exploit had been a valuable experience which Italian Intelligence would build upon, but it could only indirectly be described as a triumph of the Allies' propaganda campaign. Crewe House implied erroneously that the sabotage had been the work of Czechs who were still members of the Austrian army. It tied in rather well with their view that the offensive had witnessed major examples of insubordination in the Austrian forces: that a Czech company had tried to desert en masse or that a fervently Yugoslav commander had succeeded in bringing his whole company over to Italy.[188] What was the truth in these rumours? Certainly, as we have seen, the offensive provided an opportunity for seemingly reliable Austrian troops to be captured easily by the Italians. Others, if they had not specifically refused to go into the front line, had revolted passively. One Austrian corps command, for instance, discovered that in the first two days of the offensive most units were reporting a startling deficit of 75–80 per cent of their manpower due to shirkers who had rejoined their units only when the 'coast was clearer'.[189] Yet there appear to have been few cases of mass desertion to the enemy. According to Delmé-Radcliffe, writing on 21 June:

> There have been indications of the desire of bodies of troops and individuals to come over, but hitherto the action taken by us has failed to produce practical results on a large scale. As a whole the enemy troops on the Piave and Montello especially, are fighting with great determination. If the Austrian army continues to fail in obtaining successes, desertions on a large scale may be expected, perhaps also open mutinies.[190]

Coming from a 'Czech enthusiast' like Radcliffe, such an idea was overoptimistic. The offensive showed in fact that, despite the Austro-Hungarian army's growing material and ideological crisis, it was still welded together by its officers and by the large number of soldiers who were ready to fulfil their duties. Those involved in Italy's propaganda campaign exaggerated the potential for unrest in June 1918 just as they boasted about the fruits of their labours after only a few months of the campaign. Thus Steed was quick to point out that a mass revolt by 'Yugoslav' troops had only been prevented because of Sonnino's anti-Yugoslav stance at Versailles in early June; but for that, 'the Piave battle would probably have ended in a complete Austro-Hungarian disaster and the war would have been shortened by some months'.[191] With this idea, Steed, of course, presumed that most soldiers of southern Slav nationality were 'nationally conscious'. He also presumed too much of the power of Allied manifestos. Polish prisoners who were interrogated by the Italians, for example, were found to have little knowledge of Allied propaganda or even of the Versailles Declaration in favour of Polish independence.[192]

Front propaganda therefore had so far only had a moderate impact. Its significance lay in what the Italian and Austrian military *thought* it had achieved or could achieve, rather than what it had actually contributed to the Piave *débâcle*. As a final balance to some of the propagandists' own extreme claims it is worth quoting a perceptive analysis drawn up by British military Intelligence on the state of the enemy after the battle:

> From the large number of prisoners and deserters who have been examined, and from the letters, diaries and army orders which have been captured during the last offensive it is evident that except in some isolated instances Allied propaganda is not having the immediate effect which had been hoped for. It has not stimulated desertion to any extent; it cannot be said to have had any great influence on the morale of the troops. The reason for this is that a large number of Austro-Hungarian soldiers whom it is desired to influence are ill-educated and apathetic, they do not know much about the causes of the war and do not care much about its consequences. They are all tired of fighting and long to have done with it, but the path of least resistance is to take things as they find them and to obey orders. The tradition of the army is a force not altogether spent and there is undoubtedly a feeling that, after all, the Habsburg Empire, whatever may be thought of it, is an institution which has lasted so long that it must have some good points; and that as long as rations are enough to support life and conditions not too intolerable, desertion, disgrace and loss of citizenship are hardly worthwhile.[193]

Yet from the experience of June 1918 it was indeed the supposed benefits of psychological warfare which convinced the Italian CS that their propaganda campaign should be intensified. The opposite was true for the AOK. The Austrians were suddenly confronted with the fact that their campaign had not been as effective as they assumed. They decided immediately to shelve their own efforts and end the propaganda duel; only in the last month of the war would it be revived. In the weeks before the June offensive, the duel had been at its height. On 26 April at a meeting to discuss front propaganda, the AOK had decided to intensify its efforts during the month before the attack.[194] This was to mean an increase in the number of leaflets distributed by plane, rocket and patrol. Direct fraternization with the enemy, which the Austrian military had always viewed as the most efficient way to wield the weapon, was now to cease in view of Italian counter-measures, in view of the need to keep Austria's plans secret, and because such work necessitated exceptionally reliable propaganda personnel.[195] Instead, personal traffic with the enemy was to be limited to handing over manifestos. The work would be fully supported by troop commanders who should dispel any idea that propaganda activity was 'unfair' and ensure that its personnel received the full cooperation of the Intelligence Service and conventional forces. As for the content of manifestos, the AOK issued new guidelines which differed little in substance from those circulated earlier in the year.[196] The spring in the tail was that during the offensive a mass distribution would continue, assuring the Italians that it was an 'offensive of peace', while after the offensive's 'successful conclusion' the enemy would immediately be bombarded with proclamations which called for 'peace in 1918'.[197] Thus propaganda would help to make the offensive a success, but must then be prepared to follow up that success with powerful arguments.

In keeping with Baden's instructions, in May the army commands significantly increased their propaganda output. KISA, for example, which had distributed 98 500 leaflets in March and 150 000 in April, sent out about 500 000 in May.[198] Distribution continued to pose some problems. The Allies were now masters of the air, some Austrian divisions still possessed no propaganda personnel,[199] and in the plains KISA and the 6AK continued to find the Piave an obstacle which could only be surmounted at low-water level. But despite this, and despite increasing signs that the Italians were no longer as responsive as previously, the AOK appear to have believed that the fruit of its campaign was beginning to ripen. After all, in May the number of Italian deserters increased and some of the deposited material was still being picked up; in a few places the local commanders even permitted some fraternization with the Italians.[200] Elsewhere it was taken as a positive sign that the enemy was more alert and nervous and had increased his 'counter-propaganda' in response to Austrian efforts. The AOK, therefore, like its Italian counterparts, expected that its campaign would facilitate success in the June offensive, and publicly the Austrians prophesied a second Caporetto. On 11 June Arz's deputy, Alfred von Waldstätten, sent Conrad a propaganda map for duplication during the attack; it showed how far Austrian troops had advanced into Italian territory.[201]

The fact that Austria-Hungary's propaganda campaign was a failure only became clear during the offensive itself. It was not just that the Italian lines stood relatively firm. Of 26 000 Italian soldiers taken prisoner by the Isonzo army, only three possessed Austrian manifestos.[202] Moreover, in a survey of a sample 5000 Italians taken prisoner, it was found that while 376 had read some Austrian propaganda and 707 had seen but not read it, 3917 had no knowledge of it whatsoever. As in the Austrian ranks the high degree of illiteracy among Italian soldiers had undoubtedly proved to be an obstacle; of the 5000 examined, 1546 could not read or write. But the survey also showed that the Italian military since the spring had managed very successfully to counter Austria's campaign, both by intervening to seize propaganda material and by presenting effective defensive arguments to their own men. One powerful argument was the Italian material situation which at the front had greatly improved since Caporetto. Another was to instil a conviction that, since the Austrians were ill-treating civilians in Venetia, it was vital to reconquer the occupied province and destroy the Monarchy. Many of the Italians captured seemed to be confident that with American help this could be achieved, and rather than being depressed or even affected by Austria's campaign they simply viewed it as a sign of the enemy's own war-weariness.[203]

The AOK reacted quickly to the knowledge that the results of the campaign in no way corresponded to its efforts (over three million leaflets). On 5 July, blaming its failure on Italian vigilance and counter-propaganda, Baden advised the army commanders 'in the future to continue propaganda on a more limited scale with the aim of combatting enemy propaganda'.[204] The army commands totally agreed. KISA replied that, in spite of distributing over a million leaflets since January, 'the effect of our propaganda on the enemy is not noticeable. The Italian soldier is under too strict a control, while the Italian officer is reliable and too nationally disposed for peace propaganda to be able to take firm roots at the front.' If the campaign had had no success prior to the offensive it would have even less now and 'would on the contrary only provoke and advance even more Italy's defensive propaganda'.[205] The 6AK, similarly, felt that because of strict discipline and good food in the trenches, and the absence of a strong revolutionary movement in the Italian hinterland, Austrian propaganda could not be expected to reap any benefits.[206] The 11AK went even further, advising that any recommencement of Austria's campaign in the foreseeable future would be 'completely pointless'. In analyzing why the campaign had failed, the 11AK reasoned with hindsight that the most favourable moment for intensive propaganda against Italy had been immediately after Caporetto, but it had been neglected and in the 11th army sector had only been organized in late January: 'then it was already too late. The fighting spirit of the Italian soldier had already recovered from the blows of our offensive, the units were already organized, disciplined and firmly in the hands of their superiors.' Just when Austria's campaign had been starting to have some success, the enemy officers had managed to thwart it.[207]

In retrospect some might argue that the Austrians had been defeatist in effectively halting their campaign in early July.[208] At the time all were in agreement. Henceforth there was to be only small-scale leaflet distribution, so as to keep up some pressure on the enemy, but the main aim would be to defend Austro-Hungarian morale against Italy's poisonous efforts. After all, the Italian military had set a good example of how important defensive measures could be against hostile propaganda. Thus it was that the June offensive, which was a permanent blow to the Habsburg forces' morale, was also a significant turning-point in the competing propaganda campaigns of 1918. After the offensive, the Austrians placed themselves on the defensive with regard to psychological warfare. The propaganda duel was at an end, or at least for the AOK, any continuation had been shelved until the military situation changed again in the Monarchy's favour.

## Notes

1. Edmund von Glaise-Horstenau, *The Collapse of the Austro-Hungarian Empire* (London and Toronto, 1930) p. 123.
2. The most thorough account is Richard Plaschka, Horst Haselsteiner and Arnold Suppan, *Innere Front. Militärassistenz, Widerstand und Umsturz in der Donaumonarchie 1918*, 2 vols (Vienna, 1974) I, pp. 59ff.
3. KA, EvB 1918, Fasz.5743/2790, Arz to Na.Abt, Pers.Geh.Nr 11, 26 January 1918.
4. Ibid., Fasz.5743/4041, Stöger-Steiner to AOK, Präs. Nr 672, 8 February; Plaschka, Haselsteiner, Suppan, *Innere Front*, I, pp. 260–1.
5. KA, EvB, Fasz.5742/1707, Militärkanzlei im Kriegsministerium [successor to KÜA] to EvB, Nr 9922, 12 January; Fasz.5743/2792, AOK to all military commands, 13 February 1918.
6. For a collection of such material, see KA, EvB, Fasz.5745/7417.
7. KA, EvB, Fasz.5743/2792 and 5745/6649. The *Times* report was sent into the AOK by the 10th army on 20 January.
8. KA, EvB, Fasz.5742/1935 (Copy also in HIL, Hadifelügyeleti Bizottság [HFB], Fasz.4470, Nr 777); Ronge, *Kriegs- und Industriespionage*, p. 341.
9. Ibid., p. 340. See also HIL, Honvéd Minisztérium [HM] 1918, Fasz.537(B), Nr 4102, Arz to Szurmay, Op.Nr 49946, 15 February 1918.
10. Erich Feigl, *Kaiserin Zita. Legende und Wahrheit* (Vienna and Munich, 1977) p. 336.
11. *Pester Lloyd*, 18 February (Abend). Cf. the *Neue Freie Presse* which gave news of Northcliffe's appointment no prominence: Nr 19213, 19 February 1918 (Morgenblatt), p. 6.
12. *Stenographische Protokolle*, III, 70.Sitzung, 7 March 1918, p. 3544: speech in response to an interpellation by Wilhelm Miklas and others on 22 February (ibid., p. 3269).
13. KA, EvB, Fasz.5744/4899, report and minutes by Hptm Novak, 21 February 1918.
14. KA, EvB, Fasz.5747/9459, Ronge to various military authorities, 5 April 1918.
15. KA, Feindespropaganda-Abwehrstelle [FAst], Fasz.5994, Res.86, EvB to FAst, Nr 10683, 3 May 1918.
16. Andrea Torre and G.A. Borgese were mentioned.
17. 'Northcliffes bezahltes Propagandameeting', *Bosnische Post* (Sarajevo), 11 April; 'Trumbićeva Jugoslavija', *Hrvatska* (Zagreb), broj 2021, 13 April. See also *Glas Slovenaca Hrvata i Srba*, broj 113, 10 June 1918.
18. KA, EvB, Fasz.5751/14973, EvB to various military authorities, 25 May 1918: 'Anglo-Amerikanische Propaganda'.
19. Ibid., Fasz. 5756/22824, Protocol of meeting on 18 July (Ronge with Intelligence officers from Bohemia and northern Hungary).
20. See, for example, ibid., Fasz.5758/25618, MilKmdo Pozsony [Bratislava] Gstbs Abt to EvB, Gstb Nr 974/Na, 20 August 1918.
21. Ibid., Fasz.5755/21672, Philipp Gaiger (journalist) to EvB, 18 July 1918.
22. For the Swiss border, see KA, Zensurstelle Feldkirch, Fasz.5952, Polizeiliche Nachrichten 70, MJ12 144 – Statth.Präs.3589; Polizeiliche Nachrichten 71, MilKmdo Innsbruck 3721 res – Statth.Präs.15/805. Some hints of the reality can be gleaned from E. Voska and W. Irwin, *Spy and Counterspy: The Autobiography of a Master Spy* (London, 1941) pp. 223ff, although in general Voska's account is also littered with inaccuracy. For the eastern borders, see HIL, M.V.in Rumänien: k.u.k. Sektion bei der politischen Polizei OKR, Fasz.13, Na Nr 4275/18, 'Bericht über Entente Agitation und Propaganda in der Moldau und in Bessarabien', 23 August 1918; KA, EvB, Fasz.5757/

24357, Na Lemberg to EvB, Na Nr 4800 res, 8 August (report for July 1918); and ibid., Fasz.5756/23557 and Fasz.5758/25212, Beilage 4.

23. Janko Pleterski, *Prvo Opredeljenje Slovenaca za Jugoslaviju* (Belgrade, 1976) p. 402.
24. Stephen Burián von Rajecz, *Austria in Dissolution* (London, 1925) pp. 451–2; Feigl, *Kaiserin Zita*, p. 336.
25. *Tribune de Genève*, quoted in KA, 11AK Gstbs Abt 1918, Fasz.449, Pr.2350: KPQ report on 'propaganda activity', July 1918, pp. 5–6.
26. KA, EvB, Fasz.5759/28977, Military attaché The Hague to Na.Abt AOK, Res 530/17, 3 September 1918.
27. KA, 11AK Gstbs Abt 1918, Fasz.264, Op.Nr 1400/18, 55ID Kmdo to I KK, Na Nr 180, 22 May 1918, referring to the period 22 April–22 May. Of these, about 800 publicized the Czechoslovak army, 900 appealed to the South Slavs not to fight for Germany, and 1300 called on all soldiers to desert.
28. KA, 11AK, Fasz.449, Pr.2252, 2303 (I KK).
29. KA, 11AK Op.Abt 1918, Fasz.446, Na Nr 1106, 10AK propaganda report, June 1918.
30. The general context of Sarkotić's views is discussed in Cornwall, 'The Experience of Yugoslav Agitation in Austria-Hungary 1917–1918'. See also particularly Sarkotić's reports in AHZ, Sarkotić MSS, Sarkotić to AOK, Op.Nr 751, 12 February; KA, EvB, Fasz.5751/15181/18, Sarkotić to AOK Na Abt, Op.Nr 2669, 18 May 1918. For the leaflets sent out by the Cattaro mutineers, see above Chapter 5, p. 153.
31. Manifesto 17, 'Jugosloveni! Draga braćo Srbi, Hrvati i Slovenci!' (KA, EvB, Fasz.5756/22782 and 5752/16897/6). The word 'Mitteleurope' is in the original Croat text.
32. Manifesto 16, 'Hrvati, Srbi i Slovenci!'. Jambrišak had in fact been concerned about having his name publicized in enemy territory: see AJA, JO 35/252, Jambrišak to Banjanin, 7 June 1918.
33. For the reception, see KA, EvB, Fasz.5756/22782; AJA, JO 35/247, Jambrišak notes; and for copies of the photographs, PRO, AIR 1/2127/207/80, no. 7. Ojetti gives his reaction in *La Propaganda sul Nemico*, p. 130.
34. Quoted in 'Die Luftpostbriefe des Dr Trumbić', *Reichspost*, Nr 276, 19 June 1918 (p. 4). See also 'Proglasi Dra Trumbića', in the radical *Glas Slovenaca Hrvata i Srba* which quoted extracts from the leaflets: broj 123, 21 June (p. 1).
35. Pleterski, *Prvo Opredeljenje*, pp. 253–4. For the context of Korošec's behaviour, see Cornwall, 'The Experience of Yugoslav Agitation'.
36. The AOK felt that Tavčar's own behaviour was opportunistic, carefully calculated so that he would not forfeit his influence either with the radicals or with the government: see KA, AOK Op.Abt 1918, Fasz.376, Nr 112303, 20 September 1918.
37. BL, Northcliffe MSS, vol.X, Add.Mss 62162, minutes of the 6th EPD Committee meeting, 9 July 1918. Pivko also recalls that Šušteršić's moves were known to Italian Intelligence (see *Val Bella*, p. 78).
38. For example, KA, EvB, Nrs 16895, 17003, 18306, 19447, 21352, 23510, 24959, 27664, 28248, 31651, 32552, 23749 (Lublin: manifesto 55), 33024 (Bratislava: manifesto 89), 33993 (Graz: manifesto 252).
39. KA, EvB, Fasz.5760/31223, NaSt.MilKmdo Nagyszeben to EvB, Na Nr 8478 res, 2 October 1918. The newssheet was manifestos 44/45/46/49.
40. Ibid., Fasz.5757/24326, Arz to various military authorities, 24 August 1918. For Bolshevik or Russian leaflets (most of which emanated from Ukraine) see EvB Nrs 17217, 17625, 18560, 18735, 22471, 23681, 24258, 24779, 26128, 26715, 28147, 31840. For manifestos of the POW (Polska Organizacja Wojskowa), see EvB Nrs 2340, 23510 (pp. 10, 41, 46), 24131, 24156, 26107.

41. Ibid., Fasz.5759/28207, MilKmdo Prague Gstbs Abt to EvB, Na Nr 1454, 8 September 1918.
42. Ibid., Fasz.5744/5125/I, Protocol of Ronge's discussions with leaders of the Intelligence service, 21–2 May 1918; Ronge, *Kriegs- und Industriespionage*, pp. 346–7.
43. KA, 11AK Gstbs Abt, Fasz.272, 4–6/2, 11AK to corps, Op.Nr 1423, 2 March 1918; Arz, *Zur Geschichte des Grossen Krieges*, p. 135.
44. KA, EvB, Fasz.5742/2477; Fasz.5743/3584 (the idea of a mass search, which took place also in military units in the hinterland on 15 March, seems to have originated with the Hungarian Minister of the Interior); Fasz.5749/11092, Arz to various military authorities, 27 May 1918.
45. Ronge, *Kriegs- und Industriespionage*, pp. 327–31. See also KA, AOK Op.Abt 1918, Fasz.376, Nr 112226, Beilage 3: 'Heimkehrer-Standesbewegung'; and for the May rebellions, Plaschka *et al.*, *Innere Front*, I, pp. 324ff. The Padua Commission only picked up a few details of the revolts from a Bavarian newspaper, and it could arguably have exploited them more fully: see, for example, manifesto 74, *Jugoslavia* no. 4; manifesto 114, *Neamul Românesc* no. 5 (KA, 11AK Fasz.451 'Flugzettel I').
46. KA, EvB, Fasz.5743/4041, Stöger-Steiner to AOK Na.Abt, Präs.Nr 672, 8 February 1918.
47. Richard Plaschka, 'Contradicting Ideologies: the Pressure of Ideological Conflicts in the Austro-Hungarian Army of World War I', in R.A. Kann, B.K. Király and P.S. Fichtner (eds), *The Habsburg Empire in World War I* (New York, 1977) pp. 108–11.
48. KA, 11AK 1918, Fasz.449, Pr.2145, 11AK Op.Nr 1766, 25 March 1918: 'Maßnahmen gegen ital. Propaganda'.
49. Ibid., Fasz.448, Pr.2087, AOK to 11AK, Op.Nr 140286, 23 February; Pr.2099, AOK to 11AK, Op.Nr 140566, 7 March 1918, enclosing first editions of *Heimat*.
50. KA, FAst 1918, Fasz.5994, Res.80, Waldstätten to AOK Op.Abt, 8 May 1918.
51. By June *Heimat* had 1020 private subscribers, *Üzenet* 480 and *Domov* only 340 (KA, HGK Conrad, Fasz.66, Na 400a/395). This was somewhat offset by the large number of copies which were sent out direct to the military commands: by late June, 30 000 copies of each edition of *Heimat* and *Üzenet* were being dispatched and 15 000 copies of *Domov* (KA, FAst, Fasz.5998, Res.705/2). For details of the free editions sent out from September, see ibid., Fasz.5997, Res.569. Cf. the phenomenon of unofficial 'trench journalism' in the French army: Stéphane Audoin-Rouzeau, *Men at War 1914–1918: National Sentiment and Trench Journalism in France during the First World War* (Providence and Oxford, 1992).
52. Later, Glaise-Horstenau, who was involved with the new body, specifically mentioned the German example: OULK, VII, p. 99. See Max Ronge's reports on the Germans' organization which was subject to their KPQ and the Prussian War Ministry: KA, FAst 1918, Fasz.5994, Res.40, Ronge to Waldstätten, EvB Nr 7241, 21 March; Res.101, Ronge to KPQ, EvB Nr 11279, 29 April. In the latter report, he extolled the virtues of cinema for propaganda purposes, but Eisner-Bubna, head of KPQ, commented that regrettably the Monarchy did not have enough modern equipment available to match the Germans.
53. For some recent thoughts on Germany's failure in the field of patriotic instruction, see Wilhelm Deist, 'The German Army, the Authoritarian Nation-State and Total War', in John Horne (ed.), *State, Society and Mobilization in Europe during the First World War* (Cambridge, 1997) pp. 168ff.
54. KA, EvB, Fasz.5745/6187, KPQ P.Nr 4400, January report on 'propaganda activity'.
55. See, for example, KA, KISA Gstbs Abt 1918, Fasz.4, Op.Nr 770, Obst Pitreich to KISA, Op.Nr 306/1, 17 February; KA, HGK Conrad, Fasz.66, Na Nr 400a/59, AOK to

Conrad, Boroević, etc., Op.Nr 766/34, 12 February; ibid., Na Nr 400a/82, Boroević to Conrad, Op.Nr 300/416, 28 February (enclosing two articles from the *Corriere della Sera*).

56. KA, FAst, Fasz.5994, Res.14a, Petrović to 'Anton', 23 January 1918 (enclosing order of GM Viktor von Severus, and seven pages of 'suggestions for patriotic instruction').
57. Ibid., Res.18, Arz Op.Geh.Nr 1219, 'Aufklärungsarbeit in der Wehrmacht', 14 March 1918.
58. Ibid., Res.13, KPQ to FAst, Adj.Nr 11612, minutes of meeting held on 20 March 1918.
59. Ibid., Res.25, 30 and 35. Kraus's pun was actually on the words *chlorreichen* ('rich in chlorine') and *erfolgreich* ('successful'), but my translation captures the essential wit more accurately. See Timms, *Karl Kraus*, p. 355.
60. KA, FAst, Fasz.6003, AOK zu Op.Nr 141676: 'Richtlinien für vaterländischen Unterricht und Abwehr des Feindespropaganda'.
61. Ibid., Fasz.5994, Res.18.
62. See Edmund von Glaise-Horstenau, *Ein General im Zwielicht*, ed. Peter Broucek, 3 vols (Vienna, 1980–8) I, p. 497.
63. KA, FAst, Fasz.5994, Res.46, Werkmann to FAst, 21 April 1918.
64. Ibid., Fasz.5995, Res.278/I, *Vaterländische Bildungsarbeit, Mitteilungen der FAst*, Nr 1, 10 July 1918, pp. 4–6, 8–9. FAst and KPQ representatives met together on 25 May to discuss cooperation (Fasz.5994, Res.121).
65. Ibid., Fasz.5994, Res.267, MGG/S to FAst, Präs.Nr 22678, 6 July 1918. For details of the mutiny of IR71, caused largely by disgruntled homecomers, see Plaschka *et al.*, *Innere Front*, I, pp. 385–400.
66. Ibid., Res.273/8, MilKmdo Kraków to FAst, Präs.Nr 5942/FA, 29 July 1918.
67. Ibid., Fasz.5994, Res.124, Hptm Franz Zeidner to FAst, 28 May and 6 June 1918.
68. Ibid., Res.8a, HGK Conrad Na.Abt to AOK Op.Abt, Na Nr 400a/81, 'Aufklärende Propaganda', 9 March 1918. Here it was suggested that such information should be discussed in Slav editions of *Heimat*.
69. Ibid., Fasz.5995, Res.273/6, 42HID (Oberlt Juraj Šušnjak) to XIII KK, 20 June 1918.
70. Ibid., Fasz.5994, Res.22, 59, 105; Res.212, Waldstätten to AOK Op.Abt, 25 June 1918. For FA instructions about the railways, see Res.39/1 and 170; and for responses to requests from Sarkotić and the 11AK: Res.170/1 and 170/2. For displeasure at the information courses, see Res.214, where Major Franz Hočevar complained to the FAst that his three-week visit to Vienna from Zagreb had cost him 124 Kronen since only one meal was provided on the course.
71. Ibid., Fasz.5997, Res.513. Only in October 1918 was a 'translation group' established at the KPQ to service both the AOK and FAst (Fasz.5998, Res.853).
72. Ibid., Fasz.5994, Res.155, FAst to AOK Op.Abt, Tätigkeitsbericht, 11 June 1918.
73. Ibid., Res.187/3, 245, 263.
74. Ibid., Res.263, Gablenz to Waldstätten, 1 July 1918.
75. OULK, VII, pp. 94, 99.
76. See Miklós Komjáthy (ed.), *Protokolle des Gemeinsamen Ministerrates der Österreichisch-Ungarischen Monarchie 1914–1918* (Budapest, 1966) pp. 593, 605ff: meetings of the Council on 24 September and 28 October 1917, which illustrate well the clash of views among the authorities. Landwehr's memoirs, *Hunger. Die Erschöpfungsjahre der Mittelmächte 1917–18* (Zurich, Leipzig and Vienna, 1931) are essential to understand the options available (see pp. 142–8).
77. KA, MKSM 1918, 25–1/9, AOK Q.Nr 119083, Beilage 3: 'Darstellungen der materiellen Lage der Armee im Felde'; Arz, *Zur Geschichte*, p. 195.

78. Requisitioning in Hungary is well described in Plaschka *et al.*, *Innere Front*, I, pp. 209–31; Landwehr, *Hunger*, pp. 150ff, 176ff.
79. Ottokar Czernin, *Im Weltkriege* (Berlin and Vienna, 1919) p. 345.
80. On Austrian problems in Ukraine, see Alfred Krauss and Franz Klingenbrunner, 'Die Besetzung der Ukraine 1918', in Hugo Kerchnawe (ed.), *Die Militärverwaltung in den von den österreichisch-ungarischen Truppen besetzten Gebieten* (Vienna, 1928); and Wolfdieter Bihl, *Österreich-Ungarn und die Friedenschlüsse von Brest-Litovsk* (Vienna, Cologne and Graz, 1970) pp. 120ff.
81. Josef Redlich, *Schicksalsjahre Österreichs 1908–1919. Das politische Tagebuch Josef Redlichs*, ed. Fritz Fellner, 2 vols (Graz and Cologne, 1953–4) I, p. 263.
82. Landwehr, *Hunger*, pp. 189ff.
83. See ibid., pp. 201, 229ff; HHStA, PA I/505, Liasse XLVII/3/24, Karl to Wilhelm II, June 1918.
84. AHZ, Sarkotić MSS, Archduke Eugen to Sarkotić, 30 December 1917.
85. See Hermann Leidl, 'Die Verwaltung des besetzten Gebietes Italiens, November 1917 bis Oktober 1918', in Kerchnawe (ed.), *Die Militärverwaltung*, pp. 342–5. The grape harvest in 1918 was disappointing and over half the cultivatable land was given over to maize which could not be harvested until October.
86. KA, KISA Gstbs Abt 1918 Op.Akten, Fasz.6, Op.Nr 2034, KISA Q.Op.Nr 15600/V.A., Zusammenfassender Darstellung, 14 March 1918.
87. For conditions for the 10ID, see the reports in: ibid., Fasz.2, Op.Nr 444 and Fasz.3, Op.Nr 571. In March the number who reported sick in the KISA zone as a whole rose from 9436 to 12 868, most of whom had bronchial catarrh or stomach/bowel afflictions (Fasz.5, Op.Nr 982).
88. Ibid., Fasz.4, Op.Nr 768, Boroević to Arz, t.Op.Nr 379, 17 February (quoted also in OULK, VII, pp. 184–5).
89. KA, KISA, Fasz.4, Op.Nr 891, HGK Boroević to AOK, Nr 5764/Mat., 28 February 1918.
90. OULK, VII, p. 202. See also KA, 6AK 1918 Qu.Abt, Fasz.1, Nr 39, Boroević to 6AK, Op.Nr 1100/98, 20 May 1918.
91. KA, HGK Conrad, Fasz.13, 10AK Qu.Abt to Conrad, t.Nr 2450, 13 January; ibid., Conrad to AOK Qu.Abt, t.Nr 1663, 14 January 1918.
92. KA, FAst, Fasz.5994, Res.113, Krobatin to AOK, Op.Nr 3346, 16 April, enclosing letter: Korporal Wasyl to Lynda Pazia, 27 March 1918. At the FAst, it was noted that Petrović might use this material in one of his lectures.
93. KA, HGK Conrad, Fasz.13, 12–51/2–6, Scheuchenstuel to Conrad, t.Op.Nr 585, 16 January; ibid., 12–51/2–10, Scheuchenstuel to Conrad, t.Nr 5167, 29 January 1918.
94. Ibid., 12–51/1–4, Conrad to AOK Qu.Abt, t.Nr 1663, 14 January 1918.
95. Peter Fiala, *Die letzte Offensive Altösterreichs. Führungsprobleme und Führerverantwortlichkeit bei der öst.-ung. Offensive in Venetien, Juni 1918* (Boppard am Rhein, 1967) p. 82.
96. KA, 11AK, Fasz.269, 1–17/15–7/30, Op.Nr 2500/30, GM Vidale to VI KK, Res.2158, 13 June 1918. Of 950 horses expected by the division in late May, only 150 had arrived.
97. OULK, VII, p. 203.
98. KA, FAst, Fasz.5994, Res.6, Waldstätten to Arz, 23 March 1918.
99. Ibid., Fasz.6003, 'Vaterländischer Unterricht Heft Nr 1 – Einleitungsvortrag zum 1.Informationskurs, von Oberst Egon Frh. von Waldstätten', p. 6.
100. Gustav Spann, *Zensur in Österreich während des 1.Weltkrieges 1914–1918*, Ph.Diss. (Vienna, 1972) pp. 220–1; Ronge, *Kriegs- und Industriespionage*, pp. 285–6.

101. On 15 August 1917, when Eisner-Bubna (head of KPQ) had met representatives of the KÜA and the HFB to discuss censorship, he had divided news items simply into these two categories: Spann, *Zensur*, p. 219.
102. Ibid., pp. 71ff, 76ff.
103. See, for example, the comments of the military attaché in Switzerland: KA, FAst, Fasz.5994, Res.130, 16 May 1918; and the FAst's own conclusions about the domestic press on 11 June (ibid., Res.155, Beilage 11), that it conducted 'not exactly a beneficial activity'[!].
104. Ibid., Res.89, Alfred von Waldstätten to FAst, Op.Nr 766/107, 10 May: section III, 'Mittel zur Bekämpfung der fdl. Propaganda'.
105. See ibid., Res.103, AOK to FAst, Op.Nr 766/136, 16 May 1918 (eight of the daily press extracts are enclosed).
106. Ibid., Res.159, Arz to FAst, AOK Op.Nr 143027/II, 11 June. See also comments by the FAst: Res.211, FAst to Arz, 24 June, enclosing further newspaper extracts to illustrate the deficiencies of the censor.
107. By October 1918, for example, *Hrvatska Država, Právo Lidu, Illustrowany Kurjer Codzienny, Innsbrucker Volkszeitung* and others had been added to the list, while some (*Slovenec, Világ*) had been dropped because of 'loyal' behaviour: ibid., Fasz.5998, Res.754.
108. See, for example, Spann, *Zensur*, p. 371.
109. See Cornwall, 'The Experience of Yugoslav Agitation in Austria-Hungary 1917–1918', pp. 664–6.
110. KA, FAst, Fasz.5994, Res.64, Rudolf Peerz to Waldstätten, 26 April; Res.228: Peerz's proposal for a FAst in the Ministry of the Interior.
111. See ibid., Res.143, 11AK to Conrad, Op.Nr 1766/3, 4 May; Res.262, 'Studie über Innenpropaganda-Organisation' by Hptm Josef Weber (11AK); Fasz.5995, Res.273/8, MilKmdo Kraków to FAst, Präs.Nr 5942, 29 July 1918.
112. Ibid., Res.85, EvB to FAst, Nr.12892, 7 May 1918, enclosing study by Hptm Otto Wittmayer for an *Österreichischer Völkerverein*.
113. A number of historians have highlighted this event. See, for example, Karel Pichlík, 'Der militärische Zusammenbruch der Mittelmächte im Jahre 1918', in R. Plaschka and K. Mack (eds), *Die Auflösung des Habsburgerreiches. Zusammenbruch und Neuorientierung im Donauraum* (Munich, 1970) p. 260.
114. Richard Spence, 'The Yugoslav Role in the Austro-Hungarian Army, 1914–1918', in B. Király and N. Dreisziger (eds), *East Central European Society in World War I* (New York, 1985) p. 360.
115. HIL, 42HID, Fasz.1659, Report by Hptm Rupnik, 30 January 1918.
116. KA, AOK Op.Abt 1918, Fasz.377, Op.Nr 112745, 42HID to VI KK, Op.Nr 4520/5, 21 April 1918. In February, for example, 24 Croats who were due at the front having attended a machine-gun school in Požega managed to escape from the transport taking them from Požega to Zagreb (HIL, 42HID, Fasz.1660, Op.Nr 4327).
117. The usual official Austro-Hungarian terminology when describing Italy.
118. Ibid., Op.Nr 4329, GM Mihaljević, special divisional order no. 5 [in Croat], 9 February 1918.
119. The following discussion is largely based on the 42HID records in HIL, Fasz.1659–67. See also KA, 11AK Gstbs Abt, Fasz.270, Op.Nr 2847/2 Soretić to 11AK, Op.Nr 4806/7, 9 July 1918.
120. KA, 11AK Gstbs Abt, Fasz.449, Pr.2222, Rittmeister Ernst Hackl to 11AK, 6 May, with minutes by Mihaljević and Frydman; Pr.2232; Pr.2242, XIII KK to 11AK,

t.Op.Nr 450/3, 27 May 1918: 500 copies of nine different manifestos had been deposited in May.

121. AHZ, 42 Domobranska pješadijska divizija (1916–1918) [42HID records], 482/Fasc.2, Verzeichnis über Deserteure.

122. Five boxes of Belošević's papers are in the Croatian State Archives (AHZ, no. 789), but they largely discuss the Carzano plot and were used by Belošević in his article, 'Uloga Ljudevita Pivka u talijanskom napadu kod Karcanca 17.Septembra 1917. godine', *Vojnoistorijski Glasnik*, 20 (1969), pp. 231–40.

123. Pivko, *Val Bella*, pp. 23–8. In late June 1918, the radical paper *Hrvatska Država* would publish a statement by Jewish university students in favour of Yugoslav unification.

124. See HIL, 42HID, Fasz.1659, Rupnik report, 30 January 1918. A *Sturmbatallion* had been created in every division in February 1917. Details of the 42nd *Sturm* course in April 1918 are to be found in AHZ, 42HID, Fasc.2.

125. Pivko, *Informatorji*, p. 100; Pivko, *Val Bella*, p. 23; KA, AOK Op.Abt 1918, Fasz.377, Op.Nr 112745, Soretić to XIII KK, Na Nr 172, 5 June; ibid., 42HID court, R.1068–18, 'Referat', 29 May 1918. For Yugoslav colours among military in the hinterland, see Cornwall, 'The Experience of Yugoslav Agitation', p. 668; and Franjo Barac (ed.), *Croats and Slovenes – Friends of the Entente in the World War* (Paris, 1919) pp. 69, 74.

126. Pivko, *Val Bella*, p. 47.

127. KA, 11AK Gstbs Abt, Fasz.449, Pr.2242. Kostrenčić himself told the Italians that in early 1918 he had been appointed as a propaganda officer to the 83rd Brigade (42HID), but a table of 11th army propaganda officers of 27 March does not contain his name, and certainly he was never one of the two divisional propaganda officers nor one of their 'interpreters' (ibid., Pr.2120, Beilage 13). The propaganda officer on leave at the time of Kostrenčić's desertion was Rittmeister Ernst Hackl who had only recently been appointed as head of *Nachrichtentruppen* no. 1 (83rd Brigade) as well as propaganda leader for the whole division. *Nachrichtentruppen* no. 2 (84th Brigade) in the Val Bella sector had been led since March by Lt Ludwig Zendron.

128. See KA, 11AK, Fasz.272, 4–6/2, 11AK to corps, Op.Nr 1423, 2 March 1918: two Czechs or two Serbs were now forbidden to be on sentry duty together.

129. KA, AOK Op.Abt, Fasz.377, Op.Nr 112745, 42HID court report, 29 May. The deserters' arrival was announced on the Italian side: see PRO, WO 157/636, DIS no. 167, 15 May 1918.

130. KA, AOK, Op.Nr 112745, 42HID court report, 29 May.

131. Pivko, *Val Bella*, pp. 47–9; *Informatorji*, pp. 98–9. Kostrenčić's information was used extensively by Mate Nikolić for an Intelligence summary of conditions in Austria-Hungary.

132. PRO, FO 371/3136, WO 'Notes on the situation in Austria-Hungary no. 3 – August 1918', paragraph 34.

133. KA, 11AK Gstbs Abt, Fasz.449, Pr.2267, 11AK to XV KK, 5 June. Copies in Czech also existed and were assumed by the Austrians to have been written by Štětina (ibid., Pr.2257).

134. KA, EvB 1918, Fasz.5753/19017/3, HGK Conrad to AOK, Na Nr 2000/4, 14 June, enclosing purple leaflet found in the Assa gorge, signed by Belošević, Kostrenčić and Štětina (dated 19 May).

135. Pivko, *Val Bella*, p. 25: manifesto, 'Jugoslav brothers! Croats, Serbs, Slovenes!' (signed by the three officer-deserters). Eugen Kvaternik (1825–71) was, ironically, a Great Croat nationalist who had led a revolt against the Habsburgs in 1871. The

later individuals referred to were heroes from the legendary Serbian struggle against the Turks which had ended at the battle of Kosovo in 1389. However, they were also key figures from a common South Slav epic poetry, and therefore potentially had a deeper cultural significance for many 'Yugoslavs'. See Andrew B. Wachtel, *Making a Nation, Breaking a Nation: Literature and Cultural Politics in Yugoslavia* (Stanford, 1998) pp. 33ff.

136. Pivko, *Val Bella*, pp. 26–8, 74: two leaflets, one signed by all four deserters, the other only by Kostrenčić. Pivko suggests that the latter manifesto had 'sensational success' on the front from early June.
137. KA, AOK Op.Abt, Fasz.377, Op.Nr 112745, HIR27 to 42HID, Op.Nr 314, 27 May. Pivko mentions that Zvonarević in August was due to be punished, but does not specify the crime committed: Pivko, *DRUP* (Maribor, 1928) p. 71.
138. KA, AOK, Fasz.377, Op.Nr 112745, 42HID court, Na Nr 143/18 (R.1242–18/16), 'Referat', 28 May; ibid., HIR27 to 42HID, Op.Nr 314, 27 May.
139. KA, AOK, Fasz.377, Op.Nr 112745, 42HID court record, 28 May; ibid., 42HID to XIII KK, Na Nr 172, 5 June 1918. Svetec too had links to Štětina's fiancée, Milica Popović, who was subsequently arrested.
140. See Pivko, *Naši Dobrovoljci u Italiji*, pp. 42–3; and for the arrival of the deserters in Italy: PRO, WO 157/636, DIS no. 180, 28 May 1918. On Val Bella, the work of one of Pivko's patrols, led by Veselko-Sedlecký, seems to have begun just after 26 May: Pivko, *Informatorji*, p. 95.
141. See KA, 11AK Gstbs Abt, Fasz.268, Op.Nr 2752/3, XIII KK to 11AK, 11 July, enclosing table of deserters during the period 1–15 June. Three were Serbs, the rest Croats.
142. KA, 11AK Gstbs Abt, Fasz.449, Pr.2242, XIII KK to 11AK, t.Op.Nr 450/3, 27 May 1918.
143. Ibid., Fasz.272, 4–6/8–2, 35 I Brigade Kmdo to VI KK, Op.Nr 527/7 Phonogram, 27 May; HIL, 42HID, Fasz.1667, 84 HI Brigade to 42HID, t.Op.Nr 527/1–b, 27 May 1918.
144. KA, AOK, Fasz.377, Op.Nr 112745, 42HID court, Na Nr 143/18, 'Referat', 28 May 1918.
145. Ibid., HIR27 to 42HID, Op.Nr 345, 2 June. For a vivid defence of the division's reputation, see also the 26th regiment's report: HIR26 to XIII KK, Res.476, 1 June.
146. KA, 11AK Gstbs Abt, Fasz.270, Op.Nr 2847/2, 42HID (Soretić) to 11AK, Op.Nr 4806/7, 9 July 1918.
147. See the 36ID judicial records in KA, Feldgerichte Akten 1918, Fasz.565, 3753, 4302, 3260, 8812. The case of Martin Maljak is typical. He returned from leave in Croatia to his regiment (IR116) two months late, giving as his reason that his wife was ill, he had to care for their two children, but that when she recovered an epidemic had broken out in the locality and he himself had fallen ill (Fasz.3260, K767/18). Hungarian courts martial records from the interior present a similar picture. Many of the records from Szeged in early 1918 deal with desertion or excessive leave in the hinterland: see for instance HIL, Szegedi Hadbíróság 1918, Box 268 Hb (cases 715–765), which is almost entirely about such incidents.
148. KA, AOK, Fasz.377, Op.Nr 112745, HIR27 to 42HID, Op.Nr 345, 2 June 1918.
149. Ibid., XIII KK to 11AK, Aw.Nr 481, 12 June; 42HID to XIII KK, Na Nr 153/1, 5 June; HIR28 to 42HID, Res.500, 31 May 1918.
150. Ibid., German translation of Obstlt Nádasdy's report about the state of the 42HID (zu Gstb Nr 81) [August? 1918].

151. KA, AOK Op.Abt, Fasz.378, Nr 113167, 42HID to XXVI KK, Op.Nr 5017/10, 20 September 1918 (and minute by Boroević).
152. Plaschka, Haselsteiner, Suppan, *Innere Front*, II, p. 78.
153. OULK, VII, pp. 245, 301, 303.
154. HIL, 42HID, Fasz.1659, Kampfstand der 42HID, 30 January; KA, XIII KK 1918, Fasz.182, Op.Nr 501, 1 May; HIL, Fasz.1668, Op.Nr 4811, 42HID to XVIII KK, Op.Nr 4792/12, 28 June 1918.
155. KA, XIII KK Op.Abt 1918, Fasz.184, Op.Nrs 617, 619.
156. KA, 11AK Gstbs Abt 1918, Fasz.270, Op.Nr 2847/2, 42HID (Soretić) to 11AK, Op.Nr 4806/7, 9 July 1918. (Draft of this is in HIL, 42HID, Fasz.1668.)
157. HIL, 42HID, Fasz.1668, Op.Nr 4826, 11AK to 42HID, Op.Nr 8070/15c, 24 July 1918. The ringleader, Korporal Stjepan Liković, was sentenced to 20 days' solitary confinement by the divisional court.
158. KA, AOK Op.Abt, Fasz.381, Nr 114315, Boroević to AOK, t.Op.Nr 1471, [27?] October 1918; OULK, VII, pp. 592, 630.
159. BL, Northcliffe MSS, vol. X, Add.Mss.62162, minutes of 2nd Committee meeting at Crewe House, 27 May 1918.
160. AJA, JO 35/252, Jambrišak to Banjanin, 7 June 1918.
161. Ojetti, *Lettere alla Moglie*, pp. 534–5. See also Zanotti-Bianco, *Carteggio 1906–1918*, p. 632, for Ojetti's confidence after a month of work.
162. Steed, *Through Thirty Years*, II, p. 215.
163. PRO, FO 371/3136, WO 'Notes on the situation in Austria-Hungary, no. III – August 1918'.
164. Ibid.
165. KA, 11AK Gstbs Abt, Fasz.272, 4–6/12, HGK Conrad to 11AK, Op.Nr 26300/13, 8 June 1918. The proportions are equally clear from corps records: from the Ist corps sector there were 28 known deserters during May, of whom 11 had deserted to Italy (ibid., 4–6/11). For the trend in desertions, see also KA, 10AK 1918, Fasz.441, R.366, Krobatin to corps, Op.Nr 4167/2, 15 May; and PRO, FO 371/3136, WO 'Notes'.
166. SWP, *Draft EPD Report*, p. 38; Stuart, *Secrets of Crewe House*, pp. 40, 168.
167. Hanzal, *S Výzvědčíky*, pp. 123, 284, 312.
168. PRO, WO 106/852, Cavan to CIGS, 27 May 1918; Ojetti, *Lettere alla Moglie*, p. 527; OULK, VII, p. 266.
169. For the case of Paprskař, see the reports (including the captured Italian interrogation of Paprskař) in KA, 6AK Na-Stelle, Fasz.16, Na Nr 4086; Hanzal, *S Výzvědčíky*, p. 284. The Austrians were more sceptical than the Italians about the quality of the information betrayed, feeling that Paprskař had imparted a lot of gossip.
170. Finzi, *'I.T.O.'*, pp. 229–40; Pivko, *Val Bella*, p. 70 note; Marchetti, *Ventotto Anni*, pp. 355–6; Hanzal, *S Výzvědčíky*, p. 176, for desertions near Lake Garda; Paulová, *Jugoslavenski Odbor*, pp. 444–5 evaluates the perhaps crucial role of a Bosnian Serb deserter on the evening of 14 June.
171. CCC, Cavan MSS, 1/3, part 1, 'Italy', p. 12.
172. See VHA, Fond ČSNR-Štefánik, 35/3/4, Šeba to Štefánik, 26 June 1918. Šeba was told the same thing by Pecori-Giraldi, commander of the Ist army.
173. Pivko, *Informatorji*, p. 95.
174. Ronge, *Kriegs- und Industriespionage*, p. 391.
175. Glaise-Horstenau, *Ein General im Zwielicht*, I, p. 471.
176. On this subject, see especially Peter Fiala, *Die letzte Offensive Altösterreichs*; OULK, VII, pp. 190–207. See also Boroević's fiery letter to Franz von Bolgar (19 June 1918),

published in *Neue Freie Presse*, Nr 20377, 23 May 1921; and in its uncensored and damning version: *Neue Freie Presse*, Nr 23128, 3 February 1929.

177. See KA, FAst 1918, Fasz.5996, Res.487, Beilage zu AOK Op.Nr 146329; KA, 11AK, Fasz.446, Nr 1100, 'Verhalten der öst-ung. Truppen in der Kämpfen vom 15–30 Juni 1918'; and 'Slawische Verrätereien an der italienischen Front', in *Neue Freie Presse*, Nr 19368, 28 July 1918 (Morgenblatt), p. 4.
178. Stuart, *Secrets of Crewe House*, p. 168; *Seton Correspondence*, I, no. 221, p. 330.
179. BL, Northcliffe MSS, vol. X, Add.Mss.62162, Minutes of 8th EPD Committee meeting, 6 August 1918; Stuart, *Secrets of Crewe House*, p. 45.
180. IWM, Wilson MSS, 22/10, Delmé-Radcliffe to Wilson, 10 June 1918.
181. Ojetti, *Lettere alla Moglie*, p. 541; Ojetti, *La Propaganda sul Nemico*, p. 129; and his comments too to Zanotti-Bianco: *Carteggio 1906–1918*, p. 634.
182. PRO, WO 106/825, Radcliffe to DMO, B.M.452/42, 24 June; Ojetti, *Lettere*, p. 541; AJA, JO 35/103, Jambrišak report, July 1918 (sent to the French ambassador in Rome).
183. Marchetti, *Ventotto Anni*, p. 338.
184. Stuart, *Secrets of Crewe House*, p. 44; PRO, WO 106/824, Radcliffe to DMO, B.M.452/40, 21 June 1918.
185. Hanzal, *S Výzvědčíky*, p. 204.
186. Pivko, *Val Bella*, pp. 49–52, 55; Pivko, *DRUP*, pp. 21–4.
187. Finzi, *'I.T.O.'*, pp. 235–6, 250–1.
188. SWP, *Draft EPD Report*, p. 37; Stuart, *Secrets of Crewe House*, p. 44.
189. See KA, 11AK Gstbs Abt, Fasz.269, 1–17/15–33, Op.Nr 2745, Csanády (XIII KK) to 11AK, Op.Nr 628/6, 29 June; and for an example of refusal to move into the front line: KA, XIII KK, Fasz.184, Op.Nr 618.
190. PRO, WO 106/824, Radcliffe to DMO, B.M.452/40, 21 June 1918. Some historians have contributed to the 'propaganda myth' by misinterpreting statistics; thus Luciano Tosi (*La Propaganda Italiana*, p. 188) interprets the Italian figures of prisoners taken during the offensive as figures for 'mass desertion'.
191. Steed, *Through Thirty Years*, II, p. 215; Stuart, *Secrets*, pp. 40,42. Jambrišak, Kujundžić and Gallenga all publicized this idea as well: see DRP, File 'Private letters out', Radcliffe to Lord Stamfordham, 10 July; PRO, WO 106/817, Radcliffe to DMO, SBM 249, 2 August 1918.
192. PRO, CAB 23/6, W.C.436, 26 June 1918.
193. PRO, FO 371/3136, WO 'Notes on the situation in Austria-Hungary, no. III – August 1918'. Radcliffe too recorded the general apathy of prisoners who 'when questioned as to open revolt, ask what they can do with a resigned and hopeless air' (PRO, WO 106/824, Radcliffe to DMO, B.M.452/40, 21 June).
194. KA, FAst 1918, Fasz.5994, Res.89, AOK to FAst, Op.Nr 766/107, 10 May: 'Sitzung am 26 April 1918. Frontpropaganda'.
195. That the AOK's fears were well-founded was to be clear from Kostrenčić's desertion, and also the desertion of a propaganda patrol of IR75 (Czech) in late May (KA, HGK Conrad, Fasz.72, Na Nr 400a/322).
196. KA, 11AK Gstbs Abt, Fasz.449, Pr.2218, AOK to 11AK, 10AK, 6AK, KISA, etc., Op.Nr 766/120, 'Richtlinien für die Feindpropaganda', 10 May 1918.
197. Ibid., Pr.2242, 11AK Beilage zum Monatsbericht über den Feind pro Mai 1918. For the 11AK 'peace offensive' leaflet, see ibid., Fasz.448, Pr.2204/34, 'Vi portiamo la pace! Non vogliamo prendervi le vostre terre!'
198. KA, 11AK, Fasz.445, Na Nrs 609 (KISA Beilage 8), 756 (KISA Beilage 11); Fasz.446, Na Nr 889.

199. For example, in the 11AK sector: 52ID, 28ID, 39HID, 16ID, 74HID, 5ID, etc. (ibid., Fasz. 449, Pr.2208).
200. For Italian desertions, see ibid., Fasz. 446, Na Nr 891. Fontana Secca (55ID) was a spot where fraternization was actually continuing into late May (ibid., Fasz. 449, Pr.2242) with the permission of the 11AK propaganda officer.
201. KA, HGK Conrad, Fasz.66, Na Nr 400a/342, AOK to Conrad, Op.Nr 766/189, 11 June 1918.
202. KA, FAst, Fasz.5995, Res.403, KISA to AOK, Op.Nr 6847/1, 28 July 1918.
203. KA, HGK Erzherzog Joseph 1918, Fasz.65, F.E.G.Nr 48850/17, AOK Op.Nr 766/345, 'Untersuchungen und statistische Daten über 5000 während der Kämpfe vom 15 bis 30 Juni an der Piave eingebrachten Kriegsgefangenen'. A few prisoners remarked that Austria might more effectively have concentrated their efforts upon the Italian hinterland, especially Reggio Emilia, Ferrara and Turin.
204. KA, 11AK Gstbs Abt, Fasz.449, Pr.2308.
205. KA, FAst, Fasz.5995, Res.403, KISA Gstbs Abt to AOK, Op.Nr 6847/1, 28 July 1918.
206. KA, 11AK Op.Abt, Fasz.447, Na Nr 1359, 6AK to 11AK, Op.Nr 977/Ev, 31 July, Beilage 14.
207. Ibid., Fasz.449, Pr.2308, 11AK to AOK, 11 July 1918.
208. Ronge, *Kriegs- und Industriespionage*, p. 346.

# 8
# The Climax of Italian Psychological Warfare

## 8.1 The pressure of Crewe House and the Italian obstacle

In his memoirs, Tullio Marchetti employed a number of vivid metaphors to describe the disintegrating Habsburg Empire, including that of a tree assaulted by rotten plants. In this vein he wrote that until the battle of the Piave 'the decomposing seeds scattered with our propaganda had germinated quite well though with irregularity', but that the events of June 1918 were 'the best manure for beginning a luxuriant and uniform vegetation'.[1] Marchetti and the other Intelligence officers felt after the battle that their campaign ought to be intensified in order to prepare the ground for the time when Italy launched a final offensive. This could not be too early. For although Intelligence sources suggested that cracks in the enemy structure were steadily widening, there were equally signs, as Finzi noted in mid-July, that the tree still had 'a solid bark'.[2]

Italian Intelligence therefore tended to back the mood which prevailed at the CS over the summer. Diaz and Badoglio were always inclined, notwithstanding news of the enemy's low morale, to postpone any unilateral Italian offensive. Their reasoning was usually the delicate numerical balance on the Italian Front, but any anxiety about a new Caporetto was certainly heightened by persistent rumours in these months that Germany was about to transfer forces to that theatre to aid its ally. Better then to launch a full-scale attack on the Monarchy only when the western Allies could provide extra military support.[3] For Italy's allies, however, attention was fully concentrated on dramatic events in the West, so the CS requests for more British or American troops for a 'knock-out blow' were always refused. Thus it was that the summer months witnessed a marked lull in military operations on the Italian Front, with occasional raids by Allied forces in the mountains, and a planned limited attack on the Asiago plateau taking the place of that full-scale offensive which the French in particular were urging and the Austrians were always expecting. The relative inactivity was characterized well by the British commander, Lord Cavan. He moved his headquarters to a cave nearer the front line and 'slept on gentians every night': 'The views from here were superb and I spent many hours with my stalking glasses watching the enemy across the plateau and gazing at the distant Dolomites.'[4]

During this period of calm, however, Italy's campaign of psychological warfare against Austria-Hungary was at its height. The CS backed the enthusiasm of both Ugo Ojetti and the Intelligence heads since it perceived that propaganda, having played its part in the Piave *débâcle*, could now form a similar prelude to a last Italian military offensive and victory. The summer months saw the Italian propagandists elaborating ever further the techniques which they had learnt earlier in the year. The number of manifestos raining down on the Austrian positions was on an unprecedented scale. The themes of the manifestos were of an unprecedented sophistication, specially tailored by Padua to suit each nationality and (partly because of this agenda) exceeding in quality anything which was being issued by the British EPD for the Western Front. If new targets at the front included Magyar soldiers, who were sent social as well as nationalist arguments to revolt, Ojetti was also eager to build on the successful propaganda flights which had been made to Ljubljana and Zagreb. Therefore, he gave full backing to the idea of the poet Gabriele D'Annunzio that the next adventure should be to Vienna itself. D'Annunzio's flight over the imperial capital in August 1918 was the most celebrated episode in Italy's whole campaign, a daring and dramatic feat which only exacerbated the Austrian authorities' paranoia about ubiquitous 'Entente propaganda' and its secret links to traitors in the hinterland. It was at the same time very much an integral part of Ojetti's campaign. This time it was the Viennese who were being targeted, with arguments which were not simply triumphalist (as Manfried Rauchensteiner has suggested[5]) but also liberating in the spirit of those manifestos distributed over Zagreb and Ljubljana.

Equally dramatic, but far less well publicized except in Czech and Slovene literature after the war, were the continued exploits of Slav propaganda troops on the Italian Front. They were being used ever more extensively by Italian Intelligence, their 'propaganda remit' widening to include espionage behind enemy lines and even combat in the front line: here was new evidence for both the Austrian and Italian armies that Czech troops in particular were reliably committed to the Entente cause. The Austrians in response would, as we will see, try to counter such poisonous propaganda by cleverly arousing Italian qualms about employing such 'unreliable Austrians' in sections of the Intelligence network. Although their efforts did not succeed they are significant, first in demonstrating that the Monarchy's psychological struggle against Italy was not completely terminated by the Piave offensive; and second, in revealing that for many leading Italian officers their commitment to a 'nationality policy' was at worst nominal, at best simply a tool to produce the victory which had proved so elusive with conventional weapons.

At Crewe House this Italian ambiguity over commitment to the oppressed nationalities was seen as the major obstacle to the effectiveness of propaganda against Austria-Hungary. Because of its perceived and actual repercussions for front propaganda, the ambiguity is worth repeating. It was personified in the Italian government by Orlando himself who, for the purpose of defeating Austria and giving Italy a 'moral edge' in western eyes, wished to espouse nationality politics, but at the same time believed in upholding the 'imperialist' Treaty of London which conflicted with Yugoslav aspirations. As we have seen, Crewe House and their Italian supporters always exaggerated the degree to which Yugoslav propaganda could influence enemy Croats, Serbs or Slovenes: a 'Yugoslav consciousness', in the idealistic sense propagated by Ante Trumbić, was rarely to be found in the enemy trenches. But it was true that any Italian arguments aimed at educated Croat and Slovene troops were substantially weakened because of Italy's alternative agenda in 1918. It was also the case that official Italy's reservation towards the Yugoslavs had damaging repercussions for their cause, however idealistic the latter may have been. It limited progress towards a Yugoslav legion and, as had been shown at Versailles on 3 June, it prevented any joint Allied declaration of commitment to the destruction of Austria. Thus Italy's qualms not only meant that the 'Yugoslav evidence' available to the Padua Commission for propaganda purposes was rather patchy (in a way that Czech evidence was not). It also had a broader impact, since the Allies could never make a common statement including the Yugoslavs which Padua could then employ in propaganda material for all of the opposing nationalities.

Yet if a joint Allied statement was now a dead letter, the Allies on 3 June had agreed that they would be free to issue separate supplements to the Versailles Declaration 'as suitable occasions arose'. In the following weeks and months it was especially the Austro-Hungarian section of Crewe House, the official guise for the many activities of Steed and Seton-Watson, which aided the national émigrés in pressing for such supplementary statements. As far as the campaign against the Monarchy was concerned, Crewe House continued to have a broader propaganda remit than the Padua Commission, fashioning policy rather than practice. Steed and his collaborators were trying above all to circumscribe Allied policy towards Austria-Hungary, tying an Allied victory to the Monarchy's dismemberment. While this work would increasingly benefit the campaign on the Italian Front, Crewe House had sensed early on, not least from Granville Baker's regular complaints, that the campaign there was not the Allied venture which Lord Northcliffe's organization claimed to have done so much to coordinate. Rather, Ojetti seemed to be working unilaterally and in a way which smelt too strongly of an Italian imperialist attitude, an 'obstructionist tendency' similar to Orlando's government. From the early summer, Steed on several occasions sought to reimpose a more active role for the British

EPD in the campaign by trying to reconvert the Padua Commission into an Allied body. At the same time, in August, Crewe House organized an inter-Allied conference in London which, among other things, tried to weaken Italian particularism and strengthen a common Allied position with regard to propaganda against the Monarchy.

While much of this effort would be in vain, Crewe House's major success in the early summer was in altering British and French official policy towards Austria-Hungary. On 6 June, on learning of the Versailles statement, Steed had immediately drafted a letter for Northcliffe to send to the British Foreign Office, deploring its weakness and emphasizing the urgent need for supplementary statements by the British and French governments. The letter continued rather pompously: 'Unless these declarations are made, I greatly fear that the propaganda organizations I have set up in Italy may get out of hand or break down entirely.'[6] Replying to Northcliffe, Balfour explained that it was Sonnino's scepticism which had caused the weak Versailles Declaration, but he noted that the French were planning to make a supplementary declaration when President Poincaré presented colours to Czechoslovak troops. Although no such convenient opportunity seemed to exist at present for an equivalent British statement, Balfour had asked Beneš to publish the letter in which Britain had recognized the Czechoslovak National Council as 'the supreme organ' of the Czechoslovak movement in Allied countries.[7] On 11 June, as a further sign of encouragement to the Czech and Yugoslav émigrés, Robert Cecil spoke in Parliament about the abundant evidence of Czech and Yugoslav national feeling and the help which their troops were lending to the Allied cause.[8]

These moves gave some consolation to Crewe House. Steed and Seton-Watson were concerned, in the absence of an adequate joint Allied declaration, that individual Allied statements should give equal satisfaction to all the oppressed nationalities. Thus when Seton-Watson learnt in Paris on 11 June that Poincaré was to present colours to Czech and Polish troops and make 'whole-hog declarations' for these nationalities, but to do nothing comparable for the Yugoslavs, he immediately stressed to Paris and London 'the disastrous effects of this omission'; it would benefit the enemy and damage the Yugoslav movement in Austria-Hungary. In the absence of Steed (who had been in a road accident and was out of circulation for a month), Seton-Watson managed to persuade the Foreign Office to urge upon the French the need for some reference to the Yugoslavs.[9] As a result, the French postponed the presentations. When they were made a few weeks later, Poincaré, in speaking to the Polish and Czech forces, also mentioned the Yugoslavs. Meanwhile on 29 June, Pichon, the Foreign Minister, in a crucial government statement to Beneš recognizing the Czech National Council as 'the first basis of the future government', further expressed the hope that the Czechoslovak state would become 'with Poland and the Yugoslav state an insurmountable barrier to Germanic aggressions'.[10]

This declaration, which had been indirectly influenced by Crewe House as well, was the most far-reaching commitment made by an Allied country to the Czechoslovak but also to the Yugoslav cause. For the first time, one of the Allies had publicly mentioned a future 'Yugoslav state'. In Padua, Bogoljub Kujundžić assured Granville Baker that for that reason the statement was 'exceptionally important': 'besides its political importance, which is without doubt enormous, it also has a practical side in that through it one will eliminate all those notes of mistrust which were spread intentionally or in good faith about the Versailles Declaration'.[11] It is surprising therefore that Pichon's announcement seems to have been omitted from Padua's Yugoslav material altogether, something which might suggest that Ojetti himself was sensitive to its implications, or at least that Kujundžić was unable to control was what printed in the Commission's Yugoslav propaganda.[12]

While Pichon's statement was an isolated event, Kujundžić hoped rather optimistically that the Entente Powers would now 'give a collective declaration in which they will precisely and simply state, *Austria est delenda*'. This was Crewe House's ideal as well, but for the present they had to be content with satisfactory statements from the British and American governments which kept up a certain momentum; Seton-Watson had continued to badger the Foreign Office for more. On 1 July, Balfour duly sent a public telegram to the French, associating Britain with Poincaré's declaration and expressing pleasure that Czechoslovaks, Yugoslavs and Poles were fighting at the side of the Allies for the cause of freedom. It was, as Steed informed the EPD Committee, 'the best [British] declaration yet made', even if it found rather limited use in Padua's manifestos.[13] More impressive certainly was a second major statement by Robert Lansing on 28 June. When the Serbian minister in Washington complained to him that the Austrian press, notably the *Neue Freie Presse*, was scorning the weak Versailles Declaration, Lansing responded with a definite American commitment to destroy Austria-Hungary: 'all branches of the Slav race should be completely freed from German and Austrian rule'. As Steed again informed Crewe House, these were words which 'had the effect of taking the leadership out of the hands of Italy, where it had been placed by the Rome Congress, and of putting it into the hands of the United States'. Ojetti duly realized their importance and publicized them rather more widely than Lansing's limp statement of sympathy a month earlier.[14]

By July, therefore, all the Allies except Italy had made some further public commitment to the Czechs and Yugoslavs to offset the weakness of the Versailles Declaration. As far as the Yugoslav Committee was concerned, Crewe House had been anxious to reassure them. Steed had advised their officials in London to submit to the Foreign Office a memorandum, indicating the strength of the Yugoslav movement in the Monarchy and requesting an 'open and decisive declaration' by the Allies to benefit that movement as well as the Allied cause. At the same time, Baker when in Paris in mid-June had assured De Giulli that he would personally work in Italy to secure for the Yugoslavs the same kind of benefits accruing to the Czech movement.[15] When the Entente Powers then made further commitments at the turn of the month, it seemed quite likely that the Yugoslav Committee would soon be following the trail blazed by the Czechs. In particular, at the Paris 'Congress of Oppressed Nationalities', being organized for 26–28 July, it might be possible to proclaim an important Allied statement on the Yugoslav question. This in turn would please Fournol and Franklin-Bouillon, who wanted their French congress to be as great a propaganda success as that in Rome, so as to underline France's leading role as patron of the oppressed nationalities.

In the days before the Congress, moreover, the British and French foreign ministers committed themselves further to the Yugoslavs. On 24 July, the fourth anniversary of the Austrian ultimatum to Serbia, at a Mansion House meeting, the British Foreign Secretary gave a significant speech which Steed expected to have great propaganda value (although again it was never exploited in Ojetti's manifestos).[16] In it, as Steed recorded later, Balfour 'criticized Austria-Hungary more frankly than any other British minister had hitherto done, and recognized the Austrian problem as the key to European reconstruction, and the case of Yugoslavia as a test case of Allied sincerity in regard to its solution'. He 'had said enough to make it clear that the full Yugoslav programme had the sympathy and support of the British Government'.[17] For Trumbić, who was already in Paris for the Congress, this was confirmation of what the French had told him a week earlier. Trumbić had stressed to Pichon that the Yugoslavs wanted the same concessions as the Czechs and Poles, whereupon Pichon had assured him that both France and Britain were 'without qualification' on the side of the Yugoslav Committee. He advised Trumbić simply to draw up a statement of recognition, as Beneš had done for the Czechs, which could then be agreed to by the Allies.[18]

This sounded a simple procedure, but as usual there were fundamental obstacles. It was highly unlikely that either Italy or the Serbian government-in-exile would agree to any Allied recognition of the Yugoslav Committee.[19] While in these circumstances the Yugoslav cause could only made slow progress, the Czechoslovak National Council had no rivals and could achieve much more. In the wake of the Anglo-French declarations, Beneš by July hoped especially to push the British further.[20] Constantly advised by Steed in his talks with the Foreign Office, Beneš could emphasize the Czechs' military contribution on three Allied fronts, and the 'evident maturity' of the Czech nation in Austria, revealed most recently by the creation of a national council in Prague. With the latter allegedly just waiting to take power as Beneš argued, British recognition of the Czechoslovaks and their army as allies could have an 'explosive effect' in Bohemia as well as 'an immense and beneficent influence on the Poles and Yugoslavs'. Beneš was anxious to gain full Allied recognition for the Czech cause before Austria-Hungary disintegrated. For the British, the propaganda aspect (the 'explosive effect') seems to have played its small part in breaking down Balfour's initial reservations, even if Beneš's arguments about the Czechs' military role were the most decisive.[21] The upshot was Balfour's declaration on 9 August: Great Britain recognized the 'Czechoslovaks' as an Allied people, the three Czechoslovak armies as 'one allied and belligerent army' and the Czechoslovak National Council as 'the present trustee of the future Czechoslovak government'. All the émigrés recognized the great value of this statement, which for the first time recognized Czechs and Slovaks, peoples wholly subject to the Habsburgs, as Allies of the West. Trumbić labelled it as *Finis Austriae*.[22] It implied that the British intended to dismember the Habsburg Empire, even if it did not bind them to that course. The Padua Commission too was not slow to realize the sharp edge to Balfour's statement: it seemed to be the most useful piece of propaganda from the Allied side since the start of Padua's campaign (see page 353).

The new declaration further highlighted Britain's leading role in support of the oppressed nationalities, in contrast to Italy's lack of initiative since the Rome Congress. This was something which loyal Italian supporters of a nationality policy found hard to swallow. For example, Leonida Bissolati viewed the declaration as a humiliation for his country which was lagging behind the other Allies and might now even be pre-empted by Britain over the sensitive Yugoslav question.[23] The propagandists, whether at Padua or Crewe House, had equally been concerned for some time at the attitude of 'official Italy'. From the early summer they, together with those like Bissolati who were sincere adherents of a nationality policy, were trying to push Italy along the path to which they felt it had publicly committed itself at the Rome Congress. Ultimately this meant that either Sonnino would have to follow what was felt by many to be the alternative 'Orlando–Bissolati' policy, or Orlando would have to remove Sonnino and his partisans from influence.

When Steed had learnt of Sonnino's behaviour at Versailles he had decided to communicate personally with Orlando. In early June the EPD had taken over responsibility for British propaganda in Italy from the Ministry of Information, and Steed now used this as an excuse for writing direct to Orlando.[24] In his letter of 15 June, Steed pointed out that the British government had asked Northcliffe to assume responsibility for 'good relations' between Britain and Italy, that a small committee had been organized for this, but that the work necessitated 'the continual coordination between English policy with regard to Italy and Anglo-Italian policy against Austria-Hungary'. The latter policy, as evidenced especially in the work of the Padua Commission, had unfortunately been obstructed of late by tendencies which were 'not completely in harmony with the spirit of the Rome Congress'; indeed, they might be connected to 'a somewhat reactionary wind blowing for some weeks in sundry Italian political circles'. Since nationality politics had already brought Italy great benefits and was the only one which could give it 'security, development and independence', Steed pressed Orlando for assurances that he was still committed to the principles of April 1918.[25]

Orlando's reply and his general behaviour in mid-June seemed reassuring. While informing Steed that his policy would remain that agreed upon in April 'whatever the consequences may be', he closed a debate in the Italian chamber on 16 June with a reaffirmation of his government's commitment to oppressed peoples.[26] This was seized upon by Trumbić who, while thoroughly disillusioned by the Versailles Declaration, chose now to exploit and reaffirm Orlando's commitment. On 18 June, he stated in the Italian press that the Prime Minister had 'understood the importance of the Austro-Hungarian question... and he enjoys our confidence'.[27] Whether or not Trumbić really believed this, his public trust in Orlando seemed to be justified when a week later he and a deputation of the Yugoslav Committee were granted an official audience, a meeting which found full expression in one of Ojetti's Yugoslav newssheets for the enemy. On this occasion Trumbić congratulated Orlando on 'the great victory of Italian arms...on the shores of the bloody and sacred Piave' and reminded him that Italy which had been 'the first among the oppressed nations to snub Habsburg rule' was now fulfilling its noble mission of destroying the Habsburg state and opening the road to freedom for the oppressed peoples of Austria-Hungary.[28] He concluded rather sycophantically that 'Your Excellency knew with a clear vision how to establish a policy of mutual trust between Italy and the Yugoslav nation'. Orlando in his reply was no less enthusiastic, confirming that Italy's role was that prophesied by Mazzini, to act on behalf of oppressed peoples and in fraternity with the 'great Slav family'.[29]

Such language encouraged the Yugoslav émigrés to continue believing that there were two currents in Italian governmental and public opinion, that of Orlando–Bissolati representing the Mazzini tradition and that of Sonnino representing himself.[30] Nor were the émigrés by any means alone in misrepresenting Orlando's outlook. Bissolati himself continued to believe that Orlando was sincerely sympathetic to nationality politics while Sonnino was the real obstacle to the execution of that policy. Others like Delmé-Radcliffe, having heard personally from Orlando of his displeasure at the Versailles Declaration, only naturally came to the same conclusion.[31] In fact Orlando's commitment to the policy was one of pure expediency, to make an Italian victory on the basis of the Treaty of London more likely. He wished to preserve a façade of vague support for the oppressed, while at the same time maintaining Italy's earlier war aims. The fact that 'appearance' was all important to Orlando is clear from remarks to his ambassador in Paris who had warned him in mid-June that Italy should not fall behind in statements of sympathy for the nationalities since certain French circles were trying to win the role of protector exclusively for France. Orlando replied that the Versailles Declaration had indeed been a mistake, but not so much because it had been too 'cold', rather because it had made Italy look guilty.[32] A few weeks later, he stressed to a delegation of Italian irredentists tha the had only adopted the nationality policy because of Italy's precarious situation after Caporetto. The policy was important simply as an instrument for Italy and did not signify that he had renounced any of Italy's territorial claims.[33]

In the light of these remarks it might be expected that after the Piave battle, with the prospect of victory over Austria more likely, Orlando would feel less anxious about maintaining the façade. This was to some extent the case, for as the summer progressed he drew openly closer to Sonnino. He was nevertheless still concerned to avoid any government crisis on the eve of victory, and this perpetuated his desire to maintain a compromise in governmental policy, to try to pacify Bissolati as well as Sonnino. For the role of mediator he was perhaps ideally suited since, in Ojetti's view, he had the *deformazione professionale* of a lawyer: the ability to agree with everyone.[34] Yet his attitude was not one which the Allied propagandists were prepared to tolerate. Both Crewe House and Ugo Ojetti moved to counter a tendency which they felt was weakening their propaganda efforts.

In spite of Orlando's 'nice speeches' which had given some satisfaction to Steed and Seton-Watson, they were still determined to bring pressure to bear upon the man whom they considered the real villain of the piece – Sonnino. On 20 June, Seton-Watson had attacked Sonnino in his journal *The New Europe*, describing him as 'the benumbing influence'.[35] It was an article which seemed to hit its mark, fuelling rumours in Italy that Sonnino was about to resign or be removed from office. But it also brought criticism upon Crewe House itself, from the British embassy in Rome and from Gaetano Salvemini's *L'Unità*, both of which considered the attack as blatant interference in Italian politics.[36] Crewe House's interference however did not stop there: in late June it sent to Italy the secretary of its 'Italian Committee', Gerald O'Donovan.[37] O'Donovan made a controversial tour of the country, publicly chastising the Italians for wavering from the nationality principle, and sending back firm recommendations to Crewe House and the Foreign Office. On his departure from Italy, for example, he advised that 'unless something is done very soon to define position of Allies towards the subject races of Austria-Hungary, suspicions of motives of more than one of the Allies will be intensified'.[38] O'Donovan therefore added his voice to those emanating from the Italian Front or the EPD who were increasingly alerting the Allies to the danger of Italy's ambiguous attitude, pressing them to formulate a clear Allied policy which might, not least, prove more useful and effective for the purposes of psychological warfare against Austria-Hungary.

These voices naturally included Ojetti himself as well as Salvemini and Bissolati, men who as sincere proponents of a nationality policy viewed with alarm the way in which an ultra-nationalist and anti-Yugoslav agitation had emerged in the Italian press after the Versailles Declaration.[39] Already on 6 June, *La Stampa* of Turin had congratulated Sonnino on his opposition to the Yugoslavs, alleging that they had yet to prove themselves to be anti-Habsburg or of any help to the Allies. It was an article which encouraged Bissolati to complain to Orlando that the Consulta was supporting ultra-nationalist propaganda, pushing the Yugoslavs into the arms of Austria.[40] If Orlando's speeches in the next two weeks did something to offset the impact of Versailles, the strange ambiguity of Italy's policy was nevertheless well portrayed on 30 June by *Epoca*, a newspaper which had particular connections to Orlando. It praised his policy of Italian–Slav agreement in the spirit of 1848 or 1866, but went on to warn its readers of a 'secret organization' which was spreading poisonous propaganda with the purpose of ruining Italian–Slav friendship. On 1 July a much publicized specimen of such 'poison' duly appeared in the Bolognese *Il Resto del Carlino*. An article by Francesco Coppola contrasted the supposed 'treacherous' behaviour of Yugoslavs (against Austria) with the actual conduct of two (allegedly) 'Yugoslav' Austrian divisions, the 10ID and 12ID, whom he asserted to have fought loyally for their Habsburg masters during the battle of the Piave.[41]

Coppola's article produced a strong reaction. At Salvemini's suggestion,[42] Ojetti replied with a public refutation of the allegations. He had already demonstrated over the Caburi incident in May that he did not believe that attacks on the nationality policy should go unanswered. And in his first report on the work of the Padua Commission, written itself on 1 July and possibly influenced by Coppola's article, he numbered among the tasks still to be completed the need 'to reconcile propaganda against the enemy army with the political action, so far dispersed and contradictory, of the Italian press which is read, quoted and discussed daily not only by neutrals and allies but also by the enemy'. Italian propaganda at home and abroad had to follow the same principles as front propaganda, so that the Austrians could not take advantage of discrepancies in Italy's public pronouncements and assert that 'we are talking like this out of pure and short-sighted opportunism'.[43] Ojetti was naturally sensitive to the role of the press since he himself was exploiting the radical Austro-Hungarian press to such advantage. In his reply to Coppola, published in *Il Resto del Carlino* on 5 July, he gave full rein to his exasperation. Despite the Rome Congress and Orlando's statements, a 'tiny minority' were continuing to attack the Yugoslav émigrés, thereby doing the greatest service to the Austrians to the benefit of their propaganda campaign against Italy. He challenged the accuracy of Coppola's statements. While the 10th and 12th divisions hardly contained any Yugoslav soldiers, he himself had recently visited Yugoslav prisoners in the 3rd army zone and become convinced from their behaviour that the Yugoslav Committee did indeed have the support of the 'Yugoslav people'.[44] This was rather a wild statement, however enthusiastic the welcome which Ojetti and Jambrišak had received among Serb and Croat prisoners (on 21 June); but Ojetti was only too aware that he had to oppose Coppola's arguments with positive generalizations of his own.

Coppola replied on 10 July, describing Ojetti's views as an 'epidemic of blindness which for three or four months has been massacring Italian political intelligence'.[45] He asserted, with some justification, that the 42HID, the predominantly Slav 12ID, as well as Bosnian troops had been fighting valiantly against Italy. He then listed some rather tendentious evidence to prove that the Yugoslav movement was really anti-Italian and pro-Austrian; most examples referred to the way in which Yugoslavs in Austria and Italy were publicly laying claim to the Adriatic coastline.[46] At the core of Coppola's argument was the fact that Yugoslavs were opposed to the Treaty of London; he himself felt that the treaty embodied the sole criterion for which Italy was waging the war, namely the 'rights of Italy', and that any discussion of Mazzini's principles was 'useless and anachronistic'. He denied Ojetti's claim that those of his persuasion were a 'tiny minority'. Rather, they represented the *totalità degli italiani*, out to stop the 'cheap trick' of a few foreign intriguers and many naïve Italians by exposing the real attitude of the Yugoslavs of Austria-Hungary. To do so, he argued, could not benefit the Austrians since the Yugoslavs were already in their camp!

Ojetti was extremely irritated by this second article from Coppola, feeling that it had been directly inspired or even drafted by the Consulta itself.[47] Since Orlando seemed incapable of removing Sonnino from office, Ojetti urged Albertini to begin another campaign in the columns of *Corriere della Sera*, this time to topple Sonnino and his adherents. But such desperate tactics were not yet acceptable to Albertini who still trusted Orlando's commitment to the oppressed nationalities. He preferred, rather than being responsible for creating a government crisis, to use more subtle means to twist Orlando's arm.[48] Ojetti therefore reluctantly agreed to be patient and await a meeting with his two mentors, Orlando and Albertini, in the war zone. There they would put their cards on the table and if Orlando was found to be hesitant or frivolous over nationality politics, Ojetti vowed that he would ask to be relieved of his post. On his own admission, the only thing which was keeping him at Padua was pressure from Albertini, Bissolati and Salvemini. Having been appointed by Orlando to propagate the nationality policy from the war zone, he felt it dishonourable to remain while the 'see-saw policy' of Orlando and Sonnino continued.[49] After all, as he had pointed out in his first propaganda report, Italy's ambiguous stance was not only seriously hampering the effectiveness of psychological warfare. It was, as he told Albertini on 14 July, causing the work at Padua to become 'disjointed and weakened'. At the CS the blatant Slavophobes had retaken the upper hand, with Siciliani himself preaching that the nationality policy had failed, while the national delegates at Padua were naturally becoming suspicious and disheartened.[50] Ojetti was furthermore characteristically anxious about Italy losing its position as the leading patron amongst the Allies of the oppressed peoples. Since the British and French were already emphasizing to their advantage the contradictions in Italian policy, Ojetti feared that the Paris Congress, instead of being a valuable sequel to the Rome Congress, would simply show up Italy in a poor light. He warned Albertini: 'that congress, which ought to reaffirm the need for Austria's decomposition, will perhaps only endorse our political incapacity to smash her'.[51]

That this might indeed be the result seemed all the more likely because of Sonnino's attitude to the Paris Congress. Compared to Orlando, who contemplated Italy's image and favoured a good number of influential Italians attending the event, Sonnino saw everything through the prism of Italy's London treaty. He was not only averse to any more joint Allied statements about the subject races, but also refused to grant diplomatic passports to Salvemini, Amendola, Torre and others so that they could attend the Congress. Although in the end he yielded to pressure from Orlando, it was not, unfortunately, before the Congress had been postponed to September (it never met). At the last moment Crewe House had advised a delay. Steed reasoned that Allied disharmony would be only too evident at the event since no Yugoslav declaration was ready to be made public. This, combined with the practical hurdles which Sonnino had set up, sabotaged the chance of the Paris Congress repeating the propaganda coup of its Roman predecessor. The French, with good reason, placed the full blame for the postponement on the Italians.[52]

Meanwhile, the passport incident had contributed to fomenting the long-expected crisis in the Italian government. It centred entirely around the contradictions in official policy, personified by Sonnino on the one hand, and Bissolati and Gallenga Stuart on the other. Ever since the Rome Congress, Gallenga, with the support of Orlando, had been propagating the nationality policy in allied and neutral countries, while Sonnino had been advancing his own views abroad through Italian nationalist groups as well as diplomatic channels.[53] The two ministers and their representatives had repeatedly clashed, and finally, on 28 July, after Sonnino had recalled two employees of Gallenga's ministry to the Consulta, Gallenga's patience snapped and he submitted his resignation. Like Ojetti, he hoped by such a move to clarify the ambiguity. Either it would strengthen Orlando's hand, enabling him to take 'a decision which it is known he wished to take' of clear commitment to the Yugoslav cause, or it would set Gallenga free to exercise pressure independently inside and outside Parliament in favour of the Yugoslavs. In the event, Gallenga's move led to neither result. Orlando managed to persuade him that Italy's policy towards the Yugoslavs was still an issue which he hoped to conclude successfully, not a matter suitable to provoke a cabinet crisis. Gallenga thereupon withdrew his resignation on condition that a Yugoslav legion be formed, and that he himself would be admitted to meetings of the Italian War Council.[54]

It was clear that the governmental crisis had only been deferred. When Orlando met Ojetti and Albertini at Padua in early August and gave them similar assurances to those made to Gallenga, Albertini warned him that there would be a press campaign against Sonnino if the matter was not resolved very quickly.[55] Orlando was also still under mounting pressure from within his own cabinet, notably from Bissolati who was especially incensed at Sonnino's initial refusal to grant passports to the Paris delegates. Egged on by Ojetti, he too was threatening to resign unless the Prime Minister shook off his 'timidity' and forced Sonnino to change his stance over the Yugoslavs. Bissolati was not at all optimistic that Orlando would manage to do this, but on 12 August he informed Trumbić that in a few days there was to be an important meeting between himself, Orlando and Sonnino, followed by a ministerial conference as a result of which the question would be resolved one way or the other.[56] The impression was that Italian obstacles to 'effective propaganda', which Crewe House had failed to shift, might finally be dismantled by the Italians themselves.

## 8.2 An Italian or an Allied campaign?

Among the Italian obstacles which Steed and Seton-Watson were trying to surmount from London, the Padua Commission itself was always perceived as part of the problem. From the start it had failed to function harmoniously as an Allied concern. Ojetti's methods of control had immediately alienated Granville Baker, while progressively irritating the national delegates who, in the case of the Yugoslavs and Poles, had expected their own delimited sphere of influence in the campaign. Admittedly, by the time of Austria's offensive Ojetti's relations with the Yugoslav delegates had somewhat improved. This was due partly to Delmé-Radcliffe's intervention, but also to the CS which had decided to allow Jambrišak and Kujundžić to visit and agitate among 'Yugoslav' prisoners in the war zone. Nevertheless, when in mid-June Baker returned to Padua after a visit to London, he failed to detect any change in the environment since he was repeatedly reminded that his own role was to be strictly advisory. On 18 June, he warned Crewe House: 'everything is being done to deprive this commission of its inter-Allied character'. Ojetti, whom Baker pictured as the tool of Sonnino, was still insisting on a purely Italian organization; the Yugoslav delegates in turn were champing at the bit since, according to Baker at least, Ojetti insisted on the Treaty of London and prohibited any reference to the Corfu Declaration.[57] It was a lurid assessment and it brought a speedy and characteristic response. In his reply, sent to Delmé-Radcliffe, Northcliffe strongly condemned the drift towards a purely Italian organization or any slighting of the Yugoslavs:

> I cannot acquiesce in Baker's intercourse with the representatives of the subject nationalities being limited in any way, as the establishment of the Inter-Allied Commission was due to my initiative. I shall find means of making representations to the competent Italian authorities to this effect. Please inform Col. Siciliani and Capt. Ojetti, in the meantime, that unless the original arrangement is adhered to, we shall have [to] reconsider the whole position carefully as the whole work which was begun at my initiative would evidently be wrecked if they persist in the present alleged tendencies.[58]

At the same time, Crewe House contacted Borgese in Berne, asking him to support the EPD's efforts to counteract 'this deplorable tendency' in Padua. Borgese found the information 'extremely painful'. While sensing that Baker's own personality and interpretation were largely to blame, he advised Albertini to caution patience on Ojetti: 'we must think how useful for the policy we desire has been the action of Northcliffe and Steed towards the English government and especially towards Balfour'. A rupture with Crewe House now would do great damage at a time when, Borgese suggested, Austria was organizing large-scale propaganda against Italy.[59] Albertini, however, took a more cynical view of British behaviour. The facts seemed to be that Italy was genuinely committed to the oppressed nationalities, as shown for instance by Orlando's meeting with Trumbić (26 June), while Crewe House was constantly questioning Italy's commitment. The discrepancy of viewpoint could be explained by the British seeking to undermine Italy's leading role in the nationality cause to benefit themselves and promote Yugoslav aspirations at the expense of Italian. Albertini's theory seemed to tally quite well with the prevailing conflict in the Padua Commission. There, he felt, Ojetti was doing an excellent job with the enthusiastic backing of the national delegates, running a campaign which was naturally going to be largely an Italian affair. In contrast, Baker's attitude was inflexible and 'rather ambiguous even if he is not a complete idiot'. It was Baker, not Ojetti, who ought to be dismissed.[60]

Albertini's outlook entirely chimed with that of Ojetti. Ojetti would never accept Steed's idea that the Commission was an Allied body. As we have seen, the two concepts of an Italian or Allied campaign had their precise origins earlier in the year when both the Italians and British had separately come to the conclusion that psychological warfare ought to be more tightly coordinated against Austria-Hungary. Steed had, until April at least, erroneously worked on the premise that little had been done by Italy; while Ojetti had always been aware of previous Italian efforts, envisaging that his role was to work from an established Italian base, producing front propaganda of quality which would highlight Italy's nationality policy in the enemy trenches. To this end, he expected to run an Italian organization, assisted closely by the national delegates but with only occasional reference to Allied 'advisers'. From the start he had been irritated by Baker, who seemed to regard himself as something more than a British adviser. The scale of the irritation can be measured by his gripe to Albertini that Baker kept his office locked when away from Padua. Baker had insisted that all facilities be put at his disposal, but then at the Commission had done nothing but disparage Italy, treating it like 'the republic of Guatemala', alleging that the campaign had been imposed on the Italians by Britain, and above all encouraging mistrust among the Yugoslav delegates. This had done some damage to what Ojetti believed to be his generally harmonious relationship with his *balcanici*; particularly, he felt it had pushed Jambrišak to complain to Delmé-Radcliffe in early June. Therefore it was not surprising in the political climate of the early summer, with Ojetti himself anxious to clarify Italy's nationality policy, that he viewed Baker as an obstacle to good Italo-Yugoslav relations and even suggested that in this way the British were supporting Sonnino.[61]

Ironically, this was, of course, the very accusation which Baker was levelling at Ojetti. Baker continued to misinterpret Ojetti's determination to run an Italian campaign, his caution on the issue of Italo-Yugoslav aspirations, as proof of his personal support for the Treaty of London. Undoubtedly Baker confused Ojetti's views with those of Siciliani who was indeed a 'Sonnino man' whom Ojetti himself considered something of a liability.[62] On the other hand, Baker's complaints were not unfounded, nor did they result wholly from his own wounded pride or a certain aloofness. The evidence suggests that the national delegates were increasingly unhappy at being treated as mere translators, with their own writings subject to intensive Italian scrutiny and censorship.[63] Indeed, it was the excessive level of Italian control which led Jan Zamorski, the Polish delegate, to quit the Commission from mid-July. Officially, Zamorski departed at that time with the purpose of attending the Paris Congress. But it is clear that the Pole had precise grievances. He had been informed by the Italians that he had to keep regular office hours in Padua. For the headstrong Zamorski, who in Baker's words objected to 'interference by any military authority with his work which he does under orders of his National Committee', it was the last straw. He left in a huff and refused to return until he could be assured of his own independence; his place was taken by his deputy, Antoni Szuber. Ojetti seems to have blamed Siciliani but also Zamorski himself for this 'irreparable loss' to the Commission.[64] In fact the incident was an outcome which logically developed out of the ill-defined spheres of influence in Padua, where the national delegates usually had their own agenda and found Italian and military discipline as irksome as each other. By August, the Romanian Cotruş was itching to leave too. And in the middle of the month,

Trumbić would withdraw Jambrišak because of deadlock over Italy's attitude to the issue of Yugoslav volunteers.[65] In this way the Padua Commission was becoming a lone Italian instrument, and one where only the more submissive national delegates would remain.

Crewe House naturally challenged any such tendency. As Steed had reminded Albertini in early July, the Commission was supposed to be an inter-Allied body, set up to propagate the anti-Austrian ideas of those who alone understood the Austrian mentality, namely the national delegates. Steed optimistically hoped that that ideal might be achieved if both Baker and Ojetti could show some spirit of conciliation and collaboration.[66] But in the following weeks, Baker's constant complaints suggested that nothing had changed, while from what the EPD learnt from Albertini and O'Donovan it was clear that Baker himself, even if he appeared good on paper, was tactless and inflexible; on 20 July, Seton-Watson noted in his diary 'that both Ojetti and Baker must go'.[67] In the end Crewe House decided on a more defensive course. After O'Donovan had failed to arrange a meeting of reconciliation for Baker and Ojetti, the British simply recalled Baker to London for a month's counselling.[68]

It would be wrong, however, to suggest that Crewe House could only deal with the problem defensively and at arm's length. An alternative method was to exploit the aura which had surrounded the EPD since its inception in order to influence a change in propaganda technique among the Allies. In other words, the EPD would seek to draw the threads of 'Allied propaganda' together in its hands, using the occasion to put some pressure especially on the Italians. This was the purpose of the inter-Allied conference on Enemy Propaganda which Northcliffe convened in London in the middle of August. It was always undertaken partly in view of Crewe House's anxiety about Italy's ambiguous policy and Italian exclusiveness at Padua. But in addition there was now pressure for better Allied coordination from a different quarter, the United States.[69] From July 1918, the American Committee on Public Information [CPI] which had previously only had observers in Europe, began to establish itself more seriously in Allied countries. It appointed James Keeley, former editor of the *Chicago Herald*, as director of all CPI propaganda against the enemy, while a young Harvard lecturer named G.H. Edgell was designated the American delegate to the Padua Commission.[70]

The Americans were quite aware that inter-Allied cooperation was in its infancy. Since the propaganda conferences in Paris and London in March, the only real development had been the Padua Commission (which had occasionally been sent some data by the CPI agent in Rome). But the small Allied committee which Northcliffe's conference in March 1918 had proposed to set up 'to regulate a combined policy on enemy propaganda' had never materialized.[71] One reason was that establishing the centre at Padua had taken precedence. Another key reason was that the French since the spring had been reorganizing their propaganda machinery, and only by June was A. Klobukowski, the French envoy to Belgium, appointed to head it. Moreover, Commandant Chaix who by July was in charge of the Centre d'Action de Propagande contre l'Ennemi in Paris, displayed an attitude remarkably akin to Ojetti's in that he wished to run a purely French organization with only a few Allied advisers.[72] The upshot was that when James Keeley reached Europe he reported back to the CPI in Washington:

> We expected to find three organized and working Inter-Allied Propaganda Boards, one in Paris, one in London and one in Padua, which would be landmarks in the fields with which we would have to deal and to which we would immediately designate liaison officers. These boards are ghosts...[73]

This was a slight exaggeration, and all the more so if one compares Allied propaganda links with the paucity of any substantial coordination among the Central Powers for their propaganda campaigns. Nor was Keeley quite accurate in judging that 'there is considerable stirring of the ground but no clear and scientific ploughing'. On the contrary, one might argue that the actual techniques being used on the Italian Front constituted a major breakthrough in the field of psychological warfare. Keeley's impressions had the hint of a Steed before he had visited Italy in the spring. But likewise, the Americans' arrival in Europe suggested a reinvigoration of what had previously been attempted, with this time the inter-Allied conference acting as the first step to something new.

The conference was presided over by Northcliffe himself, whose recovery in health had undoubtedly accelerated its convening as his name gave weight to a serious British input. About 40 delegates gathered at Crewe House between 14 and 17 August. The British contingent included Steed, Seton-Watson, Granville Baker, Campbell Stuart, S.A. Guest, and representatives from military Intelligence; the French included Klobukowski and the famous propagandist Emil Haguenin; the Americans arrived under Keeley with four officers of US military Intelligence. Ironically, it was the Italian delegation which was the weakest. Northcliffe had hoped that Gallenga himself would attend, but the latter felt unable to do so due to the political crisis at home and instead, with Orlando's approval, he delegated the dependable Borgese. More significantly, no Italian representative came from the Padua Commission (although Gallenga had thought of designating Siciliani), so that the centre of much inter-Allied tension had no real voice. Nor were envoys of the subject peoples present who might have leant their weight in pressurizing the Italians; Crewe House had urged Trumbić and Jambrišak to attend, but Trumbić mistakenly continued to feel that more could be achieved by staying in Italy.[74] These weaknesses in representation in London only served to weaken the impact which the conference could have upon Italian front propaganda.

In his opening speech to the conference on 14 August, Northcliffe ran through the results already believed to have been achieved in the campaign against Austria-Hungary: they included the mythical 'victory' of delaying one Austrian offensive in April and sabotaging another in June. He then singled out for attention the crucial connection between effective propaganda and agreed policy, emphasizing that the time had come for greater Allied coordination in the campaign against the Central Powers. For this purpose, he suggested that the conference divide into four committees which would discuss and report on propaganda policy (the most important aspect), distribution by military and civil means, propaganda material, and prisoners of war.[75]

As far as Austria-Hungary was concerned, the decisions on 15 August of the policy committee were by far the most significant.[76] When this committee discussed Austria, Steed related recent history: the importance of the Rome Congress, the damage done at Versailles which had been recouped to a certain extent by Lansing's statement and British recognition of the Czechoslovaks; and he stressed the need at last for a joint Allied statement of recognition of the subject peoples' independence in time for the next Congress. Crewe House's view was best expressed in a memorandum which Seton-Watson had prepared for the conference:

> It is obvious that from the Propagandist standpoint what is most needed and certain of the maximum effect is, so to speak, the codification of Allied pronouncements regarding Austria-Hungary and its nationalities. The present position is that the Allied Governments have completely compromised themselves in certain directions but have hesitated to draw the full advantage from their action, like a bather who undresses but remains standing on the bank.[77]

Steed now particularly probed at Italy's ambiguous stance. He proposed that the conference should ask the British, French and American governments to press Rome to take the initiative in making a collective Allied declaration in favour of a Yugoslav state as one of the conditions of a just and lasting peace. Such a statement should also say that any secret treaty which seemed to be an obstacle to the creation of Yugoslavia would have to be modified.[78]

Guglielmo Emanuel, the *Corriere* correspondent in London, interpreted this as 'a real and directly frontal attack upon Italian foreign policy'.[79] It was left to Borgese to reply. Although Borgese supported the creation of Yugoslavia and in no way approved of the full implementation of the Treaty of London, he vigorously and eloquently objected to Steed's proposal. Viewing it as blatant interference by the Allies in a distinctly Italian sphere of influence, he also significantly rejected the idea that Italy could abandon the treaty. He pointed to the lack of consensus on the Yugoslav side: there was a history of 'Yugoslavs' questioning Italy's just aspirations to Trieste and the Littoral.[80] And at the same time Trumbić's Committee did not constitute an authoritative enough Yugoslav body with which Italy might finalize a territorial settlement (a statement which, coming from a 'Yugophile' like Borgese, was a damning comment on the Committee). Under these circumstances, he argued, it would be madness to renounce the treaty; to do so would be to play into Austria's hands and deprive Italy of an important safeguard for the future. In the end, Borgese was able to convince the policy committee of his views, probably through having French backing which placed Steed in a minority.[81] Indeed, the committee approved one motion which advised Yugoslavs to avoid controversial discussion of the Italian–Yugoslav borders (alleging openly that the Italian press had shown such discretion!); and another which recognized Italy's 'imprescriptible' right to union with 'the cities and regions of Trento and Trieste and the other regions of Italian character'. These motions were a quid pro quo for the Italians accepting a watered-down version of Steed's original proposal. Yet Borgese still ensured that there would be no direct Allied pressure on Rome for a Yugoslav declaration. Instead, the resolution read out to the conference on 16 August bowed to Italian judgement:

> The Policy Committee of the Inter-Allied Propaganda Conference resolves to suggest that the Italian Government take the initiative in promoting a joint and unanimous public declaration that all the Allies regard the establishment of a free and united Jugo-Slav state, embracing Serbs, Croats and Slovenes, as one of the conditions of a just and lasting peace, and of the rule of right in Europe.[82]

It was for Borgese and his Italians a subtle victory over Steed's onslaught. It was also tantamount to an admission by the British EPD that, in the propaganda campaign against Austria-Hungary, Italian dominance was a reality.

In his closing speech to the conference on 17 August, Northcliffe duly urged Borgese to bring the resolution as quickly as possible to the attention of the Italian government, since its effect might 'hasten the process of disintegration in the Austro-Hungarian Army'. Borgese concurred, reminding the British in his reply that it was Italy which had always been the pioneer in the crusade against Austria. Now, while pushing forward from a pro-Yugoslav platform, it had been essential to give Italy some extra guarantees as security for the future; they had been given, and would make the Italian propagandists' task a little easier. As a result, and in view of the new Allied coordination, Borgese felt optimistic that 'not only the technical but the political proposals that have arisen at our Conference will exercise the greatest possible influence upon the development of events'.[83] The EPD could only hope that this would be true as far as Rome was concerned.

If in this way the conference was exercising indirect pressure on Orlando, through trying to raise the whole subject of propaganda to an Allied level, it had done little in practical terms to inject a greater Allied dimension to the campaign organized on the Italian Front. The issue of the Padua Commission had been totally ignored to the benefit of a discussion of policy, admittedly the field in which the British EPD had always been most actively engaged. It is true that the conference finally resolved to set up a permanent inter-Allied body at Crewe House to coordinate 'Allied purpose and organization' in the campaigns against the enemy.[84] But even if this idea had not been still-born (because of the sudden end to the war) it seems doubtful, given the experience of the conference in August, that such a body would have had any quick influence in Padua. As we have seen, the campaign in the Italian theatre had been aided by, but always somewhat detached from, British or Allied influences, and this remained its character throughout. Northcliffe's conference revealed the limits of British influence, and the distance which would have to be travelled to create a truly Allied effort.

None the less, the conference played its part in forcing Italy to clarify its official stance towards a Yugoslav state. In that way it indirectly aided Ojetti, who undoubtedly wished to demonstrate a clearer Italian position in his Yugoslav manifestos. Even before the end of the conference Borgese had warned Orlando that Italy ought to take the initiative in the Yugoslav question, for otherwise others would do so, inflicting what he termed a 'diplomatic Caporetto' on the country.[85] As we have seen, those Italians who shared Borgese's concern were already sure that Britain's recognition of the Czechoslovaks as Allies had seriously compromised Italy's claim to be the leading protector of the oppressed. It was this which finally persuaded Albertini to begin a new crusade in the *Corriere della Sera* against Sonnino and the contradictions of Italian foreign policy.[86] On 17 August, the first article in the campaign appeared, written by Giovanni Amendola and entitled '*La politica anti-austriaca in Inghilterra e in Italia*'. It recalled Britain's Czech declaration, lamenting Italy's failure of initiative since the Rome Congress: 'It seems to us that the hour has come to set aside uncertainty and ambiguity and to give back to the nationality policy that tone and certainty which it should never have lost.' In the next fortnight the *Corriere* repeatedly attacked Sonnino for his rigid adherence to the Treaty of London and his belief that it could be implemented without the destruction of the Habsburg Empire. He was the main obstacle to Italy's 'new course', a course which in the spirit of Mazzini envisaged not territorial renunciations but rather an emphasis upon support for the oppressed. The nationality policy would not only guarantee that Italy defeated the enemy but would have long term benefits too, ensuring considerable Italian influence in the New Europe after the war. The *Corriere* arguments, although supported by most of the interventionist and nationalist press (including Mussolini's *Popolo d'Italia*), were fiercely rejected by Sonnino's mouthpiece, the *Giornale d'Italia*.[87] By September, as many leading politicians feared, the effect of the campaign seemed to be to place Sonnino more firmly in the saddle than ever. At the CS anyway, most officers had little sympathy for the *Corriere* ideas, viewing them as rather academic and still at variance with their own perception of the 'Austrian' enemy. Equally, much of educated Italian public opinion was still not in tune with the 'new course', responding more readily to the crude simplicity sounded by the *Giornale*. Despite this, Albertini had not totally missed his target. The campaigners had been, in Amendola's words, the 'disturbers of public calm', highlighting the ambiguity of Italian policy and increasing the pressure on Orlando to act.[88]

In fact Orlando himself was convinced by the argument that Britain's recognition of the Czechoslovaks had marginalized Italy. He realized the need to respond in some way to the chief resolution of Northcliffe's conference so as to restore some credibility to his nationality policy. At the same time he still wished to preserve a balance in his cabinet, to avoid a government crisis by not offending too much the 'porcupine Sonnino'[89] with whose views he secretly sympathized. He consequently felt the *Corriere* crusade to be inopportune, since it was raising the temperature of the foreign policy debate and making his chances of mediation more difficult; his perpetual vacillation was quite apparent to Ojetti whom he met again in the war zone in late August.[90] But his hopes of proceeding at a leisurely pace were dashed. Bissolati since mid-August had been expecting a meeting *à trois* with Sonnino to settle the Yugoslav question. When the weeks passed and it failed to occur, he threatened to resign if his two demands, a pro-Yugoslav declaration and a Yugoslav legion, were not discussed in cabinet. It required repeated threats from Bissolati, pressure from Borgese, and American recognition of the Czechoslovak National Council as a *de facto* government (3 September), before Orlando conceded the need to bring the issue before the full cabinet. On 8 September, after three lively sessions at which Bissolati was supported by Nitti, Gallenga and the Prime Minister himself,[91] Sonnino suddenly accepted a resolution which went some way towards that recommended by the Northcliffe conference:

> The Italian Government regards the movement of the Jugo-Slav peoples for the conquest of their independence and for their constitution in a free state as corresponding to the principles for which the Entente is fighting and also to the aims of a just and lasting peace.[92]

Bissolati viewed this as 'complete victory'. He urged Ojetti to assure the national delegates in Padua that Italy was now set on a steadfast course; the battle had been rough but the Sonninos had been overcome.[93] Ojetti duly proceeded, as we will see, to use the Italian statement to full advantage in his

Yugoslav manifestos from late September. Yet victory was really on the side of Orlando and Sonnino. Orlando had managed to perpetuate his Janus-like stance by making a concession to the Yugoslavs while at the same time clinging on to both Sonnino and the Treaty of London. In the following weeks, although continuing to assert Italy's support for the nationalities, he moved increasingly towards a full realignment with the view of his foreign minister. As for Sonnino, he had, in the face of the opposition on 8 September, made a minor concession to nationality politics, but had altered none of his opinions about the probable survival of Austria-Hungary; as he observed to the CPI agent in Rome, 'the bear should be caught before the hide is divided'.[94] His behaviour in cabinet had simply been a tactical manoeuvre. Thus, together with Orlando, he tried to prevent publication of the new pro-Yugoslav statement. Only after Steed had published the text in *The Times*, and after another shouting-match with Bissolati in cabinet, was it finally issued on 25 September by the Italian news agency. Even then, its impact was diminished by the press announcing, to Bissolati's disgust, that the declaration in no way abrogated the Treaty of London.

Although in appearance Italy had moved in the direction favoured by Northcliffe's conference, the ambiguity in Italy's position remained and would do so until the end of the war. It perpetuated tension between Rome and the Italian propagandists for whom the nationality policy had always been the bedrock of their campaign: they wanted an unequivocal Italian statement that their country was fighting for the freedom of all nationalities under the Habsburg yoke. However, it should be emphasized that the propagandists themselves were never prepared to back the Yugoslav cause unreservedly. Ojetti, Borgese or Bissolati might want Italy to make an open commitment to Yugoslav unity for immediate and long-term benefits; but, as is clear from Borgese's remarks at the August conference, they were quite aware of the dangers of spelling out how the territorial settlement would affect Italy. In particular, although they believed in distributing 'Yugoslav propaganda' against the enemy, they always seem to have retained a core of doubt about it. There were obvious signs that a Yugoslav state might adversely affect Italian aspirations in the future.

There were also signs (which we know to be accurate) that the image publicized by the Yugoslav Committee of all Serbs, Croats and Slovenes as 'Yugoslav' was a flawed one. On this subject, Ojetti and others were rather more realistic than Crewe House which wholeheartedly embraced the Yugoslav ideal. Nevertheless, the Padua Commission did not stop issuing material which lauded the work of the Yugoslav Committee and its 'good relations' with Italy, even though one might argue that to work with such an openly Yugoslav agenda (rather than appealing to Serbs, Croats and Slovenes separately) was probably self-defeating. After all, Ante Trumbić did not have the full trust of Italy's government or military, and in the enemy trenches the degree of specifically 'Yugoslav' consciousness was always questionable. It was perhaps the ultimate irony that Steed and his colleagues, who talked repetitively about a tight link between propaganda and truth, were always pressing upon Padua a Yugoslav agenda which did not reflect a 'Yugoslav reality' either in Italy or in the Austro-Hungarian trenches. This whole issue, apart from the problem of whether the campaign was an Italian or Allied affair, was the one which consistently bedevilled Ugo Ojetti's work at Padua. But it did not deflect him from energetically pursuing his aim over the summer, and it to this which we must now turn.

## 8.3 Padua's summer campaign: the 'Oppressed Nationalities'

Notwithstanding the tensions at Padua, over the summer Ojetti and the national delegates still managed to compose hundreds of new leaflets. From mid-June to mid-September 375 different manifestos were composed,[95] while the Italian Intelligence offices issued separately a variety of leaflets to publicize crucial events of the war or news of interest to their own sector of the front. The momentum reflected CS enthusiasm about the potential of psychological warfare. In late July, General Diaz himself told Ojetti that he was concerned about the ambiguity of Italian policy, and wrote to Orlando, asking him to increase the number of Slavophile manifestations which were so valuable for propaganda.[96]

Even during the Austrian offensive in June, the distribution of Italian propaganda over the enemy had not diminished. Padua had issued some special material, including a leaflet from 'Trumbić' which spelt out the choice for Croats and Slovenes:

> The decisive battle has begun. Either justice will conquer and the sun of freedom for all nations will shine, or the coarse, brutal force of German militaristic barbarism will conquer, which would signify: further slavery. At this great moment it is the duty of every Serb, Croat and Slovene not only not to fight on the Austrian side, but to thrust their bayonets into Magyar and German chests.[97]

As the offensive progressed, Italian propaganda kept the enemy so regularly informed about the course of events that its news reached them almost at the same time as the official Austrian reports. Rumours that Conrad's troops had reached the plains were refuted, while Diaz's daily war bulletins were distributed to prove the strength of Italian resistance.[98] Not all the material, however, kept within the bounds of reality. Ojetti was clearly irritated when he discovered that some Intelligence offices had been issuing leaflets which announced that revolution had broken out in the Monarchy and that Boroević's forces were marching there to restore order. His reaction suggests that he (rightly) perceived certain limits which could not be exceeded if the material was to be believed.[99] The same sentiments seem to have coloured his view on what was suitable to publish after the offensive. Baker was only too ready to report to London that the Italians had distributed 'songs of exultation over Italy's great victory'. In fact, while a few leaflets had more than a hint of chauvinism (that Italy was fighting for 'freedom and culture'), Ojetti was more concerned to rub a little salt into the wounds than to brag excessively about Italy's victory.[100] The manifestos more subtly contrasted the Austrian military's promise of booty and peace on the eve of the offensive with the miserable results (allegedly 300 000 casualties).[101] They also turned particular attention towards 'Germany's role' in the fiasco. While the Austrian socialist *Arbeiter-Zeitung* could be quoted to show that blood had been spilt for Germany alone,[102] Padua eagerly pounced on some inaccurate intelligence according to which General von Below, one of the German commanders at Caporetto, had been appointed commander of all Austrian forces in the Italy. The 'arrogant Prussian war-lord' was even now planning to send Austrian troops to the slaughter again in a 'wonderful new offensive'.[103]

In the following months, besides returning occasionally to the decisive Piave defeat, Ojetti directed at soldiers of all nationalities a number of key themes to prove that the war was lost for the Central Powers. It was a mirror image of what Austrian propaganda had proclaimed about Italy in the spring of 1918. Padua's message of despair might at times be over-dramatic, but it now seemed to reflect accurately the vivid unfolding of events on the Western Front where Germany had launched a last offensive on 15 July. Indeed, it was events in the West, and then in the Balkans, which now most bluntly illustrated the concept of defeat on the battlefield, for there was no such drama to match it in the Italian theatre in the summer. Some leaflets ascribed Ludendorff's offensive in the West to German anger at the Piave defeat:

> The waters of the Piave, dyed red with your blood, were still muddy and the corpses of many tens of thousands of your comrades had scarcely started to putrify when the German Emperor, furious at the defeat of the Austro-Hungarian army on the Piave, ordered a decisive offensive against the Anglo-French armies. Kaiser Wilhelm II ordered his lunch to be served in Paris on 14 July [*sic*], the anniversary of French freedom.[104]

Instead, the Kaiser was taught 'a bloody lesson' on the river Marne. Padua's manifestos were able regularly to report, often with detailed maps, the steady German retreat before General Foch's counter-offensive on 18 July and the successful Anglo-French attack west of Amiens on 8 August. The victorious advance continued, bringing the Allies thousands of prisoners while making the German people ever more disillusioned and pessimistic. Radical German newspapers could be quoted to show that 'an awful abyss yawns under the feet of the German people', and that Habsburg soldiers ought to break their own chains immediately if they were not to suffer the same dismal fate.[105] Certainly (and here Ojetti's use of the 'German threat' was turned on its head) the Austrians could no longer expect any help from Germany on the Italian Front. Rather, like 'a drowning man grasping at a straw to keep above water', Germany had demanded that its ally send troops to the West.[106] The reality in fact was that the AOK had only reluctantly agreed in late June to dispatch two infantry divisions (the lst and 35th) to the Western Front.[107] But for Padua, the issue of Austria's full subservience to Germany was always a major theme to be set out in the starkest colours. Thus: 'The faithful servant of Germany, Emperor Karl, has already sent some of his starving divisions to the French Front to rescue Germany and pan-Germanism'; other divisions would be following to be treated by Hindenburg as cannon-fodder, 'driven to the butcher's slab by the manic madness of the German and Austrian Emperors'.[108]

Nor was there any prospect of a change in fortune for the Central Powers. A second supra-national theme in Allied propaganda during the summer was the vastness of American resources. Already by 1 July, according to a much-publicized correspondence between President Wilson and his Secretary of War, there were a million Americans in France; with 10 000 new soldiers reaching Europe every day, the number would total two-and-a-half million by Christmas and four million by spring 1919.[109] In contrast to the exhausted troops of the Central Powers, the American soldiers were 'young and robust men of 20–25 years of age. They fight like lions and are certainly the best soldiers in Europe.'[110] They were only the tip of the iceberg of what the United States could and would contribute to the Allied cause of freedom and justice, disproving the earlier claims of Austrian propaganda that the war would be won before the Americans could make an impact. In manifesto 269 entitled 'What all America contributes to annihilate the militarism of Germany and Austria-Hungary' (the information for which appears to have been telegraphed to Padua by Crewe House), enemy soldiers were reminded that America was replacing for the Entente what had been lost through Russia's withdrawal from the war. The speech of nine Congressmen visiting London was quoted to show America's resolve to fight until militarism was crushed and its capability of doing so: namely, its stock of 20 million troops, its endless food supplies, its 25 000 planes, its daily production of 720 000 shells.[111] Well might the *Arbeiter-Zeitung* (a favourite source for Padua) comment that America's entry into the war dissolved the Central Powers' hope of a victory through arms, for it now appeared that the reserves of the whole world were at the Allies' disposal. Even distant Siam was doing its bit in the crusade against Prussian militarism by supplying 500 aviators to the European battlefields.[112]

Such a united front could easily be contrasted with the Monarchy's blatant inability to continue the war for much longer. Borgese's bureau in Berne did not have to search the Austrian press too thoroughly to supply Padua with good examples of the appalling food crisis in the empire. At the same time that American ships were bringing daily supplies to the Allies, the mayor of Vienna was publicly accusing the Germans of not fulfilling their promises of grain; there were hunger riots in Galicia; civilians were eating grass in Bosnia; and, allegedly, even the Viennese Reichsrat had to be adjourned in late July because the parliamentary buffet had run out of food![113] Nor was there the remotest possibility that the authorities would find grain supplies in Ukraine as they had bragged earlier. As Padua regularly reminded its readership, events in the East were chaotic and now running counter to the Monarchy's interests. The Russian people was rising up against the Bolshevik regime and its hated German supporters; German representatives such as Mirbach and Eichhorn had been assassinated;[114] and the shock of Allied military success in Russia had allegedly been so great as to cause Kaiser Wilhelm to fall ill. Thus Lenin's regime, portrayed by Ojetti as 'the tyranny of a few Jewish profiteers', was rapidly nearing its end: instead of grain supplies, the Central Powers were allegedly finding a new front being set up against them in the East.[115]

Simultaneously with this theme of the inevitable defeat of Austria-Hungary, Padua broadcast to the different nationalities a message of hope: that the Allies were fighting for a just peace and liberty for all peoples. This message could be individually packaged for each nationality, and it carried increasing weight in these months, firstly because of the West's public commitment to the nationality principle, and secondly because of the extent to which radical nationalism was taking firm root in the Monarchy itself. This is not to deny that Padua's arguments were stronger for some nationalities than others (for the Czechs more than the Romanians, for the Poles far more than the Ruthenes), reflecting in itself the respective progress made by each national movement at home and abroad. Even so, Ojetti still managed to focus his data quite effectively in order to match the prevailing range of ethnic mentalities. It was a fact which was duly acknowledged by the Habsburg authorities, making them feel all the more beleaguered.

With regard to propaganda directed specifically at 'Yugoslav' soldiers or civilians, the Commission produced from mid-June to mid-September 54 new manifestos (about five million copies) and 12 editions of the weekly newssheet *Jugoslavija* (1 400 000 copies). This was about 20 per cent of the total production in this period.[116] Most of it, signed by the 'Yugoslav Committee' and containing far fewer spelling and typographical errors than before, was in the Croat language, possibly again an indication that Padua wanted to stress a Yugoslav uniformity, or perhaps simply a sign that typesetting in the Cyrillic script was more difficult. There was also now an increasing amount of material in the Slovene language, including Slovene passages in the newssheet, due to the active participation of Stojan Lasić whom Kujundžić described as 'loquacious but very industrious and useful'.[117]

Much of the Yugoslav propaganda proclaimed the vague ideal (with no mention of the Corfu Declaration or territorial issues) of a free, united and independent state of Serbs, Croats and Slovenes. According to one special newssheet, manifesto 203, published to commemorate the outbreak of war between Serbia and Austria, 'Now we are split up, separated like fingers on a hand, we must concentrate them into one so that from weak digits there becomes a strong fist.' This, the pamphlet maintained, should not be feared as a 'Bolshevik dream', for the Serbs, Croats and Slovenes were one nation of 12 million people who desired a Yugoslav state and had the firm backing of the Allied Powers.[118] In view of the confusion over the Yugoslav issue in Allied lands, it was naturally a lot easier for Padua to make these vague pronouncements of Allied commitment than to give concrete evidence of that pledge. The leaflets asserted that an independent Yugoslav state was one of the Entente's conditions for peace, even though the only real proof of this was given in Robert Lansing's statement of 28 June, and in a declaration by the American Senator Henry Cabot Lodge on 24 August.[119] Even so, as we have noted, Padua also did not make the most of the 'evidence' that was available. Its output appears to have contained no reference to Pichon's statement of 29 June, nor to Balfour's Mansion House speech which Steed had expected to be 'excellent material for propaganda'.

However, in the early summer in particular, the theme of warm Italian–Yugoslav cooperation continued to be a regular motif in the manifestos. During the Piave offensive, 'Trumbić', while urging his compatriots to revolt, assured them that 'relations between us and the Italians are first-rate and we have also told each other that in the future we will live as the best of neighbours and friends'.[120] It was a message which seemed to be confirmed by accounts of his official meeting with Orlando, or by the celebrations in Rome on 28 June to mark the anniversary of the battle of Kosovo. At the latter event Trumbić had spoken of the Allies' solidarity and of his enthusiastic reception at the prison camp of Nocera Umbra the previous day, while Andrea Torre had read out a telegram from Orlando, reminding the audience that in spite of two defeats on Kosovo field the Serbian people had never been conquered; like Italy, they too would rise again to take part in a brilliant future.[121] In similar vein, though without the Italian link, the 'Yugoslav Committee' spoke directly to enemy soldiers of Serb nationality in one of the few leaflets printed in Cyrillic script:

> Kosovo became the symbol of our national Golgotha, but was at the same time a horribly expensive lesson which today especially we must make use of...Now is the time when, learning by our experience, we must avoid a new Kosovo which would bury for ever our freedom and unity. We will avoid it if, with that same sacrifice with which the knights of old fought 'for the holy cross and golden freedom', we fight for our unity and freedom.[122]

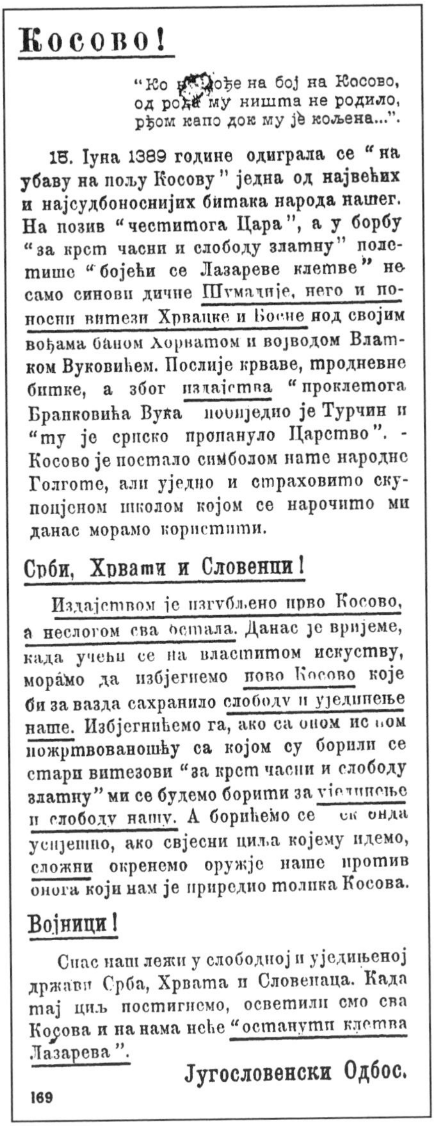

**Косово!**

"Ко [illegible]ође на бој на Косово,
од рода му ништа не родило,
рђом капо док му је кољена...".

15. Іуна 1389 године одиграла се "на убаву на пољу Косову" једна од највећих и најсудбоноснијих битака народа нашег. На позив "честитога Цара", а у борбу "за крст часни и слободу златну" полетише "бојећи се Лазареве клетве" не само синови дичне <u>Шумадије, него и поносни витези Хрвацке и Босне</u> под својим вођама баном Хорватом и војводом Влатком Вуковићем. Послије крваве, тродневне битке, а због <u>издајства</u> "проклетога Бранковића Вука" побиједио је Турчин и "ту је српско пропануло Царство". - Косово је постало симболом наше народне Голготе, али уједно и страховито скупоцјеном школом којом се нарочито ми данас морамо користити.

**<u>Срби, Хрвати и Словенци!</u>**

<u>Издајством је изгубљено прво Косово, а неслогом сва остала.</u> Данас је вријеме, када учени се на властитом искуству, морамо да избјегнемо <u>ново Косово</u> које би за вазда сахранило <u>слободу и уједињење наше.</u> Избјегнићемо га, ако са оном истом пожртвованошћу са којом су борили се стари витезови "за крст часни и слободу златну" ми се будемо борити за <u>уједињење и слободу нашу.</u> А борићемо се [illegible] онда успјешно, ако свјесни циља којему идемо, <u>сложни</u> окренемо оружје наше против онога који нам је приредио толика Косова.

**<u>Војници!</u>**

Спас наш лежи у слободној и уједињеној држави Срба, Хрвата и Словенаца. Када тај циљ постигнемо, осветили смо сва Косова и на нама неће <u>"остануги клетва Лазарева".</u>

**Југословенски Одбос.**

169

*Illustration 8.1* Manifesto 169: Serbs should reflect on the lessons of Kosovo (KA)

That Italy was still committed to this same ideal, and was helping to avenge Kosovo and banish the 'curse of Prince Lazar' (killed at the fateful battle in 1389), might be deduced also from the way in which the Italians were treating Yugoslav prisoners. Manifestos composed in the early summer continued to mention the 'extraordinarily kind' treatment of prisoners, of how they were united with their compatriots and were cared for by delegates from the Yugoslav Committee:

> On the 14th [July] two delegates of the Yugoslav Committee visited our prisoners. They could not recognize them as they had made such a good recovery. One Bosnian declared that, *after reading our newspaper he deserted because he saw where the truth lay*. Now he is not sorry, as not only has he saved himself but he does not have to fight anymore for the Krauts and Magyars, the greatest murderers of our people.[123]

Not surprisingly, in view of Italian sensitivity about Yugoslav prisoners, such visits could not be described in later leaflets, nor could Padua dwell as in its Czech material on the presence of a strong volunteer force at the front. There could be hints that a Yugoslav legion was in the making, that prisoners in Italy could volunteer to fight against Austria (and were not compelled to do so as the Austrians disgracefully suggested). But generally Ojetti had to make the most of references to Yugoslav forces in Russia or America. The realities of the situation in Italy therefore limited Padua's arguments on this subject, as also on the broader theme of Italo-Yugoslav cooperation to which there were few references in the propaganda material composed in August.[124]

While vaguely supporting a free and united Yugoslav state, Padua continued to emphasize as its antithesis the oppression of the South Slavs which was a major aim of the German and Magyar races of the Monarchy. This contrast was perhaps most vividly illustrated by manifesto 101, an open letter from Trumbić to FM Boroević dated 23 June. It was actually written by Jambrišak by mid-June and, after a thorough vetting by Ojetti, was distributed widely over the front and southern Slav regions.[125] According to Delmé-Radcliffe, Padua did not expect the leaflet to influence Boroević himself, but hoped that it would 'produce a considerable sensation among the population'.[126] In the leaflet Trumbić begged to say a few words to the Field Marshal at 'this critical moment for the development of all mankind'. At a time when the Yugoslav people wished to be master of its own house and the Allies, especially Italy through the historic resolutions of the Rome Congress, had shown their commitment to this ideal, why was Boroević, instead of acting as a liberator for the Yugoslavs, leading the flower of the nation to destruction? Did he not realize that he was fighting for 'an obsolete anachronistic principle', for Germany, against whom the whole world had arisen since 'the very essence of German authority and culture is a misfortune for humanity'?:

> A culture which in every way systematically brings immorality to all non-German peoples, a culture which develops the lowest instincts in the non-German masses, isolates them and causes dissension amongst them, and

> then with its brutal military hand subjects everything to its service – there! that is the present German culture, that is the picture of Mittel-Europa. Knowledge, science, technology, everything had and has to serve the German plan to rule the world. One should remember the German ways and methods in Russia and among the oppressed peoples of Austria-Hungary. The spread of alcoholism, the spread of pornographic literature, corruption, the destruction of family morality amongst the nations, those are the methods and fruits of German culture.

Those were the aims which Boroević was serving, falling into the same error as Ban Jelačić, the Croatian hero of 1848, who had served Vienna only to have a brutal absolutism imposed on his people in the 1850s. History, warned 'Trumbić', was merciless in its judgement: Boroević had started on a course which could result in his replacing Vuk Branković (the traitor of Kosovo) in future Yugoslav ballads.

This diatribe against all things German, which at the same time tried to appeal to a hazy Yugoslav history encompassing both Croat and Serb traditions, drew the particular attention of the Austrian authorities in view of its direct attack on Boroević. Max Ronge thought it worthy of mention in his memoirs, while the FAst was quick to condemn Trumbić in one of its circulars, praising Boroević as 'the better son of his people' for knowing that the only real enemy of the South Slavs was Italian imperialism.[127] For Padua, it was only the start of a mass of leaflets which sought to display the reality of German and Magyar oppression in the Monarchy, based on a far wider range of information than previously possible. The Empire was described as being, since Karl's 'Canossa' to Spa in May 1918, another version of Turkey, completely subordinate to Germany. In military terms this did not only mean that Habsburg troops on the Italian Front were dying at the German Kaiser's command, but was given a more sinister twist:

> According to reliable news, German troops are already to be found in the Monarchy and are disguised in Austrian uniform. Others are concentrated on the border and they expect at any moment the order to march in. In Budapest, where German troops arrived with the excuse of creating order and peace, the people are unusually excited. Bloody conflicts are the order of the day, and at night attacks on German patrols are so frequent that the government has adopted the strictest measures to prevent them. So the Monarchy suffocates already with a fatal death-rattle.[128]

This story was sheer fabrication, but was let through by Ojetti as a simple exaggeration of underlying realities. It was matched by manifestos alleging that on 30 April hundreds of Magyar troops had invaded Zagreb, brutally attacking the homes of two Croat MPs and finally occupying the Croatian assembly itself. As one newssheet concluded: 'Drunken Magyar hordes are smashing and violating all that you hold sacred. Tell each other secretly what you need to do.'[129]

More reliably, Borgese's bureau in Switzerland was able to extract from the Austrian press the news of two damning declarations which spoke volumes about the real mentality of some German leaders in Austria. On 16 July, the Viennese Reichsrat had reconvened for the first time since March. The Prime Minister, Ernst von Seidler, in a speech which one deputy warned would be of great value to the Entente's propaganda offensive,[130] had bowed to German-Austrian pressure and recognized his government's 'German course', that one could not rule against the interests of the Germans in Austria as they formed the backbone of the Monarchy.[131] In seizing upon Seidler's open partiality for the Germans, Padua proceeded to link his 'internal offensive' in the Reichsrat against the Slav–Latin majority of Austria with the renewed German offensive on the Western Front against the Allies. Convinced that Germany's attack would be successful, Seidler had prematurely dropped his Austrian mask to reveal his pan-German face. Then, Padua maintained, when Germany was rebuffed in the West, Seidler had been forced to resign as Prime Minister by a desperate Austrian elite who were now on the defensive themselves.[132]

If further proof were needed that Austrian policy was serving pan-Germanism, Padua could recount appeals by the Germans of Vienna, demanding a 'German course' against all Czech and Yugoslav aspirations, and particularly the striking declaration of a notorious German radical deputy, Friedrich Wichtl.[133] Wichtl's speech, in Styria on 12 July, was published in the Maribor daily *Straža*, was unashamedly racist, and for that reason came in for some criticism even from military quarters.[134] Answering his own question as to what should be done with the Slavs, he said: 'We must decimate their number and break up their unity, otherwise they really will become extraordinarily dangerous for the German race.' Asserting that war was the best means to achieve this goal, he gave figures to show how the Germans had successfully exterminated 20 million Slavs in the previous four years, predicting that with another two years of war the Czechs could be completely destroyed. However, he warned, the Yugoslavs as a compact mass, not surrounded by Germans, were more threatening than the Czechs and should at all costs be prevented from creating Yugoslavia:

> We must seek to decimate the Yugoslav people. We have the means for achieving this goal: German schools, war, lack of food or, in other words, starvation. The alliance with Germany must correspond to German desires. The alliance must be a common German house in which we will speak only German, think only German and wage war only in the German way. Thus Germany and Austria will form only one state: a Greater Germany.[135]

It was not difficult for Padua to portray Wichtl's dream as nearing reality. Apart from the alleged military and political subordination of the Monarchy to Germany, the same message could be stressed in economic terms. To give one example, the governor of Trieste seemed to be following 'the perfidious recipe of the notorious Slav-devouring [*slavoždera*]' Wichtl when he ordered requisitioning among the already famished population of Istria and the Croatian islands.[136]

In these circumstances Padua's manifestos stressed that it was not enough for a good Yugoslav soldier simply to declare 'in merry company with a glass of wine' that he hated the Kraut and Magyar. Rather, now was the time to follow the example of legendary 'Yugoslav' heroes like Zrinjski or Matija Gubec, to turn all weapons against the tyrants, against 'that monster which is called Austria-Hungary'.[137] Those Yugoslav troops who still hesitated to act because of loyalty to the Habsburgs were reminded that Karl as King of Croatia had himself trampled on his oath to the Croats and Serbs by permitting Magyar oppression in Croatia. 'Credible' rumours were also now circulating in the Monarchy, accusing the imperial family, and Empress Zita in particular, of treachery and espionage to the benefit of the enemy: crimes in other words, for which thousands of Yugoslavs had been executed during the war. Reproducing this gossip from the Austrian press was the nearest that Padua ever got to openly attacking the imperial couple apart from briefly describing Karl as a liar (because of the Sixtus Affair) or as the servant of Kaiser Wilhelm. It was a sign that, in contrast to the latter who could be vilified at every opportunity, the Austrian Emperor was rarely viewed as a worthy target.[138]

For Yugoslav soldiers, the path which they should follow had been mapped out by their heroic historic predecessors. But they could also emulate their contemporary leaders in the hinterland, many of whom by the summer months were moving into a new phase of grass-roots mobilization on behalf of South Slav unity and opposition to the Habsburgs. To illustrate this radical shift, Ojetti again had far more material to hand than previously. He was able for example to reproduce 'ten rules for the true Croat, Serb and Slovene' which seem to have first appeared in mid-July in *Volja Naroda*, a radical new paper being published in Varaždin; the Zagreb military authorities had tried to prevent it reaching troops in the war zone.[139] But Padua was also able, mainly from information secured via Berne, to give hints and sometimes more specific information about the real progress of Yugoslav agitation in the Monarchy. In keeping with the actual state of affairs,[140] little could be said about the political movement in Croatia where the Serb–Croat Coalition continued to maintain an opportunistic stance until October 1918. Only the Coalition's opponents could be quoted as having demanded in the Sabor (27 June) that the Yugoslav question should be settled on the basis of national self-determination as recognized by all free and democratic states of the world.[141]

However, with regard to the more radical movement in Slovene regions, where plans were afoot in the early summer to establish in Ljubljana a National Council which would eventually be a branch of a central Yugoslav Council in Zagreb, useful details of the mounting agitation filtered through to the Allied propagandists. They could report important resolutions made by Slovene socialists about self-determination and Yugoslav unity, as well as news from the Swiss *Neue Züricher Zeitung* according to which on 1 June a National Council of all Slovene political parties had been founded in Ljubljana. This was actually inaccurate, since on 1 June the Slovene leaders had only discussed future organization of such a council (and socialists had declined to join it).[142] But when it came to the actual event, the so-called Slav Days of 16–18 August at which a Slovene National Council was created in Ljubljana, Padua was fully alert to its significance and proclaimed: 'Greetings to you, white Ljubljana, capital of Slovenia, northern seat of Yugoslavia! . . . An important chapter in the history of your people is written today in your house!'

Subsequent manifestos stressed that the Slav Days were vital not only as proof of the awakened consciousness of all Yugoslavs, for Slovene, Croat and Serb leaders had all participated; but also, as Anton Korošec himself intended, as a further manifestation of solidarity between the Yugoslav, Czech and Polish nations. For just like the celebrations in Prague in May 1918, so in Ljubljana in August, distinguished Czech and Polish representatives joined with Yugoslav politicians in calling for freedom and national unification.[143] These meetings had been convened on a date which coincided with the Emperor's birthday and had taken place despite police prohibition; there had been little regard for the authorities' demand for strict censorship in press coverage of the events.[144] Padua was easily able to acquire the main details and hammer them home in its manifestos. Indeed, the Slav Days aptly reflected the crumbling state of Habsburg authority in the summer of 1918, something which the Padua Commission summed up in one of its most vivid passages in the Slovene language:

> Germany and Austria lit the conflagration, but they did not think that there would accumulate in Austria in the course of time so much fuel to be able to inflame the whole house if it caught fire. The oppressed Austrian peoples are that fuel and that enormous mass has now been set alight, and all the German and Magyar firemen are not able to extinguish the conflagration engulfing the old Austrian house. 'Fire! Fire!' cry the frightened firemen. They mobilize all the Austrian hose-pipes of the old and new systems, but the blaze spreads ever further. In vain are all your efforts, German and Magyar firemen! You should have thought about the possibility of fire before. Now it is too late! Your house is burning to the ground, and we are building a new one according to our plan and without you.[145]

As with the Yugoslav material, propaganda in the Czech, Romanian and Polish languages in the summer emphasized a simple polarization of the ideological struggle in Europe. On the one hand was the imminent victory of the national struggle for freedom, the struggle being successfully waged both by the West and in the Monarchy; on the other hand, the tyranny and misery which any German victory would entail. Czechoslovak propaganda, none of which was in Slovak, could of course give far more proof than the Yugoslav about the vitality of the Czechoslovak cause in Allied countries. It consistently played on the existence of the Czech Legions. In Russia, where Czech troops were fighting against Bolshevism along the Trans-Siberian railway, they could be praised as making a major contribution to both the Allied cause and the cause of Czech recognition.[146] Nearer home, Padua's manifestos were often signed by 'soldiers of the Czechoslovak army in Italy'; they dwelt as usual on their excellent treatment, but particularly now on their heroism during the June offensive when Czechs and Italians had spilt blood for a common ideal.[147] A constant refrain, that Czechs should not fight against their own countrymen, was most poignantly transmitted in manifesto 243, 'Brothers! Brothers!' This described an actual incident which had occurred on Monte di Val Bella in June, when two brothers from the opposing trenches had encountered one another. The leaflet colourfully illustrated their embrace, while reminding Czechs that they all had a fraternal bonding from their Hussite and Sokol heritage, were sons of the same Bohemia, and were viewed by Italy as sons of a fraternal nation.[148]

If Italy's commitment to the Czech cause was implicit in the presence of the Legion, and more openly espoused by Orlando after the Piave victory, Czech propaganda could further offset any perceived weakness of the Versailles Declaration through the British, French and American statements which had flowed out in the early summer.[149] The most crucial, as we have seen, was Balfour's declaration of 9 August. This British recognition of the Czechoslovaks was given the widest publicity by Padua, more so than any other Allied statement in 1918, in almost all languages of the Monarchy. It was trumpeted not only as signifying de facto independence for a Czechoslovak state, but also, as even the German press warned, as tantamount to *Delenda Austria*: 'the decay and end of the hitherto existing Habsburg Empire'.[150] Quite correctly, the Austrian authorities could be alarmed, for the Czech leaders at home and abroad now felt fully justified in proclaiming their cause as an 'international' issue which could only be solved at the peace conference.

As in the southern Slav regions, the Czech movement at home also began to crystallize in the early summer. Padua duly reported that on 13 July a National Council had been created in Prague which called for self-determination for the Czechoslovak nation. This could be set alongside newly strident speeches from the Czech Club in the Reichsrat. On the 22nd, Adolf Stránský, in a speech which one army command rightly suspected would be exploited by enemy

*Illustration 8.2* Manifesto 243: Two Czech brothers meet on Val Bella (KA)

propaganda, condemned Seidler for embarking on a German course which would divide up Bohemia along national lines. Four days later, the leader of the Czech Club, František Staněk, boasted to the Parliament:

> Never was a people more united and ready for battle, never so certain of victory as at this moment. The whole Czech nation is united in an unshakeable determination no longer to be subject to a foreign yoke under foreign colours...The Czechoslovak state is a fact which is inevitably approaching realization. On that point, nobody, neither here nor in Budapest, is still in doubt.[151]

Even the faint stirrings of Slovak politicians from May 1918 were noticed by Padua just as they were noticed by the military authorities in Hungary. The manifestos briefly mentioned the important declaration by Vavro Šrobár at Liptovský Sväty Mikuláš (1 May) calling for self-determination for the Hungarian Slovaks; as well as Slovak participation at the Prague theatre celebrations after which the Hungarian authorities had moved against them.[152] Thus the fate of the Slovaks under a Magyar yoke was clearly, if briefly, portrayed as being on a par with that of the Czechs in German-dominated Austria.

In keeping again with the opportunistic character of domestic Czech agitation at this time, Padua did not have many Staněk-type speeches to relay back across the front. Ojetti was better served by Czech comments from the Allied side. But the manifestos compensated for this by amply reporting the miserable economic crisis in Bohemia, contrasting the 'famine' in Prague with the food shortages in Vienna. The German authorities were portrayed as 'bloody-thirsty rogues' who thought nothing of shooting starving women and children in the streets of Plzeň; thus, one leaflet in only a slight flight of fancy concluded that 'Czech blood has already flowed at home and still flows in streams'.[153] The main example for Czechs to follow was that of their brothers in Italy, but Ojetti also resurrected the image of Jan Hus as a worthy predecessor who had suffered similar torment. Czech soldiers were told to take heart from Hus, who was pictured in a saintly pose in his cell, and assume their natural role as 'fighters for truth, right, justice and all the greatest ideals of mankind'.[154] Even more than Yugoslav propaganda, Czech propaganda was imbued with a deeply moralistic and sacrificial streak which drew its strength from the blood which Czechs were allegedly shedding everywhere for the national ideal.

Padua illustrated the comparable suffering endured by Romanians by taking examples especially from the Romanian kingdom which the Central Powers had occupied since 1916. The harsh peace treaty which they had imposed in May 1918 had, according to Padua, transformed Romania into a prison. Under the puppet government of Alexandru Marghiloman and with 300 000 German soldiers in control, the country was being bled of its resources of oil and grain. Civilians, at the mercy of these 'barbarous hordes', had even been forced to remove from public places all pictures of the pro-Entente politician, Take Ionescu. It was in this deplorable situation that a great Transylvanian poet, Gheorghe Coşbu, had died in Bucharest.[155] If further proof were needed of the oppression, it could come from the lips of Take Ionescu himself. Having obtained permission to go abroad, where some believed he would do less harm than in Romania, Ionescu arrived in Switzerland on 2 July and gave a long interview to an Italian newspaper; his description of conditions at home was reproduced in Padua's weekly *Neamul Românesc* under the caption, 'Terrible German rule in Romania'.[156] Yet as usual, Padua's message was not wholly

Nechť Vás posílí pohled na velkého mučedníka

M. JANA HUSA!

On nezná váhání ani pochyb. Silná duše a pevná vůle Jeho nepřipouštějí vteřiny slabosti; jeho cesta jasně vytčena. Jen do vzdálené vlasti, k milovanému národu zalétají Jeho vzpomínky a drahým Čechům piše svůj poslední vzkaz....

Nyní národ náš staví nejdůstojnější pomník svému Hledateli Pravdy, neboť oživen Jeho duchem jde neohroženě, hotov ke všem obětem, za poznanou Pravdou.

Dnes, silou poměrů a osudu, největší pravdou pro nás jest, že národ musí se zbaviti poroby a do vlastních rukou vzíti správu svých osudů!

Celý národ poznal pravdu, mluví pravdu a stojí v poznané pravdě! To dosvědčují historické dny české - 6. leden, 13. duben a 16. květen t. r.

Statisíce nových Božích bojovníků vyvstalo, jimž kostnické plameny jsou majákem na bouřném postupu za Pravdou.

Odvrzte od sebe Lež i Vy, bratři, lež habsburskou a rakouskou!

Dokažte i Vy činně, že není Čecha, který by bránil klam a násilí, nýbrž že jeho místo bylo, jest a bude vždy mezi bojovníky

za pravdu, právo, spravedlnost
a všechny nejvyšší ideály Lidstva.

*V Italii, dne 6. července 1918.*

131

*Illustration 8.3* Manifesto 131: Czechs ought to follow the example of Jan Hus (KA)

pessimistic. Ionescu, who was to be Romanian foreign minister after the war, alleged that 99 per cent of Romanians believed that the Entente would win the war. Other evidence suggested that there was spirited defiance in occupied Romania. The peasantry were said to be resisting, frequently murdering German soldiers; prominent politicians had protested in parliament against the charges being brought against the former premier, Ion Brătianu, for taking Romania into the war.[157] And even the royal family was setting a good example. King Ferdinand was keeping his promise that on the attainment of peace the landed estates would be divided up amongst the peasantry. Queen Marie, confident of an Entente victory, had, according to an outraged Hungarian newspaper, made a dramatic tour of the regions ceded to Hungary by the Peace of Bucharest, assuring local inhabitants that she would 'see them again soon!'[158]

Publicizing a similar level of resistance among the Romanians of Hungary was not so easy. This accurately reflected the stagnation of political life in Transylvania, where there was strict censorship and little effective Romanian leadership.[159] The manifestos could enumerate Magyar atrocities in Transylvania, alleging that 15 000 Romanians had been executed during the war, as well as condemn the treacherous pro-Magyar behaviour of Metropolitan Mangra of Nagyszeben.[160] They could also give some brief examples of Romanians on trial in Kolozsvár for nationalist activity, such as Dr Aristotele Banciu who had edited a newspaper called 'Greater Romania' and now received a jail sentence of seven years.[161] But when it came to reproducing subversive speeches, akin to those of a Korošec or Staněk, only one example was forthcoming: that of Ştefan Cicio Pop, speaking in early July in a debate on electoral reform in the Hungarian Parliament. In response to Count István Bethlen, who had remarked that only 'living nations' (like the Magyars) should have rights, Pop had condemned the proposed reform, saying that it would only further subject the oppressed peoples of Hungary to the ruling classes. He went on, to cries from one deputy that all Romanians should be executed, to compare the parliament of 1918 where there were only four Romanians with that of 1868 which had contained 30 non-Magyar deputies. Padua commented that the Magyars viewed themselves as the 'chosen people of God' and the Romanians as cattle or cannon-fodder; in revenge, Romanian soldiers should desert to Italy where there were many brothers waiting to welcome them.[162]

While Magyars and Germans were stifling the rights of Romanians, the Allies were fighting for their freedom and unity in a greater Romania. Apart from vague statements to that effect[163] (and it seems questionable whether many Romanians in the Austrian trenches shared such an ideal), Padua's manifestos provided somewhat limited evidence. For instance, Take Ionescu had been received in France by President Poincaré and interviewed by Italian and English newspapers. Albert Thomas, 'an enlightened Frenchman who knows and loves our nation', had usefully observed that Romanians had been omitted from the Versailles Declaration and advised the Allies to listen to those voices protesting against the Peace of Bucharest.[164] More striking was the proof which Padua regularly supplied of Italy's special commitment to the Romanian cause. Although some notable events such as the founding of an 'Action Committee' under Simeon Mîndrescu in mid-June received no mention, Ojetti did include references to festivities in Rome in May, Genoa in June, and Rome again in August; the latter were organized by Mîndrescu's group together with Maria Rygier's 'Pro-Romeni' committee and centred on Trajan's column: one historic symbol of Italian–Romanian fraternity.[165]

Something could also be made of the growing presence of Romanian forces in the Italian war zone. As in Czech propaganda, many of the Romanian leaflets were signed by 'Romanian volunteer officers and soldiers in Italy' who called upon their compatriots to join them in creating a new legion. *Neamul Românesc* duly informed its readers that in June a small nucleus of Romanian volunteers had been formed near the front at a ceremony at which a local dignatory proclaimed the common origin of Italians and Romanians in the 'golden age of Trajan'; the company had then been trained and officially presented with its colours.[166] Few other details were forthcoming in the following months. Padua therefore vaguely tried to suggest a movement comparable to the Czech Legions, observing that 'from all sides the Romanians are taking up arms against the Germans and Hungarians: in Siberia, America and Italy'. In Russia, there were 30 000 volunteers, in America a similar number had been recruited, soon to be transported to the French and Italian theatres. Romanian soldiers needed to be vigilant, for they could be shooting at Romanians and therefore into the hearts of their children and grandchildren.[167]

Padua's Romanian propaganda undoubtedly suffered because we know that Ojetti diverted Cotruş into writing Hungarian material as well. It was a contrast to Polish propaganda which was more inventive and abundant, with twice as many leaflets distributed (overall in the campaign, 14 million as opposed to seven million Romanian manifestos).[168] This Polish trend continued despite Zamorski's abrupt departure, an indication that his deputy, Antoni Szuber, was not only diligent but had learnt much from Zamorski's example. As in the earliest leaflets, those of the summer months made frequent appeals to Poles to desert or revolt. They also occasionally contained a distinctive religious tinge. This was generally absent from other propaganda where at most the national cause was associated with martyrdom, as in the case of Jan Hus, or in the Yugoslavs being described as a people 'nailed to the cross, awaiting the moment of deliverance'.[169] Poles in contrast were assured that the Pope supported Polish independence, and were urged to pray to God for deliverance from slavery; with His help they would create a free Poland, raising to heaven the glorious hymn, 'Glory be to God on High and on earth peace, goodwill towards men'.[170] Polish material, however, resembled the Yugoslav and Romanian, and differed from the Czech, in dwelling far more on the 'oppressive regime' of the Central Powers than on new evidence of Allied commitment to the oppressed nationalities. In the case of the Poles, of course, that commitment had been confirmed in the Versailles Declaration, and Padua had made some use of it. But little attention was paid to the activities of the Polish National Committee since that link was clearly much weaker with Zamorski absent. The Committee's branch in Rome might well assure Poles in the Austrian trenches that prisoners in Italy were well-treated,[171] but otherwise, since there was no substantial Polish volunteer force in Italy, Padua was forced to report Polish military aid on other fronts to fill up the columns in its weekly newssheet *Polak*. In Siberia, Poles could be found organizing themselves in the Czechoslovak forces, or even as far east as Harbin; and much could be made of Polish valour in France where General Haller had arrived from the East to become commander-in-chief of the Polish army.[172]

As for evidence of the miserable conditions in Galicia or the occupied regions of Poland, Padua was supplied by Borgese's bureau with a wealth of information from the enemy press. Anti-Viennese newspapers such as *Illustrowany Kurjer Codzienny*, *Kurjer Lwowski* (both of which were on the AOK index) and the socialist *Naprzód* were frequently quoted to illustrate the realities of life for soldiers' families. For example, in Kraków, food prices were exorbitant, with a kilogram of butter now costing 50 crowns, instead of 4½ in 1914, and a kilogram of beetroot costing 5 crowns instead of half a crown; robbery and profiteering were rife, and even criminals had to be released from prison because of the lack of food there.[173] Padua's seventh edition of the weekly *Polak* alleged that a cordon had been set up around L'viv to prevent the importing of food, while at the same time the Austrians and Prussians were requisitioning and exporting food from Galicia to feed their German populations. Conditions were no better for Poles living under the heel of imperial Germany. According to a Polish deputy in the German Reichstag, Polish workers from Silesia, 'Poland' and Lithuania were treated abominably by the German authorities while the latter's behaviour in the occupied regions, their arrest of the bishop of Vilna for example, was on a par with the excesses of Tsarism.[174] Padua also mentioned German persecution of the Jews, but did not feel it necessary to be consistent on that subject, reporting in other material that Jews were benefiting economically at Polish expense in Galicia. More important was to emphasize to Polish Catholics the simple brutality of the regime for which they were dying, a regime which viewed the Pole not as a human being but as 'a miserable worm, to be trampled under foot at their pleasure'.[175]

With the Central Powers still quarrelling about the status of Poland, any Polish future under the Germans or Austrians seemed a dismal prospect. Rather than adopting the Austro-Polish solution (linking Polish regions to the Monarchy in a new entity) or creating a free and united Poland (the aim of the Entente) there were, according to one of Padua's more emotional leaflets, German schemes afoot to set up a Polish kingdom as had been planned by Frederick the Great and by 'the Russian harlot of German descent, Catherine II'. It would be a satellite state of the Central Powers where they would possess unlimited supremacy for 50 years.[176] As for Galicia, the government in Vienna was allegedly planning to divide it into three parts, one of which would be incorporated into Austrian Silesia and germanized, while another would fall to the Ukrainians, a race 'even more oppressive than the Russians'[!]. The latter prospect, heralded through Count Czernin's famous 'Bread Peace' with Ukraine in February 1918, had produced demonstrations in Galicia and ended with the trial, publicized by Padua from scanty information, of Polish legionaries at Máramarossziget.[177] It had also turned most Polish deputies in the Reichsrat against the Seidler government. Having reported the Polish Club's resolve to oppose Seidler when the Reichsrat reopened in July, and observing correctly that this would lead to Seidler's resignation (since he relied on them for his majority in the chamber), Ojetti was then able to quote at length the speeches of Polish deputies, condemning Austrian policy and Seidler in particular ('a stubborn foe of the Poles').[178] The speeches on 17 July by Tertil, Daszyński and Głąbiński sharply criticized Seidler's 'German course' and especially his supposed renunciation of the Austro-Polish solution through his secret deal with Ukraine. Ignacy Daszyński went on to advise Ruthene deputies in the Reichsrat to fight for their own national rights and not to put their trust in Vienna, for 'a bankrupt can promise absolutely nothing and this government is bankrupt'.[179] It was a message entirely in tune with that of the Allied propagandists. They could bluntly answer their own question as to whether Polish soldiers should continue to defend Austria: 'the best representatives of the Polish nation say, NO!'[180]

The richness of propaganda material in Polish, something noted by the Austrian 10AK in August, stood in striking contrast to the meagre number of manifestos in the Ukrainian language (only 25 types produced).[181] This was largely due to Polish control over the material.[182] In particular, since the Polish émigrés aimed to include all of Galicia in an independent Poland, the Ruthenes of eastern Galicia could never be promised their own independence. Zamorski, however, had been keen from the start to send some appeals to Ruthene soldiers. In mid-May he had written to Antoni Szuber, who was working in Polish prison-camps near Naples, asking if he knew of a Polish officer from eastern Galicia who could write manifestos 'in a manner tuned to the Ruthene psychology'. Since Szuber signalled that he himself was competent, he was called to the Padua Commission in early June. The Versailles Declaration had now strengthened the Polish case. Zamorski and Szuber were therefore able to persuade Ojetti that Ruthenes should not be offered independence (which the Allies were silent about anyway) but only general slogans about Austrian oppression.[183] Szuber's Ruthene material deliberately tried to avoid the 'national issue', or what he termed 'blowing at the embers' of the Polish–Ruthene question in Galicia. Yet as we have seen, he was not wholly averse to exploiting Ruthene loyalty to Vienna in order to reinforce his Polish propaganda.

When Zamorski had left Padua, Szuber naturally concentrated on his Polish leaflets. And according to what had been agreed, Ukrainian propaganda was always limited in scope to reminders about German and Austrian brutality in the East. Thus, while the destitute townspeople were 'living on grass and the roots of trees...perishing by the thousand from hunger', police in L'viv on 8 June had fired on starving women and children.[184] In Ukraine meanwhile, the Central Powers, having invaded ostensibly to chase out the Russians, had proceeded to behave 'like a tapeworm eating an organism from within', quite prepared to 'let the Ukrainians perish so that the accursed Germans in Vienna and Berlin' could 'scoff sausage and cabbage with a glass of beer!'[185] Ruthene soldiers were asked to consider whether their service in the Austrian trenches was not equivalent to behaving like 'Cain' against their brothers in distant Ukraine. For there, rather than obeying passively, 'more than 75 000 well-armed villagers under the leadership of valiant commanders are moving on golden-roofed Kiev', rebelling against the barbarism of German rule and declaring their own independence.[186]

Padua's material in Italian was on an even smaller scale, consisting only of some general manifestos issued in other languages, and reflecting perhaps Italy's awareness that there were few Italian-Austrian soldiers on the south-western front.[187] Instead, the Italian Intelligence offices continued to publish, notably in the wake of the June offensive, their own emotional appeals to civilians in Venetia. These warned them about having too much truck with the occupying forces, since 'these snakes can poison with breath and word the air which you breathe', polluting the purity of one's patriotism. The civilians were assured, with personal messages from relatives in Italy, that the day of resurrection was approaching: 'the clearest light of tomorrow will be for those who have kept hope in the darkness of foreign domination'.[188] In response, many Venetian civilians appear to have dutifully collected and concealed the propaganda leaflets, either out of simple curiosity, or deliberately, like the mayor of one town who in late July was found to have 200 manifestos stored in his house.[189] They also generally followed Italy's advice. Most Austrian official reports from Venetia, from June until November, observed that the civilians were maintaining a passive and reserved attitude towards the occupying regime, confident that Italy would soon launch a new offensive to bring them liberty and sustenance.[190]

## 8.4 Padua's summer campaign: the Magyars and German–Austrians

While it was a core aim of Padua's propaganda to appeal to the traditional 'oppressed nationalities' (the Slav and Latin races), Ojetti also increasingly targeted those of Hungarian or German–Austrian nationality as well. They too could be portrayed as oppressed in their own way, both nationally and politically. Magyar soldiers in particular were viewed as a major target during the summer. Before the June offensive the Italian military had regarded Magyars as too reliable to merit much attention from their propaganda; and Padua, lacking a suitable translator, had duly published only two texts in Hungarian (totalling 315 000 copies).[191]

However, a change of attitude occurred after the offensive by which time Cotruş had joined the Commission. Apart from the outcry from Budapest by radical Hungarian politicians and newspapers at the 'needless slaughter' on the Piave, there was now strong evidence from the statements of Magyar deserters and prisoners that many of them too shared misgivings about the war and the Germans, and might well be receptive to Allied propaganda.[192] On 14 July, Granville Baker reported to Northcliffe that, although as yet Padua's Magyar propaganda had had no 'decisive effect', he had noticed when visiting Magyar prisoners that they were much more willing to talk; he concluded that 'propaganda may be pushed on now with more hope of success'.[193] Ojetti clearly agreed, for from mid-June to mid-September the amount of material produced in Hungarian, 62 new texts totalling six million copies, was only marginally less than the amount directed at Yugoslav soldiers. Ojetti, when writing his final propaganda report at the end of the war, would explain why Magyars had been the target for over nine million manifestos:

> Because these people began to understand that they were now tied to a corpse and they sensed, every day more clearly, that their salvation depended solely on their total separation from the alliance with Germany and the union with Austria, and then on their economic and social revival on sincerely democratic bases in opposition to the feudal oligarchy of noble or ennobled latifundists.[194]

These at least were the two major arguments employed in Padua's Magyar material by Cotruş.

The first argument, that of appealing to Magyar nationalism, continued to be the principal theme of the leaflets in the tradition begun by Italian Intelligence officers in the spring. It was displayed perhaps most ingeniously in manifesto 109, which referred back to the *Waffenbund* or military alliance cemented between Germany and Austria-Hungary in May 1918; despite containing a number of errors, it continued to be distributed well into the summer. The leaflet was edged in black and inscribed with the words:

Here lies
**Hungary**
and her children
**Freedom and Independence**
born in 1848,
died after fighting for 4 years
on the Italian front
for Germany, Austria and Turkey.
Burial will take place at Spa in the
'Waffenbund' cemetery at Germany's expense.

It was dated at Spa (the German military headquarters), and signed by 'Wilhelm II Hohenzollern, Europe's chief funeral director' and 'Karl III Habsburg, private secretary'.[195]

By July 1918 some Austrian commanders were noting this new tendency of enemy propaganda to launch appeals at Hungarian troops, one observing that they would have to be energetically countered if found to have links to the Hungarian hinterland or press.[196] Such connections were soon quite apparent, for radical Budapest newspapers were Padua's best source of information, as usual reinforcing the truth of what was being propagated. Organs such as *Az Est* and *Világ* could regularly be used to condemn the German alliance, that it was creating a *Mitteleuropa* where Hindenburg would be master: 'your children and grandchildren would not be learning about Rákóczi or Petőfi or Kossuth but about the great deeds of him and Kaiser Wilhelm!'[197] Such concern could now be echoed in detailed speeches reproduced from the Hungarian Parliament. There on 21 June, in a particularly lively session, a vociferous opposition deputy, Nándor Urmánczy, had attacked the Minister of Defence for permitting discrimination against Magyars in the army, and demanded a government bill to establish an independent Hungarian army. A like-minded colleague, László Fényes, proceeded to denounce the German alliance for its economic and military exploitation of Hungary.[198]

The same sources were repeatedly quoted by Padua to illustrate the enormous and futile sacrifices made by Magyars for German interests during the Piave offensive. There had been a storm of protest in Budapest at the conduct of the war. According to vivid reports from *Az Est*, most of the 10 000 lost on the Piave had been Magyars who had died like martyrs on foreign soil.[199] It was a point reiterated by Fényes in several blistering attacks on the Hungarian government; and by Urmánczy who, on 24 July, in a speech which the AOK tried to prevent from reaching the war zone, heaped blame on the

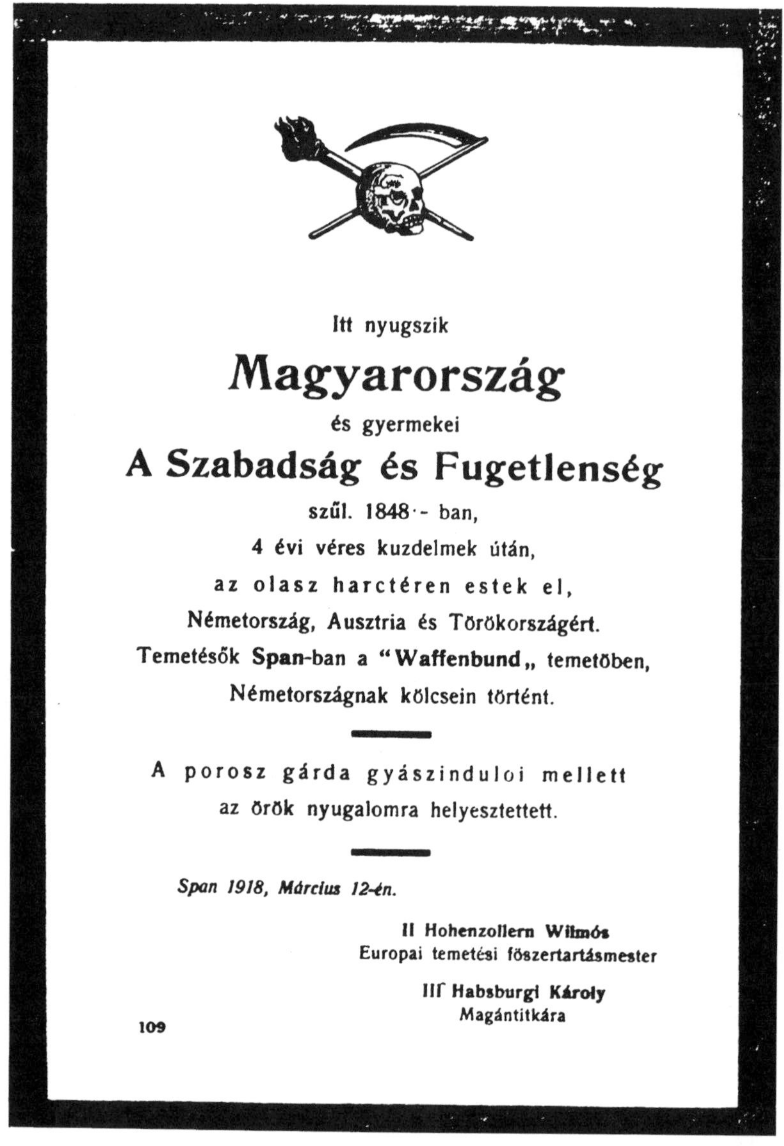

Itt nyugszik

**Magyarország**

és gyermekei

**A Szabadság és Fugetlenség**

szűl. 1848·- ban,

4 évi véres kuzdelmek után,

az olasz harctéren estek el,

Németország, Ausztria és Törökországért.

Temetésők **Span**-ban a "**Waffenbund**„ temetőben,

Németországnak kölcsein történt.

A porosz gárda gyászinduloi mellett

az örök nyugalomra helyesztettett.

*Span 1918, Március 12-én.*

II Hohenzollern Wilmós
Europai temetési főszertartásmester

III Habsburgi Károly
Magántitkára

109

*Illustration 8.4* Manifesto 109: The death of Hungary is announced (KA)

Austrian commanders and called for them to be investigated.[200] As a fellow deputy sarcastically observed, instead of being properly punished Conrad von Hötzendorf had been created a Count after the battle, whereas 'somebody who gets married at the age of 64 is more fit to be put into care'.[201] Padua duly agreed that the Magyars had been pure cannon-fodder: 'The Germans and Austrians like a bankrupt stock-exchange speculator are trying to save their own future, at the cost of your blood and national existence, spending it as if it were money obtained by theft or fraud.' In the past the Hungarian attitude had been different:

> Petőfi's great poem 'Talpra Magyar' was declaimed, and every true Magyar rushed to the frontiers to fight for liberty and against tyranny. But nowadays in a four-year long bloody war the noble and free Magyar nation is falling and perishing, and not in order to fight an enemy that threatens its hearth and freedom.[202]

On the contrary, it was Italy and her allies who were fighting in the spirit of Kossuth and Garibaldi for freedom, peace and independence for all nations. This, Padua implied, meant freedom for the Magyars too: freedom from the German and Austrian yoke, and freedom to establish their own independent Hungarian state.[203]

The second key point of attack in Padua's Magyar material was against the landowning elite of Hungary, who, in league with Vienna and Berlin, were said to be exploiting the Hungarian masses. It was an argument, the legitimacy of which was to be queried but approved at the inter-Allied propaganda conference in August, but Ojetti had already been using it effectively well before that date.[204] Since the early summer witnessed a general strike in Hungary, as well as the climax of the wartime struggle for electoral reform, Padua had fertile soil to plough. As usual, its main source of information was the radical and socialist Hungarian press. Indeed, Crewe House may well have managed at this time to insert its own articles into *Világ* and other papers through the agencies of S.A. Guest and possibly the *Világ* correspondent in Switzerland.[205] Padua's manifestos detailed the miserable situation of civilians in Hungary, where corrupt officials and profiteers were rife, where mothers were told to cut their children's throats if they could not feed them, where even Budapest now looked 'incredibly dreary and bare'; if previously only newspaper vendors had called out in the streets of the city, now it was the empty shop windows which cried out with hunger. The exorbitant prices for basic commodities were destroying the families of Hungarian soldiers, but the situation was simply condoned by a 'tyrannical government' which had nothing but contempt for working people:

> The demonstrations of the working masses draw today only regretful and disdainful smiles from the faces of the ministers... The feudal and capitalist reactionaries, who reached the peak of their power during the war, have in all walks of political and economic life pitilessly and slyly brought Hungarian social democracy to the grave.[206]

This manifesto 288 was one of the few issued by Padua on the subject of social democracy in Hungary, an indication that the Allied propagandists always shied away from openly supporting socialist (as opposed to nationalist) parties in the Monarchy, even if there was clear ambiguity in their regular use of *Arbeiter-Zeitung*. The manifesto quoted had somewhat reinforced an earlier leaflet which had made use of *Népszava*, the radical SD newspaper. Writing at the height of the mass strike in Budapest, *Népszava* had called for the resignation of the 'dishonest and reactionary' Hungarian government which had 'never been that of the toilers of the fields but rather a government of the landowners... It has stood in the way of democracy in a guilty fashion and in the way of the social policy promised by the King.'[207]

But if the Prime Minister, Sándor Wekerle, and his government had irretrievably compromised the country's interests, they were, according to Padua, no more than an 'automatic toy' in the hands of the real culprit, Count István Tisza. As *Arbeiter-Zeitung* observed, Tisza was still protecting the 'rights' of the agrarian elite, the rights for which Hungary had gone to war and sacrificed so much, for he had managed to prevent the degree of electoral reform demanded by the parliamentary opposition and promised by Karl in 1917.[208] Padua explained that Tisza

> knew very well that once the people have got the right to vote they would sweep him and his miserable flunkies away. He can only rule over slaves, and it is his obsession always to remain in power. He therefore brought down the Esterházy government [September 1917] and helped Wekerle into the Prime Minister's chair so that he and his party could dictate, cunningly and invisibly, to the cowardly Wekerle from behind the scenes, the Viennese and Berlin lessons for your complete disenfranchisement. So the bill for the extension of the franchise has failed, and in its place an Act of Slavery has been passed.[209]

The reactionary count had thereupon departed for the Italian Front, a move which produced more derisory comments from *Arbeiter-Zeitung* on 25 July:

> For many months Tisza has fought in his own fatherland with the rank of a colonel against the new franchise programme. Now he has gloriously finished the fight on the electoral front and his courage, which knows no bounds, has egged him on to new battles. Tremble O Italians!

Ironically, this particular leaflet, which ended with a reminder that 'the fight which Tisza is in the process of winning is directed not against Italy but against you', seems to have been one which Tisza himself came across during his short stay in the Italian theatre in the summer.[210] It was a type of propaganda which the Padua Commission seems to have viewed as successful, responsible according to Granville Baker for an increase in desertions by lower-class Hungarian soldiers.

The number of manifestos directed at German-Austrians also increased during the summer but, with 26 texts in three million copies, it was still less than 10 per cent of the total produced in these months and half of that directed at the Magyars. Under Ojetti's firm control, it was written largely by the 'phenomenal polyglot' Stojan Lasić.[211] It tended to contain only the more general demoralizing arguments present in Padua's other propaganda, namely the strength of Allied forces, their successes in battle or in sinking the Austrian dreadnought *Szent-István*; the abundance of food in Italy compared to the hunger and misery among civilians in Austria.[212] Only a few appeals were made to German-Austrian soldiers on the express basis of their separate nationality or identity (notably that they were fighting for Germany's interests), even though the idea of doing so was certainly mooted by some of the Allied propagandists.

On 6 August there was a discussion at Crewe House about a memorandum by a French journalist, Marcel Ray, who had had talks in Zurich with a Dr Friedrich Hertz of Vienna. Ironically, and unbeknown to the British EPD, Hertz had been giving some lectures on FA courses in Austria. But he had told Ray that he was particularly worried about Austria becoming a mere vassal of Germany, suggesting to him that, with the aid of the Entente, he might set up an anti-Prussian organization which would issue not revolutionary or defeatist material but positive propaganda to turn German-Austrians against the German Empire. The idea seems to have appealed to Crewe House, but it is unclear whether it was pursued further.[213] Possibly one of Hertz's opinions, that the West should not issue revolutionary material, had some influence upon a decision made at Northcliffe's propaganda conference, that the Allies would only circulate the Austrian proletariat's literature and not produce 'Bolshevik propaganda' of their own. Such distribution, if it occurred, would have been carried out through secret channels from Switzerland, where one British diplomat noted at this time: 'we now have admirable means for supplying material from Switzerland, even in bulk, to Vienna and elsewhere in the Dual Monarchy [but] the present difficulty is distribution'.[214] In contrast, on the Italian Front, there was little sign of the Allies spreading any socialist propaganda.

Indeed, only a few of Padua's German manifestos directly attacked the rulers in Vienna, warning for instance that the West, though very keen to make peace, would only do so with the German people, not with the absolutist regimes of Vienna and Berlin. German-Austrians were urged, like the Magyars, to throw off the 'medieval despotism' which governed Austria, where archdukes, great property owners and others were enriching themselves at the expense of the state and of those starving in the trenches.[215] Otherwise, the message was to be

Band XXVI. — Nr. 667 Wien, 11. Juli 1918. Preis 60 Heller, 50 Pf., 50 Cts.

DIE MUSKETE

Alle Rechte vorbehalten
Nachdruck verboten

Humoristische Wochenschrift

Ausweisleiſtung. (Zeichnung von K. A. Wilke.)



„Ihre Papiere lauten ja auf verſchiedene Namen! Einmal heißen Sie da Gewiſſenloſigkeit, einmal Schlamperei, dann wieder Hunger —"

»Stimmt ſcho, ſtimmt ſcho! Das is nämli in Oeſterreich immer genau daſſelbe.«

228

*Illustration 8.5* Manifesto 228: Austria's identity papers are marked 'Unscrupulousness', 'Slovenliness' and 'Hunger' (KA)

one of despair. Austria was most vividly portrayed as a 'hideous and dirty old hag' who had three different names on her identity papers: 'unscrupulousness', 'slovenliness' and 'hunger'. This was not an image invented by Padua, but one taken directly from a cartoon in the Viennese satirical journal *Die Muskete*; ironically, the AOK had already used this paper as a source of propaganda for its own campaign against Italy. Padua now reproduced one of the journal's title pages with the cartoon and a suitable commentary. A copy of the leaflet duly found its way to the FAst in Vienna which immediately warned the editors of *Die Muskete*: 'it shows how enemy propaganda knows how to pick up any clues from our press and use them to its advantage'.[216]

The Padua Commission's most notable appeal to the German-Austrians, however, and probably the most celebrated deed of the whole campaign, was the propaganda flight made over Vienna on 9 August by the legendary poet-adventurer, Gabriele D'Annunzio. Already in August 1915 this modern-day Aeschylus had scattered messages of encouragement to the populations of Trieste and Trento, and later in the year had first mentioned the idea of a dramatic flight to Vienna itself. Two years later such a plan was technically feasible, for in September 1917 D'Annunzio made a successful nine-hour test flight over a thousand kilometres of Italian territory, and proceeded to think of bombing the palace at Schönbrunn as well as broadcasting contemptuous messages to Vienna's inhabitants.[217] But only by the summer of 1918 was the CS receptive to the idea. By then, the 87th squadron, established in February to carry out bombing raids deep in the Austrian hinterland, had made its successful propaganda flights over Ljubljana and Zagreb: a similar expedition to Vienna was viewed by the Padua Commission as the next logical step.[218]

Indeed, the flight on 9 August was not just, as the *Corriere della Sera* asserted the next day, 'a gesture of heroism and magnanimity' to prove Italian superiority over the enemy. It was also very much an integral part of Padua's overall campaign. After Diaz had approved the idea, apparently through pressure from D'Annunzio, Ugo Ojetti had sat down on 24 June to write the manifestos.[219] The first, manifesto 128, with the text printed over a colour picture of the Italian flag, reminded the Viennese that instead of bombs the planes were bringing them 'a greeting of the tricolour of freedom' since Italy was not fighting Austrian civilians but the Austrian government, the 'enemy of national freedom'. As Ojetti told his wife, he did not want to throw out insults when addressing civilians, but simply to 'show our moral stature and a little of our appeal'. The leaflet, after warning that the absolute victory promised by the Prussian generals was as illusionary as bread from Ukraine, ended with cries of exaltation for freedom, Italy and the Entente.[220] Ojetti's second manifesto set out the Allies' political vision and was of more substance. It condemned the unjust 'Prussian peaces' of Brest-Litovsk and Bucharest, urging the Viennese to shake off Germany; all of Italy was now united, and was joined by the whole of the civilized world in fighting in the mid-nineteenth-century Italian spirit for the freedom of all nations. The Viennese should remember 13 March 1848, when their cries for liberty were echoed in Paris, Venice and Milan, and liberate themselves.[221]

The two manifestos were approved by Orlando and Diaz (the latter in fact wanting to submit a tactless leaflet of his own composition), and to them was added a third, personally composed by D'Annunzio in Italian. It proclaimed in exotic language that the Italian planes were the sign of an approaching destiny, of certain victory for the Allied Powers.[222] D'Annunzio himself was determined to be a member of the propaganda flight, but otherwise it was composed of 11 experienced pilots of the 87th squadron, many of whom had already taken part in raids on Innsbruck, Ljubljana and Zagreb. At 5.50 a.m. on 9 August, after a week's delay because of bad weather, the squadron of Capronis took off from Padua to travel across over 800 kilometres of enemy territory. They were equipped with leaflets and photographic equipment but no bombs because of fear of reprisals. Three of the squadron had to turn back very quickly because of engine trouble. One was forced to land near Wiener Neustadt. But at 9.20 a.m., seven of the planes reached Vienna, showering the population with 150 000 manifestos.

Although the Austrian authorities had some prior warning that a raid would be made on Vienna, the actual event took them completely by surprise.[223] It was especially embarrassing for those responsible for air defence in the hinterland that enemy planes, having crossed the front, were able to reach the capital with so little inconvenience. While the squadron had been aided by a thick band of cloud between Graz and Wiener Neustadt, its progress was also eased by the incompetence of local air defence officials. One particular sinner, Lt Oskar Schlosser, who supervised air defence at Bruck an der Mur, had taken more than two hours to report the squadron to military authorities at Graz as he thought that it 'could be' Austrian. By this time the flight was already over Vienna, and although at 9.30 a defence squadron was launched from Wiener Neustadt, it failed to intercept the Italians who were only fired at over Ljubljana on their return journey to Padua.[224]

The presence of Italian planes over Vienna aroused curiosity and excitement among the inhabitants rather than fear. According to one observer, who was peering at the aircraft through opera glasses, the Viennese gathered at windows, on roofs and in the street, and generally acted contrary to official instructions about the proper behaviour on such an occasion.[225] The police, in agreement with the military, immediately began to collect and destroy the manifestos, conducting widespread searches, for example in a home for refugees which they believed to have been a special target of the aviators since it allegedly housed some suspicious Italian characters.[226] The FAst meanwhile promptly told the AOK that the manifestos were 'extraordinarily harmful to the morale of less sensible people'; it sensed that they probably stemmed from the 'Czechoslovak section of Italian propaganda' and might even have been smuggled into Austria and distributed by rascals of the Austrian airforce itself (!). As counter-measures, the FAst recommended censorship of all reports in the Austrian press, and the immediate distribution over Vienna of a red 'counter-leaflet' urging the population to remain true to their fatherland and their allies in the face of a treacherous enemy which, having failed to win the war by arms, had now resorted to a 'poison of lies and deceit'. Such a leaflet was never produced, but the authorities did try to ensure that newspapers toed the official line and reproduced manifesto 128 only with a suitable commentary.[227] The loyalist *Neue Freie Presse* duly obliged, writing that the behaviour of the Viennese had been 'really splendid' with no sign of panic; the Italian appeals were generally to be scorned and the whole incident dismissed: 'The Italians' propaganda flight can indeed, apart from the political motives lying behind it which are obviously intended as a substitute for the lack of military success in Albania, be declared as a sporting exercise of no significance.'[228]

Despite this, the authorities were anxious to avoid a repeat performance. On 13 August the Minister of War, General Stöger-Steiner, decided that captured enemy pilots who had distributed propaganda which incited civilians against the state would, as in the war zone, be put on trial for a crime which carried the death penalty. This idea worried the Foreign Minister, Count Burián, who feared the international repercussions. Already Burián had been concerned when the AOK had publicized the execution of captured Czech legionaries after the June offensive, fearing that the Italians would simply turn on their Austrian prisoners.[229] Stöger-Steiner therefore convened a meeting at the War Ministry for 28 August. There it soon became clear that while the Ballhausplatz held one view and the AOK the opposite (namely that the law should be tightened), the War Ministry itself was anything but united over what needed to be done. Consequently, to the AOK's annoyance, Stöger-Steiner's original decision was revoked.[230] The authorities contented themselves with tightening hinterland defences against future enemy air attacks, especially in Budapest which it was feared might well be the next target. In fact, just as an Austrian counter-raid on Rome appears to have been abandoned due to technical difficulties, so a second propaganda flight which D'Annunzio was indeed dreaming of making over Budapest failed to materialize.[231] The Vienna raid was destined to be an isolated exploit of Padua's campaign, but one which, if nothing else, had alarmed and further demoralized the Austrian authorities.

If the Padua Commission could feel suitably elated, announcing to troops opposite that 'it had seemed an impossibility but it became a reality',[232] it was elation which concealed Ojetti's real frustration with the Italian airforce. His campaign depended on mass distribution from the air, usually by Italian planes although by August the British too were undertaking some propaganda flights.[233] He was trying to average 500 000 leaflets per day.[234] But from late August this could not be maintained, partly due to bad weather in the last two months of the war, partly the result of tensions with the Italian airforce. Already during the Piave offensive both Ojetti and Marchetti had despaired that the aeronautical command under General Luigi Bongiovanni did not attach the same importance to propaganda raids as to bombing raids. In early July, with the help of Badoglio, Ojetti had secured from Bongiovanni an equalizing of propaganda and bombing flights which continued fairly smoothly for the next two months. By September, however, Ojetti was again to find that the airforce was deviating from the arrangement and only distributing 90 000 manifestos per day; again it required Badoglio's intervention before Bongiovanni would agree with Padua to try to issue a daily minimum of 300 000.[235] Nor was this Ojetti's only distribution problem. A further irritant, resulting from official Italy's ambiguous policy, was the fact that the naval authorities under Thaon di Revel, a supporter of Sonnino, still refused to distribute Padua's Yugoslav manifestos over the Dalmatian coast. Thaon would only agree to throw out such material over the naval bases at Pula and Cattaro and over Austrian troops in Albania, while reserving for Dalmatia his own propaganda in Italian, especially 'suitable' newspapers such as the Sonnino-mouthpiece *Giornale d'Italia*.[236] Despite Ojetti's protests to Orlando about this, including the usual threat of resignation, the naval authorities continued to act largely independently of the Padua Commission and certainly did little to further the Yugoslav cause in Dalmatia.[237]

The Austrian authorities remained oblivious to these spanners in their enemy's propaganda machine. For them, the threat appeared to be increasingly serious and ubiquitous, seeping across the frontiers, striking at the imperial capital, as well as swamping the armed forces in the war zone. During the summer the Austrian military regularly complained about the Italians' obvious superiority in the air, enabling them to scatter manifestos en masse. As the 10AK noted in its propaganda report for July,

> *The Italian counter-propaganda*, which clearly forms one of the most dangerous lines of attack of the *Entente propaganda* directed at the solid structure of the Austro-Hungarian armed forces, is as previously very strong even if it varies on different parts of the front... *Plane propaganda* has become even more intensive than earlier. Almost every day planes appear and shower not only the front but also the rear areas with a host of leaflets.[238]

All of the army commands viewed this activity with alarm. As one pointed out, the manifestos were, in addition to the food crisis, an 'eminent danger' to troop morale. They now seemed to be infinitely varied and inventive, skilfully composed by authors who were well informed and well versed in the mentalities of the different nationalities; they were following a systematic plan which was most notable in mirroring that of agitators in the Monarchy itself.[239]

Indeed, for the Austrian military, the most striking characteristic was the degree to which the Italians were using the Austrian press as a major source for their arguments. With the enemy simply delighting in reproducing 'hot-blooded speeches' by MPs like Wichtl, Stránský or Fényes, Boroević observed with a degree of resignation that the most effective material for enemy propaganda was supplied by the 'miserable internal state of the Monarchy', which was being reliably broadcast to the enemy by a largely unpatriotic press.[240] Archduke Joseph (who had succeeded Conrad) concurred, protesting more forcefully to Baden that the press was virtually the Entente's servant, uncritically publishing reports from Reuters and even publicizing the leaflet distributed by D'Annunzio over Vienna. It was absolutely vital, he warned, to take energetic steps against this kind of journalism, for all patriotic instruction was pointless 'if the enemy manages to spread with such incredible speed the speeches of a Stránský etc'.[241] Yet the AOK could do little to satisfy these complaints from the front. They could, with their 'index', prevent unpatriotic newspapers from reaching the war zone to a certain extent, but were unable to take more direct action. They could not unilaterally impose a stricter censorship on the press, not least because there was no uniformity to press censorship in different parts of the Empire anyway; nor could they remove parliamentary immunity from those deputies who made inflammatory statements.[242] The diversity and independence of the press was accurately reflecting the chaotic conditions in the hinterland. And since there seems to have been no ban on the export of Austro-Hungarian newspapers to neutral lands like Switzerland, there remained few obstacles to the Allied propagandists in their task of exploiting and publicizing the mood of the Habsburg Empire.

## 8.5 New trials in trench propaganda

The last months of the war also meant an unprecedented level of activity for the propaganda units, supervised by Italian Intelligence, as they entered what Cesare Finzi termed 'a phase rich in movement and manoeuvre'.[243] The Intelligence offices especially used their Czech units ever more skilfully to target Czech troops in the Austrian trenches, with some notoriously successful outcomes. At the same time, the propaganda efforts of Italian Intelligence kept pace with Padua's campaign. Just as Padua's material was penetrating ever further into the Monarchy, so Czech volunteers were occasionally being called upon to agitate not just in the front line but across the front, in the Austrian war zone itself.

There was a new boldness and danger in this which matched the exploits of D'Annunzio. If Tullio Marchetti was one who naturally inclined to employing Slavs in the Tyrol for purposes of espionage or sabotage, some of the volunteers were keen to take on these new tasks which would prove their worth in the eyes of Italy while reinforcing their own national pride. Even more, however, many of the propaganda troops were eager to engage in activities where they would be used in combat rather than simple propaganda; they would thereby gain the kind of recognition in 'conventional warfare' which the rest of the Czech Legion was acquiring. As the summer progressed, there was an increasing tendency for Czech propaganda and Intelligence duties to become merged with some combat experience, a sign that the Italian military were not only trusting the volunteers but viewing their role more flexibly. It was also significant that, despite a number of disasters which befell the units, and a steady level of Italian mistrust which the Austrians would cleverly seek to exploit, the volunteer movement continued to expand in the Italian war zone. It formed, at least in the Czech case, a real vitalized alternative to set against the stale future offered by Austrian officers in the trenches opposite.

During the June offensive, the real commitment of Czech legionaries to the ideal which they were propagating had been severely tested from both sides of the front. When dozens of Czechs were captured or killed on the Piave, it enabled the Italians and Austrians to publicize respectively the glorious or shabby reality of the Czech ideal. Undoubtedly it was the Austrians, seeking to besmirch the Czechs' reputation, who were more successful in the short term, for their arguments seemed to reflect quite accurately the volunteers' less than glorious behaviour or fate. On the Italian 4th army front, Czech scouts who had continued to operate during the offensive had torn off their badges in fear that they might be captured by the enemy. On the Montello, 35 Intelligence troops of the 8th army had been surprised and taken prisoner, 25 of whom were tried and executed in a deliberately sordid manner. Those who met their fate at Conegliano for example were shot, two at a time, so that they would see the deaths of their comrades; some of the bodies were hung up along with placards marked 'Czechoslovak traitors of the fatherland'.[244]

Jan Šeba, the Czech National Council representative responsible for coordinating the Legion in Italy, bitterly reproached Major Dupont and 8th army Intelligence for what had happened. Šeba at least managed to persuade Diaz not to employ the regular Czech division in combat during June because of its lack of training. Only the 3rd army commanders, in a fit of rash enthusiasm for exploiting the Czechs, managed to secure a battalion from the Legion. They proceeded to put it into battle and the results amply justified Šeba's warnings. 62 were killed, a dozen of whom suffered the ignominious fate of their comrades of the 8th army.[245] While the Austrians could publicize this disgrace as a warning to Czechs on both sides of the front, the impact of such scare-tactics, which had certainly worked in the past, was diminishing in line with the fact that the Czech national cause was becoming more of a reality at home and abroad. Indeed, in view of this, as Czech propagandists were keen to point out, the executions could have the opposite effect to that desired, implying that the Austrian military were acting brutally and out of fear in the face of a noble and victorious cause. This side of the coin was naturally propagated by Padua whose leaflets eulogized the Czechs' heroic behaviour (on the anniversary of Jan Hus's death) while pointing to the Austrians' cowardice in hanging up the corpses and so abusing the dead heroes.[246]

In any case, these Czech sacrifices were somewhat recouped when, on 29 June, Slav propaganda troops of the 6th army successfully participated in the capture of Monte di Val Bella.[247] Although for the Italian Intelligence offices it had been prescriptive that their Slav patrols should refrain from actual combat, the commander of the 14th division, General Pantano, having witnessed Ljudevit Pivko's units at work in his sector, had suggested to Pivko on 13 June that he ought not to be content with mere propaganda. In Pantano's words, 'warfare is a matter which must not be clumsy, or ossified in the same mould from day to day, but elastic, adapted to the position and moment'. Since it would boost the reputation of his volunteers, Pivko readily agreed to Pantano's request that he supply two units for an attack north of Val Bella and quickly secured Finzi's approval for the action. A few days later the plan had changed to recapturing Val Bella itself which had just been taken by the Austrians. For this purpose some Czech and Yugoslav scouts under respectively Pajger and Belošević were dispatched to the front line to investigate the terrain and the opposing forces; they were discovered to contain a significant number of Croats. On the night of 23–24 June, the scouts engaged in some reconnaissance and propaganda work, listening to the garrisons' conversation, and informing them orally and by leaflet about the Austrian defeat on the Piave and 'the outbreak of revolution in the hinterland'.[248]

The next morning the scouts led a small force of *arditi* in an initial strike at Val Bella which secured 73 prisoners. The main assault, however, occurred on 29 June when, as Pivko vividly describes in his memoirs, about 160 of his volunteers helped Italian troops to wrest the summit from the enemy. Pivko's evidence seems here to be more reliable than the Austrian official history which maintains that Val Bella was voluntarily evacuated only on 1 July.[249] But the achievement was certainly less clear-cut than both sides liked to portray it. For a start, the conquest had been made at a price, since 19 of Pivko's unit were killed, including the hero of Carzano, Karel Mlejnek, while 60 had been wounded. Nor had one Czech volunteer who was captured, Bohumil Vácha, behaved very heroically, since before his trial and execution he betrayed copious details to the Austrians including the suggestion that he had been forced into the Legion. As his death was publicized in an Austrian propaganda leaflet, the Czech legionaries could portray him as a hero.[250] On the other hand, the operation does appear to have benefited considerably from the volunteers' propaganda (in Croat) during the assault, and among the 800 prisoners taken were a number of 'Yugoslavs' who volunteered to join Pivko's unit. Most importantly, the episode further enhanced the reputation of the Slav volunteers.[251] In retrospect, General Graziani would consider the '*energica e valorosa azione'* on Val Bella as the best deed of the Czech legionaries in Italy. And on 4 July at Bassano, when a review of Czech forces took place before King Victor Emanuel and other dignatories, Milan Štefánik, who was making a short visit to Italy, met and congratulated Pivko as an 'apostle of the Czechoslovak idea': his action on Val Bella, he said, had struck not only at foreign enemies but also at the enemies in Italy.[252]

The example which Val Bella set, of propaganda troops not simply agitating but playing some fuller role in an armed action, was one which was to be repeated on many occasions in the final months of the war. From July to October 1918 it was the Czech units which were the most active and most integrated into Italy's army. At the request of the Czechoslovak National Council, the Czech propaganda companies serving under the six Italian armies were now linked together as a 39th or *Výzvědný* (reconnaissance) regiment, which gave them a greater sense of cohesion (they all took an oath to the Council), even if they still remained divided up and subordinate to the Italian Intelligence offices. Their typical daily tasks remained constant: to assess the nature of the forces opposite and, where possible, to entice them by means of leaflets, alluring speeches or nationalist songs, occasionally broadcast by gramophone.[253] While as usual the terrain both in the mountains and on the river Piave was often a barrier to any personal contact, it is clear from Austrian evidence that in the summer the Czech units remained a brooding presence in most sectors, and simply by existing were making a psychological impact opposite. On the Lower Piave, for example, KISA's propaganda report for August was typical, complaining about enemy patrols

> who have not only made appeals for desertion with reference to better food and good treatment in Czech, Ukrainian, Polish and Croat, but have even agitated in the Hungarian language. The enemy also employs his propaganda patrols in order to discover the character of troops opposite. The patrols are very sensitive to gunfire, and immediately stop their agitation, only to start it again the following day in another spot.[254]

In many sectors it seems clear that the Austro-Hungarian troops obeyed their superiors and responded to the propaganda with bursts of gunfire. But, there were certainly a few notorious incidents where individuals decided to desert to the enemy. Such a case was three Czech officers from IR75 (stationed east of Lake Garda), who deserted in mid-August, leaving behind a note saying that they had gone not because of bad conditions or cowardice but in order to fight for their independence.[255] Another instance occurred in late July from the Polish IR113 (based on Col del Rosso); in the space of a week, 20 Poles deserted to the enemy propagandists, and then wrote letters which were shot back over the Austrian trenches:

*Table 8.1* Propaganda and Reconnaissance Units, June–November 1918[256]

| *Army sector* | *Czechoslovak (39th reg.)* | *Yugoslav* | *Intelligence head* |
|---|---|---|---|
| 7 | | | |
| Swiss Border-Lake Garda | Vojtěch Hanzal (1/39) | Oton Kovačić* | Vecchiarelli |
| 1 | | | |
| Garda-Vallarsa | Rudolf Vyčital (2/39: *Reparto Avio* or *Borghetto*) | Hugo Plhak* (*Reparto Posina*) | Tullio Marchetti |
| Vallara-V.D'Assa | Alexandr Prejda (3/39: *Reparto Astico*) | | |
| 6 | | | |
| V.D'Assa-Brenta | František Jirsa (5/39) Jindřich Felix (6/39) | Stane Vidmar* | Cesare Finzi |
| 4 | | | |
| Brenta-Piave | Jaroslav Nedvěd (7/39) (later Antonín Basl) | Delemir Vuletić | Attilio Vigevano |
| 8 | | | |
| Upper Piave-Montello | Emanuel Ambrož (9/39) | Ante Drobac | Dupont |
| 3 | | | |
| Lower Piave | Antonín Zeman (10/39) Josef Grác (11/39) | Guglievié and (from September) Bogoljub Popadić | Ercole Smaniotto |

*Note*: * Overall administration by Ljudevit Pivko.

> Dear comrades! I'm writing to you to ask you not to be stupid but to leave Austria, for Austria is a Sodom and Gomorrah and the Germans are in control. You have nothing to do with Austria. Just come to Italy. Here you'll find everything you want. The Germans and Magyars are butchering you for they are not men but murderers, who murder the Polish people and children. We have to survive in this world and here in Italy you'll find everything. [Signed *Franz Vozniak*].[257]

These desertions were certainly perceived by the Austrians to have been caused by the enemy, and as a result the regiment was transferred to the Eastern Front. But it is worth emphasizing that neither of these cases seem to have been a common occurrence, although they were naturally given prominence by the Allied propagandists. Far more common was for the propaganda patrols to have an indirect impact opposite, acting as a catalyst and adding invisibly to the demoralization which was stirring in the Austrian trenches.

When the Czech propaganda units took part in combatant action, akin to Val Bella, it was always the result of circumstances where their propaganda skills could be exploited further in order to secure precise military objectives. For the rest of the Czechoslovak Legion in Italy a combatant role was, of course, expected, even though, after being stationed on a quiet sector of the front next to Lake Garda, the Legion witnessed little action until attacked by the Austrians on Dosso Alto in late September.[258] For the dispersed 39th regiment, however, a merging of its propaganda duties with more conventional military tasks was a novel phenomenon, reflecting the Italian army's new trust in their abilities, as well as a desire over the summer to make a series of raids into enemy positions in the mountains. One small example was a raid by Czech volunteers of the 4th army into positions of the Czech IR28.[259] The 4th army unit had few obvious successes in these months due to its nervous opponents as well as the inhospitable terrain which included Monte Grappa. But an opportunity arose when IR28 was moved forward on Monte Asolone, and a Czech officer, Václav Kýhos, deserted to Italy declaring that he had been on leave in Prague and experienced the growing national enthusiasm there. On 28 July, Kýhos led a group of Czech volunteers back under the wires and, largely with his help, two *Feldwache* or sentry units were taken prisoner. Although the evidence showed that few Czechs had wanted to follow Kýhos's example, the incident unnerved the Austrians to the extent that they put 50 men into a 'disciplinary unit' and warned that the regiment could never again be wholly trusted.[260]

In September, a similar but more substantial operation was undertaken by Marchetti's Czech units of the lst army (the so-called *Reparti Astico* and *Avio*). As with IR28, the action resulted from some close liaison work across the front line, and the belief that propaganda troops could be used to capture units opposite. When cavalry regiment 8 (6KD) was discovered in the front line at Cima Tre Pezzi, and a group of Czechs led by corporal Josef Jelínek showed themselves eager to desert, Marchetti decided instead that these new *Carzanci* should stay in position in order to make a much bigger operation possible.[261] For Jelínek and his colleagues, it was a nerve-wracking experience which smacked of Pivko's a year earlier, when the danger of discovery was always threatening. For Marchetti's Czech scouts it was a welcome opportunity to use their skills to win a more concrete prize: to capture a whole garrison. On 23 September, under Alexandr Prejda's direction, a group of 60 scouts crept out and hid under a cliff beneath the Austrian positions; one was even able to meet Jelínek who escorted him around the sector in order to be fully prepared for a 'night attack into the bowels of the Austrians'. Then in the evening, during a violent storm, the unit moved slowly forward and took the garrison prisoner. Although the operation as a whole revealed that liaison between the propaganda troops and the Italian artillery was still inadequate, for the latter's flanking fire began too early to the annoyance of the Czechs, the exploit of Cima Tre Pezzi netted 80 prisoners with minimal losses to the volunteers. On this occasion the Austrians do not appear to have suspected betrayal; they had even been making some propaganda of their own against the Italians in this very place.[262]

They could not suspect either that the operation had had an extra dimension. It allowed, as we shall see, two Czechs to creep across into the Austrian war zone on a mission of espionage and sabotage.

While the Czech units had a ready supply of new volunteers from deserters or the prison camps, the Yugoslav propaganda units were consistently weakened by a lack of manpower until the end of the war. If this reflected in part a lesser enthusiasm by Croats or Slovenes to volunteer, it was principally exacerbated by political circumstances: the inability of the Italian government and the Yugoslav Committee to agree upon the status of the units because of the postwar implications. Trumbić stayed in Italy for most of the summer, trying to resolve the matter according to the Czechoslovak example so that all Yugoslav soldiers in Italy would be treated as allies. He could feel pleased that they were being concentrated together in the prison-camps and allowed access from members of the Committee. But the next step was for enlistment to begin for a Yugoslav legion, with volunteers given a free choice of whether to serve on the Italian or Salonika Fronts and (an essential condition) obliged to become members of the Serbian army, wearing Serbian uniform and taking an oath to King Petar. Orlando was only too willing to raise more volunteers, since as he told Trumbić 'the Italian army has gained significant benefits from the present propaganda at the front'; but he balked at the conditions which Trumbić laid down.[263] If all volunteers took an oath to the King of Serbia it might well imply that their area of origin was to form part of a future Yugoslav state. Similarly, the establishment of a Yugoslav legion would signal full Italian commitment to Yugoslavia, the kind of signal which Orlando was never prepared to give. On 13 August, when Orlando met Trumbić, he would only repeat what he had agreed with the Allies at Versailles, namely that 'Serbian volunteers' in Italy might be recruited for the Serbian army (and depart for Salonika), but that 'Yugoslav prisoners' should simply be organized in 'national units' to serve on the Italian Front. Orlando was fudging the issue so that, as with the propaganda campaign as a whole, Italy secured the maximum military benefits without the political commitments (sacrificing the Treaty of London). Trumbić could rightly be suspicious of the distinction which Orlando made between Serbian and Yugoslav, for it smelt strongly of Sonnino's influence. It particularly left unresolved the Committee's insistence that all volunteers in Italy had to take an oath to the King of Serbia.[264]

Since moreover the Committee had already been given the right of access to Yugoslav prisoners, it was now able to frustrate Italian efforts to recruit at will. Yugoslav officers in the camp at Nocera Umbra refused to enlist unless they could become members of the Serbian army.[265] In the war zone, the Committee introduced similar obstacles. In June, Trumbić had agreed with Ojetti the correct procedure for enlisting volunteers, and Ojetti had subsequently finalized the new conditions at Padua with Jambrišak and Kujundžić; a smooth transition on Czechoslovak lines had seemed a possibility.[266] But in the absence of Italian political sanction, any progress had immediately ground to a halt. Increasing friction emerged because while Jambrišak and Kujundžić proceeded to publicize the Committee's conditions on recruitment among volunteers and prisoners in the war zone, the Italian military were determined to use their Yugoslavs along the old lines even if the question of the oath was unresolved. While the CS itself had initially been prepared to accept the Committee's conditions, military priorities were naturally uppermost for Diaz, and this was a view shared not only by the Italian Intelligence officers but also by Ljudevit Pivko.

The friction was particularly apparent in the eastern army sectors where Pivko's influence was weakest. In the west, Pivko's Yugoslav units appear to have worked quite effectively, often contributing, as at Val Bella, to propaganda actions where it was the Czechs who predominated. Ironically, much less is known about Yugoslav propaganda in these westerly sectors. Oton Kovačić's unit in the 7th army was, according to Pivko, exemplary in its standard of discipline, and achieved 'many brilliant successes' on the icy heights north of Tonale.[267] In the lst army sector, the work of the *Reparto Posina* seems to have been appreciated by its Czech equivalents.[268] And for the 6th army, the largest Yugoslav unit under Stane Vidmar continued to conduct 'extraordinarily lively and successful' propaganda, singing Serbian and Croatian songs and even calling out misleadingly that '80 000 Croats' were fighting in France for southern Slav freedom.[269]

For Yugoslav volunteers in the 4th, 8th and 3rd army sectors, however, it was a different story. The Committee had secured more influence there, retaining in the 8th army a loyal contact (Nikola de Marchi) until late July. When Pivko visited the 8th army in early August he had to listen to complaints from the army commander, General Pennella, about the 'politicizing' of the Yugoslav unit at Noventa.[270] Pennella blamed the Yugoslav delegates in Padua for introducing politics and weakening discipline among the volunteers, a view which was shared by Ottavio Dinale, the Italian commander of the unit. A few weeks earlier Dinale had written to Trumbić, setting out the military priorities which would then 'inevitably' have political repercussions; rather than waiting for volunteers to take an oath, he argued, the Committee ought to arrange for extensive recruitment so that by sheer numbers a legion would spring into being.[271] This was the view of Pivko too (even if he made some attempts to get volunteers to take the oath). But the Committee was adamant and it added another strain to the tense Italian–Yugoslav relationship at Padua. Finally, on 10 August in the Padua Commission's building, at a meeting attended by Finzi, Pivko, Jambrišak and Ojetti, Jambrišak refused to adopt a more conciliatory line until all volunteers had taken the oath. The next day he was informed that he and the other Yugoslav delegates were henceforth banned from visiting or agitating among the volunteer units. Trumbić reacted by withdrawing Jambrišak from the Padua Commission altogether, a futile gesture which only weakened further the degree of Yugoslav influence in the propaganda campaign. Ugo Ojetti might well feel that all those at the meeting had had 'no flexibility in their hard heads', but it is clear that on this occasion he himself viewed the Yugoslavs as the main culprits for they seemed to be placing needless obstacles in front of the propaganda priority.[272]

For Pivko, who wanted to expand the Yugoslav force along the lines advocated by the Italian military, there were a few other options, but none of them were successful. At Badoglio's request, he made a tour of the three eastern sectors in order to try to secure greater control over the Yugoslav units. But the 4th army unit in particular had already been detrimentally influenced, and by September the Committee had persuaded it to give up any propaganda duties: Vidmar's unit took over that sector as well.[273] Pivko faced the same rebuff with his dream of setting up a Yugoslav brigade of 200 officers and 10 000 men. Having gained a CS blessing, he visited Trumbić in late August hoping that he too would agree and would persuade the officers of Nocera Umbra to change their mind. Trumbić, however, although he was prepared to approve the work of existing volunteers, would not countenance any new units until the question of the oath had been settled. With this deadlock, Pivko was abruptly forced to abandon a site on Lake Garda which he had been preparing as an ideal training ground for the new force.[274]

Trumbić's attitude meant that any expansion of the existing Yugoslav units could only come from newly captured prisoners or deserters. For instance, 80 per cent of the 3rd army unit had been captured in early July and enrolled as volunteers a month later (having escaped the influence of the Committee).[275] Perhaps the most notable example of deserters joining the volunteer units was that of five reserve officers of BHIR8 who deserted at Val dei Concei on 9 July. This sector west of Lake Garda was a favourite spot for the Czech propagandists or a 'real thorn in Austria's eye' as Vojtěch Hanzal describes it. The group of three 'Yugoslavs' (Bogoljub Popadić, Ante Čurić and Martin Fedel) and two Czechs (Josef Mikulík and Ladislav Jung) appear to have been led by Popadić, a teacher in civilian life. He had only just arrived at the front and just happened to be the half-brother of Bogoljub Kujundžić whom he knew, perhaps from Padua's manifestos, to be a member of the Yugoslav Committee. Whether the other deserters needed much persuading seems questionable. After all, Fedel, summed up by the Austrians as 'stupid and cowardly', also had a Yugoslav link since he was the nephew of the head of the Committee's Rome office, Dinko Trinajstić. And Čurić and Mikulík, even though decorated for bravery, had given some hints of their intentions by requesting to be left at the front rather than transferred to the hinterland.[276] After crossing the lines on 9 July, in a manner very reminiscent of the 42HID desertions in May, the five officers immediately composed a manifesto for distribution to their comrades, assuring them that they had deserted due to bitterness at the way Bosnians were treated at the front and urging them to follow their example.[277] A number duly did so, including one of their own servants who brought with him a heavy suitcase.

On both sides there were important repercussions from this. The Austrian 10th army commander, FM Alexander Krobatin, personally visited the battalion. Noting with satisfaction that no men had followed the officer-deserters [!], he warned the assembled officers that the elder and more experienced among them needed to oversee constantly the behaviour of younger and newer arrivals.[278] Meanwhile in the front line, troops from the divisional *Sturmbatallion* were ordered to ambush the Czech propaganda unit which was still functioning opposite. They succeeded in doing this on the night of 22–3 July, and captured one Czech legionary, Josef Sobotka, who was tried and executed in full view of the Italian trenches. As usual it was not the heroic end which Hanzal's history would later proclaim, for Sobotka was quite ready to claim that he had been coerced into the Legion. But Hanzal is on surer ground when he argues that the 'martyrdom' only strengthened the cause of the propagandists and their supporters.[279] One Czech legionary had been executed, but all five of the officer-deserters had been eager to volunteer for propaganda work on the Italian side. While Mikulík and Jung joined the Czech unit of the 7th army, the Yugoslavs were sent to Stane Vidmar's company; Čurić would soon be employed on the Asiago plateau, while Popadić (a mark of the trust placed in him) was eventually assigned by Pivko to command the Yugoslav unit of the 3rd army.[280]

This pattern of recruiting deserters for the Yugoslav units continued until the end of the war, though rarely with such significant achievements. Even in the last weeks of hostilities Pivko was to be found touring the camps where new deserters or prisoners were temporarily housed, urging them to volunteer while calming any fears that they might never return to their families in the Monarchy with the assurance that 'the French and English will protect us'.[281] In view of the state of the Yugoslav cause in Italy, the attitude of the Committee, and the uncertain allegiance of many prisoners, it was no easy task. Because of this, some of Pivko's officers were not averse to recruiting under false pretences. Mate Nikolić, for example, who continued to work for 6th army Intelligence at Mirabella, interrogating prisoners and composing propaganda leaflets from their statements, omitted to tell some prospective officer-recruits about the camp at Nocera Umbra when urging them to join the 'Yugoslav legion'. He even told them that the volunteer units were working in complete harmony with the Yugoslav Committee. Thus one Bosnian officer only learnt about Nocera Umbra from a Committee supporter, but he was already suspicious of 'Nikolić and friends' and had refused to volunteer; he noted contemptuously, 'Nikolić gave me the impression of being an Italian mercenary who has all means at his disposal to achieve his aim, which is to get as many volunteers as possible for the legion.'[282] In contrast, Pivko appears to have been more open. In late September, for instance, he was prepared to tell one Croat officer-deserter about Nocera Umbra whereupon, after composing the usual leaflet for distribution, the officer opted to go to the camp rather than join a Yugoslav unit.[283] Thus it cannot be said that official Italy's attitude was the only reason for the paucity of Yugoslav units. It also reflected, in contrast to the Czechs, some basic realities about the Yugoslav movement. Many Serbs, Croats and Slovenes had different perceptions about their future, and were less willing to cooperate under the guidance of Italy or the Yugoslav Committee for a vague Yugoslav ideal. The result was that, while the Czech Legion grew steadily to 17 000 by October 1918, the number of Yugoslav volunteers eventually totalled only 943. Of these, as one might expect in view of Italy's territorial aspirations, 637 were Serb, with 176 Croats and 130 Slovenes; almost half the volunteers were Serbs from Bosnia-Hercegovina.[284]

Marchetti would write later that the Yugoslav units had achieved almost nothing.[285] This was an excessive judgement, not substantiated by Pivko's evidence, but it was one made chiefly in comparison to Czech exploits. The Italian Intelligence offices faced no political dilemmas when employing the Czechs, and in the last months of the war were confident enough to send some on secret operations into the Austrian war zone itself. Such missions, which had been started in June, are important firstly because they show that the Allied propagandists were now daring to penetrate physically into the Empire, and secondly because they provoked an ingenious counter-propaganda by the Austrian 10AK over the summer.

From May 1918 at least, Marchetti had been planning to send a group of Czechs behind the enemy lines at Lake Garda.[286] If he envisaged their role chiefly in propaganda terms, to publicize the Czech cause in the rear-areas and have a simple 'moral' impact, they were also to commit sabotage and gather Intelligence. Four Czechs were chosen from Rudolf Vyčítal's unit: Alois Štorch, František Tobek, Leopold Jeřábek and Jan Šmarda, the first two of whom had deserted from artillery regiment [FAR] 13 in late May. Since Štorch and Tobek were well acquainted with the 'Abschnitt Riva' opposite, the plan was that Tobek and Šmarda would go to Riva to try and convert men of the naval detachment, while Štorch and Jeřábek would proceed to Nago, since Štorch had friends there in FAR13 and could easily spread propaganda and organize agents to work for Italian Intelligence. Depending on the possibilities, the group would then either return to Italy or go on to Bohemia.

At midnight on 2–3 July the four, disguised as soldiers of FAR13 with pistols, hand grenades, false papers and adhesive moustaches, left Malcesine on a motorboat bound for the northern shore of Lake Garda. Most of the lake was in Italian hands, enabling them to approach 100 metres from the Austrian shoreline. But there they were suddenly surprised by enemy gunfire. Tobek managed to swim away, but Jeřábek was shot dead. Štorch and Šmarda were taken prisoner. Marchetti would later surmise that the Austrians had been alerted coincidentally at this time to expect the return from Italy of some escaped Austrian prisoners.[287] But Austrian evidence now reveals that their vigilance was most probably due to the confession of Bohumil Vácha (captured on Val Bella) who had confessed before execution that 30 spies were about to be dressed in Austrian uniform and sent over to commit sabotage.[288] The same crumbling under interrogation was evident with the new captives. Both Štorch and Šmarda confessed surprisingly copious details of their mission, stressing that they had only undertaken it in order to return home, having originally been forced to join the Czech Legion. This argument may have saved Šmarda from the gallows for in addition he would argue at his court martial that he had not deserted but been taken prisoner in October 1915. Possibly, as Hanzal suggests, he was 'turned' by the Austrians, but it seems more likely in the absence of new evidence that at his trial he was simply successful in renouncing the Czech Legion and disclaiming any personal responsibility.[289] In contrast, the Austrians executed Štorch and gave the event the widest publicity on both sides of the front. Friends and contacts whom the two had implicated in their confessions were rounded up and sent to an inhospitable part of the mountain front. In retrospect, Marchetti asserted that although the expedition had failed, it had achieved the 'moral impact' he had envisaged, particularly because it had been publicized by the Austrians themselves; their counter-propaganda had proved counter-productive, and had led according to Marchetti to an increase in desertions to Italy. In fact, this was only partially true. The expedition also backfired on Marchetti, due to some subtle Austrian counter-propaganda which actually hit its target.

Following the Riva expedition the 10AK propaganda office began a new campaign of disinformation to make the Czech Legion suspect in Italian eyes. It sent over to the Italians, by leaflet and wireless, coded messages in Czech which referred mysteriously to an organization entitled 'D.R.U.P.'.[290] The messages implied that D.R.U.P. was an association of Austrian spies hidden among the Slav volunteers, and that while Štorch had been a 'true legionary' and therefore been executed, Jan Šmarda had escaped that fate because he was a 'drupan' or Austrian agent. The 10AK followed up this communication, ostensibly sent out for the benefit of their 'drupani' in Italy, with a second message which announced that Popadić, Mikulík and the other officers who had deserted at Val dei Concei on 9 July were all 'drupani' who had been sent to the '7th eagle's nest' and needed to be 'well hatched' (presumably 'instructed').[291] With these methods the Austrians were moving beyond their previous propaganda technique of warning the Italians openly by leaflet, or frightening the Czech legionaries with public executions. They were cleverly exploiting the persistent misgivings which many of the Italian military retained about the Slavs' actual reliability.

If such misgivings were fuelled by a deep-seated mistrust of Yugoslav aspirations, they seem to have been intensified in some quarters after an incident in early June when eight Czech legionaries had rebelled against their officers and been over-hastily executed by General Graziani.[292] Indeed, despite Pivko's frequent assurances to the contrary, it was untrue to suggest that all volunteers were 100 per cent reliable. We know from Czech sources that dozens of Czech officers who were in Italian prison camps were of an 'Austrian mentality'. Some Czechs had certainly felt pressurized into joining the Legion; some were judged unreliable after recruitment, so that already by June 120 had been expelled.[293] In the last months of the war there were even some cases of Czechoslovak legionaries deserting back to Austria.[294] It was therefore not surprising that when the D.R.U.P. messages appeared, and were decoded, the CS was initially anxious about unreliable or 'Austrian' volunteers. In early August, it warned the army and also its allies at Versailles:

> Information has been received from a reliable source that the introduction on a large scale among Czecho-Slovak troops on the Italian Front of defeatist and pacifist elements and spies is being organized by the Austro-German secret propaganda service.[295]

When Pivko made a tour of the various army sectors in early August he quickly learnt about D.R.U.P. and sensed correctly, from talking to the Intelligence heads, that a certain degree of suspicion had surfaced again in military circles:

> Every day I detect new traces of untiring enemy propaganda against the Czechoslovaks and I would justifiably conclude that the Comando Supremo has issued confidential instructions that the Czechoslovak volunteers should be controlled and their movement at the front restricted.[296]

This seems to have been true. According to Finzi, the CS had ordered that the Legion should not be used at the front again until D.R.U.P. had been properly investigated.

The whole deception was finally exposed on 15 August at a meeting in the 1st army sector attended by Pivko, Finzi and other Italian officers.[297] Pivko defended those who were accused of being 'drupani', including Šmarda since it seemed unlikely that he could have dissimulated for almost three years in the Italian war zone. Indeed, Pivko went further, alleging that those 'primitive Slavs' who continued to fight for Austria were motivated by 'primitive duty' to the Emperor and lacked the intelligence to be capable of espionage. Although those present undoubtedly never shared Pivko's straight division of Slavs into 'primitives' and 'idealists', they agreed that D.R.U.P. was an Austrian invention to throw suspicion on the volunteer units. One Italian officer remarked, 'we are dealing here with clever and yet clumsy propaganda'. The clumsiness in fact seemed evident only now that the trick had been exposed.

The Austrians could not know this, and in the final months of hostilities the 10AK continued to issue the coded messages, relying for their content principally upon the statements of captured Czech legionaries. A third D.R.U.P. message, sent over in September, advised Czech prisoners who had been coerced into the Legion to enter D.R.U.P. where they would be 'rendering the best and most valuable service to the fatherland'. A fourth message, deciphered by Italian Intelligence in early October, announced that Andrej Ruziak (a Slovak legionary who had deserted back to Austria) had been a 'drupan', and also tried to throw suspicion upon Yugoslav volunteers whose 'drupani' allegedly had links to socialists.[298] These efforts were now falling on deaf ears, but the D.R.U.P. disinformation had nevertheless had some impact in August, ensuring perhaps that Italy used the Czech units less efficiently in that month. It was one example in the last months that the propaganda duel between Italy and Austria-Hungary was not completely dead. The Austrians, basing their arguments on what they believed to be true, had subtly tested Italy's attitude to the Slav volunteers, and had discovered a surprising number of chinks in the Italian armour.

By September, the strength of Italian propaganda when compared to the Austrians' had been reaffirmed, and the faith of Italian Intelligence in their Slavs had been steadied. It was evident in the intensive practice of trench propaganda, but especially in Italy's use of Czech volunteers to penetrate again into the enemy war zone, an activity which (despite the D.R.U.P. claims) was significantly not practised by the Austrians. The most successful Italian expedition was linked to a Czech attack which took place, as described above, in late September on Cima Tre Pezzi in the lst army sector. As an extra benefit from liaising with the Czech cavalry regiment opposite, Marchetti was able to smuggle two Czech agents across the lines on a mission of sabotage and espionage in the rear.[299] Václav Vopálenský and Rudolf Petr, equipped with false papers and bombs disguised as jars of marmalade, moved forward along Val d'Assa and, after blowing up two munition dumps, a *teleferiche*, and some aircraft hangers, finally reached Trento itself. There they found far tighter controls on their movement than they had anticipated, but they managed to return on the same route and reported back to Marchetti having survived 'five days in the crater of an active volcano'.[300] It was an example which the other Intelligence heads were keen to emulate. In the last weeks of the war, 3rd army Intelligence sent a Czech and an Italian on a joint mission into the rear of the Lower Piave; reaching their destination by boat, they mixed with disgruntled Italian civilians and were able to dispatch pigeons which carried their information back to Italy.[301]

Such journeys into the occupied zone of Venetia had certainly been occurring since August. Under British supervision, the Italians over the summer had learnt how to drop agents by parachute into enemy territory (rather than the aeroplane needing to land). It was a development still in its infancy, but some Italians and also some Slav volunteers seem to have participated in the experiment, being set down in the war zone and 'obtaining useful results' which they despatched back to Italy by 'pigeon-post'.[302] The Austrian authorities were not unaware that such infiltration was occurring. Parachutes had been discovered as well as baskets of carrier pigeons; one 'carrier' had even been shot down in flight.[303] But while they vainly sent out orders for increased vigilance, the Italian Intelligence heads were one step ahead, confidently experimenting with new techniques and often turning to their propaganda troops to carry them out.

From afar in London, Henry Wickham Steed over the summer had been keeping the British EPD informed about the campaign on the Italian Front. He suggested to the EPD Committee that, while there had been major successes in June, the campaign had then been frustrated and allowed to weaken because of Italy's political vacillation over the cause of the oppressed nationalities. In addition, what Steed called the 'spirit of propaganda' at the front had been affected because the Italians were not keen to make a decisive attack on Austria-Hungary without Allied military support.[304] Both of Steed's statements were not quite accurate in view of what we now know about the campaign in Italy. Although the struggle over Italian official policy had continued unabated, had caused frictions at the Padua Commission and hampered the creation of a Yugoslav legion, it had not prevented the Italian military from continuing the propaganda campaign quite intensively in these months.

Nor had the 'spirit of propaganda' lost its attraction for the Italians, except perhaps temporarily during the D.R.U.P. affair. On the contrary, all the indications are that they viewed front propaganda as a viable substitute for an orthodox military offensive at a time when the Monarchy might still be strong enough to resist. As Finzi asked Orlando on one occasion, 'should one now give a violent shake without being certain that the pear, perhaps not completely ripe, will fall from the tree?': better, undoubtedly, to wait and help in the process of ripening the fruit.[305] This policy over the summer was pursued with a new sophistication, both by manifesto and propaganda patrol, aiming at all the opposing nationalities, even the Magyars and Germans, and thereby reaching new psychological and geographical targets in the heart of the Monarchy. The campaign's major strength, as the Austrians recognized, was that it mirrored and interacted with the social and political crisis in the Empire, acting as a catalyst upon existing moods and currents. Clearly, it also had its weaknesses which the Austrians occasionally tried to exploit. But the reality of trends in Austria-Hungary and in the wider war meant that the Austrians' outlook in the final months was largely defensive. They felt besieged by a superior enemy propaganda which seemed to be permeating everywhere.

## Notes

1. Tullio Marchetti, *Ventotto Anni nel Servizio Informazioni Militari* (Trento, 1960) p. 365.
2. Cesare Finzi, *'I.T.O'. Note di un Capo del Servizio Informazioni d'Armata 1915–1918* (Milan, 1934) p. 253.
3. See IWM, Wilson MSS, 22/14, Delmé-Radcliffe to Wilson, no. SBM 248, 1 August; 22/15, Radcliffe to Wilson, no.SBM 250, 2 August 1918; Marchetti, *Ventotto Anni*, pp. 370ff. The Minister of the Treasury, Francesco Nitti (a long associate of Diaz's), was also constantly urging Diaz to be cautious: Alberto Monticone, *Nitti e la Grande Guerra 1914–1918* (Milan, 1961) pp. 282–7.
4. CCC, Cavan MSS, 1/3, 'Italy', pp. 13–14.
5. See Manfried Rauchensteiner, *Der Tod des Doppeladlers. Österreich-Ungarn und der Erste Weltkrieg* (Graz, Vienna and Cologne, 1993) p. 591.
6. PRO, FO 800/212, Northcliffe to Balfour, 6 June 1918. The EPD during June was receiving regular telegrams from Delmé-Radcliffe about the Padua Commission.
7. PRO, FO 800/329, Balfour to Northcliffe, 8 June 1918.
8. *The Times*, 12 June 1918.
9. *Seton Correspondence*, I, nos. 218–19.
10. PRO, FO 371/3135, Derby to Balfour, t.741, 15 June; BL, Northcliffe MSS, vol. X, Add.Mss 62162, Minutes of the 6th EPD Committee meeting, 9 July 1918. Beneš, *Světová Válka*, II, p. 233 terms this 'perhaps the most important' diplomatic act by the French on behalf of the Czechoslovak cause in view of its consequences.
11. AJA, JO 60E/III/1(1), Kujundžić to Trumbić, 2 July 1918.
12. Pichon's statement appears to have been mentioned only in the Czech newssheet, manifesto 159: *Československá Samostatnost* no. 7, 21 July (KA, 11AK Fasz.451, 'Flugzettel I').
13. See, for example, manifesto 159, *Československá Samostatnost* no. 7; BL, Northcliffe MSS, vol. X, Add.Mss 62162, Minutes of 6th EPD Committee meeting.
14. Manifesto 139, 'Češi a Slováci!' (Czech/Croat with no. 138, 'Polacy!' on reverse: KA, 11AK Fasz.451, 'Flugzettel I'). Lansing's statement was also used explicitly to refute Austrian scorn at the Versailles Declaration: manifesto 179, *Jugoslavija* no. 8, 27 July (AJA, JO 111/4). For background to the statement, see Paulová, *Jugoslavenski Odbor*, pp. 460–1; Živojinović, *America, Italy and the Birth of Yugoslavia*, pp. 148–9.
15. PRO, FO 371/3135, C.J. Phillips to Drummond, 15 June, enclosing memorandum by Mičić; Janković and Krizman (eds), *Gradja*, I, no. 161 and note 13, p. 217; AJA, JO 27/72, De Giulli to Trumbić, 17 June 1918.
16. In late July Crewe House was preparing a Croat translation of Balfour's speech with the aid of a JO member Miće Mičić (SWP, 'Crewe House Activities', 26 July). But the only mention of the meeting in Padua's propaganda appears to be manifesto 237 in Czech: *Československá Samostatnost* no. 10, 10 August. News of it did, however, reach Zagreb via a different route: see *Glas Slovenaca Hrvata i Srba*, broj 158, 2 August 1918, p. 2, quoting a report from the Berne *Tagespost*.
17. Steed, *Through Thirty Years*, II, pp. 230–1.
18. AJA, JO 31/50, Trumbić notes, 19 July 1918. The commitment was unequivocal: Trumbić noted Pichon's words as 'we are unreservedly supporting you'.
19. For Pašić's view, see Paulová's perceptive comments: *Jugoslavenski Odbor*, pp. 469–70.
20. For the following, see Beneš, *Světová Válka*, II, pp. 260ff; and the documents in PRO, FO 371/3135, notably Beneš to Steed, 16 July 1918.
21. Beneš, *Světová Válka*, p. 280.

22. Ibid., p. 290. See Guglielmo Emanuel's article, 'Il *Delenda Austria* dell'Inghilterra', in *Corriere della Sera*, 15 August 1918.
23. AJA, JO 19/56, Notes by Trumbić on conversation with Bissolati in Rome, 16 August 1918.
24. Steed's key role in ensuring that propaganda in Italy was transferred to Crewe House seems clear from BL, Northcliffe MSS, vol. XCIV, Add.Mss 62246, Steed to Northcliffe, 31 May; and by early June the transfer was complete (ibid., Northcliffe to Steed, 2 June). Cf. Steed, *Through Thirty Years*, II, p. 216.
25. TTA, Steed MSS, Steed to Orlando, dated 24 June 1918 (but the copy in Steed's private papers is dated the 15th as in his memoirs).
26. PRO, FO 371/3228, Rodd to Balfour, d.202, 16 June 1918.
27. Šepić, *Italjia, Saveznici i Jugoslavensko Pitanje*, p. 329. Trumbić's remarks were intercepted by the Austrians from a British radio station: see HHStA, PA I/771, Generalia XII Slawische Umtriebe 1918.
28. Trumbić sent a similar message at this time to Diaz, but it was bolder in declaring that Italy was fighting for the freedom of the Yugoslav race: AJA, JO 35/104, Trumbić to Diaz [undated]. It was not mentioned in Padua's propaganda.
29. Quotes from manifesto 135, *Jugoslavija* no. 6, which gave in full the speeches made by Trumbić and Orlando on 26 June (KA, 11AK, Gstbs Abt 1918, Fasz.451, File 'Flugzettel I').
30. AJA, JO 28/66, Kujundžić to Yugoslav Committee Rome, 8 August; JO 31/50, Trumbić notes on talk with Pichon, 19 July 1918.
31. Malagodi, *Conversazioni della Guerra*, II, p. 369; PRO, WO 106/825, Radcliffe to DMO, no. BM 452/42, 24 June 1918; DRP, File 'Private letters out', Radcliffe to Lord Stamfordham, 10 July 1918.
32. Šepić, *Italija, Saveznici*, p. 327.
33. Tosi, *La Propaganda Italiana*, pp. 197–8.
34. Albertini, *Epistolario*, II, no. 870, p. 946.
35. *The New Europe*, no. 88, 20 June 1918. See also *Seton Correspondence*, I, no. 219.
36. PRO, FO 170/1145, Rodd to Balfour, pte t., 10 July; FO 800/203, Rodd to Balfour, pte, 14 July; Seton-Watsons, *The Making of a New Europe*, pp. 295–6.
37. For the organization of Crewe House's Italian Committee, see BL, Northcliffe MSS, vol. LXXXVIII, Add.Mss. 62240, chart 2 attached to Stuart to Northcliffe, 24 June 1918.
38. PRO, FO 371/3228, Erskine to Balfour, t.548, 23 July 1918. See also O'Donovan's report on his Italian tour: BL, Northcliffe MSS, vol. XI, Add.Mss 62163.
39. For Salvemini's view, see especially his letter to Ojetti of 5 July: Salvemini, *Carteggio 1914–1920*, p. 400.
40. Šepić, *Italija, Saveznici*, p. 325; Tosi, *La Propaganda Italiana*, p. 198. Delmé-Radcliffe noted how papers loyal to Sonnino (such as *Il Resto del Carlino*) were increasingly writing articles which insisted on Italy's right to Dalmatia: PRO, FO 371/3474, Radcliffe to DMI, t.10440, 9 June.
41. Pivko, *DRUP*, pp. 8–10; Albertini, *Venti Anni di Vita Politica*, III, p. 352.
42. This at least was Pivko's view according to what Salvemini informed him in writing (*DRUP*, p. 8). It is not evident from Salvemini's published correspondence, but he later replied himself to Coppola in *L'Unità* (see *Carteggio 1914–1920*, pp. 403ff).
43. Ojetti, *La Propaganda sul Nemico*, in G. Amendola *et al.*, *Il Patto di Roma* (Rome, 1919), p. 131.

44. Pivko, *DRUP*, p. 9; Albertini, *Venti Anni*, III, pp. 352–3. Ojetti's exasperation is also blatant in a letter to his wife: Ojetti, *Lettere alla Moglie*, p. 552.
45. 'Il settimana all'estero', *Il Resto del Carlino*, 10 July 1918.
46. On 24 May, for example, members of the Yugoslav Committee had not felt able to participate fully in the anniversary celebrations in Rome because of the presence of Italian flags from 'exclusively Yugoslav regions': see Dinko Trinajstić's account in AJA, JO 35/128, 24 May 1918.
47. AJA, JO 19/168, Trumbić notes on meeting with Ojetti (Hotel Regina, Rome), 12 July; DRP, File 'Private letters out', Radcliffe to Stamfordham, 10 July.
48. Albertini, *Epistolario*, II, nos. 841 p. 939, 851 p. 950, 852 p. 952.
49. Ojetti, *Lettere alla Moglie*, pp. 560, 563–4; Albertini, *Epistolario*, II, no. 851, p. 951.
50. Ibid., no. 855, p. 953.
51. Ibid., no. 851, p. 951; Tosi, *La Propaganda Italiana*, p. 237 note 132: Ojetti to Orlando, 26 June and 27 July 1918.
52. Ojetti, *Lettere*, pp. 559ff, 561–2; PRO, FO 371/3228, Erskine to Balfour, t.547, 23 July. Steed's reasoning (which took into account other perceived Italian obstacles such as disharmony in the Padua Commission) is clear from Ante Mandić's report to Trumbić in AJA, JO 8/14a, 25 July 1918. See also Salvemini's letters to Ojetti of 22 and 26 July (*Carteggio*, pp. 408–13) for a sharp impression of Orlando's 'fence-sitting'.
53. For a thorough study of this rivalry, see Tosi, *La Propaganda Italiana*, pp. 191ff. Sonnino was now gradually setting aside his former indifference to propaganda and public opinion.
54. See PRO, WO 106/817, Delmé-Radcliffe to DMO, no. SBM 249, 2 August; no. SBM 271, 11 August.
55. Ojetti, *Lettere*, pp. 570–1.
56. AJA, JO 19/56, Trumbić notes on talks with Bissolati. See also PRO, WO 106/817, Radcliffe to DMO, no. SBM 271, 11 August; WO 106/1384, Radcliffe to DMO, t.10684, 12 August.
57. Bodleian Library, Oxford, Milner MSS, Box 108, Delmé-Radcliffe to DMI, t.10474, 18 June 1918. I am grateful to Christopher Seton-Watson for this reference.
58. AJA, JO 19/139, DMI to Delmé-Radcliffe, t.60750 cipher, 22 June 1918.
59. Albertini, *Epistolario*, II, no. 839, p. 937.
60. Ibid., nos. 840, 841, pp. 938–40 (Albertini's letters to Borgese and Emanuel).
61. Ibid., no. 848, pp. 947–9: Ojetti to Albertini, 8 July 1918.
62. See for example ibid., no. 844, p. 943; Ojetti, *Lettere*, p. 553.
63. Baker's view: PRO, WO 106/817, Baker to Secretary of Enemy Propaganda Committee, no. BM 452/62, 21 July. Jambrišak's view: AJA, JO 19/116, Jambrišak to Trumbić, 18 June 1918.
64. PRO, WO 106/817, Baker to Secretary of Enemy Propaganda Committee, no. BM 452/62, 21 July; Antoni Szuber, *Walka o Przewagę Duchową*, pp. 125–6, for Zamorski's own explanation; Ojetti, *Lettere*, pp. 559, 562–3.
65. Umberto Zanotti-Bianco, *Carteggio 1906–1918* (Rome and Bari, 1987) p. 645. Unravelling the misunderstandings at Padua was no easy matter. By late July, for example, Jambrišak was complaining to Diaz not about Ojetti, but about the British (Radcliffe was singled out) whom he alleged to be slandering him in their propaganda. Steed could not understand Jambrišak's reasoning: see AJA, JO 8/14a, Mandić to Trumbić, 25 July.
66. Albertini, *Epistolario*, II, no. 842, pp. 940–1.

67. Seton-Watsons, *The Making of a New Europe*, p. 306 note 35.
68. PRO, FO 371/3474, Erskine to Balfour, t.543, 21 July; and the correspondence of O'Donovan with Phillips and Delmé-Radcliffe in July in FO 170/1145.
69. PRO, FO 170/1145, Balfour to Rodd, t.1022, 12 July; SWP, *Draft EPD Report*, p. 48. There is no evidence that the conference was planned in response to propaganda from the Central Powers as Tosi suggests: 'Romeo A. Gallenga Stuart e la propaganda di guerra all'estero', *Storia Contemporanea*, II (1971) p. 534.
70. James R. Mock and Cedric Larson, *Words that Won the War: The Story of the Committee on Public Information 1917–1919* (Princeton, 1939) pp. 256–8.
71. Documents in PRO, FO 371/3474 detail Crewe House's attempts from March to secure the official appointment of a French and American delegate for the committee; Steed and Borgese were to serve on behalf of Britain and Italy.
72. See Chaix to Colonel Le Roy Lewis, 20 July, in PRO, FO 371/3474, Derby to Balfour, d.588, 27 July 1918; Mock and Larson, *Words that Won the War*, p. 258; A. Klobukowski, *Souvenirs de Belgique 1914–1918* (Brussels, 1928) pp. 10, 265.
73. Mock and Larson, *Words that Won the War*, pp. 258–9.
74. AJA, JO 35/45(2), JO Paris to Trinajstić, 5 August; PRO, WO 106/817, Radcliffe to DMO, no. SBM 249, 11 August. For the full list of participants at the conference, see SWP, *Draft EPD Report*, pp. 90–1.
75. Stuart, *Secrets of Crewe House*, pp. 151–2.
76. The other three committees all agreed on the need for more Allied exchange of information, but made few important decisions with regard to Austria. On the 'prisoners' committee' the Italian delegate simply announced that most prisoners in Italy were 'Austrians'! (report in BL, Northcliffe MSS, vol. XI, Add.Mss. 62163).
77. *Seton Correspondence*, I, no. 221, p. 331.
78. Albertini, *Epistolario*, II, no. 862, p. 965: Emanuel's report.
79. For the following, see ibid., pp. 966–7. Emanuel's account, as related to him by Borgese, is valuable in revealing the passion with which the debate in the policy committee unfolded.
80. Most recently the Slovene leader, Anton Korošec, had been among those who made such speeches to that effect in Trieste on 30 May 1918 (a point which had been taken up also by Francesco Coppola in his article of 10 July in *Il Resto del Carlino*): see Šepić, *Italija, Saveznici*, p. 328.
81. Šepić's account (*Italija, Saveznici*, p. 338) adds substance since he used Borgese's final report to Gallenga. Šepić, however, interprets Borgese's stance during the discussion as insincere, simply adopted in order to defeat Steed; this seems improbable for Borgese had always been a realist (like Albertini) and was only too conscious of disunity in the Yugoslav camp.
82. Stuart, *Secrets of Crewe House*, pp. 173–6. The full committee reports submitted to the Allied governments can be found in PRO, CAB 24/61, G.T.5492 (and in HLRO, Beaverbrook MSS, BBK E/3/44).
83. SWP, *Draft EPD Report*, pp. 108–11.
84. Stuart, *Secrets of Crewe House*, pp. 183–4, 199.
85. Albertini, *Epistolario*, II, pp. 968–9.
86. The following account of the *Corriere* polemic is based largely on Albertini, *Venti Anni di Vita Politica*, III, pp. 355–70.
87. For an Austrian view of this polemic, and its possible use in 'patriotic instruction' among troops of southern Slav nationality, see KA, FAst 1918, Fasz.5997, Res.550.

88. Albertini, *Epistolario*, II, no. 869, p. 980; Ojetti, *Lettere*, p. 576. Later, Albertini would even judge that the *Corriere* had won the polemic (ibid., p. 1013). Both Trumbić and the British ambassador felt the opposite at the time: AJA, JO 19/173; HLRO, Lloyd George MSS, F/56/29, Rodd to Lloyd George, pte, 25 September.
89. Malagodi's term: Malagodi, *Conversazioni della Guerra*, II, p. 383. For Orlando's outlook, see especially his conversation with Malagodi, pp. 371–3.
90. Ojetti to Albertini, 28 August: Albertini, *Epistolario*, II, no. 870, p. 982.
91. Gallenga was all the more motivated to join forces against Sonnino as the latter, having found out about the Allied propaganda conference, had complained to Orlando and demanded that Gallenga's ministry be made subordinate to his own: see Tosi, *La Propaganda Italiana*, pp. 211–13. Nitti appears to have been convinced by Amendola's advice that the best way to avoid crisis was to shift the balance in the cabinet towards Bissolati: see Albertini, *Epistolario*, II, no. 873, p. 987.
92. Malagodi, *Conversazioni della Guerra*, II, pp. 385–8. See also Trumbić's notes of 27 August in AJA, JO 19/173.
93. Albertini, *Epistolario*, II, pp. 1066–7 note 440.
94. For Sonnino's continued influence from September, see Tosi, *La Propaganda Italiana*, pp. 214ff; and his remarks to Charles Merriam: PRO, FO 371/3137, Merriam to Sisson, 9 September 1918.
95. AJA, JO 28/48(1), 'Pregled rada, Manifesti sul nemico'; JO 28/48(2), 'Giornali sul nemico'.
96. Ojetti, *Lettere*, p. 560; Albertini, *Epistolario*, II, no. 855, p. 953.
97. Manifesto 90, 'Srbi, Hrvati i Slovenci!' (Croat and Slovene: KA, EvB 5758/26661).
98. Manifesto 99 [issued in most languages], 'Soldaten! (KA, EvB, Fasz.5758/26661, 5744/4538; OHM, sz.1485, 1415/10; AJA, JO 19/95); Diaz war bulletins of 18 June and 6 July (OHM, sz.1353/1/2/3; OHM, sz.1264/1).
99. Zanotti-Bianco, *Carteggio 1906–1918*, p. 635. For the leaflets, see: 'Soldaten des oesterreich-ungarischen Heeres' (KA, EvB, Fasz.5753/19324); 'Soldaten! In Oesterreich und in Ungarn ist die Revolution ausgebrochen!' (OHM sz.7354; in Croat: HIL, Fasz.4517 'Propaganda Anyag'). For an Austrian reaction to 'these tendentious lies': KA, 11AK Gstbs Abt, Fasz.449, Pr.2295.
100. SWP, *Draft EPD Report*, p. 40. See, for example, manifesto 99 [Italian and German editions], 'Soldati combattenti per l'Austria-Ungheria!' (OHM, sz.1415/10, 1485); manifesto 94 [Romanian], 'Ostaşi români! (AJA, JO 19/94; IWM, 3(45) File 39); and manifesto 170, 'Soldaten! Zehntausende von eurem Brüdern sind an der Piave und den Montellomassiv gefallen' (rare leaflet, only discovered in VHA collection).
101. Manifesto 108 [issued in most languages], 'Ai soldati combattenti...' (numerous copies in OHM, sz.1252; KA, Flugzettel Sammlung; AHZ, Dobrovoljački Arhiv, etc.). The actual Austrian losses appear to have been half this figure but for Padua's claims: manifesto 112, *Polak* no. 5, 6 July (KA, 11AK Fasz.451, 'Flugzettel I').
102. Manifesto 168, 'Jugoslaveni!' (KA, Flugzettel Sammlung). The same message was the subject of manifesto 165, 'Magyar Katonák!' (KA, 11AK Fasz.451, 'Flugzettel I'); manifesto 173, 'Jaký dojem v Rakousku...' (ibid.); and manifesto 167, 'Polacy!' (KA, EvB, Fasz.5761/31651).
103. Much was made of Below's 'appointment': see manifestos 165; 161, 'Magyar Katonák!' (OHM, sz.01188); and the following, all in KA, 11AK Fasz.451, 'Flugzettel I': 153, Ukraïn'ci! [Ruthene]; 152, 'Polacy!'; 154, 'Srbi, Hrvati i Slovenci!'; 147, 'Soldaţi Români!'; 163, 'Češi a Slováci!'. That false intelligence about Below was widespread on the Allied side is clear from American sources: Challener (ed.), *United States*

*Military Intelligence 1917–1927* (New York and London, 1978) IV, 20 July, p. 5; 27 July, pp. 13–14.

104. Manifesto 215, 'Magyar Katonák!' (OHM sz.1486). Manifesto 303, 'Magyar Katonák!', refuted claims that the Germans had reached Paris (KA, 11AK Fasz.451, 'Flugzettel I'). A number of leaflets wrongly dated the start of the offensive as 14 July and Foch's counter-offensive as the 16th.

105. Manifesto 286, 'Oesterreichisch-ungarische Soldaten!' (issued in German, Magyar, Slovene, Polish: copies in OHM sz.1325–7; VHA; KA, 11AK Fasz.451, 'Flugzettel I'); manifesto 330, 'Graphischer Aufriss der grossen Entent-Offensive in Frankreich' (issued in German, Magyar, Croat: KA, 11AK Fasz.451, 'Flugzettel II'; VHA; Stuart, *Secrets of Crewe House*, opposite p. 48). Reports about the Western Front formed regular items in Padua's four weekly newssheets.

106. Manifesto 317, 'Soldaten!' (OHM sz.80.20.1).

107. See OULK, VII, pp. 336–7, 433ff, for the divisions' despatch and their deployment at Verdun.

108. Manifesto 318, 'Slovenci, Hrvati in Srbi' (Slovene: KA, 11AK Fasz.451, 'Flugzettel I and II'); manifesto 319, 'Zhovnïri-Ukraïn'cï!' (Ukrainian: KA, 11AK Fasz.448, Pr.2000); manifesto 215, 'Magyar Katonák!'.

109. Manifesto 148, 'Die erste Million amerikanischer Soldaten ist schon in Frankreich' (OHM sz.1250; HIL, Fasz.4517; KA, EvB 1918 Fasz.5755/26619), and copies also in Magyar (manifesto 174), Czech (164), Slovene (149), Romanian (150) and Polish (151). On this theme, see also manifestos 267, 'Srbi, Hrvati i Slovenci!' (KA, Flugzettel Sammlung) and 361, which depicted an American soldier bawling out '4 Millionen Amerikaner...' (VHA; and in Polish in Žipek (ed.), *Domov za Války*, V, p. 93).

110. Manifesto 235, *Jugoslavija* no. 10, 10 August (section in Slovene: KA, 11AK Fasz.451, 'Flugzettel III').

111. Manifesto 269, 'Was alles Amerika beiträgt...' (copies in German, Italian, Polish, Ukrainian: KA, EvB Fasz.5761/32114; IWM, 3(45)/39; OHM, sz.1212); BL, Northcliffe MSS, vol. X, Add.Mss 62162, Minutes of the 8th EPD Committee meeting, 6 August 1918.

112. Manifesto 252, 'Soldaten die ihr für Deutschland und Österreich-Ungarn kämpft' (German, Magyar: OHM sz.1555; IWM, 3(45)/39); manifesto 235 (section in Croat); manifesto 208, *Jugoslavija* no. 9 (AJA, JO 111/4; KA, 11AK Fasz.451, 'Flugzettel I').

113. See manifesto 323, 'Glad' (Croat and Czech editions: KA, 11AK Fasz.451, 'Flugzettel III'; KA, EvB Fasz.5762/33878); manifesto 125, 'Nachrichten über den Hunger' (German, Italian, Polish, Romanian: IWM, 3(45)/39; OHM sz.1248); manifesto 143, 'Głód w Austryi' (Polish and Romanian: KA, 11AK Fasz.451, 'Flugzettel I'); manifesto 112, *Polak* no. 5.

114. Respectively German ambassador (on 6 July) and German commander in Ukraine (on 30 July): see manifesto 178, *Československá Samostatnost* no. 8, 27 July (AJA, JO 111/4); and manifestos 257, 267 and 275.

115. Manifesto 237, *Československá Samostatnost* no. 10, 10 August (HIL, Fasz. 4517); manifesto 258, *Jugoslavija* no. 11, 17 August (AJA, JO 111/4); manifesto 263, 'Magyar Katonák!' (OHM sz.78.41.1): 'you Magyar soldiers, instead of Russian grain, are likely to receive an order to start this Russian war again thanks to Kaiser Wilhelm and his Junkers'.

116. Figures in AJA, JO 28/48(1), 28/48(2), 28/48(3). It is not clear whether the figures quoted refer to the number of leaflets composed *or* printed *or* distributed during

these months. Certainly, leaflets printed before June continued to be distributed along with new, more topical, material.

117. AJA, JO 60E/III/1(1), Kujundžić to Trumbić, 2 July 1918.
118. Manifesto 203, *Jugoslavija*, July 1918 [special illustrated edition]: copies in AJA, JO 111/4; KA, EvB Fasz.5755/26619; OHM sz.3508.
119. Manifesto 199, 'Uslovi mira Sila Sporazuma' (also issued in seven other languages: KA, Flugzettel Sammlung). For Lodge's speech: manifesto 309, *Jugoslavija* no. 14, 10 September (section in Slovene: AJA, JO 111/4) and manifesto 341, Soldaţi români!' (printed in Romanian, Italian, Polish and Czech editions: KA, 11AK Fasz.451, File 'Unerledigt').
120. Manifesto 90, 'Srbi, Hrvati, Slovenci!' (Croat and Slovene).
121. Manifestos 135 and 158. See also manifesto 203 which recounted a speech by Mihajlović (secretary at Serbia's Rome embassy) at Kosovo celebrations in Milan; Mihajlović emphasized Croatian–Italian links from 1848.
122. Manifesto 169, 'Kosovo!' (KA, 11AK Fasz.449, Pr.2323); also reprinted in manifesto 135.
123. Manifesto 208, *Jugoslavija* no. 9. On this theme, see also manifesto 142, 'Bezumne optužbe austriske o rdjavom postupanju sa zarobljenicima' (Croat/Czech/Polish/ Romanian: HIL, Fasz.4517. Manifesto 232 is exactly the same: KA, 11AK Fasz.451, 'Flugzettel I'); and manifestos 115, 135, 158.
124. For the Yugoslav forces in Russia and America: manifestos 179, 258, 135, 158, 208, 309. Surprisingly, Padua made no mention of Trumbić's official audience with the King of Italy in the war zone on 14 August.
125. Manifesto [101], 'Njegovoj ekselenciji maršalu Svetozaru Borojeviću od Bojne' (KA, EvB Fasz.5758/26661; OHM sz.1256; HIL, Fasz.4517. Reproduced also in Pivko, *Val Bella*, pp. 73–4). That the leaflet was no. 101 is clear from the Italian translation in AJA, JO 19/104 (Ojetti ordered 200 Italian copies to be printed). Jambrišak's draft is in AJA, JO 19/102.
126. PRO, WO 106/825, Delmé-Radcliffe to DMO, no.BM 452/42, 24 June 1918.
127. Max Ronge, *Kriegs- und Industriespionage*, p. 370; KA, FAst 1918, Fasz. 6003, *Vaterländische Bildungsarbeit. Mitteilungen der FAst*, no. 3, 15 August, p. 13.
128. Manifesto 235, *Jugoslavija* no. 10. The same 'reliable news' was relayed in manifestos 224, 'Krajané bratři!', and 222, 'Polacy!' (both in KA, 11AK Fasz.451 'Flugzettel I'), and has even been propagated by one modern historian: see Alan Sked, *The Decline and Fall of the Habsburg Empire 1815–1918* (London and New York, 1989) p. 260.
129. Manifesto 183, 'Srbi, Hrvati i Slovenci!' (white leaflet in dark blue type: KA, 11AK Fasz.451, 'Flugzettel I'). See also manifestos 235, 135, and 208.
130. *Stenographische Protokolle über die Sitzungen des Hauses der Abgeordneten des Österreichischen Reichsrates*, XXII Session, III (Vienna, 1918) p. 3900: 75.Sitzung, 16 July 1918, speech by the Czech Social Democrat, Vlastimil Tusar.
131. Ibid., p. 3897. Glaise-Horstenau for one was worried about the wisdom of making such a speech at this time: *Ein General im Zwielicht*, I, p. 480. The best study of this trend in Austrian politics remains Helmut Rumpler, *Max Hussarek. Nationalitäten und Nationalitätenpolitik in Österreich im Sommer des Jahres 1918* (Graz and Cologne, 1965).
132. Manifesto 223, 'Slovenci, Hrvati in Srbi' (Slovene: OHM sz.1438/1). In Padua's Polish propaganda, a more accurate assessment of Seidler's fall from power was given.

133. For the Viennese appeals: manifestos 110, 'Srbi, Hrvati i Slovenci!'; and 184, 'Srbi, Hrvati i Slovenci!' (both in KA, 11AK Fasz.451, 'Flugzettel I').
134. See the complaints of the 6ID command: KA, FAst 1918, Fasz. 5997, Res.645, 6ID Kmdo to FAst, Na Nr 1507, 11 September 1918. The speech also provoked an interpellation in the Reichsrat on 19 July by Verstovšek, Brenčić and others; but the AOK privately rejected their idea that German-Austrian soldiers had been given special treatment during the war: see KA, AOK Op.Abt 1918, Fasz.375, Op.Nr 111966, 18 September.
135. Manifesto 295, 'Srbi, Hrvati i Slovenci!' (OHM sz.1440); manifesto 291, *Jugoslavija* no. 13, 3 September (AJA, JO 111/4). For a Czech version: manifesto 297, 'Valečné cíle rakouských Němců' (KA, 11AK Fasz.448, Pr.2000; Polish version, manifesto 294, on reverse). Wichtl's rabid view of the Czechs had already been publicized widely through his brochure, *Dr Karel Kramarsch, der Anstifter des Weltkrieges* (Vienna and Munich, 1918). It came to the attention of Padua who noted in its Czech propaganda that the work had quickly sold out (to German readers) when published: see manifesto 159, *Československá Samostatnost* no. 7 (KA, 11AK Fasz.451, 'Flugzettel I').
136. Manifesto 291, *Jugoslavija* no. 13. For an Italian discussion of Wichtl's views, see *Corriere della Sera,* 19 August 1918. The reality of famine in Istria is assessed in Cornwall, 'The Experience of Yugoslav Agitation', p. 661.
137. Manifesto 304, 'Srbi, Hrvati i Slovenci!' (KA, 11AK Fasz.451, 'Flugzettel II'); manifesto 313, 'Srbi, Hrvati i Slovenci!' (OHM sz.7351; KA, EvB Fasz.5761/32114), which is probably the work of Kujundžić.
138. See manifestos 313 and 331, 'Vojnici Austro-Ugarske' (Croat, Polish, German and Magyar editions: KA, Flugzettel Sammlung). For the 'court scandal' which erupted after the Piave defeat, see manifestos 158, 179, 258; and Karl Freiherr von Werkmann, *Deutschland als Verbündeter. Kaiser Karls Kampf um den Frieden* (Berlin, 1931) p. 277.
139. Manifesto 291, *Jugoslavija* no. 13; KA, EvB 1918, Fasz.5758/27382, Ronge to AOK Op.Abt, 14 September 1918.
140. In English, the course of events is analyzed fully in Cornwall, 'The Experience of Yugoslav Agitation'.
141. Manifesto 235, *Jugoslavija* no. 10. See Bogdan Krizman, *Hrvatska u Prvom Svetjskom Ratu. Hrvatsko-Srpski Politički Odnosi* (Zagreb, 1989) p. 182.
142. Manifesto 115, *Jugoslavia* no. 5 (passage in Slovene); manifesto 179, *Jugoslavija* no. 8; see Janko Pleterski, *Prvo Opredeljenje Slovenaca za Jugoslaviju* (Belgrade, 1976) pp. 335–6. For socialist resolutions: manifestos 135 and 275 (sections in Slovene); and for context: Vlado Strugar, *Jugoslavenske Socialdemokratske Stranke 1914–1918* (Zagreb, 1963) pp. 289–90.
143. Manifesto 291, *Jugoslavija* no. 13 (leading section in Slovene); manifesto 308, 'Srbi, Hrvati i Slovenci!' (KA, 11AK Fasz.451, 'Flugzettel I'); and manifesto 309, *Jugoslavija* no. 14, 10 September (AJA, JO 111/4), which listed who was present at the celebrations and also detailed some of the events such as the uncovering of a monument to the former Slovene leader, Janez Krek.
144. HIL, HFB Fasz.4473/1925, MK/KM to HFB, Nr 32110 (telephone communication), 10 August 1918. See Lojze Ude, 'Declarijsko gibanje na Slovenskem', in Vasa Čubrilović, Ferdo Čulinović and Marko Kostrenčić (eds), *Naučni Skup u Povodu 50-Godišnjice Raspada Austro-Ugarske Monarhije i Stvaranja Jugoslavenske Države* (Zagreb, 1969) p. 156.
145. Manifesto 203, *Jugoslavija* [special edition].

146. See, for example, manifesto 87, 'Československé vojsko na pochodu do Vladivostoku' (VHA collection); the same leaflet recorded that Count Czernin was now desperately trying to sell his estates in Bohemia. The Czech army in Russia was also briefly discussed in manifestos 137, 178, 210, 237, 274.
147. Manifesto 229, 'Bratři Češi a Slováci!' (KA, Flugzettel Sammlung); manifesto 324 'Češi a Slováci!' (enclosed with KA, 11AK Fasz.448, Pr.2004); manifesto 78, 'Přehlídka československého vojska J.V. králem Italským' (AJA, JO 111/4), telling of the King of Italy's review of Czech forces.
148. Manifesto 243, 'Bratři! Bratři!' (VHA; KA, 11AK Fasz.451, 'Flugzettel I'). See also Pivko, *Val Bella*, p. 116, who records the truth of the incident.
149. Of Balfour, Cecil, Pichon and Lansing: see manifestos 80, 113, 139, 159. Manifesto 137 recorded the effusive congratulations which passed between Orlando and Štefánik in early July.
150. Manifesto 285, 'Anglická vláda uznala samostatnost a svrchovanost českého národa' (editions in most languages: OHM sz.1313; HIL, Fasz.4516; IWM, 3(45)/39). See also manifesto 289, *Československá Samostatnost* no. 13, 3 September (AJA, JO 111/4) which recorded Beneš's views; and the bright red leaflet [unnumbered and in 8 languages including French], 'Engleska vlada priznala je Čeho-Slovake savezničkom narodom' (VHA; OHM sz.3498. Probably issued by one of the Italian Intelligence offices).
151. Manifesto 237 and 257, *Československá Samostatnost* no. 11, 17 August (AJA, JO 111/4). For the speeches by Stránský and Staněk, see *Stenographische Protokolle*, III, pp. 4134ff, 4244. The view of the 11AK: KA, 11AK 1918 Gstbs Abt, Fasz.449, Pr.2317, 11AK Propaganda report.
152. Manifesto 210, *Československá Samostatnost* no. 9, 3 August (AJA, 111/4); and for the Hungarian military view: KA, EvB Fasz.5756/222824, Beilage I.
153. Manifesto 224, 'Krajané, bratři!'. See also manifestos 237, 159, 178; and 323, 'Kronika hladu' (KA, 11AK Fasz.451, 'Flugzettel III'). For the actual food protests and bloodshed in Plzeň, see Plaschka *et al.*, *Innere Front*, II, pp. 49–50.
154. Manifesto 131, 'Necht' Vas posílí pohled na velkého mučedníka – M. JANA HUSA!' (KA, Flugzettel Sammlung; and reproduced in Szuber, *Walka o Przewagę Duchową*).
155. Manifestos 277, 'Soldaţi români!'; 305, 'Soldaţi români!'; 238, *Neamul Românesc* no. 10, 10 August; 136, *Neamul Românesc* no. 6, 15 July; 276, *Neamul Românesc* no. 12, 26 August (all in KA, 11AK Fasz.451, 'Flugzettel I').
156. Manifesto 156, *Neamul Românesc* no. 7, 21 July (KA, 11AK Fasz.451, 'Flugzettel I'. See Ronge's view in *Kriegs- und Industriespionage*, p. 356.
157. Manifesto 260, *Neamul Românesc* no. 11, 17 August (AJA, JO 111/4); manifesto 238; manifesto 209, *Neamul Românesc* no. 9, 3 August (AJA, JO 111/4).
158. Manifestos 209; and 290, *Neamul Românesc* no. 13, 3 September (AJA, JO 111/4). See also Hannah Pakula, *The Last Romantic: A Biography of Queen Marie of Romania* (London, 1996) p. 249.
159. See Ronge's summary of 'Romanian Irredenta' in KA, MKSM 1918, 28–3/18, AOK to MKSM, EvB Nr 29230, 7 October 1918.
160. On Mangra, see R.W. Seton-Watson, *A History of the Roumanians* (Cambridge, 1934) p. 523. And manifestos 75, *Neamul Românesc* no. 4, 25 June (OHM sz.3507; AJA, JO 19/66); and 311, *Neamul Românesc* no. 14, 10 September (AJA, JO 111/4).
161. Manifestos 238 and 276, repeating extract from *Neue Pester Journal*.

162. Manifesto 209; 192, 'Soldaţi români!' (HIL, Fasz.4517), quoting *Budapesti Hirlap* of 6 July. The speech was also the subject of another leaflet (possibly no. 182) of which only the German translation remains: 'Rumänische Soldaten! Das ungar. Blatt *A Nap*...' (KA, 11AK Gstbs Abt, Fasz.448, Pr.2000). Manifestos 260 and 276 gave extracts from two Hungarian newspapers of the 1890s to illustrate Magyar hatred of the 'Romanian savages'.
163. See 'Soldaţi români!' (OHM sz.1591); manifesto 247, 'Soldaţi Români!' (KA, Flugzettel Sammlung); and manifesto 199, 'Condiţiile de pace ale Aliaţilor' (issued in all languages: KA, 11AK Fasz.451, 'Flugzettel I').
164. See manifestos 156, 260, 276. Crewe House proceeded to meet Ionescu when he visited London, as part of its general cultivation of Romanian émigrés: see SWP, memorandum of 'Crewe House Activities', 27 July, 4 August, 8 August.
165. Manifesto 260, *Neamul Românesc* no. 11. For the 'Romanian Days' in Rome (on 30 May), see manifesto 75; for a Romanian contribution in Genoa (25 June), see manifesto 136, *Neamul Românesc* no. 6, 15 July (KA, EvB, Fasz.5761/31651).
166. Manifesto 290, *Neamul Românesc* no. 13. Manifesto 311, *Neamul Românesc* no. 14, gave a long, very emotional speech by a 'Lt Dr A.C.B' on the occasion of the founding of an officer corps for the Romanian Legion in Italy.
167. See manifestos 206, 'Soldaţi Români!' (OHM sz.1414); 311; 181, 'Soldaţi români!' (KA, 11AK Fasz.451, 'Flugzettel III').
168. Szuber, *Walka o Przewagę Duchową*, pp. 155–6.
169. Manifesto 309, *Jugoslavija* no. 14. For Ojetti's desire to play the religious card with the Poles, see Zanotti-Bianco's request for material from the Catholic lawyer Attilio Begey: *Carteggio 1906–1918*, p. 638
170. Manifesto 251, 'Ojciec Święty dla Połski' (KA, 11AK Fasz.451, 'Flugzettel III'; IWM, 3(45)/39); manifesto 244, 'Żołnierze-Ludu Polski!' (IWM, 3(45)/39). See also manifesto 265, 'Modlitwa uciśnionych synów': a bombastic sermon to the Poles (KA, 11AK, Fasz.448 Pr.2000; IWM, 3(45)/39).
171. Manifesto 322, 'Żołnierze-Polacy!' (HIL, Fasz.4515, 'Propaganda Anyag'). Szuber notes (*Walka*, p. 139) that this was the only leaflet composed in the name of the Polish National Committee. See also the statement by Polish prisoners in the camp at Santa Maria Capua Vetere: manifesto 231, 'Zołnierze Polacy! (contains many typographical errors: IWM, 3(45)/39).
172. Manifestos 259, *Polak* no. 11, 17 August (AJA, JO 111/4); 262, 'Polacy!' (OHM sz.1328); 236, *Polak* no. 10, 10 August (HIL, Fasz.4517; KA, 11AK Fasz.451, 'Flugzettel III'). Manifestos 259; 273, *Polak* no. 12, 26 August (AJA, JO 111/4); and 310, *Polak* no. 14, 10 September (AJA, JO 111/4) gave details of Haller's career and activity in France.
173. Manifesto 259, *Polak* no. 11, quoting *Illustrowany Kurjer Codzienny* of 11 July; manifesto 157, *Polak* no. 7, 21 July (KA, 11AK Fasz.451, 'Flugzettel I') gave similar figures from *Naprzód*. See also manifestos 187, 'Polacy!' (KA, 11AK Fasz.451, 'Flugzettel III'); and 197, 'Wojna i głód' (KA, Flugzettel Sammlung).
174. Manifesto 193, 'Jak Niemcy prześladują...' (OHM sz.1454/1). On German behaviour in Lithuania, see manifestos 177, *Polak* no. 8, 27 July (AJA, JO 111/4); 207, *Polak* no. 9, 3 August (AJA, JO 111/4); and 273.
175. Manifesto 307, 'Żołnierze Polacy' (KA, 11AK Fasz.451, 'Flugzettel III'). For the ambiguous attitude to Jews, see manifestos 207, 273, 292; and 283, 'Polacy!', quoting *Kurjer Poznański* of 3 July.

176. Manifesto 160, 'Polacy!' (KA, EvB Fasz.5755/26619). For a more moderate view: manifesto 293, 'Polacy!' (KA, Flugzettel Sammlung).
177. Manifesto 186, 'Polacy' (KA, FAst, Fasz.5996, Res.486/28); manifesto 272, 'Polacy!' (IWM, 3(45)/39), signed by the Polish People's Party in Lublin; manifesto 259, *Polak* no. 11, which contained an address by officers being tried at Máramarossziget.
178. The propaganda also reported those who criticized the Polish Club for not taking a more determined stance (see manifesto 217, 'Polacy!' in OHM sz.1452). This undoubtedly unintentional ambiguity in Padua's argument reflected in fact the reality of the situation, for when Seidler resigned, his successor Max von Hussarek still gained some support from conservative members of the Club to approve the budget.
179. Manifesto 221, 'Polacy' (OHM, sz.1442). For similar criticism, see manifestos 218, 'Bracia Polacy z Galicyi!' (KA, EvB, Fasz.5755/26619) and 198, 'Polacy!' (KA, EvB, Fasz.5744/4538). For a full record of the speeches: *Stenographische Protokolle*, III, 76. Sitzung, 17 July, pp. 3950ff, 3982ff, 3994ff.
180. Manifesto 240, 'Polacy!' (KA, EvB, Fasz.5755/26619).
181. KA, HGK Conrad 1918, Fasz.66, Na Nr 400a/400, 10AK Propaganda report, 28 August 1918.
182. See Szuber, *Walka o Przewagę Duchową*, pp. 147–50.
183. Thus the Ukrainian version of manifesto 199, 'Uslovya mira deržav – "Porozum lïnya"', offered Ruthene soldiers no particular peace conditions (OHM sz.79.77.1). Many other leaflets were not Ukrainian-specific: 99, 153, 269, 285, 319.
184. Manifesto 88, 'Ukraïn'cï!'; and also manifesto 91, 'Ukraïn'cï, za kogo polivazte krov?' (both in KA, EvB, Fasz.5758/26661).
185. Manifesto 88; manifesto 112, *Polak* no. 5: referring especially to an Austrian propaganda newspaper, *Ukaïn'ska Gazeta*, founded in Kiev.
186. Manifesto 239, 'Zhovnïrci-Ukraïn'ckii Narode!' (KA, EvB, Fasz.5755/26619).
187. For example, manifestos 98, 99, 108, 125, 199, 269, 285, 341.
188. Leaflet, 'Fratelli in guardia' (KA, EvB, Fasz.5758/26661); leaflet, 'Corriere delle Terre Invase, n. 3, 21 Luglio 1918' (KA, 11AK Fasz.451, 'Flugzettel III'): with personal messages and a picture of civilians gathering the distributed leaflets. See also leaflets, 'Posta aerea per le familiglie dei territori invasi' (OHM sz.1238) and 'Alle forti popolazioni delle terre momentaneamente invase' (KA, EvB, Fasz.5756/23149). Messages were also sent to Russian prisoners of war employed in the Austrian war zone, urging them to stop work: leaflet in KA, 11AK Fasz.451, 'Flugzettel I'.
189. KA, 6AK Na-Stelle 1918, Fasz.16, Na Nr 2203, N.Offizier Pordenone to Na-Stelle Boroević, Na Nr 64, 28 July 1918.
190. For example, KA, 6AK, Fasz.16, N-Offiz. Spilimbergo to Na Offiz. 6AK, Na Nr 233, 25 August; Na Nr 149/2 (Geheim), 6AK to Na Stelle Udine, 24 August: which noted that civilian morale in Venetia had also been raised by Entente advances on the Western Front and Gabriele D'Annunzio's propaganda flight over Vienna.
191. AJA, JO 19/186, Trumbić notes [June 1918]; AJA, JO 28/48(4).
192. Ojetti, *La Propaganda sul Nemico*, p. 129; Ojetti, *Lettere alla Moglie*, p. 554. See also PRO, WO 157/637, DIS no. 209, 26 June: statements by Magyar prisoners. On several occasions Padua informed Romanian soldiers that even Magyars were now deserting: see manifesto 95, 'Mîndri ostaşi români!' (IWM, 3(45)/39); manifestos 114 and 238.

193. PRO, WO 106/817, Baker to Northcliffe, no.BM 452/58, 14 July 1918.
194. Ojetti, *La Propaganda sul Nemico*, p. 133.
195. Manifesto 109, 'Itt nyugszik Magyarország' (OHM sz.79.71.1; KA, EvB Fasz.5759/27687: thrown out on 22 August). Errors included 'Karl III' instead of 'Karl IV', and the dating of the *Waffenbund* as 12 March instead of May.
196. KA, FAst 1918, Fasz.5994, Res.260/XXIV, 6AK to AOK, Fa Nr 21, 18 July 1918.
197. Manifesto 117, 'Magyar honfiak-Katonák!' (KA, Flugzettel Sammlung).
198. Manifesto 133, 'A magyar képviselöház ülése' (OHM sz.3499/2). See also manifesto 126, 'Magyar Katonák!' (KA, 11AK, Fasz.451, 'Flugzettel I').
199. Manifesto 171, 'Magyar halál az olasz frontón' (OHM sz.78.441; IWM, 3(45)/39); manifesto 172, 'Magyar Katonák!' (KA, 11AK, Fasz.451, 'Flugzettel I'); manifesto 166, 'Magyar Katonák!' (OHM sz.73.1.1; KA, EvB, Fasz.5758/26766: distributed over Dalmatia).
200. Manifesto 180, 'Interpelláció az olasz offenziváról a magyar képviselöházban' (KA, 11AK, Fasz.449 Pr.2323/1: sent in by the 42HID). For the AOK view: HIL, HFB Fasz.4473/1796, AOK to HM, t., 25 July; and Fasz.4473/1797, MK/KM to HFB, Nr 30094 (telephone), 25 July. KISA subsequently complained about the press reporting Urmánczy's speech: KA, FAst, Fasz.5995, Res.403.
201. Manifesto 254, 'Magyar Katonák!' (OHM sz.74.6.1). After several years of gossip about his private life, Conrad had finally married his mistress in October 1915 when he was almost 63 years of age.
202. Manifesto 250, 'Szegény lelkivaksággal megvert magyarok!' (OHM sz.01158); manifesto 216, 'Magyar Katonák!' (KA, 11AK Fasz.451, 'Flugzettel I').
203. For this implication, see manifesto 285, 'Magyar Katonák!' (HIL, Fasz.4516, BI 4/51) about Balfour's Czech declaration; and manifesto 199, 'Az Antant békeföltételei!' (OHM sz.76.219.1: thrown out by a British plane north of Asiago on 22 August), which was more explicit, noting that Magyars would be given full liberty to set up their own state.
204. Stuart, *Secrets of Crewe House*, p. 194.
205. See SWP, 'Crewe House Activities' memorandum: '31 July, Guest re *Világ*'; SWP, 'Report on Switzerland', p. 4; PRO, FO 371/3133, Rumbold to Balfour, d.284, 8 April 1918: telling of *Világ* and talks with its Swiss correspondent.
206. Manifesto 288, 'Magyar Katonák!' (KA, 11AK Fasz.451, 'Flugzettel I'). See also for economic misery: manifestos 270, 'Magyar Katonák!' (KA, 11AK Fasz.451, 'Flugzettel II'); 255, 'Magyar Katonák!' (OHM sz.3388); 301 [?], 'Magyar Katonák!' (a German translation only is preserved in KA, 11AK, Fasz.448 Pr.2000, but the original seems to be no. 301).
207. Manifesto 145, 'Magyar Katonák!' (OHM sz.1185/1).
208. Manifesto 241, 'Grof Tiszáról van szó!' (OHM sz.01183; HIL, Fasz.4517); manifesto 302, 'Magyar Katonák!' (OHM sz.01184). Granville Baker noted on 14 July (PRO, WO 106/817, no.BM 452/58) that efforts were being made in propaganda to separate Austria and Hungary, 'the German financier and the Magyar agriculturalist'. In fact very little of Padua's material was used specifically for this purpose. But for an anti-Austrian message, see manifesto 264, 'Magyar Katonák!' (OHM sz.74.8.1); and manifesto 270, which notes how Austria dictates and the Hungarian government obeys [!] 'with the obsequiousness of a slave'.
209. Manifesto 249, 'Magyar Katonák!' (OHM sz.79731, 00189). For an assessment of the watered-down franchise bill, passed on 19 July, see József Galántai, *Hungary in the First World War* (Budapest, 1989) pp. 296–7.

210. Manifesto 241. See Gustav Erényi, *Graf Stefan Tisza* (Vienna and Leipzig, 1935) pp. 354–5; and Tisza's own article commenting on manifesto 199: 'A veszedelem érzetének elmulása', in *Igazmondó* no. 35, 7 September 1918, p. 2.
211. Szuber, *Walka o Przewagę Duchową*, p. 120.
212. See for instance, manifesto 79, 'Zwei mächtige österreichische Panzerschiffe...' (similar text in Hungarian on reverse: IWM, 3(45)/39; AHZ, 'Dobrovoljački Arhiv' II/3); manifesto 234, 'Was man in den freien Schweiz über Oesterreich-Ungarn denkt!' (OHM sz.1320; KA, Flugzettel Sammlung). A good summary of the hopeless situation was manifesto 202, 'Denkt über folgende drei tatsachen nach' [in faltering German]: VHA collection.
213. See Ray's memorandum, 'Note sur l'Utilité, la Méthode et les Moyens d'une Propagande Méthodique en Allemagne et en Autriche', 12 July, in PRO, FO 371/3474, Percy Bennett to Balfour, no. 80, 19 July; SWP, 'Crewe House Activities', 6 August.
214. PRO, FO 371/3474, Percy Bennett (Consul General in Zurich) to Balfour, no. 80, 19 July 1918. See also Rumbold to Balfour, t.1345, 10 August; and Stuart, *Secrets of Crewe House*, p. 194.
215. Manifesto 331, 'Österreichische Soldaten!' (KA, Flugzettel Sammlung) was surprisingly one of the few manifestos which made some reference to Karl and the Sixtus Affair; manifesto 190, 'Sonderfriedensgerüchte...' (KA, 11AK Fasz.451 'Flugzettel I'); leaflet [unnumbered], 'Oesterreichische, deutsche Soldaten!' (OHM sz.1553; IWM 3(45)/47).
216. Manifesto 228, 'Wer ist diese hässliche und schmutzige Hexe?' (VHA; KA, EvB Fasz.5758/26619); *Die Muskete*, Nr 667, 11 July 1918. See also KA, AOK 1918 Op.Abt, Fasz.586, Op.Nr 766/112, AOK to 10AK (Prop.Gruppe), 3 May; KA, FAst, Fasz.5996, Res.486/12, re-EvB Nr 2777, 9 September 1918.
217. Denise Cles, 'Die Propagandatätigkeit Gabriele D'Annunzios gegen Oesterreich-Ungarn 1914–1918', *Mitteilungen des Oesterreichischen Staatsarchiv*, XXVIII (1974) pp. 368–9, 376–7.
218. Ojetti, *La Propaganda sul Nemico*, p. 130.
219. Ojetti, *Lettere alla Moglie*, p. 545.
220. There were two versions of the leaflet although the text was the same: see manifesto 128, 'Wiener!' (KA, MKSM 1918, 11–2/10; HIL, HFB, Fasz.4473/1920). Most of it is reproduced in Anthony Rhodes, *The Poet as Superman* (London, 1959) p. 162. Ojetti, *Lettere alla Moglie*, pp. 545, 548–9: the tone of the leaflet was also designed to appeal to the Italian pilots who would distribute it, and on Diaz's insistence, did not mention the Emperor.
221. Manifesto 129, 'Es ist nicht wahr' (HIL, HFB Fasz.4473/1920; KA, MKSM 1918, 11–2/10).
222. Manifesto 130 [?: unnumbered], 'In questo mattino d'agosto...' (copied edition only: HIL, HFB Fasz.4473/1920; KA, MKSM 1918, 11–2/10). Cles mentions a fourth leaflet, but this is not confirmed from any other source. For Ojetti's view, and his exasperation with Diaz: *Lettere alla Moglie*, pp. 548–9, 567, 569–71; Albertini, *Epistolario*, II, no. 844, pp. 943–4.
223. See HIL, HFB 1918, Fasz.4473/1920, Barkóczy-Klopsch to HFB, 2648 szám, 10 August 1918.
224. KA, MKSM 1918, 11–2/10: especially 11–2/10–6 which contains Schlosser's report; and 11–2/10–2, MKSM to KM, Nr 5479, 16 August.
225. *Neue Freie Presse*, Nr 19381 (Morgenblatt), 10 August, p. 4.

226. KA, MKSM 1918, 11-2/10 ad I, MilKmdo Wien to MKSM, Präs.Nr 18016/Ia, 9 August; AVA, Ministerium des Innern 1918, 48459/18.
227. KA, FAst 1918, Fasz.5995, Res.404, FAst to AOK, Op.Abt, 9 August (10 a.m.) enclosing two leaflets for counter-propaganda. The FAst also composed a clever parody of manifesto 128 for use in 'patriotic instruction': see *Vaterländische Bildungsarbeit. Mitteilungen der FAst* Nr. 4, 1 September, p. 22 (KA, FAst, Fasz.6003). For pressure on the press, see HIL, HFB 1918, Fasz.4473/1920, MK/KM to HFB (telephone), 9 August; and as a result: the report in the Zagreb loyalist daily *Hrvatska*, broj 2111, 10 August 1918.
228. *Neue Freie Presse*, Nr 19380 (Abendblatt), 9 August, p. 1; Nr 19381 (Morgenblatt), 10 August, pp. 2–3. Austrian troops in Albania had recently made some advances.
229. KA, AOK Op.Abt, Fasz.372, Op.Nr 110694, Stöger-Steiner to AOK, Abt.5 Nr 7341 res., 13 August; Trauttmansdorff to AOK, Nr 31900, 15 August; Fasz.370, Op.Nr 109805, Trauttmansdorff to AOK Op.Abt, Nr 31488, 29 July.
230. KA, AOK Op.Abt, Fasz.372, Op.Nr 110777; Fasz.374, Op.Nr 111475.
231. Albertini, *Epistolario*, II, no. 866, p. 976: D'Annunzio to Albertini, 19 August. For concerns in Budapest: *Népszava*, 17 September 1918 (quoted in PRO, AIR 1/207/81/1, summary of air Intelligence no. 10).
232. Manifesto 274, *Ceskoslovenská Samostatnost* no. 12. See also manifesto 278, 'Austria-Magyarország Katonái!' (OHM sz.1487).
233. See PRO, AIR 1/1570/204/80/59, 34th squadron record book, August–November 1918. A few propaganda flights were made in August by the 'D-Flight' of the 34th squadron which was temporarily attached to the Italian 4th army (thus on such flights it was an Italian observer who dropped the leaflets). However, in September the 34th squadron dropped a lot more propaganda (usually with bombs as well) without any Italian assistance.
234. Ojetti, *Lettere alla Moglie*, pp. 592–3. Stuart, *Secrets of Crewe House*, p. 47 is a clear exaggeration.
235. Ojetti, *Lettere*, pp. 554–5, 591–3; Marchetti, *Ventotto Anni*, pp. 333–6.
236. Albertini, *Epistolario*, II, pp. 977–8; Tosi, *La Propaganda Italiana*, p. 190. Some material in Hungarian was certainly distributed over Dalmatia (manifesto 166: KA, EvB Nr 26766); and for Italian propaganda raids over Albania, particularly in August, see PRO, ADM 137/2204, reports of Commodore Kelly.
237. Ojetti, *Lettere*, pp. 576, 578, 581; Albertini, *Epistolario*, II, p. 983.
238. KA, 11AK Gstbs Abt, Fasz.447, Fd.Ev.Nr 1346, 10AK propaganda report for July; see also Fd.Ev.Nr 1603, Boroević to 11AK, Op.Nr 301/2292, 12 September 1918.
239. KA, 11AK Gstbs Abt, Fasz.449, Pr.2318 and 2337, 11AK propaganda reports for July and August 1918.
240. KA, 11AK Gstbs Abt, Fasz.447, Fd.Ev.Nr 1415, Boroević to 11AK, Op.Nr 301/1907 monthly report, 12 August 1918.
241. KA, HGK Conrad (HGK Joseph), Fasz.66, Na 400a/400, HGK report, 4 September 1918; KA, 11AK Gstbs Abt, Fasz.447, Fd.Ev.Nr 1346, HGK GO Erzherzog Joseph to 11AK, FEG Nr 35650/13, propaganda report for July 1918.
242. As suggested by Krobatin on 10 September: KA, AOK Op.Akten, Fasz.376, Op.Nr 112195, Krobatin to Archduke Joseph (Op.Nr 5495) pp. 23–5.
243. Finzi, '*I.T.O.*', p. 256.
244. Hanzal, *S Výzvědčíky od Švýcarských Ledovců až po Moře Adriatické*, pp. 264, 284–93.
245. VHA, Fond ČSNR-Štefánik, Karton 1, 35/3/4, Šeba to Štefánik, 26 June 1918. See also Pivko, *Val Bella*, pp. 68–70.

246. Manifesto 124, 'Český prapor v bitvě u Fossetty na Piavě' (Czech/Croat/Romanian/Polish: IWM, 3(45)/39; KA, 11AK Fasz.451, 'Flugzettel I').
247. For the following, see Pivko's vivid description in *Val Bella*, pp. 82–126.
248. See KA, 11AK Gstbs Abt, Fasz.449, Pr.2300, Edelweiss Div.Kmdo to VI KK, Op.Nr 259/36, 28 June, enclosing report about Czech calls opposite. The 11AK was alarmed that one speech had been allowed to last 15 minutes. The Croats opposite would appear to belong to the 36ID.
249. OULK, VII, pp. 349–50.
250. KA, 11AK Gstbs Abt, Fasz.446, Na Nr 1086, VI KK to 11AK, t.Na Nr 704/5, 4 and 5 July. For the leaflet printed in Italian and Czech: KA, 11AK, Fasz.448, Pr.2004/36; and for Hanzal's erroneous view of Vácha's bravery: *S Výzvědčíky*, p. 252.
251. See the article in *Corriere della Sera*, 2 July 1918.
252. Pivko, *DRUP* (Maribor, 1928) pp. 5–6, 11–15.
253. A supply of gramophone records was organized by Granville Baker when in London in August, but the Italians also turned to American suppliers: see BL, Northcliffe MSS, vol. X, Add.Mss 62162, Minutes of the 8th EPD Committee meeting, 6 August; Marchetti, *Ventotto Anni*, p. 313; Hanzal, *S Výzvědčíky*, p. 210.
254. KA, 11AK Gstbs Abt, Fasz.447, Na Nr 1597, KISA propaganda report (Beilage 11). For comparable activity opposite the 10AK: KA, HGK Conrad, Fasz.66, Na 400a/400, 10AK propaganda report for August.
255. KA, AOK Op.Akten, Fasz.374, Op.Nr 111371, HGK GO Erzh.Joseph to AOK, Op.Nr 40.800/8, 29 August; Marchetti, *Ventotto Anni*, p. 339; Hanzal, *S Výzvědčíky*, p. 203: which reproduces the leaflet composed by the deserters and shot back over to the Austrians.
256. Based on Pivko, *DRUP*, p. 16; and Hanzal, *S Výzvědčíky*.
257. KA, 11AK Gstbs Abt, Fasz.449, Pr.2319, 5ID to VI KK, Na Nr 946, 24 July. For the regiment's transfer after this see: KA, AOK Op.Akten, Fasz.370, Op.Nr 109881.
258. Josef Logaj, *Československé Legie v Italii* (Prague, 1922) pp. 104–8. Cf. the suspect official Austrian account (OULK, VII p. 474) which claims that at Dosso Alto the Czechs suffered heavy casualties (they lost about half a dozen).
259. Hanzal, *S Výzvědčíky*, pp. 266–70.
260. KA, 11AK Gstbs Abt, Fasz.272, 4–6/15–1/3, XXVI KK to 11AK, Op.Nr 727/5, 8 August. The 11AK wanted the regiment moved to Albania (like the unreliable Czech IR88 in March), but the HGK insisted that it had to be disciplined within the corps sector. The AOK was still concerned about this whole incident – the 'desertion' of two *Feldwache* – in late October: KA, AOK Org.Gruppe 1918, Fasz.371, Op.Nr 114114.
261. Hanzal, *S Výzvědčíky*, pp. 190, 213–15, 224–31; Marchetti, *Ventotto Anni*, pp. 376–7.
262. KA, 11AK Gstbs Abt, Fasz.449, Pr.2400, 6KD to III KK, Na Nr 921/1, 20 September; KA, HGK Erzh.Joseph, Fasz.64, Fd.Ev.Nr 45950 [?], Archduke Joseph to AOK, Op.Nr 46000/25, 25 September, which simply records that 68 members of the regiment were 'prisoners of the enemy'.
263. AJA, JO 59/4, Trumbić memorandum to Orlando, 25 June 1918; and notes by Trumbić on his audience with Orlando the next day (JO 154/18).
264. AJA, JO 19/56, Trumbić notes on talk with Orlando, 13 August. For the meeting at Versailles, and the behaviour of Orlando and Sonnino, see HLRO, Lloyd George MSS, F/121/1, I.C.71, 4 July.
265. AJA, JO 28/47, Officers at Nocera Umbra to Yugoslav Committee at Rome, 6 July. See also Franc Grafenauer, 'Od Gorlice do Soluna', in E. Turk, J. Jeras and R. Paulin

(eds), *Dobrovoljci Kladivarji Jugoslavije 1912–1918* (Ljubljana, 1936) pp. 694–6, which describes Trumbić's visit to the camp.
266. AJA, JO 35/158, Trumbić notes on talk with Ojetti, 7 June; Ojetti, *Lettere*, p. 536; Albertini, *Epistolario*, II, no. 836, p. 934.
267. Pivko, *Naši Dobrovoljci u Italiji*, p. 44; *DRUP*, pp. 17, 33, 36.
268. Hanzal, *S Výzvědčíky*, pp. 208–9, 231.
269. Pivko, *Naši Dobrovoljci u Italiji*, p. 47. As an example of their activity opposite the Croat 36ID: KA, 36ID records, Fasz.60, Na Nr 699, 72 Brigadekmdo to 36ID, Op.Nr 226/12–I, 15 August 1918. In late July, Vidmar's unit moved from Tugurio to a new base at Longa di Schiavòn near Maróstica.
270. Pivko, *DRUP*, pp. 50–3. For the Committee's agitation in the 3rd army zone, see AJA, JO 35/210b, 'Zapisnik' made by Vilko Gecan at Nocera Umbra, 12 October 1918; and for futile attempts in the 6th army: Finzi, '*I.T.O.*', pp. 259–60.
271. AJA, JO 19/120, Dinale to Trumbić, 15 July 1918.
272. Pivko, *DRUP*, p. 67; AJA, JO 28/45, Ojetti to Jambrišak, Nr 935, 11 August; AJA, JO 19/56, Trumbić notes on talk with Orlando, 13 August 1918.
273. Pivko, *DRUP*, pp. 16, 44ff; *Naši Dobrovoljci u Italiji*, p. 46.
274. Pivko, *Naši Dobrovoljci u Italiji*, pp. 38–9. Pivko vainly also visited the officers at Nocera Umbra.
275. AJA, JO 28/52, 'Jedinačni spisak odela Eksploratora 3e Armije': over half of these were Serbs of IR96 (58ID).
276. See the Austrian report: KA, AOK, Op.Akten, Fasz.371, Op.Nr 110028, FM Müller to AOK, Res.No 33822, 20 July, enclosing 49ID Kmdo to XX KK, Op.Nr 1035/3, 10 July 1918; Pivko, *DRUP*, p. 82; Hanzal, *S Výzvědčíky*, p. 149.
277. Leaflet, 'Hrvati, Srbi i Slovenci!' in Pivko, *DRUP*, pp. 83–5. See also Padua's manifesto 220, 'Srbi, Hrvati i Slovenci!', which was a general appeal signed among others by Čurić, Popadić and Mikulík (KA, 11AK Gstbs Abt, Fasz.448, Pr.2000).
278. KA, AOK Op.Akten, Fasz.371, Op.Nr 110028, minutes by Krobatin.
279. Hanzal, *S Výzvědčíky*, pp. 150–5. See Sobotka's detailed statement on interrogation: KA, 11AK Gstbs Abt, Fasz.442, Na Nr 1306.
280. Pivko, *DRUP*, pp. 34–5, 80.
281. Jože Logar, '1:16', in *Dobrovoljci Kladivarji Jugoslavije*, pp. 725–6. See also in the same work the accounts by Franjo Košmerl, 'Čez fronto na fronto', p. 716; and Josip Klavžar, 'Železni "rožni venec"', p. 724.
282. AJA, JO 28/77, statement by Pavao Tvrtković-Senjić, 26 August; statement by Marko Spitzer, 23 August 1918.
283. AJA, JO 35/210b, statement by Stjepan Štaufel of IR79. See the leaflet, 'Časnici, momci, braćo Slaveni!', handwritten and signed by Štaufel, Řehak and Kračmar, which was shot over to the enemy by rocket: KA, EvB, Fasz.5744/4538. The background to their desertion is described in KA, AOK Op.Abt, Fasz.378, Op.Nr 113087.
284. Pivko, *Naši Dobrovoljci u Italiji*, pp. 41–2.
285. Marchetti, *Ventotto Anni*, p. 318.
286. The following is based mainly on Marchetti's account, 'Un tragico Episodio di Guerra nautica sul Fronte trentino', *Trentino. Rivista delle Legione Trentina*, IV/4 (April 1928) pp. 108–14, 149–60; Marchetti, *Ventotto Anni*, pp. 319–29; and the official Austrian investigation, in KA, 11AK Gstbs Abt, Fasz.442, Na Nr 1167, 10AK Beilagen zu Op.Nr 5047/8 Fd., 5 July 1918: Beilage 1, 'Bericht über die Einvernahme der tschechischen Legionäre Alois Storch und Smarda'.

287. Marchetti, *Ventotto Anni*, pp. 323–5. These were Austrian naval officers who in April had taken part in a raid on Ancona and been captured.
288. See KA, 11AK Gstbs Abt, Fasz.446, Fd.Ev.Nr 1086, VI KK to 11AK, t.zu Na Nr 704/5, 5 July; KA, 6AK Qu.Abt 1918, Fasz.3, Qu.Op.Nr 60799/1b, 6AK Qu.Abt to all district commands, etc., July 1918.
289. Hanzal, *S Výzvědčíky*, pp. 185–8 for a discussion of Šmarda; Marchetti, 'Un tragico Episodio', p. 156.
290. KA, 11AK Gstbs Abt 1918, Fasz.447, Fd.Ev.Nr 1346, 10AK propaganda report for July: small Czech dictionaries were also deposited with certain letters mysteriously underlined.
291. Pivko, *DRUP*, pp. 27–33, 72–4.
292. See, for example, Pivko, *DRUP*, pp. 46–7; Logaj, *Československé Legie*, p. 106.
293. See VHA, Fond ČSNR-Štefánik, Karton 1, 34/2/17, Rudolf Gabriš to Štefánik, 29 July; 35/3/3, Šeba to Štefánik, 4 June 1918.
294. For example, the cases of a Czech, Franz Rozsypal, and a Slovak, Georg Illuschak (the names germanized) who deserted from Dosso Cassina on 16 September as they did not want to fight against their 'fatherland' and longed for their families: KA, 11AK Gstbs Abt, Fasz.442, Na Nr 1674. Illuschak stressed to his captors that Slovaks in particular had not wanted to enter the Legion, something which the Austrians sensed from other captured legionaries as well. See the statement (Na Nr 1725) of a captured Slovak, Martin Badinka, who allegedly deserted back to Austria, and told of Czech bullying of the Slovaks; the 11AK on 6 October 1918 noted for the AOK that the actual 'reality' of Czech–Slovak fraternity might be usefully publicized in the Austro-Hungarian press.
295. PRO, AIR 1/2296/209/77/20, Supreme War Council: Italian section to French, British and American sections, no. 3571, 7 August; Pivko, *DRUP*, pp. 67–8.
296. Pivko, *DRUP*, pp. 38, 86. See the concerns expressed at the time by Marchetti (p. 25) and Smaniotto (pp. 59ff).
297. Pivko, *DRUP*, pp. 71–91. Finzi's memoirs make no mention of D.R.U.P.
298. Pivko, *DRUP*, pp. 91–2. For Ruziak, see: KA, 11AK Gstbs Abt, Fasz.442, Na Nr 1493; KA, AOK Op.Abt, Fasz.381, Op.Nr 114127.
299. Hanzal, *S Výzvědčíky*, pp. 218–23.
300. Marchetti, *Ventotto Anni*, p. 379.
301. Hanzal, *S Výzvědčíky*, pp. 316–24 for the mission of Rudolf Šárka. Similar missions from the 7th and 8th army fronts were unsuccessful: pp. 156–7, 299–300. The claims made by the Czech-American Emanuel Voska about his role in such missions are unsubstantiated from other sources and probably exaggerated: Emanuel Voska and Will Irwin, *Spy and Counterspy: The Autobiography of a Masterspy* (London, 1941) pp. 234–40. Sanders and Taylor, *British Propaganda*, p. 128, certainly overrate Voska's importance.
302. For details of dropping agents, see especially Captain Wedgwood Benn, *In the Side Shows* (London, 1919) pp. 278ff; and PRO WO 106/1550, C.H. Mitchell report on the Intelligence service in Italy, 30 May 1919, pp. 111–13; Pivko, *DRUP*, p. 24, notes the dispatch of a Croat agent as well.
303. See KA, 6AK 1918, Fasz.16, Na Nrs 2797, 2857, 4159, 4553, 4601, 4847, for Austrian discoveries and counter-measures.
304. BL, Northcliffe MSS, vol. X, Add.Mss 62162, Steed's comments at the 8th and 12th EPD Committee meetings.
305. Finzi, *'I.T.O.'*, p. 268.

# 9
# Disintegration

## 9.1 The failure of patriotic instruction

As the end of hostilities appeared on the horizon in October 1918, one Austrian commander in the Tyrol observed that while the enemy in its propaganda was exploiting what was happening in the Austro-Hungarian hinterland, what was far more dangerous for army morale was the wretched reality of what was actually occurring there.[1] It might be seen as a repetition of what had happened in Russia a year earlier. Then, the AOK had viewed Russia's domestic chaos as a crucial element in undermining the cohesion of the Russian armed forces, enabling the Central Powers' propaganda campaign to play its part in maintaining a close interaction between front and hinterland. In the autumn of 1918, the same process was at work in the Habsburg Empire with the mood of front and hinterland often mirroring each other, and being reflected in turn in the themes of Italy's psychological offensive. Although the Austrian commanders until the very end tended to see the hinterland as the source of most evils, infecting their otherwise blameless and reliable forces, any such attempt to delimit military and civilian spheres, or indeed to suggest that the 'poison' was only acting in one direction, was highly questionable by August 1918.[2] Rather, the final months of the war witnessed an interaction, with ideas not only flowing into the war zone, but a mass desertion into the interior by troops who passed on their experiences (and their perceptions of the enemy) to friends and relatives.

In these circumstances it could not be said that the armed forces were standing firm on the Italian Front, even though most military reports gave that impression, fuelling a widespread myth in the postwar years about the army's wartime loyalty. A steady weakening of the troops was occurring, sometimes imperceptible, but usually evident in the way that divisional conditions were described. In the face of major material deficiencies which could not be alleviated, the AOK still vainly tried to maintain 'patriotic instruction' in these months, while at the same time launching a last propaganda offensive at the Italians. If these moves seemed to indicate that the military leaders were stoical to the end, the purpose of both of them was now largely defensive, with the final propaganda gasp against Italy aiming principally to secure peace before the army disintegrated. The Habsburg Empire therefore fought a last propaganda duel. Then its troops, responding to rumours of chaos in the interior which were echoed in Padua's manifestos, began to mutiny and retreat before the Italian army.

All historians agree that the morale of the Austrian army never recovered after the battle of the Piave. One divisional commander spoke for many when in mid-July he observed 'on all sides, regardless of nationality, rank or intelligence, a mental and physical depression'.[3] The defeat left the troops feeling perpetually inferior to the Italians in their artillery and in the air. And the demoralization was sustained over the summer by news of Germany's retreat in the West, the growing national polarization in the Monarchy and, most significantly, by an unabated material crisis in the war zone. It was notably the latter which led General Arz in mid-August to call on his German ally to end the war as soon as possible for, he predicted, the army could not survive beyond December. The food crisis was hardly alleviated, for the harvests in Hungary and Romania had been poor and the grain from Ukraine still remained an illusion, leading by late August to a critical few weeks in the 11AK sector. It was exacerbated by a clothing crisis which in turn fed illness and disease, and by increasing burdens on an army which was consistently short of manpower. From 1 July to 1 October the army on the Italian Front (in the front and rear lines) shrank from 650 000 to 400 000, largely due to illness or desertion.[4]

The combined effect of these demoralizing factors can be illustrated through a series of reports which were made by AOK officers who visited various corps at the front in the final months. When Captain Bauer surveyed the XV corps (11th army) in early August, he found the troops in the isolated mountainous terrain in an exhausted condition. Undernourishment was commonplace so that a man's average weight in one division was 50 kg; the corps doctor predicted that nearly half of those aged 19 to 21 would get tuberculosis. Bauer observed that the younger soldiers in particular were tolerating the physical and psychological hardships less well: 'In some sectors there are almost daily desertions. In most cases the reason for this is to be found not in treasonable or political tendencies but in the bad food conditions and general war-weariness.'[5]

A month later, when Captain Géza Schwarz visited the VII corps on the Lower Piave, he discovered a section of the front which was weakly manned (reminding him of the Eastern Front), where enemy aircraft constantly swarmed over the positions. If there were the usual complaints about food (the lack of meat, the hatred of dried vegetables), the absence of clothing was particularly alarming, feeding a dramatic increase in malaria, dysentery and influenza:

> I saw young officers with thin shirts which they will have to wear during the winter as they are not entitled to any more uniforms until the spring. I also saw men with totally ripped shirts and even some without shirts! Even the washing of uniforms has to be strictly limited so that their material does not become worn out.[6]

It was an everyday crisis. While some troops were returning from hospital in the rear with little bodily protection at all, a clothing survey on the mountain front had found that hundreds of troops lacked boots or underwear. In one regiment, for instance, 800 men were without boots and 400 without an undergarment.[7]

When another AOK officer inspected the XX corps (10th army) he too noted the clothing shortage and the small rations which were insufficient at such a high altitude. But he gave an extra slant to his report:

> Enthusiasm for the war is completely missing. Most of the men are apathetic, but they will fulfil their duty bravely and unflaggingly, and will according to their commanders hold out for another year or longer if it is demanded. The longing for peace is widespread... [Morale is especially affected] by conditions in the hinterland. Again and again one hears complaints among the officers or in the ranks about the total disorganization of the hinterland and the inability of the government to remedy the economic and political misery. Efforts of the company commanders to put heart into the ranks by patriotic instruction are unsuccessful largely because of news which they receive from the hinterland or the impressions which they bring back from their time on leave.[8]

These themes were steadily repeated in other reports which the AOK was receiving by October.[9] The constant impression was of an army which was maintaining its discipline, was regularly reported to be reliable by its commanders, but was nevertheless in a deep depression due to the food crisis and concern about the hinterland. In early October, after Bulgaria had collapsed and asked for an armistice, a new element was creeping into the reports. As FM Krobatin noted on 6 October, those who were intelligent were increasingly concerned about the future of the state and whether all the sacrifices had been in vain. Their lack of confidence in the face of the enemy was now accompanied by increased anxiety about their own future.[10]

Krobatin's report, like so many others, implied that the troops were generally *kaisertreu* and reliable. Yet other evidence flew in the face of such a judgement, suggesting as usual that many commanders were concerned not to besmirch the name of their regiments, or were simply determined to make the best of a pessimistic situation. Most notably, there was the steady increase in desertion which must have been apparent to all. Krobatin himself had discussed this issue in a lengthy report on 10 September to Archduke Joseph, who had succeeded Conrad as commander of troops in the Tyrol. He indicated as the key reasons for desertion, first the effect of the hinterland (war-weariness and nationalist agitation) and second the permanent food and clothing crisis, two evils which he felt to be stimulated and nurtured by 'enemy propaganda'.[11] Krobatin could rightly assume that the propaganda stemming from Italy was causing a steady trickle of deserters across the front; for those few who had openly idealistic motives, there were many more who responded to the Italians' allurement out of largely material reasons.[12] Yet, as is clear from 11AK statistics for September 1918, the bulk of desertions in the final months was not to the enemy but in the direction of the hinterland (Table 9.1).

These figures cannot be taken as wholly reliable, but they enable certain conclusions to be drawn. They show that the number of deserters to the enemy from the Tyrol was steady but still moderate a month before the collapse; and that Czechs tended to form the largest percentage of that number. They also reveal, not surprisingly, that the hinterland was the chief destination for those who refused to fight any longer. Here, however, the figures concealed a more alarming picture about the hundreds if not thousands of soldiers who were exceeding their leave and making a decision not to return to their units. Their number by the autumn has been set as high as 250 000, roughly the same as the number of troops actually serving in the front line in the south-west.[13]

*Table 9.1* Desertions from the Austrian 11th Army, 1–30 September 1918[14]

| *Direction* | *Nationality** | | | | | | | | | | | *Total* |
|---|---|---|---|---|---|---|---|---|---|---|---|---|
| | *Cz* | *P* | *R* | *M* | *G* | *U* | *Sk* | *Sl* | *Cr* | *S-Cr* | *Other* | |
| Enemy | 4 | 2 | 4 | 3 | – | 1 | 1 | – | – | – | 8 | 23 |
| Probably to enemy | 3 | 1 | – | – | 1 | – | – | – | – | – | 1 | 6 |
| Hinterland | 6 | 7 | 2 | 8 | 15 | – | – | 5 | 2 | 1 | 9 | 55 |
| Probably to hinterland | 3 | 2 | – | 1 | 5 | – | – | – | – | – | – | 11 |
| Unknown | 2 | – | – | – | 4 | – | – | – | – | – | – | 6 |
| Total | 18 | 12 | 6 | 12 | 25 | 1 | 1 | 5 | 2 | 1 | 18 | 101 |
| Total who deserted to enemy from HGK** | 55 | 15 | 11 | 7 | 11 | 11 | – | 16 | 5[+] | 2 | – | 133 |

*Notes*:
*Cz (Czech), P (Polish), R (Romanian), M (Magyar), G (German), U (Ukrainian; Ruthene), Sk (Slovak), Sl (Slovene), Cr (Croat) S-Cr (Serbo-Croat: *sic*).
**These were the figures supplied by the *Heeresgruppekommando* of Archduke Joseph for September: i.e. its figures for the 10th and 11th army sectors.
[+] Includes one soldier specified as a 'Dalmatian'.

In view of this, the fact that there were no open mutinies at the front until late October simply suggests that a certain cohesion and discipline was being maintained in the front line, but not that the army as a whole was 'standing firm'. The real warning signs over the summer had been the increasing disturbances in march-formations bound for the front; in one incident in Galicia, 550 soldiers had deserted from a train heading towards the Italian theatre. By October, the number of instances of insubordination was rising in the rear of the war zone itself. One can also question the commanders' assurances of reliability, that their troops would 'fulfil their duty bravely and unflaggingly'. The propagandists in Italy felt that the fruit of their efforts might not be immediately clear, but that the 'yeast was fermenting' and would eventually produce a reaction during the next offensive if not earlier. It is impossible to judge how many units had been infected by October, but there are sufficient hints, not least the behaviour of troops during the final offensive, to show that a hidden fermentation was occurring. More and more units, with an eye on the hinterland, were certainly developing a particularist or 'national' outlook which was wholly at odds with any efforts by their commanders to instil in them patriotic instruction.[15]

This was not for want of any commitment by the FAst or the *Unterrichtsoffiziere* in the armed forces for, ironically, the last four months of the war were the high point of patriotic instruction. In July, the AOK, on the advice of the FAst leaders, and referring to Germany and Russia as notable examples of success and failure in this regard, had urged the armies to build up their instruction network.[16] Egon von Waldstätten and his new deputy, Major Eugen von Höberth, proceeded energetically with new initiatives.[17] They organized over the summer another three training courses in Vienna (the last one in late September to train a reserve of suitable instructors); they issued a range of patriotic material including a regular package of information for instructors known as the *Vaterländische Bildungsarbeit*; they tried to stifle unpatriotic newspapers and warn of subversives in the hinterland; and they even experimented with a competition whereby a prize of 200 crowns would be awarded to the best lecture submitted on a patriotic theme.[18]

It was very much part of Waldstätten's thinking to encourage the flow of ideas and suggestions around the 'network'. Indeed, the impetus to advance patriotic instruction after the June offensive had come as much from FA personnel themselves as from the centre in Vienna. The 6AK *Unterrichtsreferent* was typical, writing on 6 July that a full organization was now being created in the army sector with all divisions having their own *Unterrichtsoffiziere*. They were beginning to visit the men, enjoying their trust through acting as spokesmen for their material concerns, while warning them about the content of enemy manifestos; the only problems, the *Referent* noted, were the damaging rumours from the hinterland and the lack of sufficient patriotic reading.[19] Some instructors were able to compensate for the latter by producing their own material, but for most of them the same problems would persist until the end. This is clear from two examples. In mid-August Dr Karl Lukács, the *Unterrichtsoffizier* of the half-Czech 12SchD, reported to the FAst that although he had been using FA material in his work and was about to tell the troops about the fate of the deserter Alois Štorch, he was hampered by a paper shortage and could not reproduce FA leaflets for distribution. While everyday, thousands of enemy manifestos were being brought in (for a reward of ten heller per leaflet), the division was receiving few leaflets from the FAst: 'How good it would be to have, here and there, a few uplifting words, a few historic maxims from our great statesmen and writers to distribute in thousands of copies to the officers and men!'[20]

A similar report, which illustrated the fierce competition of ideas at the front, came to the FAst in September from the 6ID, a division with a strong Slovene element. The divisional commander wrote that the Slovene newspaper *Straža* had just been banned since its anti-German articles were on a par with the arguments of enemy manifestos. He appealed for more material in Slovene, which would emphasize Slovene loyalty to the Habsburgs on the one hand, and the danger which Italy and southern Slav unity posed to Slovene security on the other. In this case, as in that of the 12SchD, the FAst was unable to provide sufficient literature because of the Monarchy's paper shortage (at less than 40 per cent of its prewar production), while other ideas were reaching the troops from the domestic press or enemy leaflets. One can argue in fact that the FA local instructors were sometimes left too much to their own devices, with insufficient guidance from the centre. And this was not only apparent in the paucity of material. The FAst, for example, would later criticize the 6ID *Unterrichtsoffizier* for the lectures which he delivered in Slovene, for they exaggerated Slovene Catholic feeling to the detriment of any Protestants who might be listening.[21] The incident is testament to the instructors' persistent dilemma of how precisely to engage with each nationality.

In terms of the basic arguments which the FAst centre supplied to the network, it is true that they were quite successful in challenging many of the presumptions behind Padua's manifestos. But at their core, when discussing the Monarchy's future, they came far too late to compete with the reality of what was happening in the hinterland. On 13 July at the War Ministry, at a meeting between military and civilian ministries to discuss FA work, it had been agreed that the FAst, the Foreign Ministry and the KPQ would coordinate their propaganda work more closely, so that similar arguments would be exchanged and circulated.[22] It was a rare example of closer liaison between the Austrian authorities in the battle of ideas. For the FAst, a key theme in its material was to attack the enemy's claim of superior morality, that they were standing for 'culture and humanity' against the militarism and oppression of the Central Powers. For the reality was the exact opposite. It was not Germany which was militaristic but America, ruled by the dictator President Wilson, which, as enemy manifestos showed, was steadily building up its armaments. It was not Germany which was striving for world domination but Great Britain which already dominated 80 per cent of the earth. It was the Allies who were the real barbarians: witness the Americans who lynched their Blacks; the Italians who maltreated Austrian prisoners and forced them to fight against their own fatherland; and the English who liked killing for sport and still maintained flogging as a punishment in their army.[23] That the Allies were prepared to stoop to any unscrupulous methods to achieve their imperialist ends was verified by their implication in seven major murders during the war![24] As for the Allied slogan of self-determination for the peoples of Austria-Hungary, the FA officers could present this with some justification as hypocritical and insincere. It was only too evident from the *Corriere* campaign against Sonnino in late August that Italy did not really believe in self-determination for the South Slavs but was simply using them as a means to fulfil imperialist ambitions. It was also 'clear', though the FAst had far fewer arguments to hand, that Italy was using the Czechs simply as cannon-fodder. The English too were complete hypocrites who would never apply self-determination to Ireland or India. Rather, for the Allies, the idealistic slogan was a way to destroy the Monarchy, and faced with this aggression the Austro-Hungarian army had to continue its defensive war until an honourable peace was secured.[25]

It was when the FA officers turned from attacking the enemy to defending the position and character of Austria-Hungary that their arguments looked decidedly weak. As they repeatedly reminded their superiors, they could not compete with the food crisis or the domestic turmoil which was publicized in the daily press. Their patriotic instruction was only offering a defence of the old Imperial system, emphasizing in particular the advantages of living in a large state, the 'national and cultural freedom' which allegedly existed, and the unviability of small nation-states. They themselves offered no viable alternative solution to the South Slav, Polish or Czech questions, not only because they had none (since none of the issues had been resolved politically), but because it remained a principle of the instruction never to engage in any political discussion which might introduce politics into the army. This gave the instruction an air of unreality when it was conducted against the background of a radicalized hinterland which seemed fully in tune with enemy propaganda. In the same way, the FA personnel, for all their personal contact with their pupils, could not fight the reality of the shattering defeat in June, the food and material crisis, or the increasingly gloomy military situation on the Western and Balkan Fronts. They might claim optimistically that all was not lost, that as in previous years there could be a sudden change of fortune, but such claims were increasingly at variance with the truth about an Empire which could not fight for much longer.[26]

When in late September Bulgaria collapsed, and the Central Powers (on 4 October) made a joint peace offer to America on the basis of Wilson's 'Fourteen Points', the possibility of defeat dawned on many in Austria-Hungary for the first time. The AOK's position was clear. Admitting finally that the front could not be hermetically sealed from the hinterland, they sent out a special directive for use in patriotic instruction. The key theme of the directive was that the troops should keep calm and stand firm until an honourable peace was achieved. Wilson's 'formula' might well be a basis for peace, but it was acceptable only so far as it did not endanger the vital interests of the Monarchy. It was also to be acknowledged at last (the AOK in its own words no longer favoured an 'ostrich policy'), that a big transformation was occurring in the Empire. But while Austria-Hungary would certainly have a different character after the war, it would also definitely preserve its unity and be the entity for which the armed forces had fought from the beginning. To avoid the kind of anarchy which had occurred in Russia was vital, all the more so as the soldiers would thereby be preserving some security for their loved ones at home.[27]

The FA officers at the front seem to have energetically pursued these themes in the final month of the war, spurred on by the FAst to hold fast at 'this critical moment'. Waldstätten instructed the network that, since events were moving so quickly, they would need to use their own initiative even more, adapting material as required and being constantly flexible.[28] It might be viewed as a final positive and realistic approach under the circumstances. What was clear, however, was that the subjects of their instruction were every day vacillating more in their allegiance, under the impression of what was happening in the hinterland. On 23 October, on the eve of Italy's last offensive, KISA's *Unterrichtsreferent* was quite candid about the obstacles faced by his subordinates. After the collapse of Bulgaria all were convinced that victory was impossible and that little was to be gained by fighting any longer. The troops might still be under control, but the ideological challenge from the hinterland was mounting daily:

> Since the national consciousness of all peoples of the Monarchy, even the Germans, has not only come to the fore but can be openly displayed, we are bound to face up to the threat from our newspapers and the links which exist between front and hinterland (which cannot be broken now). On top of this, there is general dissatisfaction, anxiety about life at home, the inadequate food made less palatable by the absence of fat, and the lack of clothes and undergarments: blatant facts which can only accelerate the process of disintegration... If before the start of the armistice we are to avoid and prevent the catastrophe of our army facing a similar fate to that of the Russian

army . . . the authorities will have to behave and make decisions unreservedly according to the spirit of the times [*Zeitgeist*]. There would be the most awful consequences for those responsible if they closed their eyes to the nationalist movements or tried to postpone taking decisions connected with the [army's] dissolution.[29]

If the FA network was finally being forced to bow to the realities of the hinterland, it revealed all the more starkly that in the previous years neither the military or political authorities had coordinated any effective patriotic instruction in Austro-Hungarian society as a whole. As we have seen, the official work of the KPQ and the KA had been limited in scope, and probably most effective (if at all) in the German-Austrian regions of the Monarchy. As for non-official patriotic initiatives by individuals or various groups in society, they had steadily been eclipsed, more quickly in some regions than others, by simple apathy towards the war effort or by nationalist initiatives which had their own agenda. The celebrations in Prague for the 50th anniversary of the Czech National Theatre, for instance, were on a scale which pushed into the shade any pro-Habsburg rallies (such as that by Catholics in Vienna in July 1918).[30] In this environment, the authorities' regular campaigns for war-bond subscriptions might continue, sometimes with a flourish, as when Habsburg planes threw out leaflets publicizing war bonds over Croatia in mid-1918 (a counter-propaganda perhaps to Padua's efforts).[31] But any wider idea of patriotic instruction was missing and was, arguably, impossible to implement anyway simple because its ideals could never match the realities on the ground. FA work in itself had always been envisaged as a strictly military operation, indicating clearly the military's strong sense of its own sphere of influence which was separate from the civilian. Thus, in contrast to Britain, Austria-Hungary had no ministry of information under a Lord Beaverbrook, and in contrast to Italy, there was no Gallenga Stuart to coordinate propaganda at home and abroad. It can justifiably be argued as a key weakness of the Monarchy that while from 1917 its enemies abroad were pursuing an effective secondary mobilization in their societies, in Austria-Hungary a counter-mobilization was allowed to occur. Many civilians were indeed re-mobilizing, but with a nationalist, socialist or pacifist agenda of their own, not on behalf of the Habsburg war effort.

In the face of this, as we have seen, the Austrian military's usual reaction was negative, to repress or censor wherever possible, a policy which was found to be inadequate under the constitutional government of 1917–18. There were some lone voices such as Ludwig Goiginger, commander of the XXIV corps, who opined that FA work would come to nothing unless there was a 'general propaganda mobilization' of the hinterland. The FAst, in turn, was certainly pleased when the Catholic episcopacy, or lecturers from the University of Vienna, offered their services to boost patriotism among soldiers from pulpit or lectern.[32] But the political authorities, at least in Austria, were very slow to act with any complementary civilian action. At the FA ministerial discussions on 13 July, a representative from the office of the Austrian Prime Minister had at best been able to say that a civil action was 'imminent', although purely of a private, non-official character. A month later, the FAst complained to Baden that nothing had yet materialized, yet now was the ideal moment since enemy aeroplanes had just showered Vienna with manifestos; this needed to be countered with a methodical campaign of 'resistance-propaganda' in which all organizations and classes, all nationalities and parties of the hinterland would take part.[33] It slowly emerged that the Austrian Ministry of Interior was beginning to plan such a campaign but was constrained by financial considerations. By late September the lack of progress had reached the ears of the press. Taking up the baton which the *Corriere della Sera* had run with in Italy eight months earlier, the Vienna *Reichspost* proclaimed that it was time to move beyond the preparatory stage by setting up an 'Austrian propaganda centre':

> It will be a responsible position which the propaganda chief assumes. If he understands his job, he can do more for Austria than ten ministers or one army, in other words he can spare Austria the blood of a whole army. We seek Austria's salvation not in lies, like England when it appointed Northcliffe – the world master of lies – as its agent, but in truth, in the Austrian truth. The truth has to be preserved so that it does not drown in the enemy's flood of lies.[34]

It was the kind of statement which Northcliffe himself might have made. It showed that, among Austrian journalists at least, Northcliffe retained a powerful reputation as the man who had the predominant role in enemy propaganda because of his newspaper empire. The *Reichspost* repeated a rumour that an Austrian newspaper editor, Leopold von Chlumecky, might be about to assume the role of a 'Northcliffe' for the Monarchy. The reality was that, with a million crowns finally placed at its disposal, the Austrian Ministry of Interior had decided to organize everything under its own auspices, appointing an official, *Hofrat* Robert Davy, to head a 'civilian propaganda centre'. On 8 October, the AOK agreed that Egon von Waldstätten, Max Ronge and the head of the KPQ, Eisner-Bubna, would help Davy to set up a propaganda committee.[35]

At this late stage few of those involved were under many illusions. As Eisner-Bubna observed, 'in order to begin suitable domestic propaganda, a clear political goal must first be established', and they would inevitably be bowing before existing realities:

> Priests, teachers, writers and politicians of the different nationalities are all contributing to a situation where the nationalist goals of the native races

take precedence over the imperial ideal... Considering the degree of disorganization already present, the goal of domestic propaganda can only be to hold the various nationalities together in a looser association. It can certainly not be a goal of domestic propaganda to try to preserve existing conditions, for this would rapidly cause internal antagonism.[36]

The leaders of patriotic instruction, whether in the hinterland or the war zone, were therefore hoping that they might still appeal to some latent concept of *Staatsgedanken* among broad swathes of the population. Then at least, even if the main goal of *Vaterländischer Unterricht* had failed (as they recognized), it might yet be possible to preserve public order and perhaps even some form of Habsburg state entity.

## 9.2 A final duel in front propaganda

Just as the Austrian military had tended to view Italy's campaign of 1918 as really 'counter-propaganda' to the campaign which they had started after Caporetto, so they always felt that to continue their own efforts against Italy was a necessary extra dimension to their 'enemy propaganda defence'. The battle of ideas across the front could never be wholly surrendered to the enemy, even if temporarily one side might be in a more advantageous position. Thus, although the Austrian military had acknowledged after the June offensive that their campaign had failed and would accordingly be scaled-down as more effort was put into ideological defence, it would not be abandoned altogether. As Baden explained in new guidelines issued to the armies on 4 August, 'the effect of propaganda changes according to the momentary military and moral situation. At present its basis is unfavourable for us, but the time may come when the propaganda weapon employed so successfully in other theatres of war may also render good service against Italy.' The chief aim was to maintain some pressure on the Italians, by encouraging thoughts of peace, while waiting for a change in fortune for the Central Powers. As usual one might also hope that front propaganda would then (as in Russia) have some indirect impact in the Italian hinterland.[37]

With these thoughts in mind, all the Austrian armies continued some propaganda against Italy over the summer, working largely on their own initiative while following the basic AOK directive. Their efforts, however, were to be limited as much by technical obstacles as by their own self-imposed restraints. Since Italian vigilance was so strong, the AOK forbade personal contact; and the depositing of material, a favourite method of the past, was also viewed as less promising. Instead the material was to be spread from the air, where the Austrians were distinctly inferior, or by special rockets which were always in short supply to the propaganda personnel. Given too the shortage of paper available to the armies, and even though it was common practice for the propaganda officers to exchange their material with neighbouring armies, it was not surprising that the distribution in these months was minuscule. In August, while KISA sent out 15 300 pieces of propaganda (in comparison to 500 000 in May), the 11AK was even more hesitant with only 2450 pieces to its name. The 10AK might muster a figure of 100 000 for the same month, but this should be compared with the 100 000 or more leaflets which the Italians were scattering every day.[38]

If the Austrians' material was not reaching its target, their arguments were nevertheless quite sound and, as the AOK rightly noted, might have been capable of bearing fruit if Italy's military position had been weaker. In line with the guidelines, they paid particular attention to the issue of the Czecho-slovak Legion, not simply through 'disinformation' with the D.R.U.P. messages, but also by openly appealing to the Italian soldier's sense of honour and decency in permitting himself to rub shoulders with such individuals 'of base and vile character'.[39] Those Italians who were under the illusion that they were fighting for 'freedom' or the 'oppressed nationalities' could be given the same argument as that of Austria's patriotic instruction, that the Allies were hypocrites. A leaflet from the 6AK, for example, reported a declaration by Indian nationalists criticizing Theodor Roosevelt for urging freedom for peoples in central Europe while making no mention of the 'oppressed and tyrannized Indians, Irish, Egyptians, African Boers, Philippinos, Koreans, etc'.[40] Alongside this, the material tried to suggest the real bleakness of 'Italy's war', recalling a host of arguments which had been used earlier in the year. Italy had lost over two million men and 50 000 million lira, and was now continuing the war simply to satisfy the imperialist ambitions of the English and American capitalists. The country was fast becoming an Allied colony, for already 'Sonnino and Orlando have to dance to the tune of Wilson's and Lloyd George's orchestra'.[41]

If the Austrians felt justifiably that there was still some potential in this line of argument on the basis of their own Intelligence sources, their assertion that Italy and its Allies were about to lose the war had naturally lost its force after July 1918 as the Germans retreated on the Western Front. There might be a few hopeful signs, such as General Pflanzer-Baltin's brief success in Albania,[42] but otherwise the Austrian propagandists had insufficient material to work with. Despite many subtle touches in their leaflets, they could never secure from the Italian press the same kind of subversive evidence which Padua was able to exploit so fully for its own purposes. Similarly, any propaganda which dwelt too heavily upon Austria-Hungary's own strengths or stability had begun to sound hollow by the late summer; such was a leaflet widely circulated from the 11th army sector which tried to suggest that the Monarchy with its peoples 'united and well-fed', would not be destroyed in a hundred years.[43] A more profitable line, undoubtedly, was simply to dwell on the Italian soldier's desire for peace, emphasizing that Austria-Hungary wanted a peace which was just and lasting; it could be made immediately, as the Monarchy was fighting a defensive war with no claims upon Italian territory.[44]

These efforts became more urgent from mid-September as Austria-Hungary began to make concrete proposals for peace to the enemy. The campaign was stepped up and returned to the overall control of Max Ronge's Intelligence section. Until then Ronge had only been responsible, in propaganda terms, for smuggling material into the Italian hinterland via Switzerland, a route which had always been difficult to keep open; but it was perhaps especially due to Ronge's experience with 'peace propaganda' on the Eastern Front that the AOK now expanded his mandate. In his memoirs, Ronge tells how he quickly set up a special propaganda centre in Baden, sensing that the desire for peace in the enemy camp would offer several clear 'lines of attack' with the propaganda weapon.[45] In fact, the main aim of Austria's revitalized campaign had now changed. Its purpose was not so much to demoralize the Italians as a prelude to some future military success, but to achieve an end to the war as soon as possible before the Monarchy itself disintegrated.

On 5 September, the Foreign Minister Count Burián, with an eye on the deteriorating economic situation, had informed Germany that Austria-Hungary could not wait 'until the roasted dove of peace flies into our mouth'. On 14 September, despite German protests, he went ahead and dispatched to all belligerent states a note proposing discussions for peace.[46] At the front, Austrian planes and propaganda patrols began to spread manifestos reporting this 'sincere offer' made in accordance with the wishes of 'the people', and pressing Italian soldiers to demand that their government accept the proposal; after all, was it not time to end a war which 'neither side could win'?[47] The Austrians were anxious to find out whether their arguments were having some immediate effect, but because of the lack of fraternization, or of Italian prisoners or deserters, such an inquiry proved impossible.[48] In fact, news of Burián's note, whether learnt from Austrian propaganda or from the Italian press, seems to have caused quite a stir in Italian military circles. Ugo Ojetti was worried lest 'naïve talk of an armistice' might lead to another Caporetto. He himself speedily composed for enemy troops some blunt replies which reflected, or perhaps even anticipated, the Allied governments' rejection of Burián's offer: the Habsburg Monarchy, 'the originator of the world conflagration ... penitently strews its head with ashes and asks for peace. However, the first question which strikes every decent man is, can one pardon a criminal who has no equal in history?' The hand which Austria offered was the 'hand of an imposter which even at this critical moment has not laid aside his inborn shifty habits'. The Entente would not make peace with the old Austria, those who wanted to impose a new type of Brest-Litovsk peace, but only with true representatives of the people, those who were fighting for freedom and national independence. For this reason, Padua declared, 'the hour of peace has not yet struck'.[49]

Responding to this, Austrian propaganda attacked the Italian government for failing to meet the wishes of its own people, and the English and Americans for hypocrisy. The latter, the first to officially reject Burián's note, were portrayed as fat American Indians who greedily plucked feathers from the Austrian dove of peace in order to adorn their own headdresses (see Illustration 9.1).[50] From 4 October, however, Austria's 'peace propaganda' had some new substance as the Central Powers sent a joint note to Wilson, requesting peace on the basis of his 'Fourteen Points'. In a final set of guidelines issued a week later, Ronge stressed that it was vital at this stage not to renounce what was the 'most modern weapon of warfare'. While the chances of an impact were not too favourable, given the state of Italy's morale, it simply meant that 'peace

*Illustration 9.1* America rejects Burián's peace offer: Austria's final effort at propaganda against Italy (KA)

propaganda' had to be more subtly put across; the idea of peace had to be carefully nurtured, building bridges to the Italians without arousing any resentment, and doing so through a resumption of 'oral contact' across the trenches.[51] The importance which the military leadership attached to this last burst of front propaganda very much reflected the vain hopes which the rest of the Habsburg elite were placing on a favourable reply from President Wilson. When it did not come, and Wilson only replied to Germany, the front propagandists still interpreted this as an acceptance of Austria's offer, pending the solution of 'a few details'; no mention was made of the crucial absence of any reply to Vienna.[52]

Yet the manifestos assumed a more critical tone as the days went by. From mid-October Ronge was sending out to the armies material which expressly blamed the English and French for sabotaging Wilson's programme, while highlighting the 'pacifist demonstrations' which were allegedly occurring in Allied countries.[53] Although these leaflets were distributed until the eve of Italy's offensive (24 October) few appear to have reached their goal, nor was there much time for any oral contact. For at the front it was the Allies' propaganda campaign which held sway. The Padua Commission duly treated the Central Powers' offer of 4 October with the same disdain as Burián's earlier note. At first Ojetti was rather anxious, since Wilson's answer, if it adhered too much to the 'Fourteen Points', might seriously affect Italian territorial aspirations. But he eventually anticipated the American reply altogether and repeated his claim that Wilson would only deal with the peoples, never with the old rulers of Austria-Hungary.[54] It was a valid prediction, for on 19 October when Wilson finally replied he effectively told the Habsburg elite that the future lay in the hands of the Monarchy's various national leaders. With this announcement, the Austrians' peace programme through which they desperately hoped to save the Monarchy at the eleventh hour lay in ruins. Their propaganda campaign on the Italian Front, weak as it was, had also lost all impact, for the Italians knew that they could achieve a victory over Austria-Hungary before the war came to an end.

In the propaganda duel in these final weeks of hostilities, the advantages which Italy's campaign possessed in comparison to Austria-Hungary's could be measured in almost every field. Although there were some on the Allied side who worried that Italian troops might be too receptive to news of an imminent peace (as the Austrians hoped),[55] the arguments in Padua's propaganda were far more numerous and 'newsworthy'. They were propagated widely, because Italy controlled most of the avenues of distribution, and they were better coordinated because Italy's propaganda machine was largely centralized in one place. It remained, moreover, Italy's campaign despite all the efforts of Crewe House. By September, some new Allied representatives had been delegated to the Padua Commission: the American G.H. Edgell and the Serbian liaison officer Major

Filip Hristić (this, perhaps, a reflection of Serbia's increasing influence to the detriment of the Yugoslav Committee). But they appear to have had little more impact than Baker and Gruss; even when Ojetti was absent for a few weeks, his faithful lieutenants Donati and Zanotti-Bianco held the fort quite competently. Ojetti himself appears to have written many of the manifestos in the final months, using the national delegates largely as translators or advisers. They in turn (lacking the vociferous Jambrišak or Zamorski) seem to have fallen in docilely or, to be more precise, fallen ill one after the other.[56] Ojetti's overall control was further aided by the departure of Granville Baker in mid-October. With the collapse of Bulgaria, a wider front had been opened against the Monarchy, and Crewe House once again took the initiative by transferring Baker to Salonika in order to establish a new propaganda commission on the Balkan Front. On arrival there, Baker began to play the role which Ojetti had successfully assumed in Padua. He had at last secured his own sphere of influence, with a staff who would have included Jambrišak. But it was a dream soon overtaken by events.[57]

Yet Ojetti himself was far from satisfied in the last months of the war. Apart from a personal concern (his daughter, who was seriously ill), he had two major interlocking anxieties which affected the efficiency of his work. First, he was exasperated by the continuing ambiguity of Italian official policy. He had fully supported the *Corriere* campaign against Sonnino and repeatedly pressed Orlando to remove his foreign minister and conclude a special pact with America for the destruction of Austria. The lack of a clear line, especially on the Yugoslav issue, was enabling the naval and air authorities to obstruct leaflet distribution, while at Padua some renewed tension was occurring with the anti-Yugoslav Colonel Siciliani (officially head of the Commission) whom Ojetti suspected of trying to assume control over his liaisons with the national councils, the CS and the Intelligence offices.[58] On 23 September, at a war council, Orlando furiously defended Ojetti to Sonnino and Diaz as his 'confidant' who was carrying out excellent work, and suggested that Siciliani should be moved elsewhere; the attack appears to have weakened the latter's position at Padua.[59] Yet Orlando's own 'balancing act' in the Italian cabinet persisted. His delay in publishing Italy's Yugoslav declaration or in advancing the case for a Yugoslav legion, and his refusal to speak out more decisively in Parliament for the destruction of Austria as Ojetti requested – all these elements combined, in Ojetti's view, to weaken the potential of Padua's campaign, as well as weakening Italy's prime role as Allied leader of the oppressed nationalities.[60]

Ojetti's second major frustration was closely linked to this last point. By the autumn he was increasingly concerned at the CS's delay in launching another offensive against the enemy. The danger was that the Austrians might collapse completely before Italy had attacked and gained the main credit for defeating them. Ironically, therefore, near the end of the war, Ojetti – the propagandist – wanted more traditional warfare to take over before the weapon of propaganda should have too great an impact upon the enemy; the new weapon, in his eyes, was a supplement but not a substitute for an armed attack which would 'prove' Italy's victory to the world. As it was, the Italians were discrediting themselves with Britain and France, who were both pressing the CS to attack and complement the successful offensive on the Western Front. In response, the CS in September hesitated to act until Allied reinforcements, or a major setback for the enemy on other fronts, could offset what they viewed as Austria's numerical superiority against them. Diaz told Lord Cavan, 'the Austrian is not ready to fall down and be trampled on. He has shown good fighting qualities on several occasions since his defeat in June.' This view persisted at the CS despite the steady collapse of Bulgaria from mid-September.[61] One British officer on 25 September characterized well the mood in the war zone: 'To sum up, the offensive will probably not take place, but on the other hand it may. Equally it may be ordered and again cancelled.'[62] Only in early October, after the Bulgarian armistice and clear signs of success in the West, did Diaz and Badoglio finally decide on an offensive. They may have been critically swayed by Italian Intelligence sources. On 2 October, Tullio Marchetti, brimming with confidence after his two Czech agents had returned from their adventure in Trento, presented the CS and Orlando with a vivid picture of the reality behind the enemy façade:

> The Austrian army in line is still strong but it cannot be supported from the rear which is infected. It is like a pudding which has a crust of roasted almonds and is filled with cream. The crust which is the army in the front line is hard to break.[63]

But if a hole was pierced in the crust at a suitable point, the cream or reserve would be reached and the whole Austro-Hungarian army would melt away. It was a fairly accurate prediction of what would happen three weeks later. Even so, the Italian attack, delayed into late October because of rain which caused the river Piave to swell, still came too late. As Ojetti, Orlando and others feared, the confusion in the Monarchy had by then progressed too far for the Italians to be able to claim convincingly that their offensive was the 'decisive battle which sealed the fate of Austria'.[64]

In Italy's postwar history the myth of the traditional military victory (Vittorio Veneto) would predominate. But at the time, in 1918, Italy's military and political leaders had felt able to acknowledge the role which propaganda had played in the *débâcle*. As in June, so in September, the CS viewed propaganda as a valuable preparation for Italy's attack as well as a temporary substitute for taking too many risks. Therefore the period of mid-September onwards witnessed an intensification of Padua's campaign, with the Commission producing

264 new leaflets in about 15 million copies, twice the number issued in the previous month but on a par with figures for the period during and immediately after the June offensive.[65] How far this material reached its targets is unclear. The paucity of copies of the later manifestos surviving in the archives may suggest not only that many were lost in the chaos of the final retreat, but that Austrian troops were failing to surrender the leaflets to the authorities. We know, for example, that in the 10th army sector the average daily 'intake' of leaflets by September was only about 2000, while for the 11th army it was at best 150–200. Ojetti at the end of the war was delighted when he came across a battalion of captured Hungarians who retained a mass of his leaflets in their possession.[66]

In this final phase, the main theme of Padua's propaganda was Allied military success in other theatres of the war. The material directed to different nationalities appears to have become more uniform, and it is tempting to suggest that this was due to Ojetti's dominance and his relegation of those national delegates who previously had given the manifestos a more native stamp. It meant in fact that the summer months had been the highpoint of inventiveness for the material, but that time had now passed as the war of movement took over and Padua found it more difficult to keep up with events. Great play was especially made of Bulgaria's collapse and the armistice signed on 29 September with General Franchet d'Esperay. In one commentary, Slovene soldiers were supplied with a common metaphor:

> When the ship sinks all the rats abandon it. Only Austria clings to the wreckage of Germany. Only the Austrian rat is so mad that she does not want to leave the sinking German ship on which she embarked to sail through the rough seas of discontent of her peoples. In the end this is not surprising: for she is old and stupid. It is better she dies.[67]

Bulgaria's defeat opened the way for a rapid Allied advance into Serbia towards the Hungarian frontier, enabling Padua to hint at the 'threat' or 'liberation' which was about to ensue for Serbs, Romanians or Hungarians. At the same time Turkey's links with the Central Powers had been severed. Since British troops under Allenby were racing through Palestine, seizing Damascus and 75 000 prisoners by late September (one of Padua's more wild estimates), it was 'obvious' that the Ottomans were about to follow the Bulgarians' example.[68]

In the West the news was equally gloomy for the Central Powers, causing the German people to realize suddenly that they had been led by a 'lunatic of degenerate stock' who had the 'fantasies of a diseased imperial mind'.[69] In early September British troops had pierced the 'Wotan line', recovering all the territory taken by Germany since the March offensive. On 12 September, American forces in one day had captured the St Mihiel salient, taking according to Padua 5320 prisoners of the Austro-Hungarian 35ID (which incidentally now became a target for Allied propaganda on that front, as Arz himself had feared).[70] On 26 September, Marshal Foch had attacked the supposedly impenetrable 'Hindenburg line' in four places, broken through, and taken 40 000 prisoners in two days.[71] Padua portrayed the German retreat in the West as being virtually uninterrupted since July. And in view of the success on other fronts, not to mention the Italian advance in Albania or Bolshevik-German reverses in Russia, the manifestos could justifiably proclaim that the 'day of wrath' (*dies irae*) had arrived for the enemy: 'From east to west the victorious song of the Allies overflows.'[72]

The encirclement of the Monarchy and its inevitable defeat as 'millions' of Americans joined the fray were forceful realities which could still be balanced with the idealistic message that victory for the Allies would mean freedom and justice for all peoples in Europe. For the Yugoslavs, Italy's official statement which Crewe House had managed to secure in September, was portrayed by Ojetti as a 'historic declaration... perhaps more important than any other event of the war'. It was displayed in tricolour leaflets in Slovene, Croatian and Serbian, which stated boldly that the Italians had now adopted as a war aim the destruction of Austria-Hungary and the creation of a free and independent Yugoslavia. Trumbić himself was quoted as usual, thanking Orlando for a statement which represented 'a new era in the relations of both peoples'.[73]

Although this was indeed a new departure for Padua's Yugoslav propaganda, the reality behind it was very different. Orlando remained ambivalent, while Trumbić would soon perceive that Italy's words were just another example of 'throwing dust in the eyes of the Allies' for propaganda purposes: the Yugoslavs had not been officially recognized by any of the western Powers as allies.[74] It suited the Italian government to perpetuate this ambivalent stance, giving lip-service to the Yugoslav cause, while aiming to implement the Treaty of London as soon as the war ended. In the last days of hostilities, it was a trend in policy which speeded up. Some, like Gallenga Stuart, were inclined in the sight of victory to fall in with the Orlando–Sonnino camp. Others like Borgese were shocked at Italy's increasing divergence from the nationality policy of which he had been a sincere adherent. In mid-November he would resign from the Berne office as he refused to be the propagator abroad of a policy which would set Italy at odds with America and the new nationalist states of eastern Europe.[75] Yet at the front, Padua's Yugoslav propaganda had always been more clearly defined than was warranted by Italian policy. The discrepancy between Italian policy and propaganda in 1918, the mask which Orlando had donned after Caporetto to ease the path to victory, stored up a mass of resentment for the future. It would erupt in earnest at the Paris Peace Conference, when the claims of Italy and Yugoslavia were placed on an international stage, and it bedevilled relations between the two countries for the next 20 years.

With its Czech, Polish and Romanian material, the Padua Commission had always been on surer ground. In the final weeks Ojetti challenged head-on the suggestion in Austrian propaganda that the Czech Legion was a minor force made up of individuals who were forced to join, for if such was the case why had captured legionaries been executed? Why too had the enemy thought it necessary to launch an attack on the Legion on Dosso Alto in late September? On that occasion, the Austrians had been given 'a good hiding', while the Legion's exploits had called forth a range of eulogies from Beneš, Masaryk and the Italian government.[76] The Czechs could thus be presented in the manifestos as a fully Allied nation, all the more so as both America and Japan had given them such a status in early September.[77] Poles too could be reassured, from the mouth of Clemenceau himself, that France was determined after victory to create a free Poland with its historic frontiers.[78] And Romanians could finally be told about discussions in the émigré community in Paris, which culminated on 3 October in the formation of a Romanian National Council dedicated to creating a 'greater Romania' at the end of the war.[79]

While trumpeting the Allied principle of 'democracy', the manifestos continued to labour the themes of Prussian militarism or Austrian imperial autocracy. Material in Hungarian remained quite ingenious, using the Budapest press to warn Magyar soldiers that their country faced bankruptcy not due to the war but because Austrians and Germans were stripping it of funds. Sándor Petőfi's poetic tirade of 1849 against Austria was reproduced in full to indicate the honourable course which Hungarians should follow.[80] Similarly, Poles when told about Germany's plans to exploit and violate Polish soil in the postwar period, were supplied with the words of the poet Adam Mickiewicz, 'Everyone who does not serve his country will perish'.[81] But for inspiration from nationalist contemporaries within the Monarchy, Padua was less well supplied with information during these final weeks. Perhaps largely due to the speed of events, little could be said about the various national councils assuming authority in Zagreb, Prague and elsewhere, and nothing at all about the Emperor's Manifesto of 16 October which sought to impress the West with a last-minute federalization of Austria. Most useful for Padua appears to have been the turbulent session in the Vienna Reichsrat on 2 October, when the outlook of Max von Hussarek, the Austrian Prime Minister, was effectively condemned by Slav deputies; the Poles spoke on behalf of the 'Polish nation' to demand an independent Polish state, while for the Czechs František Staněk gave a notorious speech, claiming that the defeat of Austria fully met the wishes of the Czech people who would be represented separately at the peace conference.[82] This news, however, was only being distributed from Italian planes three weeks later, by which time Ojetti was also announcing the full break-up of the Empire and urging soldiers to hurry home to help their brothers achieve liberty.[83]

# Magyarok !

**Emlékezetetekbe hossuk legnagyobb forradalmi költőtök, *Petőfi Sándor* egyik költeményét arról az Ausztriaról, amelynek parancsszavára már négy éve ontjàtok véreteket csak azért, hogy azoknak a Habsburgoknak nagyhatalmi vàgyait szolgàljàtok, kikkel szemben oly nagy gyülölettel volt eltelve vilàghirü költőtök s a kiket mà is oka volna gyülölni teljes szivébol minden igaz magyarnak. Olvassàtok!**

## AUSZTRIA !

Miként elpusztult Jeruzsàlem,
El fogsz pusztulni Ausztria,
S miként Jeruzsàlemnek lakói,
Földönfutók lesznek csaszàrjaid,
Földönfutók és üldözöttek !

Készüljetek,
Ti fölfuvalkodott félistenek,
Az óra kondúl s futnotok kell.
Hogy el ne zùzzanak
Az omló trónus romjai....
Ott veszni nem szabad ti nektek,
Ti nektek élni, hosszan élni kell
Bukàs utàn
Nyemorban, végtelen nyomorban!

Hiàba mossàtok kezeiteket,
Ti Pontius Pilàtusok,
Àmithatjàtok a vilàgot,
De làt az isten s ismer bennetek,
S nincs szà motokra többé kegyelem;
Vagy érdemeltek - e
Csak annyit is az ég kegyéből,
A mennyitől egy hajszàl meghajol ?
Nem ! - Birodalmatok
A szabadsàg kalvàriàja,
Uralkodàs volt minden vàgyatok,
Ezért emeltetek Munkàcsokat,
Hogy a szellem vilàgàt, melegét,
A rabbilincsek e fölolvasztójàt

Elrejtsétek mélységes föld alà,
S fölötte a sötétségben buján
Tenyèszhessék a zsarnokok viràga,
a test - s lélekzsibbaszto butasàg....
Elrablottàtok nép jogàt
És elloptàtok kincseit,
Ti biboros haramjàk,
Ti koronàzott tolvajok !

De a lopott vagyont
El nem viszitek magatokkal;
Félmeztelen
Fognak kiverni titeket
A fölemelkedett alattvalók,
Mint a tüzkardos angyal
Àdàmot s Evàt a paradicsomból.
Kolduljatok, miként
Koldultak milliók miattatok !
Koldulni fogtok és
Nem nyertek alamizsnàt,
Mert a kihez fordultok, az mind
Gazsàgitoknak àldozatja volt,
Ràtok köp, elrùg bennetteket,
Es undorodva fordul el !
S ha ekkép éhen vesztetek,
Dögtestetekre hollók szàllanak,
Mert nem lesz és ne légyen ember az
Utàlat miatt, a ki eltemessen ;
A hollók gyomra lesz majd sirotok
És szemfödötök a népeknek àtka !

352. **Petőfi Sàndor.**

*Illustration 9.2* Manifesto 352: A poem of Sándor Petőfi to inspire the Magyars (OHM)

The little material which survives from late October suggests that Ojetti finally turned on the German-Austrians, the most loyal troops, as a special target. With a delicious irony, they were told to demand from their officers that they be shown their own newspapers, so as to read why it was pointless to fight for something which no longer existed. As proof, Padua reproduced articles from the *Arbeiter-Zeitung* showing that nobody believed any longer that Austria-Hungary would survive the war; the dynasty, the church, the common army were now incapable of holding together a state which had lost the allegiance of its peoples. Recalling the way in which the Habsburg elite in July 1914 had attacked the Serbians for refusing to submit to an Austrian judicial investigation on their soil, the newspaper quipped that at the end of hostilities it was the whole Habsburg Empire which would be subject to a full investigation at the hands of foreigners.[84] In a final proclamation, scattered over the retreating troops, the futility of resistance was driven home:

> THE END!
>
> Thoughts of an Austro-Hungarian soldier.
>
> Wilson has declared that he cannot recognize the Austro-Hungarian government. The Allies are delivering their last blows to Germany and Austria-Hungary. Bloody Count Tisza has declared that the war is lost.[85] Who can number our enemies? When I look over to the enemy positions I see Italians, French, English, Americans, Czechs, South Slavs, Romanians, Poles...! Terrible! The whole world stands opposed to the house of Habsburg, even its 'loyal peoples'! Hungary has declared independence. The Czechs, Poles and South Slavs have done the same. The Romanians of Austria-Hungary want to unite with Romania. Even the Germans of Austria have left the disintegrating Empire and want to unite with Germany. The Emperor has announced that Italian territory must be ceded to Italy.
>
> The clergy are not standing by the state but going with the people. The Pope has renounced any further help.
>
> *I alone am standing here and allowing myself to be butchered! What for? Austria-Hungary is lost; there is no point risking my life for a former Empire.*
>
> *It only remains for me to save my skin.*[86]

It was a cry of despair, reflecting fairly accurately the fact that among the nationalities it was the German-Austrians who, in the face of the Italian offensive, showed particular 'combative spirit'. Slav units were much quicker to revolt, learning of the news of independence in Prague and Zagreb (which Ojetti too proclaimed); Hungarians had been called back to Budapest by the new Károlyi regime there. But German-Austrian soldiers were the most unsure of what might await them in the future as the other peoples deserted the Monarchy.[87]

By early November the propaganda organizations of the belligerents were moving into a phase of liquidation. In Vienna, Waldstätten, who until the end was calling for discipline and order, and hoping that his network might still have some peacetime educational or welfare role, was ordered by the AOK to dissolve the FAst.[88] In London, the British EPD, the organization which Vienna always believed to be the key centre of 'enemy propaganda', also came to an end when Lord Northcliffe quarrelled with Lloyd George and submitted his resignation. Like Waldstätten, Henry Wickham Steed too had been thinking that his organization at Crewe House might have a peacetime role to play, to educate the German people about the Allies' ideals, but the folding of the EPD removed the platform from under him.[89]

Meanwhile on the Italian Front, the machinery of front propaganda had lost its purpose. Yet even on 27 October the AOK was still sending out 'propaganda concepts' for use against the Italians.[90] Four days later, with the Austrians suing for an armistice, Ojetti asked the Comando Supremo for permission to end the work of the Padua Commission. It was significant, and wholly in keeping with the impression which he had stamped on the Commission during its six months of existence, that Ojetti's final leaflet was not aimed at the enemy at all: it was scattered over the liberated cities of Trento, Trieste and Pula, proclaiming to 'brothers of the new Italy' that 'in the name of Rome, liberty has been resurrected on the sacred graves of our dead'. It was a suitable finale to what Ojetti saw as Italy's mission, something expressed on 1 November when he gathered the national delegates together for the last time and told them that their work had been creative as well as destructive; with watery eyes, the group shook hands and departed. If Ojetti, despite all his frustrations, felt the campaign had been a success, he was seconded in that view by the CS and the Intelligence heads.[91] During the Austrian retreat, the latter had once again employed their Czech and Yugoslav patrols as guides, interpreters or propagandists, using their skills as a supplement to more conventional weapons. Many accompanied the Italian troops as far as Trento or Bolzano. On 4 November, Cesare Finzi too made the journey northwards over the Asiago plateau, passing the former enemy trenches, the roads cluttered with Austrian prisoners, in order to enter liberated Trento. He then returned down Val Sugana and stopped at Carzano. The site which had opened his eyes to the potential of the propaganda weapon was now a ghost town and completely silent.[92]

## Notes

1. KA, 11AK Op.Abt 1918, Fasz.270, 1–17/50–4/9, III KK (GO Martiny) to 11AK, Op.Nr 262/11, 2 October 1918.
2. Karel Pichlík, 'Das Ende der österreichisch-ungarischen Armee', *Österreichische Osthefte*, V (1963) p. 363.
3. KA, XIII KK 1918, Fasz.182, 48ID Kmdo (GM Gärtner) to I KK, Op.Nr 707/16, 10 July 1918.
4. OULK, VII, p. 361.
5. KA, AOK 1918 Op.Akten, Fasz.372, Op.Nr 110531, 13 August 1918.
6. KA, AOK Op.Abt, Fasz.377, Op.Nr 112802, 21 September 1918.

7. See the photographs in KA, AOK Op.Akten, Fasz.373, Op.Nr 110848; KA, 11AK Qu.Abt, Fasz.811, Q.Abt 11AK I.Nr 55105, XXVI KK to 11AK Qu.Abt, 13 August: the last supply of undergarments had been in May 1918.
8. KA, AOK Org.Gruppe, Fasz.380, Op.Nr 113801, Report of Hptm Alfred von Marquet [undated], who visited the XX corps in early September 1918.
9. Hugo Kerchnawe, *Der Zusammenbruch der österr.-ungar. Wehrmacht im Herbst 1918* (Munich, 1921) pp. 21–33.
10. KA, AOK Org. Gruppe, Fasz.379, Op.Nr 113639, 10AK to HGK Joseph, Op.Nr 8012/1, 6 October 1918.
11. KA, AOK Op.Akten, Fasz.376, Op.Nr 112195, Krobatin to HGK GO Erzherzog Joseph, Op.Nr 5495, 10 September 1918.
12. See, for example, the case in July of BHIR2, where 22 men seem to have deserted largely to escape their critical material situation: KA, AOK Op.Akten, Fasz.371, Op.Nr 110295, BHIR2 to 55ID Kmdo, Nr 169/1, 23 July 1918.
13. For a detailed discussion of the phenomenon of desertion in the interior, see Plaschka, Haselsteiner, Suppan, *Innere Front*, II, pp. 63ff, 101.
14. KA, 11AK Gstbs Abt, Fasz.272, 4–6/12–2, 11AK to corps, Op.Nr 3581, 4 October 1918.
15. See the view of the 6AK, 29 September, which singled out Czech, Polish and Ruthene regiments as rather suspect: Kerchnawe, *Der Zusammenbruch*, pp. 22–3.
16. KA, FAst 1918, Fasz.5994, Res.263, AOK Op.Nr 146335, 19 July 1918.
17. Höberth arrived from KISA on 1 July, and took over from Dušan Petrović who went to be chief of staff of the 33ID on the Lower Piave. Höberth was later praised by Waldstätten as being 'thoroughly correct and very military in his behaviour' (FAst, Fasz.5999, Res.987).
18. KA, FAst, Fasz.5995, Res.441. Separate FA training courses were held in Budapest, on 8–20 July and 29 July–10 August (the lecture titles were much the same as in Vienna).
19. KA, FAst, Fasz.5995, Res.330, 6AK to AOK, Op.Nr 900/Ev-4, 6 July; the same urgency was felt by the 10AK and 11AK: see Res.273/4 and 273/6.
20. KA, FAst, Fasz.5995, Res.436, 12 rt.SchD Kmdo to FAst, Na Nr 938, 14 August 1918.
21. KA, FAst, Fasz.5997, Res.645, 6ID Kmdo to FAst, Na.Nr 1507, 11 September. See also Fasz.5998, Res.726; and Res.792 for FAst criticism.
22. KA, FAst, Fasz.5994, Res.254, Waldstätten to AOK, 18 July, enclosing protocol of meeting on 13 July 1918.
23. KA, FAst, Fasz.6003, *Vaterländische Bildungsarbeit. Mitteilungen der FAst*, Nr 4, pp. 18–19; Nr 5, pp. 18–21; Nr 6, pp. 20–1; Nr 7, p. 16.
24. Namely, Archduke Franz Ferdinand, Jean Jaurès, Roger Casement, Rasputin, Mirbach, Eichhorn and Tsar Nicholas II: Fasz.5999, Res.962, 11AK 'Beitrag' Nr 8 (F.A.174).
25. KA, FAst, Fasz.6003, *Vaterländische Bildungsarbeit*, Nr 2, p. 14; Nr 4, p. 20; Nr 6, pp. 3–6.
26. Ibid., Nr 2, p. 6; Nr 4, pp. 4–5; Nr 6, Nachtrag p. 2.
27. KA, FAst, Fasz.5998, Res.825, AOK to FAst, Op.Nr 148428, 8 October 1918, enclosing guidelines.
28. KA, FAst, Fasz.5998, Res.869, FAst to FA network, 14 October; Res.875, 'Gegenwartsaufgaben der vaterländischen Unterrichtes' [drafted by 15 October]. For army responses: Res.872/1, 6AK to FAst, F.A.Nr 107/1, 14 October; and Res.892, 11AK to AOK, F.A.Nr 158, 13 October: the 11AK set out various options for 'instruction' depending on whether an armistice was agreed.

29. KA, FAst, Fasz.5998, Res.872/5, FA Referent KISA to FAst, F.A. Nr 169, 23 October 1918.
30. According to the German ambassador in Vienna, by mid-July two-thirds of the 'Austrian public' assumed that the enemy would win the war: John W. Boyer, *Culture and Political Crisis in Vienna: Christian Socialism in Power, 1897–1918* (Chicago and London, 1995), p. 438.
31. This incident, in which Austrian planes distributed leaflets over the town of Vukovar in Croatia, was mentioned in Padua's manifesto 258, *Jugoslavija* no. 11.
32. KA, FAst, Fasz.5994, Res.223, FAst to Apostolische Feldvikariat, 2 July; Plaschka, Haselsteiner, Suppan, *Innere Front*, II, pp. 134–5, 140–1.
33. KA, FAst, Fasz.5995, Res.423, FAst to AOK, 14 August 1918 [drafted by Ernst Keil]. In mid-September the War Ministry also urged both the Austrian and Hungarian governments to begin such an action: Fasz.5997, Res.662, KM Präs. Nr 32650, 15 September 1918.
34. 'Eine Österreichische Propagandastelle', *Reichspost*, 25 September 1918, p. 3.
35. KA, FAst, Fasz.5998, Res.747, Arz to FAst, Op.Nr 147866, 25 September; Res.841, AOK to Ministry of Interior, Op.Nr 148279, 8 October 1918.
36. KA, FAst, Fasz.5998, Res.839, Eisner-Bubna (KPQ) to FAst, Adj.Nr 14600, 7 October 1918.
37. KA, 11AK Gstbs Abt 1918, Fasz.449, Pr.2328, AOK to armies, Op.Nr 766/270, 4 August: 'Neue Weisungen für die Feindpropaganda gegen Italien'.
38. Propaganda reports for August in: KA, 11AK Gstbs Abt, Fasz.447, Fd.Ev.Nr 1597, KISA Op.Nr 8600, Beilage 11; KA, 11AK Gstbs Abt, Fasz.448, Pr.2337, 11AK Beilage 9; KA, HGK Conrad/Joseph, Fasz.66, Na Nr 400a/400, 10AK Op.Nr 5771/2 Prop., 28 August 1918.
39. 6AK leaflet, 'Soldati italiani! Nuovamente sono comparsi...' (KA, 11AK Gstbs Abt, Fasz.448). Only in October would the HGK Joseph produce a leaflet specifically directed at Czechoslovak legionaries, urging them to return home without fear of execution; it was a clear change of tactic based on the evidence of one captured legionary as to what might appeal most to his former comrades (see leaflet, 'Češi a Slováci!' in KA, 11AK Fasz.449, Pr.2429; and the statement by Franz Rozsypal in KA, 11AK Fasz.442, Na Nr 1674). Moreover, it was significant for the confusion which might be generated, that the 11AK also distributed this leaflet to the enemy in Italian.
40. 6AK leaflet, 'La Risposta dei nazionalisti indiani a Roosevelt!' (KA, 11AK, Fasz.448); see also the 10AK propaganda brochure issued in September, 'Inghilterra e le piccoli nazioni' (ibid.).
41. See 10AK leaflet, 'I successi dell'Italia in tre anni di Guerra italiana'; 6AK leaflet, 'L'Inutilità della Guerra Italiana'; 10AK leaflet, 'La colpa del prolungamento della guerra è dell'Inghilterra!' (all in KA, 11AK, Fasz.448). In one newssheet, Lloyd George was depicted as a man who was fast going senile: *Il Piccolo Corriere*, 24 July (issued by the HGK Joseph: KA, HGK Conrad, Fasz.66, Na 400a/404).
42. 6AK leaflet, 'Comunicato ufficiale austriaco del 26 Agosto 1918' (KA, 11AK Fasz.448).
43. 11AK leaflet, 'Come s'inganna il soldato italiano!' (KA, 11AK, Fasz.448, Pr.2004/37).
44. 6AK leaflet, 'Soldati italiani! L'Austria-Ungheria non mai desiderato...' (KA, 11AK, Fasz.448).
45. Ronge, *Kriegs- und Industriespionage*, p. 373.
46. HHStA, PA I/505, Liasse XLVII/3/26, notes of Burián's meeting with the German Foreign Minister (Paul von Hintze), 5 September; Stephen Burián von Rajecz, *Austria in Dissolution* (London, 1925) pp. 388–92.

47. KISA leaflet, 'In alto i cuori, apunta l'alba di pace'; 6AK leaflet, 'Soldati italiani! L'Austria-Ungheria ha fatto ieri...' (both KA, 11AK Fasz.448); 11AK leaflets: 'Basta Sangue' (Fasz.448, Pr.2004/39); 'Ancora un inverno in guerra?' (Pr.2004/40).
48. KA, HGK Conrad/Joseph, Fasz.66, Na Nr 400a/414, 10AK to HGK Joseph, t. Op.Nr 8138/3 prop., 3 October.
49. Manifesto 375, 'Srbi, Hrvati i Slovenci!' (OHM, sz.1434); manifesto 385, 'Hodina míru dosud neudeřila' (KA, EvB, Fasz. 5762/33878). See Ojetti, *Lettere alla Moglie*, p. 585.
50. Leaflet, 'L'America spela la nota pacifista dell'Austria-Ungheria' (KA, 11AK Fasz.452, '1918 11AK Na. Feindespropaganda'); 6AK leaflet, 'Soldati italiani! Il governo italiano ha respinto la nostra proposta di pace' (KA, 11AK Fasz.448).
51. KA, FAst, Fasz.5998, Res.863, AOK Na.Abt to Fast etc, Na Nr 22823/P, 10 October: 'Weisungen für die Feindpropaganda'.
52. KISA leaflet, 'La pace, sospiro dell'umanità, è imminente!' (KA, 11AK Fasz.451, 'Flugzettel III'); 11AK leaflets: 'Italiani!' (KA, 11AK Fasz.448, Pr.2004/44); 'Le trattative di pace iniziate' (Pr.2004/45); 'Perchè fate ancora assalti?' (Pr.2004/46).
53. AOK leaflet, 'I Falsari!' (KA, 11AK Fasz.452); leaflet, 'Ultime Nuove. La vittoria dell'unione pacifista al congresso dei socialisti francesi' (OHM, sz.72409); and see also the draft leaflets in KA, 11AK Fasz.449, Pr.2456, 2460.
54. Manifesto 431, 'Pace orî Războiu?' (Romanian: KA, Flugzettel Sammlung; German: VHA); Ojetti, *Lettere alla Moglie*, pp. 600, 617: Admiral Thaon di Revel complained to Orlando about this leaflet.
55. IWM, Wilson MSS, 28B/11, Cavan to Wilson, 13 October 1918.
56. Kujundžić, Lasić and Szuber all fell ill in October, as did Zanotti-Bianco who had only moved from Rome to Padua in early September on Ojetti's instruction: Ojetti, *Lettere*, pp. 584, 612; Zanotti-Bianco, *Carteggio 1906–1918*, p. 653.
57. For details see BL, Northcliffe MSS, vol.X, Add.Mss 62162, minutes of 13th and 14th EPD Committee meetings.
58. Albertini, *Epistolario*, II, no. 876, p. 989, and pp. 1067–8 note 441: Ojetti to Orlando, 16 September 1918.
59. Albertini, *Epistolario*, II, no. 879, p. 992; Ojetti, *Lettere*, pp. 594, 600, 611: Siciliani was also to be laid low with influenza.
60. On the opening of Parliament on 3 October, Orlando made a speech recording Italy's recognition of the movement for independence of the oppressed nationalities, but it did not go far enough for Ojetti, who viewed it as 'mediocre, nothing more than rhetoric' (*Lettere*, p. 598; PRO, FO 371/3228, Rodd to Balfour, t.712, 3 October).
61. PRO, WO 106/852, Cavan to CIGS, 9 September. See also Colonel Repington's talks with Diaz and Badoglio on the 27th: Repington, *The First World War 1914–1918*, 2 vols (London, 1920) II, pp. 422–5.
62. PRO, WO 106/852, H.B. Walker to CIGS, 25 September 1918.
63. Marchetti, *Ventotto Anni*, pp. 380–2, 385.
64. Ibid., p. 386.
65. Finzi, *'I.T.O.'*, p. 273; AJA, JO 28/48, 'Pregled rada'. The usual caution is needed in evaluating these figures, but the general trend is confirmed by Szuber in his data for Padua's Polish manifestos: Szuber, *Walka o Przewagę Duchową*, p. 147.
66. Ojetti, *Lettere*, p. 625. KA, 11AK 1918, Fasz.449, Pr.2367, HGK Joseph to 11AK, Na Nr 2000/138, 11 September 1918.
67. Manifesto 411, *Jugoslavija* no. 19, 19 October (section in Slovene: AJA, JO 111/4). See also for Bulgaria's collapse: manifestos 390(a), 'Soldaţi Români!' (OHM, sz.1563) and

391(a), 'Slovenci, Hrvati in Srbi' (KA, EvB 1918, Fasz. 5762/33878): both with maps on the reverse; 399, 'Bugarska kapitulacija' (ibid.); 404, 'Bulharsko přijalo podminký Dohody' (ibid.). Many others gave the same details (400, 405, 406).

68. For Allenby's advance, see manifesto 391(b), 'Slovenci, Hrvati in Srbi' with map on reverse (KA, EvB Fasz.5762/33878); manifesto 401, 'Turecká fronta v Palestýně' (VHA); manifesto 408, *Polak* no. 19, 19 October (AJA, JO 111/4). Other leaflets issued by the Intelligence offices gave maps showing Allied advances in Palestine and the Balkans (KA, 11AK Fasz.451, 'Flugzettel III').

69. Manifesto 364, *Československá Samostatnost* no. 17, 4 October (KA, EvB Fasz.5762/ 33878).

70. Manifesto 360, 'Vitězství Spojenců u Saint Mihiel' (VHA); manifesto 365, *Neamul Românesc* no. 17, 4 October (KA, EvB Fasz.5762/33878). For American propaganda against the 35ID (which significantly received no material from the FAst), see Heber Blankenhorn, *Adventures in Propaganda: Letters from an Intelligence Officer in France* (Boston and New York, 1919) pp. 49, 125; Zoltán Szende, *Die Ungarn im Zusammenbruch. Feldheer/Hinterland* (Oldenbourg, 1931) p. 112. For Arz's fears: *Zur Geschichte des Grossen Krieges*, p. 280.

71. See, for example, manifesto 402, 'Nové porážky německé ve Francii' (OHM, sz.1339); and for advances in early September: manifesto 336, 'Zapadni front. Pregledna karta bitke u Flandriji i Pikardiji' (IWM, 3(45)/39).

72. Manifesto 425, *Jugoslavija* no. 20, 24 October; and 426, *Polak* no. 20 (both in AJA, JO 111/4).

73. Manifesto 411, *Jugoslavija* no. 19: [large headline], 'Istoriska izjava talijanske vlade'; manifesto 396, 'Srbi, Hrvati i Slovenci' (OHM sz.1437; KA, EvB Fasz.5762/33878; Stuart, *Secrets of Crewe House*, opposite p. 49); manifesto 425, *Jugoslavija* no. 20.

74. AJA, JO 27/208, Trumbić to Yugoslav Committee, Washington, 26 October 1918. Trumbić in October tried in vain with the aid of the British EPD to achieve the allied recognition which had been accorded the Czechoslovaks.

75. Tosi, *La Propaganda Italiana*, pp. 215ff. It was significant that by December Gallenga's ministry had been absorbed by Sonnino.

76. Manifesto 409, *Československá Samostatnost* no. 19, 19 October (AJA, JO 111/4); manifesto 420, 'Poselství prof.Masaryka československému vojsku v Italii' (Stuart, *Secrets of Crewe House*, opposite p. 177). See Beneš, *Světová Válka*, III, documents 161–7.

77. Manifesto 376, 'Také Japonsko uznává samostatnost československého národa' (OHM sz.1318); hand-written leaflet [of an Intelligence office], 'Čechové Slováci!' (KA, 11AK Fasz.451, 'Flugzettel I').

78. Manifesto 380, 'Polacy! Ważne oświadczenia w sprawie polskiej' (Szuber, *Walka o Przewagę Duchową*, p. 129).

79. Manifestos 410 and 428, *Neamul Românesc* nos.19 and 20 (both in AJA, JO 111/4). For the background, see Miron Constantinescu and Ştefan Pascu (eds), *Unification of the Romanian National State: The Unification of Transylvania with Old Romania* (Bucharest, 1971) pp. 138–9.

80. Manifesto 352, 'Magyarok!' (OHM sz.802481); manifesto 370, 'Austria-Magiarország háboru-adosságai' (KA, 11AK Fasz.451, 'Flugzettel Unerledigt').

81. Manifesto 363, *Polak* no. 17 (KA, EvB, Fasz. 5762/33878); manifesto 426, *Polak* no. 20 (AJA, JO 111/4).

82. Manifesto 427, *Československá Samostatnost* no. 20 (AJA, JO 111/4); manifesto 426, *Polak* no. 20. For the full speeches which caused a storm of protest: *Stenographische*

*Protokolle*, IV, 85.Sitzung, pp. 4312, 4315–16. The divergent outlook of individuals in the Monarchy as peace approached is the subject of my article, 'Austria-Hungary' in H. Cecil and P. Liddle (eds), *At the Eleventh Hour: Reflections, Hopes and Anxieties at the Closing of the Great War, 1918* (London, 1998) pp. 285–300.

83. Manifesto 455, 'Soldaten!' (German: VHA; Romanian: OHM sz.1624).
84. Manifesto 487, 'Österreichisch-ungarische Soldaten!' (VHA collection), quoting articles from the *Arbeiter-Zeitung* on 11 and 12 October.
85. Tisza made the statement on 15 October in the Budapest Parliament, and while this seems to be the only mention in Padua's propaganda, it had already probably had a major impact on the morale of Hungarian troops. See Glaise-Horstenau, *The Collapse of the Austro-Hungarian Empire*, pp. 212–13.
86. Manifesto 492, 'Das Ende!' (VHA); manifesto 486, 'Trpěti a umírati! Proč?' (VHA) summarized such thoughts for Czechs.
87. See Fritz Weber, *Das Ende der Armee* (Leipzig, Vienna and Berlin, 1931) p. 69; PRO, WO 157/641, DIS no. 328, 31 October 1918: 'Morale of prisoners'.
88. KA, FAst 1918, Fasz.5999, Res.969, FAst to AOK/KM, 30 October; Res.988, FAst to AOK Op.Abt etc., 4 November 1918.
89. Steed, *Through Thirty Years*, II, pp. 247–50. On the EPD's peace propaganda, see also Seton-Watsons, *The Making of a New Europe*, pp. 315ff.
90. KA, 11AK Gstbs Abt, Fasz.449, Pr.2470.
91. Ojetti, *Lettere alla Moglie*, pp. 633–7, 642; AJA, JO 35/132, Trinajstić to Trumbić, 12 November, for the outlook of the Yugoslav Committee.
92. Finzi, '*I.T.O.*', pp. 280–2. The work of propaganda patrols during the final offensive is described briefly in Hanzal, *S Výzvědčíky*; and Pivko, *Naši Dobrovoljci*, pp. 44, 47. Finzi also ('*I.T.O.*', p. 277) used some agents for sabotage on the Asiago plateau.

# 10
# Conclusion

Despite the vast historiography which exists about the First World War, the phenomenon of front propaganda has remained either unexplored or trapped amidst a range of myths fashioned on all sides in the 1920s. To investigate such psychological warfare means not simply to discuss the wielding of a weapon which by the last year of the war came to be an integral part of each belligerent's armoury. It reveals much about the mentalities on either side of the front, the hopes and fears which could be aroused in different individuals, the important interaction between front and hinterland, and the perceptions and prejudices which existed or evolved between enemies but also between supposed allies. In the case of Austria-Hungary, by assessing various 'national mentalities', how they were perceived and how the stereotypes matched the 'realities', it is possible to gain a fuller insight into the reasons for the Empire's disintegration in 1918.

From this study it is also clear that front propaganda was not the special preserve of the British or French, as many historians have assumed. On the contrary, the Central Powers and the Italians were pioneers in various aspects of the weapon. On the Eastern Front in 1917, it was the Central Powers who pursued the first fully coordinated campaign of its kind, one which acquired a mythical reputation due to the way that Russia collapsed. Against Austria-Hungary in 1918, it was the Italians who were engaged in the most sophisticated example of front propaganda, a campaign which may have been given focus by British advisers but always retained a solid Italian base and outlook. With its network of Intelligence centres, its carefully considered arguments and its sheer methodical production of material, Ugo Ojetti's Padua Commission might well earn the epitaph supplied by one of its officials as 'the greatest propaganda forge of the world'.[1] Yet such language should equally instil caution. One of the key necessities in evaluating front propaganda is to strip away the myth – indeed the propaganda – surrounding the phenomenon, much of which was consciously or unconsciously manufactured by the propagandists themselves or their opponents.

While all of the belligerents dabbled with some front propaganda in the early years of the war, it required a coincidence of factors for proper campaigns to emerge in 1917. After 30 months of warfare all sides were at a turning-point, having to think more carefully about the purpose of hostilities and about new ways to achieve a quicker end to the war (thus the general announcement of war aims or Germany's U-Boat offensive of early 1917). With the fall of the Tsarist regime in March 1917, the Russian armed forces suddenly appeared more receptive to their enemies' overtures for peace. Out of these hints on the Eastern Front there developed a major propaganda offensive which, notwithstanding any questions about its actual effectiveness, had a crucial impact on the further evolution of front propaganda. The Austro-Hungarian military, on the basis of the benefits which seemed to accrue from the campaign in the East, turned to employ their 'new weapon' on the Italian and Balkan Fronts. At the same time, the reputation which enemy propaganda secured in the Russian *débâcle* was one of the decisive factors in the creation of Lord Northcliffe's 'Enemy Propaganda Department' in Britain. It was thus an initiative by the Central Powers which snowballed and caused an accelerated response in the Allied camp. Admittedly, the Italian military did not simply take lessons from others in their use of front propaganda; their more enlightened Intelligence officers had slowly begun to practise some effective psychological warfare from 1916. But the elaborate campaign which was launched in April 1918 on the Italian Front was still, in part, a reflex action to Austria-Hungary's own efforts in that theatre in the previous six months. Thus the belligerents from 1917 were interacting as they created their own organizations of front propaganda, learning as much from the 'cunning' behaviour of the enemy as from their own teething problems with the weapon.

Just as each campaign of front propaganda caused an offensive reaction in the enemy camp, so it bred defensive responses as well. The Italian military's shock after Caporetto, a trauma which was surrounded by rumours of enemy propaganda and domestic subversion, led to systematic action in the Italian war zone to improve morale. It was a move which, arguably, played its part in immunizing the troops against an Austrian propaganda campaign which in early 1918 seemed to be well-tuned to the hopes and fears in the Italian trenches. The Austrian High Command's comparable defence, its Feindespropaganda-Abwehrstelle, was set up because, even more than the Italians, the AOK felt that it knew what could be achieved through propaganda and had learnt lessons from what the other belligerents were doing. Germany had begun patriotic instruction in mid-1917, the Italian army was known to be 'regenerating' itself through defensive propaganda. On the other hand, Russia served as a constant example to the Austrian military of what could happen if an empire's psychological defences were left unmanned. When they perceived that the poison of Bolshevism was seeping into the Monarchy, as revealed in the domestic unrest of January 1918, and when one of their enemies, the British, openly announced that they would try to subvert the Central Powers by propaganda, the Austrian military finally turned their thoughts to some coordinated defensive propaganda of their own. It is clear that the AOK in the last year of the war was fully alert, if not paranoid, in the face of 'enemy propaganda'. This anxiety was a by-product from Austria-Hungary's own use of the weapon from 1917, but the sense of helplessness which seemed to grow in 1918 was also caused in part by an ill-defined and nebulous interpretation of the phenomenon. Despite this, the Austrian military retained a principally offensive perception of front propaganda until June 1918 when it was clear that their campaign against Italy had failed and ought to be temporarily shelved. Only then, when it was far too late, was the defensive propaganda organized by the FAst given a clearer priority. In this way the 'primacy of the offensive', which was always one of Conrad von Hötzendorf's maxims, was evident too in the field of psychological warfare and had very damaging consequences for Austria-Hungary.

In each theatre of the war, those who practised front propaganda had common experiences and learnt similar lessons. But the fact that the weapon was wielded in a variety of ways indicates that the propagandists had to adapt their work on the different fronts. The same methods could not always be used, nor did the targets have the same characteristics, and in the creation or coordination of propaganda machinery there were difficulties peculiar to each belligerent or theatre. On all sides among the military there was always a certain amount of scepticism about the new weapon. The view of one British commander, General Herbert Plumer, that it was an 'unfair' activity which was no substitute for 'proper fighting', was by no means a purely British trait.[2] It was equally commonplace in the Italian forces, where it was entrenched because many remained deeply suspicious about the Slav agenda of Italy's front propaganda and never fully trusted the Czech or Yugoslav volunteers who were operating in the front line. A similar mistrust was evident in the Austrian military hierarchy where local commanders tended to use the English word 'unfair' to describe an interloper who seemed to be debasing the chivalrous conduct of war.[3] As in the Italian army, Austrian scepticism about front propaganda was fuelled all the more by a fear among the Monarchy's conservative leadership that such a subversive weapon might be double-edged and, simply by being used, might be harmful to discipline in the Austro-Hungarian ranks. Emperor Karl himself expressed such anxiety about Austria's campaign in the East, but seems also to have shared the general irritation of Conrad and other commanders at the idea of introducing propaganda or 'advertising' into military or Imperial affairs in order to shape people's minds. If we are to believe one observer, the Emperor commented on one occasion that thoughts and ideas 'could not be recommended like laxatives, toothpaste and foodstuffs'.[4]

There were thus always those who from different prejudices resisted front propaganda, whether it be local commanders who neglected to coordinate their operations with propaganda personnel in the front line, or airmen who refused to distribute 'dishonourable' manifestos. Alongside them, however, there emerged groups of enthusiasts, or those who increasingly felt that the new weapon should not be neglected or left solely in enemy hands. Intelligence officers like Tullio Marchetti, Cesare Finzi or Max Ronge came naturally to appreciate what might be achieved through 'throwing out the seeds of future discord'.[5] In turn, some like Delmé-Radcliffe or Captain Frydman, the head of 11AK propaganda, were enthused to perceive front propaganda as 'an essential, modern weapon of warfare' because of their close involvement in its genesis. Others in the Allied camp, such as the grouping around the *Corriere della Sera*, the propagandists of Crewe House or the delegates of Slav émigré organizations, all had their own political agendas which they brought to bear when participating in Italy's campaign. Their input gave that campaign a special colouring which was symptomatic of the fresh political-military mobilization which took place in Italy after Caporetto; they were trying to inject more political arguments into a largely military phenomenon. Yet it was the commitment of the military, particularly the High Commands, which was crucial to advancing front propaganda. It may have been due to pressure from their subordinates, and a set of particular circumstances on the fronts, that the AOK and the CS realized in early 1917 and early 1918 respectively that front propaganda ought to be fully sanctioned. Thereafter, they took initiatives which facilitated the comprehensive organization of the weapon; they did much to set new targets for front propaganda, on the premise that it was indeed producing significant results.

From being an isolated activity associated with Intelligence work, front propaganda by the end of the war had secured a place within each army's overall strategy. It always retained its Intelligence dimension. The Austrians' *Nachrichtentruppen*, who distributed material but also acted as Intelligence scouts, acquired their more dangerous counterpart in the form of the Italians' Slav patrols; and deserters who came from the enemy with useful information were an indirect Intelligence benefit of psychological warfare. But by 1917–18, front propaganda came to have a wider strategic significance for military operations, and this was common to the campaigns against Russia, Italy and Austria-Hungary. In each case, the military leaders gradually viewed front propaganda as a valuable precursor to any offensive, expecting that after sustained subjection to the weapon, the enemy troops would show their true moral weakness when attacked. The propagandists assured their military leaders that this process had occurred successfully during the Galician battle of July 1917, at

Caporetto in October, and in Austria-Hungary's last offensive in June 1918. In each case, against Russia, Italy and Austria-Hungary, the propagandists then intensified their efforts after the battle with the view that propaganda could perform a coup de grâce upon a disillusioned and demoralized enemy. If this did not immediately occur (and it did not), the military leaders still came to see clear benefits from continuing a psychological campaign, not least the fact that the offensive of words or ideas could be a substitute for standard military operations which were often likely to waste precious manpower. This perception is clear in all of the campaigns, and it frustrated those, like Lord Cavan or General Alfred Krauss, who always gave primacy to conventional weaponry. Those who believed in the power of front propaganda always felt that the fruits which they were nurturing in the enemy camp might take a long time to ripen. But the effects were always expected to be clearer during the next major military engagement. Hence the Austrians' disappointment when their propaganda failure was exposed in June 1918. Hence the Italians, after their 'success' in this propaganda duel, persisted with their efforts and again expected to see the results in their autumn offensive.

The propagandists were therefore not particularly worried if demoralization seemed to be a slow process, although occasional glimmers of success were vital to their own credibility. Indeed, since in each campaign it was an accepted premise that propaganda in the enemy trenches was interacting with an unstable enemy hinterland, long periods of sustained propaganda work could be exactly what was required so that the 'common yeast' could ferment and have an impact. A collective trait in the three campaigns against Russia, Italy and the Habsburg Empire was a belief that enemy soldiers, steadily subject to propaganda, would take the subversive messages back into the hinterland, where they would have an impact which would rebound on the front. The AOK believed that this had happened in Russia, and was overconfident in expecting that the same process would occur in Italy. Some of Italy's propagandists seem to have learnt a similar 'lesson' from Russia's collapse, namely that effective propaganda at the front could interact fatally with unrest in the hinterland. The evidence shows that such a process was indeed occurring in Austria-Hungary in 1918, with Padua's manifestos having some small impact. By the last months of the war, moreover, the Italians themselves were taking their propaganda direct to the Austrian hinterland. With sheer bravado, Italian pilots flew over Vienna, Zagreb and Ljubljana, importing a subversive message directly to the rear in a way which the Austrians could only theorize about attempting in Italy.

It might be argued that the Austrians were less imaginative in their methods of propaganda distribution. But it would be more correct to say that they were increasingly circumscribed by the reality of the Monarchy's military and political weaknesses. From its Eastern campaign against the Russians, the AOK judged that oral propaganda was the most effective of techniques since personal contact with the enemy, despite its obvious dangers, enabled well-trained propagandists to be flexible in their approach as well as being a particularly effective touchstone for the actual state of enemy morale. These benefits were absent when propaganda was made simply with the written word. Therefore for the AOK, manifestos or newspapers were the preferred medium only when the Eastern Front was moving or when the opposing forces were hostile to any personal approach. The type of literature then distributed was a combination of pictures and slogans with longer factual newssheets, thereby appealing to the Russians' wide range of tastes, their levels of literacy and particularly their curiosity about the turmoil in the Russian hinterland.

However, when the AOK turned to apply these 'proven techniques' elsewhere it faced major obstacles which, if partly the result of technical difficulties, were also symptomatic of the Monarchy's military inferiority. True, the evidence suggests that in its Serbian campaign, although hampered by a lack of Serbo-Croat Intelligence troops, the AOK was quite able to adapt the techniques which had been used against Russia. But on the Italian Front, the type of oral contact which the AOK envisaged was impossible because of the terrain, and the 'secondary method' of spreading written material, even if ingenious ways were explored, tended to founder because the Italian opponents were not receptive enough. The propaganda duel which developed on the Italian Front in 1918 revealed not that the Austrians were less imaginative than the Italians; indeed, many characteristics of Austrian propaganda, such as their newssheets or even their front-line patrols, were an example which the enemy tended to copy. Rather, the Austrian campaign was noticeably limited in its resources and hampered by enemy strengths. The AOK was only too aware that mass distribution from the air would be an asset (it had successfully explored that dimension in the East), but on the Italian Front it was the Allies who controlled the air space. As Padua's manifestos were daily disseminated from the air, the Austrians were persistently reminded of their military inferiority, so that the constant phenomenon of enemy propaganda raining down was perhaps more psychologically destructive than any arguments contained in the leaflets. While the Austrians could never respond in kind from the air, their weakness in oral propaganda also indicates more fundamental problems. It was not simply the terrain which was a barrier, but the growing weakness of their overall campaign when compared to the enemy's. Their arguments across the trenches could rarely match those used by Italy's Czech and Yugoslav propaganda troops. It was the latter who came to dominate 'trench propaganda'. It was also they who confirmed by their results that oral propaganda, the method so favoured by the Austrians, could under the right circumstances be the most effective way of practising front propaganda.

From this one can justifiably infer that, however sophisticated the mechanics of any propaganda machinery, what was most important was the type of material which the propagandists could distribute and its ability to resonate among the target audience. If a consistent 'resonance' occurred, it meant that the propaganda campaign was pushing at an open door, or in other words the weapon could be usefully employed to act as a catalyst upon existing unrest in the enemy camp. In each of the three major campaigns which we have studied, a certain resonance had sounded, but only in those directed against Russia and Austria-Hungary was it consistent and incremental. The arguments which Austria employed against Italy from late 1917 might seem highly suited to the desperate mood after Caporetto when many of the Italian rank and file assumed that the war was over or that Italy's allies were needlessly prolonging it; the Austrians also had extra cards to play in the shape of their peace with Ukraine, or the enticement which went with their occupation of Venetia. Yet after only a few months Austria's propaganda arguments, notably the messages of despair, had lost much of their vitality; a certain Italian remobilization had been achieved while rumours about Austria-Hungary's own domestic instability began to circulate in Italy. With the substantial 'truths' of their propaganda weakened in this way, the Austrians found that the weapon had lost its edge: it could never function effectively as a lone instrument. They could not wield it as on the Eastern Front, where over a period of many months they had played successfully upon the Russian aspirations to peace and land, adding their voice to others like the Bolsheviks who were proclaiming the reality of turmoil in the Russian interior. Instead, as some of the Austrian propagandists always feared, it was their own Empire rather than Italy which increasingly began to assume disintegrating 'Russian characteristics' and prove a suitable target for the propaganda weapon.

The strength of Italy's campaign against Austria-Hungary lay in the degree of resonance which its front propaganda could maintain, playing consistently on a set of mounting grievances in a way wholly reminiscent of the Central Powers' campaign on the Eastern Front. What sharpened Italy's weapon, however, was the fact that it not only exploited pacifist or social discontent but, in Finzi's words, 'spread dissension and mistrust among the various races'.[6] Striking in this way at 'Austria's real weakness', the propaganda campaign used arguments which threatened the very existence of the Habsburg Empire, and did so often from sources within the Monarchy itself. Contrary to one recent view of the phenomenon, here was an example of 'propaganda for foreign consumption' which was indeed closely linked to 'the actual conditions or prevailing sentiments within a given state'.[7] Via the bureau run by Borgese in Switzerland, the Padua Commission was able to secure a steady supply of news thanks to the freer flow of information in Austria-Hungary. Suitable items were then selected for each nationality, the premise being that although the Austro-Hungarian forces had common hopes and anxieties, the troops of different nationality always retained parochial concerns, including their own strong cultural identities. Each might be lured in a particular way: the Poles with news of Galicia and a Catholic slant, the Czechs with evidence of national resistance at home and memories of past martyrdom, the Magyars with pointed remarks about Count Tisza's elitism or suggestions that they were abandoning their own heroic traditions from 1848.

If Padua's arguments about national polarization in the Monarchy were often exaggerated (and assumed too much of a politicized national consciousness in the recipients), they were still firmly rooted in the reality of domestic disintegration, communicating and reinforcing perceptions which were already current. Indeed, the propaganda campaign highlighted for the Habsburg army commanders and many of their troops the ideological struggle in which the Empire was now engaged. Many of those targeted by Padua in the trenches were undoubtedly indifferent in the face of enemy propaganda, just as they were apathetic towards any patriotic instruction from the FAst network. But evidence from the clash of the FAst's instruction with Padua's message shows that both of these 'propagandas' could garner adherents in the Austro-Hungarian army in 1918. Even so, it was the FAst which had the steeper hill to climb. The organization was very much on the defensive, suddenly trying to reinvent an image of the Empire which for many educated soldiers was absent even in 1914, an image also now challenged by obvious realities in the hinterland, where the Habsburg authorities had effectively lost control.

If Italy's front propaganda could mirror developments in the Monarchy fairly faithfully, it was on somewhat shakier ground when it discussed Italian or Allied commitments to the various nationalities. It is true that the presence of the Czechoslovak Legion was a powerful symbol of that commitment, perhaps in itself the single most important piece of Italy's front propaganda. It is also the case that with the depressing or uplifting news of Allied military advances from July 1918, it probably mattered little if Padua's manifestos contained only vague Allied promises for the nationalities' future. Certainly, the basic Allied commitment to the Czechs and Poles was evident in Italy's propaganda and, partly via this medium, such 'morally disturbing information' must have reached many in the Austrian trenches.[8] Even so, official Italy's perpetual ambiguity over the Yugoslav question was important for a number of reasons. To some extent, it hampered the work of the Padua Commission since it soured relations between various employees who queried the type of Yugoslav propaganda which was being issued; these tensions dovetailed with others which owed much to Ugo Ojetti's view that he was running an Italian, not an Allied, campaign. The Yugoslav issue also regularly surfaced to reveal that all was not what it seemed in the Italian or Yugoslav camp in 1918. If many Italians in positions of authority were cynically donning the mask of 'nationality politics' in order to win the war, the evidence from Italy's front propaganda shows that they were right to be rather sceptical about the idea of a burgeoning Yugoslav consciousness in the enemy trenches or territory. The reality was that in 1918 a 'Yugoslav mentality' was not at all as prevalent as some tried to insist (witness Ljudevit Pivko's vain attempts to recruit for his volunteer force among Croats and Slovenes). Those propagandists like Steed or Ojetti who suggested otherwise were trying to shape propaganda far ahead of reality.

At the same time, it is clear that Italy's ambiguous stance could only tarnish its reputation among potential allies and hinder a clearer (even if more idealistic) message in front propaganda. The Yugoslav issue remained Italy's Achilles' heel in the campaign of 1918, one which the Austro-Hungarian authorities might have done a lot more to attack at the front, or at least actively challenge with some domestic propaganda in the Croat and Slovene regions of the Monarchy. As an Achilles' heel, this was an issue similar to that of Germany's annexationist goals in 1917 which had threatened to weaken the viability of the Central Powers' propaganda against Russia. Both cases showed that there could be serious repercussions, both among allies and in the theoretical effectiveness of front propaganda, if the latter tried to perpetuate an image which diverged too far from reality.

Yet under the circumstances, official Italy's ambiguous stance over the Yugoslav question becomes more understandable, being rooted not simply in the Treaty of London but also in certain realities about the concept of a 'Yugoslav nationality'. In assessing both the official Italian and Yugoslav standpoints, we can see that the uneasy interaction of 1918 served as a significant prelude to the bitter clashes between the two sides at the 1919 Paris Peace Conference. The Yugoslavs felt all the more deceived in 1919 when Orlando fully threw off the mask of 'nationality politics', labelled the Croats and Slovenes as enemy peoples, and insisted on the London treaty with its territorial prizes on the eastern Adriatic coast. By June, when he fell from power on a vote of parliamentary confidence having failed in his objectives, Orlando had done much to feed the roots of fascism in Italy and much to sour the relationship with Yugoslavia. In turn, the Yugoslav leaders in 1919 continued to demonstrate many of their wartime weaknesses, including their lack of any firm Allied support for their cause, and those basic ethnic divisions which existed under the 'Yugoslav label'.[9] As a result, after 1919, the hopes of neither Italian or Yugoslav propagandists involved in Padua's campaign became a reality. Those like Borgese or Albertini, who had expected to win Italy a prime place of influence on the ruins of Austria-Hungary, were disillusioned. So were those like Trumbić or Jambrišak, who had proclaimed a Yugoslavia which would be harmoniously united together and closely associated with an Italian ally. The ideals of Italian–Yugoslav friendship or of a Yugoslav utopia had been temporarily propagated in 1918. But both then succumbed to underlying 'realities' when the common danger of Austria-Hungary had disappeared.

If it is doubtful whether Padua's Yugoslav propaganda had much impact (although we have noted the potential in a sample Croat division and some clear results from the flights over Zagreb and Ljubljana), a more taxing question is the overall effect of the campaigns of front propaganda. Could they or did they significantly influence enemy behaviour? The propagandists themselves were, of course, the first to triumph their own success, that front propaganda had helped to 'break Russia' or had caused an 'unprecedented disruption' of the Austro-Hungarian army.[10] More realistically, the evidence suggests that the role of this weapon was to act as a small catalyst upon prevailing moods in the enemy war zone, at times provoking a few desertions, but usually contributing some 'yeast' to a general fermentation which was lowering morale. The overriding factors which determined the state of morale in the Austro-Hungarian trenches were the food and material situation; the cohesion and camaraderie within each military unit as part of a hierarchical structure; the relationship with life in the hinterland; and the overall perception of whether the war was worth fighting. While a combination of these determined the behaviour of individuals or military units, enemy propaganda can only ever be viewed as a secondary, extra ingredient.

Even so, it is clear that 'trench propaganda', by patrols on the Italian or Eastern Fronts, did have a strong psychological impact when in the right hands, besides also producing valuable Intelligence benefits. When Czech soldiers were found to be serving in the front line against their co-nationals in the Habsburg forces, the underlying reason why the Monarchy was waging war was directly challenged. The Austrian military's attempts to weaken the impact of such Czech forces, though sometimes quite ingenious, increasingly backfired because Czech propaganda from outside the Monarchy had a strong resonance in Bohemia-Moravia. Czech soldiers in the Austrian trenches gradually learnt of nationalist agitation in front of them and behind them, and this certainly influenced the behaviour of some individuals (even if many only challenged Habsburg authority in the final days of the war).

In contrast, the actual effect of Padua's manifestos is far more difficult to gauge. We have seen that the potential to persuade was most promising because Padua was skilfully utilizing the Monarchy's press and trying to invade a 'news quarantine' in the Austrian war zone. It supplied not just slogans to the various nationalities, but accurate items of news which dovetailed neatly with rumours reaching the war zone from the hinterland. For those who were politically minded, Padua's material might fill an information vacuum which FAst material was unable to handle; all the more so since, in contrast to Allied armies, there appear to have been few 'trench newspapers', composed by the soldiers themselves, which did not stem from official Austrian sources. Padua's propaganda was also carefully tailored to meet the supposed outlook of each nationality, here again gaining its potency from the news sources it used from the

Monarchy. In this way, and by employing 'national delegates' at Padua, the manifestos to some extent avoided propagating simple nationalist stereotypes. Not that the latter were wholly absent: but alongside material which was short, crude and colourful, there were messages which tried to appeal more deeply to an historic 'national patriotism'. For many soldiers these arguments were still perhaps too sophisticated (or idealistic in the Yugoslav case), especially since they were rarely pictorial and usually in written form. Indeed, in questioning the direct effects of the leaflet propaganda upon troop morale, one can never ignore the major practical obstacles which always existed. One was illiteracy, another was the basic problem of matching a leaflet's language to the recipient's; finally, there was the issue of whether those who read a leaflet would give its arguments any serious consideration anyway. In view of this, it is difficult to ascribe to Padua's manifestos more than a minor role of persuasion in the Austro-Hungarian trenches.

Yet it has been argued in this study that the phenomenon of front propaganda is still important in itself for what it reveals about the perceptions of those who wielded it. The Italian military anticipated definite results, the Austrian military feared them: on both sides, there were many who believed at the time that the new weapon was having a dangerous impact. Moreover, by viewing the Habsburg Empire through the prism of front propaganda we can draw some clear conclusions as to why the Monarchy collapsed in 1918. The 'primary reason' was internal. During the war, the Austro-Hungarian authorities lost the battle for hearts and minds to those who believed in new state structures and new forms of government. Not only did the Empire fail to propagate its own *raison d'être* sufficiently. Even if it had done so, the evidence suggests that its own propaganda would have been wholly inadequate and ill-matched to deal with the many unresolved political and national issues from the prewar period. These issues festered increasingly during the war, exacerbated by war-weariness and the critical food situation. They formed the essential domestic basis which enabled outside forces, the 'secondary reason', to contribute to the Monarchy's dissolution. Whether in the shape of Allied pronouncements (such as recognition of the Czechoslovaks as allies), or through the work of Czech legionaries on the Italian Front, these external influences had the effect of spurring on domestic nationalists, so that they made crucial moves away from the Empire at an opportune moment, when it was clear that the war was lost. Only in this way might one agree with Henry Wickham Steed's 'modest' conclusion: on 29 October 1918, he told the EPD that Allied propaganda 'could claim credit not for the actual breaking up, but for very materially accelerating the break-up of Austria'.[11] But even this statement seems excessive. At best it can be said that the undermining of Austria-Hungary depended on a consistent interaction between internal and external factors, but the decisive ones were domestic.

In this process, front propaganda had only a small role to play. Yet because it was often impossible to verify rumours, the stories about Russia's collapse, about Lord Northcliffe's appointment or the Czechoslovak Legion, combined to give 'enemy propaganda' a mythical quality even before the war had ended. Any reality about the phenomenon was thus quickly engulfed in a myth, a propaganda of its own. This could then be nurtured after the war, used by Czech nationalists or Hitler for example, to support different interpretations of the wartime experience. It ensured that front propaganda, as a tried and tested weapon, would be resurrected and wielded in all successive conflicts of the twentieth century.

## Notes

1. Antoni Szuber, *Walka o Przewagę Duchową. Kampanja Propagandowa Koalicji 1914–1918* (Warsaw, 1933) p. ix.
2. See Steed, *Through Thirty Years*, II, p. 208.
3. For example, KA, FAst 1918, Fasz.5994, Res.89, minutes of AOK meeting to discuss front propaganda, 26 April 1918.
4. Ludwig Windischgrätz, *Helden und Halunken. Selbsterlebte Weltgeschichte* (Vienna, Munich and Zurich, 1965) pp. 134–5.
5. Finzi, '*I.T.O.*', p. 140.
6. Ibid., p. 119.
7. Cf. Aviel Roshwald and Richard Stites (eds), *European Culture in the Great War: The Arts, Entertainment and Propaganda, 1914–1918* (Cambridge, 1999) p. 350.
8. Cf. István Deák, *Beyond Nationalism: A Social and Political History of the Habsburg Officer Corps, 1848–1918* (Oxford and New York, 1992) p. 200.
9. See Andrej Mitrović, *Jugoslavija na Konferenciji Mira 1919–1920* (Belgrade, 1969); René Albrecht-Carrie, *Italy at the Paris Peace Conference* (New York, 1966 reprint).
10. Szuber, *Walka o Przewagą Duchowę*, p. 104.
11. BL, Northcliffe MSS, vol.X, Add.Mss 62162, Minutes of 14th EPD Committee meeting, 29 October 1918. To be precise, Steed made this claim on behalf of 'Crewe House', not 'Allied propaganda'.

# Appendix: Manifestos Issued by the Padua Commission, May–November 1918

This appendix lists all the leaflets written by the Padua Commission during its seven-month existence which have been discovered in archives in Vienna, Budapest, Zagreb, Prague and London. Those marked with an asterisk (*) have been located only in Antoni Szuber's work. Manifestos with more than one language in the same leaflet are indicated thus: C/Cz; otherwise the leaflets were issued separately in different languages (with some occasionally issued on the obverse and reverse of a single sheet). The spelling of the titles has been left as in the original.

| Language Key: | *C* | *Croat* | *P* | *Polish* |
|---|---|---|---|---|
| | *Cz* | *Czech* | *R* | *Romanian* |
| | *G* | *German* | *S* | *Serb* [*Cyrillic*] |
| | *I* | *Italian* | *Sl* | *Slovene* |
| | *M* | *Magyar* | *U* | *Ukrainian* |

| | | |
|---|---|---|
| 1. | Hrvati, Srbi i Slovenci! | *C* |
| 2. | Polacy! | *P* |
| 3. | *Unlocated* | |
| 4. | Srbi, Hrvati i Slovenci! | *C* |
| 5. | *Unlocated* | |
| 6. | Mândre catane Române! | *R* |
| 7. | Vojáci Rakousko-Uherska! | *Cz C G M P R* |
| 8. | [Title unknown]* | *Cz C G M P R* |
| 9. | Drazi bratři Čechoslováci! | *Cz* |
| 10. | Polacy! | *P* |
| 11. | Krajané Čechoslováci! | *Cz* |
| 12. | Legioniści polscy! | *P* |
| 13. | *Unlocated* | |
| 14. | *Unlocated* | |
| 15. | Vojíni Čechoslováci, Poláci... | *Cz C P R* |
| 16. | Hrvati, Srbi i Slovenci! | *C* |
| 17. | Jugosloveni! Draga braćo Srbi, Hrvati i Slovenci! | *C* |
| 18. | Bitka na zapadnom frontu! | *C* |
| 19. | *Jugoslavija* (no. 1) | *C* |
| 20. | Soldaten der deutschen und magyarischen Nazionalität | *G* |
| 21. | *Československá Samostatnost* (no. 1) | *Cz* |
| 22. | *Neamul Românesc* (no. 1) | *R* |
| 23. | *Polak* (no. 1) | *P* |
| 24. | *Unlocated* | |

| | | |
|---|---|---|
| 25. | Polacy! | *P* |
| 26. | Srbi, Hrvati i Slovenci! | *C* |
| 27. | Bratri Čechoslováci! | *Cz* |
| 28. | Polacy! | *P* |
| 29. | Hrvati, Srbi i Slovenci! | *C* |
| 30. | Čechové a Slováci! | *Cz* |
| 31. | Polacy! | *P* |
| 32. | Soldaţi romani! | *R* |
| 33. | *Jugoslavija* (no. 2) | *C* |
| 34. | *Československá Samostatnost* (no. 2) | *Cz* |
| 35. | *Polak* (no. 2) | *P* |
| 36. | *Neamul Românesc* (no. 2) | *R* |
| 37. | Srbi, Hrvati i Slovenci! | *C/P* |
| 38. | Gospodarska važnost jugoslovanske deklaracije | *Sl* |
| 39. | Srbi, Hrvati i Slovenci! | *C* |
| 40. | Żołnierzu Polaku! | *P* |
| 41. | Magyar Katonák! | *M* |
| 42. | Legioniści polscy! | *P* |
| 43. | Żołnierze – Polacy, Legioniści! | *P* |
| 44. | *Polak* (no. 3) | *P* |
| 45. | *Jugoslavija* (no. 3) | *C* |
| 46. | *Neamul Românesc* (no. 3) | *R* |
| 47. | *Unlocated* | |
| 48. | Bratři! Češi! Slováci! | *Cz* |
| 49. | *Československá Samostatnost* (no. 3) | *Cz* |
| 50. | Srbi, Hrvati i Slovenci! | *C* |
| 51. | Polacy! | *P* |
| 52. | Bratři Češi a Slováci! | *Cz* |
| 53. | Polacy! | *P* |
| 54. | Mândre catane române! | *R* |
| 55. | Österreichische Soldaten! | *G* |
| 56. | Srbi, Hrvati i Slovenci! | *C* |
| 57. | Srbi, Hrvati i Slovenci! | *C* |
| 58. | Polacy! | *P* |
| 59. | Polacy! | *P* |
| 60. | Polacy! | *P* |
| 61. | Polacy! | *P* |
| 62. | Bracia żołnierze! | *P* |
| 63. | *Unlocated* | |
| 64. | *Unlocated* | |
| 65. | Polacy! | *P* |
| 66. | Národní Listy rakouskou vládou zastaveny | *Cz* |
| 67. | Z 13. čísla Československé Samostatnosti | *Cz* |
| 68. | Österreichischer Begriff von Hochverrat | *G* |
| 69. | *Unlocated* | |
| 70. | Österreichische Soldaten! | *G* |
| [71–3 | *Unlocated*] | |
| 74. | *Jugoslavija* (no. 4) | *C* |
| 75. | *Neamul Românesc* (no. 4) | *R* |

76. *Polak* (no. 4) *P*
77. *Československá Samostatnost* (no. 4) *Cz*
78. Prehlidka československého vojska J.V. králem *Cz I*
79. Az olaszok elsülyesztették két nagy... hadihajot *G M*
80. Československé vojsko uznáno anglickou vládou *Cz*
81. Unutrašnje prilike u Austriji *C*
82. Polacy z pod zaboru austyackiego w opozycyi *P*
83. Representanţii Societţilor ungureşti din America *R*
84. Opozycya Polaków zaostrza przesilenie wewnętrzne *P*
85. Jugoslovenski pokret *C*
86. Politia militar nemţeasc din Romania *R*
87. Československé vojsko na pochodu do Vladivostoku *Cz*
88. Ukraïn'cï! *U*
89. Magyar Katonák! Miért harcoltok ti? *M*
90. Srbi, Hrvati, Slovenci! *C Sl*
91. Polacy! Za kogo walczycie? *P U*
92. Čechové a Slováci, položili jste si otázku *Cz*
93. Mândri ostaşi români! *R*
94. Ostaşi români! *R*
95. Mndri ostaşi români! *R*
96. Derék magyar katonák!... *M*
97. Klamstwa niemieckiej prasy *P*
98. Talijanski demokrate iredentiste *C/Cz/I/Sl*
99. Srbi, Hrvati, Slovenci! *C Cz G I M P R U*
100. Nic jim nevěřte! *Cz*
101. Njegovoj ekselenciji maršalu Svetozaru Borojeviću *C*
[102–7 *Unlocated*]
108. Češi a Slováci! *Cz G I M P R Sl*
109. Itt nyugszik Magyarország *M*
110. Srbi, Hrvati i Slovenci! *C*
111. Zatím co na frontě čěsti... *Cz*
112. *Polak* (no. 5) *P*
113. *Československá Samostatnost* (no. 5) *Cz*
114. *Neamul Românesc* (no. 5) *R*
115. *Jugoslavija* (no. 5) *C*
116. Derék Magyar Katonák! *M*
117. Magyar honfiak-Katonák! *M*
118. Srbi, Hrvati i Slovenci! *C*
119. Srbi, Hrvati i Slovenci! *C*
120. *Unlocated*
121. Soldaten! *G*
122. *Unlocated*
123. *Unlocated*
124. Češko-slovački bataljon u bitci kod Fossette *C/Cz/P/R*
125. Nachrichten über den Hunger in Oesterreich-Ungarn *C Cz G I P R*
126. Magyar Katonák! *M*
127. *Unlocated*
128. Wiener! *G*
129. Es ist nicht wahr *G*

| | |
|---|---|
| 130. In questo mattino d'agusto... | *I* |
| 131. Necht' Vás posílí na velkého mučedníka M.Jana Husa! | *Cz* |
| 132. *Unlocated* | |
| 133. A magyar képviselöház ülése | *M* |
| 134. *Polak* (no. 6) | *P* |
| 135. *Jugoslavija* (no. 6) | *C/S/Sl* |
| 136. *Neamul Românesc* (no. 6) | *R* |
| 137. *Československá Samostatnost* (no. 6) | *Cz* |
| 138. Polacy! | *P* |
| 139. Češi a Slováci! | *C/Cz* |
| 140. Polacy! | *P* |
| 141. Polacy! / Ukraïn'cï! | *P/U* |
| 142. Bezumne optužbe austriske o rdjavom postupanju | *C/Cz/P/R* |
| 143. Głód w Austryi | *P R* |
| 144. *Unlocated* | |
| 145. Magyar katonák! | *M* |
| 146. Magyar katonák! | *M* |
| 147. Soldaţi Români! | *R* |
| 148. Die erste Millionen amerikanischer Soldaten | *G* |
| 149. Prvi miljon amerikanskih vojakov | *Sl* |
| 150. Uriaşele pregtiri de rzboi ale Americii | *R* |
| 151. Milion żołnierzy amerykańskich | *P* |
| 152. Polacy! | *P* |
| 153. Ukraïn'cï! | *U* |
| 154. Srbi, Hrvati i Slovenci! | *C* |
| 155. Soldaten! Die Folgen des neuen Bündnisses... | *G* |
| 156. *Neamul Românesc* (no. 7) | *R* |
| 157. *Polak* (no. 7) | *P* |
| 158. *Jugoslavija* (no. 7) | *C* |
| 159. *Československá Samostatnost* (no. 7) | *Cz* |
| 160. Polacy! | *P* |
| 161. Magyar katonák! | *M* |
| 162. Soldaţi români! | *R* |
| 163. Jugosloveni! | *C Cz* |
| 164. Ohromné válečné přípravy výkony | *Cz* |
| 165. Magyar katonák! | *M* |
| 166. Magyar katonák! | *M* |
| 167. Polacy! | *P* |
| 168. Jugosloveni! | *C* |
| 169. Kosovo! | *S* |
| 170. Soldaten! Zehntausende von euren Brüdern... | *G* |
| 171. Magyar halál az olasz frontón | *M* |
| 172. Magyar katonák! | *M* |
| 173. Jaký dojem v Rakousku vyvolalo přiznání | *Cz* |
| 174. Oriási hadikészülödés Amerikában | *M* |
| 175. Soldaţi români! | *R* |
| 176. *Neamul Românesc* (no. 8) | *R* |
| 177. *Polak* (no. 8) | *P* |
| 178. *Československá Samostatnost* (no. 8) | *Cz* |

| | | |
|---|---|---|
| 179. | *Jugoslavija* (no. 8) | *C* |
| 180. | Interpelláció az olasz offenziváról... | *M* |
| 181. | Soldaţi români! | *R* |
| 182. | ? Soldaţi români! | *R* |
| 183. | Srbi, Hrvati i Slovenci! | *C* |
| 184. | Srbi, Hrvati i Slovenci! | *C* |
| 185. | *Unlocated* | |
| 186. | Polacy! | *P* |
| 187. | Polacy! Prezydent miasta Krakowa... | *P* |
| 188. | *Unlocated* | |
| 189. | Żołnierze! | *P* |
| 190. | Sonderfriedensgerüchte und Sonderfriedenstatsachen | *G* |
| 191. | Soldaţi români! | *R* |
| 192. | Soldaţi români! | *R* |
| 193. | Jak Niemcy prześladują lud polski | *P* |
| 194. | Polacy! Wiecie, że wasi bracia z Brazylji...* | *P* |
| 195. | Polacy! | *P* |
| 196. | *Unlocated* | |
| 197. | Válka a Hlad | *Cz M P R* |
| 198. | Polacy! | *P* |
| 199. | Uslovi mira Sila Sporazuma | *C Cz G I M P R U* |
| 200. | Polacy! | *P* |
| 201. | Polacy! | *P* |
| 202. | Denkt über folgende drei tatsachen nach... | *G* |
| 203. | *Jugoslavija* | *C/Sl* |
| 204. | Polacy! | *P* |
| 205. | Polacy! | *P* |
| 206. | Soldaţi Români! | *R* |
| 207. | *Polak* (no. 9) | *P* |
| 208. | *Jugoslavija* (no. 9) | *C/Sl* |
| 209. | *Neamul Românesc* (no. 9) | *R* |
| 210. | *Československá Samostatnost* (no. 9) | *Cz* |
| 211. | Polacy! | *P* |
| 212. | Srbi, Hrvati i Slovenci! | *C* |
| 213. | Soldaţi români! | *R* |
| 214. | Češi a Slováci! | *Cz* |
| 215. | Magyar Katonák! | *M* |
| 216. | Magyar Katonák! | *M* |
| 217. | Polacy! | *P* |
| 218. | Bracia Polacy z Galicyi! | *P* |
| 219. | Soldaten! Der deutsche Staatssekretär... | *G* |
| 220. | Srbi, Hrvati i Slovenci! | *C* |
| 221. | Polacy! | *P* |
| 222. | Polacy! | *P* |
| 223. | Slovenci, Hrvati in Srbi! | *Sl* |
| 224. | Krajané, bratři! | *Cz* |
| 225. | Jugosloveni! | *C* |
| 226. | Soldaţi români! | *R* |
| 227. | Soldaţi Români! | *R* |

| | | |
|---|---|---|
| 228. | wer ist diese hässliche und schmutzige Hexe | *G* |
| 229. | Bratři Češi a Slováci! | *Cz* |
| 230. | *Unlocated* | |
| 231. | Zołnierze Polacy! | *P* |
| 232. | Bezumne optužbe austriske o rdjavom postupanju | *C/Cz/P/R* |
| 233. | *Unlocated* | |
| 234. | Magyar Katonák! | *G M* |
| 235. | *Jugoslavija* (no. 10) | *C/Sl* |
| 236. | *Polak* (no. 10) | *P* |
| 237. | *Československá Samostatnost* (no. 10) | *Cz* |
| 238. | *Neamul Românesc* (no. 10) | *R* |
| 239. | Zhovnïri-Ukraïn'skii Narode! | *U* |
| 240. | Polacy! | *P* |
| 241. | Gróf Tiszáról van szó! | *M* |
| 242. | Magyar Katonák! | *M* |
| 243. | Bratři! Bratři! | *Cz* |
| 244. | Żołnierze – Ludu Polski! | *P* |
| 245. | Żołnierze – Polacy! Powiedzcie, dlaczego? | *P* |
| 246. | Polacy! | *P* |
| 247. | Soldaţi Români! | *R* |
| 248. | [Serb leaflet]* | *S* |
| 249. | Magyar Katonák! | *M* |
| 250. | Szegény lelkivaksággal megvert magyarok! | *M* |
| 251. | Ojciec Święty dla Polski | *P* |
| 252. | Soldaten, die ihr für Deutschland... kämpft | *G M R* |
| 253. | *Unlocated* | |
| 254. | Magyar Katonák! | *M* |
| 255. | Magyar katonák! | *M* |
| 256. | *Unlocated* | |
| 257. | *Československá Samostatnost* (no. 11) | *Cz* |
| 258. | *Jugoslavija* (no. 11) | *C/Sl* |
| 259. | *Polak* (no. 11) | *P* |
| 260. | *Neamul Românesc* (no. 11) | *R* |
| 261. | Magyar Katonák! | *M* |
| 262. | Polacy! | *P* |
| 263. | Magyar Katonák! | *M* |
| 264. | Magyar Katonák! | *M* |
| 265. | Modlitwa uciśnionych synow Polski | *P* |
| 266. | *Unlocated* | |
| 267. | Srbi, Hrvati i Slovenci! | *C* |
| 268. | *Unlocated* | |
| 269. | Was alles Amerika beiträgt | *G I P U* |
| 270. | Magyar Katonák! | *M* |
| 271. | *Unlocated* | |
| 272. | Polacy! | *P* |
| 273. | *Polak* (no. 12) | *P* |
| 274. | *Československá Samostatnost* (no. 12) | *Cz* |
| 275. | *Jugoslavija* (no. 12) | *C/Sl* |
| 276. | *Neamul Românesc* (no. 12) | *R* |

277. Soldaţi români! *R*
278. Austria-Magyarország Katonái! *M*
279. Polacy* *P*
280. Co czyni Ameryka dla *P*
281. Polacy! *P*
282. Magyar Katonák! *M*
283. Polacy! *P*
284. *Unlocated*
285. 'Delenda Austria!' *Cz G I M P U*
286. Österreichisch-ungarische Soldaten! *G Cz M P R Sl*
287. Soldaţi români! *R*
288. Magyar Katonák! *M*
289. *Československá Samostatnost* (no. 13) *Cz*
290. *Neamul Românesc* (no. 13) *R*
291. *Jugoslavija* (no. 13) *C/Sl*
292. *Polak* (no. 13) *P*
293. Polacy! *P*
294. Polacy! *P*
295. Srbi, Hrvati i Slovenci! *C*
296. Srbi, Hrvati i Slovenci! *C*
297. Válečné cíle rakouských Němců *Cz*
298. *Unlocated*
299. *Unlocated*
300. Vzešlý již dnové odplaty strašné... *Cz*
301. ? Magyar Katonák! *M*
302. Magyar Katonák! *M*
303. Magyar Katonák! *M*
304. Srbi, Hrvati i Slovenci! *C*
305. Soldaţi Români! *R*
306. *Unlocated*
307. Żołnierze Polacy! *P*
308. Srbi, Hrvati i Slovenci! *C*
309. *Jugoslavija* (no. 14) *C/Sl*
310. *Polak* (no. 14) *P*
311. *Neamul Românesc* (no. 14) *R*
312. *Československá Samostatnost* (no. 14) *Cz*
313. Srbi, Hrvati i Slovenci! *C*
314. Slovenci, Hrvati in Srbi! *Sl*
315. Srbi, Hrvati i Slovenci! *C G I M R*
316. *Unlocated*
317. Soldaten! Das Lied klingt aus *G*
318. Slovenci, Hrvati in Srbi! *Sl*
319. Żołnierze-Polacy! *P U*
320. Magyar Katonák! *M*
321. *Unlocated*
322. Żołnierze-Polacy! *P*
323. Glad *C Cz*
324. Češi a Slováci! *Cz*
325. ? *Jugoslavija* (no. 15) *C/Sl*

| | | |
|---|---|---|
| 326. | ? *Polak* (no. 15) | *P* |
| 327. | ? *Československá Samostatnost* (no. 15) | *Cz* |
| 328. | ? *Neamul Românesc* (no. 15) | *R* |
| 329. | *Unlocated* | |
| 330. | Graphischer Aufriss der grossen Entent-Offensive | *C G M* |
| 331. | Vojnici Austro-Ugarske | *C G M P* |
| 332. | Miliardy, Miliardy...* | *P* |
| [333–5 | *Unlocated*] | |
| 336. | Zapadni front. Pregledna karta bitke u Flandriji | *C Cz R* |
| 337. | *Unlocated* | |
| 338. | Polacy! | *P* |
| 339. | [Czech leaflet]* | *Cz* |
| 340. | *Unlocated* | |
| 341. | *Čechové a Slováci!* | *Cz I P R* |
| 342. | ? *Jugoslavija* (no. 16) | *C/Sl* |
| 343. | ? *Polak* (no. 16) | *P* |
| 344. | ? *Československá Samostatnost* (no. 16) | *Cz* |
| 345. | ? *Neamul Românesc* (no. 16) | *R* |
| [346–51 | *Unlocated*] | |
| 352. | Magyarok! | *M* |
| 353. | Ludendorff und Wilson | *G* |
| 354. | Vojáci rakousko-uherští! | *Cz* |
| [355–9 | *Unlocated*] | |
| 360. | Vitězství Spojenců u Saint Mihiel | *Cz G* |
| 361. | 4 Millionen Amerikaner | *G P* |
| 362. | *Jugoslavija* (no. 17) | *C/Sl* |
| 363. | *Polak* (no. 17) | *P* |
| 364. | *Československá Samostatnost* (no. 17) | *Cz* |
| 365. | *Neamul Românesc* (no. 17) | *R* |
| 366. | Magyar Katonák! | *M* |
| 367. | Polacy!* | *P* |
| 368. | Lloyd George o výkonech československého vojska* | *Cz* |
| 369. | *Unlocated* | |
| 370. | Austria-Magiarország háboru-adosságai | *M* |
| [371–4 | *Unlocated*] | |
| 375. | Srbi, Hrvati i Slovenci | *C* |
| 376. | Také Japonsko uznává samostatnost | *Cz* |
| [377–9 | *Unlocated*] | |
| 380. | Polacy! Ważne oświadczenia w sprawie polskiej* | *P* |
| 381. | ? *Jugoslavija* (no. 18) | *C/Sl* |
| 382. | ? *Polak* (no. 18) | *P* |
| 383. | ? *Československá Samostatnost* (no. 18) | *Cz* |
| 384. | ? *Neamul Românesc* (no. 18) | *R* |
| 385. | Hodina míru dosud neudeřila | *Cz* |
| 386. | Polacy* | *P* |
| [387–9 | *Unlocated*] | |
| 390a. | Soldaţi Români! | *R* |
| 390b. | Soldaţi Români! | *R* |
| 391a. | Slovenci, Hrvati in Srbi! | *Sl* |

| | | |
|---|---|---|
| 391b. | Slovenci, Hrvati in Srbi! | *Sl* |
| [392–5 | *Unlocated*] | |
| 396. | Srbi, Hrvati i Slovenci | *C S Sl* |
| 397. | *Unlocated* | |
| 398. | *Unlocated* | |
| 399. | Bugarska kapitulacija | *C* |
| 400. | Soldaţi Români! | *R* |
| 401. | Turecká fronta v Palestyně | *Cz* |
| 402. | Nové porážky německé ve Francii | *Cz* |
| 403. | Mięknie i rozsypuje się w drazgi centralny blok* | *P* |
| 404. | Bulharsko přijalo podmínky Dohody | *Cz* |
| 405. | Magyar Katonák! | *M* |
| 406. | Soldaţi Români! | *R* |
| 407. | *Unlocated* | |
| 408. | *Polak* (no. 19) | *P* |
| 409. | *Československá Samostatnost* (no. 19) | *Cz* |
| 410. | *Neamul Românesc* (no. 19) | *R* |
| 411. | *Jugoslavija* (no. 19) | *C/S/Sl* |
| [412–7 | *Unlocated*] | |
| 418. | Soldaten! | *G* |
| 419. | *Unlocated* | |
| 420. | Poselství prof. Masaryka československému vojsku | *Cz* |
| 421. | *Unlocated* | |
| 422. | Az Antant győzelmei Szakadatlanul folytatod... | *M* |
| 423. | Deutsches Volk! Die zwölfte Stunde schlägt! | *G* |
| 424. | Magyar Katonák! | *M* |
| 425. | *Jugoslavija* (no. 20) | *C/Sl* |
| 426. | *Polak* (no. 20) | *P* |
| 427. | *Československá Samostatnost* (no. 20) | *Cz* |
| 428. | *Neamul Românesc* (no. 20) | *R* |
| 429. | *Unlocated* | |
| 430. | *Unlocated* | |
| 431. | KRIEG ODER FRIEDEN? | *Cz G R* |
| 432. | *Unlocated* | |
| 433. | *Unlocated* | |
| 434. | 'Den Besiegten muss man nur die Augen lassen...' | *G* |
| 435. | *Unlocated* | |
| 436. | Österreichisch-ungarische Soldaten! | *G* |
| [437–8 | *Unlocated*] | |
| 439. | Srbi, Hrvati i Slovenci!* | *S* |
| [440–53 | *Unlocated*] | |
| 454. | Magyar Katonák! | *M* |
| 455. | Soldaten! | *G R* |
| [456–85 | *Unlocated*] | |
| 486. | Trpěti a umírati! Proč? | *Cz* |
| 487. | Österreichisch-ungarische Soldaten! | *G* |
| [488–91 | *Unlocated*] | |
| 492. | Das Ende! | *G* |

# Bibliography

## A Primary sources

### I Archives

#### *1 Austria (Vienna)*

ÖSTERREICHISCHES STAATSARCHIV, KRIEGSARCHIV (KA – War Archives)
*Army High Command* (AOK)
Evidenzbüro (EvB)
Feindespropaganda-Abwehrstelle (FAst)
Operations Section (Op.Abt)
Verbindungsoffizier Oberost, 1917

*Army, Corps and Divisional Command records*
Heeresgruppekommando Conrad (HGK Conrad)
2nd Army Command (2AK)
Isonzo Army Command (KISA)
6th Army Command (6AK)
10th Army Command (10AK)
11th Army Command (11AK)
6th Corps Command (VI KK)
10th Corps Command (X KK)
13th Corps Command (XIII KK)
36th Divisional Command and Court records (36ID)

*Other records*
Flugzettel Sammlung
Militärkanzlei Seiner Majestät (MKSM)
Zensurstelle Feldkirch

ALLGEMEINES VERWALTUNGSARCHIV (AVA)
Ministry of Interior files

HAUS-HOF-UND STAATSARCHIV (HHStA)
Politisches Archiv I, XL

#### *2 Croatia (Zagreb)*

ARHIV HRVATSKE (AHZ – Croatian States Archives)
Mirko Beloševič MSS (789)
Maximilian Csicserics MSS (792)
Julije Gazzari MSS (798)
Stjepan Sarkotić MSS
Ratni Arhiv (477)
42. Domobranska Pješadijska Divizija, 1916–18 (482)
Propaganda leaflet collection (907)

ARHIV JUGOSLAVENSKE AKADEMIJE ZNANOSTI I UMJETNOSTI (AJA – Archive of the Yugoslav Academy)
Arhiv Jugoslavenskog Odbora (JO – Yugoslav Committee):
America (1); Czechoslovaks (24); England (2); France (31); Milivoj Jambrišak, Yugoslav Committee in Rome (35); Ante Mandić (8); Miscellaneous reports (136); Northcliffe (85); Paris Congress (46); Prisoners in Italy (59); Propaganda leaflets (111); Rome Congress (19); Henry Wickham Steed (9); Dinko Trinajstić (84); Ante Trumbić (60, 76); Volunteer question in Italy (28); Yugoslav Committee in Paris (27)

## 3 *Czech Republic (Prague)*

ARCHÍV NÁRODNÍHO MUZEA (ANM – Archive of the National Museum)
František Hlaváček MSS

VOJENSKÝ HISTORICKÝ ARCHÍV (VHA – Military History Archive)
Czechoslovak National Council papers (ČSNR)
Propaganda leaflets 1915–18
Records of the 39th Regiment
Lev Sychrava MSS

## 4 *Great Britain*

BRITISH LIBRARY London (BL)
Northcliffe MSS

CHURCHILL COLLEGE Cambridge (CCC)
Earl of Cavan MSS
Maurice Hankey MSS
Henry Rawlinson MSS

HOUSE OF LORDS RECORD OFFICE (HLRO)
Beaverbrook MSS
Lloyd George MSS

IMPERIAL WAR MUSEUM London (IWM)
Charles Delmé-Radcliffe: diary and papers (DRP)
L.I.L. Ferguson MSS
F.C. Pritchard MSS
L.A.E. Price-Davies MSS
V.G. Ricketts MSS
Campbell Stuart MSS
Henry Wilson MSS
Propaganda leaflet collection (1914–18)

PUBLIC RECORDS OFFICE London (PRO)

| | |
|---|---|
| Admiralty Files (ADM) | 137 |
| Air Ministry Files (AIR) | |
| Foreign Office Files (FO) | 170 – Consular |
| | 371 – Political |
| | 383 – Prisoners |
| | 395 – News, Miscellaneous |
| | 800 – Balfour MSS |
| War Cabinet Files (CAB) | |
| War Office Files (WO) | 79, 106, 157, 158 |

School of Slavonic and East European Studies London (SSEES)
R.W. Seton-Watson MSS (SWP)

The Times Archive London (TTA)
W.K. McClure MSS
Northcliffe MSS
Henry Wickham Steed MSS

### 5 *Hungary (Budapest)*

Hadtörténeti Intézet és Levéltár (HIL – Hungarian Military Archives)
Army and Divisional Command records: KISA, 6AK, 42HID, IR25.
Hadifelügyeleti Bizottság (HFB – War Surveillance Commission)
Honvéd Ministerium (1918)
'Propaganda Anyag'
Szeged and Miskolc court martial records

Országos Hadtörténeti Múzeum (OHM – National Military History Museum)
Propaganda leaflet collection

### 6 *Italy (Padua)*

Archivio di Stato di Padova (State Archives)
Gabinetto Prefettura

## II Newspapers and journals

*Bosnische Post* (Sarajevo)
*Corriere della Sera* (Milan)
*Glas Slovenaca Hrvata i Srba* (Zagreb)
*Hrvatska* (Zagreb)
*Neue Freie Presse* (Vienna)
*The New Europe* (London)
*Österreichische Wehrzeitung* (Vienna)
*Pester Lloyd* (Budapest)
*The Times* (London)

## III Official documents and government publications

Browder, Robert and Kerensky, Alexander (eds), *The Russian Provisional Government 1917: Documents*, 3 vols (Stanford, 1961).

Challener, Richard D. (ed.), *United States Military Intelligence 1917–1927*, vols 1–5 (New York and London, 1978).

Comando Supremo of the Royal Italian Army, *The Battle of the Piave, June 15–23 1918* (London, 1921).

Komjáthy, Miklós (ed.), *Protokolle des Gemeinsamen Ministerrates der Österreichisch-Ungarischen Monarchie 1914–1918* (Budapest, 1966).

Janković, Dragoslav and Krizman, Bogdan (eds), *Gradja o Stvaranju Jugoslavenske Države*, 2 vols (Belgrade, 1964).

Ludendorff, Erich (ed.), *Urkunden des Obersten Heeresleitung über ihre Tätigkeit 1916–18* (Berlin, 1922).

*Papers relating to the Foreign Relations of the United States 1918. Supplement 1. The World War*, vol. 1 (Washington, 1933).

*Papers relating to the Foreign Relations of the United States. The Lansing Papers 1914–1920*, vol. 2 (Washington, 1940).
*Relazione della Commissione d'Inchiesta. Dall'Isonzo al Piave, 24 Ottobre–9 Novembre, 1917*, 2 vols (Rome, 1919).
*Stenographische Protokolle über die Sitzungen des Hauses der Abgeordneten des Österreichischen Reichsrates*, XXII Session, vols 4–5 (Vienna, 1918).
Zeman, Z.A.B., *Germany and the Revolution in Russia 1915–1918: Documents from the Archives of the German Foreign Ministry* (Oxford, 1958).

## IV Published letters, diaries and contemporary writings

Albertini, Luigi, *Epistolario 1911–1926*, ed. Ottavio Barie, 3 vols (Verona, 1968).
Alessi, Rino, *Dall'Isonzo al Piave. Lettere Clandestine di un Corrispondente di Guerra*, ed. Arnoldo Mondadori (Milan, 1966).
Amendola, G., Borgese, G.A., Ojetti, U. and Torre, A., *Il Patto di Roma* (Rome, 1919).
Barac, Franjo (ed.), *Croats and Slovenes – Friends of the Entente in the World War* (Paris, 1919).
Bissolati, Leonida, *Diario di Guerra*, ed. G. Einaudi (Turin, 1935).
Bocou, Sévère, *Les Legions Roumaines de Transylvanie. L'Irrédentisme Roumain* (Paris, 1918).
Goldsmid, C.H., *Diary of a Liaison Officer in Italy in 1918* (London, 1920).
Kafka, Franz, *The Diaries of Franz Kafka 1910–1923*, ed. Max Brod (Penguin, 1972).
Korošec, Anton, *Les Yougoslaves et la Conférence de Brest-Litovsk* (Geneva, 1918).
Malagodi, Olindo, *Conversazioni della Guerra 1914–1919*, ed. B. Vigezzi, 2 vols (Milan, 1960).
Ojetti, Ugo, *Lettere alla Moglie 1915–1919*, ed. Fernanda Ojetti (Florence, 1964).
Kobald, Karl (ed.), *Kriegsalmanach 1914–1916* (Vienna, 1916).
Kokoschka, Olda, and Marnau, Alfred (eds), *Oskar Kokoschka Letters 1905–1976* (London, 1992).
Popović, Nikola (ed.), *Jugoslovenski Dobrovoljci 1914–1918. Zbornik Dokumenata* (Belgrade, 1980).
Redlich, Josef, *Schicksalsjahre Österreichs 1908–1919. Das politische Tagebuch Josef Redlich*, ed. Fritz Fellner, 2 vols (Graz and Cologne, 1953–4).
Salvemini, Gaetano, *Carteggio 1914–1920*, ed. Enzo Tagliacozzo (Rome and Bari, 1984).
Seton-Watson, R.W., *R.W. Seton-Watson and the Yugoslavs: Correspondence 1906–1941*, eds. Hugh and Christopher Seton-Watson, Ljubo Boban, Mirjana Gross, Bogdan Krizman, Dragovan Šepić, 2 vols (London and Zagreb, 1976).
Sonnino, Sidney, *Diario 1916–1922*, 3 vols (Bari, 1972).
Wichtl, Friedrich, *Dr Karel Kramarsch, der Anstifter des Weltkrieges* (Vienna and Munich, 1918).
Zanotti-Bianco, Umberto, *Carteggio 1906–1918*, ed. V. Carinci (Rome and Bari, 1987).

# B Secondary sources

## I Memoirs

Albertini, Luigi, *Venti Anni di Vita Politica. Parte Seconda. L'Italia nella Grande Guerra*, 3 vols (Bologna, 1950–3).
Arz von Straussenburg, Arthur, *Kampf und Sturz der Mittelmächte* (Vienna, 1935).
Arz von Straussenberg, Arthur, *Zur Geschichte des Großen Krieges 1914–1918* (Vienna, 1924).

Auffenberg-Komarów, Moritz, *Aus Österreichs Höhe und Niedergang. Ein Lebensschilderung* (Munich, 1921).
Bardolff, Carl Freiherr von, *Soldat im alten Österreich. Erinnerungen aus meinem Leben* (Leipzig, 1938).
Benedikt, Heinrich, *Damals im alten Österreich. Erinnerungen* (Vienna and Munich, 1979).
Beneš, Edvard, *Světová Válka a naše Revoluce. Vzpomínky a Úvahy z Bojů za Svobodu Národa*, 3 vols (Prague, 1927).
Benn, Captain Wedgwood, *In the Side Shows* (London, 1919).
Blankenhorn, Heber, *Adventures in Propaganda: Letters from an Intelligence Officer in France* (Boston and New York, 1919).
Borgese, G.A., *Goliath: the March of Fascism* (London, 1938).
Brancaccio, Nicola, *In Francia durante la Guerra* (Milan, 1926).
Burián von Rajecz, Stephen, *Austria in Dissolution* (London, 1925).
Cockerill, George, *What Fools We Were* (London, 1944).
Conrad von Hötzendorf, Franz, *Private Aufzeichnungen. Erste Veröffentlichungen aus den Papieren des k.u.k. Generalstabs-Chefs*, ed. Kurt Peball (Vienna and Munich, 1977).
Cramon, August von, *Unser österreich-ungarischer Bundesgenosse im Weltkriege* (Berlin, 1920).
Creel, George, *How we Advertised America* (New York, 1972).
Crosse, E.C., *The Defeat of Austria as seen by the Seventh Division* (London, 1919).
Czernin, Ottokar, *Im Weltkriege* (Berlin and Vienna, 1919).
Finzi, C.P.L., *Il Sogno di Carzano* (Bologna, 1926).
Finzi, Cesare P.L., *'I.T.O.' Note di un Capo del Servizio Informazioni d'Armata 1915–1918* (Milan, 1931; 2nd edn: Milan, 1934).
Gladden, Norman, *Across the Piave: A Personal Account of the British Forces in Italy, 1917–1919* (London, 1971).
Glaise-Horstenau, Edmund von, *Ein General im Zwielicht*, ed. Peter Broucek, 3 vols (Vienna, 1980–8).
Gomoll, Wilhelm Conrad, *Im Kampf gegen Russland und Serbien* (Leipzig, 1916).
Hajšman, Jan, *Česká Mafie. Vzpomínky na Odboj Doma*, 2nd edn (Prague, 1934).
Hajšman, Jan, *Mafie v Rozmachu. Vzpomínky na Odboj Doma* (Prague, 1933).
Hansi [Jean Jacques Waltz] and Tonnelat, Henri, *Á Travers les Lignes Ennemies* (Paris, 1922).
Hanzal, Vojtěch, *S Výzvědčíky od Švýcarských Ledovců až po Moře Adriatické* (Prague, 1938).
Hanzal, Vojtěch, *Výzvědčíci v Italii a na Slovenskem* (Prague, 1928).
Hlaváček, František, 'Činnost dra Ed. Beneše za Války v Italii a moje Spolupráce s ním', *Naše Revoluce*, XII (Prague, 1936).
Károlyi, Michael, *Gegen eine ganze Welt. Mein Kampf um den Frieden* (Munich, 1924).
Károlyi, Michael, *Memoirs of Michael Károlyi: Faith without Illusion* (London, 1956).
Klobukowski, A., *Souvenirs de Belgique 1911–1918* (Brussels, 1928).
Knox, Alfred, *With the Russian Army 1914–1917*, 2 vols (London, 1921).
Krauss, Alfred, *Die Ursachen unserer Niederlage. Erinnerungen und Urteile aus dem Weltkrieg* (Munich, 1920).
Landwehr von Pragenau, Ottokar, *Hunger. Die Erschöpfungsjahre der Mittelmächte 1917–18* (Vienna, 1931).
Ludendorff, Erich, *My War Memories 1914–1918*, 2 vols (London, 1919).
Mandić, Ante, *Fragmenti za Historiju Ujedinjenja* (Zagreb, 1956).
Marchetti, Tullio, *Luci nel Buio. Trentino Sconosciuto 1872–1915* (Trento, 1934).
Marchetti, Tullio, *Ventotto Anni nel Servizio Informazioni Militari* (Trento, 1960).
Marchetti, Tullio, 'Un tragico Episodio di Guerra nautica sul Fronte trentino', *Trentino. Rivista delle Legione Trentina*, IV/4 (April 1928).

Meštrović, Ivan, *Uspomene na Političke Ljude i Dogadjaje* (Zagreb, 1969).
Mironescu, G.G., *Aperçus sur la Question Roumaine* (Paris, 1919).
Nicolai, Walter, *Geheime Mächte: Internationale Spionage und ihre Kämpfung im Weltkriege und heute* (Leipzig, 1924).
Papírník, Antonín, 'U Národní Rady v Římě', *Naše Revoluce*, XII (Prague, 1936).
Pivko, Ljudevit, *Carzansko Noč* (Maribor, 1924).
Pivko, Ljudevit, *DRUP* (Maribor, 1928).
Pivko, Ljudevit, *Informatorji* (Maribor, 1925).
Pivko, Ljudevit, *Jablane med Frontama* (Maribor, 1924).
Pivko, Ljudevit, *Naši Dobrovoljci u Italiji* (Maribor, 1924).
Pivko, Ljudevit, *Proti Avstriji 1914–1918* (Maribor, 1991).
Pivko, Ljudevit, *Seme* (Maribor, 1924).
Pivko, Ljudevit, *Val Bella* (Maribor, 1928).
Pivko, Ljudevit, *Vulkanska Tla* (Maribor, 1924).
Pivko, Ljudevit, *Zeleni Odred* (Maribor, 1925).
Polzer-Hoditz, Arthur, *Kaiser Karl. Aus der Geheimmappe seines Kabinettschefs* (Zurich, Leipzig and Vienna, 1929).
Rodd, James Rennell, *Social and Diplomatic Memories. 3rd Series. 1902–1919* (London, 1925).
Ronge, Max, *Kriegs- und Industriespionage. Zwölf Jahre Kundschaftsdienst* (Zurich, Leipzig and Vienna, 1930).
Simpson, J.Y., *The Self-Discovery of Russia* (London, 1916).
Stebbing, E.C., *From Czar to Bolshevik* (London, 1918).
Steed, Henry Wickham, *Through Thirty Years 1892–1922: A Personal Narrative*, 2 vols (London, 1924).
Strobl, Karl Hans, *Die Weltgeschichte und das Igelhaus: von Nachmittag des Lebens* (Budweis and Leipzig, 1944).
Stuart, Campbell, *Secrets of Crewe House: The Story of a Famous Campaign* (London, 1920).
Stuart, Campbell, *Opportunity Knocks Once* (London, 1952).
Trevelyan, G.M., *Scenes from Italy's War* (London, 1919).
Turk, Ernest, Jeras, Josip and Paulin, Rajko (eds), *Dobrovoljci Kladivarji Jugoslavije 1912–1918* (Ljubljana, 1936).
Voska, E. and Irwin, W., *Spy and Counterspy: The Autobiography of a Masterspy* (London, 1941).
Vošnjak, Bogumil, *U Borbi za Ujedinjenu Narodnu Državu* (Ljubljana, Belgrade and Zagreb, 1928).
Weber, Fritz, *Das Ende der Armee* (Leipzig, Vienna and Berlin, 1931).
Werkmann, Karl Freiherr von, *Deutschland al Verbündeter. Kaiser Karls Kampf um den Frieden* (Berlin, 1931).
Windischgrätz, Ludwig, *Helden und Halunken. Selbsterlebte Weltgeschichte 1899–1964* (Vienna, Munich and Zurich, 1965).
Windischgrätz, Ludwig, *My Memoirs* (London, 1921).
Zeman, Adolf (ed.), *Cestami Odboje (Jak žily a kudy táhly Čs. Legie)*, 5 vols (Prague, 1927).
Žipek, Alois (ed.), *Domov za Války*, 5 vols (Prague, 1929–31).

## II Other secondary literature

Acković, Aleksandar (ed.), *Politički Zivot Jugoslavije 1914–1945* (Belgrade, 1973).
Almann, Klaus and Lengauer, Hubert (eds), *Österreich und der Große Krieg 1914–1918* (Vienna, 1989).

Andrássy, Gyula, *Diplomacy and the War* (London, 1921).

Antongini, Tom, *D'Annunzio* (London, 1938).

Baker, B. Granville, *The Danube with Pen and Pencil* (London, 1913).

Baker, B. Granville, *The German Army from Within by a British Officer who has Served in it* (London, 1914).

Baker, B. Granville, *Old Cavalry Stations* (London, 1934).

Baker, B. Granville, *The Passing of the Turkish Empire in Europe* (London, 1913).

Balfour, Michael, *Propaganda in War 1939–1945: Organizations, Policies and Publics in Britain and Germany* (London, 1979).

Baumann, Gerhard, *Grundlage und Praxis der internationalen Propaganda* (Essen, 1941).

Bednařík, František, *V Boj! Obrázkova Kronika Československého Revolučního Hnutí v Italii 1915–1918* (Prague, 1927).

Bihl, Wolfdieter, *Österreich-Ungarn und die Friedensschlüsse von Brest-Litovsk* (Vienna, Cologne and Graz, 1970).

Boyer, John W., *Culture and Political Crisis in Vienna: Christian Socialism in Power 1897–1918* (Chicago and London, 1995).

Bruntz, George G., *Allied Propaganda and the Collapse of the German Empire in 1918* (Stanford, 1938; reissued New York, 1972).

Calder, Kenneth J., *Britain and the Origins of the New Europe 1914–1918* (Cambridge, 1976).

Candeloro, Giorgio, *Storia dell'Italia Moderna*, 4th edn, vol. 8 (Milan, 1993).

Constantinescu, Miron and Pascu, Ştefan (eds), *Unification of the Romanian National State: The Union of Transylvania with Old Romania* (Bucharest, 1971).

Cornwall, Mark (ed.), *The Last Years of Austria-Hungary: Essays in Political and Military History 1908–1918* (Exeter, 1990; 2nd edn, 2000).

Čulinović, Ferdo, *1918 na Jadranu* (Zagreb, 1951).

Dan, Maria Masau, and Porcedda, Donatella (eds), *L'Arma della Persuasione. Parole ed Immagini di Propaganda nella Grande Guerra* (Gorizia, 1991).

Daniel, Ute and Siemann, Wolfram (eds), *Propaganda. Meinungskampf, Verführung und politische Sinnstiftung 1789–1989* (Frankfurt am Main, 1994).

Deák, István, *Beyond Nationalism: A Social and Political History of the Habsburg Officer Corps, 1848–1918* (Oxford, 1992).

Debo, Richard K., *Revolution and Survival: The Foreign Policy of Soviet Russia 1917–18* (Liverpool, 1979).

DeGroot, Gerald, *Blighty: British Society in the Era of the Great War* (London and New York 1996).

Deist, Wilhelm (ed.), *Militär und Innenpolitik im Weltkrieg 1914–1918*, 2 vols (Dusseldorf, 1970).

Della Volpe, N., *Esercito e Propaganda nella Grande Guerra* (Rome, 1989).

Djordjević, Dimitrije (ed.), *The Creation of Yugoslavia 1914–1918* (Santa Barbara and Oxford 1980).

Doob, Leonard W., *Propaganda: Its Psychology and Technique* (New York, 1935).

Edmonds, J.E. and Davies, H.R., *Official History of the War: Military Operations Italy 1915–1919* (London, 1949).

Erényi, Gustav, *Graf Stefan Tisza. Ein Staatsmann und Märtyrer* (Vienna and Leipzig, 1935).

Ernst, Wilhelm, *Die antideutsche Propaganda durch das Schweizer Gebiet im Weltkrieg speziell die Propaganda in Bayern* (Munich, 1933).

Fava, Andrea, *Fronte Interno. Propaganda e Mobilitazione Civile nell'Italia della Grande Guerra* (Rome, 1988).

Feigl, Erich, *Kaiserin Zita. Legende und Wahrheit* (Vienna and Munich, 1977).
Felger, Friedrich (ed.), *Was wir von Weltkrieg nicht wissen* (Berlin, 1929).
Ferguson, Niall, *The Pity of War* (London, 1998).
Fest, Wilfried, *Peace or Partition: The Habsburg Monarchy and British Policy 1914–1918* (London, 1978).
Fiala, Peter, *Die letzte Offensive Altösterreichs. Führungsprobleme und Führerverantwortlichkeit bei der öst.-ung. Offensive in Venetien, Juni 1918* (Boppard am Rhein, 1967).
Fischer, Fritz, *Germany's Aims in the First World War* (London, 1977).
Foerster, Wolfgang (ed.), *Kämpfer an vergessenen Fronten* (Berlin, 1931).
Führ, Christoph, *Das k.u.k. Armeeoberkommando und die Innenpolitik in Österreich 1914–1917* (Graz, Vienna and Cologne, 1968).
Fyfe, Hamilton, *Northcliffe* (London, 1930).
Galántai, József, *Hungary in the First World War* (Budapest, 1989).
Glaise-Horstenau, Edmund von, *The Collapse of the Austro-Hungarian Empire* (London and Toronto, 1930).
Glaise-Horstenau, Edmund von and Kiszling, Rudolf (eds), *Österreich-Ungarns letzter Krieg 1914–1918* [OULK], 7 vols (Vienna 1930–8).
Gratz, Gustav and Schüller, Richard, *Die wirtschaftliche Zusammenbruch Österreich-Ungarns. Die Tragödie der Erschöpfung* (Vienna, 1930).
Hanak, Harry, *Great Britain and Austria-Hungary during the First World War: A Study in the Formation of Public Opinion* (Oxford, 1962).
Hanks, Ronald, *Il Tramonto di un'Istitutizione. L'Armata Austro-Ungarica in Italia, 1918* (Milan, 1994).
Hargrave, John, *Words win Wars: Propaganda the Mightiest Weapon of All* (London, 1940).
Herwig, Holger, *The First World War: Germany and Austria-Hungary 1914–1918* (London, 1997).
Hitchens, Keith, *Rumania 1866–1947* (Oxford, 1994).
Höglinger, Felix, *Ministerpräsident Heinrich Graf Clam-Martinic* (Graz and Cologne, 1964).
Horne, John (ed.), *State, Society and Mobilization in Europe during the First World War* (Cambridge, 1997).
Hrabak, Bogumil, *Jugosloveni Zarobljenci u Italiji i njihovo Dobrovoljačko Pitanje 1915–1918* (Novi Sad, 1980).
Isnenghi, Mario, *Giornali di Trincea 1915–1918* (Turin, 1977).
Jackall, Robert (ed.), *Propaganda* (New York, 1995).
Jeřábek, Rudolf, *Potiorek. General im Schatten von Sarajevo* (Graz, 1991).
Jones, H.R., *The War in the Air*, vol. 6 (Oxford, 1937).
Kalvoda, Josef, *The Genesis of Czechoslovakia* (New York, 1986).
Kann, R.A., Király, B.K., and Fichtner, P.S. (eds), *The Habsburg Empire in World War I* (New York, 1977).
Kerchnawe, Hugo (ed.), *Die Militärverwaltung in den von österreichisch-ungarischen Truppen besetzten Gebieten* (Vienna, 1928).
Kerchnawe, Hugo, *Der Zusammenbruch der österr.-ungar. Wehrmacht im Herbst 1918* (Munich, 1921).
Kiraly, Béla and Dreisziger, Nándor (eds), *East Central European Society in World War I* (New York, 1985).
Klecanda, Vladimír, *Bitva u Zborova. Vojensko Historická Studie o Bojích Československé Brigády v Haliči roku 1917* (Prague, 1927).
Knesebeck, Ludolf Gottschalk von dem, *Die Wahrheit über den Propagandafeldzug und Deutschlands Zusammenbruch* (Munich, 1927).

Krause, Gerhard, *Die britische Auslandspropaganda. Organisation, Methoden, Inhalt 1914–1940* (Berlin, 1940).
Krizman, Bogdan, *Hrvatska u Prvom Svjetskom Ratu. Hrvatsko-Srpski Politički Odnosi* (Zagreb, 1989).
Lasswell, Harold, *Propaganda Technique in World War I* (New York, 1927).
Logaj, Josef, *Československé Legie v Italii* (Prague, 1922).
Lorenz, Reinhold, *Kaiser Karl und der Untergang der Donaumonarchie* (Graz, Vienna and Cologne, 1959).
Marchetti, Odoardo, *Il Servizio Informazioni dell'Esercito Italiano nella Grande Guerra* (Rome, 1937).
May, A.J., *The Passing of the Hapsburg Monarchy 1914–1918*, 2 vols (Philadelphia, 1966).
Melograni, Piero, *Storia Politica della Grande Guerra 1915–1918* (Bari, 1972).
Messinger, Gary S., *British Propaganda and the State in the First World War* (Manchester and New York, 1992).
Mock, James and Larson, Cedric, *Words that Won the War: The Story of the Committee on Public Information 1917–1919* (Princeton, 1939).
Monticone, Alberto, *Nitti e la Grande Guerra 1914–1918* (Milan, 1961).
Moroïanu, George, *Les Luttes des Roumains Transylvains pour la Liberté et l'Opinion Européene* (Paris, 1933).
Nowak, Karl Friedrich, *Der Sturz der Mittelmächte* (Munich, 1921).
Nowak, Karl Friedrich, *Der Weg zur Katastrophe* (Berlin, 1926).
Opočenský, Jan, *Konec Monarchie Rakousko-Uherské* (Prague, 1928).
Page, T.N., *Italy and the World War* (London, 1921).
Palla, Luciana, *Il Trentino Orientale e la Grande Guerra* (Trento, 1994).
Paulová, Milada, *Jugoslavenski Odbor* (Zagreb, 1925).
Pichlík, Karel, Klípa, Bohumír and Zabloudilova, Jitka, *Českoslovenští Legionáři, 1914–1920* (Prague, 1996).
Pieri, Piero and Rochat, Giorgio, *Pietro Badoglio* (Turin, 1974).
Pilch, Jenő, *A hírszerzés és kémkedés története*, 3 vols (Budapest, 1937).
Plaschka, Richard, *Cattaro-Prag. Revolte und Revolution* (Graz and Cologne, 1963).
Plaschka, Richard, Haselsteiner, Horst, and Suppan, Arnold, *Innere Front. Militärassistenz, Widerstand und Umsturz in der Donaumonarchie 1918*, 2 vols (Vienna, 1974).
Plaschka, Richard and Mack, Karl-Heinz (eds), *Die Auflösung des Habsburgerreiches. Zusammenbruch und Neuorientierung im Donauraum* (Munich, 1970).
Pleterski, Janko, *Prvo Opredeljenje Slovenaca za Jugoslaviju* (Belgrade, 1976).
Pound, Reginald and Harmsworth, Geoffrey, *Northcliffe* (London, 1959).
Procacci, Giovanna, *Soldati e Prigionieri Italiani nella Grande Guerra* (Rome, 1993).
Rauchensteiner, Manfried, *Der Tod des Doppeladlers. Österreich-Ungarn und der Erste Weltkrieg* (Graz, 1993).
Redlich, Joseph, *Emperor Francis Joseph of Austria: a Biography* (New York, 1929).
Redlich, Joseph, *Österreichische Regierung und Verwaltung im Weltkriege* (Vienna, 1925).
Regele, Oskar, *Feldmarschall Conrad. Auftrag und Erfüllung 1906–1918* (Vienna and Munich, 1955).
Regele, Oskar, *Gericht über Habsburgs Wehrmacht* (Vienna and Munich, 1968).
Rhodes, Anthony, *The Poet as Superman* (London, 1959).
Roetter, Charles, *The Art of Psychological Warfare 1914–1945* (New York, 1974).
Roshwald, Aviel and Stites, Richard (eds), *European Culture in the Great War: The Arts, Entertainment and Propaganda, 1914–1918* (Cambridge, 1999).
Rothenburg, Gunther, *The Army of Francis Joseph* (West Lafayette, 1976).

Rumpler, Helmut, *Max Hussarek. Nationalitäten und Nationalitätenpolitik in Österreich im Sommer des Jahres 1918* (Graz and Cologne, 1965).

Sanders, M.S. and Taylor, P.M., *British Propaganda in the First World War 1914–1918* (London, 1982).

Schubert, Peter, *Die Tätigkeit des k.u.k. Militärattachés in Bern während des Ersten Weltkrieges* (Osnabruck, 1980).

Schuster, Peter, *Henry Wickham Steed und die Habsburgermonarchie* (Vienna, Cologne and Graz, 1970).

Schwabe, Matthias, *Die französische Auslandspropaganda. Ihre Grundlagen und Voraussetzungen* (Berlin, 1939).

Šepić, Dragovan, *Italija, Saveznici i Jugoslavensko Pitanje 1914–1918* (Zagreb, 1970).

Seton-Watson, Hugh and Christopher, *The Making of a New Europe: R.W. Seton-Watson and the Last Years of Austria-Hungary* (London, 1981).

Seton-Watson, R.W., *A History of the Czechs and Slovaks* (London, 1943).

Seton-Watson, R.W., *A History of the Roumanians* (Cambridge, 1934).

Shanafelt, Gary, *The Secret Enemy: Austria-Hungary and the German Alliance 1914–1918* (New York, 1985).

Sked, Alan, *The Decline and Fall of the Habsburg Empire 1815–1918* (London and New York, 1989).

Squires, J.D., *British Propaganda at Home and in the United States from 1914 to 1917* (Cambridge, 1935).

Steed, Henry Wickham, *The Fifth Arm* (London, 1940).

Steglich, Wolfgang, *Die Friedenspolitik der Mittelmächte 1917–18* (Wiesbaden, 1964).

Stone, Norman, *The Eastern Front 1914–1917* (London, 1974).

Strugar, Vlado, *Jugoslavenske Socijaldemokratske Stranke 1914–1918* (Zagreb, 1963).

Szende, Zoltán, *Die Ungarn im Zusammenbruch. Feldheer/Hinterland* (Oldenbourg, 1931).

Szuber, Antoni, *Walka o Przewagę Duchową. Kampanja Propagandowa Koaliciji 1914–1918* (Warsaw, 1933).

Taylor, Philip M., *British Propaganda in the Twentieth Century: Selling Democracy* (Edinburgh, 1999).

Taylor, Philip M., *Munitions of the Mind: A History of Propaganda from the Ancient World to the Present Day*, 2nd edn (Manchester, 1995).

Taylor, Philip M., *War and the Media: Propaganda and Persuasion in the Gulf War* (Manchester, 1992).

*The Times History of the War*, vol. XXI (London, 1920).

Thimme, Hans, *Weltkrieg ohne Waffen* (Stuttgart and Berlin, 1932).

Timms, Edward, *Karl Kraus. Apocalyptic Satirist. Culture and Collapse in Habsburg Vienna* (New Haven and London, 1989).

Tobolka, Zdeněk, *Politické Dějiny Československého Národa od r.1848 až do Dnešní Doby*, 4 vols (Prague, 1932–7).

Tosi, Luciano, *La Propaganda Italiana all'Estero nella Prima Guerra Mondiale. Rivendicazioni Territoriali e Politica delle Nazionalità* (Udine, 1977).

Tosti, Amedeo, *Come ci vide l'Austria Imperiale. Dall'Ultimatum alla Serbia a Villa Giusti* (Milan, 1930).

Valiani, Leo, *The End of Austria-Hungary* (London, 1973).

Vermes, Gábor, *István Tisza: the Liberal Vision and Conservative Statescraft of a Magyar Nationalist* (New York, 1985).

Viazzi, Luciano, *I Diavoli dell'Adamello. La Guerra a Quota Tremila 1915–1918* (Milan, 1981).

Villari, Luigi, *The War on the Italian Front* (London, 1932).

Wachtel, Andrew B., *Making a Nation, Breaking a Nation: Literature and Cultural Politics in Yugoslavia* (Stanford, 1995).
Wanderscheck, Hermann, *Bibliographie zur englischen Propaganda im Weltkrieg* (Stuttgart, 1935).
Wanderscheck, Hermann, *Weltkrieg und Propaganda*, 2nd edn (Berlin, 1939).
Wheeler-Bennett, *Brest-Litovsk: The Forgotten Peace. March 1918* (London, 1963).
Wildman, Alan, *The End of the Russian Imperial Army: The Old Army and the Soldiers' Revolt, March–April 1917* (Princeton, 1980).
Wildman, Alan, *The End of the Russian Imperial Army: The Road to Soviet Power and Peace* (Princeton, 1987).
Williamson, Samuel R. and Pastor, Peter (eds), *Essays on World War I: Origins and Prisoners of War* (New York, 1983).
Wilson, Trevor, *The Myriad Faces of War: Britain and the Great War, 1914–1918* (Cambridge, 1986).
*Zborov, 1917–1937. Památník k Dvacátém Výročí Bitvy u Zborova. 2 Července 1917* (Prague, 1937).
Zell, A. von, *Warum haben wir den Weltkrieg verloren?* (Klagenfurt, n.d.).
Zeman, Z.A.B., *The Break-Up of the Habsburg Empire 1914–1918* (Oxford, 1961).
Zeman, Z.A.B., *Nazi Propaganda*, 2nd edn (London, Oxford and New York, 1973).
Živojinović, Dragan, *America, Italy and the Birth of Yugoslavia 1917–1919* (New York, 1972).

## III Articles

Angerer, Thomas, 'Henry Wickham Steed, Robert William Seton-Watson und die Habsburgermonarchie', *Mitteilungen des Instituts für Österreichische Geschichtsforschung*, vol. 99, 3/4 (1991).
Belošević, Mirko, 'Uloga Ljudevita Pivka u talijanskom napadu kod Karcanu 17.Septembra 1917. godine', *Vojnoistorijski Glasnik*, no. 20 (1969).
Broucek, Peter, 'Aus den Erinnerungen eines Kundschaftsoffiziers in Tirol 1914–1918', *Mitteilungen des Österreichischen Staatsarchivs*, vol. 33 (1980).
Cles, Denise, 'Die Propagandatätigkeit Gabriele D'Annunzios gegen Österreich-Ungarn 1914–1918', *Mitteilungen des Österreichischen Staatsarchivs*, vol. 27 (1974).
Cornwall, Mark, 'Austria-Hungary', in Hugh Cecil and Peter Liddle (eds), *At the Eleventh Hour: Reflections, Hopes and Anxieties at the Closing of the Great War, 1918* (London, 1998).
Cornwall, Mark, 'The Experience of Yugoslav Agitation in Austria-Hungary 1917–1918', in Hugh Cecil and Peter Liddle (eds), *Facing Armageddon: The First World War Experienced* (London, 1996).
Cornwall, Mark, 'Morale and Patriotism in the Austro-Hungarian Army 1914–1918', in John Horne (ed.), *State, Society and Mobilization in Europe during the First World War* (Cambridge, 1997).
Cornwall, Mark, 'News, Rumour and the Control of Information in Austria-Hungary 1914–1918', *History*, vol. 77 no. 249 (1992).
Jedlicka, Ludwig, 'Das Ende der Monarchie in Österreich-Ungarn', in Hellmuth Rössler (ed.), *Weltwende 1917. Monarchie, Weltrevolution, Demokratie* (Göttingen, 1965).
Opačić, Petar, 'Solunski Front 1917. godine', in Slavenko Terzić (ed.), *Srbija 1917. Godine. Naučni Skup* (Belgrade, 1988).
Peball, Kurt, 'Literarische Publikationen des Kriegsarchivs im Weltkrieg 1914 bis 1918', *Mitteilungen des Österreichischen Staatsarchivs*, vol. 14 (1961).
Pichlík, Karel, 'Das Ende der österreichisch-ungarischen Armee', *Österreichische Osthefte*, 5 (1963).

Plaschka, Richard, 'Contradicting Ideologies: the Pressure of Ideological Conflicts in the Austro-Hungarian Army of World War I', in R.A. Kann, B.K. Király and P.S. Fichtner (eds), *The Habsburg Empire in World War I* (New York, 1977).
Plaschka, Richard, 'Zur Vorgeschichte des Überganges von Einheiten des Infanterieregiments Nr.28 an der russischen Front 1915', in *Österreich und Europa. Festgabe für Hugo Hantsch zum 70. Geburtstag* (Vienna, 1965).
Pleterski, Janko, 'Koroški Slovenci med Prvo Svetovno Vojno', in Janko Pleterski, Lojze Ude and Tone Zorn (eds), *Koroški Plebiscit. Razprave in Članki* (Ljubljana, 1970).
Sándorné, Gábor, 'Az oroszországi forradalmi mozgalmak visszhangja a magyar dolgozók hadifoglyokhoz írt leveleiben', *Párttörténeti Közlemények*, no. 2 (1958).
Šepić, Dragovan, 'Oktobarska Revolucija i jugoslavensko pitanje u Austro-Ugarskoj 1917–18', *Historijski Zbornik*, XI–XII (1958–9).
Simonetti, M., 'Il Servizio "P" al Fronte', *Riforma della Scuola* (August–September 1968).
Tosi, Luciano, 'Giuseppe Antonio Borgese e la Prima Guerra Mondiale (1914–1918)', *Storia Contemporanea*, IV/2 (1973).
Tosi, Luciano, 'Romeo A. Gallenga Stuart e la propaganda di guerra all'estero (1917–1918)', *Storia Contemporanea*, II (1970).
Ude, Lojze, 'Deklaracijsko gibanje na Slovenskem', in Vasa Čubrilović, Ferdo Čulinović and Marko Kostrenčić (eds), *Naučni Skup u Povodu 50–Godišnjice Raspada Austro-Ugarske Monarhije i Stvaranja Jugoslavenske Države* (Zagreb, 1969).

## IV Theses and dissertations

Holzer, Barbara, *Die politische Erziehung und der vaterländische Unterricht in Österreich zur Zeit des Ersten Weltkrieges*, Diploma Diss. (Vienna, 1987).
Klein, Signe, *Freiherr Sarkotić von Lovćen. Die Zeit seiner Verwaltung in Bosnien–Hercegovina von 1914 bis 1918*, Ph.Diss. (Vienna, 1969).
Mayer, Klaus, *Die Organisation des Kriegspressequartiers beim AOK im Ersten Weltkrieg 1914–1918*, Ph.Diss. (Vienna, 1963).
Schiel, Wolfgang, *Die Flugblatt- und Flugschriftpropaganda der Entente im Ersten Weltkrieg 1914–1918*, Ph.Diss. (Vienna, 1979).
Schmölzer, Hildegund, *Die Propaganda des Kriegspressequartiers im Ersten Weltkrieg 1914–1918*, Ph.Diss. (Vienna, 1965).
Spann, Gustav, *Zensur in Österreich während des 1. Weltkrieges 1914–1918*, Ph.Diss. (Vienna, 1972).

# Index

AH = Austria-Hungary
PC = Padua Commission
*For propaganda campaigns, see under fronts*: Balkan Front, Eastern Front, Italian Front, etc.